The Notary Signing Agent's
Loan Documents Sourcebook

The Notary Signing Agent's illustrated guide
to common and uncommon forms
and how to notarize them

Published by:

National Notary Association
9350 De Soto Avenue
Chatsworth, CA 91311-4926
Telephone: (818) 739-4000
Fax: (818) 700-0920
Website: NationalNotary.org
Email: nna@NationalNotary.org

Third Edition ©2022
First Edition ©2005
ISBN: 978-1-59767-299-3

Table of Contents

APPENDIX

Milton G. Valera

"Some people have greatness thrust upon them.
Very few have excellence thrust upon them."

— John W. Gardner
U.S. Secretary of Health, Education, and Welfare, 1965–1968

In these early years of the fledgling Notary Signing Agent vocation, it is already evident that Notary Signing Agents must demonstrate an unswerving commitment to excellence, for success is not often granted upon easier terms.

Everyone who aspires to be a Notary Signing Agent must start at the same place. Agents must gain a working knowledge of mortgage loans, loan terms and documents, lending practices, and know how the real property recording and title industries operate.

At the closing table itself, Agents must exude confidence in helping borrowers execute any of the myriad papers that may comprise a closing documentation package.

There are no shortcuts here. Your chosen career field demands that you cultivate your knowledge and never stop learning.

The Notary Signing Agent's Loan Documents Sourcebook provides a wealth of information for the beginner and veteran alike. Five separate Notary Signing Agent transactions are explained and illustrated, including the refinance loan and the home equity line of credit, purchase and sale transactions, the increasingly popular "reverse" mortgage, and the purely commercial transaction. Next are explained the instruments that are typically encountered in documentation packages for these transactions, followed by helpful tips for presenting and notarizing the applicable instruments.

In addition, separate chapters of this *Sourcebook* contain several examples each of various affidavits, conveyance deeds, security instruments, and other common and uncommon forms Notary Signing Agents routinely encounter.

Never before has such a breadth of diverse real property and mortgage documents been compiled in a single volume with the needs of the Notary Signing Agent in mind. It would take considerable real-world experience to gain exposure to the forms in this *Sourcebook*.

You are to be commended for recognizing that the excellence of which John W. Gardner speaks comes only as the result of an investment of time, dedication, and sacrifice, and taking the initiative to broaden your knowledge and sharpen your skills.

Milton G. Valera
Chairman
National Notary Association

About This Sourcebook

The venerable Mark Twain, who was once a Notary, quipped: *"All you need in this life is ignorance and confidence, and then success is sure."*

Any Notary Signing Agent will agree that confidence is critical for success. Ignorance, however, is simply not an option.

To receive assignments from a title office, escrow agent, or signing service, Notary Signing Agents must demonstrate knowledge of how to conduct a home loan signing ceremony. In interviews and on written examinations submitted with an application, Agents are pre-screened by contracting companies for their knowledge of loan signing procedures and the documents they will present to borrowers.

The importance of Notary Signing Agents acquiring knowledge of particular loan documents was impressed upon the author at an informational meeting of Agents seeking work with a signing service. All were present by invitation and had some experience with loan signings, including a working knowledge of many of the standard documents.

The signing service representative leading the meeting passed out an instructional test to the Agents in attendance. There was quite a lively discussion about the questions on the handout, but silence fell upon the room when the following question was asked: "Which major lender requires the 'Notice of Right to Cancel' form to be initialed by the borrower, but not signed?"

Contracting companies require Notary Signing Agents to be thoroughly versed in the documents they handle, even if they never explain them to a borrower.

Knowledge, as important as it is, is only half the battle.

At the appointment itself, the Agent will sit across the table from perfect strangers with a briefcase full of documents the Agent may feel ill-equipped to present. Add to this the uncertainty of not knowing what the borrower will say or ask next and it is apparent that only one word can quell the insecurities that are the product of inexperience.

Confidence.

Notary Signing Agents need confidence in presenting documents as much as they need knowledge of the documents themselves.

This book was written upon the premise that, to be successful, Notary Signing Agents must possess both knowledge and confidence. The best way to achieve both is through years of experience conducting loan signings. In the case of beginners, of course, this is not possible.

The purpose of this book is to instill a measure of needed knowledge and confidence in not only the beginner, but also the veteran encountering a particular form for the first time.

Part I attempts to bridge the gap of inexperience by reprinting full and complete loan document packages from seven actual refinance, home equity line of credit (HELOC), home equity conversion mortgage (HECM, otherwise known as a "reverse" mortgage), purchase and commercial transactions.

A review of these complete document sets will yield an enhanced knowledge of standard loan documents, a recognition that loan packages can vary from lender to lender and from signing to signing, and perhaps most important, an increased familiarity with loan documents, which results in confidence ("familiarity breeds confidence").

While the complete sets of loan documents comprise the bulk of the present volume, Notary Signing Agents who have conducted only a few signings have already learned that not only can loan packages vary from signing to signing, the individual documents themselves can vary in format. The sheer number of possible combinations of forms that may appear in a document package defies any definitive attempt to anticipate, classify, or present them in a book of this size, due to the fact that each individual lender or title company may require different forms, a specific loan program may require certain documents, or a borrower's unique financial or life circumstances may necessitate inclusion of one or more particular documents to be included in a loan package.

Notwithstanding this limitation, Part II of this book presents several examples of each of the more common forms found in residential loan document packages, including the most commonly notarized documents. By examining several similar forms, Signing Agents can more readily be prepared to quickly recognize and differentiate between one lender's forms and another's. Above all — and this is critical for confidence — Agents will have had exposure to the subtle variations and will feel better prepared to proceed.

In particular, chapters in Part II discuss and illustrate the following instruments:

• Occupancy affidavits;

• Compliance agreements;

• Signature and name affidavits;

• Deeds used to convey title to real property;

• Promissory notes and security instruments;

• Notice of right to cancel forms (including the document that was the source of the test question in the above-mentioned example);

• Customer Identification Program (CIP) forms required under the "Uniting and Strengthening America by Providing Appropriate Tools Required to Intercept and Obstruct Terrorism" (PATRIOT) Act of 2001; and

• Affidavits used for various purposes in the mortgage and title industry.

We include in an Appendix the current draft of the SPW Code of Conduct for Notary Signing Agents, an ethical code of conduct for Notary Signing Agents.

Finally, a word of caution. The forms reproduced in this book are provided solely to aid in comprehending Notary Signing Agent practices and procedures. State laws universally prohibit Notaries Public and nonattorneys from engaging in the unauthorized practice of law. Notary Signing Agents should not use this book to recommend or draft a particular document for, or to provide legal counsel about, any document to borrowers. Agents should advise borrowers to have their specific legal questions answered by their loan officer, escrow agent or attorney. ■

Part I
SIGNING AGENT TRANSACTIONS

Part I of this book illustrates seven complete sets of loan document packages from the most common Notary Signing Agent transactions — refinance loans, home equity lines of credit, purchase transactions and reverse mortgages — and sets from less common commercial transactions. These packets will illustrate the various lender, title, and tax forms common to these transactions.

We have attempted to include document packages which contain elements unique to each transaction, so the reader will be exposed to as broad a variety of instruments as possible. Forms that are unique to a particular type of transaction will be noted in accompanying marginal notes.

Marginal notes also will appear in places where the documents raise issues or questions of interest to the Notary Signing Agent, such as how exactly the forms should be notarized.

Since these forms are reproductions of documents used in actual loan transactions, all company and individual names, addresses, phone numbers, and identification data used throughout have been altered.

The security instrument (deed of trust or mortgage) is abridged in most cases due to the length of the instrument and the fact that much of the content of these documents is "boilerplate" text.

1

Refinance Loans

INTRODUCTION

One of the Notary Signing Agent's staples is the home refinance transaction, which, according to industry analyst accounted for the majority of the record volume of over $4.1 trillion in new loans originated in 2020. Low interest rates and high home values kept the gold rush going in 2021. While the number of refinances has trended downward in the first quarter of 2022, refinance transactions are still an important part of a Signing Agent's workload.

As the mortgage origination numbers suggest, when refinance transactions are up, Notary Signing Agents are extremely busy. At the height of the recent lending boom in 2019–2021, Notary Signing Agents made it possible for title and escrow companies to handle the increased volume of closings.

In leaner times, when interest rates creep higher and the number of refinance loans drop, lenders begin to more aggressively market adjustable rate refinance and HELOC loans for debt consolidation, remodeling, and funding college education. They also introduce new programs to woo first-time buyers and consumers who cannot afford a traditional mortgage, such as interest-only or zero-interest loans.

Clearly, as market shifts occur, the types of loans Notary Signing Agents handle will change.

The two complete sets of refinance papers presented in this chapter represent two types of refinance loans, an FHA fixed rate and conventional adjustable rate mortgage (ARM). They illustrate documents found in virtually every refinance loan package as well as forms which are dictated by a particular type of lender or transaction.

Forms in Sample Set 1 — Pages

The full list of documents comprising Sample Set 1 follows. Refer to the marginal notes on the samples for additional comments on these forms.

Notarized Forms in Sample Set 1   Pages

The documents in Sample Set 1 that must be notarized are listed below, along with the type of notarization required (in parentheses). Refer to the marginal notes for additional comments and guidelines for notarizing these forms.

Forms in Sample Set 2   Pages

The full list of documents comprising Sample Set 2 follows. Refer to the marginal notes for additional comments on and guidelines for notarizing these forms.

Notarized Forms in Sample Set 2

The documents in Sample Set 2 that must be notarized are listed below.
Refer to the marginal notes for additional comments and guidelines for
notarizing these forms.

Refinance Loans

Sample Set 1

Uniform Residential Loan Application

Verify and complete the information on this application. If you are applying for this loan with others, each additional Borrower must provide information as directed by your Lender.

Section 1: Borrower Information. This section asks about your personal information and your income from employment and other sources, such as retirement, that you want considered to qualify for this loan.

1a. Personal Information

Name *(First, Middle, Last, Suffix)*

Alternate Names – *List any names by which you are known or any names under which credit was previously received (First, Middle, Last, Suffix)*

Social Security Number _____ – ___ – _____
(or Individual Taxpayer Identification Number)

Date of Birth   **Citizenship**
(mm/dd/yyyy)   ○ U.S. Citizen
____ / ____ / _____ ○ Permanent Resident Alien
                      ○ Non-Permanent Resident Alien

Type of Credit
○ I am applying for **individual credit.**
○ I am applying for **joint credit.** Total Number of Borrowers: _
   Each Borrower intends to apply for joint credit. **Your initials:** _____

List Name(s) of Other Borrower(s) Applying for this Loan
(First, Middle, Last, Suffix) – Use a separator between names

---

NOTES

Borrower(s) sign Section Six. If applying for joint credit, borrower initials Section One.

Dependents *(not listed by another Borrower)*
Number __
Ages _____

owed, Civil Union, Domestic Partnership, Registered
Relationship)

Contact Information
Home Phone (____) ____ – _____
Cell Phone (____) ____ – _____
Work Phone (____) ____ – _____   **Ext.** _____
Email _____

Street _____   Unit # _____
City _____   State _____ ZIP _____   Country _____
How Long at Current Address? ___ Years ___ Months **Housing** ○ No primary housing expense ○ Own ○ Rent ($_____/month)

If at Current Address for LESS than 2 years, list Former Address   ☐ *Does not apply*
Street _____   Unit # _____
City _____   State _____ ZIP _____   Country _____
How Long at Former Address? ___ Years ___ Months **Housing** ○ No primary housing expense ○ Own ○ Rent ($_____/month)

Mailing Address – *if different from Current Address*   ☐ *Does not apply*
Street _____   Unit # _____
City _____   State _____ ZIP _____   Country _____

1b. Current Employment/Self-Employment and Income   ☐ *Does not apply*

Employer or Business Name _____   Phone (____) ____ – _____
Street _____   Unit # _____
City _____   State _____ ZIP _____   Country _____

Position or Title _____
Start Date ____ / ____ / ____ *(mm/dd/yyyy)*
How long in this line of work? ___ Years ___ Months

Check if this statement applies:
☐ I am employed by a family member, property seller, real estate agent, or other party to the transaction.

☐ **Check if you are the Business Owner or Self-Employed**
○ I have an ownership share of less than 25%. **Monthly Income (or Loss)**
○ I have an ownership share of 25% or more. $_____

Gross Monthly Income
Base	$_____	/month
Overtime	$_____	/month
Bonus	$_____	/month
Commission	$_____	/month
Military Entitlements	$_____	/month
Other	$_____	/month
TOTAL $	0.00	/month

Section 6: Acknowledgments and Agreements. This section tells you about your legal obligations when you sign this application.

Acknowledgments and Agreements

Definitions:
- "Lender" includes the Lender's agents, service providers, and any of their successors and assigns.
- "Other Loan Participants" includes (i) any actual or potential owners of a loan resulting from this application (the "Loan"), (ii) acquirers of any beneficial or other interest in the Loan, (iii) any mortgage insurer, (iv) any guarantor, (v) any servicer of the Loan, and (vi) any of these parties' service providers, successors or assigns.

I agree to, acknowledge, and represent the following:

(1) The Complete Information for this Application
- The information I have provided in this application is true, accurate, and complete as of the date I signed this application.
- If the information I submitted changes or I have new information before closing of the Loan, I must change and supplement this application, including providing any updated/supplemented real estate sales contract.
- For purchase transactions: The terms and conditions of any real estate sales contract signed by me in connection with this application are true, accurate, and complete to the best of my knowledge and belief. I have not entered into any other agreement, written or oral, in connection with this real estate transaction.
- The Lender and Other Loan Participants may rely on the information contained in the application before and after closing of the Loan.
- Any intentional or negligent misrepresentation of information may result in the imposition of:
    (a) civil liability on me, including monetary damages, if a person suffers any loss because the person relied on any misrepresentation that I have made on this application, and/or
    (b) criminal penalties on me including, but not limited to, fine or imprisonment or both under the provisions of Federal law (18 U.S.C. §§ 1001 *et seq.*).

(2) The Property's Security
The Loan I have applied for in this application will be secured by a mortgage or deed of trust which provides the Lender a security interest in the property described in this application.

(3) The Property's Appraisal, Value, and Condition
- Any appraisal or value of the property obtained by the Lender is for use by the Lender and Other Loan Participants.
- The Lender and Other Loan Participants have not made any representation or warranty, express or implied, to me about the property, its condition, or its value.

(4) Electronic Records and Signatures
- The Lender and Other Loan Participants may keep any paper record and/or electronic record of this application, whether or not the Loan is approved.
- If this application is created as (or converted into) an "electronic application", I consent to the use of "electronic records" and "electronic signatures" as the terms are defined in and governed by applicable Federal and/or state electronic transactions laws.
- I intend to sign and have signed this application either using my:
    (a) electronic signature; or
    (b) a written signature and agree that if a paper version of this application is converted into an electronic application, the application will be an electronic record, and the representation of my written signature on this application will be my binding electronic signature.
- I agree that the application, if delivered or transmitted to the Lender or Other Loan Participants as an electronic record with my electronic signature, will be as effective and enforceable as a paper application signed by me in writing.

(5) Delinquency
- The Lender and Other Loan Participants may report information about my account to credit bureaus. Late payments, missed payments, or other defaults on my account may be reflected in my credit report and will likely affect my credit score.
- If I have trouble making my payments I understand that I may contact a HUD-approved housing counseling organization for advice about actions I can take to meet my mortgage obligations.

(6) Authorization for Use and Sharing of Information
By signing below, in addition to the representations and agreements made above, I expressly authorize the Lender and Other Loan Participants to obtain, use, and share with each other (i) the loan application and related loan information and documentation, (ii) a consumer credit report on me, and (iii) my tax return information, as necessary to perform the actions listed below, for so long as they have an interest in my loan or its servicing:
    (a) process and underwrite my loan;
    (b) verify any data contained in my consumer credit report, my loan application and other information supporting my loan application;
    (c) inform credit and investment decisions by the Lender and Other Loan Participants;
    (d) perform audit, quality control, and legal compliance analysis and reviews;
    (e) perform analysis and modeling for risk assessments;
    (f) monitor the account for this loan for potential delinquencies and determine any assistance that may be available to me; and
    (g) other actions permissible under applicable law.

Borrower Signature _____ Date *(mm/dd/yyyy)* ____ / ____ / _____

Additional Borrower Signature _____ Date *(mm/dd/yyyy)* ____ / ____ / _____

Borrower Name: _____
Uniform Residential Loan Application
Freddie Mac Form 65 • Fannie Mae Form 1003
Effective 1/2021

The Escrow Palace
23161 Lake Drive, Suite 120
Any City, AS 00000
(000) 380-9701 Fax (000) 380-7899
Web Site: http://www.escrowpalace.com, E-Mail: info@escrowpalace.com

Escrow No. <u>52944</u>   Date: <u>October 3, 20XX</u>

Re: 1000 Anywhere St., Any City, AS 00000

To: The Escrow Palace - BEVERLY CLOSER

My previous instructions in the above numbered escrow are hereby modified -supplemented in the following particulars only:

LENDER, RATE & TERMS:

A new Conventional Trust Deed loan in favor of ANPAC FUNDING CORP. DBA ANPAC LENDING GROUP, in the principal amount of $166,500.00 bearing interest at the rate of 6.375% per annum, for a term of 30 years. Borrower(s) signature on loan documents shall constitute full acceptance and approval of all lender terms and conditions and shall be Escrow Holder's authorization to comply with all terms and conditions contained therein.

All parties signing this instruction acknowledge receipt of a copy of same. All other terms and conditions of this escrow shall remain the same.

Borrower's Signature

_____   _____
Barbara Borrower   Barry Borrower

American Land Title Association	ALTA Settlement Statement - Borrower/Buyer

File No./Escrow No.: 52944 Print Date & Time: Officer/ Escrow Officer: Settlement Location:	**The Escrow Place** **23161 Lake Dr.** **Any City, AS 00000**	Title Company Logo

Property Address: 1000 Anywhere St.,
Any City, AS 0000
Buyer: Barry Borrower, Barbara Borrower
Seller:
Lender:

Settlement Date:
Disbursement Date:
Additional dates per state requirements:

Description	Borrower/Buyer	
	Debit	Credit
Financial		
Sales Price of Property		
Personal Property		
Deposit including earnest money		
Loan Amount		
Existing Loan(s) Assumed or Taken Subject to _____		
Seller Credit		
Excess Deposit		
Prorations/Adjustments		
School Taxes from (date) to (date)		
County Taxes from (date) to (date)		
HOA dues from (date) to (date)		
Seller Credit		
Loan Charges to (lender co.)		
Points		
Application Fee		
Origination Fee		
Underwriting Fee		
Mortgage Insurance Premium		
Prepaid Interest		

Refinance Loans

Other Loan Charges		
Appraisal Fee to _____		
Credit Report Fee to _____		
Flood Determination Fee to _____		
Flood Monitoring Fee to _____		
Tax Monitoring Fee to _____		
Tax Status Research Fee to _____		
Impounds		
Homeowner's Insurance _____ mo @ $ _____/mo		
Mortgage Insurance _____ mo @ $ _____/mo		
City/town taxes _____ mo @ $ _____/mo		
County Taxes _____ mo @ $ _____/mo		
School Taxes _____ mo @ $ _____/mo		
Aggregate Adjustment		
Title Charges & Escrow / Settlement Charges		
Owner's Title Insurance ($ amount) to _____		
Owner's Policy Endorsement(s) _____		
Loan Policy of Title Insurance ($ amount) to _____		
Loan Policy Endorsement(s) _____		
Title Search to _____		
Insurance Binder to _____		
Escrow / Settlement Fee to _____		
Notary Fee to _____		
Signing Fee to _____		
Commission		
Real Estate Commission to _____		
Real Estate Commission to _____		
Other		
Government Recording and Transfer Charges		
Recording Fees (Deed) to _____		
Recording Fees (Mortgage/Deed of Trust) to _____		
Recording Fees (Other) to _____		
Transfer Tax to _____		
Transfer Tax to _____		
Payoff(s)		
Lender: Payoff Lender Co.		
Principal Balance ($ amount)		
Interest on Payoff Loan ($ amount/day)		
Additional Payoff fees/Reconveyance Fee/Recording Fee/Wire Fee		
Lender: Payoff Lender Co.		
Principal Balance ($ amount)		

File #
Printed on (date) at (time)

	Debit	Credit
Interest on Payoff Loan ($ amount/day)		
Additional Payoff fees/Reconveyance Fee/Recording Fee/Wire Fee		
Miscellaneous		
Pest Inspection Fee to _____		
Survey Fee to _____		
Homeowner's insurance premium to _____		
Home Inspection Fee to _____		
Home Warranty Fee to _____		
HOA dues to _____		
Transfer fee to Management Co.		
Special Hazard Disclosure		
[Utility] Payment to _____		
Assessments		
School Taxes		
City/town taxes		
County Taxes/County Property taxes		
Buyer Attorney fees to _____		
Seller Attorney fees to _____		
	Debit	**Credit**
Subtotals		
Due From/To Borrower		
Due From/To Seller		
Totals		

Acknowledgement

We/I have carefully reviewed the ALTA Settlement Statement and find it to be a true and accurate statement of all receipts and disbursements made on my account or by me in this transaction and further certify that I have received a copy of the ALTA Settlement Statement. We/I authorize _____ *title company name* _____ to cause the funds to be disbursed in accordance with this statement.

_____
Barry Borrower

_____
Barbara Borrower

_____
Escrow Officer

File #
Printed on (date) at (time)

SECOND NATIONAL
Crucial Data Proof Sheet

Prepared for:
ANPAC FUNDING CORP. D/B/A ANPAC LENDING GROUP
1401 COVE STREET, SUITE 100
NEWPORT BEACH, CALIFORNIA 92660
FHA/VA #:
Refinance?: 00 Yes
Loan number: 2500020183
Loan Type: CONVENTIONAL

Borrower #1: **BARRY BORROWER**
Manner of Title: **AND**
AKA: POA:

Borrower #2: **BARBARA BORROWER**
Manner of Title: **HUSBAND AND WIFE AS COMMUNITY PROPERTY**
AKA: POA:

Borrower #3:
Manner of Title:
AKA: POA:

Borrower #4: Manner of Title:
AKA: POA:

Borrower #5:
Manner of Title:
AKA: POA:

Borrower #6:
Manner of Title:
AKA: POA:

Property Address: 1000 ANYWHERE STREET, ANY CITY, AS 00000

Mailing Address: 1000 ANYWHERE STREET, ANY CITY, AS 00000

Prior Address:

Sellers:

Loan closing in the name of: ANPAC FUNDING CORP. D/B/A ANPACT LENDING GROUP, A CALIFORNIA CORPORATION

Address: 1401 COVE STREET, SUITE 100, NEWPORT BEACH, CALIFORNIA 92660

State of incorporation: THE STATE OF CALIFORNIA
Investor (if applicable): ANPAC FUNDING CORPORATION

Loan Amount: $ 166,500.00	Interest rate: 6.37500%	1st payment date: 12/01/XX
Sale price: $	Appraised value: $185,000.00	Closing/document date: 10/02/XX
Late charge: 5.000%	Maturity date: 11/01/XX	Disbursement date: 10/07/XX
Actual term: 360 mos.	Amortized term: 360 mos.	Rescission date:

Settlement agent: ESCROW PALACE   Settlement county:
Settlement address: 23161 LAKE DR. STE.120, ANY CITY, AS 00000
Property county: LOS ANGELES   Riders: **X** ARM   ____Condo   ____PUD   ____GPM
____1-4 Family   ____VAAssumptn   ____Other
Legal Description:
THE LAND REFERRED TO IN THIS DESCRIPTION SITUATED IN THE STATE OF CALIFORNIA,
COUNTY OF LOS ANGELES, CITY OF LOS ANGELES AND IS DESCRIBED AS FOLLOWS:

Condo/PUD name:
PUD description: COVENANTS, CONDITIONS & RESTRICTIONS OF RECORD

Trustee(s): RON MORRISON - GENERAL COUNSEL

Trustee address(es): 1401 COVE STREET, SUITE 100, NEWPORT BEACH, CALIFORNIA 92660

P&I:	$ 884.53					ARM (if applicable)	
MIP/PMI:	173.43	X				Change period: 6 months	
Haz. Ins.:	52.73	X	11	mos. escrow = $	580.03	1st change date: MAY, 20XX	
Flood Ins.:		X		mos. escrow = $		Index: 1.68900	
Cnty taxes:	106.09	X	4	mos. escrow = $	424.36	Margin: 2.75000	
City taxes:		X		mos. escrow = $		Rate cap: 1.00000	
Other taxes:		X		mos. escrow = $		Lifetime cap: 6.00000	
Other taxes:		X		mos. escrow = $			
						Buydown (if applicable):	
Total PITI:	$ 1,216.78					Rate P&I B/D	
						1st:	
						2nd:	
						3rd:	
						Total buydown amount: $	

(See also: TIL Worksheet. HUD-1 and Itemization.)

To Settlement Agent: ESCROW PALACE
23161 LAKE DR. STE. 120
ANY CITY, AS 00000

Attn: GEORGIA Phone No. (000) 380-7899
Fax No. 1-949-380-7899
Escrow/Closing No. 52944

From Lender:
ANPAC FUNDING CORP. D/B/A ANPAC
1401 COVE STREET, SUITE 100 NEWPORT
BEACH, CALIFORNIA 92660

Funder: EMAIL, A
Phone No. 949-567-4174
E-mail Addr: AEMAIL@ANPAC.COM
Fax No. 949-475-3962
Loan No. 2500020183

CLOSING INSTRUCTIONS

You are engaged to close this loan in accordance with these Closing Instructions. If there are any discrepancies; if any of the closing conditions and/or requirements cannot be met; or if the loan does not close as scheduled contact the Lender immediately and return funds disbursed by Lender unless Lender has extended closing in writing.

You may not impose any additional charges on the Lender's behalf without obtaining the Lender's prior approval.

Scheduled Closing Date: OCTOBER 02, 20XX
Scheduled Disbursement Date: OCTOBER 07, 20XX

Borrower: BARRY BORROWER AND BARBARA BORROWER
Seller:

Property Address: 1000 ANYWHERE STREET, ANY CITY, AS 00000

Loan Type: Conventional   Loan Amount $ 166,500.00   Interest Rate: 6.37500
                                                        Second Home ____ Yes __X_ No

Rescindable: _X_ Yes ____ No   Owner-occupied _X_ Yes ____ No
HUD-1 to be prepared by Settlement Agent and faxed to 949-475-3962.

Section I: LENDER CLOSING INSTRUCTIONS

The following are lender closing conditions to be satisfied prior to loan closing. If you have any questions about any of these conditions, please contact the lender as soon as possible. Please collect the required document(s) and fax to the lender for lender's approval prior to closing.

Brokers checks will be held, in all wet funding states, until Funder has confirmed receipt of all original documentation.

NOTE: Any changes to the terms of the closing must be prior approved by ANPAC lending, if not the Closer and/or Title may be liable.

1   BORROWER(S) MUST INITIAL EACH PAGE OF THE DEED/MORTGAGE, RIDERS, AND THE NOTE, PER INVESTORS REQUIREMENTS.
2   CLOSING AGENT IS AUTHORIZED TO COMPLETE VESTING PER STATE REQUIREMENTS.
3   PRIOR TO FUNDS BEING DISBURSED, EXECUTED DOCUMENTS MUST BE RECEIVED BY ANPAC FOR All RESCINDABLE TRANSACTIONS.
4   ILG REQUIRES AN INDEPENDENT 3RD PARTY TO SUPERVISE AND NOTARIZE ALL LOAN DOCUMENTS AT CLOSING.
5   ORIGINAL SIGNED INITIAL GFE & TIL IN ACCORDANCE WITH CALIFORNIA AB 795 PRIOR TO FUNDING.
6   HAZARD INSURANCE SUFFICIENT TO COVER LOAN AMOUNT/REPLACEMENT COST
7   FINAL 1003 WITH CORRECT TERMS OF LOAN AMOUNT, NOTE RATE, INS, TAXES. MI, ETC..SIGNED BY BORROWER & INTERVIEWER - BROKER TO PROVIDE. **NEED CORRECT EMPLOYMENT INFO.**
8   ESTIMATED HUD/SETTLEMENT STATEMENT TO INCLUDE ALL CLOSING AGENT FEES ** RECD CLOSING TO REVIEW **
9   COPY OF CURRENT DEMANDS (2) FOR REVIEW ** RECD CLOSING TO REVIEW **
10 THE FOLLOWING DEBT TO BE PAID IN FULL - BALANCES TO BE VERIFIED BY PAYOFF STATEMENT: CHASE MANHATTAN MTG ($114,666) IRWIN HOME EQUITY   ($39,452)

Section II   HAZARD INSURANCE/FLOOD INSURANCE

X_____   Collect original fire and extended coverage insurance policy or other evidence of insurance for not less than the loan amount or the replacement cost of improvements, together with evidence of payment for all purchase money transactions.

X_____   Mortgagee clause must indicate the following:
ANPAC Funding Corporation
c/o Lender Funding, Inc.
P O Box 57018 Irvine, CA 92619-7018
1-888-281-3681

X_____   Collect Notice of Flood Insurance Requirement.

X_____   Collect executed application for flood insurance, together with evidence of payment or all purchase money transactions.

Section III   SURVEY

X_____   Collect Survey (2 copies required if applicable)

Section IV   POWER OF ATTORNEY

ALL POWERS OF ATTORNEY MUST BE PRIOR APPROVED BY LENDER.

X_____   Collect Specific Power of Attorney (original) to be recorded.

Section V   RESCISSION

X_____   Deliver 2 copies of Notice of Right to Cancel to each person whose ownership in their principal residence will be subject to the Security Instrument.

X_____   Deleting or removing an existing mortgagor from title as a direct result of this transaction requires the removed mortgagors signature on the Notice of Right to Cancel.

X_____   Closer is required to add a date that is 3 days after the date the borrower signs the Notice of Right to Cancel form in the "How to Cancel" section of the Notice of Right to Cancel form.

X_____   Obtain an acknowledgement of receipt from each person receiving a Notice of Right to Cancel.

X_____   Prior to disbursing the loan on the Closer must reconfirm with all parties to the transaction, including the ANPAC Lending under that the ANPAC Lending loan is to close.

Section VI   TAXES/ASSESSMENTS

X_____   Obtain tax certificate or other evidence of payment indicating payment of all real estate taxes due and payable at time of closing.

X_____   Obtain tax certificate, a signed statement from an authorized representative of the assessment district or other evidence of payment indicating payment of all special assessments or special district taxes due and payable at closing, together with an assumption of liability for all special assessments or special district taxes not yet due and payable. Collect a statement from the water and/or sewer district or other evidence of payment indicating payment of all water and sewer charges due and payable.

Section VII   TITLE INSURANCE COMMITMENT/POLICY

X_____   Prior to disbursement, update title commitment to the date of closing.

X_____   Fax written update to lender prior to closing.

X_____   Within 120 days after loan closing, mail a final Title Policy to: ANPAC FUNDING CORP. D/B/A ANPAC LENDING GROUP 1401 COVE Street, Suite 100, Document Control Newport Beach, CA 92660

X_____   ALTA Policy must contain endorsements 100, 116, 8.1 and 111.5

X_____   Collect payment for all listed endorsements and include in final ALTA policy.

X_____   Liability subject only to: General taxes and special taxes for fiscal year MUST BE CURRENT

X_____   Funds may be used for account of the vestees, and you will record all instruments when you comply with the following:
    X   The vesting should read as follows: - BARRY BORROWER AND BARBARA BORROWER HUSBAND AND WIFE AS COMMUNITY PROPERTY
    X   Issue said form of policy showing title vested as shown above.
    X   ALTA policy must cover $ 166,500.00
    X   Issue said form of ALTA policy free from encumbrances except items: 3, 6, and 7 of preliminary Title Report dated 07-30-XX
    ___ Secondary financing in the amount of $ NOT ALLOWED

Section VIII.   ESCROW ACCOUNTING

X_____   Prior to releasing the wired funds the Closer must updated estimated HUD-1.

X_____   Insert an aggregate escrow adjustment amount of $ -52.82 in the last line of the 1000 series of the HUD-1 Settlement Statement.

Section IX. RECORDING INSTRUCTIONS

X_____   Record the following documents with the Clerk and Recorder of **LOS ANGELES** County State of **CALIFORNIA** order and within the necessary timeframes for issuance of a Title Policy meeting Lender's closing conditions/requirements.

_____   Specific Power of Attorney for Seller
_____   Deed from Seller vesting title in Borrower
_____   Specific Power of Attorney for Borrower
_____   Security Instrument, with any Riders
_____   Assignment to ANPAC FUNDING CORPORATION
_____   Return address for Security Instrument and any Riders sent for recording should be: ANPAC FUNDING CORP. D/B/A ANPAC LENDING GROUP 1401 COVE Street, Suite100, Document Control Newport Beach, CA 92606
_____   Return address for assignment sent for recording should be: ANPAC FUNDING CORP. D/B/A ANPAC LENDING GROUP 1401 COVE Street, Suite100, Document Control Newport Beach, CA 92606
_____   Return address for Borrower's Power of Attorney sent for recording should be:
_____   Return address for Seller's Power of Attorney sent for recording should be:

Section X. DISBURSEMENT REQUIREMENTS

X_____   **When the transaction is a rescindable transaction, do not disburse and/or deposit any funds until the expiration of the rescission period.** The Closer must reconfirm with all parties to the transaction, including the ANPAC Lending Funder that the ANPAC Lending loan is to close.

X_____   Funds for this transaction shall be delivered in the form of a wire transfer. *If funds are not disbursed within 48 hours of receipt said funds must be returned to Lender and may be subject to penalty.*

Return wiring instructions:

Bank: *Banker's Trust Company*
Address: *New York, N.Y. 10006*
ABA#:   *0000000000*
Acct#:   *00000000*
Acct Name: *ANPAC/CDC 00000*
Credit To: *0000000000*

X_____   **Broker checks will be held, in all wet funding states, until Funder has confirmed receipt of all original documentation.**

X_____   If an invoice is provided, disburse directly to the service provider as instructed on HUD-1 Settlement Statement.

Section XI. DELIVERY OF DOCUMENTATION

X_____   Within 48 hours of funding the following documents must be delivered to lender by next day overnight at: ANPAC lending Group 1401 COVE Street, Suite 100, FUNDING Newport Beach, CA 92606

X_____   When the transaction is a rescindable transaction all loan documents must be returned and reviewed by the lender prior to funding.

NOTE: All documents must show signatures and dates. All signatures on documents must exactly match names as typed and as appear in recorded documents. All documents must be signed in person, after you have obtained proper identification, and signatures must be acknowledged by a notary public if there is an acknowledgement block included in a document.

ALL FEDERAL TRUTH-IN-LENDING DISCLOSURES MUST BE EXECUTED PRIOR TO EXECUTION OF THE NOTE, SECURITY INSTRUMENT AND OTHER LOAN DOCUMENTS.

Documents to be collected from Borrower:
X__   Evidence of completion of all lender closing conditions listed in Section I above.
X__   Hazard insurance policy or certificate of insurance.
___   Flood insurance application, together with evidence of payment of flood insurance premium.
___   Survey.

Section XI. DELIVERY OF DOCUMENTATION (cont.)

Documents to be provided by Lender:

X	Original and/or certified copies of Note, with any Riders.
	X certified copies of Security Instrument, with any Riders.
	X certified copies of Assignment.
	X certified copies of Deed, with any Riders.
X	Original Truth-in-Lending Disclosure and copy of any requested Financed.
X	Compliance Agreement
X	Acknowledgement of Receipt of Notice of Right to cancel.
X	I.R.S. Form W-9 or W-8.
X	Name Affidavit.
X	Initial Escrow Account Statement.
X	First Payment Letter.
X	Occupancy Affidavit.
X	Notice of Transfer of Servicing.
X	State of California requires Borrowers to execute the Truth and Lending documents.
_____	
_____	
_____	
_____	

Documents to be provided by Settlement Agent:

X	Copies of the following disbursement checks:
	_____ Mortgage Insurance Premium
	_____ Hazard Insurance Premium
	_____ Broker Fee
	_____
	_____
	_____
X	Certified copy of Specific Power of Attorney for Borrower & Seller, as applicable
X	Original HUD-1 Settlement Statement with 2 certified copies
X	Original Buyer/Seller Statements Lien Affidavit
X	Copy of Payoffs
X	Copy of Tax Information Form
X	Copy of Tax Agreement(s) and Tax certificate.
_____	
_____	
_____	
_____	
X	When the transaction is a rescindable transaction all loan documents must be returned and reviewed by the Lender prior to funding.
X	Delivery of the warehouse/collateral package, including original Note, according to instructions previously provided by Lender.
X	**DELIVERY OF DOCUMENTS TO LENDER IS AT SETTLEMENT AGENTS EXPENSE.**

Section XII. MISCELLANEOUS

On _____, I/we have closed this loan in accordance with these Closing Instructions. In addition, all required documentation is included in this closing package.

_____   _____
BY: Title

2500020183

BORROWER
1277 ANYWERE STREET
ANY CITY, AS 00000

ANPAC FUNDING CORP.
D/B/A ANPAC LENDING GROUP,
A CALIFORNIA CORPORATION

PRIVATE MORTGAGE INSURANCE TERMINATION DISCLOSURE
(Adjustable Rate, Not High Risk)

We (Lender) require that you (Borrower) maintain private mortgage insurance ("PMI") in connection with your mortgage loan. PMI protects lenders and others against financial loss if borrowers default. Federal law provides that, under certain circumstances, you may have the right to cancel PMI. Federal law also establishes when PMI must be terminated. This Disclosure describes those cancellation and termination rights.

Please note that PMI is not the same as property/casualty insurance, which may protect you against damage to your property, and cancellation or termination of PMI does not affect any types of insurance.

I. BORROWER CANCELLATION.

You have the right to request cancellation of PMI at any time on or after:

(1) the date on which the principal balance of the loan, based solely on the amortization schedule then in effect, is first scheduled to reach 80% of the original value of the property securing the loan. [If your mortgage loan is a balloon loan, this date may not be reached before your loan matures.]; or

(2) the date on which the principal balance of the loan, based solely on actual payments made, reaches 80% of the original value of the property securing the loan.

You will be notified when these dates are reached.

"Original value" means the lesser of the sales price or the appraised value of the property securing the loan. If this is a refinance loan, "original value" means the appraised value relied on by us to approve your loan.

PMI shall then be cancelled if you meet all of the following requirements:

(1) You must submit your cancellation request in writing to the servicer of your loan.

(2) You must have a good payment history on your loan. "Good payment history" means that you have not made a mortgage payment that was 60 days or longer past due during the 24 months preceding the later of the cancellation date or the date of your last cancellation request and that you have not made a mortgage payment that was 30 days or longer past due during the 12 months preceding the later of the cancellation date or the date of your cancellation request.

(3) You must be current on your mortgage loan payments as required by the terms of your mortgage loan.

Page 1

(4) You must have satisfied the note holder's requests for:

(a) evidence that the value of the property securing the note has not declined below its original value; and

(b) certification that you do not have a subordinate lien on the equity in the property.

2. AUTOMATIC TERMINATION

If you are current on your mortgage loan payments, PMI will automatically terminate when the principal balance of your loan is scheduled to reach, based solely on the amortization schedule then in effect, 78% of the original value, unless you will earlier reach 75% of the original appraised value of the property. [If your mortgage loan is a balloon loan, this date may not be reached before your loan matures.) If, on that date, you are not current on your mortgage loan payments, PMI will automatically terminate on the first day of the first month after the date on which you become current.

3. EXEMPTIONS

There are certain exemptions to the right to cancellation and automatic termination of PMI. These exemptions relate to certain mortgage loans with higher risks associated with the extension of credit. These exemptions do not apply to your loan transaction.

4. STATE LAW

If your property is located in California, Minnesota or New York, state law may require that PMI on your loan be terminated earlier than the Borrower Cancellation and Automatic Termination dates described above. If you have any questions about the applicability of state law to PMI on your loan, please contact the servicer of your loan.

_____

BARRY BORROWER

_____

BARBARA BORROWER

BORROWER
1277 ANYWHERE STREET
ANY CITY, AS 00000

ANPAC FUNDING CORP.
D/B/A ANPAC CORPORATION

California Private Mortgage Insurance Cancellation Disclosure

We will require that you obtain and maintain private mortgage insurance in connection
loan.

_____ If this box is checked, you do not have the right to cancel the privat
insurance.

__XX__ If this box is checked, you may have the right to cancel the private
insurance. Cancellation may be based on various factors, including
in property value based on a current appraisal. Cancellation is als
the following conditions:

I. You must make your request in writing and address It to: ANPAC FUNDING CORP. D/B/A
ANPAC LENDING GROUP, A CALIFORNIA CORPORATION

1401 COVE STREET, SUITE 100 NEWPORT BEACH, CALIFORNIA 92660

If the servicing of your loan is transferred, you must send your request to your new loan servicer at
the address for written customer service inquiries that will be given to you at the time the servicing is
transferred.

2. Your request must include a statement that you wish to cancel your private mortgage insurance,
your name as it appears in the lender's records, the property address and your loan number.

3. It must be at least 2 years since your loan closed.

4. The unpaid principal balance of the loan must be reduced to 80% or less of either:

   (a) the original purchase price, provided the current fair market value is equal to or greater than
   the original appraised value used at origination; or

   (b) the current fair market value. If the note holder requires a new appraisal, you must pay for
   the appraisal and the appraisal must be performed by an appraiser selected by the note holder.

5. All monetary obligations of your loan must be current at the time of your request, and you must
not have been delinquent in payments more than one time over the 24-month period immediately
preceding your request.

6. No other defaults under the terms of your deed of trust may have occurred during the 12-month
period immediately preceding your request.

Page 1

7. No notice of default has been recorded against your property as a result of non-monetary default by you during the 24-month period immediately preceding your request.

8. You must satisfy the criteria for cancellation of private mortgage insurance of any subsequent purchasers of your note or the note holder's successors and assigns.

AUTOMATIC TERMINATION

Private mortgage insurance will be automatically canceled when the principal balance of your loan reaches 75% of the lessor of (1) the sales price of the property (if the loan was for the purchase of the property) or (2) the original appraised value of the property, provided that all of the following conditions are met:

> **A.** You occupy the property as your primary or second residence.

> **B.** All monetary obligations of your loan are current and you have not been more than 30 days delinquent in payments or have been assessed more than one late penalty over the 12-month period immediately preceding the termination date.

> **C.** No other defaults under the terms of your mortgage may have occurred during the 12-month period immediately preceding the cancellation date.

> **D.** No notice of default may have been recorded against your property as a result of non-monetary default by you during the 12-month period immediately preceding the termination date.

If you do not occupy the property as your primary or secondary residence, your rights to cancel mortgage insurance will vary depending on the note holder's requirements. The requirements of the note holder are subject to change, and the note may be transferred to a new note holder. Consequently, if at any time you want to determine whether you may cancel your mortgage insurance, you should contact your loan servicer to determine the cancellation requirements in effect at that time.

By signing below, you acknowledge receiving a copy of this Disclosure.

_____   _____
BARRY BORROWER   **DATE**

_____   _____
BARBARA BORROWER   **DATE**

Page 2

After Recording Return To:
ANPAC FUNDING CORP. D/B/A ANPAC LENDING GROUP
1401 COVE STREET, SUITE 100
NEWPORT BEACH, CALFORNIA 92660

Recording Requested By:
ANPAC FUNDING CORP. D/B/A ANPAC LENDING GROUP
1401 COVE STREET, SUITE 100
NEWPORT BEACH, CALFORNIA 92660

_____[Space Above This Line For Recording Data]_____

DEED OF TRUST

DEFINITIONS

Words used in multiple sections of this document are defined below and other words are defined in
13, 18, 20 and 21. Certain rules regarding the usage of words used in this document are also provide

(A) "**Security Instrument**" means this document, which is dated **OCTOBER 02, 20XX,**
Riders to this document.
(B) "**Borrower**" is **BARRY BORROWER AND BARBARA BORROWER HUSBAND**
COMMUNITY PROPERTY
Borrower is the trustor under this Security Instrument.
(C) "**Lender**" is **ANPAC FUNDING CORP. D/B/A ANPAC LENDING**
CALIFORNIA CORPORATION
Lender is a **CORPORATION** organized and existing under the laws of **THE STATE OF CALIFC**
Lender's address is **1401 COVE STREET, SUITE 100 NEWPORT BEACH, CALFORNIA 926**
Lender is the beneficiary under this Security Instrument.
(D) "**Trustee**" is **VAN MORRISON -- GENERAL COUNSEL**
1401 COVE STREET, SUITE 100 NEWPORT BEACH, CALFORNIA 92660
(E) "**Note**" means the promissory note signed by Borrower and dated **OCTOBER 02, 20XX**
that Borrower owes Lender **ONE HUNDRED SIXTY SIX THOUSAND FIVE HUNDRD AND 0**
Dollars (U.S. $166,500.00) plus interest. Borrower has promised to pay this debt in regular Period
to pay the debt in full not later than **NOVEMBER 01, 20XX**.
(F) "**Property**" means the property that is described below under the heading "Transfer
Property."
(G) "**Loan**" means the debt evidenced by the Note, plus interest, any prepayment charges and late charges due
under the Note, and all sums due under this Security Instrument, plus interest.
(H) "**Riders**" means all Riders to this Security Instrument that are executed by Borrower. The following
Riders are to be executed by Borrower [check box as applicable]:

_X_ Adjustable Rate Rider	___ Condominium Rider	___ Second Home Rider☒
___ Balloon Rider	___ Planned Unit Development Rider	___ Other(s) [specify] ___ ___
___ 1-4 Family Rider	___ Biweekly Payment Rider	_____

CALIFORNIA--Single Family--**Fannie Mae/Freddie Mac UNIFORM INSTRUMENT**   Form 3005   1/01   *(page 1 of 11 pages)*

NOTES

The security instrument ("Deed of Trust" or "Mortgage") may, depending upon the transaction, appear slightly different.

The full "Deed of Trust" is reprinted for this loan, but subsequent security instruments are abridged for space considerations.

Note that under Item H, the checkbox "Adjustable Rate Rider" is selected. The Notary Signing Agent should ensure this rider is found in the documentation package. Absence of a rider that is flagged in the security instrument constitutes a "blank space" in the instrument. The security instrument (and any other notarized document) should never be notarized without all referenced attachments and exhibits present.

Borrower needs to sign on page 11 of document. This is also where the acknowledgment certificate appears.

Refinance Loans

(I) **"Applicable Law"** means all controlling applicable federal, state and local statutes, regulations, ordinances and administrative rules and orders (that have the effect of law) as well as all applicable final, non-appealable judicial opinions.

(J) **"Community Association Dues, Fees, and Assessments"** means all dues, fees, assessments and other charges that are imposed on Borrower or the Property by a condominium association, homeowners association or similar organization.

(K) **"Electronic Funds Transfer"** means any transfer of funds, other than a transaction originated by check, draft, or similar paper instrument, which is initiated through an electronic terminal, telephonic instrument, computer, or magnetic tape so as to order, instruct, or authorize a financial institution to debit or credit an account. Such term includes, but is not limited to, point-of-sale transfers, automated teller machine transactions, transfers initiated by telephone, wire transfers, and automated clearinghouse transfers.

(L) **"Escrow Items"** means those items that are described in Section 3.

(M) **"Miscellaneous Proceeds"** means any compensation, settlement, award of damages, or proceeds paid by any third party (other than insurance proceeds paid under the coverages described in Section 5) for: (i) damage to, or destruction of, the Property; (ii) condemnation or other taking of all or any part of the Property; (iii) conveyance in lieu of condemnation; or (iv) misrepresentations of, or omissions as to, the value and/or condition of the Property.

(N) **"Mortgage Insurance"** means insurance protecting Lender against the nonpayment of, or default on, the Loan.

(O) **"Periodic Payment"** means the regularly scheduled amount due for (i) principal and interest under the Note, plus (ii) any amounts under Section 3 of this Security Instrument.

(P) **"RESPA"** means the Real Estate Settlement Procedures Act (12 U.S.C. §2601 et seq.) and its implementing regulation, Regulation X (24 C.F.R. Part 3500), as they might be amended from time to time, or any additional or successor legislation or regulation that governs the same subject matter. As used in this Security Instrument, "RESPA" refers to all requirements and restrictions that are imposed in regard to a "federally related mortgage loan" even if the Loan does not qualify as a "federally related mortgage loan" under RESPA.

(Q) **"Successor in Interest of Borrower"** means any party that has taken title to the Property, whether or not that party has assumed Borrower's obligations under the Note and/or this Security Instrument.

TRANSFER OF RIGHTS IN THE PROPERTY

This Security Instrument secures to Lender: (i) the repayment of the Loan, and all renewals, extensions and modifications of the Note; and (ii) the performance of Borrower's covenants and agreements under this Security Instrument and the Note. For this purpose, Borrower irrevocably grants and conveys to Trustee, in trust, with power of sale, the following described property located in the **COUNTY** of **LOS ANGELES**

[Type of Recording Jurisdiction]   [Name of Recording Jurisdiction]

THE LAND REFERRED TO IN THIS DESCRIPTION SITUATED IN THE STATE OF ANY STATE, COUNTY OF ANY COUNTY, CITY OF ANY CITY AND IS DESCRIBED AS FOLLOWS:

which currently has the address of **1000 ANYWHERE STREET**

[Street]

ANY CITY, AS **00000**   ("Property Address"):

[City]   [Zip Code]

TOGETHER WITH all the improvements now or hereafter erected on the property, and all easements, appurtenances, and fixtures now or hereafter a part of the property. All replacements and additions shall also be covered by this Security Instrument. All of the foregoing is referred to in this Security Instrument as the "Property."

BORROWER COVENANTS that Borrower is lawfully seised of the estate hereby conveyed and has the right to grant and convey the Property and that the Property is unencumbered, except for encumbrances of record. Borrower warrants and will defend generally the title to the Property against all claims and demands, subject to any encumbrances of record.

THIS SECURITY INSTRUMENT combines uniform covenants for national use and non-uniform covenants with limited variations by jurisdiction to constitute a uniform security instrument covering real property.

CALIFORNIA--Single Family--**Fannie Mae/Freddie Mac UNIFORM INSTRUMENT**   **Form 3005**   1/01   *(page 2 of 11 pages)*

UNIFORM COVENANTS. Borrower and Lender covenant and agree as follows:

1.   Payment of Principal, Interest, Escrow Items, Prepayment Charges, and Late Charges. Borrower shall pay when due the principal of, and interest on, the debt evidenced by the Note and any prepayment charges and late charges due under the Note. Borrower shall also pay funds for Escrow Items pursuant to Section 3. Payments due under the Note and this Security Instrument shall be made in U.S. currency. However, if any check or other instrument received by Lender as payment under the Note or this Security Instrument is returned to Lender unpaid, Lender may require that any or all subsequent payments due under the Note and this Security Instrument be made in one or more of the following forms, as selected by Lender: (a) cash; (b) money order; (c) certified check, bank check, treasurer's check or cashier's check, provided any such check is drawn upon an institution whose deposits are insured by a federal agency, instrumentality, or entity; or (d) Electronic Funds Transfer.

Payments are deemed received by Lender when received at the location designated in the Note or at such other location as may be designated by Lender in accordance with the notice provisions in Section 15. Lender may return any payment or partial payment if the payment or partial payments are insufficient to bring the Loan current. Lender may accept any payment or partial payment insufficient to bring the Loan current, without waiver of any rights hereunder or prejudice to its rights to refuse such payment or partial payments in the future, but Lender is not obligated to apply such payments at the time such payments are accepted. If each Periodic Payment is applied as of its scheduled due date, then Lender need not pay interest on unapplied funds. Lender may hold such unapplied funds until Borrower makes payment to bring the Loan current. If Borrower does not do so within a reasonable period of time, Lender shall either apply such funds or return them to Borrower. If not applied earlier, such funds will be applied to the outstanding principal balance under the Note immediately prior to foreclosure. No offset or claim which Borrower might have now or in the future against Lender shall relieve Borrower from making payments due under the Note and this Security Instrument or performing the covenants and agreements secured by this Security Instrument.

2.   Application of Payments or Proceeds. Except as otherwise described in this Section 2, all payments accepted and applied by Lender shall be applied in the following order of priority: (a) interest due under the Note; (b) principal due under the Note; (c) amounts due under Section 3. Such payments shall be applied to each Periodic Payment in the order in which it became due. Any remaining amounts shall be applied first to late charges, second to any other amounts due under this Security Instrument, and then to reduce the principal balance of the Note.

If Lender receives a payment from Borrower for a delinquent Periodic Payment which includes a sufficient amount to pay any late charge due, the payment may be applied to the delinquent payment and the late charge. If more than one Periodic Payment is outstanding, Lender may apply any payment received from Borrower to the repayment of the Periodic Payments if, and to the extent that, each payment can be paid in full. To the extent that any excess exists after the payment is applied to the full payment of one or more Periodic Payments, such excess may be applied to any late charges due. Voluntary prepayments shall be applied first to any prepayment charges and then as described in the Note.

Any application of payments, insurance proceeds, or Miscellaneous Proceeds to principal due under the Note shall not extend or postpone the due date, or change the amount, of the Periodic Payments.

3.   Funds for Escrow Items. Borrower shall pay to Lender on the day Periodic Payments are due under the Note, until the Note is paid in full, a sum (the "Funds") to provide for payment of amounts due for: (a) taxes and assessments and other items which can attain priority over this Security Instrument as a lien or encumbrance on the Property; (b) leasehold payments or ground rents on the Property, if any; (c) premiums for any and all insurance required by Lender under Section 5; and (d) Mortgage Insurance premiums, if any, or any sums payable by Borrower to Lender in lieu of the payment of Mortgage Insurance premiums in accordance with the provisions of Section 10. These items are called "Escrow Items." At origination or at any time during the term of the Loan, Lender may require that Community Association Dues, Fees, and Assessments, if any, be escrowed by Borrower, and such dues, fees and assessments shall be an Escrow Item. Borrower shall promptly furnish to Lender all notices of amounts to be paid under this Section. Borrower shall pay Lender the Funds for Escrow Items unless Lender waives Borrower's obligation to pay the Funds for any or all Escrow Items. Lender may waive Borrower's obligation to pay to Lender Funds for any or all Escrow Items at any time. Any such waiver may only be in writing. In the event of such waiver, Borrower shall pay directly, when and where payable, the amounts due for any Escrow Items for which payment of Funds has been waived by Lender and, if Lender requires, shall furnish to Lender receipts evidencing such payment within such time period as Lender may require. Borrower's obligation to make such payments and to provide receipts shall for all purposes be deemed to be a covenant and agreement contained in this Security Instrument, as the phrase "covenant and agreement" is used in Section 9. If Borrower is obligated to pay Escrow Items directly, pursuant to a waiver, and Borrower fails to pay the amount due for an Escrow Item, Lender may exercise its rights under Section 9 and pay such amount and Borrower shall then be obligated under Section 9 to repay to Lender any such amount. Lender may revoke the waiver as to any or all Escrow Items at any

CALIFORNIA--Single Family--**Fannie Mae/Freddie Mac UNIFORM INSTRUMENT**   Form 3005   1/01   *(page 3 of 11 pages)*

time by a notice given in accordance with Section 15 and, upon such revocation, Borrower shall pay to Lender all Funds, and in such amounts, that are then required under this Section 3.

Lender may, at any time, collect and hold Funds in an amount (a) sufficient to permit Lender to apply the Funds at the time specified under RESPA, and (b) not to exceed the maximum amount a lender can require under RESPA. Lender shall estimate the amount of Funds due on the basis of current data and reasonable estimates of expenditures of future Escrow Items or otherwise in accordance with Applicable Law.

The Funds shall be held in an institution whose deposits are insured by a federal agency, instrumentality, or entity (including Lender, if Lender is an institution whose deposits are so insured) or in any Federal Home Loan Bank. Lender shall apply the Funds to pay the Escrow Items no later than the time specified under RESPA. Lender shall not charge Borrower for holding and applying the Funds, annually analyzing the escrow account, or verifying the Escrow Items, unless Lender pays Borrower interest on the Funds and Applicable Law permits Lender to make such a charge. Unless an agreement is made in writing or Applicable Law requires interest to be paid on the Funds, Lender shall not be required to pay Borrower any interest or earnings on the Funds. Borrower and Lender can agree in writing, however, that interest shall be paid on the Funds. Lender shall give to Borrower, without charge, an annual accounting of the Funds as required by RESPA.

If there is a surplus of Funds held in escrow, as defined under RESPA, Lender shall account to Borrower for the excess funds in accordance with RESPA. If there is a shortage of Funds held in escrow, as defined under RESPA, Lender shall notify Borrower as required by RESPA, and Borrower shall pay to Lender the amount necessary to make up the shortage in accordance with RESPA, but in no more than 12 monthly payments. If there is a deficiency of Funds held in escrow, as defined under RESPA, Lender shall notify Borrower as required by RESPA, and Borrower shall pay to Lender the amount necessary to make up the deficiency in accordance with RESPA, but in no more than 12 monthly payments.

Upon payment in full of all sums secured by this Security Instrument, Lender shall promptly refund to Borrower any Funds held by Lender.

4.   **Charges; Liens.** Borrower shall pay all taxes, assessments, charges, fines, and impositions attributable to the Property which can attain priority over this Security Instrument, leasehold payments or ground rents on the Property, if any, and Community Association Dues, Fees, and Assessments, if any. To the extent that these items are Escrow Items, Borrower shall pay them in the manner provided in Section 3.

Borrower shall promptly discharge any lien which has priority over this Security Instrument unless Borrower: (a) agrees in writing to the payment of the obligation secured by the lien in a manner acceptable to Lender, but only so long as Borrower is performing such agreement; (b) contests the lien in good faith by, or defends against enforcement of the lien in, legal proceedings which in Lender's opinion operate to prevent the enforcement of the lien while those proceedings are pending, but only until such proceedings are concluded; or (c) secures from the holder of the lien an agreement satisfactory to Lender subordinating the lien to this Security Instrument. If Lender determines that any part of the Property is subject to a lien which can attain priority over this Security Instrument, Lender may give Borrower a notice identifying the lien. Within 10 days of the date on which that notice is given, Borrower shall satisfy the lien or take one or more of the actions set forth above in this Section 4.

Lender may require Borrower to pay a one-time charge for a real estate tax verification and/or reporting service used by Lender in connection with this Loan.

5.   **Property Insurance.** Borrower shall keep the improvements now existing or hereafter erected on the Property insured against loss by fire, hazards included within the term "extended coverage," and any other hazards including, but not limited to, earthquakes and floods, for which Lender requires insurance. This insurance shall be maintained in the amounts (including deductible levels) and for the periods that Lender requires. What Lender requires pursuant to the preceding sentences can change during the term of the Loan. The insurance carrier providing the insurance shall be chosen by Borrower subject to Lender's right to disapprove Borrower's choice, which right shall not be exercised unreasonably. Lender may require Borrower to pay, in connection with this Loan, either: (a) a one-time charge for flood zone determination, certification and tracking services; or (b) a one-time charge for flood zone determination and certification services and subsequent charges each time remappings or similar changes occur which reasonably might affect such determination or certification. Borrower shall also be responsible for the payment of any fees imposed by the Federal Emergency Management Agency in connection with the review of any flood zone determination resulting from an objection by Borrower.

If Borrower fails to maintain any of the coverages described above, Lender may obtain insurance coverage, at Lender's option and Borrower's expense. Lender is under no obligation to purchase any particular type or amount of coverage. Therefore, such coverage shall cover Lender, but might or might not protect Borrower, Borrower's equity in the Property, or the contents of the Property, against any risk, hazard or liability and might provide greater or lesser coverage than was previously in effect. Borrower acknowledges that the cost of the insurance coverage so obtained might significantly exceed the cost of insurance that Borrower could have obtained. Any amounts disbursed by Lender under this Section 5 shall become additional debt of Borrower secured by this Security

CALIFORNIA--Single Family--**Fannie Mae/Freddie Mac UNIFORM INSTRUMENT**   **Form 3005**   **1/01**   *(page 4 of 11 pages)*

Instrument. These amounts shall bear interest at the Note rate from the date of disbursement and shall be payable, with such interest, upon notice from Lender to Borrower requesting payment.

All insurance policies required by Lender and renewals of such policies shall be subject to Lender's right to disapprove such policies, shall include a standard mortgage clause, and shall name Lender as mortgagee and/or as an additional loss payee and Borrower further agrees to generally assign rights to insurance proceeds to the holder of the Note up to the amount of the outstanding loan balance. Lender shall have the right to hold the policies and renewal certificates. If Lender requires, Borrower shall promptly give to Lender all receipts of paid premiums and renewal notices. If Borrower obtains any form of insurance coverage, not otherwise required by Lender, for damage to, or destruction of, the Property, such policy shall include a standard mortgage clause and shall name Lender as mortgagee and/or as an additional loss payee and Borrower further agrees to generally assign rights to insurance proceeds to the holder of the Note up to the amount of the outstanding loan balance.

In the event of loss, Borrower shall give prompt notice to the insurance carrier and Lender. Lender may make proof of loss if not made promptly by Borrower. Unless Lender and Borrower otherwise agree in writing, any insurance proceeds, whether or not the underlying insurance was required by Lender, shall be applied to restoration or repair of the Property, if the restoration or repair is economically feasible and Lender's security is not lessened. During such repair and restoration period, Lender shall have the right to hold such insurance proceeds until Lender has had an opportunity to inspect such Property to ensure the work has been completed to Lender's satisfaction, provided that such inspection shall be undertaken promptly. Lender may disburse proceeds for the repairs and restoration in a single payment or in a series of progress payments as the work is completed. Unless an agreement is made in writing or Applicable Law requires interest to be paid on such insurance proceeds, Lender shall not be required to pay Borrower any interest or earnings on such proceeds. Fees for public adjusters, or other third parties, retained by Borrower shall not be paid out of the insurance proceeds and shall be the sole obligation of Borrower. If the restoration or repair is not economically feasible or Lender's security would be lessened, the insurance proceeds shall be applied to the sums secured by this Security Instrument, whether or not then due, with the excess, if any, paid to Borrower. Such insurance proceeds shall be applied in the order provided for in Section 2.

If Borrower abandons the Property, Lender may file, negotiate and settle any available insurance claim and related matters. If Borrower does not respond within 30 days to a notice from Lender that the insurance carrier has offered to settle a claim, then Lender may negotiate and settle the claim. The 30-day period will begin when the notice is given. In either event, or if Lender acquires the Property under Section 22 or otherwise, Borrower hereby assigns to Lender (a) Borrower's rights to any insurance proceeds in an amount not to exceed the amounts unpaid under the Note or this Security Instrument, and (b) any other of Borrower's rights (other than the right to any refund of unearned premiums paid by Borrower) under all insurance policies covering the Property, insofar as such rights are applicable to the coverage of the Property. Lender may use the insurance proceeds either to repair or restore the Property or to pay amounts unpaid under the Note or this Security Instrument, whether or not then due.

6. **Occupancy.** Borrower shall occupy, establish, and use the Property as Borrower's principal residence within 60 days after the execution of this Security Instrument and shall continue to occupy the Property as Borrower's principal residence for at least one year after the date of occupancy, unless Lender otherwise agrees in writing, which consent shall not be unreasonably withheld, or unless extenuating circumstances exist which are beyond Borrower's control.

7. **Preservation, Maintenance and Protection of the Property; Inspections.** Borrower shall not destroy, damage or impair the Property, allow the Property to deteriorate or commit waste on the Property. Whether or not Borrower is residing in the Property, Borrower shall maintain the Property in order to prevent the Property from deteriorating or decreasing in value due to its condition. Unless it is determined pursuant to Section 5 that repair or restoration is not economically feasible, Borrower shall promptly repair the Property if damaged to avoid further deterioration or damage. If insurance or condemnation proceeds are paid in connection with damage to, or the taking of, the Property, Borrower shall be responsible for repairing or restoring the Property only if Lender has released proceeds for such purposes. Lender may disburse proceeds for the repairs and restoration in a single payment or in a series of progress payments as the work is completed. If the insurance or condemnation proceeds are not sufficient to repair or restore the Property, Borrower is not relieved of Borrower's obligation for the completion of such repair or restoration.

Lender or its agent may make reasonable entries upon and inspections of the Property. If it has reasonable cause, Lender may inspect the interior of the improvements on the Property. Lender shall give Borrower notice at the time of or prior to such an interior inspection specifying such reasonable cause.

8. **Borrower's Loan Application.** Borrower shall be in default if, during the Loan application process, Borrower or any persons or entities acting at the direction of Borrower or with Borrower's knowledge or consent gave materially false, misleading, or inaccurate information or statements to Lender (or failed to provide Lender with material information) in connection with the Loan. Material representations include, but are not limited to, representations concerning Borrower's occupancy of the Property as Borrower's principal residence.

CALIFORNIA--Single Family--**Fannie Mae/Freddie Mac UNIFORM INSTRUMENT**   Form 3005   1/01   *(page 5 of 11 pages)*

9.   Protection of Lender's Interest in the Property and Rights Under this Security Instrument. If (a) Borrower fails to perform the covenants and agreements contained in this Security Instrument, (b) there is a legal proceeding that might significantly affect Lender's interest in the Property and/or rights under this Security Instrument (such as a proceeding in bankruptcy, probate, for condemnation or forfeiture, for enforcement of a lien which may attain priority over this Security Instrument or to enforce laws or regulations), or (c) Borrower has abandoned the Property, then Lender may do and pay for whatever is reasonable or appropriate to protect Lender's interest in the Property and rights under this Security Instrument, including protecting and/or assessing the value of the Property, and securing and/or repairing the Property. Lender's actions can include, but are not limited to: (a) paying any sums secured by a lien which has priority over this Security Instrument; (b) appearing in court; and (c) paying reasonable attorneys' fees to protect its interest in the Property and/or rights under this Security Instrument, including its secured position in a bankruptcy proceeding. Securing the Property includes, but is not limited to, entering the Property to make repairs, change locks, replace or board up doors and windows, drain water from pipes, eliminate building or other code violations or dangerous conditions, and have utilities turned on or off. Although Lender may take action under this Section 9, Lender does not have to do so and is not under any duty or obligation to do so. It is agreed that Lender incurs no liability for not taking any or all actions authorized under this Section 9.

Any amounts disbursed by Lender under this Section 9 shall become additional debt of Borrower secured by this Security Instrument. These amounts shall bear interest at the Note rate from the date of disbursement and shall be payable, with such interest, upon notice from Lender to Borrower requesting payment.

If this Security Instrument is on a leasehold, Borrower shall comply with all the provisions of the lease. If Borrower acquires fee title to the Property, the leasehold and the fee title shall not merge unless Lender agrees to the merger in writing.

10.   Mortgage Insurance. If Lender required Mortgage Insurance as a condition of making the Loan, Borrower shall pay the premiums required to maintain the Mortgage Insurance in effect. If, for any reason, the Mortgage Insurance coverage required by Lender ceases to be available from the mortgage insurer that previously provided such insurance and Borrower was required to make separately designated payments toward the premiums for Mortgage Insurance, Borrower shall pay the premiums required to obtain coverage substantially equivalent to the Mortgage Insurance previously in effect, at a cost substantially equivalent to the cost to Borrower of the Mortgage Insurance previously in effect, from an alternate mortgage insurer selected by Lender. If substantially equivalent Mortgage Insurance coverage is not available, Borrower shall continue to pay to Lender the amount of the separately designated payments that were due when the insurance coverage ceased to be in effect. Lender will accept, use and retain these payments as a non-refundable loss reserve in lieu of Mortgage Insurance. Such loss reserve shall be non-refundable, notwithstanding the fact that the Loan is ultimately paid in full, and Lender shall not be required to pay Borrower any interest or earnings on such loss reserve. Lender can no longer require loss reserve payments if Mortgage Insurance coverage (in the amount and for the period that Lender requires) provided by an insurer selected by Lender again becomes available, is obtained, and Lender requires separately designated payments toward the premiums for Mortgage Insurance. If Lender required Mortgage Insurance as a condition of making the Loan and Borrower was required to make separately designated payments toward the premiums for Mortgage Insurance, Borrower shall pay the premiums required to maintain Mortgage Insurance in effect, or to provide a non-refundable loss reserve, until Lender's requirement for Mortgage Insurance ends in accordance with any written agreement between Borrower and Lender providing for such termination or until termination is required by Applicable Law. Nothing in this Section 10 affects Borrower's obligation to pay interest at the rate provided in the Note.

Mortgage Insurance reimburses Lender (or any entity that purchases the Note) for certain losses it may incur if Borrower does not repay the Loan as agreed. Borrower is not a party to the Mortgage Insurance.

Mortgage insurers evaluate their total risk on all such insurance in force from time to time, and may enter into agreements with other parties that share or modify their risk, or reduce losses. These agreements are on terms and conditions that are satisfactory to the mortgage insurer and the other party (or parties) to these agreements. These agreements may require the mortgage insurer to make payments using any source of funds that the mortgage insurer may have available (which may include funds obtained from Mortgage Insurance premiums).

As a result of these agreements, Lender, any purchaser of the Note, another insurer, any reinsurer, any other entity, or any affiliate of any of the foregoing, may receive (directly or indirectly) amounts that derive from (or might be characterized as) a portion of Borrower's payments for Mortgage Insurance, in exchange for sharing or modifying the mortgage insurer's risk, or reducing losses. If such agreement provides that an affiliate of Lender takes a share of the insurer's risk in exchange for a share of the premiums paid to the insurer, the arrangement is often termed "captive reinsurance." Further:

(a)   Any such agreements will not affect the amounts that Borrower has agreed to pay for Mortgage Insurance, or any other terms of the Loan. Such agreements will not increase the amount Borrower will owe for Mortgage Insurance, and they will not entitle Borrower to any refund.

CALIFORNIA--Single Family--Fannie Mae/Freddie Mac UNIFORM INSTRUMENT   Form 3005   1/01   *(page 6 of 11 pages)*

(b)   Any such agreements will not affect the rights Borrower has - if any - with respect to the Mortgage Insurance under the Homeowners Protection Act of 1998 or any other law. These rights may include the right to receive certain disclosures, to request and obtain cancellation of the Mortgage Insurance, to have the Mortgage Insurance terminated automatically, and/or to receive a refund of any Mortgage Insurance premiums that were unearned at the time of such cancellation or termination.

11.   Assignment of Miscellaneous Proceeds; Forfeiture. All Miscellaneous Proceeds are hereby assigned to and shall be paid to Lender.

If the Property is damaged, such Miscellaneous Proceeds shall be applied to restoration or repair of the Property, if the restoration or repair is economically feasible and Lender's security is not lessened. During such repair and restoration period, Lender shall have the right to hold such Miscellaneous Proceeds until Lender has had an opportunity to inspect such Property to ensure the work has been completed to Lender's satisfaction, provided that such inspection shall be undertaken promptly. Lender may pay for the repairs and restoration in a single disbursement or in a series of progress payments as the work is completed. Unless an agreement is made in writing or Applicable Law requires interest to be paid on such Miscellaneous Proceeds, Lender shall not be required to pay Borrower any interest or earnings on such Miscellaneous Proceeds. If the restoration or repair is not economically feasible or Lender's security would be lessened, the Miscellaneous Proceeds shall be applied to the sums secured by this Security Instrument, whether or not then due, with the excess, if any, paid to Borrower. Such Miscellaneous Proceeds shall be applied in the order provided for in Section 2.

In the event of a total taking, destruction, or loss in value of the Property, the Miscellaneous Proceeds shall be applied to the sums secured by this Security Instrument, whether or not then due, with the excess, if any, paid to Borrower.

In the event of a partial taking, destruction, or loss in value of the Property in which the fair market value of the Property immediately before the partial taking, destruction, or loss in value is equal to or greater than the amount of the sums secured by this Security Instrument immediately before the partial taking, destruction, or loss in value, unless Borrower and Lender otherwise agree in writing, the sums secured by this Security Instrument shall be reduced by the amount of the Miscellaneous Proceeds multiplied by the following fraction: (a) the total amount of the sums secured immediately before the partial taking, destruction, or loss in value divided by (b) the fair market value of the Property immediately before the partial taking, destruction, or loss in value. Any balance shall be paid to Borrower.

In the event of a partial taking, destruction, or loss in value of the Property in which the fair market value of the Property immediately before the partial taking, destruction, or loss in value is less than the amount of the sums secured immediately before the partial taking, destruction, or loss in value, unless Borrower and Lender otherwise agree in writing, the Miscellaneous Proceeds shall be applied to the sums secured by this Security Instrument whether or not the sums are then due.

If the Property is abandoned by Borrower, or if, after notice by Lender to Borrower that the Opposing Party (as defined in the next sentence) offers to make an award to settle a claim for damages, Borrower fails to respond to Lender within 30 days after the date the notice is given, Lender is authorized to collect and apply the Miscellaneous Proceeds either to restoration or repair of the Property or to the sums secured by this Security Instrument, whether or not then due. "Opposing Party" means the third party that owes Borrower Miscellaneous Proceeds or the party against whom Borrower has a right of action in regard to Miscellaneous Proceeds.

Borrower shall be in default if any action or proceeding, whether civil or criminal, is begun that, in Lender's judgment, could result in forfeiture of the Property or other material impairment of Lender's interest in the Property or rights under this Security Instrument. Borrower can cure such a default and, if acceleration has occurred, reinstate as provided in Section 19, by causing the action or proceeding to be dismissed with a ruling that, in Lender's judgment, precludes forfeiture of the Property or other material impairment of Lender's interest in the Property or rights under this Security Instrument. The proceeds of any award or claim for damages that are attributable to the impairment of Lender's interest in the Property are hereby assigned and shall be paid to Lender.

All Miscellaneous Proceeds that are not applied to restoration or repair of the Property shall be applied in the order provided for in Section 2.

12.   Borrower Not Released; Forbearance By Lender Not a Waiver. Extension of the time for payment or modification of amortization of the sums secured by this Security Instrument granted by Lender to Borrower or any Successor in Interest of Borrower shall not operate to release the liability of Borrower or any Successors in Interest of Borrower. Lender shall not be required to commence proceedings against any Successor in Interest of Borrower or to refuse to extend time for payment or otherwise modify amortization of the sums secured by this Security Instrument by reason of any demand made by the original Borrower or any Successors in Interest of Borrower. Any forbearance by Lender in exercising any right or remedy including, without limitation, Lender's acceptance of payments from third persons, entities or Successors in Interest of Borrower or in amounts less than the amount then due, shall not be a waiver of or preclude the exercise of any right or remedy.

CALIFORNIA--Single Family--**Fannie Mae/Freddie Mac UNIFORM INSTRUMENT**   **Form 3005**   **1/01**   *(page 7 of 11 pages)*

13.   Joint and Several Liability; Co-signers; Successors and Assigns Bound. Borrower covenants and agrees that Borrower's obligations and liability shall be joint and several. However, any Borrower who co-signs this Security Instrument but does not execute the Note (a "co-signer"): (a) is co-signing this Security Instrument only to mortgage, grant and convey the co-signer's interest in the Property under the terms of this Security Instrument; (b) is not personally obligated to pay the sums secured by this Security Instrument; and (c) agrees that Lender and any other Borrower can agree to extend, modify, forbear or make any accommodations with regard to the terms of this Security Instrument or the Note without the co-signer's consent.

Subject to the provisions of Section 18, any Successor in Interest of Borrower who assumes Borrower's obligations under this Security Instrument in writing, and is approved by Lender, shall obtain all of Borrower's rights and benefits under this Security Instrument. Borrower shall not be released from Borrower's obligations and liability under this Security Instrument unless Lender agrees to such release in writing. The covenants and agreements of this Security Instrument shall bind (except as provided in Section 20) and benefit the successors and assigns of Lender.

14.   Loan Charges. Lender may charge Borrower fees for services performed in connection with Borrower's default, for the purpose of protecting Lender's interest in the Property and rights under this Security Instrument, including, but not limited to, attorneys' fees, property inspection and valuation fees. In regard to any other fees, the absence of express authority in this Security Instrument to charge a specific fee to Borrower shall not be construed as a prohibition on the charging of such fee. Lender may not charge fees that are expressly prohibited by this Security Instrument or by Applicable Law.

If the Loan is subject to a law which sets maximum loan charges, and that law is finally interpreted so that the interest or other loan charges collected or to be collected in connection with the Loan exceed the permitted limits, then: (a) any such loan charge shall be reduced by the amount necessary to reduce the charge to the permitted limit; and (b) any sums already collected from Borrower which exceeded permitted limits will be refunded to Borrower. Lender may choose to make this refund by reducing the principal owed under the Note or by making a direct payment to Borrower. If a refund reduces principal, the reduction will be treated as a partial prepayment without any prepayment charge (whether or not a prepayment charge is provided for under the Note). Borrower's acceptance of any such refund made by direct payment to Borrower will constitute a waiver of any right of action Borrower might have arising out of such overcharge.

15.   Notices. All notices given by Borrower or Lender in connection with this Security Instrument must be in writing. Any notice to Borrower in connection with this Security Instrument shall be deemed to have been given to Borrower when mailed by first class mail or when actually delivered to Borrower's notice address if sent by other means. Notice to any one Borrower shall constitute notice to all Borrowers unless Applicable Law expressly requires otherwise. The notice address shall be the Property Address unless Borrower has designated a substitute notice address by notice to Lender. Borrower shall promptly notify Lender of Borrower's change of address. If Lender specifies a procedure for reporting Borrower's change of address, then Borrower shall only report a change of address through that specified procedure. There may be only one designated notice address under this Security Instrument at any one time. Any notice to Lender shall be given by delivering it or by mailing it by first class mail to Lender's address stated herein unless Lender has designated another address by notice to Borrower. Any notice in connection with this Security Instrument shall not be deemed to have been given to Lender until actually received by Lender. If any notice required by this Security Instrument is also required under Applicable Law, the Applicable Law requirement will satisfy the corresponding requirement under this Security Instrument.

16.   Governing Law; Severability; Rules of Construction. This Security Instrument shall be governed by federal law and the law of the jurisdiction in which the Property is located. All rights and obligations contained in this Security Instrument are subject to any requirements and limitations of Applicable Law. Applicable Law might explicitly or implicitly allow the parties to agree by contract or it might be silent, but such silence shall not be construed as a prohibition against agreement by contract. In the event that any provision or clause of this Security Instrument or the Note conflicts with Applicable Law, such conflict shall not affect other provisions of this Security Instrument or the Note which can be given effect without the conflicting provision.

As used in this Security Instrument: (a) words of the masculine gender shall mean and include corresponding neuter words or words of the feminine gender; (b) words in the singular shall mean and include the plural and vice versa; and (c) the word "may" gives sole discretion without any obligation to take any action.

17.   Borrower's Copy. Borrower shall be given one copy of the Note and of this Security Instrument.

18.   Transfer of the Property or a Beneficial Interest in Borrower. As used in this Section 18, "Interest in the Property" means any legal or beneficial interest in the Property, including, but not limited to, those beneficial interests transferred in a bond for deed, contract for deed, installment sales contract or escrow agreement, the intent of which is the transfer of title by Borrower at a future date to a purchaser.

If all or any part of the Property or any Interest in the Property is sold or transferred (or if Borrower is not a natural person and a beneficial interest in Borrower is sold or transferred) without Lender's prior written consent,

CALIFORNIA--Single Family--**Fannie Mae/Freddie Mac UNIFORM INSTRUMENT**   Form 3005   1/01   *(page 8 of 11 pages)*

Lender may require immediate payment in full of all sums secured by this Security Instrument. However, this option shall not be exercised by Lender if such exercise is prohibited by Applicable Law.

If Lender exercises this option, Lender shall give Borrower notice of acceleration. The notice shall provide a period of not less than 30 days from the date the notice is given in accordance with Section 15 within which Borrower must pay all sums secured by this Security Instrument. If Borrower fails to pay these sums prior to the expiration of this period, Lender may invoke any remedies permitted by this Security Instrument without further notice or demand on Borrower.

19.   Borrower's Right to Reinstate After Acceleration. If Borrower meets certain conditions, Borrower shall have the right to have enforcement of this Security Instrument discontinued at any time prior to the earliest of: (a) five days before sale of the Property pursuant to any power of sale contained in this Security Instrument; (b) such other period as Applicable Law might specify for the termination of Borrower's right to reinstate; or (c) entry of a judgment enforcing this Security Instrument. Those conditions are that Borrower: (a) pays Lender all sums which then would be due under this Security Instrument and the Note as if no acceleration had occurred; (b) cures any default of any other covenants or agreements; (c) pays all expenses incurred in enforcing this Security Instrument, including, but not limited to, reasonable attorneys' fees, property inspection and valuation fees, and other fees incurred for the purpose of protecting Lender's interest in the Property and rights under this Security Instrument; and (d) takes such action as Lender may reasonably require to assure that Lender's interest in the Property and rights under this Security Instrument, and Borrower's obligation to pay the sums secured by this Security Instrument, shall continue unchanged. Lender may require that Borrower pay such reinstatement sums and expenses in one or more of the following forms, as selected by Lender: (a) cash; (b) money order; (c) certified check, bank check, treasurer's check or cashier's check, provided any such check is drawn upon an institution whose deposits are insured by a federal agency, instrumentality or entity; or (d) Electronic Funds Transfer. Upon reinstatement by Borrower, this Security Instrument and obligations secured hereby shall remain fully effective as if no acceleration had occurred. However, this right to reinstate shall not apply in the case of acceleration under Section 18.

20.   Sale of Note; Change of Loan Servicer; Notice of Grievance. The Note or a partial interest in the Note (together with this Security Instrument) can be sold one or more times without prior notice to Borrower. A sale might result in a change in the entity (known as the "Loan Servicer") that collects Periodic Payments due under the Note and this Security Instrument and performs other mortgage loan servicing obligations under the Note, this Security Instrument, and Applicable Law. There also might be one or more changes of the Loan Servicer unrelated to a sale of the Note. If there is a change of the Loan Servicer, Borrower will be given written notice of the change which will state the name and address of the new Loan Servicer, the address to which payments should be made and any other information RESPA requires in connection with a notice of transfer of servicing. If the Note is sold and thereafter the Loan is serviced by a Loan Servicer other than the purchaser of the Note, the mortgage loan servicing obligations to Borrower will remain with the Loan Servicer or be transferred to a successor Loan Servicer and are not assumed by the Note purchaser unless otherwise provided by the Note purchaser.

Neither Borrower nor Lender may commence, join, or be joined to any judicial action (as either an individual litigant or the member of a class) that arises from the other party's actions pursuant to this Security Instrument or that alleges that the other party has breached any provision of, or any duty owed by reason of, this Security Instrument, until such Borrower or Lender has notified the other party (with such notice given in compliance with the requirements of Section 15) of such alleged breach and afforded the other party hereto a reasonable period after the giving of such notice to take corrective action. If Applicable Law provides a time period which must elapse before certain action can be taken, that time period will be deemed to be reasonable for purposes of this paragraph. The notice of acceleration and opportunity to cure given to Borrower pursuant to Section 22 and the notice of acceleration given to Borrower pursuant to Section 18 shall be deemed to satisfy the notice and opportunity to take corrective action provisions of this Section 20.

21.   Hazardous Substances. As used in this Section 21: (a) "Hazardous Substances" are those substances defined as toxic or hazardous substances, pollutants, or wastes by Environmental Law and the following substances: gasoline, kerosene, other flammable or toxic petroleum products, toxic pesticides and herbicides, volatile solvents, materials containing asbestos or formaldehyde, and radioactive materials; (b) "Environmental Law" means federal laws and laws of the jurisdiction where the Property is located that relate to health, safety or environmental protection; (c) "Environmental Cleanup" includes any response action, remedial action, or removal action, as defined in Environmental Law; and (d) an "Environmental Condition" means a condition that can cause, contribute to, or otherwise trigger an Environmental Cleanup.

Borrower shall not cause or permit the presence, use, disposal, storage, or release of any Hazardous Substances, or threaten to release any Hazardous Substances, on or in the Property. Borrower shall not do, nor allow anyone else to do, anything affecting the Property (a) that is in violation of any Environmental Law, (b) which creates an Environmental Condition, or (c) which, due to the presence, use, or release of a Hazardous Substance,

CALIFORNIA--Single Family--**Fannie Mae/Freddie Mac UNIFORM INSTRUMENT**   Form 3005   1/01   *(page 9 of 11 pages)*

creates a condition that adversely affects the value of the Property. The preceding two sentences shall not apply to the presence, use, or storage on the Property of small quantities of Hazardous Substances that are generally recognized to be appropriate to normal residential uses and to maintenance of the Property (including, but not limited to, hazardous substances in consumer products).

Borrower shall promptly give Lender written notice of (a) any investigation, claim, demand, lawsuit or other action by any governmental or regulatory agency or private party involving the Property and any Hazardous Substance or Environmental Law of which Borrower has actual knowledge, (b) any Environmental Condition, including but not limited to, any spilling, leaking, discharge, release or threat of release of any Hazardous Substance, and (c) any condition caused by the presence, use or release of a Hazardous Substance which adversely affects the value of the Property. If Borrower learns, or is notified by any governmental or regulatory authority, or any private party, that any removal or other remediation of any Hazardous Substance affecting the Property is necessary, Borrower shall promptly take all necessary remedial actions in accordance with Environmental Law. Nothing herein shall create any obligation on Lender for an Environmental Cleanup.

NON-UNIFORM COVENANTS. Borrower and Lender further covenant and agree as follows:

22. **Acceleration; Remedies.** **Lender shall give notice to Borrower prior to acceleration following Borrower's breach of any covenant or agreement in this Security Instrument (but not prior to acceleration under Section 18 unless Applicable Law provides otherwise). The notice shall specify: (a) the default; (b) the action required to cure the default; (c) a date, not less than 30 days from the date the notice is given to Borrower, by which the default must be cured; and (d) that failure to cure the default on or before the date specified in the notice may result in acceleration of the sums secured by this Security Instrument and sale of the Property. The notice shall further inform Borrower of the right to reinstate after acceleration and the right to bring a court action to assert the non-existence of a default or any other defense of Borrower to acceleration and sale. If the default is not cured on or before the date specified in the notice, Lender at its option may require immediate payment in full of all sums secured by this Security Instrument without further demand and may invoke the power of sale and any other remedies permitted by Applicable Law. Lender shall be entitled to collect all expenses incurred in pursuing the remedies provided in this Section 22, including, but not limited to, reasonable attorneys' fees and costs of title evidence.**

If Lender invokes the power of sale, Lender shall execute or cause Trustee to execute a written notice of the occurrence of an event of default and of Lender's election to cause the Property to be sold. Trustee shall cause this notice to be recorded in each county in which any part of the Property is located. Lender or Trustee shall mail copies of the notice as prescribed by Applicable Law to Borrower and to the other persons prescribed by Applicable Law. Trustee shall give public notice of sale to the persons and in the manner prescribed by Applicable Law. After the time required by Applicable Law, Trustee, without demand on Borrower, shall sell the Property at public auction to the highest bidder at the time and place and under the terms designated in the notice of sale in one or more parcels and in any order Trustee determines. Trustee may postpone sale of all or any parcel of the Property by public announcement at the time and place of any previously scheduled sale. Lender or its designee may purchase the Property at any sale.

Trustee shall deliver to the purchaser Trustee's deed conveying the Property without any covenant or warranty, expressed or implied. The recitals in the Trustee's deed shall be prima facie evidence of the truth of the statements made therein. Trustee shall apply the proceeds of the sale in the following order: (a) to all expenses of the sale, including, but not limited to, reasonable Trustee's and attorneys' fees; (b) to all sums secured by this Security Instrument; and (c) any excess to the person or persons legally entitled to it.

23. **Reconveyance.** Upon payment of all sums secured by this Security Instrument, Lender shall request Trustee to reconvey the Property and shall surrender this Security Instrument and all notes evidencing debt secured by this Security Instrument to Trustee. Trustee shall reconvey the Property without warranty to the person or persons legally entitled to it. Lender may charge such person or persons a reasonable fee for reconveying the Property, but only if the fee is paid to a third party (such as the Trustee) for services rendered and the charging of the fee is permitted under Applicable Law. If the fee charged does not exceed the fee set by Applicable Law, the fee is conclusively presumed to be reasonable.

24. **Substitute Trustee.** Lender, at its option, may from time to time appoint a successor trustee to any Trustee appointed hereunder by an instrument executed and acknowledged by Lender and recorded in the office of the Recorder of the county in which the Property is located. The instrument shall contain the name of the original Lender, Trustee and Borrower, the book and page where this Security Instrument is recorded and the name and address of the successor trustee. Without conveyance of the Property, the successor trustee shall succeed to all the title, powers and duties conferred upon the Trustee herein and by Applicable Law. This procedure for substitution of trustee shall govern to the exclusion of all other provisions for substitution.

CALIFORNIA--Single Family--**Fannie Mae/Freddie Mac UNIFORM INSTRUMENT**   **Form 3005**   **1/01**   *(page 10 of 11 pages)*

25.   Statement of Obligation Fee. Lender may collect a fee not to exceed the maximum amount permitted by Applicable Law for furnishing the statement of obligation as provided by Section 2943 of the Civil Code of California.

BY SIGNING BELOW, Borrower accepts and agrees to the terms and covenants contained in this Security Instrument and in any Rider executed by Borrower and recorded with it.

Witnesses:

_____   _____ (Seal)
                                                                       BARRY BORROWER - Borrower

_____   _____ (Seal)
                                                                       BARBARA BORROWER - Borrower

_____**[Space Below This Line for Acknowledgment]**_____

State of California   )

County of _____)

On _____ before me, _____, personally
appeared _____
_____, personally known to me (or proved to me on the basis of satisfactory
evidence) to be the person(s) whose name(s) is/are subscribed to the within instrument and acknowledged to me that
he/she/they executed the same in his/her/their authorized capacity(ies), and that by his/her/their signature(s) on the
instrument the person(s), or the entity upon behalf of which the person(s) acted, executed the instrument.

WITNESS my hand and official seal.

_____   (Seal)

CALIFORNIA--Single Family--**Fannie Mae/Freddie Mac UNIFORM INSTRUMENT**   **Form 3005**   **1/01**   *(page 11 of 11 pages)*

Chapter 1: Refinance Loans   39

Refinance Loans

2500020183

ADJUSTABLE RATE NOTE
(6-Month LIBOR Index - Rate Caps)
ssumable during Life of Loan) (First Business Day of Preceding Month Lookback)

TE CONTAINS PROVISIONS ALLOWING FOR CHANGES IN MY INTEREST RATE
MONTHLY PAYMENT. THIS NOTE LIMITS THE AMOUNT MY INTEREST RATE
NGE AT ANY ONE TIME AND THE MAXIMUM RATE I MUST PAY.

R 02, 20XX   LAKE FOREST,   CALIFORNIA
Date]   [City]   [State]

1000 ANYWHERE STREET, ANY CITY, AS 00000
[Property Address]

1.   **BORROWER'S PROMISE TO PAY**
         In return for a loan that I have received, I promise to pay U.S. **$166,500.00**   (this amount is called "Principal"), plus interest, to the order of the Lender. The Lender is **ANPAC FUNDING CORP. D/B/A ANPAC LENDING GROUP, A CALIFORNIA CORPORATION**. I will make all payments under this Note in the form of cash, check or money order.
         I understand that the Lender may transfer this Note. The Lender or anyone who takes this Note by transfer and who is entitled to receive payments under this Note is called the "Note Holder."

2.   **INTEREST**
         Interest will be charged on unpaid principal until the full amount of Principal has been paid. I will pay interest at a yearly rate of   **6.37500 %**. The interest rate I will pay will change in accordance with Section 4 of this Note.
         The interest rate required by this Section 2 and Section 4 of this Note is the rate I will pay both before and after any default described in Section 7(B) of this Note.

3.   **PAYMENTS**
         (A)   Time and Place of Payments
         I will pay principal and interest by making a payment every month.
         I will make my monthly payment on the first day of each month beginning on **DECEMBER 01, 20XX**. I will make these payments every month until I have paid all of the principal and interest and any other charges described below that I may owe under this Note. Each monthly payment will be applied as of its scheduled due date and will be applied to interest before Principal. If, on **NOVEMBER 01, 20XX**   I still owe amounts under this Note, I will pay those amounts in full on that date, which is called the "Maturity Date."
         I will make my monthly payments at **1401 COVE STREET, SUITE 100, NEWPORT BEACH, CALIFORNIA 92660** or at a different place if required by the Note Holder.

         (B)   Amount of My Initial Monthly Payments
         ~~Each of my initial monthly payments will be in the amount of U.S. $~~ ** SEE ATTACHED INTEREST-ONLY ADDENDUM . ~~This amount may change.~~
         (C)   Monthly Payment Changes
         Changes in my monthly payment will reflect changes in the unpaid principal of my loan and in the interest rate that I must pay. The Note Holder will determine my new interest rate and the changed amount of my monthly payment in accordance with Section 4 of this Note.

4.   **INTEREST RATE AND MONTHLY PAYMENT CHANGES**
         (A)   Change Dates
         The interest rate I will pay may change on the first day of   **MAY, 20XX,** and may change on that day every sixth month thereafter. Each date on which my interest rate could change is called a "Change Date."
         (B)   The Index
         Beginning with the first Change Date, my interest rate will be based on an Index. The "Index" is the six month London Interbank Offered Rate ("LIBOR") which is the average of interbank offered rates for six-month U.S. dollar-denominated deposits in the London market, as published in *The Wall Street Journal*. The most recent Index figure available as of the first business day of the month immediately preceding the month in which the Change Date occurs is called the "Current Index."
         If the Index is no longer available, the Note Holder will choose a new index which is based upon comparable information. The Note Holder will give me notice of this choice.
         (C)   Calculation of Changes
         Before each Change Date, the Note Holder will calculate my new interest rate by adding   **TWO   AND 750/1000**   percentage point(s) (**2.75000 %**) to the Current Index. The Note Holder will then round the result of

MULTISTATE ADJUSTABLE RATE NOTE-6-Month LIBOR Index (Assumable during Life of Loan) (First Business Day Lookback)--Single Family--
Freddie Mac UNIFORM INSTRUMENT   Form 5520   3/04   *(page 1 of 3 pages)*

this addition to the nearest one-eighth of one percentage point (0.125%). Subject to the limits stated in Section 4(D) below, this rounded amount will be my new interest rate until the next Change Date.

The Note Holder will then determine the amount of the monthly payment that would be sufficient to repay the unpaid principal that I am expected to owe at the Change Date in full on the Maturity Date at my new interest rate in substantially equal payments. The result of this calculation will be the new amount of my monthly payment.

(D)   Limits on Interest Rate Changes

The interest rate I am required to pay at the first Change Date will not be greater than **7.37500**   % or less than **5.37500** %. Thereafter, my interest rate will never be increased or decreased on any single Change Date by more than   **ONE AND 000/1000**   percentage point(s) (**1.00000**%) from the rate of interest I have been paying for the preceding six months. My interest rate will never be greater than   **12.37500**   %.

(E)   Effective Date of Changes

My new interest rate will become effective on each Change Date. I will pay the amount of my new monthly payment beginning on the first monthly payment date after the Change Date until the amount of my monthly payment changes again.

(F)   Notice of Changes

The Note Holder will deliver or mail to me a notice of any changes in my interest rate and the amount of my monthly payment before the effective date of any change. The notice will include information required by law to be given to me and also the title and telephone number of a person who will answer any question I may have regarding the notice.

5.   BORROWER'S RIGHT TO PREPAY

I have the right to make payments of Principal at any time before they are due. A payment of Principal only is known as a "Prepayment." When I make a Prepayment, I will tell the Note Holder in writing that I am doing so. I may not designate a payment as a Prepayment if I have not made all the monthly payments due under the Note.

I may make a full Prepayment or partial Prepayments without paying a Prepayment charge. The Note Holder will use my Prepayments to reduce the amount of Principal that I owe under this Note. However, the Note Holder may apply my Prepayment to the accrued and unpaid interest on the Prepayment amount before applying my Prepayment to reduce the Principal amount of the Note. If I make a partial Prepayment, there will be no changes in the due dates of my monthly payment unless the Note Holder agrees in writing to those changes. My partial Prepayment may reduce the amount of my monthly payments after the first Change Date following my partial Prepayment. However, any reduction due to my partial Prepayment may be offset by an interest rate increase.

6.   LOAN CHARGES

If a law, which applies to this loan and which sets maximum loan charges, is finally interpreted so that the interest or other loan charges collected or to be collected in connection with this loan exceed the permitted limits, then: (a) any such loan charge shall be reduced by the amount necessary to reduce the charge to the permitted limit; and (b) any sums already collected from me which exceeded permitted limits will be refunded to me. The Note Holder may choose to make this refund by reducing the Principal I owe under this Note or by making a direct payment to me. If a refund reduces Principal, the reduction will be treated as a partial Prepayment.

7.   BORROWER'S FAILURE TO PAY AS REQUIRED

(A)   Late Charges for Overdue Payments

If the Note Holder has not received the full amount of any monthly payment by the end of _____ calendar days after the date it is due, I will pay a late charge to the Note Holder. The amount of the charge will be   **5.000**   % of my overdue payment of principal and interest. I will pay this late charge promptly but only once on each late payment.

(B)   Default

If I do not pay the full amount of each monthly payment on the date it is due, I will be in default.

(C)   Notice of Default

If I am in default, the Note Holder may send me a written notice telling me that if I do not pay the overdue amount by a certain date, the Note Holder may require me to pay immediately the full amount of Principal which has not been paid and all the interest that I owe on that amount. That date must be at least 30 days after the date on which the notice is mailed to me or delivered by other means.

(D)   No Waiver by Note Holder

Even if, at a time when I am in default, the Note Holder does not require me to pay immediately in full as described above, the Note Holder will still have the right to do so if I am in default at a later time.

(E)   Payment of Note Holder's Costs and Expenses

If the Note Holder has required me to pay immediately in full as described above, the Note Holder will have the right to be paid back by me for all of its costs and expenses in enforcing this Note to the extent not prohibited by applicable law. Those expenses include, for example, reasonable attorneys' fees.

8.   GIVING OF NOTICES

Unless applicable law requires a different method, any notice that must be given to me under this Note will be given by delivering it or by mailing it by first class mail to me at the Property Address above or at a different address if I give the Note Holder a notice of my different address.

Any notice that must be given to the Note Holder under this Note will be given by delivering it or by mailing it by first class mail to the Note Holder at the address stated in Section 3(A) above or at a different address if I am given a notice

MULTISTATE ADJUSTABLE RATE NOTE-6-Month LIBOR Index (Assumable during Life of Loan) (First Business Day Lookback)--Single Family--
Freddie Mac UNIFORM INSTRUMENT   Form 5520   3/04   *(page 2 of 3 pages)*

Refinance Loans

of that different address.

9.   OBLIGATIONS OF PERSONS UNDER THIS NOTE

If more than one person signs this Note, each person is fully and personally obligated to keep all of the promises made in this Note, including the promise to pay the full amount owed. Any person who is a guarantor, surety or endorser of this Note is also obligated to do these things. Any person who takes over these obligations, including the obligations of a guarantor, surety or endorser of this Note, is also obligated to keep all of the promises made in this Note. The Note Holder may enforce its rights under this Note against each person individually or against all of us together. This means that any one of us may be required to pay all of the amounts owed under this Note.

10.   WAIVERS

I and any other person who has obligations under this Note waive the rights of Presentment and Notice of Dishonor. "Presentment" means the right to require the Note Holder to demand payment of amounts due. "Notice of Dishonor" means the right to require the Note Holder to give notice to other persons that amounts due have not been paid.

11.   UNIFORM SECURED NOTE

This Note is a uniform instrument with limited variations in some jurisdictions. In addition to the protections given to the Note Holder under this Note, a Mortgage, Deed of Trust, or Security Deed (the "Security Instrument"), dated the same date as this Note, protects the Note Holder from possible losses which might result if I do not keep the promises which I make in this Note. That Security Instrument describes how and under what conditions I may be required to make immediate payment in full of all amounts I owe under this Note. Some of those conditions are described as follows:

Transfer of the Property or a Beneficial Interest in Borrower. As used in this Section 18, "Interest in the Property" means any legal or beneficial interest in the Property, including, but not limited to, those beneficial interests transferred in a bond for deed, contract for deed, installment sales contract or escrow agreement, the intent of which is the transfer of title by Borrower at a future date to a purchaser.

If all or any part of the Property or any Interest in the Property is sold or transferred (or if Borrower is not a natural person and a beneficial interest in Borrower is sold or transferred) without Lender's prior written consent, Lender may require immediate payment in full of all sums secured by this Security Instrument. However, this option shall not be exercised by Lender if such exercise is prohibited by Applicable Law. Lender also shall not exercise this option if: (a) Borrower causes to be submitted to Lender information required by Lender to evaluate the intended transferee as if a new loan were being made to the transferee; and (b) Lender reasonably determines that Lender's security will not be impaired by the loan assumption and that the risk of a breach of any covenant or agreement in this Security Instrument is acceptable to Lender.

To the extent permitted by Applicable Law, Lender may charge a reasonable fee as a condition to Lender's consent to the loan assumption. Lender may also require the transferee to sign an assumption agreement that is acceptable to Lender and that obligates the transferee to keep all the promises and agreements made in the Note and in this Security Instrument. Borrower will continue to be obligated under the Note and this Security Instrument unless Lender releases Borrower in writing.

If Lender exercises the option to require immediate payment in full, Lender shall give Borrower notice of acceleration. The notice shall provide a period of not less than 30 days from the date the notice is given in accordance with Section 15 within which Borrower must pay all sums secured by this Security Instrument. If Borrower fails to pay these sums prior to the expiration of this period, Lender may invoke any remedies permitted by this Security Instrument without further notice or demand on Borrower.

WITNESS THE HAND(S) AND SEAL(S) OF THE UNDERSIGNED.

_____ (Seal)
BARRY BORROWER

_____ (Seal)
BARBARA BORROWER

_____ (Seal)
- Borrower

[Sign Original Only]

**MULTISTATE ADJUSTABLE RATE NOTE-6-Month LIBOR Index (Assumable during Life of Loan) (First Business Day Lookback)--Single Family--
Freddie Mac UNIFORM INSTRUMENT**   **Form 5520   3/04**   *(page 3 of 3 pages)*

INTEREST-ONLY ADDENDUM
TO ADJUSTABLE RATE PROMISSORY NOTE

Loan Number: **2500020183**
Property Address: **1000 ANYWHERE STREET ANY CITY, ANY STATE 0000**

THIS ADDENDUM is made this **02ND** day of **OCTOBER, 20XX** and is incorporated into and intended to form a part of the Adjustable Rate Note (the 'Note') dated the same date as the Addendum executed by the undersigned and payable to
ANPAC FUNDING CORP. D/B/A IMPAC LENDING GROUP, A CALIFORNIA CORPORATION
(the Lender).

THIS ADDENDUM supersedes Section 3(A), 3(8), 4(C) and 7(A) of the Note. None of the other provisions of the Note are changed by this Addendum.

3. PAYMENTS

(A) Time and Place of Payments

I will pay interest by making payments every month for the first **60** payments (the 'interest-only period') in the amount sufficient to pay interest as it accrues on the unpaid principal balance. I will pay principal and interest by making payments every month thereafter for the next 300 payment(s) in an amount sufficient to fully repay the unpaid principal balance of the Note at the end of the interest-only period in substantially equal monthly payments. I will make my monthly payments on the **01ST** day of each month beginning on **DECEMBER, 20XX** I will make these payments every month until I have paid all of the principal and interest and any other charges described below that I may owe under this Note. Each monthly payment will be applied as of its schedule due date and will be applied to interest before principal. If, on **NOVEMBER 01, 20XX**, I still owe amounts under this Note, I will pay those amounts in full on that date which is called the 'Maturity Date.'

I will make my payments at
1401 COVE STREET, SUITE 100
NEWPORT BEACH, CALIFORNIA 92660
or at a different place if required by the Note Holder.

(B) Amount of My Initial Monthly Payment

Each of my initial monthly payments will be in the amount of U.S. $ **884.53** based on the original principal balance of the Note. This payment amount may change.

4. INTEREST RATE AND MONTHLY PAYMENT CHANGES

(C) Calculation of Changes

Before each Change Date, the Note Holder will calculate my new interest rate by adding **TWO AND 750/1000** percentage point(s) (**2.75000**) to the current index for such Change Date. The Note Holder will then round the result of this addition to the nearest one-eighth of one percentage point (0.125%). Subject to the limits stated in Section 4(D), this rounded amount will be my new interest rate until fle next Change Date.

During the interest-only period, the Note Holder will determine the amount of the monthly payment that would be sufficient to pay accrued interest on the unpaid principal balance. This will be the amount of my monthly payment until the earlier of the next Change Date or the end of the interest-only period unless I make a voluntary prepayment of principal during such period. If I make a voluntary prepayment of principal during the interest-only period, my payment amount for subsequent payments will be reduced to the amount necessary to pay interest at the then current interest rate on the lower unpaid principal balance.

Page 1

At the end of the interest only period and on each Change Date thereafter, the Note Holder will determine the amount of the monthly payment that would be sufficient to repay in full the unpaid principal balance that I will owe in substantially equal monthly payments over the remaining term of the Note. The result of this calculation will be the new amount of my monthly payment. After the end of the interest-only period, my payment amount will not be adjusted due to voluntary principal payments until the next Change Date.

7. BORROWER'S FAILURE TO PAY AS REQUIRED

(A) Late Charge for Overdue Payments

I f the Note Holder has not received the Full amount of any monthly payment by the end of **15** calendar days after the date it is due, I will pay a late charge to the Note Holder. The amount of the charge will be 5.000 % of my overdue payment of interest for the first **60** payments, and **5.000 %** of my overdue payment of principal and interest thereafter. I will pay this late charge promptly but only once on each late payment.

DATED

_____   _____
BARRY BORROWER   **BARBARA BORROWER**

Page 2

2500020183

ADJUSTABLE RATE RIDER
(6-Month LIBOR Index - Rate Caps)

THIS ADJUSTABLE RATE RIDER is made this **02ND** day of **MAY** , **20XX**, and is incorporated into and shall be deemed to amend and supplement the Mortgage, Deed of Trust, or Security Deed (the "Security Instrument") of the same date given by the undersigned (the "Borrower") to secure the Borrow Note (the "Note") to

ANPAC FUNDING CORP. D/B/A IMPAC LENDING GROUP, A CALIFORNIA CORPORA
(the "Lender") of the same date and covering the property described in the Security Instrument and l

1000 ANYWHERE STREET, ANY CITY, ANY STATE 00000

[Property Address]

**THE NOTE CONTAINS PROVISIONS ALLOWING FOR CHANGES IN THE I
RATE AND THE MONTHLY PAYMENT. THE NOTE LIMITS THE AMO
BORROWER'S INTEREST RATE CAN CHANGE AT ANY ONE TIME AND THE N
RATE THE BORROWER MUST PAY.**

ADDITIONAL COVENANTS. In addition to the covenants and agreements made in the Security Instrument, Borrower and Lender further covenant and agree as follows:

A. INTEREST RATE AND MONTHLY PAYMENT CHANGES

The Note provides for an initial interest rate of **6.37500** %. The Note provides for changes in the interest rate and the monthly payments, as follows:

4. INTEREST RATE AND MONTHLY PAYMENT CHANGES

(A) Change Dates

The interest rate I will pay may change on the first day of **MAY**, **20XX**, and may change on that day every sixth month thereafter. Each date on which my interest rate could change is called a "Change Date."

(B) The Index

Beginning with the first Change Date, my interest rate will be based on an Index. The "Index" is the six month London Interbank Offered Rate ("LIBOR") which is the average of interbank offered rates for six-month U.S. dollar-denominated deposits in the London market, as published in *The Wall Street Journal*. The most recent Index figure available as of the first business day of the month immediately preceding the month in which the Change Date occurs is called the "Current Index."

If the Index is no longer available, the Note Holder will choose a new index which is based upon comparable information. The Note Holder will give me notice of this choice.

(C) Calculation of Changes

Before each Change Date, the Note Holder will calculate my new interest rate by adding **TWO AND 750/1000** percentage point(s) **2.7500**%) to the Current Index. The Note Holder will then round the result of this addition to the nearest one-eighth of one percentage point (0.125%). Subject to the limits stated in Section 4(D) below, this rounded amount will be my new interest rate until the next Change Date.

The Note Holder will then determine the amount of the monthly payment that would be sufficient to repay the unpaid principal that I am expected to owe at the Change Date in full on the maturity date at my new interest rate in substantially equal payments. The result of this calculation will be the new amount of my monthly payment.

(D) Limits on Interest Rate Changes

The interest rate I am required to pay at the first Change Date will not be greater than **7.37500**% or less than **5.37500**%. Thereafter, my interest rate will never be increased or decreased on any single Change Date by more than **ONE** percentage point(s) (**1.000**%) from the rate of interest I have been paying for the preceding six months. My interest rate will never be greater than **12.37500**%.

(E) Effective Date of Changes

My new interest rate will become effective on each Change Date. I will pay the amount of my new monthly payment beginning on the first monthly payment date after the Change Date until the amount of my monthly payment changes again.

(F) Notice of Changes

The Note Holder will deliver or mail to me a notice of any changes in my interest rate and the amount of my monthly payment before the effective date of any change. The notice will include information required by law to be given to me and also the title and telephone number of a person who will answer any question I may have regarding the notice.

MULTISTATE ADJUSTABLE RATE RIDER 6-Month LIBOR Index (Assumable during Life of Loan) (First Business Day Lookback)--Single Family--
Freddie Mac UNIFORM INSTRUMENT   Form 5120   3/04   *(page 1 of 2 pages)*

NOTES

"The Adjustable Rate Rider" was referenced in the "Deed of Trust" as amending or supplementing the terms of the security instrument. The Notary Signing Agent must ensure this form is included within the document package.

B. TRANSFER OF THE PROPERTY OR A BENEFICIAL INTEREST IN BORROWER

Uniform Covenant 18 of the Security Instrument is amended to read as follows:

Transfer of the Property or a Beneficial Interest in Borrower. As used in this Section 18, "Interest in the Property" means any legal or beneficial interest in the Property, including, but not limited to, those beneficial interests transferred in a bond for deed, contract for deed, installment sales contract or escrow agreement, the intent of which is the transfer of title by Borrower at a future date to a purchaser.

If all or any part of the Property or any Interest in the Property is sold or transferred (or if Borrower is not a natural person and a beneficial interest in Borrower is sold or transferred) without Lender's prior written consent, Lender may require immediate payment in full of all sums secured by this Security Instrument. However, this option shall not be exercised by Lender if such exercise is prohibited by Applicable Law. Lender also shall not exercise this option if: (a) Borrower causes to be submitted to Lender information required by Lender to evaluate the intended transferee as if a new loan were being made to the transferee; and (b) Lender reasonably determines that Lender's security will not be impaired by the loan assumption and that the risk of a breach of any covenant or agreement in this Security Instrument is acceptable to Lender.

To the extent permitted by Applicable Law, Lender may charge a reasonable fee as a condition to Lender's consent to the loan assumption. Lender may also require the transferee to sign an assumption agreement that is acceptable to Lender and that obligates the transferee to keep all the promises and agreements made in the Note and in this Security Instrument. Borrower will continue to be obligated under the Note and this Security Instrument unless Lender releases Borrower in writing.

If Lender exercises the option to require immediate payment in full, Lender shall give Borrower notice of acceleration. The notice shall provide a period of not less than 30 days from the date the notice is given in accordance with Section 15 within which Borrower must pay all sums secured by this Security Instrument. If Borrower fails to pay these sums prior to the expiration of this period, Lender may invoke any remedies permitted by this Security Instrument without further notice or demand on Borrower.

BY SIGNING BELOW, Borrower accepts and agrees to the terms and covenants contained in this Adjustable Rate Rider.

_____ (Seal)
BARRY BORROWER

_____ (Seal)
BARBARA BORROWER

MULTISTATE ADJUSTABLE RATE RIDER 6-Month LIBOR Index (Assumable during Life of Loan) (First Business Day Lookback)--Single Family--
Freddie Mac UNIFORM INSTRUMENT   Form 5120   3/04   *(page 2 of 2 pages)*

INTEREST-ONLY ADDENDUM
TO ADJUSTABLE RATE RIDER

Loan Number: **2500020183**
Property Address: **1000 ANYWHERE STREET, ANY CITY, ANY STATE 00000**

THIS ADDENDUM is made this **02ND** day of **OCTOBER,** **20XX** and is incorporated into and intended to form a part of the Adjustable Rate Rider (the "Rider") dated the same date as the Addendum executed by the undersigned and payable to: **ANPAC FUNDING CORP. D/B/A IMPAC LENDING GROUP, A CALIFORNIA CORPORATION**

THIS ADDENDUM supersedes Section 4(C) of the Rider. None of the other provisions of the Note are changed by this Addendum.

4. INTEREST RATE AND MONTHLY PAYMENT CHANGES

   (C) Calculation of Changes

   Before each Change Date, the Note Holder will calculate my new interest rate by adding **TWO AND 750/1000** percentage point(s) (2.75000) to the Current Index for such Change Date. The Note Holder will then round the result of this addition to the nearest one-eighth of one percentage point (0.125%). Subject to the limits stated in Section 4(D), this rounded amount will be my new interest rate until the next Change Date.

   During first five (5) years after loan closing ("interest-only period"), the Note Holder will determine the amount of the monthly payment that would be sufficient to pay accrued interest on the unpaid principal balance. This will be the amount of my monthly payment until the earlier of the next Change Date or the end of the interest- only period unless I make a voluntary prepayment of principal during such period. If I make a voluntary prepayment of principal during the interest-only period, my payment amount for subsequent payments will be reduced to the amount necessary to pay interest at the then current interest rate on the lower unpaid principal balance.

   At the end of the interest-only period and on each Change Date thereafter, the Note Holder will determine the amount of the monthly payment that would be sufficient to repay in full the unpaid principal balance that I am expected to owe in substantially equal monthly payments over the remaining term of the Note. The result of this calculation will be the new amount of my monthly payment. After the end of the interest-only period, my payment amount will not be adjusted due to voluntary principal payments.

DATED:

_____   _____
BARRY BORROWER   **BARBARA BORROWER**

Loan No. 2500020183

ADDENDUM TO NOTE

This addendum is made **OCTOBER 02, 20XX** and is incorporated into and deemed to amend and supplement the Note of the same date.

Covering the property described in the security instrument and located at:
1000 ANYWHERE STREET
ANY CITY, ANY STATE 00000

Amended Provisions.

In addition to the provisions and agreements made in the Note, I/we further covenant and agree as follows:

Borrower's Right to Prepay:

I have the right to make payments of principal at any time before they are due. A payment of principal only is known as "prepayment". When I make a prepayment, I will tell the Note Holder in writing that I am doing so.

Subject to the prepayment penalty specified below, I may make a full prepayment or partial prepayments of my obligation. The Note Holder will use all of my prepayments to reduce the amount of principal that I owe under this Note. If I make a partial prepayment, there will be no changes in the due date or in the amount of my monthly payment unless the Note Holder agrees in writing of those changes.

If I make prepayments of this loan during the first **FIVE** years of the Note term, beginning on the date this Note is executed, I will pay a prepayment penalty in the amount of six months' advance interest on the amount by which the aggregate prepayments made within any consecutive twelve month period exceed twenty percent (20%) of the original principal amount. No prepayment penalty will be assessed for any prepayment after the first **FIVE** years of the Note term. The Note Holder will waive this penalty if I furnish the Note Holder with documentation, in the manner and at the time reasonably specified by the Note Holder, identifying the prepayment as being in connection with the sale of the Property.

The Note Holder's failure to collect a prepayment penalty at the time a prepayment is received shall note be deemed a waiver of such penalty and any such penalty calculated in accordance with this section shall be payable on demand.

_____   _____
BARRY BORROWER   **BARBARA BORROWER**

BORROWER'S INCOME CERTIFICATION

Date: **OCTOBER 02, 20XX**

Loan No.:   **2500020183**

Borrower's Name: **BARRY BORROWER BARBARA BORROWER**

Property Address: **1000 ANYWHERE STREET**
                    ANY CITY, ANY STATE 00000

The undersigned Borrower(s) certifies to Lender that the monthly income disclosed on the Uniform Residential Loan Application (Fannie Mae Form 1003) referenced loan is true, accurate, and current as of this date.

The undersigned Borrower(s) acknowledges my/our understanding that any intentional or negligent misrepresentation(s) of the information contained in the Uniform Residential Loan Application (Fannie Mae Form l003/Freddie Mac 65) may result in civil liability and/or criminal penalties including, but not limited to, fine or imprisonment or both under the provisions of Title 18, United States Code, Section 100 I, et seq. and liability for successors and assigns, insurers and any other person who may suffer misrepresentation which I/we have made on the Uniform Residential Loan Application.

_____   _____
BARRY BORROWER   **BARBARA BORROWER**

VARIABLE RATE MORTGAGE PROGRAM DISCLOSURE

LENDER: **ANPAC FUNDING CORP. D/B/A ANPAC LENDING GROUP, A CALIFORNIA CORPORATION**

VARIABLE RATE LOAN PROGRAM   *Six (6) Month LIBOR ARM -- First 5 Years Interest-Only Payments*

This variable rate loan program disclosure describes the features of the adjustable rate mortgage ("ARM") program you are considering. Information on other ARM programs is available upon request. This is neither a contract nor a commitment to lend. If you do obtain a loan from the Lender, the Note, Security Instrument and related documents will establish your legal rights and obligations. Because the Lender may sell any loan it makes, the purchaser of the loan ("Noteholder") may enforce the terms of any loan obtained from the Lender. You will be required to make payments to the Noteholder or a Servicer the Noteholder designates. For purposes of easy reference, the term Lender is used below and refers to the initial Lender or purchaser of the Note.

HOW YOUR INTEREST RATE AND PAYMENT ARE DETERMINED
- During the period that you make payments of interest only, your payments will be based on the interest rate and loan balance. After that period, your payment will be based on the interest rate, loan balance and remaining loan term. .
- Your interest rate will be based on an index rate plus a margin. . The index upon which the interest rate will be based is the yearly average of interbank offered rate for six-month U.S. Dollar denominated deposits in the London market ("LIBOR").
- Information about the current index is published in the Wall Street Journal.
- This ARM loan may have a discount feature, and your initial interest rate may not be based on the index used to make later adjustments. Ask about our current discount rate.
- Your interest rate will equal the index rate plus your margin unless your interest rate 'caps' limit the amount of change in the interest rate.
- During the first five (5) years, interest only payments will be required to be made. This means that the regular monthly payments will not reduce the principal balance during the first five (5) years of your loan.
- Beginning in year six (6), the payment will be amortized over the remaining term and applied towards principal and interest.

HOW YOUR INTEREST RATE CAN CHANGE
- Your interest rate can change every 6 months beginning approximately 6 months after your loan closes. These are known as the "Change Dates".
- Your new interest rate will be equal to the sum of the margin and index value published on the first business day of the month in the month prior to the Change Date subject to the restrictions described below.
- Your interest rate cannot increase or decrease more than one percentage point (1.0000/0) at each adjustment thereafter (a "cap"). Your interest rate can never be less than your margin (a "cap").
- Your interest rate can never increase by more than six percentage points (6.000%) above the start rate (a "cap").
- Your interest rate will be rounded to the nearest 0.125% at each adjustment.

HOW YOUR MONTHLY PAYMENT CAN CHANGE
- Your monthly payment can increase or decrease substantially every 6 months beginning approximately 6 months after your loan closes based on changes to the interest rate. You will begin making your new monthly payments on the first payment due date after each Change Date.
- At each Change Date during the interest-only period the lender will recalculate your monthly payment to be an amount necessary to fully repay the accrued interest at the then current interest.
- If you make a voluntary prepayment of principal during the interest-only period, your payment amount for subsequent payments will be reduced to the amount necessary to pay interest at the then current interest rate on the lower unpaid principal balance.
- At each Change Date after the interest-only period, the lender will recalculate your monthly payment based on an amount necessary to fully repay the unpaid principal balance at the then current interest rate on the maturity date in substantially equal monthly payments. You will be notified in writing at least 25 calendar days before the monthly adjustment is made. This notice will contain information about your index, interest rate, payment amount and loan balance.
- For example, on a new $10,000, 30 year loan with an initial interest rate of 4.375% in effect in December, 20XX, the maximum amount that the interest rate could rise under this example is 10.375%, and the payment amount could rise from a beginning payment of $36.46 to a maximum of $86.46 in 3 years based on an interest-only payment during the 3 years. You will begin making monthly payments of principal and interest in the 6th year. (For example, the monthly payment for a mortgage amount of $60,000/$10,000 = 6; 6 x $36.46 = $218.76.) To compute the above example we used a margin value and interest rate we have used recently. Your margin value and interest rate may be different and you should ask about what is the current margin value and interest rate.

I/We hereby acknowledge receipt of this variable rate program disclosure and a copy of the Consumer Handbook on Adjustable Rate Mortgages on the date indicated below.

Date:

_____   _____
BARRY BORROWER   **BARBARA BORROWER**

_____   _____
Signature   Signature

_____   _____
Signature   Signature

COMPLIANCE AGREEMENT

Borrower(s): **Barry Borrower**
Barbara Borrower

Date: **July 25, 20XX**

Loan Number: **2500020183**

Property Address: **1277 Anywhere Street**
Any City, AS 00000

Lender: **ANPAC Funding Corp.**

The undersigned borrower(s), for and in consideration of Lender disbursing loan proceeds for the purchas[e] of, or construction of improvements on the aforementioned property, agree(s), if requested by the Len[der] acting on behalf of said Lender, to fully cooperate in adjusting for clerical errors, on any or all loan closing[s] deemed necessary or desirable in the reasonable discretion of Lender to enable Lender to sell, convey[,] or market said loan to any entity, including but not limited to, an investor, Fannie Mae (FNMA), Gove[rnment] Mortgage Association (GNMA), Freddie Mac (FHLMC), Department of Housing and Urban Developme[nt,] of Veterans Affairs or any municipal bonding authority.

The undersigned borrower(s) do hereby so agree and covenant as aforesaid in order to assure that the l[oca-] tion executed this date will conform and be acceptable in the marketplace in the instance of transfer, sale[,] by Lender of its interest in and to said loan documentation.

Dated effective this 25th day of July, 20XX.

_____
Barry Borrower   **DATE**

_____
Barbara Borrower   **DATE**

NOTES

The "Compliance Agreement" included in this sample document package is a notarized version.

Notary Signing Agents should note that a "Compliance Agreement" or any other regularly notarized form should only be notarized if there is Notary acknowledgment or jurat wording on the form, or in absence of such wording, an explicit instruction that the form should be notarized.

SIGNATURES CONTINUED ON FOLLOWING PAGE.

A notary public or other officer completing this certificate verifies only the identity of the individual who signed the document to which this certificate is attached, and not the truthfulness, accuracy, or validity of that document.

State of
County of

On _____, before me, _____
(here insert name and title of the officer), personally appeared _____, who proved to me on the basis of satisfactory evidence to be the person(s) whose name(s) is/are subscribed to the within instrument and acknowledged to me that he/she/they executed the same in his/her/their authorized capacity(ies), and that by his/her/their signature(s) on the instrument the person(s), or the entity upon behalf of which the person(s) acted, executed the instrument.

I certify under PENALTY OF PERJURY under the laws of the State of California that the foregoing paragraph is true and correct.

WITNESS my hand and official seal.

Signature_____

_____(NOTARY)

(SEAL)

Form W-9
(Rev. November 2017)
Department of the Treasury
Internal Revenue Service

Request for Taxpayer
Identification Number and Certification

▶ Go to *www.irs.gov/FormW9* for instructions and the latest information.

Give Form to the requester. Do not send to the IRS.

1 Name (as shown on your income tax return). Name is required on this line; do not leave this line blank.

Barry Borrower

2 Business name/disregarded entity name, if different from above

3 Check appropriate box for federal tax classification of the person whose name is entered on line 1. Check only **one** of the following seven boxes.

☑ Individual/sole proprietor or single-member LLC ☐ C Corporation ☐ S Corporation ☐ Partnership ☐ Trust/estate

☐ Limited liability company. Enter the tax classification (C = C corporation, S = S corporation, P = Partnership) ▶ _____

Note: Check the appropriate box in the line above for the tax classification of the single-member owner. Do not check LLC if the LLC is classified as a single-member LLC that is disregarded from the owner unless the owner of the LLC is another LLC that is **not** disregarded from the owner for U.S. federal tax purposes. Otherwise, a single-member LLC that is disregarded from the owner should check the appropriate box for the tax classification of its owner.

☐ Other (see instructions) ▶

4 Exemptions (codes apply only to certain entities, not individuals; see instructions on page 3):

Exempt payee code (if any) _____

Exemption from FATCA reporting code (if any) _____

(Applies to accounts maintained outside the U.S.)

5 Address (number, street, and apt. or suite no.) See instructions.

1000 Anywhere Street

6 City, state, and ZIP code

Any City, Any State 00000

Requester's name and address (optional)

7 List account number(s) here (optional)

Print or type.
See Specific Instructions on page 2.

Part I | **Taxpayer Identification Number (TIN)**

Enter your TIN in the appropriate box. The TIN provided must match the name given on line 1 to avoid backup withholding. For individuals, this is generally your social security number (SSN). However, for a resident alien, sole proprietor, or disregarded entity, see the instructions for Part I, later. For other entities, it is your employer identification number (EIN). If you do not have a number, see *How to get a TIN*, later.

Note. If the account is in more than one name, see the instructions for line 1. Also see *What Name and Number To Give the Requester* for guidelines on whose number to enter.

Social security numb

0 0 0 – 0 0 –

or

Employer identificati

Part II | **Certification**

Under penalties of perjury, I certify that:

1. The number shown on this form is my correct taxpayer identification number (or I am waiting for a number to be issued to me); and
2. I am not subject to backup withholding because: (a) I am exempt from backup withholding, or (b) I have not been notified by the Internal Revenue Service (IRS) that I am subject to backup withholding as a result of a failure to report all interest or dividends, or (c) the IRS has notified me that I am no longer subject to backup withholding; and
3. I am a U.S. citizen or other U.S. person (defined below); and
4. The FATCA code(s) entered on this form (if any) indicating that I am exempt from FATCA reporting is correct.

Certification instructions. You must cross out item 2 above if you have been notified by the IRS that you are currently subject to backup withholding because you have failed to report all interest and dividends on your tax return. For real estate transactions, item 2 does not apply. For mortgage interest paid, acquisition or abandonment of secured property, cancellation of debt, contributions to an individual retirement arrangement (IRA), and generally, payments other than interest and dividends, you are not required to sign the certification, but you must provide your correct TIN. See the instructions for Part II, later.

Sign Here | Signature of U.S. person ▶ | Date ▶

General Instructions

Section references are to the Internal Revenue Code unless otherwise noted.

Future developments. For the latest information about developments related to Form W-9 and its instructions, such as legislation enacted after they were published, go to *www.irs.gov/FormW9*.

Purpose of Form

An individual or entity (Form W-9 requester) who is required to file an information return with the IRS must obtain your correct taxpayer identification number (TIN) which may be your social security number (SSN), individual taxpayer identification number (ITIN), adoption taxpayer identification number (ATIN), or employer identification number (EIN), to report on an information return the amount paid to you, or other amount reportable on an information return. Examples of information returns include, but are not limited to, the following.

• Form 1099-INT (interest earned or paid)
• Form 1099-DIV (dividends, including those from stocks or mutual funds)
• Form 1099-MISC (various types of income, prizes, awards, or gross proceeds)
• Form 1099-B (stock or mutual fund sales and certain other transactions by brokers)
• Form 1099-S (proceeds from real estate transactions)
• Form 1099-K (merchant card and third party network transactions)
• Form 1098 (home mortgage interest), 1098-E (student loan interest), 1098-T (tuition)
• Form 1099-C (canceled debt)
• Form 1099-A (acquisition or abandonment of secured property)

Use Form W-9 only if you are a U.S. person (including a resident alien), to provide your correct TIN.

If you do not return Form W-9 to the requester with a TIN, you might be subject to backup withholding. See What is backup withholding, *later.*

By signing the filled-out form, you:

1. Certify that the TIN you are giving is correct (or you are waiting for a number to be issued),

2. Certify that you are not subject to backup withholding, or

3. Claim exemption from backup withholding if you are a U.S. exempt payee. If applicable, you are also certifying that as a U.S. person, your allocable share of any partnership income from a U.S. trade or business is not subject to the withholding tax on foreign partners' share of effectively connected income, and

4. Certify that FATCA code(s) entered on this form (if any) indicating that you are exempt from the FATCA reporting, is correct. See *What is FATCA reporting,* later, for further information.

Note: If you are a U.S. person and a requester gives you a form other than Form W-9 to request your TIN, you must use the requester's form if it is substantially similar to this Form W-9.

Definition of a U.S. person. For federal tax purposes, you are considered a U.S. person if you are:

• An individual who is a U.S. citizen or U.S. resident alien;

• A partnership, corporation, company, or association created or organized in the United States or under the laws of the United States;

• An estate (other than a foreign estate); or

• A domestic trust (as defined in Regulations section 301.7701-7).

Special rules for partnerships. Partnerships that conduct a trade or business in the United States are generally required to pay a withholding tax under section 1446 on any foreign partners' share of effectively connected taxable income from such business. Further, in certain cases where a Form W-9 has not been received, the rules under section 1446 require a partnership to presume that a partner is a foreign person, and pay the section 1446 withholding tax. Therefore, if you are a U.S. person that is a partner in a partnership conducting a trade or business in the United States, provide Form W-9 to the partnership to establish your U.S. status and avoid section 1446 withholding on your share of partnership income.

Ellie Mae, Inc. | Cat. No. 10231X | Form **W-9** (Rev. 11-2017) GW9C (CLS)

NOTES

While this particular "Form W-9" does not call for the signer to initial the following pages, Notary Signing Agents should be aware that some versions of "Form W-9" do require that the instructions pages be initialed.

In the cases below, the following person must give Form W-9 to the partnership for purposes of establishing its U.S. status and avoiding withholding on its allocable share of net income from the partnership conducting a trade or business in the United States.

• In the case of a disregarded entity with a U.S. owner, the U.S. owner of the disregarded entity and not the entity;

• In the case of a grantor trust with a U.S. grantor or other U.S. owner, generally, the U.S. grantor or other U.S. owner of the grantor trust and not the trust; and

• In the case of a U.S. trust (other than a grantor trust), the U.S. trust (other than a grantor trust) and not the beneficiaries of the trust.

Foreign person. If you are a foreign person or the U.S. branch of a foreign bank that has elected to be treated as a U.S. person, do not use Form W-9. Instead, use the appropriate Form W-8 or Form 8233 (see Pub. 515, Withholding of Tax on Nonresident Aliens and Foreign Entities).

Nonresident alien who becomes a resident alien. Generally, only a nonresident alien individual may use the terms of a tax treaty to reduce or eliminate U.S. tax on certain types of income. However, most tax treaties contain a provision known as a "saving clause." Exceptions specified in the saving clause may permit an exemption from tax to continue for certain types of income even after the payee has otherwise become a U.S. resident alien for tax purposes.

If you are a U.S. resident alien who is relying on an exception contained in the saving clause of a tax treaty to claim an exemption from U.S. tax on certain types of income, you must attach a statement to Form W-9 that specifies the following five items.

1. The treaty country. Generally, this must be the same treaty under which you claimed exemption from tax as a nonresident alien.

2. The treaty article addressing the income.

3. The article number (or location) in the tax treaty that contains the saving clause and its exceptions.

4. The type and amount of income that qualifies for the exemption from tax.

5. Sufficient facts to justify the exemption from tax under the terms of the treaty article.

Example. Article 20 of the U.S.-China income tax treaty allows an exemption from tax for scholarship income received by a Chinese student temporarily present in the United States. Under U.S. law, this student will become a resident alien for tax purposes if his or her stay in the United States exceeds 5 calendar years. However, paragraph 2 of the first Protocol to the U.S.-China treaty (dated April 30, 1984) allows the provisions of Article 20 to continue to apply even after the Chinese student becomes a resident alien of the United States. A Chinese student who qualifies for this exception (under paragraph 2 of the first protocol) and is relying on this exception to claim an exemption from tax on his or her scholarship or fellowship income would attach to Form W-9 a statement that includes the information described above to support that exemption.

If you are a nonresident alien or a foreign entity, give the requester the appropriate completed Form W-8 or Form 8233.

Backup Withholding

What is backup withholding? Persons making certain payments to you must under certain conditions withhold and pay to the IRS 28% of such payments. This is called "backup withholding." Payments that may be subject to backup withholding include interest, tax-exempt interest, dividends, broker and barter exchange transactions, rents, royalties, nonemployee pay, payments made in settlement of payment card and third party network transactions, and certain payments from fishing boat operators. Real estate transactions are not subject to backup withholding.

You will not be subject to backup withholding on payments you receive if you give the requester your correct TIN, make the proper certifications, and report all your taxable interest and dividends on your tax return.

Payments you receive will be subject to backup withholding if:

1. You do not furnish your TIN to the requester,

2. You do not certify your TIN when required (see the instructions for Part II for details),

3. The IRS tells the requester that you furnished an incorrect TIN,

4. The IRS tells you that you are subject to backup withholding because you did not report all your interest and dividends on your tax return (for reportable interest and dividends only), or

5. You do not certify to the requester that you are not subject to backup withholding under 4 above (for reportable interest and dividend accounts opened after 1983 only).

Certain payees and payments are exempt from backup withholding. See *Exempt payee code*, later, and the separate Instructions for the Requester of Form W-9 for more information.

Also see *Special rules for partnerships*, earlier.

What is FATCA Reporting?

The Foreign Account Tax Compliance Act (FATCA) requires a participating foreign financial institution to report all United States account holders that are specified United States persons. Certain payees are exempt from FATCA reporting. See *Exemption from FATCA reporting code*, later, and the Instructions for the Requester of Form W-9 for more information.

Updating Your Information

You must provide updated information to any person to whom you claimed to be an exempt payee if you are no longer an exempt payee and anticipate receiving reportable payments in the future from this person. For example, you may need to provide updated information if you are a C corporation that elects to be an S corporation, or if you no longer are tax exempt. In addition, you must furnish a new Form W-9 if the name or TIN changes for the account; for example, if the grantor of a grantor trust dies.

Penalties

Failure to furnish TIN. If you fail to furnish your correct TIN to a requester, you are subject to a penalty of $50 for each such failure unless your failure is due to reasonable cause and not to willful neglect.

Civil penalty for false information with respect to withholding. If you make a false statement with no reasonable basis that results in no backup withholding, you are subject to a $500 penalty.

Criminal penalty for falsifying information. Willfully falsifying certifications or affirmations may subject you to criminal penalties including fines and/or imprisonment.

Misuse of TINs. If the requester discloses or uses TINs in violation of federal law, the requester may be subject to civil and criminal penalties.

Specific Instructions

Line 1

You must enter one of the following on this line; **do not** leave this line blank. The name should match the name on your tax return.

If this Form W-9 is for a joint account (other than an account maintained by a foreign financial institution (FFI)), list first, and then circle, the name of the person or entity whose number you entered in Part I of Form W-9. If you are providing Form W-9 to an FFI to document a joint account, each holder of the account that is a U.S. person must provide a Form W-9.

a. **Individual.** Generally, enter the name shown on your tax return. If you have changed your last name without informing the Social Security Administration (SSA) of the name change, enter your first name, the last name as shown on your social security card, and your new last name.

Note: ITIN applicant: Enter your individual name as it was entered on your Form W-7 application, line 1a. This should also be the same as the name you entered on the Form 1040/1040A/1040EZ you filed with your application.

b. **Sole proprietor or single-member LLC.** Enter your individual name as shown on your 1040/1040A/1040EZ on line 1. You may enter your business, trade, or "doing business as" (DBA) name on line 2.

c. **Partnership, LLC that is not a single-member LLC, C corporation, or S corporation.** Enter the entity's name as shown on the entity's tax return on line 1 and any business, trade, or DBA name on line 2.

d. **Other entities.** Enter your name as shown on required U.S. federal tax documents on line 1. This name should match the name shown on the charter or other legal document creating the entity. You may enter any business, trade, or DBA name on line 2.

e. **Disregarded entity.** For U.S. federal tax purposes, an entity that is disregarded as an entity separate from its owner is treated as a "disregarded entity." See Regulations section 301.7701-2(c)(2)(iii). Enter the owner's name on line 1. The name of the entity entered on line 1 should never be a disregarded entity. The name on line 1 should be the name shown on the income tax return on which the income should be reported. For example, if a foreign LLC that is treated as a disregarded entity for U.S. federal tax purposes has a single owner that is a U.S. person, the U.S. owner's name is required to be provided on line 1. If the direct owner of the entity is also a disregarded entity, enter the first owner that is not disregarded for federal tax purposes. Enter the disregarded entity's name on line 2, "Business name/disregarded entity name." If the owner of the disregarded entity is a foreign person, the owner must complete an appropriate Form W-8 instead of a Form W-9. This is the case even if the foreign person has a U.S. TIN.

Line 2

If you have a business name, trade name, DBA name, or disregarded entity name, you may enter it on line 2.

Line 3

Check the appropriate box on line 3 for the U.S. federal tax classification of the person whose name is entered on line 1. Check only one box on line 3.

IF the entity/person on line 1 is a(n)...	THEN check the box for...
• Corporation	Corporation
• Individual • Sole proprietorship, or • Single-member limited liability company (LLC) owned by an individual and disregarded for U.S. federal tax purposes.	Individual/sole proprietor or single-member LLC
• LLC treated as a partnership for U.S. federal tax purposes, • LLC that has filed Form 8832 or 2553 to be taxed as a corporation, or • LLC that is disregarded as an entity separate from its owner but the owner is another LLC that is not disregarded for U.S. federal tax purposes.	Limited liability company and enter the appropriate tax classification. (P= Partnership; C= C corporation; or S= S corporation)
• Partnership	Partnership
• Trust/estate	Trust/estate

Line 4, Exemptions

If you are exempt from backup withholding and/or FATCA reporting, enter in the appropriate space on line 4 any code(s) that may apply to you.

Exempt payee code.

• Generally, individuals (including sole proprietors) are not exempt from backup withholding.

• Except as provided below, corporations are exempt from backup withholding for certain payments, including interest and dividends.

• Corporations are not exempt from backup withholding for payments made in settlement of payment card or third party network transactions.

• Corporations are not exempt from backup withholding with respect to attorneys' fees or gross proceeds paid to attorneys, and corporations that provide medical or health care services are not exempt with respect to payments reportable on Form 1099-MISC.

The following codes identify payees that are exempt from backup withholding. Enter the appropriate code in the space in line 4.

1 – An organization exempt from tax under section 501(a), any IRA, or a custodial account under section 403(b)(7) if the account satisfies the requirements of section 401(f)(2)

2 – The United States or any of its agencies or instrumentalities

3 – A state, the District of Columbia, a U.S. commonwealth or possession, or any of their political subdivisions or instrumentalities

4 – A foreign government or any of its political subdivisions, agencies, or instrumentalities

5 – A corporation

6 – A dealer in securities or commodities required to register in the United States, the District of Columbia, or a U.S. commonwealth or possession

7 – A futures commission merchant registered with the Commodity Futures Trading Commission

8 – A real estate investment trust

9 – An entity registered at all times during the tax year under the Investment Company Act of 1940

10 – A common trust fund operated by a bank under section 584(a)

11 – A financial institution

12 – A middleman known in the investment community as a nominee or custodian

13 – A trust exempt from tax under section 664 or described in section 4947

The following chart shows types of payments that may be exempt from backup withholding. The chart applies to the exempt payees listed above, 1 through 13.

IF the payment is for...	THEN the payment is exempt for...
Interest and dividend payments	All exempt payees except for 7
Broker transactions	Exempt payees 1 through 4 and 6 through 11 and all C corporations. S corporations must not enter an exempt payee code because they are exempt only for sales of noncovered securities acquired prior to 2012.
Barter exchange transactions and patronage dividends	Exempt payees 1 through 4
Payments over $600 required to be reported and direct sales over $5,000[1]	Generally, exempt payees 1 through 5[2]
Payments made in settlement of payment card or third party network transactions	Exempt payees 1 through 4

[1] See Form 1099-MISC, Miscellaneous Income, and its instructions.

[2] However, the following payments made to a corporation and reportable on Form 1099-MISC are not exempt from backup withholding: medical and health care payments, attorneys' fees, gross proceeds paid to an attorney reportable under section 6045(f), and payments for services paid by a federal executive agency.

Exemption from FATCA reporting code. The following codes identify payees that are exempt from reporting under FATCA. These codes apply to persons submitting this form for accounts maintained outside of the United States by certain foreign financial institutions. Therefore, if you are only submitting this form for an account you hold in the United States, you may leave this field blank. Consult with the person requesting this form if you are uncertain if the financial institution is subject to these requirements. A requester may indicate that a code is not required by providing you with a Form W-9 with "Not Applicable" (or any similar indication) written or printed on the line for a FATCA exemption code.

A – An organization exempt from tax under section 501(a) or any individual retirement plan as defined in section 7701(a)(37)

B – The United States or any of its agencies or instrumentalities

C – A state, the District of Columbia, a U.S. commonwealth or possession, or any of their political subdivisions or instrumentalities

D – A corporation the stock of which is regularly traded on one or more established securities markets, as described in Regulations section 1.1472-1(c)(1)(i)

E – A corporation that is a member of the same expanded affiliated group as a corporation described in Regulations section 1.1472-1(c)(1)(i)

F – A dealer in securities, commodities, or derivative financial instruments (including notional principal contracts, futures, forwards, and options) that is registered as such under the laws of the United States or any state

G – A real estate investment trust

H – A regulated investment company as defined in section 851 or an entity registered at all times during the tax year under the Investment Company Act of 1940

I – A common trust fund as defined in section 584(a)

J – A bank as defined in section 581

K – A broker

L – A trust exempt from tax under section 664 or described in section 4947(a)(1)

M – A tax exempt trust under a section 403(b) plan or section 457(g) plan

Note: You may wish to consult with the financial institution requesting this form to determine whether the FATCA code and/or exempt payee code should be completed.

Line 5

Enter your address (number, street, and apartment or suite number). This is where the requester of this Form W-9 will mail your information returns. If this address differs from the one the requester already has on file, write NEW at the top. If a new address is provided, there is still a chance the old address will be used until the payor changes your address in their records.

Line 6

Enter your city, state, and ZIP code.

Part I. Taxpayer Identification Number (TIN)

Enter your TIN in the appropriate box. If you are a resident alien and you do not have and are not eligible to get an SSN, your TIN is your IRS individual taxpayer identification number (ITIN). Enter it in the social security number box. If you do not have an ITIN, see *How to get a TIN* below.

If you are a sole proprietor and you have an EIN, you may enter either your SSN or EIN.

If you are a single-member LLC that is disregarded as an entity separate from its owner, enter the owner's SSN (or EIN, if the owner has one). Do not enter the disregarded entity's EIN. If the LLC is classified as a corporation or partnership, enter the entity's EIN.

Note. See *What Name and Number To Give the Requester*, later, for further clarification of name and TIN combinations.

How to get a TIN. If you do not have a TIN, apply for one immediately. To apply for an SSN, get Form SS-5, Application for a Social Security Card, from your local SSA office or get this form online at *www.SSA.gov*. You may also get this form by calling 1-800-772-1213. Use Form W-7, Application for IRS Individual Taxpayer Identification Number, to apply for an ITIN, or Form SS-4, Application for Employer Identification Number, to apply for an EIN. You can apply for an EIN online by accessing the IRS website at *www.irs.gov/Businesses* and clicking on Employer Identification Number (EIN) under Starting a Business. Go to *www.irs.gov/Forms* to view, download, or print Form W-7 and/or Form SS-4. Or, you can go to *www.irs.gov/OrderForms* to place an order and have Form W-7 and/or SS-4 mailed to you within 10 business days.

If you are asked to complete Form W-9 but do not have a TIN, apply for a TIN and write "Applied For" in the space for the TIN, sign and date the form, and give it to the requester. For interest and dividend payments, and certain payments made with respect to readily tradable instruments, generally you will have 60 days to get a TIN and give it to the requester before you are subject to backup withholding on payments. The 60-day rule does not apply to other types of payments. You will be subject to backup withholding on all such payments until you provide your TIN to the requester.

Note: Entering "Applied For" means that you have already applied for a TIN or that you intend to apply for one soon.

Caution: A disregarded U.S. entity that has a foreign owner must use the appropriate Form W-8.

Part II. Certification

To establish to the withholding agent that you are a U.S. person, or resident alien, sign Form W-9. You may be requested to sign by the withholding agent even if item 1, 4, or 5 below indicates otherwise.

For a joint account, only the person whose TIN is shown in Part I should sign (when required). In the case of a disregarded entity, the person identified on line 1 must sign. Exempt payees, see *Exempt payee code*, earlier.

Signature requirements. Complete the certification as indicated in items 1 through 5 below.

1. Interest, dividend, and barter exchange accounts opened before 1984 and broker accounts considered active during 1983. You must give your correct TIN, but you do not have to sign the certification.

2. Interest, dividend, broker, and barter exchange accounts opened after 1983 and broker accounts considered inactive during 1983. You must sign the certification or backup withholding will apply. If you are subject to backup withholding and you are merely providing your correct TIN to the requester, you must cross out item 2 in the certification before signing the form.

3. Real estate transactions. You must sign the certification. You may cross out item 2 of the certification.

4. Other payments. You must give your correct TIN, but you do not have to sign the certification unless you have been notified that you have previously given an incorrect TIN. "Other payments" include payments made in the course of the requester's trade or business for rents, royalties, goods (other than bills for merchandise), medical and health care services (including payments to corporations), payments to a nonemployee for services, payments made in settlement of payment card and third party network transactions, payments to certain fishing boat crew members and fishermen, and gross proceeds paid to attorneys (including payments to corporations).

5. Mortgage interest paid by you, acquisition or abandonment of secured property, cancellation of debt, qualified tuition program payments (under section 529), ABLE accounts (under section 529A), IRA, Coverdell ESA, Archer MSA or HSA contributions or distributions, and pension distributions. You must give your correct TIN, but you do not have to sign the certification.

What Name and Number To Give the Requester

For this type of account:	Give name and SSN of:
1. Individual	The individual
2. Two or more individuals (joint account) other than an account maintained by an FFI	The actual owner of the account or, if combined funds, the first individual on the account[1]
3. Two or more U.S. persons (joint account maintained by an FFI)	Each holder of the account
4. Custodial account of a minor (Uniform Gift to Minors Act)	The minor[2]
5. a. The usual revocable savings trust (grantor is also trustee)	The grantor-trustee[1]
b. So-called trust account that is not a legal or valid trust under state law	The actual owner[1]
6. Sole proprietorship or disregarded entity owned by an individual	The owner[3]
7. Grantor trust filing under Optional Form 1099 Filing Method 1 (see Regulations section 1.671-4(b)(2)(i)(A))	The grantor*

For this type of account:	Give name and EIN of:
8. Disregarded entity not owned by an individual	The owner
9. A valid trust, estate, or pension trust	Legal entity[4]
10. Corporation or LLC electing corporate status on Form 8832 or Form 2553	The corporation
11. Association, club, religious, charitable, educational, or other tax-exempt organization	The organization
12. Partnership or multi-member LLC	The partnership
13. A broker or registered nominee	The broker or nominee

For this type of account:	Give name and EIN of:
14. Account with the Department of Agriculture in the name of a public entity (such as a state or local government, school district, or prison) that receives agricultural program payments	The public entity
15. Grantor trust filing under the Form 1041 Filing Method or the Optional Form 1099 Filing Method 2 (see Regulations section 1.671-4(b)(2)(i)(B))	The trust

[1] List first and circle the name of the person whose number you furnish. If only one person on a joint account has an SSN, that person's number must be furnished.

[2] Circle the minor's name and furnish the minor's SSN.

[3] You must show your individual name and you may also enter your business or DBA name on the "Business name/disregarded entity" name line. You may use either your SSN or EIN (if you have one), but the IRS encourages you to use your SSN.

[4] List first and circle the name of the trust, estate, or pension trust. (Do not furnish the TIN of the personal representative or trustee unless the legal entity itself is not designated in the account title.) Also see *Special rules for partnerships*, earlier.

* **Note:** The grantor also must provide a Form W-9 to trustee of trust.

Note. If no name is circled when more than one name is listed, the number will be considered to be that of the first name listed.

Secure Your Tax Records From Identity Theft

Identity theft occurs when someone uses your personal information such as your name, SSN, or other identifying information, without your permission, to commit fraud or other crimes. An identity thief may use your SSN to get a job or may file a tax return using your SSN to receive a refund.

To reduce your risk:
• Protect your SSN,
• Ensure your employer is protecting your SSN, and
• Be careful when choosing a tax preparer.

If your tax records are affected by identity theft and you receive a notice from the IRS, respond right away to the name and phone number printed on the IRS notice or letter.

If your tax records are not currently affected by identity theft but you think you are at risk due to a lost or stolen purse or wallet, questionable credit card activity or credit report, contact the IRS Identity Theft Hotline at 1-800-908-4490 or submit Form 14039.

For more information, see Pub. 5027, Identity Theft Information for Taxpayers.

Victims of identity theft who are experiencing economic harm or a systemic problem, or are seeking help in resolving tax problems that have not been resolved through normal channels, may be eligible for Taxpayer Advocate Service (TAS) assistance. You can reach TAS by calling the TAS toll-free case intake line at 1-877-777-4778 or TTY/TDD 1-800-829-4059.

Protect yourself from suspicious emails or phishing schemes. Phishing is the creation and use of email and websites designed to mimic legitimate business emails and websites. The most common act is sending an email to a user falsely claiming to be an established legitimate enterprise in an attempt to scam the user into surrendering private information that will be used for identity theft.

The IRS does not initiate contacts with taxpayers via emails. Also, the IRS does not request personal detailed information through email or ask taxpayers for the PIN numbers, passwords, or similar secret access information for their credit card, bank, or other financial accounts.

If you receive an unsolicited email claiming to be from the IRS, forward this message to *phishing@irs.gov*. You may also report misuse of the IRS name, logo, or other IRS property to the Treasury Inspector General for Tax Administration (TIGTA) at 1-800-366-4484. You can forward suspicious emails to the Federal Trade Commission at: *spam@uce.gov* or report them at *www.ftc.gov/complaint*. You can contact the FTC at *www.ftc.gov/idtheft* or 877-IDTHEFT (877-438-4338). If you have been the victim of identity theft, see *www.IdentityTheft.gov* and Pub. 5027.

Visit *www.irs.gov/IdentityTheft* to learn more about identity theft and how to reduce your risk.

Privacy Act Notice

Section 6109 of the Internal Revenue Code requires you to provide your correct TIN to persons (including federal agencies) who are required to file information returns with the IRS to report interest, dividends, or certain other income paid to you; mortgage interest you paid; the acquisition or abandonment of secured property; the cancellation of debt; or contributions you made to an IRA, Archer MSA, or HSA. The person collecting this form uses the information on the form to file information returns with the IRS, reporting the above information. Routine uses of this information include giving it to the Department of Justice for civil and criminal litigation and to cities, states, the District of Columbia, and U.S. commonwealths and possessions for use in administering their laws. The information also may be disclosed to other countries under a treaty, to federal and state agencies to enforce civil and criminal laws, or to federal law enforcement and intelligence agencies to combat terrorism. You must provide your TIN whether or not you are required to file a tax return. Under section 3406, payers must generally withhold a percentage of taxable interest, dividend, and certain other payments to a payee who does not give a TIN to the payer. Certain penalties may also apply for providing false or fraudulent information.

Form **W-8BEN**

(Rev. July 2017)

Department of the Treasury
Internal Revenue Service

Certificate of Foreign Status of Beneficial Owner for United States Tax Withholding and Reporting (Individuals)

▶ For use by individuals. Entities must use Form W-8BEN-E.
▶ Go to *www.irs.gov/FormW8BEN* for instructions and the latest information.
▶ Give this form to the withholding agent or payer. Do not send to the IRS.

OMB No. 1545-1621

Do NOT use this form if: / **Instead, use Form:**

• You are NOT an individual W-8BEN-E

• You are a U.S. citizen or other U.S. person, including a resident alien individual W-9

• You are a beneficial owner claiming that income is effectively connected with the conduct of trade or business within the U.S. (other than personal services) W-8ECI

• You are a beneficial owner who is receiving compensation for personal services performed in the United States . . . . 8233 or W-4

• You are a person acting as an intermediary W-8IMY

Note: If you are resident in a FATCA partner jurisdiction (i.e., a Model 1 IGA jurisdiction with reciprocity), certain tax account information may be provided to your jurisdiction of residence.

Part I   **Identification of Beneficial Owner** (see instructions)

1 Name of individual who is the beneficial owner

Barry Borrower

2 Country of citizenship

3 Permanent residence address (street, apt. or suite no., or rural route). **Do not use a P.O. box or in-care-of address.**

1000 Anywhere Street

City or town, state or province. Include postal code where appropriate.   Country

Any City, AS 00000   United State

4 Mailing address (if different from above)

City or town, state or province. Include postal code where appropriate.   Country

5 U.S. taxpayer identification number (SSN or ITIN), if required (see instructions)

000-00-0000

6 Foreign tax identifying nu

7 Reference number(s) (see instructions)

8 Date of birth (MM-DD-YYYY) (see instructions)

04-18-1960

Part II   **Claim of Tax Treaty Benefits** (for chapter 3 purposes only) (see instructions)

9 I certify that the beneficial owner is a resident of _____ within the m

treaty between the United States and that country.

10 **Special rates and conditions** (if applicable—see instructions): The beneficial owner is claiming the provisions of Artic _____ of the treaty identified on line 9 above to claim a ____ % rate of withholding on (specify type of income): _____ .

Explain the additional conditions in the Article and paragraph the beneficial owner meets to be eligible for the rate of withholding: _____

Part III   **Certification**

Under penalties of perjury, I declare that I have examined the information on this form and to the best of my knowledge and belief it is true, correct, and complete. I further certify under penalties of perjury that:

• I am the individual that is the beneficial owner (or am authorized to sign for the individual that is the beneficial owner) of all the income to which this form relates or am using this form to document myself for chapter 4 purposes,

• The person named on line 1 of this form is not a U.S. person,

• The income to which this form relates is:

(a) not effectively connected with the conduct of a trade or business in the United States,

(b) effectively connected but is not subject to tax under an applicable income tax treaty, or

(c) the partner's share of a partnership's effectively connected income,

• The person named on line 1 of this form is a resident of the treaty country listed on line 9 of the form (if any) within the meaning of the income tax treaty between the United States and that country, and

• For broker transactions or barter exchanges, the beneficial owner is an exempt foreign person as defined in the instructions.

Furthermore, I authorize this form to be provided to any withholding agent that has control, receipt, or custody of the income of which I am the beneficial owner or any withholding agent that can disburse or make payments of the income of which I am the beneficial owner. **I agree that I will submit a new form within 30 days if any certification made on this form becomes incorrect.**

Sign Here ▶

Signature of beneficial owner (or individual authorized to sign for beneficial owner)   Date (MM-DD-YYYY)

Print name of signer   Capacity in which acting (if form is not signed by beneficial owner)

For Paperwork Reduction Act Notice, see separate instructions.   Cat. No. 25047Z   Form **W-8BEN** (Rev. 7-2017)

NOTES

"Form W-8BEN" is designed for foreign persons who are not subject to U.S. income tax withholding. If a nonresident alien of the United States, the person must provide a Form W-8BEN to:

• Establish that the nonresident alien is not a U.S. citizen.

• Claim that the nonresident alien is the beneficial owner of the income for which Form W-8BEN is being provided.

Loan package contained separate Name Affidavits for each borrower. The second form is not reprinted.

2500020183

Lender: **ANPAC FUNDING CORP. D/B/A ANPAC LENDING GROUP, A CALIFORNIA CORPORATION**

Borrower: **BARRY AND BARBARA BORROWER**

> ## NOTES
>
> The "Name Affidavit" serves two purposes:
>
> • It establishes that the borrower is the same person that is referenced in the loan documentation.
>
> • If noted, the borrower is one and the same person as other referenced names.
>
> If no other names are noted, the borrower makes the first representation only and the form may be notarized by completing the standard jurat wording. Note: the Notary Signing Agent must administer an oath or affirmation to the borrower.

ress: **1000 ANYWHERE STREET, ANY CITY, ANY STATE 00000**

:   **2500020183**

NAME AFFIDAVIT
(One and the Same Certification)

)
) ss:
)

ed hereby certifies that he/she, **BARRY BORROWER**

the loan closing documentation is one and the same as and/or is also known as

as indicated in the loan application processing, and/or closing documentation.

Date: _____

BARRY BORROWER   _____

Subscribed and sworn to before me this   day of   , .

_____
Notary Public

My commission expires:
[Seal]

Lender Escrow Account Disclosure Summary

Lender Borrower(s): BARRY AND BARBARA BORROWER

Address: 1000 ANYWHERE STREET
ANY CITY, ANY STATE 00000

Servicer: ANPAC FUNDING CORPORATION
Address: P.O. BOX 70808
CHARLOTTE, NC 28272-0808
Toll-Free Phone: (888) 934-1011

Reserve Account Entry Summary

Refer to this information for assistance in completing the Good Faith Estimate and/or HUD1 Settlement Statement.

HUD-1 Line/ Account #	Description	Months in Reserve	Monthly Amount	Total Amount
1001	HAZARD INSURANCE		52.73	580.03
1002	MORTGAGE INSURANCE	11	173.43	
1003	CITY PROPERTY TAX			
1004	COUNTY PROPERTY TAX	4	106.09	424.36
1005	ANNUAL ASSESSMEENTS			
1006	FLOOD INSURANCE			
1007				
1008	Aggregate Reserve Adjustment			-52.82
	Escrow Account Beginning Balance			951.57

Initial Escrow Account Disclosure Summary

Month	Payments to Escrow Account	Payments from Escrow Account	Description	Escrow Account Balance
			Escrow Account Beginning Balance	951.57
12/01/XX	332.25	173.43	1002 Mortgage Insurance	1,100.39
01/01/XX	332.25	173.43	1002 Mortgage Insurance	1,269.21
02/01/XX	332.25	632.70	1001 Hazard Insurance	
		173.43	1002 Mortgage Insurance	795.33
03/01/XX	332.25	173.43	1002 Mortgage Insurance	
		636.51	1004 County Property Taxes	317.64
04/01/XX	332.25	173.43	1002 Mortgage Insurance	476.46
05/01/XX	332.25	173.43	1002 Mortgage Insurance	635.28
06/01/XX	332.25	173.43	1002 Mortgage Insurance	794.10
07/01/XX	332.25	173.43	1002 Mortgage Insurance	952.92
08/01/XX	332.25	173.43	1002 Mortgage Insurance	1,111.74
09/01/XX	332.25	173.43	1002 Mortgage Insurance	1,270.56
10/01/XX	332.25	173.43	1002 Mortgage Insurance	1,429.38
11/01/XX	332.25	173.43	1002 Mortgage Insurance	
		636.51	1004 County Property Taxes	951.69

Cushion Information:	Amount	$	317.64		Months:	0 Mortgage Insurance
		$				2 Other Items
Payment Information		$	884.53			
P & I		$	332.25			
Escrow		$	0.00			
Other		$	1,216.78			
Total		$		Beginning on	**DECEMBER 01, 20XX**	

INTIAL ESCROW ACCOUNT DISCLOSURE STATEMENT

Loan #: 2500020183
PMI/MI Case #:
Disclosure Date: OCTOBER 02, 20XX

Lender Borrower(s): BARRY AND BARBARA BORROWER

Address: 1277 ANYWHERE STREET ANY CITY, AS 0000
Servicer: ANPAC FUNDING CORPORATION
Address: P.O. BOX 70808 CHARLOTTE, NC 28272-0808
Toll-Free Phone: (888) 934-1011

THIS IS AN ESTIMATE OF ACTIVITY IN YOUR ESCROW ACCOUNT DURING THE COMING YEAR BASED ON PAYMENTS ANTICIPATED TO BE MADE FROM YOUR ACCOUNT

Month	Payments to Escrow Account	Payments from Escrow Account	Description	Escrow Account Balance
Initial Deposit				951.57
12/01/XX	332.25	173.43	1002 Mortgage Insurance	1,100.39
01/01/XX	332.25	173.43	1002 Mortgage Insurance	1,269.21
02/01/XX	332.25	632.70	1001 Hazard Insurance	
		173.43	1002 Mortgage Insurance	795.33
03/01/XX	332.25	173.43	1002 Mortgage Insurance	
		636.51	1004 County Property Taxes	317.64
04/01/XX	332.25	173.43	1002 Mortgage Insurance	476.46
05/01/XX	332.25	173.43	1002 Mortgage Insurance	635.28
06/01/XX	332.25	173.43	1002 Mortgage Insurance	794.10
07/01/XX	332.25	173.43	1002 Mortgage Insurance	952.92
08/01/XX	332.25	173.43	1002 Mortgage Insurance	1,111.74
09/01/XX	332.25	173.43	1002 Mortgage Insurance	1,270.56
10/01/XX	332.25	173.43	1002 Mortgage Insurance	1,429.38
11/01/XX	332.25	173.43	1002 Mortgage Insurance	
		636.51	1004 County Property Taxes	951.69

(PLEASE KEEP THIS STATEMENT FOR COMPARISON WITH THE ACTUAL ACTIVITY IN YOUR ACCOUNT AT THE END OF THE ESCROW ACCOUNTING COMPUTATION YEAR.)

Cushion selected by servicer: $ 317.64

_____ YOUR MONTHLY MORTGAGE PAYMENT FOR THE COMING YEAR WILL BE $ OF WHICH $ WILL BE FOR PRINCIPAL AND INTEREST, $ WILL GO INTO YOUR ESCROW ACCOUNT AND $ WILL BE FOR DISCRETIONARY ITEMS (SUCH AS LIFE INSURANCE, DISABILITY INSURANCE) THAT YOU CHOSE TO INCLUDE WITH YOUR MONTHLY PAYMENT.

__XX__ YOUR FIRST MONTHLY MORTGAGE PAYMENT FOR THE COMING YEAR WILL BE $ 1,216.78 OF WHICH $ 884.53 WILL BE FOR PRINCIPAL AND INTEREST, $ 332.25 WILL GO INTO YOUR ESCROW ACCOUNT AND $ 0.00 WILL BE FOR DISCRETIONARY ITEMS (SUCH AS LIFE INSURANCE, DISABILITY INSURANCE) THAT YOU CHOSE TO INCLUDE WITH YOUR MONTHLY PAYMENT. THE TERMS OF YOUR LOAN MAY RESULT IN CHANGES TO THE MONTHLY PRINCIPAL AND INTERST PAYMENTS DURING THE YEAR.

_____   _____
BARRY BORROWER   Date

_____   _____
BARBARA BORROWER   Date

SERVICING DISCLOSURE STATEMENT

2500020183

NOTICE TO FIRST-LIEN MORTGAGE LOAN APPLICANTS: The right to collect your mortgage loan payments may be transferred. Federal Law gives you certain related rights. If your loan is made, save this statement with your loan documents. Read this statement and sign it ONLY if you understand its contents.

Because you are applying for a mortgage loan covered by the Real Estate Settlement Procedures Act (RESPA) (12 U.S.C. Section 2601 et seq.) you have certain rights under that Federal Law.

This statement tells you about those rights. It also tells you what the chances are that the servicing for this loan may be transferred to a different loan servicer. "Servicing" refers to collecting your principal, interest and escrow payments, if any. If your loan servicer changes, there are certain procedures that must be followed. This statement generally explains those procedures.

Transfer Practices and Requirements

If the servicing of your loan is assigned, sold or transferred to a new servicer, you must be given written notice of that transfer. The present loan servicer must send you notice in writing of the assignment, sale or transfer of the servicing not less than 15 days before the date of transfer. The new loan servicer must also send you notice within 15 days after the effective date of the transfer. The present servicer and the new servicer may combine this information in one notice, so long as the notice is sent to you 15 days before the effective date of the transfer. A notice of prospective transfer may be provided to you at settlement (when title of your new property is transferred to you) to satisfy these requirements. The law allows a delay in the time (not more than 30 days after a transfer) for servicers to notify you under certain business emergencies.

Notices must contain certain information. They must contain the effective date of the transfer of the servicing of your loan to the new servicer, the name, address and toll-free or collect-call telephone numbers of the servicer, and toll-free or collect-call telephone numbers of a person or department for both your present servicer and your new servicer to answer your questions about the transfer of servicing. During the 60-day period, following the effective date of the transfer of the loan servicing, a loan payment received by your old servicer before its due date may not be treated by the new loan servicer as late, and a late fee may not be imposed on you.

Complaint Resolution

Section 6 of RESPA (12 U.S.C. Section 2605) gives you certain consumer rights, whether or not your loan servicing is transferred. If you send a "qualified written request" to your loan servicer concerning the servicing of the loan, your servicer must provide you with a written acknowledgment within 20 business days of receipt of your request. A "qualified written request" is a written correspondence, other than notice on a payment coupon or other payment medium supplied by the servicer, which includes your name and account number, and your reasons for the request. Not later than 60 days after receiving your request, your servicer must make any appropriate corrections to your account, and must provide you with a written clarification regarding any dispute. During this 60-day period, your servicer may not provide information to a consumer reporting agency concerning any overdue payment related to such period of qualified written request.

A business day is any day in which the offices of the business entity are open to the public for carrying on substantially all of its business functions.

Damages and Costs

Section 6 of RESPA also provides for damages and costs for individuals or classes of individuals in circumstances where servicers are shown to have violated the requirements of that Section.

Servicing Transfer Estimates by Original Lender

The following is the best estimate of what will happen to the servicing of your mortgage loan:

1. ___X___ We do not service mortgage loans. We intend to assign, sell, or transfer the servicing of your loan to another party. You will be notified of your servicer.

   OR

   _____ We are able to service this loan and presently intend to do so. However, that may change in the future.
   _____ We are able to service this loan, but have not decided whether or not to do so. You will be notified of your servicer.

   OR

   _____ We are able to service this loan, but have decided not to do so. You will be notified of your servicer.

2. For all the loans that we make in the 12 month period after your loan is funded, we estimate that the chances that we will transfer the servicing of those loans is between:

   _____ 0 to 25% (none) _____ 26 to 50% _____ 50 to 75% ___X___ 76 to 100% (all)

This is only our best estimate and it is not binding. Business conditions or other circumstances may affect our future transferring decisions. This estimate does not include assignments, sales or transfers to affiliates or subsidiaries.

3. _____ We have previously assigned, sold, or transferred the servicing of first lien mortgages.

ANPAC FUNDING CORP. D/B/A ANPAC LENDING GROUP

_____   _____
Lender   Representative/Title

ACKNOWLEDGMENT OF MORTGAGE APPLICANT

I/We have read this disclosure form, and understand its contents, as evidenced by my/our signature(s) below. I/we understand that this acknowledgment is a required part of the mortgage loan application.

_____
BARRY BORROWER   Date

_____
BARRY BORROWER   Date

BORROWER   **2500020183**
1277 ANYWHERE STREET
ANY CITY, AS 00000
ANPAC FUNDING CORP. D/B/A ANPAC LENDING GROUP, A CALIFORNIA CORPORATION

BORROWER'S CERTIFICATION

In connection with the above identified loan which is being closed as of this date, I (we) hereby certify that my (our) financial status, employment and income are substantially the same as they were at the time I (we) made my (our) application for said loan.

_____

Borrower **BARRY BORROWER**   Date

_____

Borrower **BARRY BORROWER**   Date

OCCUPANCY STATEMENT

Lender: IMPAC FUNDING CORP. D/B/A IMPAC LENDING GROUP
Borrower Name: BARBARA & BARRY BORROWER
Loan #: 2500020183
Date:
Property Address:

Borrower hereby declares, under penalty of perjury, as follows:

☐   **Owner Occupied**
I/We will occupy the subject property as my/our principal residence within 60 days after the date of closing as required by, and in compliance with, the terms of the Deed of Trust/Mortgage/Security Instrument relating to the subject property. I/We will continue to occupy the property as my/our principal residence for at least one year after the date of occupancy, unless Lender otherwise agrees in writing.

☐   **Occupied as a Second Home**
I/We will occupy the subject property as my/our second residence as required by, and in compliance with, the terms of the Deed of Trust/Mortgage/Security Instrument relating to the subject property.

☐   **Investment Property - Will Not Occupy**
I/We will not occupy the subject property.

I/We are aware of and understand that if at any time it is determined that the foregoing statement is untrue, I/We will be subject to prosecution for fraud under applicable state laws.

I certify under penalty of Chapter 18, U.S.C. 1010 to 1014 that the statement contained herein is true and correct.

_____
– BORROWER –   – DATE –

STATE OF ————————————————

COUNTY OF:————————————————

Subscribed and sworn to before me this   day of   .

WITNESS my hand and official seal.   Signature: _____
                                          Name (typed or printed)
                                          My Commission Expires:

FLOOD INSURANCE CERTIFICATION AND NOTICE

RE: Borrower: **BARRY BORROWER AND BARBARA BORROWER**

Address: **1277 ANYWHERE STREET**

City and State: **ANY CITY, ANY STATE 00000**

Loan No.:   **2500020183**   **Flood Map No.:**

_____   The above referenced property is located in an area which has been identified by the Federal Emergency Management Agency as having special flood hazards. Flood insurance has been made available under the National Flood Insurance Program and such coverage will be obtained.

__XX__   The above referenced property is not located in an area identified by the Federal Emergency Management Agency as having special flood hazards. Federal law requires that if the Lender or its servicer determines at any time during the term of the loan that the building or mobile home and any personal property securing the loan is not adequately covered by flood insurance as required by law, the Lender or its servicer shall notify the Borrower that the Borrower should obtain flood insurance, at Borrower's expense, within 45 days after notification. If the Borrower fails to do so, the Lender or its servicer will purchase the insurance on the Borrower's behalf and charge the Borrower for the cost of premiums and fees incurred in purchasing the insurance.

ANPAC FUNDING CORP. D/B/A ANPAC LENDING GROUP
1401 COVE STREET, SUITE 100
NEWPORT BEACH, CALIFORNIA 92660

By: _____

Title: _____

_____   _____
Borrower **BARRY BORROWER**   Date

_____   _____
Borrower **BARBARA BORROWER**   Date

BORROWER   2500020183
1277 ANYWHERE STREET
ANY CITY, ANY STATE 00000
ANPAC FUNDING CORP. D/B/A ANPAC LENDING GROUP, A CALIFORNIA CORPORATION

AFFIDAVIT OF DISBURSEMENT AND FIRST LIEN LETTER

I, the undersigned Settlement Agent, do hereby state that I have closed and properly disbursed connection with the above-referenced loan.

The Security Instrument is a valid first lien on the Property with all requirements of the captioned title commitment having been satisfied; all taxes and special assessments which constitute a valid lien on the subject Property have been paid in full.

ESCROW PALACE _____
(Settlement Agent/Title Company Name)

By: _____

Title: _____

Date: _____

NOTES

The "Affidavit of Disbursement and First Lien Letter" is to be signed by the closing agent, not the Notary Signing Agent. The form should be left blank.

BORROWER   2500020183
1277 ANYWHERE STREET
ANY CITY, ANY STATE 00000
ANPAC FUNDING CORP. D/B/A ANPAC LENDING GROUP, A CALIFORNIA CORPORATION

QUALITY CONTROL RELEASE

We, the undersigned applicants, understand that our mortgage application may be selected for a Quality Control Review. This review may be performed by the Lender, the Lender's Quality Control Review Agent, and/or the Lender's Successors and Assigns. Such a review, which may occur up to one year after the closing of the loan, is aimed at producing and maintaining quality service for your borrowers and will include a reverification of the credit information and a review of the appraisal.

You are hereby authorized to release to the Lender, its Agent and/or Successors and Assigns any information required to allow for the conducting of a quality control review which will include reverification of credit documentation and appraisal information.

A photocopy of this form may be deemed as acceptable authorization for release of any of the above information or documentation requested. The original signed form is maintained by the Lender.

_____   _____
Borrower **BARRY BORROWER**   Social Security Number

_____   _____
Borrower **BARBARA BORROWER**   Social Security Number

RIGHT TO RECEIVE A COPY OF AN APPRAISAL

You have the right to a copy of the appraisal report used in connection with your application for credit. If you wish a copy, please write to us at the mailing address below. We must hear from you no later than 90 days after we notify you about the action taken on your credit application or you withdraw your application.

ANPAC FUNDING CORP. D/B/A ANPAC LENDING GROUP, A CALIFORNIA CORPORATION
1401 COVE STREET,SUITE 100
NEWPORT BEACH, CALIFORNIA 92660

_____

Borrower **BARRY BORROWER**   Date

_____

Borrower **BARBARA BORROWER**   Date

2500020183

ANPAC FUNDING CORP. D/B/A ANPAC LENDING GROUP, A CALIFORNIA CORPORATION

MAILING ADDRESS CERTIFICATION

As borrower(s), I/we plan to move into the property on or about _____.

The mailing address for the property is:

1277 ANYWHERE STREET _____

ANY CITY, ANY STATE _____ Zip **00000**

All correspondences should be sent to the following address:

_____

_____

I/We will keep you advised should there be any change in the above mailing addresses.

_____
Borrower **BARRY BORROWER**   Date

_____
Borrower **BARBARA BORROWER**   Date

NOTICE TO BORROWER(S)

**MONTHLY ESCROW PAYMENTS ARE SUBJECT
TO SIGNIFICANT INCREASES WHEN
FINANCING NEW CONSTRUCTION**

2500020183

Your initial escrow deposit and monthly escrow payments are determined in accordance with the Real Estate Settlement Procedures Act of 1974 and its implementing regulations (RESPA). Compliance with these RESPA requirements in some instances may result in significant increases in required escrow payments during the first few years of a loan, particularly with loans to finance new construction.

Your initial escrow deposit and monthly payment amounts are generally based on the most recent assessment of your property value. With newly constructed homes, the assessment may be based on unimproved or partially improved property (the construction of your home had not been started or was not fully completed). As a result, the amount of property taxes due in the first year may be less than in future years. Your loan servicer will analyze your account at least annually to determine whether your escrow account has sufficient funds and to determine whether a change in your monthly escrow payment is required.

It is likely YOUR PROPERTY TAXES WILL INCREASE SUBSTANTIALLY WITHIN THE FIRST 12 - 24 MONTHS OF YOUR LOAN when an assessment has been performed based on the fully improved value of your home. As a result, YOUR MONTHLY ESCROW PAYMENT IS LIKELY TO INCREASE SIGNIFICANTLY.

_____

The undersigned borrower(s) acknowledge(s) that I/we have read and understand this notice.

_____
Borrower **BARRY BORROWER**   Date

_____
Borrower **BARBARA BORROWER**   Date

NOTICE OF RIGHT TO CANCEL

...o Cancel

...g into a transaction that will result in a security interest in your home. You have a legal right ...aw to cancel this transaction, without cost, within three business days from whichever of the ...ts occurs last:

 the date of the transaction, which is _____; or

 the date you received your Truth in Lending disclosures; or

 the date you received this notice of your right to cancel.

...e transaction, the security interest is also cancelled. Within 20 calendar days after we ...tice, we must take the steps necessary to reflect the fact that the security interest in your home has been cancelled, and we must return to you any money or property you have given to us or to anyone else in connection with this transaction.

You may keep any money or property we have given you until we have done the things mentioned above, but you must then offer to return the money or property. If it is impractical or unfair for you to return the property, you must offer its reasonable value. You may offer to return the property at your home or at the location of the property. Money must be returned to the address below. If we do not take possession of the money or property within 20 calendar days of your offer, you may keep it without further obligation.

How to Cancel

If you decide to cancel this transaction, you may do so by notifying us in writing, at:

ANPAC FUNDING CORP. D/B/A ANPAC LENDING GROUP
1401 COVE STREET, SUITE 100
NEWPORT BEACH, CALIFORNIA 92660

You may use any written statement that is signed and dated by you and states your intention to cancel, or you may use this notice by dating and signing below. Keep one copy of this notice because it contains important information about your rights. If you cancel by mail or telegram, you must send the notice no later than midnight of _____ (or midnight of the third business day following the latest of the three events listed above). If you send or deliver your written notice to cancel some other way, it must be delivered to the above address no later than that time.

_____   Date: _____
Consumer's Signature

I acknowledge receipt of two copies of the foregoing "Notice of Right to Cancel," as well as one copy of other Truth in Lending disclosures.

_____   _____
Borrower **BARRY BORROWER**   Date

_____   _____
Borrower **BARBARA BORROWER**   Date

FIRST PAYMENT LETTER

ANPAC Funding Corporation

LOAN NO.: **2500020183**
DATE: **July 25, 20XX**
BORROWER(S): **Barry Borrower**

Barbara Borrower

ADDRESS: **1000 Anywhere Street, Any City, Any State 00000**

We are pleased to have you as a mortgage loan customer. The following is a breakdown of your initial monthly payment:

Principal and Interest	$ 884.53
Estimated Taxes	$ 106.09
Hazard Insurance	$ 52.73
Flood Insurance	$
Mortgage Insurance	$ 173.43
City Property Tax	$
	$
	$
	$
	$
TOTAL MONTHLY PAYMENT	$ 1,216.78

Your first regular payment is due **September 1, 20XX.**

Partial Payments:
- ☐ Your lender may accept partial payments you make and apply such payments to your loan.
- ☐ Your lender may hold partial payments in a separate account until you pay the remainder of the payment, and then apply the full periodic payment to your loan.
- ☒ Your lender will not accept any partial payments.

If this loan is sold, your new lender may have a different policy.

The outstanding principal balance at the time of this letter is **$166,500.00.**

The current interest rate is **6.375 %.**

Your loan **DOES NOT** have a prepayment penalty.

Housing Counselor Information: If you would like counseling or assistance, you can contact the following:

- U.S. Department of Housing and Urban Development (HUD): For a list of homeownership counselors or counseling organizations in your area, go to http://www.hud.gov/ or call 800-225-5342.

For additional information regarding your loan please contact: **ANPAC Funding Corporation**

at **314-628-2213.**

We hereby acknowledge receiving a copy of this letter.

We are aware that the total monthly payment may be subject to change each year due to increases or decreases in annual taxes and/or insurance premiums and when applicable, adjustments in accordance with the adjustable rate mortgage provisions of the Note.

_____   _____
Barry Borrower   **DATE**

_____   _____
Barbara Borrower   **DATE**

Ellie Mae, Inc.

GPT6 1015
GPT6 (CLS)

NOTICE OF ASSIGNMENT, SALE, OR TRANSFER
OF SERVICING RIGHTS

You are hereby notified that the servicing of your mortgage loan, that is, the right to collect payments from you, is being assigned, sold or transferred from:

ANPAC FUNDING CORP. D/B/A IMPAC LENDING GROUP

to: **ANPAC FUNDING CORPORATION**

effective: **DECEMBER 01, 20XX**

The assignment, sale or transfer of the servicing of the mortgage loan does not affect any term or condition of the mortgage instruments, other than terms directly related to the servicing of your loan.

Except in limited circumstances, the law requires that your present servicer send you this notice at least 15 days before the effective date of transfer, or at closing. Your new servicer must also send you this notice no later than 15 days after this effective date or at closing.

Your present servicer is: **ANPAC FUNDING CORP. D/B/A ANPAC LENDING GROUP**

If you have any questions relating to the transfer of servicing from your present servicer call:

CUSTOMER SERVICE at: **800-597-4101** during normal business hours. This is a toll-free or collect call number.

Your new servicer will be: **ANPAC FUNDING CORPORATION**

The business address for your new servicer is: **1401 COVE STREET, SUITE 100**
NEWPORT BEACH, CALIFORNIA 92606

The toll-free or collect call telephone number of your new servicer is **(800) 597-4101.**

If you have any questions relating to the transfer of servicing to your new servicer call:

CUSTOMER SERVICE at **(888) 934-1011** during normal business hours.

The date that your present servicer will stop accepting payments from you is: **DECEMBER 01, 20XX.** The date that your new servicer will start accepting payments from you is **DECEMBER 01, 20XX.** Send all payments due on or after that date to your new servicer.

The transfer of servicing rights may affect the terms of or the continued availability of mortgage life or disability insurance or any other type of optional insurance in the following manner:
N/A
and you should take the following action to maintain coverage:
N/A

You should also be aware of the following information, which is set out in more detail in Section 6 of the Real Estate Settlement Procedures Act (RESPA) (12 V.S.C. 2605):

During the 60-day period following the effective date of the transfer of the loan servicing, a loan payment received by your old servicer before its due date may not be treated by the new loan servicer as late, and a late fee may not be imposed on you.

Section 6 of RESPA (12 V.S.C. 2605) gives you certain consumer rights. If you send a "qualified written request" to your loan servicer concerning the servicing of your loan, your servicer must provide you with a written acknowledgment within 20 Business Days of receipt of your request. A "qualified written request" is a written correspondence, other than notice on a payment coupon or other payment medium supplied by the servicer, which includes your name and account number, and your reasons for the request. (If you want to send a "qualified written request" regarding the servicing of your loan, it must be sent to this address: **1401 COVE STREET, SUITE 100, NEWPORT BEACH, CALIFORNIA 92606).**

Not later than 60 Business Days after receiving your request, your servicer must make any appropriate corrections to your account, and must provide you with a written clarification regarding any dispute. During this 60 Business Day period, your servicer may not provide information to a consumer reporting agency concerning any overdue payment related to such period or qualified written request. However, this does not prevent the servicer from initiating foreclosure if proper grounds exist under the mortgage documents.

A Business Day is a day on which the offices of the business entity are open to the public for carrying on substantially all of its business functions.

Section 6 of RESPA also provides for damages and costs for individuals or classes of individuals in circumstances where servicers are shown to have violated the requirements of that Section. You should seek legal advice if you believe your rights have been violated.

_____

Borrower **BARRY BORROWER**   Date

_____

Borrower **BARBARA BORROWER**   Date

Tax Information Sheet

Instructions: This form must be completed on every loan and submitted with the closing package for review prior to funding. Complete any of the following tax authority sections that apply to this property. Taxes which are due within 30 days of closing must be paid unless tax escrows are waived. If taxes are presently past due must be paid by the closing agent. In addition, proof of payment via a paid receipt must be attached.

Borrower: **Barry and Barbara Borrower**　　　　Loan No. **2500020183**

Property Address: **1000 Anywhere Street, Any City, AS 00000**

Mailing Address: **1000 Anywhere Street, Any City, AS 00000**

Owner of Record on January 1st of Current Year: _____

Previous Owner: _____

If new property, estimated annual real estate tax: _____

If existing property, amount of last tax bill: _____

Note: If property contains more than one parcel or lot, you must provide each individual tax ID number.

City/Town Tax payable to:

Tax Authority Name: _____

Tax Authority Address: _____

Telephone: _____

Tax ID/Account #: _____

Estimated Annual Tax: _____ Improvement levy/supplemental Amount_____

Last paid date: _____ Amount paid:_____ Period covered: _____

Next due date: _____ Amount due: _____ Period covered: _____

Monthly Escrow: _____ Discount date: _____ Penalty date:_____

Required Frequency of Payment: ☐ Annually ☐ Semi-Annually ☐ Quarterly ☐ Monthly

County Tax payable to:
Tax Authority Name: _____

Tax Authority Address: _____

Tax ID/Account #: _____

Estimated Annual Tax: _____ Improvement levy/supplemental Amount:_____

Last paid date: _____ Amount paid:_____ Period covered:

Next due date: _____ Amount due: _____ Period covered:

Monthly Escrow: _____ Discount date: _____ Penalty date:

Required Frequency of Payment: ☐ Annually ☐ Semi-Annually ☐ Quarterly ☐ Monthly

Other: School/Ground Rent/Leasehold/Etc.　Tax payable to:
Tax Authority Name: _____

Tax Authority Address: _____

Tax ID/Account #: _____

Estimated Annual Tax: _____ Improvement levy/supplemental Amount:_____

Last paid date: _____ Amount paid:_____ Period covered:

Next due date: _____ Amount due: _____ Period covered:

Monthly Escrow: _____ Discount date: _____ Penalty date:

Required Frequency of Payment: ☐ Annually ☐ Semi-Annually ☐ Quarterly ☐ Monthly

Certification

I have completed this form accurately and completely and certify one of the following:

☐　A. This is to certify that I have determined the taxes to be current through the last tax period and further that taxes will next be due on _____ which is beyond the 30 day requirement.

☐　B. This is to certify that I have obtained the tax bills for the property captioned above and have paid those taxes in full in the amount of $_____ on _____ for the taxes due on _____. A tax receipt is attached. Taxes are now current and are next due on

☐　C. Taxes are due less than 30 days from closing but bills are unavailable. Payment in the amount of $_____ was collected at closing; payment will be made by Closing Agent/Lender (select one).

**Internal Use Only: SunTrust to disburse taxes ___　　Lender to disburse taxes ___

_____　　　_____
Closing Agent Signature　　　　　　　　　Date

COR 0034

Certification

The undersigned certify the following:

1. I/We have applied for a mortgage loan from **ANPAC FUNDING CORP. D/B/A ANPAC LENDING GROUP** (Lender).
    In applying for the loan, I/we completed a loan application containing various information on the purpose of the loan, the amount and source of the downpayment, employment and income information, and assets and liabilities. I/we certify that all of the information is true and complete. I/We made no misrepresentation in the loan application or other documents, nor did I/we omit any pertinent information.

2. I/We understand and agree that **ANPAC FUNDING CORP. D/B/A ANPAC LENDING GROUP** (Lender)
    reserves the right to change the mortgage loan review process to a full documentation program. This may include verifying the information provided on the application with the employer and/or the financial institution.

3. I/We fully understand that it is a Federal crime punishable by fine or imprisonment, or both, to knowingly make any false statements when applying for this mortgage loan, as applicable under the provisions of Title 18, United States Code, Section 1014.

Authorization to Release Information

To Whom It May Concern:

1. I/We have applied for a mortgage loan from **ANPAC FUNDING CORP. D/B/A ANPAC LENDING GROUP** (Lender).
    As a part of the application process, **ANPAC FUNDING CORP. D/B/A ANPAC LENDING GROUP** (Lender)
    and the mortgage guaranty insurer (if any) may verify information contained in my/our loan application and in other documents required in connection with the loan, either before the loan is closed or as of its quality control program.

2. I/We authorize you to provide to **ANPAC FUNDING CORP. D/B/A ANPAC LENDING GROUP** (Lender),
    and to any investors to whom **ANPAC FUNDING CORP. D/B/A ANPAC LENDING GROUP** (Lender)
    may sell my mortgage loan, any and all documents that they request. Such information includes, but is not limited to, employment history and income; bank, money market, and similar account balances; credit history; and copies of income tax returns.

3. **ANPAC FUNDING CORP. D/B/A ANPAC LENDING GROUP** (Lender)
    or any other investor that purchases the mortgage loan, or the mortgage guaranty insurer (if any), may address this authorization to any party named in the application.

4. A copy of this authorization may be accepted as an original.

5. Your prompt reply to **ANPAC FUNDING CORP. D/B/A ANPAC LENDING GROUP** (Lender),
    the investor that purchased the mortgage loan, or the mortgage guaranty insurer (if any) is appreciated.

6. Mortgage guaranty insurer (if any).

BARRY BORROWER (Borrower's Signature)   (Social Security Number)

BARRY BORROWER (Borrower's Signature)   (Social Security Number)

LENDER FINANCIAL SERVICES CORP
DRAFT AUTHORIZATION

WFSC SERVICE
YOUR NAME: BORROWER_____   **(LOAN) NUMBER: _____**

This completed and signed form serves as authorization my checking account for my monthly loan payment.

Please circle the type of account to be drafted: checking   or   savings

My bank account is with _____
                                                    Name of Bank

_____   _____   _____
         Branch   City   State

My bank account number is _____. The bank transit number

(nine digit number in the bottom left hand corner of checks) is _____

Date of the month payment is to be drafted_____ . You may choose a date up to 9 days after your due date. For instance, if your payment is DUE on the first of the month, regardless of your grace days, you may be drafted as late as the tenth of the month.

ADDITIONAL FUNDS TO PRINCIPAL:

I request to have an additional $_____ per month drafted from my account to be applied as principal reduction.

I understand that Lender Financial Services Corp will notify me in writing of the first effective date of the draft which will coincide with the due date. I will continue to send a check with my coupon until I am notified (Allow 6 to 8 weeks for processing).

The draft will be in effect until I notify LENDER FINANCIAL that this service is no longer desired, allowing reasonable time to act on my notification and discontinue the monthly withdrawal. If an error occurs in the processing of drafting my account, I understand that corrective debits or credits may be necessary.

I understand that LENDER FINANCIAL SERVICES CORP reserves the right to revoke this authorization and will notify me in writing if this option is exercised.

I understand that the draft will not take place if my loan is delinquent, and in such case, I must remit all payments directly to LENDER FINANCIAL SERVICES CORP, P. O. Box 26903, Greensboro, NC 27419-6903.

PLEASE ATTACH VERIFICATION A VOIDED CHECK FOR BANK TRANSIT AND ACCOUNT NUMBER VERIFICATION. NOTE: THIS AUTHORIZATION CANNOT BE PROCESSED WITHOUT SUFFICIENT BANK INFORMATION.

THIS AUTHORIZATION IS NON-NEGOTIABLE AND NON-TRANSFERABLE.

_____
Borrower **BARRY BORROWER**   Date

_____
Borrower **BARBARA BORROWER**   Date

If this request was not submitted during the application process, Please fax or forward to:
Customer Service Fax number: 336-664-1865
AceVendor Financial Services Corp, P.O. Box 26903, Greensboro, NC 27419

IMPORTANT PRIVACY CHOICES FOR CONSUMERS

You have the right to control whether we share some of your personal information.
Please read the following information carefully before you make your choices
below.

ANPAC Companies

Your Rights

You have the following rights to restrict the sharing of personal and financial information with our affiliates (companies we own or control) and outside companies that we do business with. Nothing in this form prohibits the sharing of information necessary for us to follow the law, as permitted by law, or to give you the best service on your accounts with us. This includes sending you information about some other products or services.

Your Choices

Restrict Information Sharing With Companies We Own or Control (Affiliates): Unless you say "No," we may share personal and financial information about you with our affiliated companies.

☐ NO, please do not share personal and financial information with your affiliated companies.

Restrict Information Sharing With Other Companies We Do Business With To Provide Financial Products And Services: Unless you say "No," we may share personal and financial information about you with outside companies we contract with to provide financial products and services to you.

☐ NO, please do not share personal and financial information with outside companies you contract with to provide financial products and services.

Time Sensitive Reply

You may make your privacy choice(s) at any time. Your choice(s) marked here will remain unless you state otherwise. However, if we do not hear from you we may share some of your information with affiliated companies and other companies with whom we have contracts to provide products and services.

Name: **Barry Borrower** _____

Account or Policy Number(s): _____ [to be filled in by consumer]

Signature: _____

To exercise your choices do one of the following:

[Mandatory]

(1) Fill out, sign and send back this form to us using the envelope provided (you may want to make a copy for your records)

[Optional]

(2) Call this toll-free number: **888-250-6522**

OR

(3) Reply electronically by contacting us through the following Internet option:

www.usa-mortgage.com

Ellie Mae, Inc.

CAPRIV_S 0316
CAPRIVS (CLS)

Sample Set 2

1

Subordination Agreement   U.S. Department of Housing   OMB Approval No. 2502-0598
                                and Urban Development
                                Office of Housing

Public Reporting Burden for this collection of information is estimated to average 0.5 hours per response, including the time for reviewing instructions, searching existing data sources, gathering and maintaining the data needed, and completing and reviewing the collection of information. Response to this request for information is required in order to receive the benefits to be derived. This agency may not collect this information, and you are not required to complete this form unless it displays a currently valid OMB control number. While no assurance of confidentiality is pledged to respondents, HUD generally discloses this data only in response to a Freedom of Information Act request.

Project Name: _____
HUD Project No: 621-080-000 _____

S SUBORDINATION AGREEMENT ("Agreement") is entered into this
of October _____, _20XX_ by and among (i)
___ Far East National Bank _____, a _____ ("Senior
ii) _____, a _____
ate Lender"), and (iii)
_____ ("Borrower").

Recitals

EREAS, Borrower is the owner of that certain _____ unit residential rental
nt known as "_____" ("Project"), located at
_____. Senior Lender has made or is making the senior
an as described on Schedule A hereto ("Senior Indebtedness") to
the original principal amount(s) as shown on Schedule A, evidenced by the
bed in Schedule A ("Senior Note"), and secured by, among other things,
Instrument as described in Schedule A (collectively, "Senior Security
"), covering the property described in Exhibit A attached hereto together
rovements thereon and personal property used relative thereof, all as more
described in the Senior Security Instrument ("Mortgaged Property").

EREAS, {CHOOSE ONE OF THE FOLLOWING BRACKETED OPTIONS
HERE AND THROUGHOUT THE DOCUMENT, AS APPROPRIATE} [Borrower has
requested Senior Lender to permit Subordinate Lender to make] [Subordinate Lender
made] a subordinate loan to Borrower in the amount of $ _____
ate Loan"), pursuant to the Subordinate Loan Documents as defined below,
d by, among other things, a mortgage lien against the Mortgaged Property.

EREAS, Senior Lender, with the approval of the U.S. Department of Housing
Development ("HUD"), has agreed to permit Subordinate Lender to [make the
Loan and to place a subordinate mortgage lien] [keep the Subordinate Loan
and maintain a subordinate mortgage lien] against the Mortgaged Property
l of the conditions contained in this Agreement and in accordance with
bligations. "Program Obligations" means (1) all applicable statutes and
ons issued by the Secretary pursuant thereto that apply to the Project,
including all amendments to such statutes and regulations, as they become effective,

Subordination Agreement   HUD-92420M

provided, however, that all such counterparts shall together constitute one and the same instrument.

Each signatory below hereby certifies that each of their statements and representations contained in this Agreement and all their supporting documentation thereto are true, accurate, and complete. This Agreement has been made, presented, and delivered for the purpose of influencing an official action of HUD in insuring the Loan, and may be relied upon by HUD as a true statement of the facts contained therein.

IN WITNESS WHEREOF, the parties hereto have executed this Agreement as of the day and year first written above.

SENIOR LENDER:

By: _____

Name:_____

Title:_____

SUBORDINATE LENDER:

By:_____

Name:_____

Title:_____

BORROWER:

By: John Maxell_____

Name: _____

Subordination Agreement   HUD-92420M

Title: _____

[Jurats to be added]

Warning:

Any person who knowingly presents a false, fictitious, or fraudulent statement or claim in a matter within the jurisdiction of the U.S. Department of Housing and Urban Development is subject to criminal penalties, civil liability, and administrative sanctions.

NOTES

Depending upon the timing of the transaction, the owner of the second mortgage may have already executed the "Subordination Agreement" and have had his or her signature notarized.

Subordination Agreement   HUD-92420M

Recording requested by (name):

XYZ Title

When recorded mail to
and mail tax statements to:
John A. Maxell

10116 Chevrolet Drive

Los Angeles

California, 90060

Recorder's Use Onl[y]

GRANT DEED

Assessor's Parcel No. (APN):
4316-016-000

Documentary Transfer Tax: $ 0.00
If exempt, enter R&T code: _____
Explanation: _____
_____
_____

Signature of Declarant or Agent determining tax

Declaration of Exemption From Gov't Code

☐ Transfer is exempt from fee per GC § 2738
   ☐ recorded concurrently "in connection with
      Documentary Transfer Tax
   ☐ recorded concurrently "in connection with" a transfer of
      residential dwelling to an owner-occupier
☐ Transfer is exempt from fee per GC 27388.1(a)(1):
   ☐ Fee cap of $225.00 reached   ☐ Not related to real property

For a valuable consideration, receipt of which is hereby acknowledged,

GRANTOR(S) John A. Maxell ,
      (owners who are signing deed)

a single man ,
(current owner(s) form of title)

hereby grant(s) to GRANTEE(S) John A. Maxell
      (new owners, including current owners if staying on title)

The Maxell Family Trust
(new owners, continued)

as Trustee
   (new owner(s) form of title)

the following real property in the City of Los Angeles ,

County of Los Angeles , California (insert legal description):

Lot 147 of Tract 15299, in the city of Los Angeles, County of Los Angeles, State of California as per map recorded in book 407, page(s) 6 to 9 inclusive of maps, in the office of the county recorder of said county

Date: October 18, 20XX

_____
(Signature of declarant)

_____
(Print name)

Date: _____

_____
(Signature of declarant)

_____
(Print name)

PRELIMINARY CHANGE OF OWNERSHIP REPORT

To be completed by the transferee (buyer) prior to a transfer of subject property, in accordance with section 480.3 of the Revenue and Taxation Code. A *Preliminary Change of Ownership Report* must be **filed with each conveyance in the County Recorder's office for the county where the property is located.**

ERNEST J. DRONENBURG, JR.
SAN DIEGO COUNTY ASSESSOR/RECORDER/COUNTY CLERK
1600 PACIFIC HIGHWAY, SUITE 103, SAN DIEGO, CA 92101
TELEPHONE (619) 531-5730

FOR RECORDER USE ONLY

ASSESSOR'S PARCEL NUMBER
4316-016-000

SELLER/TRANSFEROR
The Maxell Family Trust

BUYER/TRANSFEREE

NOTES

The "Preliminary Change of Owner-ship Report" is filed with the county clerk whenever there is a change or transfer of ownership of real property in California. Similar forms may be required in other states. This form is to be completed by transferee (buyer) prior to transfer of subject property.

... NUMBER

... L LOCATION OF REAL PROPERTY

...ve, Los Angeles, CA 90060

...roperty is intended as my principal residence. If YES, please indicate the date of occupancy ...nded occupancy.

MO	DAY	YEAR

...u a disabled veteran or a unmarried surviving spouse of a disabled veteran who was ...ensated at 100% by the Department of Veterans Affairs?

...TION TO (NAME)

...TION TO (ADDRESS) | CITY | STATE | ZIP CODE
...ve | Los Angeles | CA | 90060

PART 1. TRANSFER INFORMATION   *Please complete all statements.*

This section contains possible exclusions from reassessment for certain types of transfers.

YES NO

☐ ☐ A. This transfer is solely between spouses *(addition or removal of a spouse, death of a spouse, divorce settlement, etc.).*

☐ ☐ B. This transfer is solely between domestic partners currently registered with the California Secretary of State *(addition or removal of a partner, death of a partner, termination settlement, etc.).*

☐ ☐ * C. This is a transfer: ☐ between parent(s) and child(ren)   ☐ from grandparent(s) to grandchild(ren).

☐ ☐ * D. This transfer is the result of a cotenant's death. Date of death _____

☐ ☐ * E. This transaction is to replace a principal residence owned by a person 55 years of age or older. Within the same county? ☐ YES ☐ NO

☐ ☐ * F. This transaction is to replace a principal residence by a person who is severely disabled as defined by Revenue and Taxation Code section 69.5. Within the same county? ☐ YES ☐ NO

☐ ☐ G. This transaction is only a correction of the name(s) of the person(s) holding title to the property *(e.g., a name change upon marriage).* If YES, please explain: _____

☐ ☐ H. The recorded document creates, terminates, or reconveys a lender's interest in the property.

☐ ☐ I. This transaction is recorded only as a requirement for financing purposes or to create, terminate, or reconvey a security interest *(e.g., cosigner).* If YES, please explain: _____

☐ ☐ J. The recorded document substitutes a trustee of a trust, mortgage, or other similar document.

K. This is a transfer of property:

☐ ☐ 1. to/from a revocable trust that may be revoked by the transferor and is for the benefit of
   ☐ the transferor, and/or ☐ the transferor's spouse ☐ registered domestic partner.

☐ ☐ 2. to/from an irrevocable trust for the benefit of the
   ☐ creator/grantor/trustor and/or ☐ grantor's/trustor's spouse ☐ grantor's/trustor's registered domestic partner.

☐ ☐ L. This property is subject to a lease with a remaining lease term of 35 years or more including written options.

☐ ☐ M. This is a transfer between parties in which proportional interests of the transferor(s) and transferee(s) in each and every parcel being transferred remain exactly the same after the transfer.

☐ ☐ N. This is a transfer subject to subsidized low-income housing requirements with governmentally imposed restrictions, or restrictions imposed by specified nonprofit corporations.

☐ ☐ * O. This transfer is to the first purchaser of a new building containing an active solar energy system.

☐ ☐ P. Other. This transfer is to _____

* Please refer to the instructions for Part 1.

Please provide any other information that will help the Assessor understand the nature of the transfer.

THIS DOCUMENT IS NOT SUBJECT TO PUBLIC INSPECTION

PART 2. OTHER TRANSFER INFORMATION   *Check and complete as applicable.*

A. Date of transfer, if other than recording date: _____

B. Type of transfer:

☐ Purchase   ☐ Foreclosure   ☐ Gift   ☐ Trade or exchange   ☐ Merger, stock, or partnership acquisition (Form BOE-100-B)

☐ Contract of sale. Date of contract: _____   ☐ Inheritance. Date of death: _____

☐ Sale/leaseback   ☐ Creation of a lease   ☐ Assignment of a lease   ☐ Termination of a lease. Date lease began: _____

Original term in years *(including written options)*: _____   Remaining term in years *(including written options)*: _____

☐ Other. Please explain: _____

C. Only a partial interest in the property was transferred. ☐ YES ☐ NO   If YES, indicate the percentage transferred: _____ %

PART 3. PURCHASE PRICE AND TERMS OF SALE   *Check and complete as applicable.*

A. Total purchase price $_____

B. Cash down payment or value of trade or exchange excluding closing costs   Amount $_____

C. First deed of trust @ _____% interest for _____ years.   Monthly payment $_____   Amount $_____

☐ FHA (___Discount Points)   ☐ Cal-Vet   ☐ VA (___Discount Points)   ☐ Fixed rate   ☐ Variable rate

☐ Bank/Savings & Loan/Credit Union   ☐ Loan carried by seller

☐ Balloon payment $_____   Due date: _____

D. Second deed of trust @ _____% interest for _____ years. Monthly payment $_____   Amount $_____

☐ Fixed rate   ☐ Variable rate   ☐ Bank/Savings & Loan/Credit Union   ☐ Loan carried by seller

☐ Balloon payment $_____   Due date: _____

E. Was an Improvement Bond or other public financing assumed by the buyer? ☐ YES ☐ NO   Outstanding balance $_____

F. Amount, if any, of real estate commission fees paid by the buyer which are not included in the purchase price $_____

G. The property was purchased: ☐ Through real estate broker. Broker name: _____ Phone number: (___) _____

☐ Direct from seller   ☐ From a family member-Relationship _____

☐ Other. Please explain: _____

H. Please explain any special terms, seller concessions, broker/agent fees waived, financing, and any other information (e.g., buyer assumed the existing loan balance) that would assist the Assessor in the valuation of your property. _____

PART 4. PROPERTY INFORMATION   *Check and complete as applicable.*

A. Type of property transferred

☐ Single-family residence   ☐ Co-op/Own-your-own   ☐ Manufactured home

☐ Multiple-family residence. Number of units: _____   ☐ Condominium   ☐ Unimproved lot

☐ Other. Description: (i.e., timber, mineral, water rights, etc.)   ☐ Timeshare   ☐ Commercial/Industrial

B. ☐ YES ☐ NO Personal/business property, or incentives, provided by seller to buyer are included in the purchase price. Examples of personal property are furniture, farm equipment, machinery, etc. Examples of incentives are club memberships, etc. Attach list if available.

If YES, enter the value of the personal/business property: $_____   Incentives $_____

C. ☐ YES ☐ NO A manufactured home is included in the purchase price.

If YES, enter the value attributed to the manufactured home: $_____

☐ YES ☐ NO The manufactured home is subject to local property tax. If NO, enter decal number: _____

D. ☐ YES ☐ NO The property produces rental or other income.

If YES, the income is from: ☐ Lease/rent   ☐ Contract   ☐ Mineral rights   ☐ Other: _____

E. The condition of the property at the time of sale was: ☐ Good   ☐ Average   ☐ Fair   ☐ Poor

Please describe: _____

CERTIFICATION

I certify (or declare) that the foregoing and all information hereon, including any accompanying statements or documents, is true and correct to the best of my knowledge and belief.

SIGNATURE OF BUYER/TRANSFEREE OR CORPORATE OFFICER	DATE	TELEPHONE ( )
▶		

NAME OF BUYER/TRANSFEREE/PERSONAL REPRESENTATIVE/CORPORATE OFFICER (PLEASE PRINT)	TITLE	EMAIL ADDRESS

The Assessor's office may contact you for additional information regarding this transaction.

When recorded, mail to:

ABC Loan Services, Inc.
2530 S. Parker Road, Suite 600··
Aurora, CO 80014

NOTES

Section H of the "Deed of Trust" indicates the security instrument is supplemented by two riders — the "Planned Unit Development Rider" and "Prepayment Rider." Notary Signing Agents should ensure these riders are included in the documentation prior to notarizing the security instrument.

LOAN #: CHI123456

⸻ ⌐Space Above This Line for Recording Data⌐ ⸻

| FHA Case No. |
| 045-92345301-703-203B |

DEED OF TRUST

MIN   1001290-3

MERS PHONE #: 888-679-6377

DEFINITIONS
Words used in multiple sections of this document are defined below and other words are defined in Sections 3,10,12,17,19, and 21. Certain rules regarding the usage of words used in this document are also provided in Section 15.
(A) Security Instrument means this document, which is dated **Oct. 18, 20XX,** together with all Riders to this document.

(B) Borrower is   **John A. Maxell, a single man.**

Borrower's address is **10116 Chevrolet Dr. Los Angeles, CA 90060**

Borrower is the trustor under this Security Instrument.
Lender is Hunter Financial Group, Inc.

Ellie Mae, Inc.   Page 1 of 13   CAEFHA15DL 0915
                                                                                CAEDEDL (CLS)

Lender is **a Limited Liability Company,** organized and existing
under the laws of **Arizona.**
Lender's address is **3303 East Courtline Road, Gilbert, AZ 85234.**

Trustee is **XYZ Title, 1111 E. Katella Ave., Orange, Orange County, California 92867**

MERS is a Mortgage Electronic Registration Systems, Inc. MERS is a separate corporation that is acting solely as a nominee for Lender and Lender's successors and assigns. **MERS is the bene iciary under this Security Instrument.** MERS is organized and existing under the laws of Colorado, and has the address of P.O. Box 222, Flint, CO 44444-2026, tel. (877) 333-MERS.
NOTE the promissory note signed by Borrower and dated **Oct. 18, 20XX.**
Borrower owes Lender **TWO HUNDRED SIXTY SIX THOUSAND FIVE HUNDRED EIGHTY I**
* Dollars (U.S. **$26**
interest. Borrower has promised to pay this debt in regular Periodic Payments and to pay the debt in full n
Nov. 1, 20XX.
 Property means the property that is described below under the heading "Transfer of Rights in
 H Loan means the debt evidenced by the Note, plus interest, late charges due under the Note, an this Security Instrument, plus interest.
(I) "Riders" means all Riders to this Security Instrument that are executed by Borrower. The follow executed by Borrower [check box as applicable]:

☐ Adjustable Rate Rider ☐ Condominium Rider ☐ Planned Unit Development Rider
☐ Other(s) [specify]

> **NOTES**
>
> The Deed of Trust references an attached "Exhibit A" containing the legal description of the property. Since the Exhibit was not included in the loan documentation package sent to the Notary Signing Agent, the Agent must request the title company to fax or e-mail the Exhibit prior to the appointment.

 J Applicable Law means all controlling applicable federal, state and local statutes, regulations, ordinances and administrative rules and orders (that have the effect of law) as well as all applicable final, non-appealable judicial opinions.
 Community Association Dues, ees, and Assessments means all dues, fees, assessments and other charges that are imposed on Borrower or the Property by a condominium association, homeowners association or similar organization.
 L Electronic unds Transfer means any transfer of funds, other than a transaction originated by check, draft, or similar paper instrument, which is initiated through an electronic terminal, telephonic instrument, computer, or magnetic tape so as to order, instruct, or authorize a financial institution to debit or credit an account. Such term includes, but is not limited to, point-of-sale transfers, automated teller machine transactions, transfers initiated by telephone, wire transfers, and automated clearinghouse transfers.
 M Escrow Items means those items that are described in Section 3.
 N Miscellaneous Proceeds means any compensation, settlement, award of damages, or proceeds paid by any third party (other than insurance proceeds paid under the coverages described in Section 5) for: (i) damage to, or destruction of, the Property; (ii) condemnation or other taking of all or any part of the Property; (iii) conveyance in lieu of condemnation; or (iv) misrepresentations of, or omissions as to, the value and/or condition of the Property.
 O Mortgage Insurance means insurance protecting Lender against the nonpayment of, or default on, the Loan.
 P Periodic Payment means the regularly scheduled amount due for (i) principal and interest under the Note, plus (ii) any amounts under Section 3 of this Security Instrument.
 RESPA means the Real Estate Settlement Procedures Act (12 U.S.C. §2601 et seq.) and its implementing regulation, Regulation X (12 C.F.R. Part 1024), as they might be amended from time to time, or any additional or successor legislation or regulation that governs the same subject matter. As used in this Security Instrument, "RESPA" refers to all requirements and restrictions that are imposed in regard to a "federally related mortgage loan" even if the Loan does not qualify as a "federally related mortgage loan" under RESPA.
 R Secretary means the Secretary of the United States Department of Housing and Urban Development or his designee.
 S Successor in Interest of Borrower means any party that has taken title to the Property, whether or not that party has assumed Borrower's obligations under the Note and/or this Security Instrument.

TRANSFER OF RIGHTS IN THE PROPERTY

The beneficiary of this Security Instrument is MERS (solely as nominee for Lender and Lender's successors and assigns) and the successors and assigns of MERS. This Security Instrument secures to Lender: (i) the repayment of the Loan, and all renewals, extensions and modifications of the Note; and (ii) the performance of Borrower's covenants and agreements under this Security Instrument and the Note. For this purpose, Borrower irrevocably mortgages, grants and conveys to Trustee, in trust, with power of sale, the following described property located in the

County
[Type of Recording Jurisdiction]

of **Los Angeles**
[Name of Recording Jurisdiction]:

LOT 4 IN BLOCK 15432 OF MONTEREY BAY UNIT NO. 11, AS PER MAP FILED MARCH 1, 20XX IN BOOK 34 OF MAPS, PAGE 59, COUNTY RECORDS.
A CERTIFICATE OF CORRECTION RECORDED APRIL 2, 20XX UNDER RECORDER'S SERIAL NUMBER 2001-1578, COUNTY RECORD.
A CERTIFICATE OF CORRECTION RECORDED AUGUST 9, 20XX UNDER RECORDER'S SERIAL NUMBER 2001-0096, COUNTY RECORDS.
EXCEPTING UNTO THE GRANTOR THEREFROM ALL OIL, GAS, CASINGHEAD GAS, ASPHALTUM AND OTHER HYDROCARBOR AND ALL CHEMICAL GAS, NOW OR HEREAFTER FOUND, SITUATED OR LOCATED IN ALL OR ANY PART OR PORTION OF THE LANDS HEREIN DESCRIBED LYING MORE THAN FIVE FEET (500') BELOW THE SURFACE THEREOF, AND THE TIGHT TO GRANT LEASES FOR ALL OR ANY OF SAID PURPOSES, BUT WITHOUT ANY RIGHT WHATSOEVER TO ENTER UPON THE SURFACE OF SAID LANDS WITHIN FIVE HUNDRED FEET (500') VERTICAL DISTANCE BELOW THE SURFACE THEREOF.
APN #: 077-045-012-001

which currently has the address of **10116 Chevrolet Drive, Los**

Angeles, CA 90060

("Property Address"):

    TOGETHER WITH all the improvements now or hereafter erected on the property, and all easements, appurtenances, and fixtures now or hereafter a part of the property. All replacements and additions shall also be covered by this Security Instrument. All of the foregoing is referred to in this Security Instrument as the "Property." Borrower understands and agrees that MERS holds only legal title to the interests granted by Borrower in this Security Instrument, but, if necessary to comply with law or custom, MERS (as nominee for Lender and Lender's successors and assigns) has the right: to exercise any or all of those interests, including, but not limited to, the right to foreclose and sell the Property; and to take any action required of Lender including, but not limited to, releasing and canceling this Security Instrument.

    BORROWER COVENANTS that Borrower is lawfully seised of the estate hereby conveyed and has the right to mortgage, grant and convey the Property and that the Property is unencumbered, except for encumbrances of record. Borrower warrants and will defend generally the title to the Property against all claims and demands, subject to any encumbrances of record.

    THIS SECURITY INSTRUMENT combines uniform covenants for national use and non-uniform covenants with limited variations by jurisdiction to constitute a uniform security instrument covering real property.

    UNIFORM COVENANTS. Borrower and Lender covenant and agree as follows:
    1. Payment of Principal, Interest, Escrow Items, and Late Charges. Borrower shall pay when due the principal of, and interest on, the debt evidenced by the Note and late charges due under the Note. Borrower shall also pay funds for Escrow Items pursuant to Section 3. Payments due under the Note and this Security Instrument shall be made in U.S. currency. However, if any check or other instrument received by Lender as payment under the Note or this Security Instrument is returned to Lender unpaid, Lender may require that any or all subsequent payments due under the Note and this Security Instrument be made in one or more of the following forms, as selected by Lender: (a) cash; (b) money order;

Ellie Mae, Inc.   Page 3 of 13   CAEFHA15DL 0915
                                                                   CAEDEDL (CLS)

preceding sentence shall deprive the Secretary of any rights otherwise available to a Lender under this Section 24 or applicable law.

25. Reconveyance. Upon payment of all sums secured by this Security Instrument, Lender shall request Trustee to reconvey the Property and shall surrender this Security Instrument and all notes evidencing debt secured by this Security Instrument to Trustee. Trustee shall reconvey the Property without warranty and without charge to the person or persons legally entitled to it. Such person or persons shall pay any recordation costs.

26. Substitute Trustee. Lender, at its option, may from time to time appoint a successor trustee to any Trustee appointed hereunder by an instrument executed and acknowledged by Lender and recorded in the office of the Recorder of the county in which the Property is located. The instrument shall contain the name of the original Lender, Trustee and Borrower, the book and page where this Security Instrument is recorded and the name and address of the successor trustee. Without conveyance of the Property, the successor trustee shall succeed to all the title, powers and duties conferred upon the Trustee herein and by Applicable Law. This procedure for substitution of trustee shall govern to the exclusion of all other provisions for substitution.

27. Statement of Obligation Fee. Lender may collect a fee not to exceed the maximum amount permitted by Applicable Law for furnishing the statement of obligation as provided by Section 2943 of the Civil Code of California.

The undersigned Borrower requests that a copy of any Notice of Default and any Notice of Sale under this Security Instrument be mailed to Borrower at the address set forth above.

BY SIGNING BELOW, Borrower accepts and agrees to the terms and covenants contained in this Security Instrument and in any Rider executed by Borrower and recorded with it.

_____ (Seal)
John A. Maxell

_____ (Seal)

A notary public or other officer completing this certificate verifies only the identity of the individual who signed the document to which this certificate is attached, and not the truthfulness, accuracy, or validity of that document.

State of
County of

On _____, before me, _____ (here insert name and title of the officer), personally appeared _____, who proved to me on the basis of satisfactory evidence to be the person(s) whose name(s) is/are subscribed to the within instrument and acknowledged to me that he/she/they executed the same in his/her/their authorized capacity(ies), and that by his/her/their signature(s) on the instrument the person(s), or the entity upon behalf of which the person(s) acted, executed the instrument.

I certify under PENALTY OF PERJURY under the laws of the State of California that the foregoing paragraph is true and correct.

WITNESS my hand and official seal.

Signature_____

_____(NOTARY)

(SEAL)

Lender: Hunter Financial Group, Inc.
NMLS ID: 227262
Loan Originator: Michael Gracz
NMLS ID: 1160212

PLANNED UNIT DEVELOPMENT RIDER

THIS PLANNED UNIT DEVELOPMENT RIDER is made this __18th__ day of _October,___20XX__, and is incorporated into and shall be deemed to amend and supplement the Mortgage, Deed of Trust, or Security Deed (the "Security Instrument") of the same date, given by the undersigned (the "Borrower") to secure Borrower's Note to Hunter Financial Group, Inc., dba, USA Select Mortgage An Arizona Corporation (the "Lender") of the same date and covering the Property described in the Security Instrument and located at:

10116 Chevrolet Drive,
Los Angeles, California 90060
[Property Address]

The Property includes, but is not limited to, a parcel of land improved with a dwelling, together with other such parcels and certain common areas and facilities, as described in

COVENANTS, CONDITIONS, AND RESTRICTIONS

(the "Declaration"). The Property is a part of a planned unit development known as

California Country Club Estates
[Name of Planned Unit Development]

(the "PUD"). The Property also includes Borrower's interest in the homeowners' association or equivalent entity owning or managing the common areas and facilities of the PUD (the "Owners Association") and the uses, benefits and proceeds of Borrower's interest.

PUD COVENANTS. In addition to the covenants and agreements made in the Security Instrument, Borrower and Lender further covenant and agree as follows:

A. PUD Obligations. Borrower shall perform all of Borrower's obligations under the PUD's Constituent Documents. The "Constituent Documents" are the (i) Declaration; (ii) articles of incorporation, trust instrument or any equivalent document which creates the Owners Association; and (iii) any by-laws or other rules or regulations of the Owners Association. Borrower shall promptly pay, when due, all dues and assessments imposed pursuant to the Constituent Documents.

B. Property Insurance. So long as the Owners Association maintains, with a generally accepted insurance carrier, a "master" or "blanket" policy insuring the Property which is satisfactory to Lender and which provides insurance coverage in the amounts (including deductible levels), for the periods, and against loss by fire, hazards included within the term "extended coverage," and any other hazards, including, but not limited to, earthquakes and floods, for which Lender requires insurance, then: (i) Lender waives the provision in Section 3 for the Periodic Payment to Lender of the yearly premium installments for property insurance on the Property; and (ii) Borrower's obligation under Section 5 to maintain property insurance coverage on the Property is deemed satisfied to the extent that the required coverage is provided by the Owners Association policy.

What Lender requires as a condition of this waiver can change during the term of the loan.

Borrower shall give Lender prompt notice of any lapse in required property insurance coverage provided by the master or blanket policy.

In the event of a distribution of property insurance proceeds in lieu of restoration or repair following a loss to the Property, or to common areas and facilities of the PUD, any proceeds payable to Borrower are hereby assigned and shall be paid to Lender. Lender shall apply the proceeds to the sums secured by the Security Instrument, whether or not then due, with the excess, if any, paid to Borrower.

MULTISTATE PUD RIDER--Single Family--**Fannie Mae/Freddie Mac UNIFORM INSTRUMENT Form 3150** *(page1 of 2 pages)*

C. Public Liability Insurance. Borrower shall take such actions as may be reasonable to ensure that the Owners Association maintains a public liability insurance policy acceptable in form, amount, and extent of coverage to Lender.

D. Condemnation. The proceeds of any award or claim for damages, direct or consequential, payable to Borrower in connection with any condemnation or other taking of all or any part of the Property or the common areas and facilities of the PUD, or for any conveyance in lieu of condemnation, are hereby assigned and shall be paid to Lender. Such proceeds shall be applied by Lender to the sums secured by the Security Instrument as provided in Section 11.

E. Lender's Prior Consent. Borrower shall not, except after notice to Lender and with Lender's prior written consent, either partition or subdivide the Property or consent to: (i) the abandonment or termination of the PUD, except for abandonment or termination required by law in the case of substantial destruction by fire or other casualty or in the case of a taking by condemnation or eminent domain; (ii) any amendment to any provision of the "Constituent Documents" if the provision is for the express benefit of Lender; (iii) termination of professional management and assumption of self-management of the Owners Association; or (iv) any action which would have the effect of rendering the public liability insurance coverage maintained by the Owners Association unacceptable to Lender.

F. Remedies. If Borrower does not pay PUD dues and assessments when due, then Lender may pay them. Any amounts disbursed by Lender under this paragraph F shall become additional debt of Borrower secured by the Security Instrument. Unless Borrower and Lender agree to other terms of payment, these amounts shall bear interest from the date of disbursement at the Note rate and shall be payable, with interest, upon notice from Lender to Borrower requesting payment.

BY SIGNING BELOW, Borrower accepts and agrees to the terms and covenants contained in this PUD Rider.

_____(Seal)
John A. Maxell   -Borrower

_____(Seal)
                                                            -Borrower

MULTISTATE PUD RIDER--Single Family--**Fannie Mae/Freddie Mac UNIFORM INSTRUMENT Form 3150** *(page2 of 2 pages)*

Loan Number: **NCMO3780**

PREPAYMENT RIDER
(Multi-State)

     This Prepayment Rider is made this **1st** day of **November, 20XX** and is incorporated into and shall be deemed to amend and supplement the Mortgage, Deed of Trust or Security Deed (the "Security Instrument") of the same date given by the undersigned (the "Borrower") to secure Borrower's Note (the "Note") to **Hunter Financial Group, Inc., dba, USASelect Mortgage An Arizona Corporation** (the "Lender") of the same date and covering the property described in the Security Instrument and located at

10116 Chevrolet Drive
Los Angeles, CALIFORNIA 90060
(the "Property").

     Additional Covenants. Notwithstanding anything to the contrary set forth in the Note or Security Instrument, Borrower and Lender further covenant and agree as follows:

     Borrower has the right to make payments of principal at any time before they are due. A payment of principal only is known as a "prepayment." A "full prepayment" is the prepayment of the entire unpaid principal due under the Note. A payment of only part of the unpaid principal is known as a "partial prepayment."

     If, within the five (5)-year period beginning with the date Borrower executes the Note (the "Penalty Period"), Borrower makes a full prepayment, or partial prepayment in any twelve (12)-month period that exceeds 20% of the original principal loan amount, Borrower will pay a prepayment charge as consideration for the Note Holder's acceptance of such prepayment. The prepayment charge will equal the amount of interest that would accrue during a six (6)-month period on the amount prepaid that exceeds 20% of the original principal balance of the Note, calculated at the rate of interest in effect under the terms of the Note at the time of the prepayment, unless otherwise prohibited by applicable law or regulation. No prepayment charge will be assessed for any prepayment occurring after the Penalty Period.

     Notwithstanding the foregoing, in the event of a full prepayment concurrent with a bona fide sale of the Property to an unrelated third party after the rust zero (0) year(s) of the term of the Note, no prepayment penalty will be assessed. In that event, Borrower agrees to provide the Note Holder with evidence acceptable to the Note Holder of such sale.

     By signing below, Borrower accepts and agrees to the terms and covenants contained in this Prepayment Rider.

_____ (Seal)   _____ (Seal)
John A. Maxell   -Borrower   -Borrower

603B2 Multi-State Rider

Note

October 18, 20XX
[Date]

Gilbert
[City]

ARIZONA
[State]

10116 Chevrolet Drive
Los Angeles, CALIFORNIA 90060
[Property Address]

1. BORROWER'S PROMISE TO PAY

In return for a loan that I have received, I promise to pay U.S. $ **426,000.00**   (this amount is called "Principal"), plus interest, to the order of the Lender. The Lender is

Hunter Financial Group, Inc.

s under this Note in the form of cash, check or money order.

he Lender may transfer this Note. The Lender or anyone who takes this Note by transfer and who is entitled

ler this Note is called the "Note Holder."

arged on unpaid principal until the full amount of Principal has been paid. I will pay interest at a yearly rate %.

quired by this Section 2 is the rate I will pay both before and after any default described in Section 6(B) of

NOTES

Item 4 includes strike-outs and refers to an addendum outlining prepayment provisions. Note this section must be initialed by the borrowers.

3. PAYMENTS

(A) Time and Place of Payments

I will pay principal and interest by making a payment every month.

I will make my monthly payment on the **1ST**   day of each month beginning on **JANUARY 01,20XX**   . I will make these payments every month until I have paid all of the principal and interest and any other charges described below that I may owe under this Note. Each monthly payment will be applied as of its scheduled due date and will be applied to interest before Principal. If, on **SEPTEMBER 01, 2032** , I still owe amounts under this Note, I will pay those amounts in full on that date, which is called the "Maturity Date."

I will make my monthly payments at
3303 East Courtline Rd. Gilbert, ARIZONA 85234
or at a different place if required by the Note Holder.

(B) Amount of Monthly Payments

My monthly payment will be in the amount of U.S. $ **2554.09**   .

4. BORROWER'S RIGHT TO PREPAY

I have the right to make payments of Principal at any time before they are due. A payment of Principal only is known as a "Prepayment." When I make a Prepayment, I will tell the Note Holder in writing that I am doing so. I may not designate a payment as a Prepayment if I have not made all the monthly payments due under the Note.

I may make a full Prepayment or partial Prepayments without paying a Prepayment charge. The Note Holder will use my Prepayments to reduce the amount of Principal that I owe under this Note. However, the Note Holder may apply my Prepayment to the accrued and unpaid interest on the Prepayment amount, before applying my Prepayment to reduce the Principal amount of the Note. If I make a partial Prepayment, there will be no changes in the due date or in the amount of my monthly payment unless the Note Holder agrees in writing to those changes.

FIRST LIEN

FLORIDA FIXED RATE NOTE - Single Family - Fannie Mae/Freddie Mac UNIFORM INSTRUMENT
VMP ®
Wolters Kluwer Financial Services

NCMO3780
Form 3210
VMP5N(FL) (1302).00
Page 1 of 4

5. LOAN CHARGES

If a law, which applies to this loan and which sets maximum loan charges, is finally interpreted so that the interest or other loan charges collected or to be collected in connection with this loan exceed the permitted limits, then: (a) any such loan charge shall be reduced by the amount necessary to reduce the charge to the permitted limit; and (b) any sums already collected from me which exceeded permitted limits will be refunded to me. The Note Holder may choose to make this refund by reducing the Principal I owe under this Note or by making a direct payment to me. If a refund reduces Principal, the reduction will be treated as a partial Prepayment.

6. BORROWER'S FAILURE TO PAY AS REQUIRED

(A) Late Charge for Overdue Payments

If the Note Holder has not received the full amount of any monthly payment by the end of **15** calendar days after the date it is due, I will pay a late charge to the Note Holder. The amount of the charge will be **5.0000** % of my overdue payment of principal and interest. I will pay this late charge promptly but only once on each late payment.

(B) Default

If I do not pay the full amount of each monthly payment on the date it is due, I will be in default.

(C) Notice of Default

If I am in default, the Note Holder may send me a written notice telling me that if I do not pay the overdue amount by a certain date, the Note Holder may require me to pay immediately the full amount of Principal which has not been paid and all the interest that I owe on that amount. That date must be at least 30 days after the date on which the notice is mailed to me or delivered by other means.

(D) No Waiver By Note Holder

Even if, at a time when I am in default, the Note Holder does not require me to pay immediately in full as described above, the Note Holder will still have the right to do so if I am in default at a later time.

(E) Payment of Note Holder's Costs and Expenses

If the Note Holder has required me to pay immediately in full as described above, the Note Holder will have the right to be paid back by me for all of its costs and expenses in enforcing this Note to the extent not prohibited by applicable law. Those expenses include, for example, reasonable attorneys' fees.

7. GIVING OF NOTICES

Unless applicable law requires a different method, any notice that must be given to me under this Note will be given by delivering it or by mailing it by first class mail to me at the Property Address above or at a different address if I give the Note Holder a notice of my different address.

Any notice that must be given to the Note Holder under this Note will be given by delivering it or by mailing it by first class mail to the Note Holder at the address stated in Section 3(A) above or at a different address if I am given a notice of that different address.

8. OBLIGATIONS OF PERSONS UNDER THIS NOTE

If more than one person signs this Note, each person is fully and personally obligated to keep all of the promises made in this Note, including the promise to pay the full amount owed. Any person who is a guarantor, surety or endorser of this Note is also obligated to do these things. Any person who takes over these obligations, including the obligations of a guarantor, surety or endorser of this Note, is also obligated to keep all of the promises made in this Note. The Note Holder may enforce its rights under this Note against each person individually or against all of us together. This means that any one of us may be required to pay all of the amounts owed under this Note.

9. WAIVERS

I and any other person who has obligations under this Note waive the rights of Presentment and Notice of Dishonor. "Presentment" means the right to require the Note Holder to demand payment of amounts due. "Notice of Dishonor" means the right to require the Note Holder to give notice to other persons that amounts due have not been paid.

FIRST LIEN

FLORIDA FIXED RATE NOTE - Single Family - Fannie Mae/Freddie Mac UNIFORM INSTRUMENT
VMP ®
Wolters Kluwer Financial Services

NCMO3780

Form 3210
VMP5N(FL) (1302).00
Page 2 of 4

Loan Number: NCMO3780

PREPAYMENT NOTE ADDENDUM
(Multi-State)

This Prepayment Note Addendum is made this **1st** day of **November, 20XX** and is incorporated into and shall be deemed to amend and supplement the Note of the same date (the "Note") made by the undersigned (the "Borrower") to evidence indebtedness to **Hunter Financial Group, Inc., dba, USASelect Mortgage An Arizona Corporation** (the "Lender"), which debt is secured by a Mortgage or Deed of Trust or comparable security instrument (the "Security Instrument") of the same date and covering the property described in the Security Instrument and located at

10116 Chevrolet Drive
Los Angeles, CALIFORNIA 90060
(the "Property")

ADDITIONAL COVENANTS. Notwithstanding anything to the contrary set forth in the Note or Security Instrument, Borrower and Lender covenant, and agree, that the provisions of the section of the Note entitled "BORROWER'S RIGHT TO PREPAY" are amended to read as follows:

Subject to the Prepayment penalty provided below, I have the right to make payments of Principal at any time before they are due. A payment of Principal only is known as a "Prepayment." A "Full Prepayment" is the Prepayment of the entire unpaid Principal due under the Note. A payment of only part of the unpaid Principal is known as a "Partial Prepayment." When I make a Prepayment, I will tell the Note Holder in writing that I am doing so. I may not designate a payment as a Prepayment if I have not made all the monthly payments due under the Note.

If, within the five (5)-year period beginning with the date I execute the Note (the "Penalty Period"), I make a Full Prepayment, or Partial Prepayment in any twelve (12) month period that exceeds 20% of the original Principal loan amount, I will pay a Prepayment charge as consideration for the Note Holder's acceptance of such Prepayment. The Prepayment charge will equal the amount of interest that would accrue during a six (6)-month period on the amount prepaid that exceeds 20% of the original Principal balance of the Note, calculated at the rate of interest in effect under the terms of the Note at the time of the Prepayment, unless otherwise prohibited by applicable law or regulation. No Prepayment charge will be assessed for any Prepayment occurring after the Penalty Period.

Notwithstanding the foregoing, in the event of a Full Prepayment concurrent with a bona fide sale of the Property to an unrelated third party after the first zero (0) year(s) of the term of the Note, no prepayment penalty will be assessed. In that event, I agree to provide the Note Holder with evidence acceptable to the Note Holder of such sale.

The Note Holder will apply all Prepayments to reduce the amount of Principal that I owe under the Note. However, the Note Holder may apply my Prepayment to the accrued and unpaid interest on the Prepayment amount, before applying my Prepayment to reduce the Principal amount of the Note. If I make a Partial Prepayment, there will be no change in the due dates of my monthly payments unless the Note Holder agrees in writing to those changes.

If my Note is an Adjustable Rate Note, Partial Prepayments may reduce the amount of my monthly payment after the first interest rate Change Date following the Partial Prepayment. However, any reduction due to my Partial Prepayment may be offset by an interest rate increase.

The Note Holder's failure to collect a Prepayment charge at the time a prepayment is received shall not be deemed a waiver of such charge. Any Prepayment charge not collected at the time the Prepayment is received shall be payable on demand.

All other provisions of the Note are unchanged and remain in full force and effect.

NOTICE TO BORROWER - Do not sign this Addendum before you read it. This Addendum provides for the payment of a Prepayment charge if you wish to repay the loan prior to the date provided for repayment in the Note.

WITNESS THE HAND(S) AND SEAL(S) OF THE UNDERSIGNED:

_____ (Seal)	
John A. Maxell	Borrower

_____ (Seal)	
	Borrower

ACKNOWLEDGMENT OF UNDERSTANDING OF
CONDITIONAL LOAN APPROVAL

USASelect Mortgage **3303 East Courtline Road, Building 7, Suite 118** **Gilbert, AZ** **Telephone: (480) 461-1111** **FAX: (480) 654-0027**	Subject Property: 10116 Chevrolet Drive Los Angeles, CA 90060

The undersigned Applicants(s) hereby acknowledge that the signing of the loan application and/or the other documents presented to the Applicant(s), in no way constitutes, establishes nor signifies a formal loan commitment by Lender to approve the requested loan.

The undersigned Applicant(s) hereby acknowledge that the requested loan is still conditioned upon the review, investigation, approval and acceptance by the Lender of all facts, documents, representations and circumstances in connection with the requested loan -- including all subjective and objective factors such as, but not limited to the Applicant(s) credit history, property appraisals or inspections, income and employment verification, etc.

The undersigned Applicant(s) hereby acknowledge that by receiving the loan application and agreeing to review all such subjective and objective factors in order to determine whether or not to approve the requested loan, that Lender is not bound to make a loan to the Applicant(s), nor has it agreed to do so.

The undersigned Applicant(s) hereby acknowledge and understand that until such time as notification is given to Applicants(s) by Lender that the entire loan application and any and all supporting documents and verifications have been reviewed, approved and accepted by Lender, the Applicant(s) status is/are that of an individual seeking a loan, and that Lender is under no obligation to approve said loan request.

I/We have read this acknowledgment, and understand its contents:

_____   _____
John A. Maxell   Date   Date

Borrower's Certification & Authorization

Mortgage Loan Originator Hunter Financial Group	**Borrower** John A. Maxell	**Date** October 18, 20XX

Loan Number NCM003780

3303 East Courtline Rd.
Gilbert, AZ 85234

Property Address:
10116 Chevrolet Drive Los Angeles, CA 90060

Certification

The undersigned certify the following:

1. I/We have applied for a mortgage loan from the Mortgage Loan Originator. In applying for the loan, I/we completed a loan application containing various information on the purpose of the loan, the amount and source of the down payment, employment and income information, and assets and liabilities. I/We certify that all of the information is true and complete. I/We made no misrepresentations in the loan application or other documents, nor did I/we omit any pertinent information.

2. I/We understand and agree that the Mortgage Loan Originator reserves the right to change the mortgage loan review process to a full documentation program. This may include verifying the information provided on the application with the employer and/or the financial institution.

3. I/We fully understand that it is a Federal crime punishable by fine or imprisonment, or both, to knowingly make any false statements when applying for this mortgage, as applicable under the provisions of Title 18, United States Code, Section 1014.

Authorization to Release Information

To Whom It May Concern:

1. I/We have applied for a mortgage loan from the Mortgage Loan Originator. As part of the application process, the Mortgage Loan Originator may verify information contained in my/our loan application and in other documents required in connection with the loan, either before the loan is closed or as part of its quality control program.

2. I/We authorize you to provide to the Mortgage Loan Originator and to any investor to whom the Mortgage Loan Originator may sell my/our mortgage, any and all information and documentation that they request. Such information includes, but is not limited to, employment history and income; bank, money market, and similar account balances; credit history; and copies of tax returns.

3. The Mortgage Loan Originator or any investor that purchases the mortgage may address this authorization to any party named in the loan application or disclosed by any consumer credit reporting agency or similar source.

4. A copy of this authorization may be accepted as an original.

5. Your prompt reply to the Mortgage Loan Originator or the investor that purchased the mortgage is appreciated.

☐ **Notice to FHA or VA Borrowers.** This is notice to you as required by the Right to Financial Privacy Act of 1978 that the Department of Housing and Urban Development or Department of Veterans Affairs has a right of access to financial records held by financial institutions in connection with the consideration or administration of assistance to you. Financial records involving your transaction will be available to the Department of Housing and Urban Development or Department of Veterans Affairs without further notice or authorization but will not be disclosed or released by this institution to another Government Agency or Department without your consent except as required or permitted by law.

1234567890

Borrower's Certification & Authorization
Bankers Systems™ VMP ®
Wolters Kluwer Financial Services ©

VMP50 (1502).00
Page 1 of 2

Hunter Financial Group, Inc., dba, USASelect
3303 East Courtline Road, #7-118
Gilbert, AZ 85234 480-461-1111

CREDIT SCORE NOTICE

Date: November 1, 20XX
Loan Number: NCM03780
Borrower(s):   John A. Maxell   - Experian: 726,   Equifax Credit Information Services: 668
                       Trans Union: 728
                       - Experian: 0, Equifax Credit Information Services: 0, Trans Union: 0 - Experian: 0,
                       Equifax Credit Information Services: 0, Trans Union: 0   - Experian: 0,
                       Equifax Credit Information Services: 0, Trans Union: 0

Property Address: 10116 Chevrolet Drive Los Angeles, CA 90060

NOTICE TO THE HOME LOAN APPLICANT

In connection with your application for a home loan, the lender must disclose to you the score that a credit
to users and the lender used in connection with your home loan, and the key factors affecting your credit

The credit score is a computer generated summary calculated at the time of the request and based on info
bureau or lender has on file. The scores are based on data about your credit history and payment patterns
important because they are used to assist the lender in determining whether you will obtain a loan. They may also be used to
determine what interest rate you may be offered on the mortgage. Credit scores can change over time, depending on your
conduct, how your credit history and payment patterns change, and how credit scoring technologies change.

Because the score is based on information in your credit history, it is very important that you review the credit-related
information that is being furnished to make sure it is accurate. Credit records may vary from one company to another.

If you have questions about your credit score or the credit information that is furnished to you, contact the credit bureau at the
address and telephone number provided with this notice, or contact the lender, if the lender developed or generated the credit
score. The credit bureau plays no part in the decision to take any action on the loan application and is unable to provide you
with specific reasons for the decision on a loan application.

If you have questions concerning the terms of the loan, contact the lender.

One or more of the following credit bureaus will provide the credit score:

Experian   **Equifax Credit Information Services**   **Trans Union**
P.O. Box 9600   P.O. Box 740241   P.O. Box 1000
Allen, TX 75013   Atlanta, GA 30374   Chester, PA 19022
1-800-311-4769   1-800-685-1111   1-800-888-4213

Your acknowledgement below signifies that this written notice was provided to you.

_____   _____
John A. Maxell   Date   Date

NOTES

The "Credit Score Notice" illustrated on
this page actually gives the borrower's
credit scores as reported by the three
major credit reporting services.

CALIFORNIA HAZARD INSURANCE DISCLOSURE

Loan Number: NCMO3780

Loan Number: NCM03780

Borrower(s):   John A. Maxell

Property Address: 10116 Chevrolet Drive Los Angeles, CA 90060

According to California Civil Code Section 2955.5(a), *"No Lender shall require a borrower. as a condition of receiving or maintaining a loan secured by real property, to provide hazard insurance coverage against risks to the improvements on that real property in an amount exceeding the replacement value of the improvements on the property."*

By signing below, borrower signifies that this written notice was provided to you pursuant to the state statute.

_____   _____

John A. Maxell   Date   Date

CALIFORNIA IMPOUND DISCLOSURE/WAIVER

Loan Number: NCMO3780

Date: November 15, 20XX

Lender: Hunter Financial Group, Inc.

Applicant: John Maxell

For convenience, an impound account may be established on the Borrower(s) behalf with the Lender, for the payment of property taxes and hazard insurance premiums. The Lender will pay interest on money deposited into the impound account as required by applicable law.

The Lender may require an impound account:

1) where required by a state or federal regulatory authority; or
2) where a loan is made, guaranteed, or insured by a state or federal governmental lending or insuring agency; or
3) upon a failure of Borrower to pay two consecutive tax installments on the property prior to the delinquency date for such payments; or
4) where the original principal amount of such a loan is (i) 90 percent or more of the sale price, if the property involved is sold, or (ii) 90 percent or more of the appraised value of the property securing the loan; or
5) whenever the combined principal amount of all loans secured by the real property exceeds 80 percent of the appraised value of the property securing the loans; or
6) where a loan is made in compliance with the requirements for higher priced mortgage loans established in Regulation Z, whether or not the loan is a higher priced mortgage loan; or
7) where a loan is refinanced or modified in connection with a lender's homeownership preservation program or a lender's participation in such a program sponsored by a federal, state, or local government authority or a nonprofit organization.

If the Lender does not require an impound account, the Borrower(s) may still elect to establish an imp[...]
Borrower(s) should register their choice by placing an "X" below, and acknowledges this option is ava[...]
application and can be changed no more than once annually.

IMPOUNDS REQUIRED BY LENDER

[X] The undersigned understand that the establishment of an impound account for payments of real pro[...] and/or flood insurance and other related expenses is REQUIRED.

[ ] The undersigned understand that the establishment of an impound account for payments of real pro[...] and/or flood insurance and other related expenses is NOT REQUIRED.

IMPOUNDS REQUESTED BY BORROWER

[ ] The undersigned understand that the establishment of an impound account for the payment of re[...] hazard and/or flood insurance and other related expenses is NOT REQUIRED; however, Borrowe[...] an account be established.

[ ] The undersigned understand that the establishment of an impound account for the payment of re[...] hazard and/or flood insurance and other related expenses is NOT REQUIRED. Borrower is not re[...] an account be established.

If an escrow account is not established the Borrower(s) will assume full responsibility for the timely paym[...] insurance premiums for the property referenced herein, and agree to provide proof of such payment upon t[...] The Borrower(s) failure to make two such payments within 30 days of their due date will result in [...] agreement, and the establishment of an escrow/impound account to be administered by the Lender will [...]

The undersigned hereby acknowledge receipt and understanding of this disclosure.

Borrower John A. Maxell	Date	Borrower	Date
Borrower	Date	Borrower	Date
Borower	Date	Borrower	Date

CALIFORNIA IMPOUND DISCLOSURE/WAIVER
CA Civil Code 2954(a)(1)
CAIDW.MSC

NOTES

The "Impound Disclosure Waiver" is a form the borrower completes to indicate whether the borrower wishes to establish an escrow account for the payment of taxes and insurance. In this particular form, the borrower must check the appropriate box prior to signing the form, if the box has not been marked.

Some loans require establishment of an impound account as a condition for loan approval. When such an account is not required, the borrower may choose to establish an account or pay all bills for taxes and insurance as they become due.

CALIFORNIA PER DIEM INTEREST CHARGE DISCLOSURE

Pursuant to California Civ. Code § 2948.5(b)

Borrower(s): **John A. Maxell**

Date: **November 16, 20XX**

Loan Number: **NCMO3780**

Property Address: **10116 Chevrolet Drive
Los Angeles, CA 90060**

Lender: **Hunter Financial Group, Inc.**

Loan Originator: **Michael Gracz**

License #: **41DBO-45971**
NMLS #: **227262**

License #: **CA-DBO1160212**
NMLS #: **1160212**

☐ I request loan disbursement occur on a Monday or a day immediately following a bank holiday. As such, interest will commence to accrue on the business day immediately preceding the day of disbursement.

The amount of additional per diem interest that will be charged to facilitate disbursement on the day you have elected is $ 70.03.

It may be possible to avoid the additional per diem interest charge by disbursing the loan proceeds on a day immediately following a business day.

ACKNOWLEDGEMENT

I/We have read the above document and acknowledge receiving a copy by signing below.

John A. Maxell	DATE

	DATE

As a representative of the lender, my signature indicates our agreement to the disbursement of the loan proceeds occurring on a Monday or a day immediately following a bank holiday, and the additional per diem interest charge, in accordance with California Civil Code Section 2948.5. My signature also certifies that the foregoing is true and correct.

Michael Gracz
Lender Representative Name

Lender Representative Signature   Date

Ellie Mae, Inc.

CAPDID 0317
CAPDID (CLS)

COMPLIANCE AGREEMENT

Borrower(s): **John A. Maxell**   Date: **November 16, 20XX**

                                                    Loan Number: **NCMO3780**

Property Address: **10116 Chevrolet Drive**
Los Angeles, CA 90060

Lender: **Hunter Financial Group, Inc.**

The undersigned borrower(s), for and in consideration of Lender disbursing loan proceeds for the purchase or refinancing of, or construction of improvements on the aforementioned property, agree(s), if requested by the Lender or someone acting on behalf of said Lender, to fully cooperate in adjusting for clerical errors, on any or all loan closing documentation deemed necessary or desirable in the reasonable discretion of Lender to enable Lender to sell, convey, seek guaranty or market said loan to any entity, including but not limited to, an investor, Fannie Mae (FNMA), Government National Mortgage Association (GNMA), Freddie Mac (FHLMC), Department of Housing and Urban Development, Department of Veterans Affairs or any municipal bonding authority.

The undersigned borrower(s) do hereby so agree and covenant as aforesaid in order to assure that the loan documentation executed this date will conform and be acceptable in the marketplace in the instance of transfer, sale or conveyance by Lender of its interest in and to said loan documentation.

Dated effective this 16th day of November, 20XX.

_____   _____
John A. Maxell   DATE

_____   _____
                                                                            DATE

NOTES

This "Compliance Agreement" must be notarized with an acknowledgment.

For California Notaries, the acknowledgment form provided will not meet California requirements if the document is filed in California. Attachment of a "California All-Purpose Acknowledgment" form will be required.

SIGNATURES CONTINUED ON FOLLOWING PAGE.

Ellie Mae, Inc.   Page 1 of 2   GCOMCA 0315
                                                                      GCOMCA (CLS)

CALIFORNIA FINANCING LAW
STATEMENT OF LOAN DISCLOSURE

Borrower(s): **John A. Maxell**

Date: **October 18, 20XX**

Loan Number: **NCMO3780**

Property Address: **10116 Chevrolet Drive**
Los Angeles, CA 90060

Lender: **Hunter Financial Group, Inc.**
3303 East Courtline Rd.
Gilbert, AZ 85234

Broker (if any): **N/A**

License #: **41DBO-45971**
NMLS #: **227262**

This disclosure is provided to you pursuant to Cal. Fin. Code § 22337. This loan is being made pursuant to the California Finance Lenders Law, Division 9 (commencing with Section 22000) of the Financial Code.

LOAN INFORMATION
Loan Date: **October 18, 20XX**
Loan Amount: **$426,000.00**
Maturity Date: **September 1, 2032**

Interest Rate: **3.5 %**
Annual Percentage Rate (APR): **4.25 %**

REPAYMENT INFORMATION
I will repay my loan by making a payment of interest and/or principal each month beginning on **January 1, 20XX** until I have paid all of the principal and interest and any other charges. I understand I have the right to make payment in advance and in any amount on any contract of loan at any time.

SECURITY
I am giving a security interest in the property located at:
10116 Chevrolet Drive
Los Angeles, CA 90060

BROKER ACTS
Has any person performed any act as a broker in connection with the making of this loan?   ☐ Yes   ☒ No

If yes, then please indicate all sums paid/payable to the broker or other person. The Finance Lender must obtain a full statement of all sums paid or payable to the broker or other person.

Total Broker Fees:

Fee Description   **Amount**

FOR INFORMATION CONTACT THE DEPARTMENT OF BUSINESS OVERSIGHT, STATE OF CALIFORNIA.

ACKNOWLEDGEMENT
By signing below, you hereby acknowledge reading and understanding all of the information disclosed above, and receiving a copy of this disclosure on the date indicated below.

_____   DATE
John A. Maxell

_____   DATE

Ellie Mae, Inc.

CASOL 0218
CASOLJ (CLS)

Hunter Financial Group, Inc., dba, USASelect Mortgage,
3303 East Courtline Road, #7-118
Gilbert, AZ 85234

ECOA NOTICE

The Federal Equal Credit Opportunity Act prohibits creditors from discriminating against credit applicants on the basis of race, color, religion, national origin, sex, marital status, age (provided that the applicant has the capacity to enter into a binding contract): because all or part of the applicant's income is derived from a public assistance program; or because the applicant has in good faith exercised any right under the Consumer Credit Protection Act. The Federal Agency that administers compliance with this law concerning this creditor is: Federal Trade Commission, Equal Credit Opportunity, Washington, D.C. 20580.

John A. Maxell	Date	Date

OCCUPANCY STATEMENT

Borrower's Name: **John A. Maxell**

Property Address: **10116 Chevrolet Drive**
Los Angeles, CA 90060

Loan Number: **NCM03780**

I/We hereby certify that my/our intent in seeking this loan is to obtain financing for refinance or purchase of a home to be used as my/our principal residence, with occupancy to begin within 30 days after loan closing. I recognize that any loan made pursuant to this application is contingent upon owner occupancy and agree that (1) failure to occupy the property as provided in this certification shall constitute a DEFAULT under the terms of the loan, and (2) in case of such default, I must upon recall of the loan by Lender, immediately pay the full balance of the loan and any other amounts to which Lender is entitled upon default.

John A. Maxell	Date	Date

MAILING ADDRESS CERTIFICATION

_____ Our mailing address will be the property address designated above.

___X___ Our mailing address will be as follows:
10116 Chevrolet Drive
Los Angeles, CA 90060

John A. Maxell	Date	Date

HUD/FHA STATEMENT
WARNING! Section 1010 of the Title 18, V.S.C. "Federal Housing Administration Transaction", provides: Whoever for the purpose of ... influencing in any way the actions of such administration ... makes, passes, utters, or publishes any statement knowing the same to be false ... shall be fined not more than $5,000 or imprisoned not more than two years, or both.

THE HOUSING FINANCIAL DISCRIMINATION ACT OF 1977

FAIR LENDING NOTICE

IT IS ILLEGAL TO DISCRIMINATE IN THE PROVISION OF OR IN THE AVAILABILITY OF FINANCIAL ASSISTANCE BECAUSE OF THE CONSIDERATION OF:

1.   Trends, characteristics or conditions in the neighborhood or geographic area surrounding a housing accommodation, unless the financial institution can demonstrate in the particular case that such consideration is required to avoid an unsafe and unsound business practice; or

2.   Race, Color, Religion, Sex, Marital Status, National Origin of Ancestry.

IT IS ILLEGAL TO CONSIDER THE RACIAL, ETHNIC, RELIGIOUS OR NATIONAL ORIGIN COMPOSITION OF A NEIGHBORHOOD OR GEOGRAPHIC AREA SURROUNDING A HOUSING ACCOMMODATION OR WHETHER OR NOT SUCH COMPOSITION IS UNDERGOING CHANGE, OR IS EXPECTED TO UNDERGO CHANGE, IN APPRAISING A HOUSING ACCOMMODATION OR IN DETERMINING WHETHER OR NOT, OR UNDER WHAT TERMS AND CONDITIONS, TO PROVIDE FINANCIAL ASSISTANCE.

THESE PROVISIONS GOVERN FINANCIAL ASSISTANCE FOR THE PURPOSE OF THE PURCHASE, CONSTRUCTION, REHABILITATION OF REFINANCING OF ONE TO FOUR UNIT FAMILY RESIDENCES OCCUPIED BY THE OWNER AND FOR THE PURPOSE OF THE HOME IMPROVEMENT OF ANY ONE TO FOUR UNIT FAMILY RESIDENCE.

IF YOU HAVE ANY QUESTIONS ABOUT YOUR RIGHTS, OR IF YOU WISH TO FILE A COMPLAINT, CONTACT THE MANAGEMENT OF THIS FINANCIAL INSTITUTION OR:

DEPARTMENT OF REAL ESTATE	DEPARTMENT OF REAL ESTATE
320 W. 4TH STREET, SUITE 350	1515 CLAY STREET, SUITE 702
LOS ANGELES, CA 90013-1105	OAKLAND, CA 94612-1402

****

****NOTICE OF RIGHT TO APPRAISAL

You have the right to a copy of the appraisal report used in connection with your application for credit. If you wish a copy, please write to us at the address provided. We must hear from you no later than 90 days after we notify you about the action taken on your credit application or you withdraw your application. In your letter, give us the following information: name, address, property address and loan/application number.
****
****

EQUAL CREDIT OPPORTUNITY ACT NOTICE

The Federal Equal Credit Opportunity Act prohibits creditors from discriminating against credit applicants on the basis of race, color, religion, national origin, sex, marital status, age (provided that the applicant has the capacity to enter in a binding contract); because all or part of the applicant's income derives from any public assistance program; or because the applicant has in good faith exercised any right under the Consumer Credit Protection Act.

The federal agency that administers compliance with law concerning this mortgage company is:

FEDERAL TRADE COMMISSION
600 PENNSYLVANIA AVENUE, N.W.
WASHINGTON, DC 20580

I (we) hereby acknowledge that I (we) have read and received a copy of this notice.

_____	_____	_____	_____
Applicant	**Date**	**Applicant**	**Date**

Hunter Financial Group, Inc., dba, USASelect Mortgage
3303 East Courtline Road #7-118. Gilbert, AZ 85234
NCMO3780

Loan Number

First Payment Notification

Dear Homeowner:

We would like to take this opportunity to thank you for closing your mortgage loan with our company and to provide you with the following information regarding your loan:

Your loan number is **NCM03780.** Please include this number on all inquiries and correspondence to **ABC Loan Services, Inc.**

Your loan will be serviced by: **Aurora Loan Services, Inc.**

Upon receipt of the documents, the servicer will assign you a loan number and advise you of that number. All inquiries and correspondence to **ABC Loan Services, Inc.** must have your loan number.

At present and until further notice, your monthly mortgage payment is as follows:

Principal and Interest	$	2,554.09
IMPOUNDS/ESCROW:		
Hazard Insurance		
Mortgage Insurance		
City Taxes		
County Taxes (based on present information)		
TOTAL MONTHLY MORTGAGE PAYMENT:	$	2,554.09

Your first payment is due on the 1st day of each month beginning January 1, 20XX, and is to be mailed to:

REGULAR MAIL:
ABC Loan Services, Inc.
ATTENTION: Cashiering
P.O. Box 5180
Denver, CO 80217-5180

EXPRESS SERVICES:
ABC Loan Services, Inc.
ATTENTION: Cashiering
2530 S. Parker Road, Suite 601
Aurora, CO 80014

Toll Free Phone Number: 800-550-0508

You will receive payment coupons or a payment notice from the servicer. Once again, all checks, letters, etc. MUST have your loan number on them or they will be returned.

Late charge of **5.000%** will be charged on all payments received more than **15** days after the due date set forth in the Note.

I understand that my mortgage payments are due on the **1st** day of each month and would like to request that my payment coupons and all correspondence be mailed to:

10116 Chevrolet Drive
Los Angeles, CA 90060

_____   _____
John A. Maxell   Date   Date

Fannie Mae
Affidavit and Agreement
(by Borrower and Property Seller)

STATE OF ARIZONA

COUNTY OF Los Angeles

Before me, _____, a Notary Public in and for
personally appeared
John A. Maxell

(referred to herein, whether one or more persons, as "Borrower Affiant");

_____

_____

_____

NOTES

When encountering this form:

(1) Check the venue at the top of the form carefully. Notice the state of "Arizona" and county of "Los Angeles" is already typed into the form. (Note: This is how the document was actually drafted.) This will likely require correction. Line through "Arizona" and "Los Angeles" (as applicable), print the correct state and county above or alongside, and initial the corrections.

(2) Print your full official Notary name at the beginning of the form underneath the venue and print the words "the state of _____ (enter your state of commissioning) after the words, "... a Notary Public in and for..."

(3) The borrower will be responsible for the truthfulness of the representations indicated in the form (as indicated where the information is provided), as well as Sections II and III.

(4) Since the notarization to be performed is a jurat, administer an oath or affirmation to the borrower.

...hether one or more persons, as "Seller Affiant");
...n, being of lawful age and being duly sworn according to law, upon oath deposes and makes the applicable
... in Section III below; and Borrower Affiant and Seller Affiant also agree as provided in Section II below.
...SENTATIONS:
...ation No.1. That Borrower Affiant is the party named in a promissory note (referred to herein as the "Note") and a
...eed of trust, or deed to secure debt (referred to herein as the "Security Instrument"), both bearing date of
..., 2003, evidencing and securing a loan (referred to herein as the "Loan") constituting a lien on the property

10116 Chevrolet Drive, Los Angeles, CALIFORNIA 90060

... herein as the "Property"), the Loan having been made to Borrower Affiant by Fisher Financial Group, Inc., dba,
...ice Mortgage (referred to herein as the "Lender").
...ation No.2. That Seller Affiant is the seller of the Property to Borrower Affiant.
...ation No.3. That the purpose of the Loan is as shown by X in the appropriate space below:
...nce Borrower Affiant's purchase of the Property, at a purchase price of
...nce outstanding debt against the Property.
...e following purpose: _____

_____

_____

...ation No.4. That the financial terms of the transaction constituting or related to the Loan are as follows:
...the First Mortgage on the Property $_____ **426,000.00**
...y (if the Loan is not a refinancing) $_____
...ice of the Property $_____
...thly Payment under the Note $_____ **2,554.09**
... subordinate financing relating to the Property except as specifically set forth immediately below:
...ubordinate Financing

...e: Term: _____ Months
...yment:
...Name and address of the holder of such subordinate financing:
Representation No. 5. That Borrower Affiant has not given, conveyed, permitted, or contracted for, or agreed to give, convey, or permit any lien upon the Property to secure a debt or loan, except for any lien connected with subordinate financing upon the Property, as fully disclosed in Representation No.4 above, and the lien referred to in Representation No. I above.
Representation No.6. That if the Loan is for the purpose of financing Borrower Affiant's purchase of the Property, no expenses or charges relating to, or in connection with, Borrower Affiant's purchase of the Property, such as interest charges, real estate taxes, hazard insurance premiums, initial mortgage insurance premiums, or of funds to be used for renewal of mortgage insurance relating to the Loan, have been, or will be, paid, funded, or borne by Seller Affiant for or on behalf of Borrower Affiant, except as otherwise specifically stated immediately below.
Representation No.7. As indicated by X in Appropriate space adjacent to A or B below.
____   A. That (if indicated by X in the appropriate space adjacent hereto) Borrower Affiant now occupies the Property as Borrower Affiant's principal residence, or in good faith will so occupy the Property, commencing such occupancy not later than: (a) thirty (30) days after this date or (b) thirty (30) days after the Property shall first have become ready for occupancy as a habitable dwelling, whichever is later.
_X_   B. That (if indicated by X in the appropriate space adjacent hereto) Borrower Affiant does not occupy the Property as Borrower Affiant's principal residence and does not intend to do so.
Initials of Borrower Affiant: Initials of Seller Affiant:

_____   _____

II. AGREEMENT PROVISIONS:

A. Borrower Covenant. Borrower Affiant agrees that (if an X is placed in the appropriate space adjacent to Representation No.7 A of Section I above): (I) it shall be an additional covenant of the Security Instrument that Borrower Affiant occupy the property as provided in such Representation No.7 A; and (2) failure to so occupy the property shall constitute a breach of covenant under the Security Instrument that shall entitle the Lender, its successors and assigns, to exercise the remedies for breach of covenant provided in the Security Instrument.

B. Inducement Agreement. Borrower Affiant and Seller Affiant agree and acknowledge that the foregoing Borrower Covenant (if applicable), the Representations made in Section I above, and the Statements under Oath made in Section III below are made for the purpose of inducing the Lender and it assigns to make or purchase the Loan.

III. STATEMENTS UNDER OATH

A. By Borrower Affiant: Borrower Affiant hereby deposes and says upon oath that those Representations referred to and set forth in Section I above as Representations Nos. 1,3,4,5,6, and (if Applicable) Representation No. 7A are true and correct.

B. By Seller Affiant: Seller Affiant hereby deposes and says upon oath that those Representations referred to and set forth in Section I above as Representations Nos. 2 and 6 are true and correct, and that Representations Nos. 1,3,4,5, and (if applicable) Representation No.7 A, as referred to and set forth in such Section, are true and correct to the best of Seller Affiant's knowledge, information, and belief.

John A. Maxell	Borrower		Seller
	Borrower		Seller
	Borrower		Seller
	Borrower		Seller

Sworn to and subscribed before me this _____ day of _____ , .

(SEAL)

_____
Notary Public in and for

My commission expires: _____

CERTIFICATE AND ACKNOWLEDGEMENT BY LENDER

The Lender hereby represents to, and certifies for the reliance of, any party to which the Loan hereafter is sold or assigned, that all of the applicable representations and statements contained in Sections I and III above are true and correct to the best of the Lender's knowledge, information, and belief. In addition, the Lender hereby acknowledges and accepts the Borrower Covenant (if applicable) and the Inducement Agreement, set forth, respectively, in Paragraphs A and B of Section II above.

Hunter Financial Group, Inc., dba, USASelect Mortgage
Name of Lender

_____
Signature

_____
Date:

_____
Title

(This form should be executed by the borrower(s), property seller(s) and lender on the date the Loan is closed.)

ADVISORY NOTICE

If any statement in the foregoing Affidavit and Agreement is made under oath by Borrower Affiant or Seller Affiant with knowledge that such statement is false, the person making such false statement may be subject to civil and criminal penalties under applicable law.

In addition, any breach of the covenant by Borrower Affiant relating to occupancy of the Property (as set forth in Paragraph A of Section II above) will entitle the holder of the Note to exercise its remedies for breach of covenant under the Security Instrument. Such remedies include, without limitation, requiring immediate payment in full of the remaining indebtedness under the Loan together with all other sums secured by the Security Instrument, and exercise of power of sale or other applicable foreclosure remedies, to the extent and in the manner authorized by the Security Instrument.

HOLD HARMLESS SEPTIC, WELL & WATER

Date: **November 1, 20XX**

To: **Hunter Financial Group, Inc., dba, USASelect Mortgage**
3303 East Courtline Road, #7-118
Gilbert, AZ 85234

Property
Address: **10116 Chevrolet Drive**
Los Angeles, CA 90060

Gentlemen:

We are aware that the above captioned property has a well and/or septic system and we are satisfied with the conditions of these items and, therefore, **waive the need for an inspection.**

We, also, hold your institution or any assignee of the mortgage, or any other assignee and any of your individual personnel harmless and without further liability which might arise from the condition of the septic system, well, or quality of the water. This statement is made free of any duress.

_____   _____
Borrower **John A. Maxell**   Borrower

HOMEOWNER'S REAL ESTATE TAX AUTHORIZATION

Loan Number: **NCM03780**

Date: **November 1, 20XX**

Homeowner Name: **John A. Maxell**

Address: **10116 Chevrolet Drive**

City & State: **Los Angeles, CA 90060**

County: **Los Angeles**   Lot: _____

Block: _____   Tax Parcel #: **4316-016-028**

Subdivision: _____

Dear Tax Collector:

Please accept this letter as authorization to mail all future real estate tax bills on the above property to

Hunter Financial Group, Inc., dba, USASelect Mortgage
3303 East Courtline Road, #7-118
Gilbert, AZ 85234

We further authorize that, in the event the mortgage is assigned or another paying agent is established for the payment of property taxes, the tax bills be forwarded to the assignee or paying agent immediately upon receipt of such notification.

Sincerely,

Homeowner Signature(s)

_____   _____
Borrower **John A. Maxell**   Borrower

Form 4506

(September 2018)

Department of the Treasury
Internal Revenue Service

Request for Copy of Tax Return

▶ Do not sign this form unless all applicable lines have been completed.
▶ Request may be rejected if the form is incomplete or illegible.
▶ For more information about Form 4506, visit *www.irs.gov/form4506*.

OMB No. 1545-0429

Tip. You may be able to get your tax return or return information from other sources. If you had your tax return completed by a paid preparer, they should be able to provide you a copy of the return. The IRS can provide a **Tax Return Transcript** for many returns free of charge. The transcript provides most of the line entries from the original tax return and usually contains the information that a third party (such as a mortgage company) requires. See **Form 4506-T, Request for Transcript of Tax Return,** or you can quickly request transcripts by using our automated self-help service tools. Please visit us at IRS.gov and click on "Get a Tax Transcript..." or call 1-800-908-9946.

return. If a joint return, enter the name shown first.

1b First social security number on tax return, individual taxpayer identification number, or employer identification number (see instructions)

000-00-0000

spouse's name shown on tax return.

2b Second social security number or individual taxpayer identification number if joint tax return

ss (including apt., room, or suite no.), city, state, and ZIP code (see instructions)

own on the last return filed if different from line 3 (see instructions)

be mailed to a third party (such as a mortgage company), enter the third party's name, address, and telephone number.

s being mailed to a third party, ensure that you have filled in lines 6 and 7 before signing. Sign and date the form once you completing these steps helps to protect your privacy. Once the IRS discloses your tax return to the third party listed on line ver what the third party does with the information. If you would like to limit the third party's authority to disclose your return fy this limitation in your written agreement with the third party.

sted. Form 1040, 1120, 941, etc. and all attachments as originally submitted to the IRS, including Form(s) W-2, nded returns. Copies of Forms 1040, 1040A, and 1040EZ are generally available for 7 years from filing before they are . Other returns may be available for a longer period of time. Enter only one return number. If you need more than one type of return, you must complete another Form 4506. ▶ _____

Note: If the copies must be certified for court or administrative proceedings, check here . . . . ☐

7 Year or period requested. Enter the ending date of the year or period, using the mm/dd/yyyy format. If you are requesting more than eight years or periods, you must attach another Form 4506.

_____   _____   _____

_____   _____   _____

8 Fee. There is a $50 fee for each return requested. **Full payment must be included with your request or it will be rejected. Make your check or money order payable to "United States Treasury." Enter your SSN, ITIN, or EIN and "Form 4506 request" on your check or money order.**

a Cost for each return	$	50.00
b Number of returns requested on line 7		
c Total cost. Multiply line 8a by line 8b	$	

9 If we cannot find the tax return, we will refund the fee. If the refund should go to the third party listed on line 5, check here . . . . . ☐

Caution: Do not sign this form unless all applicable lines have been completed.

Signature of taxpayer(s). I declare that I am either the taxpayer whose name is shown on line 1a or 2a, or a person authorized to obtain the tax return requested. If the request applies to a joint return, at least one spouse must sign. If signed by a corporate officer, 1 percent or more shareholder, partner, managing member, guardian, tax matters partner, executor, receiver, administrator, trustee, or party other than the taxpayer, I certify that I have the authority to execute Form 4506 on behalf of the taxpayer. **Note:** This form must be received by IRS within 120 days of the signature date.

☐ **Signatory attests that he/she has read the attestation clause and upon so reading declares that he/she has the authority to sign the Form 4506.** See instructions.

Phone number of taxpayer on line 1a or 2a

Sign Here

▶ **Signature** (see instructions)   Date

▶ **Title** (if line 1a above is a corporation, partnership, estate, or trust)

▶ **Spouse's signature**   Date

For Privacy Act and Paperwork Reduction Act Notice, see page 2.   Cat. No. 41721E   Form **4506** (Rev. 9-2018)

Section references are to the Internal Revenue Code unless otherwise noted.

Future Developments

For the latest information about Form 4506 and its instructions, go to *www.irs.gov/form4506*. Information about any recent developments affecting Form 4506, Form 4506-T and Form 4506T-EZ will be posted on that page.

General Instructions

Caution: Do not sign this form unless all applicable lines have been completed.

Purpose of form. Use Form 4506 to request a copy of your tax return. You can also designate (on line 5) a third party to receive the tax return.

How long will it take? It may take up to 75 calendar days for us to process your request.

Tip. Use Form 4506-T, Request for Transcript of Tax Return, to request tax return transcripts, tax account information, W-2 information, 1099 information, verification of nonfiling, and records of account.

Automated transcript request. You can quickly request transcripts by using our automated self-help service tools. Please visit us at IRS.gov and click on "Get a Tax Transcript..." or call 1-800-908-9946.

Where to file. Attach payment and mail Form 4506 to the address below for the state you lived in, or the state your business was in, when that return was filed. There are two address charts: one for individual returns (Form 1040 series) and one for all other returns.

If you are requesting a return for more than one year or period and the chart below shows two different addresses, send your request to the address based on the address of your most recent return.

Chart for individual returns (Form 1040 series)

If you filed an individual return and lived in:	Mail to:
Alabama, Kentucky, Louisiana, Mississippi, Tennessee, Texas, a foreign country, American Samoa, Puerto Rico, Guam, the Commonwealth of the Northern Mariana Islands, the U.S. Virgin Islands, or A.P.O. or F.P.O. address	Internal Revenue Service RAIVS Team Stop 6716 AUSC Austin, TX 73301
Alaska, Arizona, Arkansas, California, Colorado, Hawaii, Idaho, Illinois, Indiana, Iowa, Kansas, Michigan, Minnesota, Montana, Nebraska, Nevada, New Mexico, North Dakota, Oklahoma, Oregon, South Dakota, Utah, Washington, Wisconsin, Wyoming	Internal Revenue Service RAIVS Team Stop 37106 Fresno, CA 93888
Connecticut, Delaware, District of Columbia, Florida, Georgia, Maine, Maryland, Massachusetts, Missouri, New Hampshire, New Jersey, New York, North Carolina, Ohio, Pennsylvania, Rhode Island, South Carolina, Vermont, Virginia, West Virginia	Internal Revenue Service RAIVS Team Stop 6705 P-6 Kansas City, MO 64999

Chart for all other returns

If you lived in or your business was in:	Mail to:
Alabama, Alaska, Arizona, Arkansas, California, Colorado, Connecticut, Delaware, District of Columbia, Florida, Georgia, Hawaii, Idaho, Illinois, Indiana, Iowa, Kansas, Kentucky, Louisiana, Maine, Maryland, Massachusetts, Michigan, Minnesota, Mississippi, Missouri, Montana, Nebraska, Nevada, New Hampshire, New Jersey, New Mexico, New York, North Carolina, North Dakota, Ohio, Oklahoma, Oregon, Pennsylvania, Rhode Island, South Carolina, South Dakota, Tennessee, Texas, Utah, Vermont, Virginia, Washington, West Virginia, Wisconsin, Wyoming, a foreign country, American Samoa, Puerto Rico, Guam, the Commonwealth of the Northern Mariana Islands, the U.S. Virgin Islands, or A.P.O. or F.P.O. address	Internal Revenue Service RAIVS Team P.O. Box 9941 Mail Stop 6734 Ogden, UT 84409

Specific Instructions

Line 1b. Enter your employer identification number (EIN) if you are requesting a copy of a business return. Otherwise, enter the first social security number (SSN) or your individual taxpayer identification number (ITIN) shown on the return. For example, if you are requesting Form 1040 that includes Schedule C (Form 1040), enter your SSN.

Line 3. Enter your current address. If you use a P.O. box, please include it on this line 3.

Line 4. Enter the address shown on the last return filed if different from the address entered on line 3.

Note: If the addresses on lines 3 and 4 are different and you have not changed your address with the IRS, file Form 8822, Change of Address. For a business address, file Form 8822-B, Change of Address or Responsible Party — Business.

Signature and date. Form 4506 must be signed and dated by the taxpayer listed on line 1a or 2a. The IRS must receive Form 4506 within 120 days of the date signed by the taxpayer or it will be rejected. Ensure that all applicable lines are completed before signing.

 You must check the box in the signature area to acknowledge you have the authority to sign and request the information. The form will not be processed and returned to you if the box is unchecked.

Individuals. Copies of jointly filed tax returns may be furnished to either spouse. Only one signature is required. Sign Form 4506 exactly as your name appeared on the original return. If you changed your name, also sign your current name.

Corporations. Generally, Form 4506 can be signed by: (1) an officer having legal authority to bind the corporation, (2) any person designated by the board of directors or other governing body, or (3) any officer or employee on written request by any principal officer and attested to by the secretary or other officer. A bona fide shareholder of record owning 1 percent or more of the outstanding stock of the corporation may submit a Form 4506 but must provide documentation to support the requester's right to receive the information.

Partnerships. Generally, Form 4506 can be signed by any person who was a member of the partnership during any part of the tax period requested on line 7.

All others. See section 6103(e) if the taxpayer has died, is insolvent, is a dissolved corporation, or if a trustee, guardian, executor, receiver, or administrator is acting for the taxpayer.

Note: If you are Heir at law, Next of kin, or Beneficiary you must be able to establish a material interest in the estate or trust.

Documentation. For entities other than individuals, you must attach the authorization document. For example, this could be the letter from the principal officer authorizing an employee of the corporation or the letters testamentary authorizing an individual to act for an estate.

Signature by a representative. A representative can sign Form 4506 for a taxpayer only if this authority has been specifically delegated to the representative on Form 2848, line 5. Form 2848 showing the delegation must be attached to Form 4506.

Privacy Act and Paperwork Reduction Act Notice. We ask for the information on this form to establish your right to gain access to the requested return(s) under the Internal Revenue Code. We need this information to properly identify the return(s) and respond to your request. If you request a copy of a tax return, sections 6103 and 6109 require you to provide this information, including your SSN or EIN, to process your request. If you do not provide this information, we may not be able to process your request. Providing false or fraudulent information may subject you to penalties.

Routine uses of this information include giving it to the Department of Justice for civil and criminal litigation, and cities, states, the District of Columbia, and U.S. commonwealths and possessions for use in administering their tax laws. We may also disclose this information to other countries under a tax treaty, to federal and state agencies to enforce federal nontax criminal laws, or to federal law enforcement and intelligence agencies to combat terrorism.

You are not required to provide the information requested on a form that is subject to the Paperwork Reduction Act unless the form displays a valid OMB control number. Books or records relating to a form or its instructions must be retained as long as their contents may become material in the administration of any Internal Revenue law. Generally, tax returns and return information are confidential, as required by section 6103.

The time needed to complete and file Form 4506 will vary depending on individual circumstances. The estimated average time is: **Learning about the law or the form,** 10 min.; **Preparing the form,** 16 min.; and **Copying, assembling, and sending the form to the IRS,** 20 min.

If you have comments concerning the accuracy of these time estimates or suggestions for making Form 4506 simpler, we would be happy to hear from you. You can write to:

Internal Revenue Service
Tax Forms and Publications Division
1111 Constitution Ave. NW, IR-6526
Washington, DC 20224.

Do not send the form to this address. Instead, see *Where to file* on this page.

Form W-9

Department of the Treasury
Internal Revenue Service

Request for Taxpayer
Identification Number and Certification

▶ Go to *www.irs.gov/FormW9* for instructions and the latest information.

Give Form to the
requester. Do not
send to the IRS.

1 Name (as shown on your income tax return). Name is required on this line; do not leave this line blank.

John A. Maxell

2 Business name/disregarded entity name, if different from above

3 Check appropriate box for federal tax classification of the person whose name is entered on line 1. Check only **one** of the following seven boxes.

☑ Individual/sole proprietor or single-member LLC ☐ C Corporation ☐ S Corporation ☐ Partnership ☐ Trust/estate

☐ Limited liability company. Enter the tax classification (C = C corporation, S = S corporation, P = Partnership) ▶ _____

Note: Check the appropriate box in the line above for the tax classification of the single-member owner. Do not check LLC if the LLC is classified as a single-member LLC that is disregarded from the owner unless the owner of the LLC is another LLC that is **not** disregarded from the owner for U.S. federal tax purposes. Otherwise, a single-member LLC that is disregarded from the owner should check the appropriate box for the tax classification of its owner.

☐ Other (see instructions) ▶

4 Exemptions (codes apply only to certain entities, not individuals; see instructions on page 3):

Exempt payee code (if any) _____

Exemption from FATCA reporting code (if any) _____

(Applies to accounts maintained outside the U.S.)

5 Address (number, street, and apt. or suite no.) See instructions.

10116 Chevrolet Drive

6 City, state, and ZIP code

Los Angeles, CA 90060

Requester's name and address (optional)

7 List account number(s) here (optional)

Print or type.
See **Specific Instructions** on page 2.

Part I **Taxpayer Identification Number (TIN)**

Enter your TIN in the appropriate box. The TIN provided must match the name given on line 1 to avoid backup withholding. For individuals, this is generally your social security number (SSN). However, for a resident alien, sole proprietor, or disregarded entity, see the instructions for Part I, later. For other entities, it is your employer identification number (EIN). If you do not have a number, see *How to get a TIN,* later.

Note. If the account is in more than one name, see the instructions for line 1. Also see *What Name and Number To Give the Requester* for guidelines on whose number to enter.

Social security number

| 0 | 0 | 0 | – | 0 | 0 | – | 0 | 0 | 0 | 0 |

or

Employer identification number

Part II **Certification**

Under penalties of perjury, I certify that:

1. The number shown on this form is my correct taxpayer identification number (or I am waiting for a number to be issued to me); and
2. I am not subject to backup withholding because: (a) I am exempt from backup withholding, or (b) I have not been notified by the Internal Revenue Service (IRS) that I am subject to backup withholding as a result of a failure to report all interest or dividends, or (c) the IRS has notified me that I am no longer subject to backup withholding; and
3. I am a U.S. citizen or other U.S. person (defined below); and
4. The FATCA code(s) entered on this form (if any) indicating that I am exempt from FATCA reporting is correct.

Certification instructions. You must cross out item 2 above if you have been notified by the IRS that you are currently subject to backup withholding because you have failed to report all interest and dividends on your tax return. For real estate transactions, item 2 does not apply. For mortgage interest paid, acquisition or abandonment of secured property, cancellation of debt, contributions to an individual retirement arrangement (IRA), and generally, payments other than interest and dividends, you are not required to sign the certification, but you must provide your correct TIN. See the instructions for Part II, later.

Sign Here Signature of U.S. person ▶ Date ▶

General Instructions

Section references are to the Internal Revenue Code unless otherwise noted.

Future developments. For the latest information about developments related to Form W-9 and its instructions, such as legislation enacted after they were published, go to *www.irs.gov/FormW9.*

Purpose of Form

An individual or entity (Form W-9 requester) who is required to file an information return with the IRS must obtain your correct taxpayer identification number (TIN) which may be your social security number (SSN), individual taxpayer identification number (ITIN), adoption taxpayer identification number (ATIN), or employer identification number (EIN), to report on an information return the amount paid to you, or other amount reportable on an information return. Examples of information returns include, but are not limited to, the following.

• Form 1099-INT (interest earned or paid)
• Form 1099-DIV (dividends, including those from stocks or mutual funds)
• Form 1099-MISC (various types of income, prizes, awards, or gross proceeds)
• Form 1099-B (stock or mutual fund sales and certain other transactions by brokers)
• Form 1099-S (proceeds from real estate transactions)
• Form 1099-K (merchant card and third party network transactions)
• Form 1098 (home mortgage interest), 1098-E (student loan interest), 1098-T (tuition)
• Form 1099-C (canceled debt)
• Form 1099-A (acquisition or abandonment of secured property)

Use Form W-9 only if you are a U.S. person (including a resident alien), to provide your correct TIN.

If you do not return Form W-9 to the requester with a TIN, you might be subject to backup withholding. See What is backup withholding, *later.*

By signing the filled-out form, you:

1. Certify that the TIN you are giving is correct (or you are waiting for a number to be issued),

2. Certify that you are not subject to backup withholding, or

3. Claim exemption from backup withholding if you are a U.S. exempt payee. If applicable, you are also certifying that as a U.S. person, your allocable share of any partnership income from a U.S. trade or business is not subject to the withholding tax on foreign partners' share of effectively connected income, and

4. Certify that FATCA code(s) entered on this form (if any) indicating that you are exempt from the FATCA reporting, is correct. See *What is FATCA reporting,* later, for further information.

Note: If you are a U.S. person and a requester gives you a form other than Form W-9 to request your TIN, you must use the requester's form if it is substantially similar to this Form W-9.

Definition of a U.S. person. For federal tax purposes, you are considered a U.S. person if you are:

• An individual who is a U.S. citizen or U.S. resident alien;

• A partnership, corporation, company, or association created or organized in the United States or under the laws of the United States;

• An estate (other than a foreign estate); or

• A domestic trust (as defined in Regulations section 301.7701-7).

Special rules for partnerships. Partnerships that conduct a trade or business in the United States are generally required to pay a withholding tax under section 1446 on any foreign partners' share of effectively connected taxable income from such business. Further, in certain cases where a Form W-9 has not been received, the rules under section 1446 require a partnership to presume that a partner is a foreign person, and pay the section 1446 withholding tax. Therefore, if you are a U.S. person that is a partner in a partnership conducting a trade or business in the United States, provide Form W-9 to the partnership to establish your U.S. status and avoid section 1446 withholding on your share of partnership income.

Ellie Mae, Inc. Cat. No. 10231X Form **W-9**
GW9C (CLS)

In the cases below, the following person must give Form W-9 to the partnership for purposes of establishing its U.S. status and avoiding withholding on its allocable share of net income from the partnership conducting a trade or business in the United States.
• In the case of a disregarded entity with a U.S. owner, the U.S. owner of the disregarded entity and not the entity;
• In the case of a grantor trust with a U.S. grantor or other U.S. owner, generally, the U.S. grantor or other U.S. owner of the grantor trust and not the trust; and
• In the case of a U.S. trust (other than a grantor trust), the U.S. trust (other than a grantor trust) and not the beneficiaries of the trust.

Foreign person. If you are a foreign person or the U.S. branch of a foreign bank that has elected to be treated as a U.S. person, do not use Form W-9. Instead, use the appropriate Form W-8 or Form 8233 (see Pub. 515, Withholding of Tax on Nonresident Aliens and Foreign Entities).

Nonresident alien who becomes a resident alien. Generally, only a nonresident alien individual may use the terms of a tax treaty to reduce or eliminate U.S. tax on certain types of income. However, most tax treaties contain a provision known as a "saving clause." Exceptions specified in the saving clause may permit an exemption from tax to continue for certain types of income even after the payee has otherwise become a U.S. resident alien for tax purposes.

If you are a U.S. resident alien who is relying on an exception contained in the saving clause of a tax treaty to claim an exemption from U.S. tax on certain types of income, you must attach a statement to Form W-9 that specifies the following five items.

1. The treaty country. Generally, this must be the same treaty under which you claimed exemption from tax as a nonresident alien.

2. The treaty article addressing the income.

3. The article number (or location) in the tax treaty that contains the saving clause and its exceptions.

4. The type and amount of income that qualifies for the exemption from tax.

5. Sufficient facts to justify the exemption from tax under the terms of the treaty article.

Example. Article 20 of the U.S.-China income tax treaty allows an exemption from tax for scholarship income received by a Chinese student temporarily present in the United States. Under U.S. law, this student will become a resident alien for tax purposes if his or her stay in the United States exceeds 5 calendar years. However, paragraph 2 of the first Protocol to the U.S.-China treaty (dated April 30, 1984) allows the provisions of Article 20 to continue to apply even after the Chinese student becomes a resident alien of the United States. A Chinese student who qualifies for this exception (under paragraph 2 of the first protocol) and is relying on this exception to claim an exemption from tax on his or her scholarship or fellowship income would attach to Form W-9 a statement that includes the information described above to support that exemption.

If you are a nonresident alien or a foreign entity, give the requester the appropriate completed Form W-8 or Form 8233.

Backup Withholding

What is backup withholding? Persons making certain payments to you must under certain conditions withhold and pay to the IRS 28% of such payments. This is called "backup withholding." Payments that may be subject to backup withholding include interest, tax-exempt interest, dividends, broker and barter exchange transactions, rents, royalties, nonemployee pay, payments made in settlement of payment card and third party network transactions, and certain payments from fishing boat operators. Real estate transactions are not subject to backup withholding.

You will not be subject to backup withholding on payments you receive if you give the requester your correct TIN, make the proper certifications, and report all your taxable interest and dividends on your tax return.

Payments you receive will be subject to backup withholding if:

1. You do not furnish your TIN to the requester,

2. You do not certify your TIN when required (see the instructions for Part II for details),

3. The IRS tells the requester that you furnished an incorrect TIN,

4. The IRS tells you that you are subject to backup withholding because you did not report all your interest and dividends on your tax return (for reportable interest and dividends only), or

5. You do not certify to the requester that you are not subject to backup withholding under 4 above (for reportable interest and dividend accounts opened after 1983 only).

Certain payees and payments are exempt from backup withholding. See *Exempt payee code*, later, and the separate Instructions for the Requester of Form W-9 for more information.

Also see *Special rules for partnerships*, earlier.

What is FATCA Reporting?

The Foreign Account Tax Compliance Act (FATCA) requires a participating foreign financial institution to report all United States account holders that are specified United States persons. Certain payees are exempt from FATCA reporting. See *Exemption from FATCA reporting code*, later, and the Instructions for the Requester of Form W-9 for more information.

Updating Your Information

You must provide updated information to any person to whom you claimed to be an exempt payee if you are no longer an exempt payee and anticipate receiving reportable payments in the future from this person. For example, you may need to provide updated information if you are a C corporation that elects to be an S corporation, or if you no longer are tax exempt. In addition, you must furnish a new Form W-9 if the name or TIN changes for the account; for example, if the grantor of a grantor trust dies.

Penalties

Failure to furnish TIN. If you fail to furnish your correct TIN to a requester, you are subject to a penalty of $50 for each such failure unless your failure is due to reasonable cause and not to willful neglect.

Civil penalty for false information with respect to withholding. If you make a false statement with no reasonable basis that results in no backup withholding, you are subject to a $500 penalty.

Criminal penalty for falsifying information. Willfully falsifying certifications or affirmations may subject you to criminal penalties including fines and/or imprisonment.

Misuse of TINs. If the requester discloses or uses TINs in violation of federal law, the requester may be subject to civil and criminal penalties.

Specific Instructions

Line 1

You must enter one of the following on this line; **do not** leave this line blank. The name should match the name on your tax return.

If this Form W-9 is for a joint account (other than an account maintained by a foreign financial institution (FFI)), list first, and then circle, the name of the person or entity whose number you entered in Part I of Form W-9. If you are providing Form W-9 to an FFI to document a joint account, each holder of the account that is a U.S. person must provide a Form W-9.

a. **Individual.** Generally, enter the name shown on your tax return. If you have changed your last name without informing the Social Security Administration (SSA) of the name change, enter your first name, the last name as shown on your social security card, and your new last name.

Note: ITIN applicant: Enter your individual name as it was entered on your Form W-7 application, line 1a. This should also be the same as the name you entered on the Form 1040/1040A/1040EZ you filed with your application.

b. **Sole proprietor or single-member LLC.** Enter your individual name as shown on your 1040/1040A/1040EZ on line 1. You may enter your business, trade, or "doing business as" (DBA) name on line 2.

c. **Partnership, LLC that is not a single-member LLC, C corporation, or S corporation.** Enter the entity's name as shown on the entity's tax return on line 1 and any business, trade, or DBA name on line 2.

d. **Other entities.** Enter your name as shown on required U.S. federal tax documents on line 1. This name should match the name shown on the charter or other legal document creating the entity. You may enter any business, trade, or DBA name on line 2.

e. **Disregarded entity.** For U.S. federal tax purposes, an entity that is disregarded as an entity separate from its owner is treated as a "disregarded entity." See Regulations section 301.7701-2(c)(2)(iii). Enter the owner's name on line 1. The name of the entity entered on line 1 should never be a disregarded entity. The name on line 1 should be the name shown on the income tax return on which the income should be reported. For example, if a foreign LLC that is treated as a disregarded entity for U.S. federal tax purposes has a single owner that is a U.S. person, the U.S. owner's name is required to be provided on line 1. If the direct owner of the entity is also a disregarded entity, enter the first owner that is not disregarded for federal tax purposes. Enter the disregarded entity's name on line 2, "Business name/disregarded entity name." If the owner of the disregarded entity is a foreign person, the owner must complete an appropriate Form W-8 instead of a Form W-9. This is the case even if the foreign person has a U.S. TIN.

Line 2

If you have a business name, trade name, DBA name, or disregarded entity name, you may enter it on line 2.

Line 3

Check the appropriate box on line 3 for the U.S. federal tax classification of the person whose name is entered on line 1. Check only one box on line 3.

IF the entity/person on line 1 is a(n)...	THEN check the box for...
• Corporation	Corporation
• Individual • Sole proprietorship, or • Single-member limited liability company (LLC) owned by an individual and disregarded for U.S. federal tax purposes.	Individual/sole proprietor or single-member LLC
• LLC treated as a partnership for U.S. federal tax purposes, • LLC that has filed Form 8832 or 2553 to be taxed as a corporation, or • LLC that is disregarded as an entity separate from its owner but the owner is another LLC that is not disregarded for U.S. federal tax purposes.	Limited liability company and enter the appropriate tax classification. (P= Partnership; C= C corporation; or S= S corporation)
• Partnership	Partnership
• Trust/estate	Trust/estate

Refinance Loans

Line 4, Exemptions

If you are exempt from backup withholding and/or FATCA reporting, enter in the appropriate space on line 4 any code(s) that may apply to you.

Exempt payee code.
- Generally, individuals (including sole proprietors) are not exempt from backup withholding.
- Except as provided below, corporations are exempt from backup withholding for certain payments, including interest and dividends.
- Corporations are not exempt from backup withholding for payments made in settlement of payment card or third party network transactions.
- Corporations are not exempt from backup withholding with respect to attorneys' fees or gross proceeds paid to attorneys, and corporations that provide medical or health care services are not exempt with respect to payments reportable on Form 1099-MISC.

The following codes identify payees that are exempt from backup withholding. Enter the appropriate code in the space in line 4.

1 – An organization exempt from tax under section 501(a), any IRA, or a custodial account under section 403(b)(7) if the account satisfies the requirements of section 401(f)(2)

2 – The United States or any of its agencies or instrumentalities

3 – A state, the District of Columbia, a U.S. commonwealth or possession, or any of their political subdivisions or instrumentalities

4 – A foreign government or any of its political subdivisions, agencies, or instrumentalities

5 – A corporation

6 – A dealer in securities or commodities required to register in the United States, the District of Columbia, or a U.S. commonwealth or possession

7 – A futures commission merchant registered with the Commodity Futures Trading Commission

8 – A real estate investment trust

9 – An entity registered at all times during the tax year under the Investment Company Act of 1940

10 – A common trust fund operated by a bank under section 584(a)

11 – A financial institution

12 – A middleman known in the investment community as a nominee or custodian

13 – A trust exempt from tax under section 664 or described in section 4947

The following chart shows types of payments that may be exempt from backup withholding. The chart applies to the exempt payees listed above, 1 through 13.

IF the payment is for...	THEN the payment is exempt for...
Interest and dividend payments	All exempt payees except for 7
Broker transactions	Exempt payees 1 through 4 and 6 through 11 and all C corporations. S corporations must not enter an exempt payee code because they are exempt only for sales of noncovered securities acquired prior to 2012.
Barter exchange transactions and patronage dividends	Exempt payees 1 through 4
Payments over $600 required to be reported and direct sales over $5,000[1]	Generally, exempt payees 1 through 5[2]
Payments made in settlement of payment card or third party network transactions	Exempt payees 1 through 4

[1] See Form 1099-MISC, Miscellaneous Income, and its instructions.

[2] However, the following payments made to a corporation and reportable on Form 1099-MISC are not exempt from backup withholding: medical and health care payments, attorneys' fees, gross proceeds paid to an attorney reportable under section 6045(f), and payments for services paid by a federal executive agency.

Exemption from FATCA reporting code. The following codes identify payees that are exempt from reporting under FATCA. These codes apply to persons submitting this form for accounts maintained outside of the United States by certain foreign financial institutions. Therefore, if you are only submitting this form for an account you hold in the United States, you may leave this field blank. Consult with the person requesting this form if you are uncertain if the financial institution is subject to these requirements. A requester may indicate that a code is not required by providing you with a Form W-9 with "Not Applicable" (or any similar indication) written or printed on the line for a FATCA exemption code.

A – An organization exempt from tax under section 501(a) or any individual retirement plan as defined in section 7701(a)(37)

B – The United States or any of its agencies or instrumentalities

C – A state, the District of Columbia, a U.S. commonwealth or possession, or any of their political subdivisions or instrumentalities

D – A corporation the stock of which is regularly traded on one or more established securities markets, as described in Regulations section 1.1472-1(c)(1)(i)

E – A corporation that is a member of the same expanded affiliated group as a corporation described in Regulations section 1.1472-1(c)(1)(i)

F – A dealer in securities, commodities, or derivative financial instruments (including notional principal contracts, futures, forwards, and options) that is registered as such under the laws of the United States or any state

G – A real estate investment trust

H – A regulated investment company as defined in section 851 or an entity registered at all times during the tax year under the Investment Company Act of 1940

I – A common trust fund as defined in section 584(a)

J – A bank as defined in section 581

K – A broker

L – A trust exempt from tax under section 664 or described in section 4947(a)(1)

M – A tax exempt trust under a section 403(b) plan or section 457(g) plan

Note: You may wish to consult with the financial institution requesting this form to determine whether the FATCA code and/or exempt payee code should be completed.

Line 5

Enter your address (number, street, and apartment or suite number). This is where the requester of this Form W-9 will mail your information returns. If this address differs from the one the requester already has on file, write NEW at the top. If a new address is provided, there is still a chance the old address will be used until the payor changes your address in their records.

Line 6

Enter your city, state, and ZIP code.

Part I. Taxpayer Identification Number (TIN)

Enter your TIN in the appropriate box. If you are a resident alien and you do not have and are not eligible to get an SSN, your TIN is your IRS individual taxpayer identification number (ITIN). Enter it in the social security number box. If you do not have an ITIN, see How to get a TIN below.

If you are a sole proprietor and you have an EIN, you may enter either your SSN or EIN.

If you are a single-member LLC that is disregarded as an entity separate from its owner, enter the owner's SSN (or EIN, if the owner has one). Do not enter the disregarded entity's EIN. If the LLC is classified as a corporation or partnership, enter the entity's EIN.

Note. See What Name and Number To Give the Requester, later, for further clarification of name and TIN combinations.

How to get a TIN. If you do not have a TIN, apply for one immediately. To apply for an SSN, get Form SS-5, Application for a Social Security Card, from your local SSA office or get this form online at www.SSA.gov. You may also get this form by calling 1-800-772-1213. Use Form W-7, Application for IRS Individual Taxpayer Identification Number, to apply for an ITIN, or Form SS-4, Application for Employer Identification Number, to apply for an EIN. You can apply for an EIN online by accessing the IRS website at www.irs.gov/Businesses and clicking on Employer Identification Number (EIN) under Starting a Business. Go to www.irs.gov/Forms to view, download, or print Form W-7 and/or Form SS-4. Or, you can go to www.irs.gov/OrderForms to place an order and have Form W-7 and/or SS-4 mailed to you within 10 business days.

If you are asked to complete Form W-9 but do not have a TIN, apply for a TIN and write "Applied For" in the space for the TIN, sign and date the form, and give it to the requester. For interest and dividend payments, and certain payments made with respect to readily tradable instruments, generally you will have 60 days to get a TIN and give it to the requester before you are subject to backup withholding on payments. The 60-day rule does not apply to other types of payments. You will be subject to backup withholding on all such payments until you provide your TIN to the requester.

Note: Entering "Applied For" means that you have already applied for a TIN or that you intend to apply for one soon.

Caution: A disregarded U.S. entity that has a foreign owner must use the appropriate Form W-8.

Part II. Certification

To establish to the withholding agent that you are a U.S. person, or resident alien, sign Form W-9. You may be requested to sign by the withholding agent even if item 1, 4, or 5 below indicates otherwise.

For a joint account, only the person whose TIN is shown in Part I should sign (when required). In the case of a disregarded entity, the person identified on line 1 must sign. Exempt payees, see Exempt payee code, earlier.

Signature requirements. Complete the certification as indicated in items 1 through 5 below.

1. **Interest, dividend, and barter exchange accounts opened before 1984 and broker accounts considered active during 1983.** You must give your correct TIN, but you do not have to sign the certification.

2. **Interest, dividend, broker, and barter exchange accounts opened after 1983 and broker accounts considered inactive during 1983.** You must sign the certification or backup withholding will apply. If you are subject to backup withholding and you are merely providing your correct TIN to the requester, you must cross out item 2 in the certification before signing the form.

3. **Real estate transactions.** You must sign the certification. You may cross out item 2 of the certification.

4. **Other payments.** You must give your correct TIN, but you do not have to sign the certification unless you have been notified that you have

previously given an incorrect TIN. "Other payments" include payments made in the course of the requester's trade or business for rents, royalties, goods (other than bills for merchandise), medical and health care services (including payments to corporations), payments to a nonemployee for services, payments made in settlement of payment card and third party network transactions, payments to certain fishing boat crew members and fishermen, and gross proceeds paid to attorneys (including payments to corporations).

5. Mortgage interest paid by you, acquisition or abandonment of secured property, cancellation of debt, qualified tuition program payments (under section 529), ABLE accounts (under section 529A), IRA, Coverdell ESA, Archer MSA or HSA contributions or distributions, and pension distributions. You must give your correct TIN, but you do not have to sign the certification.

What Name and Number To Give the Requester

For this type of account:	Give name and SSN of:
1. Individual	The individual
2. Two or more individuals (joint account) other than an account maintained by an FFI	The actual owner of the account or, if combined funds, the first individual on the account[1]
3. Two or more U.S. persons (joint account maintained by an FFI)	Each holder of the account
4. Custodial account of a minor (Uniform Gift to Minors Act)	The minor[2]
5. a. The usual revocable savings trust (grantor is also trustee)	The grantor-trustee[1]
b. So-called trust account that is not a legal or valid trust under state law	The actual owner[1]
6. Sole proprietorship or disregarded entity owned by an individual	The owner[3]
7. Grantor trust filing under Optional Form 1099 Filing Method 1 (see Regulations section 1.671-4(b)(2)(i)(A))	The grantor*

For this type of account:	Give name and EIN of:
8. Disregarded entity not owned by an individual	The owner
9. A valid trust, estate, or pension trust	Legal entity[4]
10. Corporation or LLC electing corporate status on Form 8832 or Form 2553	The corporation
11. Association, club, religious, charitable, educational, or other tax-exempt organization	The organization
12. Partnership or multi-member LLC	The partnership
13. A broker or registered nominee	The broker or nominee

For this type of account:	Give name and EIN of:
14. Account with the Department of Agriculture in the name of a public entity (such as a state or local government, school district, or prison) that receives agricultural program payments	The public entity
15. Grantor trust filing under the Form 1041 Filing Method or the Optional Form 1099 Filing Method 2 (see Regulations section 1.671-4 (b)(2)(i)(B))	The trust

[1] List first and circle the name of the person whose number you furnish. If only one person on a joint account has an SSN, that person's number must be furnished.

[2] Circle the minor's name and furnish the minor's SSN.

[3] You must show your individual name and you may also enter your business or DBA name on the "Business name/disregarded entity" name line. You may use either your SSN or EIN (if you have one), but the IRS encourages you to use your SSN.

[4] List first and circle the name of the trust, estate, or pension trust. (Do not furnish the TIN of the personal representative or trustee unless the legal entity itself is not designated in the account title.) Also see *Special rules for partnerships,* earlier.

* **Note:** The grantor also must provide a Form W-9 to trustee of trust.

Note. If no name is circled when more than one name is listed, the number will be considered to be that of the first name listed.

Secure Your Tax Records From Identity Theft

Identity theft occurs when someone uses your personal information such as your name, SSN, or other identifying information, without your permission, to commit fraud or other crimes. An identity thief may use your SSN to get a job or may file a tax return using your SSN to receive a refund.

To reduce your risk:

- Protect your SSN,
- Ensure your employer is protecting your SSN, and
- Be careful when choosing a tax preparer.

If your tax records are affected by identity theft and you receive a notice from the IRS, respond right away to the name and phone number printed on the IRS notice or letter.

If your tax records are not currently affected by identity theft but you think you are at risk due to a lost or stolen purse or wallet, questionable credit card activity or credit report, contact the IRS Identity Theft Hotline at 1-800-908-4490 or submit Form 14039.

For more information, see Pub. 5027, Identity Theft Information for Taxpayers.

Victims of identity theft who are experiencing economic harm or a systemic problem, or are seeking help in resolving tax problems that have not been resolved through normal channels, may be eligible for Taxpayer Advocate Service (TAS) assistance. You can reach TAS by calling the TAS toll-free case intake line at 1-877-777-4778 or TTY/TDD 1-800-829-4059.

Protect yourself from suspicious emails or phishing schemes. Phishing is the creation and use of email and websites designed to mimic legitimate business emails and websites. The most common act is sending an email to a user falsely claiming to be an established legitimate enterprise in an attempt to scam the user into surrendering private information that will be used for identity theft.

The IRS does not initiate contacts with taxpayers via emails. Also, the IRS does not request personal detailed information through email or ask taxpayers for the PIN numbers, passwords, or similar secret access information for their credit card, bank, or other financial accounts.

If you receive an unsolicited email claiming to be from the IRS, forward this message to *phishing@irs.gov*. You may also report misuse of the IRS name, logo, or other IRS property to the Treasury Inspector General for Tax Administration (TIGTA) at 1-800-366-4484. You can forward suspicious emails to the Federal Trade Commission at: *spam@uce.gov* or report them at *www.ftc.gov/complaint*. You can contact the FTC at *www.ftc.gov/idtheft* or 877-IDTHEFT (877-438-4338). If you have been the victim of identity theft, see *www.IdentityTheft.gov* and Pub. 5027.

Visit *www.irs.gov/IdentityTheft* to learn more about identity theft and how to reduce your risk.

Privacy Act Notice

Section 6109 of the Internal Revenue Code requires you to provide your correct TIN to persons (including federal agencies) who are required to file information returns with the IRS to report interest, dividends, or certain other income paid to you; mortgage interest you paid; the acquisition or abandonment of secured property; the cancellation of debt; or contributions you made to an IRA, Archer MSA, or HSA. The person collecting this form uses the information on the form to file information returns with the IRS, reporting the above information. Routine uses of this information include giving it to the Department of Justice for civil and criminal litigation and to cities, states, the District of Columbia, and U.S. commonwealths and possessions for use in administering their laws. The information also may be disclosed to other countries under a treaty, to federal and state agencies to enforce civil and criminal laws, or to federal law enforcement and intelligence agencies to combat terrorism. You must provide your TIN whether or not you are required to file a tax return. Under section 3406, payers must generally withhold a percentage of taxable interest, dividend, and certain other payments to a payee who does not give a TIN to the payer. Certain penalties may also apply for providing false or fraudulent information.

Refinance Loans

NAME AFFIDAVIT

LOAN INFORMATION

Date Prepared: July 28, 20XX

Application Number: NCMO3780
Borrower: John A. Maxell

Lender: Hunter Financial Group, Inc.
Lender's Address: 3303 East Courtline Road
                          Gilbert, AZ 85234

NAME AFFIDAVIT

This is to certify that I am known by the name(s) listed below and the name(s) and signature(s) are for one and the same person.

_____   _____
Print or Type Name   Signature

_____   _____
                       Signature

_____   _____
                       Signature

...LEDGMENT

State of: _____
County of: _____

_____ ("Affiant") being duly sworn by me, and named in the foregoing instrument, has stated that every statement contained therein is true to the best of his/her knowledge and belief.

Subscribed and sworn (affirmed) before me this 28th day of July, 20XX.

_____   _____
Name of Notary   Signature of Notary

_____   _____   _____
Notary Public Stamp and Seal   Commission Expires   Commission Number

---

NOTES

Here is a "Name Affidavit" that must be notarized with a jurat. Note that the borrower is representing that he is also the same individual as the names listed in the form.

Hunter Financial Group, Inc., dba, USASelect Mortgage
3303 East Courtline Road, #7-118, Gilbert, AZ 85234 - 480-461-1111

November 1, 20XX   NCM03780

NOTICE OF ASSIGNMENT, SALE OR TRANSFER OF SERVICING RIGHTS*

In accordance with Section 6 of Real Estate Settlement Procedures Act (RESPA) (12 V.S.C. 2605) you are hereby notified that the servicing of your mortgage loan, that is, the right to collect payments from you, has been assigned, sold or transferred from **Hunter Financial Group, Inc., dba, USASelect Mortgage** (Transferor) to **Hoffman Brothers Bank, F.S.B.** (Transferee).

The assignment, sale or transfer of the servicing of the mortgage loan does not affect any term or condition of the security instruments, other than tenns directly related to the servicing of your loan.

The effective date of this transfer **is January 1, 20XX.**

TRANSFEROR SERVICER - The name of an individual employed by **Hunter Financial Group, Inc., dba, USASelect Mortgage,** or a department where you may direct inquiries related to the transfer of the servicing rights of your mortgage is **THE CLOSING DEPARTMENT** and the toll-free or collect call telephone number is **480-461-1111.**

TRANSFEREE SERVICER - The name of an individual employed by **ABC Loan Services, Inc., P.O. Box 5180, Denver, CO 80217-5180,** new servicer or a department where you may direct inquiries related to the transfer of the servicing rights of your mortgage loan is The Customer Service Department and the toll-free or collect call telephone number is **800-550-0508.**

The date on which **Hunter Financial Group, Inc., dba, USASelect Mortgage,** the transferor servicer, will stop accepting payments on your mortgage loan is December 31, 20XX, and the date **that Hoffman Brothers Bank, F.S.B.,** the transferee, will begin accepting your payments is **January 1, 20XX.**

The transfer of servicing rights may affect the terms of or the continued availability of mortgage life or disability insurance or any other type of optional insurance in the following manner: _____
You should take the following action to maintain coverage: _____

You should also be aware of the following information, which is set out in Section 6 of RESPA (12 U.S.C. 2605):

During the 60-day period following the effective date of the transfer of the loan servicing, a loan payment received by your old mortgage lender in a timely fashion may not be treated by the new loan servicer as late, and a late fee may not be imposed on you. If a mortgage loan servicer receives a qualified written request (as defined in Section 6 of RESPA) from a borrower for information concerning the servicing of the loan, the servicer must provide the borrower with a written response within 20 days of receipt of the request. Not later than 60 days after receipt of the request, the servicer must make any appropriate corrections to the borrower's account, and must provide the borrower with a written clarification regarding any dispute. During this 60-day period, the servicer may not provide information concerning an overdue payment to a consumer-reporting agency.

Whoever fails to comply with the requirements set out in Section 6 of RESPA shall be liable to individuals for actual damages and, in the case of a pattern of noncompliance, shall be liable for an additional amount not to exceed $1,000. In a class action, whoever fails to comply with these requirements shall be liable for actual damages and, in the case of a pattern of noncompliance, an additional amount of $1,000 per class member, not to exceed $500,000 or 1 % of the servicer's net worth, whichever is less. The court may also award attorneys fees. A transferor or transferee of servicing shall not be liable under this section if, within 60 days of discovering an error, and before the commencement of an action and receipt of written notice of the error from the borrower, the servicer notifies the borrower of the error and makes whatever adjustment is necessary.

* (This notice must be delivered by the transferor servicer no less than 15 days before the effective date of the transfer of servicing rights, and must be sent by the transferee servicer no more than 15 days after the transfer. Delivery means placing the notice in the mail, first class postage prepaid, prior to 15 days before the effective date of transfer or prior to the 15 days after the effective date of transfer. However, this notice may be sent within 30 days of the effective date of transfer of servicing rights if assignment, sale or transfer of the contract for servicing the loan is preceded by termination of such contract for cause, commencement of proceedings for bankruptcy of the servicer, or commencement of proceedings by the Federal Deposit Insurance Corporation (FDIC) or the Resolution Trust Corporation (RTC) for conservatorship or receivership of the servicer, or an entity by which the servicer is owned or controlled.)

CERTIFICATION OF MORTGAGOR(S)

I/We hereby certify that I/we have received, read and understand the contents of this disclosure, as evidenced by my/our signatures below, this _____ day of _____, _____.

_____   _____
John A. Maxell   Date   Date

Notice to Borrower of Property in Special Flood Hazard Area

Notice is given to **John A. Maxell**, that the improved real estate described in the attached instrument is or will be located in an area designated by the Director of the Federal Emergency Management Agency as a special flood hazard area. This area is delineated on (Community Name) _____

Flood Insurance Rate Map (FIRM) or, if the FIRM is unavailable, on the Flood Hazard Boundary Map (FHBM). This has at least a 1 % chance of being flooded within any given year. The risk of exceeding the 1 % chance increases with the time periods longer than I year. For example, during the life of a 30-year mortgage, a structure located in a special flood hazard area has a 20% chance of being flooded.

Notice To Borrower about Federal Flood Disaster Assistance

(Lender Check One)

_____ Notice in Participating Communities

The improved real estate securing your loan is or will be located in a community which is participating in the National Flood Insurance Program. In the event your property is damaged by flooding in a federally declared disaster, federal disaster relief may be available. However, such relief will be unavailable if your community is not participating in the National Flood Insurance Program at the time such assistance would be approved (assuming your community has been identified as flood-prone for at least 1 year). This assistance, usually in the form of a loan with favorable interest rate, may be available for damages incurred in excess of your flood insurance.

___X___ Notice in Nonparticipating

The improved real estate securing your loan is or will be located in a community which is not participating in the National Flood Insurance Program. This means that you are not eligible for Federal Flood Insurance. In the event your property is damaged by flooding in a federally declared disaster, federal disaster relief will be unavailable (assuming your community has been identified as flood-prone for at least I year). Federal flood disaster relief will be available only if your community is participating in the National Flood Insurance Program at the time such assistance would be approved.

(Lender Check One)

_____ All or part of your property is located in a Flood Hazard Area Zone A and it is mandatory to have flood insurance to close your loan.

_____ All or part of your property is located in Flood Zone B or C and flood insurance is not mandatory to close your loan.

_____ Flood Hazard Area not mapped.

When flood insurance is required, the policy must cover the amount of the loan, or the maximum amount available under the National Flood Insurance Program.

The Undersigned Borrower(s) received a copy of this notice at least ten (10) days prior to closing.

_____   _____
John A. Maxell

_____   _____

Hunter Financial Group, Inc., dba, USASelect Mortgage

3303 East Courtline Road, #7-118, Gilbert, AZ 85234

OCCUPANCY STATEMENT

RE: Borrower"s Name: **John A. Maxell**

              Property Address: **10116 Chevrolet Drive**
                                       Los Angeles, CA 90060

              Loan Number: **NCM03780**

I/We hereby certify that my/our intent in seeking this loan is to obtain financing for refinance or p[...]
to be used as my/our principal residence, with occupancy to begin within 30 days after loan closi[...]

I recognize that any loan made pursuant to this application is contingent upon owner occupancy a[...]
failure to occupy the property as provided in this certification shall constitute a DEFAULT under [...]
loan, and (2) in case of such default, I must upon recall of the loan by Lender, immediately pay th[...]
the loan and any other amounts to which Lender is entitled upon default.

_____   _____
John A. Maxell   Date   Date

_____   _____
                             Date   Date

State of: **CALIFORNIA**_____

County of: **Los Angeles**_____

Notary Public: _____

My Commission Expires: _____

USA PATRIOT ACT INFORMATION FORM
Customer Identification Verification

To help the government fight the funding of terrorism and money laundering activities, Federal law requires all financial institutions to obtain, verify, and record information that identifies every customer. When applying for a loan, applicants will be asked for their name, address, date of birth, and other information that will allow lenders to identify them. Applicants may also be asked to show their driver's license or other identifying documents.

THE FOLLOWING CUSTOMER INFORMATION MUST BE OBTAINED TO BE IN COMPLIANCE WITH THE USA PATRIOT ACT. THIS INFORMATION MUST BE RETAINED FOR FIVE YEARS AFTER THE ACCOUNT IS CLOSED.

Borrower Name: **John A. Maxell**   Date of Birth: **September 11, 1958**

ess: **10116 Chevrolet Drive**   Tax Identification Number (SSN): **000-00-0000**
A 90060

EPARATE FORM FOR <u>EACH</u> BORROWER.

NTIFICATION: Only One form of Verification is Required.

List -	Country/State of Origin	ID Number	Issuance Date	Expiration Date
Driver License				
D Card				
d				
stration Card				
er License				

nt List -	Name of Issuer on Form	ID Number	Issuance Date	Expiration Date
y Card	U.S. Govt			
ssued Visa				
dian Driver License				
Signed Tax Returns[1]	☐ Fed ☐ State	TIN:		
Property Tax Bill		APN:		
☐ Voter Registration Card				
☐ Organizational Membership Card				
☐ Bank/Investment/Loan Statements[1]				
☐ Paycheck stub with name[1]				
☐ Most Recent W-2[1]				
☐ Home/car/renter insurance papers				
☐ Recent utility bill				

[1] Do not verify identity with documents that illustrate income and/or assets if the documentation type for this loan precludes collection of such documentation.

Comments: _____
_____
_____

I certify that I have personally viewed and accurately recorded the information from the documents identified above, and have reasonably confirmed the identity of the Borrower.

_____   _____   _____
Signature   Printed Name/Title   Date

NOTES

Here is an example of a U.S. Patriot Act identification disclosure form. See chapter 12 for a thorough discussion of Patriot Act identification forms.

Notary needs to list the two forms of identification that were presented and sign.

If there is another Patriot Act form requiring the borrower to provide ID, the Notary Signing Agent should complete this form as instructed, sign the bottom of the form, and enter the printed name, the title "Signing Agent" and date. DO NOT AFFIX THE NOTARY SEAL TO THIS FORM AND DO NOT ENTER "NOTARY" AS THE TITLE.

Ellie Mae, Inc.

G3PATRIO 0911
G3PATRIO (CLS)

IMPORTANT PRIVACY CHOICES FOR CONSUMERS

You have the right to control whether we share some of your personal information.
Please read the following information carefully before you make your choices below.

DAS Acquisition Company, LLC

Your Rights

You have the following rights to restrict the sharing of personal and financial information with our affiliates (companies we own or control) and outside companies that we do business with. Nothing in this form prohibits the sharing of information necessary for us to follow the law, as permitted by law, or to give you the best service on your accounts with us. This includes sending you information about some other products or services.

Your Choices

Restrict Information Sharing With Companies We Own or Control (Affiliates): Unless you say "No," we may share personal and financial information about you with our affiliated companies.

☐ NO, please do not share personal and financial information with your affiliated companies.

Restrict Information Sharing With Other Companies We Do Business With To Provide Financial Products And Services: Unless you say "No," we may share personal and financial information about you with outside companies we contract with to provide financial products and services to you.

☐ NO, please do not share personal and financial information with outside companies you contract with to provide financial products and services.

Time Sensitive Reply

You may make your privacy choice(s) at any time. Your choice(s) marked here will remain unless you state otherwise. However, if we do not hear from you we may share some of your information with affiliated companies and other companies with whom we have contracts to provide products and services.

Name: **John A. Maxell** _____

Account or Policy Number(s): _____ [to be filled in by consumer]

Signature: _____

To exercise your choices do one of the following:

[Mandatory]

(1) Fill out, sign and send back this form to us using the envelope provided (you may want to make a copy for your records)

[Optional]

(2) Call this toll-free number: **314-628-2000**   or **314-628-2000**
OR

(3) Reply electronically by contacting us through the following Internet option:
  www.usa-mortgage.com

Ellie Mae, Inc.

CAPRIV_S 0316
CAPRIVS (CLS)

Refinance Loans

NOTICE OF RIGHT TO CANCEL

Borrower(s): **John A. Maxell**

10116 Chevrolet Drive Los Angeles, CA 90060

in property described as: **10116 Chevrolet Drive**
Los Angeles, CA 90060

CANCEL

into a transaction that will result in a mortgage/lien/security interest on/in your home. You have a legal
al law to cancel this transaction, without cost, within three business days from whichever of the following
st:
(1) the date of the transaction, which is

July 25, 20XX; or
(2) the date you received your Truth-In-Lending disclosures;
or
(3) the date you received this notice of your right to cancel.
If you cancel the transaction, the mortgage/lien/security interest is also cancelled. Within 20 calendar days after we receive your notice, we must take the steps necessary to reflect the fact that the mortgage/lien/security interest on/in your home has been cancelled, and we must return to you any money or property you have given to us or to anyone else in connection with this transaction.

You may keep any money or property we have given you until we have done the things mentioned above, but you must then offer to return the money or property. If it is impractical or unfair for you to return the property, you must offer its reasonable value. You may offer to return the property at your home or at the location of the property. Money must be returned to the address below. If we do not take possession of the money or property within 20 calendar days of your offer, you may keep it without further obligation.

HOW TO CANCEL
If you decide to cancel this transaction, you may do so by notifying us in writing, at
Hunter Financial Group, Inc.
3303 East Courtline Road
Gilbert, AZ 85234

You may use any written statement that is signed and dated by you and states your intention to cancel, or you may use this notice by dating and signing below. Keep one copy of this notice because it contains important information about your rights.

If you cancel by mail or telegram, you must send the notice no later than midnight of **July 28, 20XX**
(or midnight of the third business day following the latest of the three events listed above.) If you send or deliver your written notice to cancel some other way, it must be delivered to the above address no later than that time.

I WISH TO CANCEL

_____
John A. Maxell   DATE

Joint owners of the property subject to the security interest may have the right to rescind the transaction. The exercise of this right by one owner shall be effective as to all owners.

I/We acknowledge receipt of two copies of <u>NOTICE OF RIGHT TO CANCEL</u>.

_____
John A. Maxell   DATE

Ellie Mae, Inc.

CUSTOMER'S STATEMENT OF NON-RESCISSION

Creditor: **Hunter Financial Group, Inc., dba, USASelect Mortgage**
3303 East Courtline Road, #7-118
Gilbert, AZ 85234

Property Address: **10116 Chevrolet Drive**
Los Angeles, CA 90060

Date of Closing: **November 1, 20XX**

Loan Number: **NCM03780**

In order to induce lender to disburse the proceeds of the loan transaction referenced above, the undersigned represent and warrant that **three (3) business days** have elapsed since the date of such transaction and the undersigned have not exercised their right to cancel the transaction.

_____   _____
John A. Maxell   Date

NOTE: All individuals having the Right to Cancel must sign.

NOTES

The "Customer's Statement of Non-Rescission" is an accessory form to the "Notice of Right to Cancel." In the event the borrower elects not to exercise the rescission option, a lender may require completion of this form. Many borrowers prefer not to sign this form at the loan signing appointment until the actual 3-day rescission period has elapsed. If the borrower elects not to sign the form, the Notary Signing Agent should place a "Post It®" Note on the form explaining why the borrower elected not to sign.

Closing Disclosure

This form is a statement of final loan terms and closing costs. Compare this document with your Loan Estimate.

Closing Information

Date Issued	10/18/20XX
Closing Date	10/18/20XX
Disbursement Date	10/18/20XX
Settlement Agent	Epsilon Title Co.
File #	12-3456
Property	10116 Chevrolet Drive Los Angeles, CA 90060
Sale Price	$426,000

Transaction Information

Borrower	John A. Maxell 10116 Chevrolet Drive Los Angeles, CA 90060
Seller	The Maxell Family Trust 10116 Chevrolet Drive Los Angeles, CA 90060
Lender	Hunter Financial Group, Inc.

Loan Information

Loan Term	30 years
Purpose	Refinance
Product	Fixed Rate
Loan Type	☐Conventional ☒FHA ☐VA ☐_____
Loan ID #	NCMO3780
MIC #	000654321

Loan Terms

		Can this amount increase after closing?
Loan Amount	$426,000	NO
Interest Rate	3.5%	NO
Monthly Principal & Interest *See Projected Payments below for your Estimated Total Monthly Payment*	$2,554.09	NO
		Does the loan have these features?
Prepayment Penalty		YES • **As high as $3,240** if you pay off the loan during the first 2 years
Balloon Payment		NO

Projected Payments

Payment Calculation	Years 1-7	Years 8-30
Principal & Interest	$1,579.34	$1,579.34
Mortgage Insurance	+ 252.25	+ 252.25
Estimated Escrow *Amount can increase over time*	+ 722.50	+ 722.50
Estimated Total Monthly Payment	$2,554.09	$2,554.09

Estimated Taxes, Insurance & Assessments *Amount can increase over time* *See page 4 for details*	$356.13 a month	This estimate includes	In escrow?
		☒ Property Taxes	YES
		☒ Homeowner's Insurance	YES
		☒ Other: Homeowner's Association Dues	NO
		See Escrow Account on page 4 for details. You must pay for other property costs separately.	

Costs at Closing

Closing Costs	$9,712.10	Includes $4,694.05 in Loan Costs + $5,018.05 in Other Costs – $0 in Lender Credits. *See page 2 for details.*
Cash to Close	$14,147.26	Includes Closing Costs. *See Calculating Cash to Close on page 3 for details.*

WAIVER OF ESCROW

Date: **November 1, 20XX**

Loan Number: **NCM03780**

Applicant(s):   **John A. Maxell**

Property Address: **10116 Chevrolet Drive Los Angeles, CA 90060**

Hunter Financial Group, Inc., dba, USASelect Mortgage,

hereby agrees to waive the requirement for the monthly deposit of escrow funds for the above referenced mortgage loan.

The undersigned applicant(s) agree(s) to be solely responsible for the timely payment of any and all property taxes, assessments, leasehold payments, ground rents, and hazard or property insurance premiums (including flood insurance premiums, if applicable), collectively referred to as the "Escrow Items" affecting the above referenced property. Further, the applicant(s) agree(s) to provide **Hunter Financial Group, Inc., dba, USASelect Mortgage** with written evidence of the payment of such items within two (2) weeks following your receipt of a written request from **Hunter Financial Group, Inc., USASelect Mortgage.**

Hunter Financial Group, Inc., dba, USASelect Mortgage shall have the right to establish or reestablish an escrow account for the payment of the Escrow Items in accordance with the terms of your loan documents in the event that during the term of the mortgage loan:

1. Applicant(s) fail(s) to pay any of the Escrow Items in a prompt and timely manner;

2. Applicant(s) fail(s) to provide **Hunter Financial Group, Inc., dba, USASelect Mortgage** with evidence of payment of the Escrow Items within two (2) weeks following your receipt of a written request from **Hunter Financial Group, Inc., dba, USASelect Mortgage;**

3. Applicant(s) is/are otherwise in default under the terms of your mortgage loan documents; or

4. It becomes necessary for Lender to advance funds to pay all or any portion of the Escrow Items.

Acknowledged and Accepted:

_____   _____
John A. Maxell   Date

Affidavit of Identity

I, _____, swear or affirm that I am the person whose identification card(s) I presented to you and I swear or affirm that I am the person appearing before you and who signed this document and am the person he (or she) claims to be.

_____
John A. Maxell

Type of Identification: _____

ID# _____   Expiration Date _____

Date of Birth

State of   )
)
County of   )

On this _____ day of _____, 20 ____, before me personally appeared _____ (name of signer), whose identity was proved to me on the basis of satisfactory evidence to be the person whose name is subscribed to this document, and who acknowledged the he/she signed the above attached document.

_____
Notary Public

Uniform Residential Loan Application

Verify and complete the information on this application. If you are applying for this loan with others, each additional Borrower must provide information as directed by your Lender.

Section 1: Borrower Information. This section asks about your personal information and your income from employment and other sources, such as retirement, that you want considered to qualify for this loan.

1a. Personal Information

Name *(First, Middle, Last, Suffix)*

Alternate Names – *List any names by which you are known or any names under which credit was previously received (First, Middle, Last, Suffix)*

Social Security Number _____ – ___ – _____
(or Individual Taxpayer Identification Number)

Date of Birth
(mm/dd/yyyy)
___ / ___ / _____

Citizenship
○ U.S. Citizen
○ Permanent Resident Alien
○ Non-Permanent Resident Alien

Type of Credit
○ I am applying for **individual credit.**
○ I am applying for **joint credit.** Total Number of Borrowers: __
Each Borrower intends to apply for joint credit. **Your initials:** _____

List Name(s) of Other Borrower(s) Applying for this Loan
(First, Middle, Last, Suffix) – Use a separator between names

Marital Status
○ Married
○ Separated
○ Unmarried
(Single, Divorced, Widowed, Civil Union, Domestic Partnership, Registered Reciprocal Beneficiary Relationship)

Dependents *(not listed by another Borrower)*
Number ___
Ages _____

Contact Information
Home Phone (___) ___ – _____
Cell Phone (___) ___ – _____
Work Phone (___) ___ – _____
Email _____

> **NOTES**
>
> Borrower(s) sign Section Six. If applying for joint credit, borrower initials Section One.

Current Address
Street _____ Unit # _____
City _____ State ____ ZIP _____ Country _____
How Long at Current Address? ___ Years ___ Months **Housing** ○ No primary housing expense ○ Own ○ Rent ($_____ /month)

If at Current Address for LESS than 2 years, list Former Address ☐ *Does not apply*
Street _____ Unit # _____
City _____ State ____ ZIP _____ Country _____
How Long at Former Address? ___ Years ___ Months **Housing** ○ No primary housing expense ○ Own ○ Rent ($_____ /month)

Mailing Address – *if different from Current Address* ☐ *Does not apply*
Street _____ Unit # _____
City _____ State ____ ZIP _____ Country _____

1b. Current Employment/Self-Employment and Income   ☐ *Does not apply*

Employer or Business Name _____ Phone (___) ___ – _____
Street _____ Unit # _____
City _____ State ____ ZIP _____ Country _____

Position or Title _____
Start Date ___ / ___ / _____ *(mm/dd/yyyy)*
How long in this line of work? ___ Years ___ Months

Check if this statement applies:
☐ I am employed by a family member, property seller, real estate agent, or other party to the transaction.

☐ **Check if you are the Business Owner or Self-Employed**
○ I have an ownership share of less than 25%. **Monthly Income (or Loss)**
○ I have an ownership share of 25% or more. $ _____

Gross Monthly Income

Base	$ _____	/month
Overtime	$ _____	/month
Bonus	$ _____	/month
Commission	$ _____	/month
Military Entitlements	$ _____	/month
Other	$ _____	/month
TOTAL	$ **0.00**	/month

Section 6: Acknowledgments and Agreements. This section tells you about your legal obligations when you sign this application.

Acknowledgments and Agreements

Definitions:
- "Lender" includes the Lender's agents, service providers, and any of their successors and assigns.
- "Other Loan Participants" includes (i) any actual or potential owners of a loan resulting from this application (the "Loan"), (ii) acquirers of any beneficial or other interest in the Loan, (iii) any mortgage insurer, (iv) any guarantor, (v) any servicer of the Loan, and (vi) any of these parties' service providers, successors or assigns.

I agree to, acknowledge, and represent the following:

(1) The Complete Information for this Application
- The information I have provided in this application is true, accurate, and complete as of the date I signed this application.
- If the information I submitted changes or I have new information before closing of the Loan, I must change and supplement this application, including providing any updated/supplemented real estate sales contract.
- For purchase transactions: The terms and conditions of any real estate sales contract signed by me in connection with this application are true, accurate, and complete to the best of my knowledge and belief. I have not entered into any other agreement, written or oral, in connection with this real estate transaction.
- The Lender and Other Loan Participants may rely on the information contained in the application before and after closing of the Loan.
- Any intentional or negligent misrepresentation of information may result in the imposition of:
  - (a) civil liability on me, including monetary damages, if a person suffers any loss because the person relied on any misrepresentation that I have made on this application, and/or
  - (b) criminal penalties on me including, but not limited to, fine or imprisonment or both under the provisions of Federal law (18 U.S.C. §§ 1001 et seq.).

(2) The Property's Security
The Loan I have applied for in this application will be secured by a mortgage or deed of trust which provides the Lender a security interest in the property described in this application.

(3) The Property's Appraisal, Value, and Condition
- Any appraisal or value of the property obtained by the Lender is for use by the Lender and Other Loan Participants.
- The Lender and Other Loan Participants have not made any representation or warranty, express or implied, to me about the property, its condition, or its value.

(4) Electronic Records and Signatures
- The Lender and Other Loan Participants may keep any paper record and/or electronic record of this application, whether or not the Loan is approved.

- If this application is created as (or converted into) an "electronic application", I consent to the use of "electronic records" and "electronic signatures" as the terms are defined in and governed by applicable Federal and/or state electronic transactions laws.
- I intend to sign and have signed this application either using my:
  - (a) electronic signature; or
  - (b) a written signature and agree that if a paper version of this application is converted into an electronic application, the application will be an electronic record, and the representation of my written signature on this application will be my binding electronic signature.
- I agree that the application, if delivered or transmitted to the Lender or Other Loan Participants as an electronic record with my electronic signature, will be as effective and enforceable as a paper application signed by me in writing.

(5) Delinquency
- The Lender and Other Loan Participants may report information about my account to credit bureaus. Late payments, missed payments, or other defaults on my account may be reflected in my credit report and will likely affect my credit score.
- If I have trouble making my payments I understand that I may contact a HUD-approved housing counseling organization for advice about actions I can take to meet my mortgage obligations.

(6) Authorization for Use and Sharing of Information
By signing below, in addition to the representations and agreements made above, I expressly authorize the Lender and Other Loan Participants to obtain, use, and share with each other (i) the loan application and related loan information and documentation, (ii) a consumer credit report on me, and (iii) my tax return information, as necessary to perform the actions listed below, for so long as they have an interest in my loan or its servicing:
  - (a) process and underwrite my loan;
  - (b) verify any data contained in my consumer credit report, my loan application and other information supporting my loan application;
  - (c) inform credit and investment decisions by the Lender and Other Loan Participants;
  - (d) perform audit, quality control, and legal compliance analysis and reviews;
  - (e) perform analysis and modeling for risk assessments;
  - (f) monitor the account for this loan for potential delinquencies and determine any assistance that may be available to me; and
  - (g) other actions permissible under applicable law.

Borrower Signature _____ Date *(mm/dd/yyyy)* ____ / ____ / _____

Additional Borrower Signature _____ Date *(mm/dd/yyyy)* ____ / ____ / _____

Borrower Name: _____
Uniform Residential Loan Application
Freddie Mac Form 65 • Fannie Mae Form 1003
Effective 1/2021

Chapter

2

Home Equity Lines of Credit

INTRODUCTION

During periods when interest rates creep higher and the refinance market slows down, lenders begin to market Home Equity Line of Credit (HELOC) loans as a means for funding a wide array of personal financial needs. Increasingly, Notary Signing Agents are taking appointments with HELOC packages, whether as a stand-alone transaction or as a second loan in a double (refinance + HELOC) signing.

A home equity line of credit is a revolving line of credit with an interest rate typically indexed to the prime rate. A homeowner accesses the credit line by writing checks provided by the lender or through an ATM card. Most HELOC loans provide a line of credit up to 85% of a home's appraised value, minus the current mortgage loan balance.

For example, if a home carries a currently appraised value of $250,000 with a first mortgage loan balance of $75,000, a credit line of $148,750 could be extended ($250,000 - $75,000 x .85).

Interest is paid only on the amount borrowed and the line of credit is available even if it is not tapped. The property secures the debt as collateral; in most cases, the home equity line of credit will become a second lien on title.

HELOC loans are attractive to homeowners for many reasons. First, the interest paid on the loan is largely tax deductible for the majority of loans.

Home Equity Lines of Credit

Second, the credit is available to be used when need arises, making it an ideal form of sourcing for home renovations, college education, unforeseen medical expenses, debt consolidation, starting a new business and other needs. In certain circumstances when the balance on the first mortgage is winding down and its interest rate is higher, a credit line with a lower adjustable rate and a low rate cap can even be used as a means of "refinancing" to pay off the first mortgage. Third, if the line of credit is not used, the borrower has no monthly payment, making it more attractive to the homeowner than a straight second mortgage. Fourth, the loan is revolved much like a credit card — but at a markedly lower rate of interest. As current debt is repaid, the available line of credit recycles.

Of course, with HELOC loans all that glitters is not gold. While the lower interest rate and higher availability of credit make equity line loans very attractive in comparison to other forms of revolving credit, a HELOC loan places an additional lien on title and secures the property as collateral for the loan. If after consolidating debt, building that new swimming pool, buying a new car, and sending the first child off to college, a homeowner cannot keep up with the monthly payment, the repercussion could be as severe as failing to make the first mortgage payment — loss of the home to a forced sale or foreclosure.

For the Notary Signing Agent, HELOC loan packages are typically smaller in size than the average refinance loan and should take a shorter time to execute, although there are exceptions. Agents will recognize the presence of many of the forms found in the typical refinance package, including a note, security instrument, various disclosures, and right to cancel forms.

However, the sample HELOC packages will illustrate that the forms can take on an entirely different "look and feel" than their refinance counterparts. In Sample Set #1 for example, the "Truth-in-Lending Statement" and "Itemization of Amount Financed" disclosures that appear in most refinance packages as separate documents are combined into a single document with the title, "Disclosure Statement." While Sample Set #1 has a traditional "Closing Disclosure Statement," Sample Set #2 lists the closing costs found on the standard settlement statement on page 1 of the 11-page "Equity Line Account Disclosure and Agreement." No separate "disclosure statement" is included.

Home Equity Lines of Credit

Notary Signing Agents in Texas may not encounter HELOC loans as frequently as Agents in other states. Home equity loans in Texas are subject to Article XVI, Section 50 of the Texas Constitution, which requires these loans to be signed and closed in the office of a lender, attorney, or title company as opposed to in a home. ■

Sample Set 1

THE HOUSING FINANCIAL DISCRIMINATION ACT OF 1977

FAIR LENDING NOTICE

IT IS ILLEGAL TO DISCRIMINATE IN THE PROVISION OF OR IN THE AVAILABILITY OF FINANCIAL ASSISTANCE BECAUSE OF THE CONSIDERATION OF:

1.   Trends, characteristics or conditions in the neighborhood or geographic area surrounding a housing accommodation, unless the financial institution can demonstrate in the particular case that such consideration is required to avoid an unsafe and unsound business practice; or

Religion, Sex, Marital Status, National Origin of Ancestry.

CONSIDER THE RACIAL, ETHNIC, RELIGIOUS OR NATIONAL ORIGIN COMPOSITION OF A GEOGRAPHIC AREA SURROUNDING A HOUSING ACCOMMODATION OR WHETHER OR NOT SUCH UNDERGOING CHANGE, OR IS EXPECTED TO UNDERGO CHANGE, IN APPRAISING A HOUSING OR IN DETERMINING WHETHER OR NOT, OR UNDER WHAT TERMS AND CONDITIONS, TO ASSISTANCE.

GOVERN FINANCIAL ASSISTANCE FOR THE PURPOSE OF THE PURCHASE, CONSTRUCTION, REFINANCING OF ONE TO FOUR UNIT FAMILY RESIDENCES OCCUPIED BY THE OWNER AND FOR THE PURPOSE OF THE HOME IMPROVEMENT OF ANY ONE TO FOUR UNIT FAMILY RESIDENCE.

IF YOU HAVE ANY QUESTIONS ABOUT YOUR RIGHTS, OR IF YOU WISH TO FILE A COMPLAINT, CONTACT THE MANAGEMENT OF THIS FINANCIAL INSTITUTION OR:

DEPARTMENT OF REAL ESTATE   DEPARTMENT OF REAL ESTATE
320 W. 4TH STREET, SUITE 350   1515 CLAY STREET, SUITE 702
LOS ANGELES, CA 90013-1105   OAKLAND, CA 94612-1402

****

****NOTICE OF RIGHT TO APPRAISAL

You have the right to a copy of the appraisal report used in connection with your application for credit. If you wish a copy, please write to us at the address provided. We must hear from you no later than 90 days after we notify you about the action taken on your credit application or you withdraw your application. In your letter, give us the following information: name, address, property address and loan/application number.

****

****

EQUAL CREDIT OPPORTUNITY ACT NOTICE

The Federal Equal Credit Opportunity Act prohibits creditors from discriminating against credit applicants on the basis of race, color, religion, national origin, sex, marital status, age (provided that the applicant has the capacity to enter in a binding contract); because all or part of the applicant's income derives from any public assistance program; or because the applicant has in good faith exercised any right under the Consumer Credit Protection Act.

The federal agency that administers compliance with law concerning this mortgage company is:

FEDERAL TRADE COMMISSION
600 PENNSYLVANIA AVENUE, N.W.
WASHINGTON, DC 20580

I (we) hereby acknowledge that I (we) have read and received a copy of this notice.

_____   _____   _____   _____
Applicant   Date   Applicant   Date

NOTES

This notice focuses on discrimination of property due to the location of the property or the racial, religious, ethnic or national origin composition of the neighborhood where the property is located.

LENDER'S CLOSING INSTRUCTIONS

THIS LOAN MUST CLOSE WHEN SCHEDULED (AS DATED) OR CONTACT JAMES B. NUTTER & CO. FOR FURTHER INSTRUCTIONS.

PLEASE FORWARD CLOSED LOAN PACKAGE TO:

Bank TEN NA
Attn: National Direct Equity
100 East Narrow Street
Columbus, OH 43271

If not closed, please overnight the entire package and return the wire promptly, or else incur a penalty fee

Loan No:	4261000000	**FHA Case No: (HECM ONLY):**	
To:	Bank TEN NA	**Closing Date:**	December 1, 20XX
	100 East Narrow Street	**Disbursement Date:**	December 6, 20XX
	Columbus, OH 43271	**Payment Plan Type:**	HECM Monthly
Phone:	(800) 555-1212	**1ˢᵗ Change Date:**	FEBRUARY 1, 20XX
Re:	BARRY BORROWER AND BARBARA BORROWER	**Interest Rate:**	6.510
Title Co:	National Direct Equity		

BORROWERS MUST EXECUTE ALL DOCUMENTS AS THEIR NAME APPEARS. THE FINAL HUD-SETTLEMENT STATEMENT WILL REQUIRE FINAL APPROVAL PRIOR TO CLOSING. PLEASE CONTACT YOUR CLOSER AT NATIONAL DIRECT EQUITY AT 800-798-3946.

*Title Company **MUST** true and certify the Mortgages/Deeds and Notes with a "live" signature – no stamps please.*

NATIONAL DIRECT EQUITY TITLE INSTRUCTIONS

A. As disbursement agent for **National Direct Equity**, you are authorized to disburse the net proceeds delivered to you only when you are in a position to comply with the following:

TITLE POLICY COVERAGE AMOUNT ON HECM LOANS IS THE MAXIMUM CLAIM AMOUNT OF: $200,160.00. TITLE POLICY MORTGAGE AMOUNT SHOWN ON THE FACE OF THE POLICY AND IN THE RECORDING INFORMATION OF SCHEDULE A OR B, TO BE THE AMOUNT AS SHOWN ON THE NOTES AND SECURITY INSTRUMENTS. THIS AMOUNT IS CALCULATED AT 150% OF THE MAXIMUM CLAIM AMOUNT (hecm only)

TITLE POLICY COVERAGE ON HOME KEEPER LOANS IS THE PRINCIPAL LIMIT X 150% WHICH IS THE MAXIMUM PRINCIPAL LIMIT. IF THIS LOAN IS A HOME KEEPER LOAN THE MAXIMUM PRINCIPAL LIMIT IS: $181,500.00 PRELIMINARY TITLE COMMITMENT IS AN ESTIMATE UNTIL FINAL FIGURES ARE DETERMINED AT CLOSING.

B. TAXES: must indicate all taxes for the current year and subsequent years are not yet due and payable.

C. PROVIDE ENDORSEMENTS BELOW (IF APPLICABLE):
    1) 6.2 NEGATIVE AMORTIZATION
    2) 8.1 ENVIRONMENTAL PROTECTION LIEN
    3) ALTA 9 SURVEY EXCEPTION ENDORSEMENT-NOT APPLICABLE ON SHORT FORM
    4) EQUITY OR REVOLVING LINE OF CREDIT/REVERSE MORTGAGE ENDORSEMENT
    5) 5.1 PUD (IF APPLICABLE)
    6) 4.1 CONDO (IF APPLICABLE)
    7) ANY OTHER STATE SPECIFIC REQUIREMENT OR ENDORSEMENT REQUIRED TO CLEAR
       TITLE: MINERAL RIGHTS, ETC. (IF APPLICABLE)

D. All conditions, restrictive covenants, building lines, and violated easements must be reflected along with affirmative coverage against monetary loss of forfeiture of Property.

E. INSURE OUR SECURITY INSTRUMENTS AS A VALID FIRST LIEN FOR THE AMOUNT OF THE PROPERTY DESCRIBED THEREIN, NAMING THE INSURED/MORTGAGEE AS FOLLOWS:

DISCLOSURE STATEMENT

Principal	Loan Date	Maturity	Loan No	Call/Coll	Account	Officer	Initials
$49,373.00	07-16-04	07-30-19	426100000000		426100000000		

References in the shaded area are for Lender's use only and do not limit the applicability of this document to any particular loan or item.
Any item above containing "****" has been omitted due to text length limitations.

Borrower: Barry and Barbara Borrower
2812 NARROW LN
SIMI VALLEY, CA 93063

Lender: Bank TEN NA
National Direct Equity (NDE)
100 East Narrow Street
Columbus, OH 43271

ANNUAL PERCENTAGE RATE The cost of your credit as a yearly rate.	FINANCE CHARGE The dollar amount the credit will cost you.	AMOUNT FINANCED The amount of credit provided to you or on your behalf.	TOTAL OF PAYMENTS The amount you will have paid after you have made all payments as scheduled.
7.765 %	$34,375.00	$49,298.00	$83,673.00

PAYMENT SCHEDULE. Borrower's payment schedule will be 180 monthly payments of $464.85 each, beginning August 20, 2004.

PROPERTY INSURANCE. I may obtain property insurance from anyone I want that is acceptable to Lender.

SECURITY. A security interest is being given in MY HOME.

LATE CHARGE. If a payment is 10 days or more late, Borrower will be charged $25.00

PREPAYMENT. If I pay off early, I will not be entitled to a refund of the prepaid finance charges, and I may have to pay a penalty.

I will look at my contract documents for any additional information about nonpayment, default, any required repayment in full before the scheduled date, and prepayment refunds and penalties.

I read and was given a completed copy of this Disclosure Statement on July 16, 2004, prior to signing the Note.

GRANTOR:

_____
BARRY BORROWER AS TRUSTEE OF THE
BORROWER FAMILY TRUST,
DATED MARCH 4, 1999

_____
BARBARA BORROWER AS TRUSTEE OF THE
BORROWER FAMILY TRUST
DATED MARCH 4, 1999

Amount Financed Itemization

Amount paid to others on Borrower's behalf		$ 49,26.00
$49,267.00 on BANK 10 MTG		
Other Charges Financed		31.00
$31.00 RECORDING FEE		
Total Financed Prepaid Finance Charges		75.00
Note Principal		49,373.00
Prepaid Finance Charges		75.00
Financed:		
$75.00 LOAN ORIGINATION	75.00	
In Cash:	0.00	
Amount Financed		$49,298.00

DISCLOSURE STATEMENT

Principal	Loan Date	Maturity	Loan No	Call/Coll	Account	Officer	Initials
$49,373.00	07-16-04	07-30-19	426100000000		426100000000		

References in the shaded area are for Lender's use only and do not limit the applicability of this document to any particular loan or item.
Any item above containing "****" has been omitted due to text length limitations.

Borrower: **Barry and Barbara Borrower**
2812 NARROW LN
SIMI VALLEY, CA 93063

Lender: **Bank TEN NA**
National Direct Equity (NDE)
100 East Narrow Street
Columbus, OH 43271

ANNUAL PERCENTAGE RATE	FINANCE CHARGE	AMOUNT FINANCED	TOTAL OF PAYMENTS
The cost of your credit as a yearly rate.	The dollar amount the credit will cost you.	The amount of credit provided to you or on your behalf.	The amount you will have paid after you have made all payments as scheduled.
7.765 %	$34,375.00	$49,298.00	$83,673.00

PAYMENT SCHEDULE. Borrower's payment schedule will be 180 monthly payments of $464.85 each, beginning August 20, 2004.

PROPERTY INSURANCE. I may obtain property insurance from anyone I want that is acceptable to Lender.

SECURITY. A security interest is being given in MY HOME.

LATE CHARGE. If a payment is 10 days or more late, Borrower will be charged $25.00

PREPAYMENT. If I pay off early, I will not be entitled to a refund of the prepaid finance charges, and I may have to pay a penalty.

I will look at my contract documents for any additional information about nonpayment, default, any required repayment in full before the scheduled date, and prepayment refunds and penalties.

I read and was given a completed copy of this Disclosure Statement on July 16, 2004, prior to signing the Note.

GRANTOR:

_____
BARRY BORROWER, Individually

_____
BARBARA BORROWER, Individually

Amount Financed Itemization

Amount paid to others on Borrower's behalf		$ 49,26.00
$49,267.00 on BANK 10 MTG		
Other Charges Financed		31.00
$31.00 RECORDING FEE		
Total Financed Prepaid Finance Charges		75.00
Note Principal		49,373.00
Prepaid Finance Charges		75.00
Financed:		
$75.00 LOAN ORIGINATION	75.00	
In Cash:	0.00	
Amount Financed		$49,298.00

HAZARD INSURANCE DISCLOSURE

Principal	Loan Date	Maturity	Loan No	Call/Coll	Account	Officer	Initials
$49,373.00	07-16-04	07-30-19	426100000000		426100000000		

References in the shaded area are for Lender's use only and do not limit the applicability of this document to any particular loan or item.
Any item above containing "****" has been omitted due to text length limitations.

Borrower: Barry and Barbara Borrower
2812 NARROW LN
SIMI VALLEY. CA 93063

Lender: Bank 10 NA
National Direct Equity (NDE)
100 East Narrow Street
Columbus, OH 43271

HAZARD INSURANCE DISCLOSURE

Made Pursuant to California Civil Code Section 2955.5

IMPORTANT

**DO NOT SIGN THIS FORM UNTIL YOU CAREFULLY
READ IT AND UNDERSTAND ITS CONTENT**

You have applied for a loan or credit accommodation that will be secured by real property. As a condition of the loan or credit accommodation, lender may require you to maintain hazard insurance coverage for the real property. California law provides that lender cannot require you, as a condition of receiving or maintaining a loan secured by real property, to provide hazard insurance coverage against risks to the property (such as fire and other perils) in an amount exceeding the replacement value of the building or structures attached to the property.

BY SIGNING BELOW, YOU ACKNOWLEDGE THAT YOU HAVE READ, RECEIVED AND UNDERSTAND THIS HAZARD INSURANCE DISCLOSURE. THIS DISCLOSURE IS DATED JULY 16, 2004.

_____
BARRY BORROWER, INDIVIDUALLY

_____
BARBARA BORROWER, INDIVIDUALLY

TRUST CERTIFICATE

Principal	Loan Date	Maturity	Loan No	Call/Coll	Account	Officer	Initials
$49,373.00	07-16-XX	07-30-XX	426100000000		426100000000		

References in the shaded area are for Lender's use only and do not limit the applicability of this document to any particular loan or item.
*Any item above containing "***" has been omitted due to text length limitations.*

Borrower: Barry and Barbara Borrower
2812 NARROW LN
SIMI VALLEY, CA 93063

Lender: Bank 10 NA
National Direct Equity (NDE)
100 East Narrow Street
Columbus, OH 43271

Trust: The Borrower Family Trust
Dated March 4, 1999
2812 NARROW LN
SIMI VALLEY, CA 93063

WE, THE UNDERSIGNED, DO HEREBY CERTIFY THAT:

CERTIFICATION OF TRUST. This Trust Certificate is given by each of the Trustees voluntarily, pursuant to Section 18100.5 of the California Probate Co
intending that the facts set forth in this Certificate be relied upon by lender as true and correct.

(A) The names of the Trustees are: BARRY AND BARBARA BORROWER

(B) The name of the Trust Settlor is: _____

(C) The powers of Trustees include the power to do, or perform, all of the acts and things on behalf of the Trust set forth in this Certificate.

(D) The trust is revocable, and the name of the person holding any power to revoke the trust is: _____
_____

(E) The trust instrument requires the signature of any 1 Trustees to exercise any powers of the Trustee.

(F) The Trust's tax or employer identification number is _____.

(G) The Trust is established under the laws of the State of California.

(H) Title to Trust assets is to be taken in the name of: _____
_____

(I) Trustees hereby certify that the Trust has not been revoked, modified, or amended In any manner which would cause the representations contained in this Certificate to be incorrect and this Certificate is being signed by all of the currently acting Trustees of the Trust. Trustees acknowledge and agree that Lender may require Trustees to provide copies of excerpts from the trust instrument and amendments which designate the Trustee and confer upon the Trustee the power to act in these transactions and that Lender may require such further identification or legal opinion supporting the Trustee authority and power as Lender shall deem necessary and prudent.

BORROWING CERTIFICATE. Trustees, for and on behalf of the Trust, are authorized and empowered on behalf of the Trust to:

Grant Security. To mortgage, pledge, transfer, endorse, hypothecate, or otherwise encumber and deliver to lender any property now or hereafter belonging to the Trust or in which the Trust now or hereafter may have an interest, including without limitation all real property and all personal property (tangible or intangible) of the Trust, as security for the payment of any loans, any promissory notes, or any other or further indebtedness of BARRY AND BARBARA BORROWER to lender at any time owing, however the same may be evidenced. Such property may be mortgaged, pledged, transferred, endorsed, hypothecated or encumbered at the time such loans are obtained or such indebtedness is incurred, or at any other time or times, and may be either in addition to or in lieu of any property theretofore mortgaged, pledged, transferred, endorsed, hypothecated or encumbered. The provisions of this Certificate authorizing or relating to the pledge, mortgage, transfer, endorsement, hypothecation, granting of a security interest in, or in any way encumbering, the assets of the Trust shall include, without limitation, doing so in order to lend collateral security for the indebtedness, now or hereafter existing, and of any nature whatsoever, of BARRY AND BARBARA BORROWER to lender. The Trustees have considered the value to the Trust of lending collateral in support of such indebtedness, and the Trustees represent to lender that the Trust is benefited by doing so.

Execute Security Documents. To execute and deliver to lender the forms of mortgage, deed of trust, pledge agreement, hypothecation agreement, and other security agreements and financing statements which lender may require and which shall evidence the terms and conditions under and pursuant to which such liens and encumbrances, or any of them, are given; and also to execute and deliver to lender any other written instruments, any chattel paper, or any other collateral, of any kind or nature, which lender may deem necessary or proper in connection with or pertaining to the giving of the liens and encumbrances. Notwithstanding the foregoing, anyone of the above authorized persons may execute, deliver, or record financing statements.

Negotiate Items. To draw, endorse, and discount with lender all drafts, trade acceptances, promissory notes, or other evidences of indebtedness payable to or belonging to the Trust or in which the Trust may have an interest, and either to receive cash for the same or to cause such proceeds to be credited to the Trust's account with lender, or to cause such other disposition of the proceeds derived therefrom as they may deem advisable.

Further Acts. To do and perform such other acts and things and to execute and deliver such other documents and agreements as the Trustees may in their discretion deem reasonably necessary or proper in order to carry into effect the provisions of this Certificate.

TERMINATION OR TRANSFER. Trustees agree that the Trustees will provide to lender written notice prior to any termination or revocation of the Trust or prior to the transfer from the Trust of any Trust asset upon which lender may be relying for repayment of the Trust's indebtedness to lender.

MULTIPLE BORROWERS. The Trust may enter Into transactions In which there are multiple borrowers or on obligations to Lender and the Trust understands and agrees that, with or without notice to the Trust, Lender may discharge or release any party or collateral securing an obligation, grant any extension of time for payment, delay enforcing any rights granted to Lender, or take any other action or inaction, without the loss to Lender of any of it rights against the Trust; and that Lender may modify transactions without the consent of or notice to anyone other than the party with whom the modification is made.

NOTICES TO LENDER. The Trustees will promptly notify Lender in writing at Lender's address shown above (or such other addresses as Lender may designate from time to time) prior to any (A) change in the Trust's name; (B) change in the Trust's assumed business name(s); (C) change in the Trustees of the Trust; (D) change in the authorized signer(s); (E) change in the Trust's state of organization; (F) conversion of the Trust to a new or different type of business entity; or (G) change in any other aspect of the Trust that directly or indirectly relates to any agreements between the Trust and Lender. No change in the Trust's name or state of organization will take effect until after Lender has received notice.

TRUST CERTIFICATE
(Continued)

THE TRUST. The BORROWER FAMILY TRUST ("the Trust") was created pursuant to a trust agreement dated MARCH 4. 1999.

FURTHER TRUST CERTIFICATIONS. The persons named above are duly appointed and acting Trustees of the Trust and are duly authorized to act on behalf of the Trust in the manner described above; we are familiar with the purpose of the Indebtedness; the Indebtedness proceeds are to be used for a legitimate trust purpose and for the benefit of the Trust and its beneficiaries.

CONTINUING VALIDITY. This Certificate shall be continuing, shall remain in full force and effect and Lender may rely on it until written notice of its revocation shall have been delivered to and received by Lender at Lender's address shown above (or such addresses as Lender may designate from time to time). Any such notice shall not affect any of the Trust's agreements or commitments in effect at the time notice is given.

IN TESTIMONY WHEREOF. We have hereunto set our hand.

We each have read all the provisions of this Certificate, and we each personally and on behalf of the Trust certify that all statements and representations made in this Certificate are true and correct. This Trust Certificate is dated July 20. 2004.

CERTIFIED TO AND ATTESTED BY:

_____

BARRY BORROWER

_____

BARBARA BORROWER

_____[Space Below This Line for Acknowledgment]_____

State of _____)

County of _____)

On _____ before me, _____personally appeared BARRY AND BARBARA

BORROWER, personally known to me (or proved to me on the basis of satisfactory evidence) to be the person(s) whose name(s) is/are subscribed to the within instrument and

acknowledged to me that he/she/they executed the same in his/her/their authorized capacity(ies), and that by his/her/their signature(s) on the instrument the person(s), or the entity upon

behalf of which the person(s) acted, executed the instrument.

WITNESS my hand and official seal.

_____   (Seal)

For space considerations, only pages 1, 8, 9 and 10 of this Deed of Trust are reprinted.

FOR RECORDER'S USE ONLY

DEED OF TRUST

THIS DEED OF TRUST is dated JULY 16, 20XX, among BARRY BORROWER and BARBARA BORROWER AS TRUSTEES OF THE BORROWER FAMILY TRUST, DATED MARCH 4, 20XX AND INDIVIDUALS, whose address is 2812 NARROW LN, SIMI VALLEY, CA 93063 ("Trustor"); Bank One, NA , whose address is National Direct Equity (NDE), 100 East Narrow Street, Columbus, OH 43271 (referred to below sometimes as "Lender" and sometimes as "Beneficiary"); and Steward Title of California, Inc., whose address is 1800 Post Office Blvd STE 100, Houston, TX 77056 (referred to below as "Trustee").

CONVEYANCE AND GRANT. For valuable consideration, Trustor irrevocably grants, transfers and assigns to Trustee in trust, with power of sale, for the benefit of Lender as Beneficiary, all of Trustor's right, title, and interest in and to the following described real property, together with all existing or subsequently erected or affixed buildings, improvements and fixtures; all easements, rights of way, and appurtenances; all water, water rights and ditch rights (including stock in utilities with ditch or irrigation rights); and all other rights, royalties, and profits relating to the real property, including without limitation all minerals, oil, gas, geothermal and similar matters, **(the "Real Property") located in VENTURA County, State of California:**

LOT 79 OF TRACT 2207-2 IN THE CITY OF SIMI VALLEY, COUNTY OF VENTURA, CALIFORNIA, AS PER MAP RECORDED IN BOOK 71, PAGES 27 THROUGH 31 OF MAPS IN THE OFFICE OF THE COUNTY RECORDER OF SAID COUNTY.

The Real Property or its address is commonly known as 2812 NARROW LN, SIMI VALLEY, CA 93063. The Assessor's Parcel Number for the Real Property is 611-0-152-080.

Trustor presently assigns to Lender (also known as Beneficiary in this Deed of Trust) all of Trustor's right, title, and interest in and to all present and future leases of the Property and all Rents from the Property. This is an absolute assignment of Rents made in connection with an obligation secured by real property pursuant to California Civil Code Section 2938. In addition, Trustor grants to Lender a Uniform Commercial Code security interest in the Personal Property and Rents.

THIS DEED OF TRUST, INCLUDING THE ASSIGNMENT OF RENTS AND THE SECURITY INTEREST IN THE RENTS AND PERSONAL PROPERTY, IS GIVEN TO SECURE (A) PAYMENT OF THE INDEBTEDNESS AND (B) PERFORMANCE OF ANY AND ALL OBLIGATIONS UNDER THE NOTE, THE RELATED DOCUMENTS, AND THIS DEED OF TRUST. THIS DEED OF TRUST IS GIVEN AND ACCEPTED ON THE FOLLOWING TERMS:

TRUSTOR'S REPRESENTATIONS AND WARRANTIES. Trustor warrants that: (a) this Deed of Trust is executed at Borrower's request and not at the request of Lender; (b) Trustor has the full power, right, and authority to enter into this Deed of Trust and to hypothecate the Property; (ct the provisions of this Deed of Trust do not conflict with, or result in a default under any agreement or other instrument binding upon Trustor and do not result in a violation of any law, regulation, court decree or order applicable to Trustor; (d) Trustor has established adequate means of obtaining from Borrower on a continuing basis information about Borrower's financial condition; and (e) Lender has made no representation to Trustor about Borrower (including without limitation the creditworthiness of Borrower).

TRUSTOR'S WAIVERS. Except as prohibited by applicable law, Trustor waives any right to require Lender to (a) make any presentment, protest, demand, or notice of any kind, including notice of change of any terms of repayment of the Indebtedness, default by Borrower or any other guarantor or surety, any action or nonaction taken by Borrower, Lender, or any other guarantor or surety of Borrower, or the creation of new or additional Indebtedness; (b) proceed against any person, including Borrower, before proceeding against Trustor; (c) proceed against any collateral for the Indebtedness, including Borrower's collateral, before proceeding against Trustor; (d) apply any payments or proceeds received against the Indebtedness in any order; (e) give notice of the terms, time, and place of any sale of any collateral pursuant to the Uniform Commercial Code or any other law governing such sale; (f) disclose any information about the Indebtedness, Borrower, any collateral, or any other guarantor or surety, or about any action or nonaction of Lender; or (g) pursue any remedy or course of action in Lender's power whatsoever. Trustor also waives any and all rights or defenses arising by reason of (h) any disability or other defense of Borrower, any other guarantor or surety or any other person; (i) the cessation from any cause whatsoever, other than payment in full, of the Indebtedness; (j) the application of proceeds of the Indebtedness by Borrower for purposes other than the purposes understood and intended by Trustor and Lender; (k) any act of omission or commission by Lender which directly or indirectly results in or contributes to the discharge of Borrower or any other guarantor or surety, or the Indebtedness, or the loss or release of any collateral by operation of law or otherwise; (l) any statute of limitations in any action under this Deed of Trust or on the Indebtedness; or (m) any modification or change in terms of the Indebtedness, whatsoever, including without limitation, the renewal, extension, acceleration, or other change in the time payment of the Indebtedness is due and any change in the interest rate.

Trustor waives all rights and defenses arising out of an election of remedies by Lender, even though that election of remedies, such as non-judicial foreclosure with respect to security for a guaranteed obligation, has destroyed Trustor's rights of subrogation and reimbursement against Borrower by the operation of Section 580d of the California Code of Civil Procedure, or otherwise.

Trustor waives all rights and defenses that Trustor may have because Borrower's obligation is secured by real property. This means among other things: (1) Lender may collect from Trustor without first foreclosing on any real or personal property collateral pledged by Borrower. (2) If Lender forecloses on any real property collateral pledged by Borrower: (Al The amount of Borrower's obligation may be reduced only by the price for which the collateral is sold at the foreclosure sale, even if the collateral is worth more than the sale price. (B) Lender may collect from Trustor even if Lender, by foreclosing on the real property collateral, has destroyed any right Trustor may have to collect from Borrower. This is an unconditional waiver of any rights and defenses Trustor may have because Borrower's obligation is secured by real property. These rights and defenses include, but are not limited to, any rights and defenses based upon Section 580a, 580b, 580d, or 726 of the Code of Civil Procedure.

Trustor understands and agrees that the foregoing waivers are waivers of substantive rights and defenses to which Trustor might otherwise be entitled under state and federal law. The rights and defenses waived include, without limitation, those provided by California laws of suretyship and guaranty, anti-deficiency laws, and the Uniform Commercial Code. Trustor acknowledges that Trustor has provided these waivers of rights and defenses with the intention that they be fully relied upon by Lender. Until all Indebtedness is paid in full, Trustor waives any right to enforce any remedy Lender may have against Borrower's or any other guarantor, surety, or other person, and further, Trustor waives any right to participate in any collateral for the Indebtedness now or hereafter held by Lender.

Loan No: 426370133454

Related Documents. The words "Related Documents" mean all promissory notes, credit agreements, loan agreements, environmental agreements, guaranties, security agreements, mortgages, deeds of trust, security deeds, collateral mortgages, and all other instruments, agreements and documents, whether now or hereafter existing, executed in connection with the Indebtedness.

Rents. The word "Rents" means all present and future leases, rents, revenues, income, issues, royalties, profits, and other benefits derived from the Property together with the cash proceeds of the Rents.

Trustee. The word "Trustee" means Steward Title of California, Inc., whose address is 1800 Post Office Blvd STE 100, Houston, TX 77056 and any substitute or successor trustees.

Trustor. The word "Trustor" means THE BORROWER FAMILY TRUST, DATED MARCH 4, 20XX; BARRY BORROWER AS TRUSTEE OF THE BORROWER FAMILY TRUST, DATED MARCH 4, 20XX AND; and BARBARA BORROWER AS TRUSTEE OF THE BORROWER FAMILY TRUST, DATED MARCH 4, 20XX.

EACH TRUSTOR ACKNOWLEDGES HAVING READ ALL THE PROVISIONS OF THIS DEED OF TRUST, AND EACH TRUSTOR AGREES TO ITS TERMS.

TRUSTOR:

THE BORROWER LIVING TRUST DATED MARCH 4,1999

By: _____
    BARRY BORROWER

By: _____
    BARRY BORROWER AS TRUSTEE OF THE
    BORROWER FAMILY TRUST, DATED MARCH 4, 20XX
    AND, Individually

By: _____
    BARBARA BORROWER

By: _____
    BARBARA BORROWER AS TRUSTEE OF THE
    BORROWER FAMILY TRUST, DATED MARCH 4, 20XX
    AND, Individually

NOTES

This "Deed of Trust" requires the borrowers to sign in an individual capacity and as trustees of the family trust.

Loan No: 426370133454

CERTIFICATE OF ACKNOWLEDGMENT

STATE OF

COUNTY OF

On _____, 20_____ before me, _____
personally appeared BARRY BORROWER AND BARBARA BORROWER OF THE BORROWER FAMILY TRUST, DATED MARCH 4,
(or proved to me on the basis of satisfactory evidence) to be the person(s) whose name(s) is/are subscribed to the within instrument
he/she/they executed the same in his/her/their authorized capacity(ies), and that by his/her/their signature(s) on the instrument the
behalf of which the person(s) acted, executed the instrument.

WITNESS my hand and official seal.

Signature _____   (SEAL)

CERTIFICATE OF ACKNOWLEDGMENT

STATE OF

COUNTY OF

On _____, 20_____ before me, _____,
personally appeared BARRY BORROWER AS TRUSTEE OF THE BORROWER FAMILY TRUST, DATED MARCH 4, 20XX, AND BARBARA BORROWER AS
TRUSTEE OF THE BORROWER FAMILY TRUST, DATED MARCH 4, 20XX, personally known to me (or proved to me on the basis of satisfactory evidence) to be
the person(s) whose name(s) is/are subscribed to the within instrument and acknowledged to me that he/she/they executed the same in his/her/their authorized
capacity(ies), and that by his/her/their signature(s) on the instrument the person(s), or the entity upon behalf of which the person(s) acted, executed the instrument.

WITNESS my hand and official seal.

Signature _____   (SEAL)

NOTES

Separate acknowledgment certificates are provided for notarizing the signatures of the borrowers individually and as trustees. Note: California Notaries cannot complete these forms because the law prohibits completion of an acknowledgment form when the Notary must certify the signer holds a particular representative capacity. The solution would be to attach one "California Acknowledgment" form and enter the names of the borrowers only into the form.

Home Equity Lines of Credit

(DO NOT RECORD)

REQUEST FOR FULL RECONVEYANCE

(To be used only when obligations have been paid in full)

To: _____ , Trustee

The undersigned is the legal owner and holder of all Indebtedness secured by this Deed of Trust. All sums secured by this Deed of Trust have been fully paid and satisfied. You are hereby directed, upon payment to you of any sums owing to you under the terms of this Deed of Trust or pursuant to any applicable statute, to cancel the Note secured by this Deed of Trust (which is delivered to you together with this Deed of Trust), and to reconvey, without warranty, to the parties designated by the terms of this Deed of Trust, the estate now held by you under this Deed of Trust. Please mail the reconveyance and Related Documents to:

_____ .

Date: _____

Beneficiary: _____

By: _____

Its: _____

NOTES

The "Request for Full Reconveyance" need not be completed at the signing assignment. It is completed later.

NOTICE OF INSURANCE REQUIREMENTS

Principal	Loan Date	Maturity	Loan No	Call/Coll	Account	Officer	Initials
$49,373.00	07-16-XX	07-30-XX	426100000000		426100000000		

References in the shaded area are for Lender's use only and do not limit the applicability of this document to any particular loan or item.
*Any item above containing "***" has been omitted due to text length limitations.*

Borrower: Barry and Barbara Borrower
2812 NARROW LN
SIMI VALLEY, CA 93063

Lender: Bank TEN NA
National Direct Equity (NDE)
100 East Narrow Street
Columbus, OH 43271

Grantor: THE BORROWER FAMILY TRUST, DATED MARCH 4, 20XX; BARRY BORROWER AS TRUSTEE OF THE BORROWER FAMILY TRUST, DATED MARCH 4, 20XX AND; and BARBARA BORROWER AS TRUSTEE OF THE BORROWER FAMILY TRUST, DATED MARCH 4, 20XX.
2812 NARROW LN SIMI VALLEY, CA 93063

TO: COUNTERINSURANCE EXCHANGE
ATTN: AAAA AUTOMOTIVE CLUB
PO BOX 25001
SANTA ANA, CA 92799

DATE: July 16, 20XX

RE: Policy Number(s): CHO100000000
Insurance Companies/Company: **COUNTERINSURANCE EXCHANGE**

Dear AUTOMOBILE CLUB: BARRY BORROWER and BARBARA BORROWER ("Borrower"), are obtaining a loan from Bank Ten, NA. Please send appropriate evidence of insurance to Bank Ten, NA, together with the requested endorsements, on the following property, which We, THE BORROWER FAMILY TRUST, DATED MARCH 4, 20XX; BARRY BORROWER AS TRUSTEE OF THE BORROWER FAMILY TRUST, DATED MARCH 4, 20XX AND; and BARBARA BORROWER AS TRUSTEE OF THE BORROWER FAMILY TRUST, DATED MARCH 4, 20XX AND ("Grantor") are giving as security for the loan.

Property: 2812 NARROW LN. SIMI VALLEY, CA 93063.
Type. Fire and extended coverage.
Amount. Full Insurable Value; however in no event greater than the value of the replacement cost of the improvements.
Basis. Replacement value.
Endorsements. Standard mortgagee's clause with stipulation that coverage will not be cancelled or diminished without a minimum of thirty (30) days prior written notice to Lender, and without disclaimer of the insurer's liability for failure to give such notice.
Comments. If your loan requires flood insurance, the maximum deductible is $1,000.00.
Deductibles. $1,000.00.
Latest Delivery Date: By the loan closing date.

IMPOUNDING FOR INSURANCE PREMIUMS. Bank Ten is not impounding for the premiums for this loan.

LIEN POSITION. This loan is in second lien position.

GRANTOR:

By: _____
    BARRY BORROWER

By: _____
    BARRY BORROWER AS TRUSTEE OF THE BORROWER
    FAMILY TRUST, DATED MARCH 4, 20XX
    AND, Individually

By: _____
    BARBARA BORROWER

By: _____
    BARBARA BORROWER AS TRUSTEE OF THE
    BORROWER FAMILY TRUST, DATED MARCH 4, 20XX
    AND, Individually

Return to:
Bank Ten, N.A.
Retail loan Servicing, KY2-1606
P.O. Box 11908 Lexington, KY 40578-1908

LOAN #: 4261000000

NOTICE OF RIGHT TO CANCEL

Borrower(s): **Barry Borrower AND Barbara Borrower**

Mailing Address: **2812 Narrow Ln., Simi Vally, CA 93063**

Security interest in property described as: **2812 Narrow Ln.**
Simi Valley, CA 93063

YOUR RIGHT TO CANCEL
You are entering into a transaction that will result in a mortgage/lien/security interest on/in your home. You have a legal right under federal law to cancel this transaction, without cost, within three business days from whichever of the following events occurs last:

(1) the date of the transaction, which is

July 25, 20XX ; or

(2) the date you received your Truth-In-Lending disclosures;
or

(3) the date you received this notice of your right to cancel.

e transaction, the mortgage/lien/security interest is also cancelled. Within 20 calendar days after we
ice, we must take the steps necessary to reflect the fact that the mortgage/lien/security interest on/in
een cancelled, and we must return to you any money or property you have given to us or to anyone else
th this transaction.

y money or property we have given you until we have done the things mentioned above, but you must
then offer to return the money or property. If it is impractical or unfair for you to return the property, you must offer its reasonable value. You may offer to return the property at your home or at the location of the property. Money must be returned to the address below. If we do not take possession of the money or property within 20 calendar days of your offer, you may keep it without further obligation.

HOW TO CANCEL
If you decide to cancel this transaction, you may do so by notifying us in writing, at
National Direct Equity
100 East Narrow Street
Columbus, OH 43271

You may use any written statement that is signed and dated by you and states your intention to cancel, or you may use this notice by dating and signing below. Keep one copy of this notice because it contains important information about your rights.

If you cancel by mail or telegram, you must send the notice no later than midnight of **July 28, 20XX**
(or midnight of the third business day following the latest of the three events listed above.) If you send or deliver your written notice to cancel some other way, it must be delivered to the above address no later than that time.

I WISH TO CANCEL

BARRY BORROWER	DATE
BARBARA BORROWER	DATE

Joint owners of the property subject to the security interest may have the right to rescind the transaction. The exercise of this right by one owner shall be effective as to all owners.

I/We acknowledge receipt of two copies of <u>NOTICE OF RIGHT TO CANCEL</u>.

BARRY BORROWER	DATE
BARBARA BORROWER	DATE

Ellie Mae, Inc.

GRT4 0418
GRT4 (CLS)

NOTICE OF RIGHT TO CANCEL

Borrower(s): **Barry Borrower AND Barbara Borrower**

Mailing Address: **2812 Narrow Ln., Simi Valley, CA 93063**

Security interest in property described as: **2812 Narrow Ln.**
Simi Valley, CA 93063

YOUR RIGHT TO CANCEL
You are entering into a transaction that will result in a mortgage/lien/security interest on/in your home. You have a legal right under federal law to cancel this transaction, without cost, within three business days from whichever of the following events occurs last:

(1) the date of the transaction, which is

July 25, 20XX; or
(2) the date you received your Truth-In-Lending disclosures;
or
(3) the date you received this notice of your right to cancel.

If you cancel the transaction, the mortgage/lien/security interest is also cancelled. Within 20 calendar day
receive your notice, we must take the steps necessary to reflect the fact that the mortgage/lien/security int
your home has been cancelled, and we must return to you any money or property you have given to us or to a
in connection with this transaction.

You may keep any money or property we have given you until we have done the things mentioned above, but you must then offer to return the money or property. If it is impractical or unfair for you to return the property, you must offer its reasonable value. You may offer to return the property at your home or at the location of the property. Money must be returned to the address below. If we do not take possession of the money or property within 20 calendar days of your offer, you may keep it without further obligation.

> **HOW TO CANCEL**
> If you decide to cancel this transaction, you may do so by notifying us in writing, at
> **National Direct Equity**
> **100 East Narrow Street**
> **Columbus, OH 43271**
>
> You may use any written statement that is signed and dated by you and states your intention to cancel, or you may use this notice by dating and signing below. Keep one copy of this notice because it contains important information about your rights.
>
> If you cancel by mail or telegram, you must send the notice no later than midnight of **July 28, 20XX**
> (or midnight of the third business day following the latest of the three events listed above.) If you send or deliver your written notice to cancel some other way, it must be delivered to the above address no later than that time.
>
> **I WISH TO CANCEL**
>
> _____   _____
> **BARRY BORROWER**   DATE
>
> _____   _____
> **BARBARA BORROWER**   DATE

Joint owners of the property subject to the security interest may have the right to rescind the transaction. The exercise of this right by one owner shall be effective as to all owners.

I/We acknowledge receipt of two copies of <u>NOTICE OF RIGHT TO CANCEL</u>.

_____   _____
BARRY BORROWER   DATE

_____   _____
BARBARA BORROWER   DATE

Ellie Mae, Inc.   GRT4   0418
                                                                                                                         GRT4 (CLS)

NOTES

The borrower receives two copies of the Notice of Right to Cancel.

AUTHORIZATION FOR PAYOFF

Principal	Loan Date	Maturity	Loan No	Call/Coll	Account	Officer	Initials
$49,373.00	07-20-XX	07-30-XX	426100000000		426100000000		

References in the shaded area are for Lender's use only and do not limit the applicability of this document to any particular loan or item.
Any item above containing "***" has been omitted due to text length limitations.

Borrower: Barry and Barbara Borrower
2812 NARROW LN
SIMI VALLEY, CA 93063

Lender: Bank Ten, NA
National Direct Equity (NDE)
100 East Narrow Street
Columbus, OH 43271

TO: BANK TEN N.A.
500 TAYLOR 6PG PAYOFF DEPARTMENT
FORT WORTH, TX 76102

RE: PAYOFF OF ACCOUNT NO. 004318200222222

I hereby authorize you to accept from Bank Ten, NA, ("Bank Ten") a payoff of the balance of the loan represented by your referenced account number. You have informed Bank Ten and me that the payoff amount is $49,267.00 and that information is being relied upon in my transaction with Bank Ten. Upon receipt of the funds from Bank Ten, you are authorized to release to it (a) any documents of title, properly endorsed and released. (b) any financing statement terminations, (c) any security agreement releases or terminations. (d) a copy of the promissory note or credit agreement marked "cancelled" or "paid" and certifying it is a true and correct copy of the original with the original sent to me; and (e) a certified copy of any release of lien with the original sent to me. These documents are to be sent to Bank Ten within 30 days of the date of this letter. You are responsible for the closing of any accounts and the release of any liens or security interests. Your negotiation of Bank Ten's check constitutes your acceptance of these terms.

If you have any questions concerning this Payoff Authorization, please contact me or contact Bank Ten. N.A., Retail Loan Servicing at P.O. Box 1606, Lexington, KY (800) 576-1606.

Borrower:

_____

BARRY BORROWER, Individually

_____

BARBARA BORROWER, Individually

RECEIPT OF AUTHORIZATION FOR PAYOFF

Receipt is hereby acknowledged of the above Authorization for Payoff on _____ , 20 _____

☐ We are enclosing all requested documents.
☐ Please contact us concerning the requested documents.
☐ Other: _____

BANK TEN, N.A.

By: _____
(Authorized Signer)

RETURN TO:
BANK TEN Retail Loan Servicing ,
P.O. Box 11606 Lexington, KY 40576-1606

THIS COPY TO BE RETURNED TO LENDER

PROMISSORY NOTE

Principal	Loan Date	Maturity	Loan No	Call/Coll	Account	Officer	Initials
$49,373.00	07-16-XX	07-30-XX	426370133454		426370133454		

References in the shaded area are for Lender's use only and do not limit the applicability of this document to any particular loan or item.
Any item above containing "****" has been omitted due to text length limitations.

Borrower: Barry and Barbara Borrower
2812 NARROW LN
SIMI VALLEY, CA 93063

Lender: Bank TEN NA
National Direct Equity (NDE)
100 East Narrow Street
Columbus, OH 43271

Principal Amount: $49,373.00   **Interest Rate: 7.740%**   **Date of Note: October 10, 20XX**

PROMISE TO PAY. I ("Borrower") jointly and severally promise to pay to Bank Ten, NA ("Lender"), or order, in lawful money of the United States of America, the principal amount of Forty-nine Thousand Three Hundred Seventy-three & 00/100 Dollars ($49,373.00), together with interest at the rate of 7.740% per annum on the unpaid principal balance from October 16, 20XX, until paid in full.

PAYMENT. I will pay this loan in 180 payments of $464.85 each payment, My first payment is due August 20, 20XX, and all subsequent payments are due on the same day of each month after that. My final payment will be due on August 20, 20XX, and will be for all principal and all accrued interest not yet paid. Payments include principal and interest. Unless otherwise agreed or required by applicable law, payments will be applied first to accrued unpaid interest, then to principal, and any remaining amount to any unpaid collection costs and late charges. Interest on this Note is computed on a 365/365 simple interest basis; that is, by applying the ratio of the annual interest rate over the number of days in a year (366 during leap years), multiplied by the outstanding principal balance, multiplied by the actual number of days the principal balance is outstanding. I will pay Lender at Lender's address shown above or at such other place and such manner as Lender may designate in writing.

PREPAYMENT. I agree that all loan fees and other prepaid finance charges are earned fully as of the date of the loan and will not be refunded to me upon early payment (whether voluntary or as a result of default), except as otherwise required by law. Upon prepayment of this Note, Lender is entitled to the following prepayment fee: If you payoff your loan in full within thirty (30) months of the date you close your loan, you will have to pay a Prepayment Fee of 1 % of the original loan amount. Except for the foregoing, I may pay all or a portion of the amount owed earlier than it is due. Early payments will be applied first as noted above in the Payment paragraph and then to my next accruing payment(s). Partial payment of any regular payment will not relieve me of my obligation to make the remainder of the partial payment when due. Rather, early payments will reduce the principal balance due and may result in my making fewer payments. I agree not to send Lender payments marked "paid in full", "without recourse", or similar language. If I send such a payment, Lender may accept it without losing any of Lender's rights under this Note, and I will remain obligated to pay any further amount owed to Lender. All written communications concerning disputed amounts, including any check or other payment instrument that indicates that the payment constitutes "payment in full" of the amount owed or that is tendered with other conditions or limitations or as full satisfaction of a disputed amount must be mailed or delivered to: Bank Ten, P.O. Box 901008 Fort Worth, TX 76101-2008.

LATE CHARGE. If a payment is 10 days or more late I will be charged $25.00.

INTEREST AFTER DEFAULT. Upon my failure to pay all amounts declared due pursuant to this section, including failure to pay upon final maturity, the total sum due under this Note will bear interest from the date of acceleration or maturity at the interest rate on this Note. The interest rate will not exceed the maximum rate permitted by applicable law.

DEFAULT. I will be in default under this Note if any of the following happen:

    Payment Default. I fail to make any payment when due under this Note.

    Break Other Promises. I break any promise made to Lender or I fail to perform promptly at the time and strictly in the manner provided in this Note or in any agreement related to this Note, or in any other agreement or loan I have with Lender.

    False Statements. Any representation or statement made or furnished to Lender by me or on my behalf under this Note or the related documents is false or misleading in any material respect, either now or at the time made or furnished.

    Death or Insolvency. Any Borrower dies or becomes insolvent; a receiver is appointed for any part of my property; I make an assignment for the benefit of creditors; or any proceeding is commenced either by me or against me under any bankruptcy or insolvency laws.

    Taking of the Property. Any creditor or governmental agency tries to take any of the property or any other of my property in which Lender has a lien. This includes taking of, garnishing of or levying on my accounts with Lender.

    Defective Collateralization. This Note or any of the related documents ceases to be in full force and effect (including failure of any collateral document to create a valid and perfected security interest or lien) at any time and for any reason.

    Collateral Damage or Loss. Any collateral securing this Note is lost, stolen, substantially damaged or destroyed and the loss, theft, substantial damage or destruction is not covered by insurance.

    Property Damage or Loss. The Property is lost, stolen, substantially damaged, sold, or borrowed against.

    Events Affecting Guarantor. Any of the preceding events occurs with respect to any guarantor, endorser, surety, or accommodation party of any of the indebtedness or any guarantor, endorser, surety, or accommodation party dies or becomes incompetent, or revokes or disputes the validity of, or liability under, any guaranty of the indebtedness evidenced by this Note.

LENDER'S RIGHTS. Upon default, Lender may declare the entire unpaid principal balance on this Note and all accrued unpaid interest immediately due, and then I will pay that amount.

EXPENSES. To the extent not prohibited by applicable law, all reasonable expenses Lender incurs that in Lender's opinion are necessary at any time for the protection of its interest or the enforcement of its rights, shall become a part of the loan payable on demand, and shall bear interest at the Note rate from the date of expenditure until repaid. Expenses covered by this paragraph include, without limitation, however subject to any limits under applicable law, Lender's expenses for bankruptcy proceedings (including efforts to modify or vacate the automatic stay or injunction) and appeals, to the extent permitted by applicable law.

GOVERNING LAW. This agreement will be governed by and interpreted in accordance with federal law and the laws of the State of California, except for matters related to interest and the exportation of interest, which matters will be governed by and interpreted in accordance with federal law (including, but not limited to, statutes, regulations, interpretations, and opinions) and laws of the State of Ohio. However, if there ever is a question about whether any provision of the agreement is valid or enforceable, the provision that is questioned will be governed by whichever state or federal law would find the provision to be valid and enforceable. The loan transaction which is evidenced by this and other related documents has been approved, made and funded, and all necessary documents have been accepted by Lender in the State of Ohio.

DISHONORED ITEM FEE. I will pay a fee to Lender of $25.00 if I make a payment on my loan and the check or pre authorized charge with which I pay is later dishonored.

COLLATERAL. I acknowledge this Note is secured by a Deed of Trust dated July 16, 2004, to a trustee in favor of Lender on real property located in VENTURA County, State of California. That agreement contains the following due on sale provision: Lender may, at Lender's option, declare immediately due and payable all sums secured by the Deed of Trust upon the sale or transfer, without Lender's prior written consent, of all or any part of the Real Property, or any interest in the Real Property. A "sale or transfer" means the conveyance of Real Property or any right, title or interest in the Real Property; whether legal, beneficial or equitable; whether voluntary or involuntary; whether by outright sale, deed, installment sale contract, land contract, contract for deed, leasehold interest with a term greater than three

(3) years, lease-option contract, or by sale, assignment, or transfer of any beneficial interest in or to any land trust holding title to the Real Property, or by any other method of conveyance of an interest in the Real Property. However, this option shall not be exercised by Lender if such exercise is prohibited by applicable law.

COLLECTION COSTS. If you are in default under the terms of this Agreement, we may take all lawful action under applicable law to collect the money you owe us. It is our intent to collect only those attorney's fees, and those expenses, court and collection costs permitted by the laws of your state and the United States (Including the bankruptcy laws of the United States). You agree to pay only those collection costs and attorney's fees that we actually incur and that we may lawfully collect from you. If the laws of your state will not let us collect all or some of these collection costs and attorney's fees from you, we will not do so. To the extent the laws of your state prohibit us from contracting with you to collect such fees or costs or prohibit us from including this provision in your agreement with us, this provision is severed from this Agreement, is of no force and effect and your contract will be read and interpreted without this provision except to the extent federal law may now or hereafter preempt the law of your state.

As collateral security for repayment of this Note and all renewals and extensions, I grant Lender a continuing security interest in, and hereby pledge and transfer to Lender all my right, title and interest in and to any and all funds that I may now and in the future have on deposit with affiliate of Bank Ten Corporation. This includes all accounts I hold jointly with someone else and certificates of deposit. It does not include IRA, deferred deposits, or any accounts in which I am acting in a fiduciary capacity for a person or entity other than myself, or in which the grant of be prohibited by applicable law. I further agree that Lender may at any time, to the extent permitted by applicable law, apply any funds that I with Lender or any Bank Ten Corporation affiliate against the unpaid balance of this Note, including principal, interest, fees, costs, expenses

Lender is Bank Ten, N.A., a national banking association with its main offices located in Columbus, Ohio.

SENT BY LENDER. Lender may, at Lender's option, declare immediately due and payable all sums secured by this Deed of Trust upon the Lender's prior written consent, of all or any part of the Real Property, or any interest in the Real Property. A "sale or transfer" means the conveyance of Real Property or any right, title or interest in the Real Property; whether legal, beneficial or equitable; whether voluntary or involuntary; whether by outright sale, deed, installment sale contract, land contract, contract for deed, leasehold interest with a term greater than three (3) years, lease-option contract, or by sale, assignment, or transfer of any beneficial interest in or to any land trust holding title to the Real Property, or by any other method of conveyance of an interest in the Real Property. However, this option shall not be exercised by Lender if such exercise is prohibited by applicable law.

INFORMATION SHARING. The Bank Ten Consumer Information Values and Privacy Policy, which has been provided to you describes our information sharing practices and gives directions on how to opt out, or direct us to limit the sharing of Personal Information (as defined in the Privacy Policy) about you with other companies or organizations. You hereby agree that, if you choose not to exercise the opt outs described in the Privacy Policy, you will be deemed to have authorized us to share any Personal Information about you including information related to any of the products or services you may have with any Bank Ten company) with other companies or other organizations.

SUPPLEMENT TO PREPAYMENT PARAGRAPH. The following sentence in the Prepayment paragraph is modified as follows: "Depending on my payment history, early payments may reduce the principal balance due and may result in my making fewer payments.".

NOTIFY US OF INACCURATE INFORMATION WE REPORT TO CONSUMER REPORTING AGENCIES. Please notify us if we report any inaccurate information about your account(s) to a consumer reporting agency. Your written notice describing the specific inaccuracy(ies) should be sent to us at the following address: Bank Ten P.O. Box 901008 Fort Worth, TX 76101-2008

GENERAL PROVISIONS. I do not agree or intend to pay, and Lender does not agree or intend to contract for, charge, collect, take, reserve or receive (collectively referred to herein as "charge or collect"), any amount in the nature of interest or in the nature of a fee for this loan, which would in any way or event (including demand, prepayment, or acceleration) cause Lender to charge or collect more for this loan than the maximum Lender would be permitted to charge or collect by federal law or the law of the State of Ohio (as applicable). Any such excess interest or unauthorized fee shall, instead of anything stated to the contrary, be applied first to reduce the principal balance of this loan), and when the principal has been paid in full, be refunded to me. Lender may delay or forgo enforcing any of its rights or remedies under this Note without losing them. I and any other person who signs, guarantees or endorses this Note, to the extent allowed by law, waive any applicable statute of limitations, presentment, demand for payment, and notice of dishonor. Upon any change in the terms of this Note, and unless otherwise expressly stated in writing, no party who signs this Note, whether as maker, guarantor, accommodation maker or endorser, shall be released from liability. All such parties agree that Lender may renew or extend (repeatedly and for any length of time) this loan or release any party or guarantor or collateral; or impair, fail to realize upon or perfect Lender's security interest in the collateral. All such parties also agree that Lender may modify this loan without the consent of or notice to anyone other than the party with whom the modification is made. The obligations under this Note are joint and several. This means that the words "I", "me", and "my" mean each and all of the persons signing below.

PRIOR TO SIGNING THIS NOTE, I, AND EACH OF US, READ AND UNDERSTOOD AII THE PROVISIONS OF THIS NOTE. I, AND EACH OF US, AGREE TO THE TERMS OF THE NOTE.

I ACKNOWLEDGE RECEIPT OF A COMPLETED COPY OF THIS PROMISSORY NOTE.

BORROWER:

_____
BARRY BORROWER, Individually

_____
BARBARA BORROWER, Individually

NOTES

The "Promissory Note" is signed by the borrowers as individuals only, since a family trust does not incur the indebtedness of loans.

Form W-9
(Rev. November 2017)
Department of the Treasury
Internal Revenue Service

Request for Taxpayer
Identification Number and Certification

▶ Go to *www.irs.gov/FormW9* for instructions and the latest information.

Give Form to the requester. Do not send to the IRS.

1 Name (as shown on your income tax return). Name is required on this line; do not leave this line blank.

Barry Borrower

2 Business name/disregarded entity name, if different from above

3 Check appropriate box for federal tax classification of the person whose name is entered on line 1. Check only **one** of the following seven boxes.

☐ Individual/sole proprietor or single-member LLC   ☐ C Corporation   ☐ S Corporation   ☐ Partnership   ☐ Trust/estate

☐ Limited liability company. Enter the tax classification (C = C corporation, S = S corporation, P = Partnership) ▶ _____

Note: Check the appropriate box in the line above for the tax classification of the single-member owner. Do not check LLC if the LLC is classified as a single-member LLC that is disregarded from the owner unless the owner of the LLC is another LLC that is **not** disregarded from the owner for U.S. federal tax purposes. Otherwise, a single-member LLC that is disregarded from the owner should check the appropriate box for the tax classification of its owner.

☐ Other (see instructions) ▶

4 Exemptions (codes apply only to certain entities, not individuals; see instructions on page 3):

Exempt payee code (if any) _____

Exemption from FATCA reporting code (if any) _____

(Applies to accounts maintained outside the U.S.)

5 Address (number, street, and apt. or suite no.) See instructions.

2812 Narrow Ln.

Requester's name and address (optional)

6 City, state, and ZIP code

Simi Valley, CA 93063

7 List account number(s) here (optional)

Print or type.
See Specific Instructions on page 2.

Part I Taxpayer Identification Number (TIN)

Enter your TIN in the appropriate box. The TIN provided must match the name given on line 1 to avoid backup withholding. For individuals, this is generally your social security number (SSN). However, for a resident alien, sole proprietor, or disregarded entity, see the instructions for Part I, later. For other entities, it is your employer identification number (EIN). If you do not have a number, see *How to get a TIN,* later.

Note. If the account is in more than one name, see the instructions for line 1. Also see *What Name and Number To Give the Requester* for guidelines on whose number to enter.

Social security number

0 0 0 – 0 0 – 0 0 0 0

or

Employer identification number

Part II Certification

Under penalties of perjury, I certify that:

1. The number shown on this form is my correct taxpayer identification number (or I am waiting for a number to be issued to me); and
2. I am not subject to backup withholding because: (a) I am exempt from backup withholding, or (b) I have not been notified by the Internal Revenue Service (IRS) that I am subject to backup withholding as a result of a failure to report all interest or dividends, or (c) the IRS has notified me that I am no longer subject to backup withholding; and
3. I am a U.S. citizen or other U.S. person (defined below); and
4. The FATCA code(s) entered on this form (if any) indicating that I am exempt from FATCA reporting is correct.

Certification instructions. You must cross out item 2 above if you have been notified by the IRS that you are currently subject to backup withholding because you have failed to report all interest and dividends on your tax return. For real estate transactions, item 2 does not apply. For mortgage interest paid, acquisition or abandonment of secured property, cancellation of debt, contributions to an individual retirement arrangement (IRA), and generally, payments other than interest and dividends, you are not required to sign the certification, but you must provide your correct TIN. See the instructions for Part II, later.

Sign Here

Signature of U.S. person ▶   Date ▶

General Instructions

Section references are to the Internal Revenue Code unless otherwise noted.

Future developments. For the latest information about developments related to Form W-9 and its instructions, such as legislation enacted after they were published, go to *www.irs.gov/FormW9*.

Purpose of Form

An individual or entity (Form W-9 requester) who is required to file an information return with the IRS must obtain your correct taxpayer identification number (TIN) which may be your social security number (SSN), individual taxpayer identification number (ITIN), adoption taxpayer identification number (ATIN), or employer identification number (EIN), to report on an information return the amount paid to you, or other amount reportable on an information return. Examples of information returns include, but are not limited to, the following.

• Form 1099-INT (interest earned or paid)
• Form 1099-DIV (dividends, including those from stocks or mutual funds)
• Form 1099-MISC (various types of income, prizes, awards, or gross proceeds)
• Form 1099-B (stock or mutual fund sales and certain other transactions by brokers)
• Form 1099-S (proceeds from real estate transactions)
• Form 1099-K (merchant card and third party network transactions)
• Form 1098 (home mortgage interest), 1098-E (student loan interest), 1098-T (tuition)
• Form 1099-C (canceled debt)
• Form 1099-A (acquisition or abandonment of secured property)

Use Form W-9 only if you are a U.S. person (including a resident alien), to provide your correct TIN.

If you do not return Form W-9 to the requester with a TIN, you might be subject to backup withholding. See What is backup withholding, *later.*

By signing the filled-out form, you:

1. Certify that the TIN you are giving is correct (or you are waiting for a number to be issued),

2. Certify that you are not subject to backup withholding, or

3. Claim exemption from backup withholding if you are a U.S. exempt payee. If applicable, you are also certifying that as a U.S. person, your allocable share of any partnership income from a U.S. trade or business is not subject to the withholding tax on foreign partners' share of effectively connected income, and

4. Certify that FATCA code(s) entered on this form (if any) indicating that you are exempt from the FATCA reporting, is correct. See *What is FATCA reporting,* later, for further information.

Note: If you are a U.S. person and a requester gives you a form other than Form W-9 to request your TIN, you must use the requester's form if it is substantially similar to this Form W-9.

Definition of a U.S. person. For federal tax purposes, you are considered a U.S. person if you are:

• An individual who is a U.S. citizen or U.S. resident alien;

• A partnership, corporation, company, or association created or organized in the United States or under the laws of the United States;

• An estate (other than a foreign estate); or

• A domestic trust (as defined in Regulations section 301.7701-7).

Special rules for partnerships. Partnerships that conduct a trade or business in the United States are generally required to pay a withholding tax under section 1446 on any foreign partners' share of effectively connected taxable income from such business. Further, in certain cases where a Form W-9 has not been received, the rules under section 1446 require a partnership to presume that a partner is a foreign person, and pay the section 1446 withholding tax. Therefore, if you are a U.S. person that is a partner in a partnership conducting a trade or business in the United States, provide Form W-9 to the partnership to establish your U.S. status and avoid section 1446 withholding on your share of partnership income.

Ellie Mae, Inc.   Cat. No. 10231X   Form **W-9** (Rev. 11-2017)
GW9C (CLS)

Home Equity Lines of Credit

In the cases below, the following person must give Form W-9 to the partnership for purposes of establishing its U.S. status and avoiding withholding on its allocable share of net income from the partnership conducting a trade or business in the United States.

• In the case of a disregarded entity with a U.S. owner, the U.S. owner of the disregarded entity and not the entity;

• In the case of a grantor trust with a U.S. grantor or other U.S. owner, generally, the U.S. grantor or other U.S. owner of the grantor trust and not the trust; and

• In the case of a U.S. trust (other than a grantor trust), the U.S. trust (other than a grantor trust) and not the beneficiaries of the trust.

Foreign person. If you are a foreign person or the U.S. branch of a foreign bank that has elected to be treated as a U.S. person, do not use Form W-9. Instead, use the appropriate Form W-8 or Form 8233 (see Pub. 515, Withholding of Tax on Nonresident Aliens and Foreign Entities).

Nonresident alien who becomes a resident alien. Generally, only a nonresident alien individual may use the terms of a tax treaty to reduce or eliminate U.S. tax on certain types of income. However, most tax treaties contain a provision known as a "saving clause." Exceptions specified in the saving clause may permit an exemption from tax to continue for certain types of income even after the payee has otherwise become a U.S. resident alien for tax purposes.

If you are a U.S. resident alien who is relying on an exception contained in the saving clause of a tax treaty to claim an exemption from U.S. tax on certain types of income, you must attach a statement to Form W-9 that specifies the following five items.

1. The treaty country. Generally, this must be the same treaty under which you claimed exemption from tax as a nonresident alien.

2. The treaty article addressing the income.

3. The article number (or location) in the tax treaty that contains the saving clause and its exceptions.

4. The type and amount of income that qualifies for the exemption from tax.

5. Sufficient facts to justify the exemption from tax under the terms of the treaty article.

Example. Article 20 of the U.S.-China income tax treaty allows an exemption from tax for scholarship income received by a Chinese student temporarily present in the United States. Under U.S. law, this student will become a resident alien for tax purposes if his or her stay in the United States exceeds 5 calendar years. However, paragraph 2 of the first Protocol to the U.S.-China treaty (dated April 30, 1984) allows the provisions of Article 20 to continue to apply even after the Chinese student becomes a resident alien of the United States. A Chinese student who qualifies for this exception (under paragraph 2 of the first protocol) and is relying on this exception to claim an exemption from tax on his or her scholarship or fellowship income would attach to Form W-9 a statement that includes the information described above to support that exemption.

If you are a nonresident alien or a foreign entity, give the requester the appropriate completed Form W-8 or Form 8233.

Backup Withholding

What is backup withholding? Persons making certain payments to you must under certain conditions withhold and pay to the IRS 28% of such payments. This is called "backup withholding." Payments that may be subject to backup withholding include interest, tax-exempt interest, dividends, broker and barter exchange transactions, rents, royalties, nonemployee pay, payments made in settlement of payment card and third party network transactions, and certain payments from fishing boat operators. Real estate transactions are not subject to backup withholding.

You will not be subject to backup withholding on payments you receive if you give the requester your correct TIN, make the proper certifications, and report all your taxable interest and dividends on your tax return.

Payments you receive will be subject to backup withholding if:

1. You do not furnish your TIN to the requester,

2. You do not certify your TIN when required (see the instructions for Part II for details),

3. The IRS tells the requester that you furnished an incorrect TIN,

4. The IRS tells you that you are subject to backup withholding because you did not report all your interest and dividends on your tax return (for reportable interest and dividends only), or

5. You do not certify to the requester that you are not subject to backup withholding under 4 above (for reportable interest and dividend accounts opened after 1983 only).

Certain payees and payments are exempt from backup withholding. See *Exempt payee code,* later, and the separate Instructions for the Requester of Form W-9 for more information.

Also see *Special rules for partnerships,* earlier.

What is FATCA Reporting?

The Foreign Account Tax Compliance Act (FATCA) requires a participating foreign financial institution to report all United States account holders that are specified United States persons. Certain payees are exempt from FATCA reporting. See *Exemption from FATCA reporting code,* later, and the Instructions for the Requester of Form W-9 for more information.

Updating Your Information

You must provide updated information to any person to whom you claimed to be an exempt payee if you are no longer an exempt payee and anticipate receiving reportable payments in the future from this person. For example, you may need to provide updated information if you are a C corporation that elects to be an S corporation, or if you no longer are tax exempt. In addition, you must furnish a new Form W-9 if the name or TIN changes for the account; for example, if the grantor of a grantor trust dies.

Penalties

Failure to furnish TIN. If you fail to furnish your correct TIN to a requester, you are subject to a penalty of $50 for each such failure unless your failure is due to reasonable cause and not to willful neglect.

Civil penalty for false information with respect to withholding. If you make a false statement with no reasonable basis that results in no backup withholding, you are subject to a $500 penalty.

Criminal penalty for falsifying information. Willfully falsifying certifications or affirmations may subject you to criminal penalties including fines and/or imprisonment.

Misuse of TINs. If the requester discloses or uses TINs in violation of federal law, the requester may be subject to civil and criminal penalties.

Specific Instructions

Line 1

You must enter one of the following on this line; **do not** leave this line blank. The name should match the name on your tax return.

If this Form W-9 is for a joint account (other than an account maintained by a foreign financial institution (FFI)), list first, and then circle, the name of the person or entity whose number you entered in Part I of Form W-9. If you are providing Form W-9 to an FFI to document a joint account, each holder of the account that is a U.S. person must provide a Form W-9.

a. **Individual.** Generally, enter the name shown on your tax return. If you have changed your last name without informing the Social Security Administration (SSA) of the name change, enter your first name, the last name as shown on your social security card, and your new last name.

Note: ITIN applicant: Enter your individual name as it was entered on your Form W-7 application, line 1a. This should also be the same as the name you entered on the Form 1040/1040A/1040EZ you filed with your application.

b. **Sole proprietor or single-member LLC.** Enter your individual name as shown on your 1040/1040A/1040EZ on line 1. You may enter your business, trade, or "doing business as" (DBA) name on line 2.

c. **Partnership, LLC that is not a single-member LLC, C corporation, or S corporation.** Enter the entity's name as shown on the entity's tax return on line 1 and any business, trade, or DBA name on line 2.

d. **Other entities.** Enter your name as shown on required U.S. federal tax documents on line 1. This name should match the name shown on the charter or other legal document creating the entity. You may enter any business, trade, or DBA name on line 2.

e. **Disregarded entity.** For U.S. federal tax purposes, an entity that is disregarded as an entity separate from its owner is treated as a "disregarded entity." See Regulations section 301.7701-2(c)(2)(iii). Enter the owner's name on line 1. The name of the entity entered on line 1 should never be a disregarded entity. The name on line 1 should be the name shown on the income tax return on which the income should be reported. For example, if a foreign LLC that is treated as a disregarded entity for U.S. federal tax purposes has a single owner that is a U.S. person, the U.S. owner's name is required to be provided on line 1. If the direct owner of the entity is also a disregarded entity, enter the first owner that is not disregarded for federal tax purposes. Enter the disregarded entity's name on line 2, "Business name/disregarded entity name." If the owner of the disregarded entity is a foreign person, the owner must complete an appropriate Form W-8 instead of a Form W-9. This is the case even if the foreign person has a U.S. TIN.

Line 2

If you have a business name, trade name, DBA name, or disregarded entity name, you may enter it on line 2.

Line 3

Check the appropriate box on line 3 for the U.S. federal tax classification of the person whose name is entered on line 1. Check only one box on line 3.

IF the entity/person on line 1 is a(n)…	THEN check the box for…
• Corporation	Corporation
• Individual • Sole proprietorship, or • Single-member limited liability company (LLC) owned by an individual and disregarded for U.S. federal tax purposes.	Individual/sole proprietor or single-member LLC
• LLC treated as a partnership for U.S. federal tax purposes, • LLC that has filed Form 8832 or 2553 to be taxed as a corporation, or • LLC that is disregarded as an entity separate from its owner but the owner is another LLC that is not disregarded for U.S. federal tax purposes.	Limited liability company and enter the appropriate tax classification. (P= Partnership; C= C corporation; or S= S corporation)
• Partnership	Partnership
• Trust/estate	Trust/estate

Line 4, Exemptions

If you are exempt from backup withholding and/or FATCA reporting, enter in the appropriate space on line 4 any code(s) that may apply to you.

Exempt payee code.

• Generally, individuals (including sole proprietors) are not exempt from backup withholding.

• Except as provided below, corporations are exempt from backup withholding for certain payments, including interest and dividends.

• Corporations are not exempt from backup withholding for payments made in settlement of payment card or third party network transactions.

• Corporations are not exempt from backup withholding with respect to attorneys' fees or gross proceeds paid to attorneys, and corporations that provide medical or health care services are not exempt with respect to payments reportable on Form 1099-MISC.

The following codes identify payees that are exempt from backup withholding. Enter the appropriate code in the space in line 4.

1 – An organization exempt from tax under section 501(a), any IRA, or a custodial account under section 403(b)(7) if the account satisfies the requirements of section 401(f)(2)

2 – The United States or any of its agencies or instrumentalities

3 – A state, the District of Columbia, a U.S. commonwealth or possession, or any of their political subdivisions or instrumentalities

4 – A foreign government or any of its political subdivisions, agencies, or instrumentalities

5 – A corporation

6 – A dealer in securities or commodities required to register in the United States, the District of Columbia, or a U.S. commonwealth or possession

7 – A futures commission merchant registered with the Commodity Futures Trading Commission

8 – A real estate investment trust

9 – An entity registered at all times during the tax year under the Investment Company Act of 1940

10 – A common trust fund operated by a bank under section 584(a)

11 – A financial institution

12 – A middleman known in the investment community as a nominee or custodian

13 – A trust exempt from tax under section 664 or described in section 4947

The following chart shows types of payments that may be exempt from backup withholding. The chart applies to the exempt payees listed above, 1 through 13.

IF the payment is for...	THEN the payment is exempt for...
Interest and dividend payments	All exempt payees except for 7
Broker transactions	Exempt payees 1 through 4 and 6 through 11 and all C corporations. S corporations must not enter an exempt payee code because they are exempt only for sales of noncovered securities acquired prior to 2012.
Barter exchange transactions and patronage dividends	Exempt payees 1 through 4
Payments over $600 required to be reported and direct sales over $5,000[1]	Generally, exempt payees 1 through 5[2]
Payments made in settlement of payment card or third party network transactions	Exempt payees 1 through 4

[1] See Form 1099-MISC, Miscellaneous Income, and its instructions.

[2] However, the following payments made to a corporation and reportable on Form 1099-MISC are not exempt from backup withholding: medical and health care payments, attorneys' fees, gross proceeds paid to an attorney reportable under section 6045(f), and payments for services paid by a federal executive agency.

Exemption from FATCA reporting code. The following codes identify payees that are exempt from reporting under FATCA. These codes apply to persons submitting this form for accounts maintained outside of the United States by certain foreign financial institutions. Therefore, if you are only submitting this form for an account you hold in the United States, you may leave this field blank. Consult with the person requesting this form if you are uncertain if the financial institution is subject to these requirements. A requester may indicate that a code is not required by providing you with a Form W-9 with "Not Applicable" (or any similar indication) written or printed on the line for a FATCA exemption code.

A – An organization exempt from tax under section 501(a) or any individual retirement plan as defined in section 7701(a)(37)

B – The United States or any of its agencies or instrumentalities

C – A state, the District of Columbia, a U.S. commonwealth or possession, or any of their political subdivisions or instrumentalities

D – A corporation the stock of which is regularly traded on one or more established securities markets, as described in Regulations section 1.1472-1(c)(1)(i)

E – A corporation that is a member of the same expanded affiliated group as a corporation described in Regulations section 1.1472-1(c)(1)(i)

F – A dealer in securities, commodities, or derivative financial instruments (including notional principal contracts, futures, forwards, and options) that is registered as such under the laws of the United States or any state

G – A real estate investment trust

H – A regulated investment company as defined in section 851 or an entity registered at all times during the tax year under the Investment Company Act of 1940

I – A common trust fund as defined in section 584(a)

J – A bank as defined in section 581

K – A broker

L – A trust exempt from tax under section 664 or described in section 4947(a)(1)

M – A tax exempt trust under a section 403(b) plan or section 457(g) plan

Note: You may wish to consult with the financial institution requesting this form to determine whether the FATCA code and/or exempt payee code should be completed.

Line 5

Enter your address (number, street, and apartment or suite number). This is where the requester of this Form W-9 will mail your information returns. If this address differs from the one the requester already has on file, write NEW at the top. If a new address is provided, there is still a chance the old address will be used until the payor changes your address in their records.

Line 6

Enter your city, state, and ZIP code.

Part I. Taxpayer Identification Number (TIN)

Enter your TIN in the appropriate box. If you are a resident alien and you do not have and are not eligible to get an SSN, your TIN is your IRS individual taxpayer identification number (ITIN). Enter it in the social security number box. If you do not have an ITIN, see *How to get a TIN* below.

If you are a sole proprietor and you have an EIN, you may enter either your SSN or EIN.

If you are a single-member LLC that is disregarded as an entity separate from its owner, enter the owner's SSN (or EIN, if the owner has one). Do not enter the disregarded entity's EIN. If the LLC is classified as a corporation or partnership, enter the entity's EIN.

Note. See *What Name and Number To Give the Requester*, later, for further clarification of name and TIN combinations.

How to get a TIN. If you do not have a TIN, apply for one immediately. To apply for an SSN, get Form SS-5, Application for a Social Security Card, from your local SSA office or get this form online at *www.SSA.gov*. You may also get this form by calling 1-800-772-1213. Use Form W-7, Application for IRS Individual Taxpayer Identification Number, to apply for an ITIN, or Form SS-4, Application for Employer Identification Number, to apply for an EIN. You can apply for an EIN online by accessing the IRS website at *www.irs.gov/Businesses* and clicking on Employer Identification Number (EIN) under Starting a Business. Go to *www.irs.gov/Forms* to view, download, or print Form W-7 and/or Form SS-4. Or, you can go to *www.irs.gov/OrderForms* to place an order and have Form W-7 and/or SS-4 mailed to you within 10 business days.

If you are asked to complete Form W-9 but do not have a TIN, apply for a TIN and write "Applied For" in the space for the TIN, sign and date the form, and give it to the requester. For interest and dividend payments, and certain payments made with respect to readily tradable instruments, generally you will have 60 days to get a TIN and give it to the requester before you are subject to backup withholding on payments. The 60-day rule does not apply to other types of payments. You will be subject to backup withholding on all such payments until you provide your TIN to the requester.

Note: Entering "Applied For" means that you have already applied for a TIN or that you intend to apply for one soon.

Caution: *A disregarded U.S. entity that has a foreign owner must use the appropriate Form W-8.*

Part II. Certification

To establish to the withholding agent that you are a U.S. person, or resident alien, sign Form W-9. You may be requested to sign by the withholding agent even if item 1, 4, or 5 below indicates otherwise.

For a joint account, only the person whose TIN is shown in Part I should sign (when required). In the case of a disregarded entity, the person identified on line 1 must sign. Exempt payees, see *Exempt payee code*, earlier.

Signature requirements. Complete the certification as indicated in items 1 through 5 below.

1. Interest, dividend, and barter exchange accounts opened before 1984 and broker accounts considered active during 1983. You must give your correct TIN, but you do not have to sign the certification.

2. Interest, dividend, broker, and barter exchange accounts opened after 1983 and broker accounts considered inactive during 1983. You must sign the certification or backup withholding will apply. If you are subject to backup withholding and you are merely providing your correct TIN to the requester, you must cross out item 2 in the certification before signing the form.

3. Real estate transactions. You must sign the certification. You may cross out item 2 of the certification.

4. Other payments. You must give your correct TIN, but you do not have to sign the certification unless you have been notified that you have

Closing Disclosure

This form is a statement of final loan terms and closing costs. Compare this document with your Loan Estimate.

Closing Information

Date Issued	4/15/20XX
Closing Date	4/15/20XX
Disbursement Date	4/15/20XX
Settlement Agent	Trans Union
File #	12-3456
Property	1218 Narrow Ln.
	Simi Valley, AS 93063
Sale Price	

Transaction Information

Borrower	Barry Borrower and Barbara Borrower
	1218 Narrow Ln.
	Simi Valley, CA 93063
Seller	
Lender	National Direct Equity

Loan Information

Loan Term	30 years
Purpose	HELOC
Product	Fixed Rate
Loan Type	☒ Conventional ☐ FHA
	☐ VA ☐ _____
Loan ID #	123456789
MIC #	000654321

Loan Terms

		Can this amount increase after closing?
Loan Amount	$49,267.00	NO
Interest Rate	3.875%	NO
Monthly Principal & Interest *See Projected Payments below for your Estimated Total Monthly Payment*	$761.78	NO

		Does the loan have these features?
Prepayment Penalty		YES • As high as $3,240 if you pay off the loan during the first 2 years
Balloon Payment		NO

Projected Payments

Payment Calculation	Years 1-7	Years 8-30
Principal & Interest	$761.78	$761.78
Mortgage Insurance	+ 82.35	+ —
Estimated Escrow *Amount can increase over time*	+ 206.13	+ 206.13
Estimated Total Monthly Payment	$1,050.26	$967.91

		This estimate includes	In escrow?
Estimated Taxes, Insurance & Assessments *Amount can increase over time* *See page 4 for details*	$356.13 a month	☒ Property Taxes	YES
		☒ Homeowner's Insurance	YES
		☒ Other: Homeowner's Association Dues	NO
		See Escrow Account on page 4 for details. You must pay for other property costs separately.	

Costs at Closing

Closing Costs	$9,712.10	Includes $4,694.05 in Loan Costs + $5,018.05 in Other Costs – $0 in Lender Credits. *See page 2 for details.*
Cash to Close	$14,147.26	Includes Closing Costs. *See Calculating Cash to Close on page 3 for details.*

CLOSING DISCLOSURE

Closing Cost Details

Loan Costs		Borrower-Paid		Seller-Paid		Paid by Others
		At Closing	Before Closing	At Closing	Before Closing	
A. Origination Charges		**$1,802.00**				
01 0.25 % of Loan Amount (Points)		$405.00				
02 Application Fee		$300.00				
03 Underwriting Fee		$1,097.00				
04						
05						
06						
07						
08						
B. Services Borrower Did Not Shop For		**$236.55**				
01 Appraisal Fee	to John Smith Appraisers Inc.					$405.00
02 Credit Report Fee	to Information Inc.		$29.80			
03 Flood Determination Fee	to Info Co.	$20.00				
04 Flood Monitoring Fee	to Info Co.	$31.75				
05 Tax Monitoring Fee	to Info Co.	$75.00				
06 Tax Status Research Fee	to Info Co.	$80.00				
07						
08						
09						
10						
C. Services Borrower Did Shop For		**$2,655.50**				
01 Pest Inspection Fee	to Pests Co.	$120.50				
02 Survey Fee	to Surveys Co.	$85.00				
03 Title – Insurance Binder	to Epsilon Title Co.	$650.00				
04 Title – Lender's Title Insurance	to Epsilon Title Co.	$500.00				
05 Title – Settlement Agent Fee	to Epsilon Title Co.	$500.00				
06 Title – Title Search	to Epsilon Title Co.	$800.00				
07						
08						
D. TOTAL LOAN COSTS (Borrower-Paid)		**$4,694.05**				
Loan Costs Subtotals (A + B + C)		$4,664.25	$29.80			

Other Costs		Borrower-Paid		Seller-Paid		Paid by Others
E. Taxes and Other Government Fees		**$85.00**				
01 Recording Fees	Deed: $40.00 Mortgage: $45.00	$85.00				
02 Transfer Tax	to Any State			$950.00		
F. Prepaids		**$2,120.80**				
01 Homeowner's Insurance Premium (12 mo.) to Insurance Co.		$1,209.96				
02 Mortgage Insurance Premium (mo.)						
03 Prepaid Interest ($17.44 per day from 4/15/13 to 5/1/13)		$279.04				
04 Property Taxes (6 mo.) to Any County USA		$631.80				
05						
G. Initial Escrow Payment at Closing		**$412.25**				
01 Homeowner's Insurance $100.83 per month for 2 mo.		$201.66				
02 Mortgage Insurance per month for mo.						
03 Property Taxes $105.30 per month for 2 mo.		$210.60				
04						
05						
06						
07						
08 Aggregate Adjustment		– 0.01				
H. Other		**$2,400.00**				
01 HOA Capital Contribution	to HOA Acre Inc.	$500.00				
02 HOA Processing Fee	to HOA Acre Inc.	$150.00				
03 Home Inspection Fee	to Engineers Inc.	$750.00			$750.00	
04 Home Warranty Fee	to XYZ Warranty Inc.			$450.00		
05 Real Estate Commission	to Alpha Real Estate Broker			$5,700.00		
06 Real Estate Commission	to Omega Real Estate Broker			$5,700.00		
07 Title – Owner's Title Insurance (optional) to Epsilon Title Co.		$1,000.00				
08						
I. TOTAL OTHER COSTS (Borrower-Paid)		**$5,018.05**				
Other Costs Subtotals (E + F + G + H)		$5,018.05				
J. TOTAL CLOSING COSTS (Borrower-Paid)		**$9,712.10**				
Closing Costs Subtotals (D + I)		$9,682.30	$29.80	$12,800.00	$750.00	$405.00
Lender Credits						

CLOSING DISCLOSURE

Calculating Cash to Close

Use this table to see what has changed from your Loan Estimate.

	Loan Estimate	Final	Did this change?
Total Closing Costs (J)	$8,054.00	$9,712.10	**YES** • See **Total Loan Costs (D)** and **Total Other Costs (I)**
Closing Costs Paid Before Closing	$0	– $29.80	**YES** • You paid these Closing Costs **before closing**
Closing Costs Financed (Paid from your Loan Amount)	$0	$0	**NO**
Down Payment/Funds from Borrower	$18,000.00	$18,000.00	**NO**
Deposit	– $10,000.00	– $10,000.00	**NO**
Funds for Borrower	$0	$0	**NO**
Seller Credits	$0	– $2,500.00	**YES** • See Seller Credits in **Section L**
Adjustments and Other Credits	$0	– $1,035.04	**YES** • See details in **Sections K and L**
Cash to Close	$16,054.00	$14,147.26	

Summaries of Transactions

Use this table to see a summary of your transaction.

BORROWER'S TRANSACTION

K. Due from Borrower at Closing	$189,762.30
01 Sale Price of Property	$180,000.00
02 Sale Price of Any Personal Property Included in Sale	
03 Closing Costs Paid at Closing (J)	$9,682.30
04	
Adjustments	
05	
06	
07	

Adjustments for Items Paid by Seller in Advance			
08 City/Town Taxes	to		
09 County Taxes	to		
10 Assessments	to		
11 HOA Dues	4/15/13 to 4/30/13		$80.00
12			
13			
14			
15			

L. Paid Already by or on Behalf of Borrower at Closing	$175,615.04
01 Deposit	$10,000.00
02 Loan Amount	$162,000.00
03 Existing Loan(s) Assumed or Taken Subject to	
04	
05 Seller Credit	$2,500.00
Other Credits	
06 Rebate from Epsilon Title Co.	$750.00
07	
Adjustments	
08	
09	
10	
11	

Adjustments for Items Unpaid by Seller		
12 City/Town Taxes 1/1/13 to 4/14/13		$365.04
13 County Taxes	to	
14 Assessments	to	
15		
16		
17		

CALCULATION	
Total Due from Borrower at Closing (K)	$189,762.30
Total Paid Already by or on Behalf of Borrower at Closing (L)	– $175,615.04
Cash to Close ☒ From ☐ To Borrower	**$14,147.26**

SELLER'S TRANSACTION

M. Due to Seller at Closing	$180,080.00
01 Sale Price of Property	$180,000.00
02 Sale Price of Any Personal Property Included in Sale	
03	
04	
05	
06	
07	
08	

Adjustments for Items Paid by Seller in Advance			
09 City/Town Taxes	to		
10 County Taxes	to		
11 Assessments	to		
12 HOA Dues	4/15/13 to 4/30/13		$80.00
13			
14			
15			
16			

N. Due from Seller at Closing	$115,665.04
01 Excess Deposit	
02 Closing Costs Paid at Closing (J)	$12,800.00
03 Existing Loan(s) Assumed or Taken Subject to	
04 Payoff of First Mortgage Loan	$100,000.00
05 Payoff of Second Mortgage Loan	
06	
07	
08 Seller Credit	$2,500.00
09	
10	
11	
12	
13	

Adjustments for Items Unpaid by Seller		
14 City/Town Taxes 1/1/13 to 4/14/13		$365.04
15 County Taxes	to	
16 Assessments	to	
17		
18		
19		

CALCULATION	
Total Due to Seller at Closing (M)	$180,080.00
Total Due from Seller at Closing (N)	– $115,665.04
Cash ☐ From ☒ To Seller	**$64,414.96**

CLOSING DISCLOSURE

Additional Information About This Loan

Loan Disclosures

Assumption

If you sell or transfer this property to another person, your lender

☐ will allow, under certain conditions, this person to assume this loan on the original terms.

☒ will not allow assumption of this loan on the original terms.

Demand Feature

Your loan

☐ has a demand feature, which permits your lender to require early repayment of the loan. You should review your note for details.

☒ does not have a demand feature.

Late Payment

If your payment is more than *15* days late, your lender will charge a late fee of *5% of the monthly principal and interest payment.*

Negative Amortization (Increase in Loan Amount)

Under your loan terms, you

☐ are scheduled to make monthly payments that do not pay all of the interest due that month. As a result, your loan amount will increase (negatively amortize), and your loan amount will likely become larger than your original loan amount. Increases in your loan amount lower the equity you have in this property.

☐ may have monthly payments that do not pay all of the interest due that month. If you do, your loan amount will increase (negatively amortize), and, as a result, your loan amount may become larger than your original loan amount. Increases in your loan amount lower the equity you have in this property.

☒ do not have a negative amortization feature.

Partial Payments

Your lender

☒ may accept payments that are less than the full amount due (partial payments) and apply them to your loan.

☐ may hold them in a separate account until you pay the rest of the payment, and then apply the full payment to your loan.

☐ does not accept any partial payments.

If this loan is sold, your new lender may have a different policy.

Security Interest

You are granting a security interest in
1218 Narrow Ln., Simi Valley, CA 93063

You may lose this property if you do not make your payments or satisfy other obligations for this loan.

Escrow Account

For now, your loan

☒ will have an escrow account (also called an "impound" or "trust" account) to pay the property costs listed below. Without an escrow account, you would pay them directly, possibly in one or two large payments a year. Your lender may be liable for penalties and interest for failing to make a payment.

Escrow		
Escrowed Property Costs over Year 1	$2,473.56	Estimated total amount over year 1 for your escrowed property costs: *Homeowner's Insurance Property Taxes*
Non-Escrowed Property Costs over Year 1	$1,800.00	Estimated total amount over year 1 for your non-escrowed property costs: *Homeowner's Association Dues* You may have other property costs.
Initial Escrow Payment	$412.25	A cushion for the escrow account you pay at closing. See Section G on page 2.
Monthly Escrow Payment	$206.13	The amount included in your total monthly payment.

☐ will not have an escrow account because ☐ you declined it ☐ your lender does not offer one. You must directly pay your property costs, such as taxes and homeowner's insurance. Contact your lender to ask if your loan can have an escrow account.

No Escrow		
Estimated Property Costs over Year 1		Estimated total amount over year 1. You must pay these costs directly, possibly in one or two large payments a year.
Escrow Waiver Fee		

In the future,

Your property costs may change and, as a result, your escrow payment may change. You may be able to cancel your escrow account, but if you do, you must pay your property costs directly. If you fail to pay your property taxes, your state or local government may (1) impose fines and penalties or (2) place a tax lien on this property. If you fail to pay any of your property costs, your lender may (1) add the amounts to your loan balance, (2) add an escrow account to your loan, or (3) require you to pay for property insurance that the lender buys on your behalf, which likely would cost more and provide fewer benefits than what you could buy on your own.

Home Equity Lines of Credit

Loan Calculations

Total of Payments. Total you will have paid after you make all payments of principal, interest, mortgage insurance, and loan costs, as scheduled.	$285,803.36
Finance Charge. The dollar amount the loan will cost you.	$118,830.27
Amount Financed. The loan amount available after paying your upfront finance charge.	$162,000.00
Annual Percentage Rate (APR). Your costs over the loan term expressed as a rate. This is not your interest rate.	4.174%
Total Interest Percentage (TIP). The total amount of interest that you will pay over the loan term as a percentage of your loan amount.	69.46%

Questions? If you have questions about the loan terms or costs on this form, use the contact information below. To get more information or make a complaint, contact the Consumer Financial Protection Bureau at **www.consumerfinance.gov/mortgage-closing**

Other Disclosures

Appraisal
If the property was appraised for your loan, your lender is required to give you a copy at no additional cost at least 3 days before closing. If you have not yet received it, please contact your lender at the information listed below.

Contract Details
See your note and security instrument for information about
- what happens if you fail to make your payments,
- what is a default on the loan,
- situations in which your lender can require early repayment of the loan, and
- the rules for making payments before they are due.

Liability after Foreclosure
If your lender forecloses on this property and the foreclosure does not cover the amount of unpaid balance on this loan,

☒ state law may protect you from liability for the unpaid balance. If you refinance or take on any additional debt on this property, you may lose this protection and have to pay any debt remaining even after foreclosure. You may want to consult a lawyer for more information.

☐ state law does not protect you from liability for the unpaid balance.

Refinance
Refinancing this loan will depend on your future financial situation, the property value, and market conditions. You may not be able to refinance this loan.

Tax Deductions
If you borrow more than this property is worth, the interest on the loan amount above this property's fair market value is not deductible from your federal income taxes. You should consult a tax advisor for more information.

Contact Information

	Lender	Mortgage Broker	Real Estate Broker (B)	Real Estate Broker (S)	Settlement Agent
Name	National Direct Equity		Omega Real Estate Broker Inc.	Alpha Real Estate Broker Co.	Epsilon Title Co.
Address	100 East Narrow Street Columbus, OH 43271		789 Local Lane Sometown, ST 12345	987 Suburb Ct. Someplace, ST 12340	123 Commerce Pl. Somecity, ST 12344
NMLS ID					
ST License ID			Z765416	Z61456	Z61616
Contact	Joe Smith		Samuel Green	Joseph Cain	Sarah Arnold
Contact NMLS ID	12345				
Contact ST License ID			P16415	P51461	PT1234
Email	joesmith@ ficusbank.com		sam@omegare.biz	joe@alphare.biz	sarah@ epsilontitle.com
Phone	123-456-7890		123-555-1717	321-555-7171	987-555-4321

Confirm Receipt

By signing, you are only confirming that you have received this form. You do not have to accept this loan because you have signed or received this form.

_____ _____ _____ _____
Applicant Signature   Date   Co-Applicant Signature   Date

CLOSING DISCLOSURE   PAGE 5 OF 5 • LOAN ID # 123456789

MORTGAGOR'S STATEMENT

Loan #: <u>426100000000</u>

Note Date: <u>JULY 16, 20XX</u>

Credit limit or

Loan Amount: <u>$ 49267.00</u>

Property Address: <u>2812 NARROW LN. SIMI VALLEY, CA 93063</u>

BARRY BORROWER and BARBARA BORROWER (hereinafter referred to as **"Borrower"** whether one or more) make this statement in connection with an extension of credit to Borrower by Bank Ten, NA ("Lender") secured by a mortgage or deed of trust ("Mortgage") on certain real property located in VENTURA County ("Property") with the intent that lender rely on it in connection with the extension of credit.

1. All information provided in Borrower's application to lender for an extension of credit was true and complete when given and still is today.

2. Borrower has received the notices and the Equal Credit Opportunity Act and the Real Estate Settlement Procedures Act.

3. Borrower has been accorded the opportunity to choose the carrier and the agent of any required hazard or flood insurance subject to approval by lender, which approval has not been unreasonably withheld.

4. As of this date, Borrower's marital status as previously reported to lender has not changed.

5. Borrower is the owner of the Property described in the mortgage and there are no other persons who have an interest in the Property.

6. The Property is free and clear of all liens, taxes, encumbrances and claims of every kind, nature, and description whatsoever, except for real estate taxes not yet due and payable, easements, agreements and restrictions of record; and the liens disclosed to Lender in writing either by Borrower or by title information obtained by Lender.

7. There have been no improvements, alterations, or repairs to the Property for which the costs remain unpaid, and there are no claims for labor or material furnished for repairing or improving these, which remain unpaid except for the following:

    _____

    _____

8. There are no mechanic's, materialmen's, or laborer's liens against the Property.

9. The Property is properly zoned and its intended use complies with the uses permitted by such zoning, all plats, covenants, or matters of record pertaining to the Property.

10. There are no violations of any laws or regulations or any plats, covenants or restrictions pertaining to the Property.

11. There is no judgement or decree which has been entered in any court of this state (or of the state where the Property is located, if different) or of the United States against Borrower which remain unsatisfied.

12. There are no encroachments on the Property, and any improvements on the Property are and will be located entirely within its boundaries.

13. In connection being executed by Borrower in favor Property with the priority expected by Lender based on its review of the title.

14. Borrower holds title to the Property subject only to those mortgage(s) and encumbrances either disclosed to lender or as shown on lender's title examination.

15. This Statement is made for the purpose of inducing Lender to extend credit to Borrower in the principal sum or credit limit of $49,267.00. Borrower agrees that the truth of the statements herein contained is a condition of making the extension of credit and that but for the truth of these statements, the extension of credit would not be made.

_____   _____
BARRY BORROWER, Individually   **BARBARA BORROWER, Individually**

NAME AND SIGNATURE AFFIDAVIT

Loan Number: 4261000000   Date: AUGUST 21, 20XX

Before me, the undersigned authority, on this day personally appeared the Borrower named below, who after being duly sworn on oath stated the following:

My correct legal name is BARRY BORROWER _____ and I am the same person named in the Note, Security Instrument and/or the other loan documents I have executed in connection with the loan from

NATIONAL DIRECT EQUITY

_____ or the Property located at

_____ ROW LANE SIMI VALLEY, CA 93063

_____ s appeared in various forms, on documents reviewed or acquired by Lender in connection with the _____ f my loan application, as listed below. Each name variation refers to and identifies me and I hereby _____ am one and the same person as:

_____ RROWER _____

_____

_____

_____

[Name Variations]

I have never used any name variation to attempt to avoid any legal obligation.

I further swear and affirm that the signature below is my true and exact signature and is a representative likeness of my usual and customary signature found on other legal documents including my legal identification and the above referenced loan documents.

I understand that this Name and Signature Affidavit is given as a material inducement to cause Lender to make a loan to me, and any false statements, misrepresentations or material omissions may result in civil and criminal penalties.

_____   -Borrower
BARRY BORROWER

STATE OF _____ , COUNTY OF _____ §

SWORN TO AND SUBSCRIBED before me on the _____ day of AUGUST   , 20XX .

_____
(Seal)   Notary Public

My Commission Expires: _____

                                                                              1234567890

JNAMEAFF (04/13)

NOTES

Be sure to complete this "Name and Signature Affidavit" and sign at the bottom. Signing this form indicates understanding of the warning in the paragraph.

AGREEMENT TO PROVIDE INSURANCE

Principal $49,373.00	Loan Date 07-16-XX	Maturity 07-30-XX	Loan No 426100000000	Call/Coll	Account 426100000000	Officer	Initials

References in the shaded area are for Lender's use only and do not limit the applicability of this document to any particular loan or item.
Any item above containing "****" has been omitted due to text length limitations.

Borrower:	Barry and Barbara Borrower 2812 NARROW LN SIMI VALLEY, CA 93063	Lender:	Bank 10 NA National Direct Equity (NDE) 100 East Narrow Street Columbus, OH 43271
Trustee:	Barry Borrower and Barbara Borrower and Barbara Bower as Trustee of the Borrower Family Trust, Dated March 4, 20XX 2812 NARROW LN., Simi Valley, CA 93063		

INSURANCE REQUIREMENTS. We, BARRY BORROWER; BARBARA BORROWER; AND BARBARA BORROWER AS TRUSTEE OF THE BORROWER FAMILY TRUST, DATED MARCH 4, 20XX AND, not personally but as Trustee of that certain Trust Agreement dated March 4, 20XX and known as trust number, understand that insurance coverage is required in connection with the extending of a loan or the providing of other financial accommodations to BARRY BORROWER and BARBARA BORROWER ("Borrower") by Lender. These requirements are set forth in the security documents for the loan. The following minimum insurance coverages must be provided on the following described collateral (the "Collateral"):

Collateral. 2812 NARROW LN, SIMI VALLEY, CA 93063.
Type. Fire and extended coverage.
Amount. Full Insurable Value; however in no event greater than the value of the replacement cost of the improvements.
Basis. Replacement value.
Endorsements. Standard mortgagee's clause with stipulation that coverage will not be cancelled or diminished without a minimum of thirty (30) days prior written notice to Lender, and without disclaimer of the insurer's liability for failure to give such notice.
Comments. If your loan requires flood insurance, the maximum deductible is $ 1,000.00.
Deductibles. $1,000.00.
Latest Delivery Date: By the loan closing date.

INSURANCE COMPANY. We may obtain insurance from any insurance company we may choose that is reasonably acceptable to Lender. We understand that credit may not be denied solely because insurance was not purchased through Lender.

FLOOD INSURANCE. Flood Insurance for the Collateral securing this loan is described as follows:

Real Estate at 2812 NARROW LN, SIMI VALLEY, CA 93063.
The Collateral securing this loan is not currently located in an area identified as having special flood hazards. Therefore, no special flood hazard insurance is necessary at this time. Should the Collateral at any time be deemed to be located in an area designated by the Director of the Federal Emergency Management Agency as a special flood hazard area, we agree to obtain and maintain Federal Flood Insurance, if available, within 45 days after notice is given by Lender that the Collateral is located in a special flood hazard area, for the full unpaid balance of the loan and any prior liens on the property securing the loan, up to the maximum policy limits set under the National Flood Insurance Program, or as otherwise required by Lender, and to maintain such insurance for the term of the loan. Flood insurance may be purchased under the National Flood Insurance Program or from private insurers.

INSURANCE MAILING ADDRESS. All documents and other materials relating to insurance for this loan should be mailed, delivered or directed to the following address:

Bank Ten, N.A.
Retail Loan Servicing, KY2-1606
P.O. Box 11908
Lexington, KY 40578-1908

FAILURE TO PROVIDE INSURANCE. We agree to deliver to Lender, on the latest delivery date stated above, evidence of the required insurance as provided above, with an effective date of July 16, 2004, or earlier. We acknowledge and agree that if we fail to provide any required insurance or fail to continue such insurance in force, Lender may do so at our expense as provided in the applicable security document. The cost of any such insurance, at the option of Lender, shall be added to the indebtedness as provided in the security document, WE ACKNOWLEDGE THAT IF LENDER SO PURCHASES ANY SUCH INSURANCE, THE INSURANCE WILL PROVIDE LIMITED PROTECTION AGAINST PHYSICAL DAMAGE TO THE COLLATERAL, UP TO AN AMOUNT EQUAL TO THE LESSER OF (1) THE UNPAID BALANCE OF THE DEBT, EXCLUDING ANY UNEARNED FINANCE CHARGES, OR (2) THE VALUE OF THE COLLATERAL; HOWEVER, OUR EQUITY IN THE COLLATERAL MAY NOT BE INSURED. IN ADDITION, THE INSURANCE MAY NOT PROVIDE ANY PUBLIC LIABILITY OR PROPERTY DAMAGE INDEMNIFICATION AND MAY NOT MEET THE REQUIREMENTS OF ANY FINANCIAL RESPONSIBILITY LAWS.

AUTHORIZATION. For purposes of insurance coverage on the Collateral, we authorize Lender to provide to any person (including any insurance agent or company) all information Lender deems appropriate, whether regarding the Collateral, the loan or other financial accommodations, or both.

GRANTOR ACKNOWLEDGES HAVING READ ALL THE PROVISIONS OF THIS AGREEMENT TO PROVIDE INSURANCE AND AGREES TO ITS TERMS. THIS AGREEMENT IS DATED JULY 16, 20XX.

GRANTOR: THE BORROWER FAMILY TRUST DATED MARCH 4, 20XX

By: _____
   BARRY BORROWER

By: _____
   BARBARA BORROWER

_____
BARRY BORROWER AS TRUSTEE OF THE
BORROWER FAMILY TRUST, DATED MARCH 4, 20XX
AND, Individually

_____
BARBARA BORROWER AS TRUSTEE OF THE
BORROWER FAMILY TRUST, DATED MARCH 4, 20XX
AND, Individually

FOR LENDER USE ONLY
INSURANCE VERIFICATION

PHONE (800) 924-6141

DATE:
AGENT'S NAME: AAAA AUTOMOTIVE CLUB
AGENCY: COUNTERINSURANCE EXCHANGE
ADDRESS: PO BOX 25001, SANTA ANA, CA 92799
INSURANCE COMPANY: INTERINSURANCE EXCHANGE
POLICY NUMBER: CHO001686188
EFFECTIVE DATES: _____

COMMENTS: _____
_____

Sample Set 2

STATE OF _____

COUNTY OF _____

AFFIDAVIT OF PAYMENT OF TAXES

DATE: _____   COMMITMENT OR POLICY NO. _____

The undersigned being first being duly sworn, deposes and says:

That we, being the owners of record described in the above numbered Title Commitment or Policy, hereby certify that the current and subsequent years Real Estate Taxes are paid in full for the subject property.

Further, we are hereby declaring the above as true and accurate to induce Entrust Title to insure over said item for the policy on the above referenced file.

We hereby hold Entrust Title harmless with respect to any and all issues that may arise should it later be confirmed that any property tax or assessment payments are unpaid.

Further, the undersigned hereby agrees to immediately satisfy any unpaid taxes or assessments immediately upon notification that paid items are due and/or delinquent. The undersigned agrees to immediately reimburse Entrust Title any reasonable attorney fees incurred.

This affidavit if given to _____
For verification of lien related issues.

Signature: _____   Date: _____

Signature: _____   Date: _____

Subscribed and sworn to me this _____ day of _____, 20____.

_____

(NOTARY SEAL)   Notary Public

MORTGAGOR'S AFFIDAVIT FOR MASTER HOME EQUITY LOAN POLICY AND CERTIFICATE PROGRAM

Mortgagor(s)/Trustor(s)/Borrower(s): _____

_____

Property Address: _____

_____

_____

Lender: _____

Loan Number: _____

Loan Amount: _____

Disbursement Date: _____

I (we) do solemnly swear that:

1. I (we) are the exclusive fee simple owner(s) of the property above described (the "Property") and that no one has questioned our ownership or right to possession.

2. I (we) confirm that all bills for real estate taxes, special assessments for municipal improvements such as sewers, sidewalks, curbs or similar improvements benefiting the property, and water, sewer, and other municipal fees are current and paid to date and are not yet due and payable.

3. I (we) confirm that there are no mortgage(s) liens, judgements, or other encumbrances on the property except for the following:

_____

_____

No other mortgage, lien, or encumbrance upon the property has been given, contracted for or agreed to be given or executed by the Mortgagor(s)/Trustor(s)/Borrower(s) to any other person.

4. All labor and material used in the construction of improvements on the above described property have been paid for and there are now no unpaid labor or material claims against the improvements of the property and that all sums of money due for the erection of improvements have been fully paid and satisfied. We are not aware that anyone has filed or intends to file a mechanic's lien relating to this property.

5. I (we) have not applied for protection under Bankruptcy statutes or any state's creditor's rights law.

6. I (we) have not violated any covenants, conditions, restrictions, or laws of any nature relating to environmental protection and that there is no notice of any investigation, claim, demand, lawsuit or other action by any governmental or regulatory agency or private party involving the above-described property with regards to any Hazardous substance or Environmental law.

7. There has been no presence, use, disposal, storage or release of any Hazardous substance(s) on the above-described property.

8. I (we) agree to subrogate and assign any rights or payments which I (we) may have or receive under any insurance policy which compensates me (us) for a loss and such loss ~~~~~~ a loss to the Lender.

~~~~ acknowledge(s) (1) that this Mortgagor's Affidavit is executed under oath for ~~~ of inducing the Lender named above to make the Entrust Title Insurance ~~~ provide insurance thereon, (2) that the Lender will rely upon this Mortgagor's ~~aking the Entrust Title Insurance Company will rely on this Mortgagor's ~~suing insurance thereon, (3) the information set out above is correct and ~~ (4) that I (we) understand that I (we) can be criminally liable for falsely so

Mortgagor(s)/Trustor(s)/Borrower(s):

Signature: _____   Date: _____

Printed Name: _____

Signature: _____   Date: _____

Printed Name: _____

Sworn to, by the above named Mortgagor(s)/Trustor(s)/Borrower(s), on this _____ day

of _____, 20_____ before me a Notary Public for the County of

_____ and State of _____.

_____

My Commission Expires: _____   (NOTARY SEAL)

EQUITY LINE ACCOUNT DISCLOSURE AND AGREEMENT

Account No.: **4212121212**

Borrower(s): **AMANDA T GEORGE**

Property Address: **8941 SMITH ST, LOS ANGELES, CA 90034 (the "Property")**

Credit Limit:	**$118,500.00**
Index:	**4.750%**
Initial Margin (if applicable)	**-2.01%**
Initial Daily Periodic Rate (if applicable)	**0.007507%**
Initial ANNUAL PERCENTAGE RATE (if applicable)	**2.740%**
(The Initial Annual Percentage Rate will vary as the Index varies)	(Index +- the Initial Margin)
Date the Initial Margin Ends and Regular Margin Begins (if applicable)	**11/8/2002**
Regular Margin:	**0.250%**
Regular Daily Periodic Rate:	**0.013699%**
Regular ANNUAL PERCENTAGE RATE:	**5.00%**
(The Regular Annual Percentage Rate will vary as the Index varies)	(Index +- the Regular Margin)
Annual Fee:	$0.00

Closing Costs, Paid by ANYBANK*

Appraisal Fee:	**$310.00**	**Recording Fee:**	**$59.00**
Credit Report Fee:	**$4.00**	**City/County Tax/Stamps**	**$0.00**
Flood Certification Fee (Finance Charge):	**$20.00**	**State Tax/Stamps**	**$0.00**
Settlement or Closing Fee (Finance Charge):	**$200.00**	**Intangible Tax:**	**$0.00**
Abstract or Title Search Fee:	**$25.00**	**Document Stamp Tax:**	**$0.00**
Title Examination Fee:	**$90.00**	**Mortgage Registration Fee:**	**$0.00**
Title Insurance Binder:	**$0.00**	**Tax Certification Fee:**	**$0.00**
Document Preparation:	**$0.00**	**Mortgage Taxes:** Borrower's Portion	**$0.00**
Overnight Postage Fee (Finance Charge):	**$32.50**	Lender's Portion	**$0.00**
Total Closing Costs:	**$740.00**		

*These charges are paid outside of the closing by Lender. However, if your loan is terminated within the first 36 months, with the exception of the Lender's Portion of the Mortgage Taxes and the Document Preparation Fee, you will be required to repay us all of these closing costs incurred on your behalf.

The undersigned Borrower(s), jointly and severally if more than one, agree to all of the terms and conditions of this Equity Source Account Agreement and Disclosure, which consists of 11 pages, and acknowledge receipt of a completed copy, along with the notice about Your Billing Rights. The date of this Agreement is the latest date next to a Borrower's signature.

_____
Borrower: AMANDA T GEORGE

_____
Borrower:

_____
Borrower:

_____
Borrower:

NOTES

The "Equity Line Account Disclosure and Agreement" functions as the promissory note in this HELOC package.

EQUITY LINE ACCOUNT DISCLOSURE AND AGREEMENT

DEFINITIONS: As used herein:

- "Account" means the Equity Source Account opened under the Agreement.
- "Agreement" means this Equity Source Account Agreement and Disclosure together with any modifications, amendments, replacements or substitutions thereto.
- "ANYBANK" means ANYBANK, F.S.B. also known as ANYBANK, Federal Savings Bank.
- "Credit Limit" means the maximum aggregate amount of the Loan Advances that may be outstanding at any given time pursuant to the Agreement.
- "Draw Period" means the ten years and 25 days from the date of the Agreement during which Loan Advances may be made.
- "Index" means the Prime Rate as published in the Money Rates section of The Wall Street Journal from time to time.
- "Initial Pricing" means that your Agreement has an Initial Margin, Initial Daily Periodic Rate, and an Initial Annual Percentage Rate. .
- "Loan Advances" means amounts drawn on your Account pursuant to the Agreement by Equity Source Account checks, or in any other way ANYBANK allows, and advances by ANYBANK pursuant to the Agreement or Mortgage to protect the Property or ANYBANK's security interest in the Property, including but not limited to advances to maintain required insurance on the Property or to pay taxes on the Property.
- "Mortgage" means the mortgage, deed of trust, deed to secure debt or cooperative security agreement which covers the Property which secures the Agreement.
- "Property" means the property described in the Mortgage which secures the Agreement.
- "Repayment Period" means the twenty years immediately following the Draw Period during which Loan Advances may not be made.
- "You," "Your" and "Yours," whether or not the first letter of the word is capitalized, means each person who signs below as Borrower, jointly and severally.

Certain other terms are defined elsewhere in this Agreement.

PROMISE TO PAY: You promise to pay to ANYBANK the total of all Closing Costs (if indicated above that Closing Costs are paid by Borrower), all Loan Advances, together with **FINANCE CHARGES** at the applicable daily periodic rate, and any other fees, charges or other **FINANCE CHARGES,** all as provided for in the Agreement.

HOW FINANCE CHARGES DUE TO DAILY PERIODIC RATE ARE IMPOSED AND DETERMINED:

- **FINANCE CHARGES** on Loan Advances at the applicable Daily Periodic Rate begin to accrue on the date the Loan Advance is posted to your Account. There is no grace period for repayment of your balance during which **FINANCE CHARGES** will not accrue. If there are any other **FINANCE CHARGES** payable under the Agreement, they will be dollar amounts itemized herein as **FINANCE CHARGES.**
- The appropriate Margin is added to the Index to deteml1ine the **ANNUAL PERCENTAGE RATE,** which will be divided by 365 (366 in leap years) to determine the Daily Periodic Rate which will be applied to the balance on which the **FINANCE CHARGE** will be computed during your monthly billing cycle.
- The Index used for a billing cycle will be the most recent Index rate published on or before the first day of the month in which the billing cycle begins.

EQUITY LINE ACCOUNT DISCLOSURE AND AGREEMENT

- If your Account has Initial Pricing:
  - The Initial Margin shown above will be in effect from the date of the Agreement until the Date the Initial Margin Ends and Regular Margin Begins shown above.
  - The Initial **ANNUAL PERCENTAGE RATE** will be in effect from the date of the Agreement and can change on the first day of your next monthly billing cycle. Thereafter the **ANNUAL PERCENT AGE RATE** can change on the first day of each following monthly billing cycle.
  - On the Date the Initial Margin Ends and Regular Margin Begins shown above, the Regular Margin shown above will go into effect. If the Index has not changed so as to affect the rate, the Regular **ANNUAL PERCENT AGE RATE** and Regular Daily Periodic Rate shown above will then be in effect.

- If your Account does not have Initial Pricing:
  - The Regular Margin shown above will be in effect from the date of the Agreement.
  - The Regular **ANNUAL PERCENTAGE RATE** will be in effect from the date of the Agreement and can change on the first day of each following monthly billing cycle.

- The **ANNUAL PERCENTAGE RATE** does not include costs other than interest. Any increase in the **ANNUAL PERCENTAGE RATE** will result in an increase in the minimum monthly payment. The **ANNUAL PERCENTAGE RATE** will not exceed 18%, no matter how much the Index increases. In the event you have authorized ANYBANK to pay your Equity Source Account bill automatically from your checking or other authorized account and you elect to discontinue the automatic payment of your bill, your **ANNUAL PERCENTAGE RATE** shall increase by ¼ of 1 %.

- You will be sent statements on a monthly cycle which will reflect your Account activity and any amounts you owe ANYBANK.

- The amount of the **FINANCE CHARGE** in your statements will be calculated by multiplying the daily periodic rate for the day by the daily balance for your Account at the end of each day in the monthly billing cycle. To determine the daily balance we take the beginning balance of your Account each day, add any new Loan Advances and other charges, and subtract any payments and credits. Late Charges, credit life insurance, if any, and unpaid **FINANCE CHARGES** will not be counted as part of the daily balance for purposes of calculating the **FINANCE CHARGE**.

FINANCE CHARGES NOT DUE TO DAILY PERIODIC RATE; CLOSING COSTS:

- If you retained a mortgage broker, the amount of the mortgage broker fee, if any, is a **FINANCE CHARGE.** The mortgage broker fee is determined by your agreement with your mortgage broker and is not required by ANYBANK or paid by ANYBANK.

- If you agreed to pay the Closing Costs for your Account, your Closing Costs include **FINANCE CHARGES** in the amounts shown on page one of this Agreement for the cost of flood and tax certifications, overnight courier fees, and the cost charged by ANYBANK's attorneys or closing agents to conduct the closing for your Account.

OTHER CHARGES: These are charges other than **FINANCE CHARGES.** These charges are not counted as part of your daily unpaid balance of Loan Advances for purposes of computing **FINANCE CHARGES:**

- There is no annual fee associated with your Account.

- If ANYBANK does not receive the full amount of any monthly payment due within 15 calendar days of the due date, you will be charged a late charge of the greater of 6% of the overdue payment or $5. However, you will not be charged a late charge on an unpaid late charge.

- If there is a Loan Advance which causes your Credit Limit to be exceeded, ANYBANK will charge you a $10 overlimit fee. . This charge will not be imposed on more than tour transactions a day. If your payment is returned unpaid for any reason, ANYBANK will charge you a $25 returned item fee.

EQUITY LINE ACCOUNT DISCLOSURE AND AGREEMENT

- If you request ANYBANK to stop payment on one of your Equity Source Account Checks, ANYBANK will charge you an $8 stop payment charge per request.

- If ANYBANK pays the Closing Costs to open your Account and, within 36 months of the date of this Agreement, you request that your Account be closed or take any other action which will result in a release of the Mortgage, you agree to pay an early closure release fee which will consist of all costs ANYBANK incurred to open your Account. These costs are disclosed as Closing Costs on the first page of this Agreement. The amount of this fee will be automatically charged to your Account in the same manner as a Loan Advance.

- If, for any purpose other than a billing error inquiry or a tax audit inquiry, you request ANYBANK to provide copies of Account documents, ANYBANK may charge you $2 per copy and a $20 per hour document research fee.

- Any charges imposed by ANYBANK, if any, in connection with your Account are disclosed above at the beginning of the Agreement.

- You agree to pay any other fees or charges provided for in the Mortgage or otherwise provided for in the Agreement.

- You agree to carry insurance on the Property which secures your Account. You may have to pay a fee to release a prior lien or security interest in the Property.

- You agree to pay any reasonable costs incurred by ANYBANK in connection with the enforcement of its rights and remedies under the Agreement and the Mortgage, including, but not limited to, any reasonable attorneys' fees and other collection costs.

SECURITY INTEREST IN PROPERTY: As security for the Agreement, you are giving ANYBANK a security interest in the Property located at the address shown above, which security interest secures all of your obligations under this Agreement and the Mortgage. This Property is more fully described in the Mortgage you will sign along with this Agreement. Collateral which secures other obligations to ANYBANK may also secure the Agreement.

PAYMENT TERMS: You agree to pay your monthly payments by the due date shown on your monthly statement. During the Draw Period, you agree to pay a minimum monthly payment, which will be shown on your monthly statement, and which will equal the sum of any past due or over Credit Limit amounts plus accrued and unpaid **FINANCE CHARGES** and other unpaid fees or charges imposed pursuant to the Agreement. Your paying this minimum monthly payment will not reduce the principal balance of Loan Advances which you owe ANYBANK, except to the extent over Credit Limit amounts are paid. During the Repayment Period, you agree to pay a monthly payment, which will be shown on your monthly statement, and which will equal the **FINANCE CHARGES** that have accrued on the outstanding balance for the billing period, plus principal equal to the greater of $50 or 1/240th of your principal balance of Loan Advances as of the end of the Draw Period, plus the sum of the following amounts when applicable: past due amounts on your Account, amount owing in excess of your Credit Limit, late charges and other charges imposed pursuant to the Agreement. On the last payment due date of the Repayment Period, any remaining unpaid amounts owed ANYBANK will be due and payable. You may prepay your Account in whole or in part at any time without penalty, but if you request that your Account be closed or take any other action which will result in a release of the Mortgage, you may owe an early closure release fee as provided for in the **OTHER CHARGES** section. Loan Advances may not be drawn to make payments on the Account, nor may payments be drawn on business accounts. ANYBANK may accept late payments or partial payments, even though marked "payment in full," without losing any of ANYBANK's rights under the Agreement.

TRANSACTION REQUIREMENTS: You may draw Loan Advances during the Draw Period up to your Credit Limit if your Account has not been closed or suspended or your Credit Limit reduced to where further Loan Advances would not be permitted.

TERMINATION OF ACCOUNT BY ANYBANK: balance in full in a single payment, if:

- You fail to meet the repayment terms of the Agreement for any outstanding balance.

- There has been fraud or a material misrepresentation by you in connection with the Account.

EQUITY LINE ACCOUNT DISCLOSURE AND AGREEMENT

- You take any action or fail to take any action which adversely affects the Property or ANYBANK's security interest in the Property, including but not limited to: a transfer of title to the Property or sale of the Property without ANYBANK's written permission; a failure to maintain any required insurance on the Property; failure to pay taxes on the Property; you permit the filing of a lien senior to that held by ANYBANK; the sole Borrower obligated on the Account dies; the Property is taken through eminent domain; a prior lien-holder forecloses; you commit waste or otherwise destructively use or fail to maintain the Property in a way that adversely affects the Property; there is illegal use of the Property which could subject the Property to seizure; one of two Co-Borrowers dies and ANYBANK's security is thereby adversely affected; or you move out of the Property and ANYBANK's security is thereby adversely affected.

- You are or become an "executive officer" of ANYBANK as defined in Federal Reserve Board Regulation 0 and ANYBANK determines to require payment in full to comply with federal regulation.

In addition to the foregoing, ANYBANK shall have the right to exercise any and all of it rights and remedies allowed by law or as set forth in this Agreement or in the Mortgage, including, but not limited to, the right to bring an action against you and the right to bring a foreclosure action against the Property.

SUSPENSION OF ACCOUNT OR REDUCTION OF CREDIT LIMIT BY ANYBANK: ANYBANK may prohibit additional extensions of credit or reduce your Credit Limit during any period in which:

- You or any of you request a suspension of the Account or reduction of the Credit Limit.

- The maximum **ANNUAL PERCENTAGE RATE** is reached.

- The value of the Property declines significantly below the Property's appraised value for purposes of the Account. As an example, if the value of the Property declines such that the initial difference between the Credit Limit and the available equity (based on the Property's appraised value) is reduced by fifty percent, such an event would constitute a significant decline in the value of the Property.

- ANYBANK reasonably believes that you will be unable to fulfill the repayment obligations under the Agreement because of a material change in your financial circumstances.

- You are in default of any material obligation under the Agreement or Mortgage.

- ANYBANK is precluded by government action from imposing the **ANNUAL PERCENT AGE RATE** provided for in the Agreement.

- The priority of ANYBANK's security interest is adversely affected by government action to the extent that the value of the security interest is less than 120% of the Credit limit.

- ANYBANK is notified by its regulatory agency that continued advances constitute an unsafe and unsound practice.

If any of the above circumstances change during the Draw Period and you want to reopen your Account or increase your Credit Limit to the original Credit Limit, you must make such a request to ANYBANK in writing and pay any bona fide and reasonable appraisal and credit report fees actually incurred by ANYBANK to investigate whether the above circumstances continue to exist. If ANYBANK suspended your Account or reduced your Credit Limit as a result of your request, the request for reinstatement must be signed by all of you.

You agree that you will not attempt to obtain any additional credit extensions once you know that your credit privileges have been terminated or suspended. As required by law, you are hereby notified that a negative credit report reflecting on your credit record may be submitted to a credit reporting agency if you fail to fulfill the terms of your credit obligations under the Agreement.

EQUITY LINE ACCOUNT DISCLOSURE AND AGREEMENT

OTHER CHANGES TO THE ACCOUNT: ANYBANK may change the Index and Margin used under the Agreement if the original Index is no longer available, the new index has an historical movement substantially similar to that of the original Index, and the new index and margin would have resulted in an **ANNUAL PERCENTAGE RATE** substantially similar to the rate in effect at the time the original Index became unavailable. ANYBANK may make a specified change to the Account if you specifically agree to the change in writing at that time. ANYBANK may make changes to the Account that will unequivocally benefit you throughout the remainder of the Account. ANYBANK may make insignificant changes in the terms of the Account, including but not limited to: changing the address to which payments are sent; minor changes to features such as the billing cycle date, the payment due date and the day of the month on which Index values are measured; changes in rounding practices within the tolerance rules allowed by applicable regulation; and changes to balance computation methods if the change produces an insignificant difference in the **FINANCE CHARGE** you pay.

PROMOTIONAL RATE OFFERS: At ANYBANK's discretion, ANYBANK may offer you a promotional rate (a promotional daily periodic rate and/or promotional margin). The period of time for which the promotional rate applies may be limited. ANYBANK will allocate your payments and credits to pay off balances at low promotional rates before paying off balances at higher periodic rates. Any promotional rate, the corresponding periodic rate, and the period of time during which it is in effect will be disclosed to you. Any promotional rate offer will be subject to the terms of the offer and this Agreement.

TAX IMPLICATIONS: You should consult a tax advisor regarding the deductibility of interest (**FINANCE CHARGES**) and other charges under the Agreement.

DELAY IN ENFORCEMENT: ANYBANK may delay the exercise of ANYBANK's rights under the Agreement or Mortgage without losing them.

PROPERTY INSURANCE: You agree to maintain insurance on the Property as provided for in the Mortgage.

CREDIT INFORMATION: You understand and agree that ANYBANK may obtain credit reports for credit applications and for updates, renewals or extensions of the credit granted. Upon request, ANYBANK will inform you if a report has been obtained and will give you the name and address of the agency that furnished the report. You also agree that ANYBANK may obtain and use credit reports and other information that ANYBANK has obtained in a lawful manner consistent with ANYBANK's privacy policies about you for subsequent solicitations or for any other lawful purpose.

FURTHER ASSURANCES: You agree that, upon ANYBANK's request, you will promptly execute, acknowledge, initial and deliver to ANYBANK any documentation ANYBANK deems necessary to replace or correct any lost, misplaced, misstated or inaccurate document signed by you at closing.

RESOLUTION OF DISPUTES BY ARBITRATION: THIS SECTION CONTAINS IMPORTANT INFORMATION ABOUT YOUR ACCOUNT. IT PROVIDES THAT EITHER YOU OR ANYBANK CAN REQUIRE THAT ANY DISPUTES BE RESOLVED BY BINDING ARBITRATION. ARBITRATION REPLACES THE RIGHT TO GO TO COURT, INCLUDING THE RIGHT TO PARTICIPATE IN A CLASS ACTION OR SIMILAR PROCEEDING. IN ARBITRATION, THE DISPUTE IS SUBMITTED TO A NEUTRAL PARTY, AN ARBITRATOR, INSTEAD OF A JUDGE OR JURY. ARBITRATION PROCEDURES ARE SIMPLER AND MORE LIMITED THAN RULES APPLICABLE IN COURT. THE DECISION OF THE ARBITRATOR IS FINAL AND BINDING.

- Agreement to Arbitrate Disputes. You agree that by opening your Account with ANYBANK, either you or ANYBANK may elect to require that any dispute between you and ANYBANK be resolved by binding arbitration.

- Disputes Covered by Arbitration. Disputes covered by arbitration include any claim relating to or arising out of your Account and any services relating to that relationship. Disputes include not only claims made directly by you, but also made by anyone connected with you or claiming through you, such as joint account holder, account beneficiary, or a representative or agent. Disputes include not only claims that relate directly to ANYBANK, but also its parent, affiliates, successors, assignees, employees, and agents, and claims for which ANYBANK may be directly or indirectly liable, even if ANYBANK is not properly named at the time the claim is made. Disputes include claims based on any theory of law, contract, statute, regulation, tort (including fraud or any intentional tort), or any other legal or equitable ground, and include claims asserted as counterclaims, cross-claims, third-party claims, interpleaders or otherwise. Disputes include claims made as part of a class action or other representative action, it being expressly understood and agreed to that the arbitration of such claims must proceed on an individual (non-class, non-representative) basis. Disputes also include claims relating to the enforceability or interpretation of any of these arbitration provisions.

EQUITY LINE ACCOUNT DISCLOSURE AND AGREEMENT

- <u>Disputes Excluded from Arbitration</u>. Disputes filed by you or by ANYBANK individually in a small claims court are not subject to arbitration, so long as the disputes remain in such court and advance only an individual claim for relief. In addition, disputes to effect a foreclosure to transfer title to the property being foreclosed are not subject to arbitration.

- <u>Commencing an Arbitration</u>. The arbitration must be filed with one of the following neutral arbitration forums: American Arbitration Association; National Arbitration Forum; or JAMS. If you initiate the arbitration, you must notify us in writing at ANYBANK, Ten Drive Road, 41rd Floor, Anycity, NY 11120. If ANYBANK initiates the arbitration, ANYBANK will notify you in writing at your last known address on file. You may obtain a copy of the arbitration rules for these forums, as well as additional information about initiating an arbitration, by contacting these arbitration forums at the following addresses:

American Arbitration Association:	355 Madison Avenue -- 10th Floor New York, NY 10017-4605 www.adr.org
National Arbitration Forum:	P.O. Box 50191 Minneapolis, MN 55405 www.arbitration-forum.com
JAMS:	1920 Main Street Suite 300 Irvine, CA 92610 www.jamsadr.com

The arbitration shall be conducted in the same city as the U.S. District Court closest to your home address, unless the parties agree to a different location.

- <u>Administration of Arbitration</u>. The arbitration shall be decided by a single arbitrator, unless either party to the arbitration requests a panel of three arbitrators in which case the arbitration shall be conducted by a panel of three arbitrators (said arbitrator or arbitrators hereinafter referred to as "the arbitrator"). The arbitrator shall decide the dispute in accordance with applicable substantive law consistent with the Federal Arbitration Act. The arbitrator shall be empowered to award any damages or other relief provided for under applicable law and will not have the power to award relief to, or against, any person who is not a party to the arbitration. The decision rendered by the arbitrator shall be in writing; however, the arbitrator need not provide a statement of his reasons unless one is requested by you or ANYBANK. The award of the arbitrator shall be final and binding, subject to judicial intervention or review only to the extent allowed under the Federal Arbitration Act. The award of the arbitrator can be entered as a judgment in any court having jurisdiction.

- <u>Costs</u>. The party initiating the arbitration shall pay the initial filing fee. If you file the arbitration and an award is rendered in your favor, ANYBANK will reimburse you for your filing fee. If there is a hearing, ANYBANK will pay the fees and costs for the first day of that hearing. If either you or ANYBANK request a panel of three arbitrators, the party making the request shall pay the fees of those additional arbitrators unless the arbitrator rules otherwise. All other fees and costs will be allocated in accordance with the rules of the arbitration forum. However, ANYBANK will advance or reimburse filing and other fees if the arbitrator rules that you cannot afford to pay them or finds other good cause for requiring ANYBANK to do so. Each party shall bear the expense of their respective attorneys, experts, and witnesses and other expenses, regardless of who prevails, except to the extent the arbitrator assesses costs of the arbitration to either you or ANYBANK.

- <u>No Class Action or Joinder of Parties</u>. You and ANYBANK agree that no class action, private attorney general or other representative claims may be pursued in arbitration, nor may such action be pursued in court if either you or ANYBANK elect arbitration. Unless mutually agreed to by you and ANYBANK, claims of two or more persons may not be joined, consolidated, or otherwise brought together in the same arbitration (unless those persons are joint account holders or beneficiaries on your Account, or parties to a single transaction or related transaction); this is so whether or not the claim may have been assigned.

EQUITY LINE ACCOUNT DISCLOSURE AND AGREEMENT

- <u>Right to Resort to Provisional Remedies Preserved</u>. Nothing herein shall be deemed to limit or constrain ANYBANK's right to resort to self-help remedies, such as the right of set-off or the right to restrain funds in an account, to interplead funds in the event of a dispute, to exercise any security interest or lien we may hold in property, or to comply with legal process, or to obtain provisional remedies such as injunctive relief, attachment, or garnishment by a court having appropriate jurisdiction.

- <u>Governing Law</u>. You and ANYBANK agree that our relationship includes transactions involving interstate commerce and that these arbitration provisions are governed by, and enforceable under, the Federal Arbitration Act. To the extent state law is applicable, the laws of the state governing this Agreement apply.

- <u>Severability, Survival</u>. These arbitration provisions shall survive (i) termination or changes to your Account, or any related services we provide; (ii) the bankruptcy of any party; and (iii) the transfer or assignment of your Account, or any related services we provide. If one or more of these arbitration provisions are deemed invalid or unenforceable, the remaining portions shall nevertheless remain valid and enforceable.

GOVERNING LAW: The Agreement will be governed by United States federal law and, to the extent the United States federal law is inapplicable, then by the laws of the State of California; except that, with regard to the perfection and enforcement of ANYBANK's security interest in the Property, the Agreement will be governed by the law of the state where the Property is located.

DUE ON SALE: If all or any part of the Property or any interest in it is sold or transferred (or if a beneficial interest in the Property is sold or transferred) without ANYBANK's prior written consent, ANYBANK may, at its option, require immediate payment in full of the outstanding balance due and owing with respect to your Account; however, ANYBANK shall not exercise this option if the exercise is prohibited by applicable law.

CHANGE IN NAME, ADDRESS OR EMPLOYMENT: You agree to notify us in writing of any change in name, address or employment.

NO WAIVER: Neither you nor ANYBANK shall be deemed to have waived any of rights, powers or remedies hereunder unless such waiver is embodied in a writing executed by either you or ANYBANK. The waiver by either you or ANYBANK of any breach or default by the other party to the Agreement in the performance of any obligation hereunder shall not constitute a waiver of any subsequent breach or default.

NOTICES: All notices provided for in the Agreement shall be in writing and shall be deemed given (a) when delivered on a business day if delivered personally, (b) on the day after deposit with any overnight courier if such date is a business day, (c) three days after deposit in the United States mail, if delivered by certified mail, return receipt requested, postage prepaid and addressed to you at the address set forth on the first page of the Agreement or addressed to the customer service address shown on your monthly statement.

INVALIDITY CLAUSE: If any provision of the Agreement shall be otherwise unlawful, void, or for any reason unenforceable, then that provision shall be enforced to the maximum extent permissible so as to effect the intent of you and ANYBANK. In either case, the remainder of the Agreement shall continue in full force and effect.

EQUITY LINE ACCOUNT DISCLOSURE AND AGREEMENT

YOUR BILLING RIGHTS (KEEP THIS NOTICE FOR FUTURE USE)

This notice contains important information about your rights and ANYBANK's responsibilities under the Fair Credit Billing Act.

Notify ANYBANK in case of errors or questions about your bill.

If you think your bill is wrong, or if you need more information about a transaction on your bill, write to ANYBANK on a separate sheet at the address listed on your bill. Write to ANYBANK as soon as possible. ANYBANK must hear from you no later than 60 days after ANYBANK sent you the first bill on which the error or problem appeared. You can telephone ANYBANK, but doing so will not preserve your rights.

In your letter, give us the following information:

- Your name and Account number.
- The dollar amount of the suspected error.
- Describe the error and explain, if you can, why you believe there is an error. If you need more information, describe the item you are not sure about.

If you have authorized ANYBANK to pay your Equity Source Account bill automatically from your checking or other authorized account, you can stop the payment on any amount you think is wrong. To stop the payment your letter must reach ANYBANK three business days before the automatic payment is scheduled to occur.

YOUR RIGHTS AND ANYBANK'S RESPONSIBILITIES AFTER ANYBANK RECEIVES YOUR WRITTEN NOTICE

ANYBANK must acknowledge your letter within 30 days, unless ANYBANK has corrected the error by then. Within 90 days, ANYBANK must either correct the error or explain why ANYBANK believes the bill was correct.

After ANYBANK receives your letter, ANYBANK cannot try to collect any amount you question, or report you as delinquent. ANYBANK can continue to bill you for the amount you question, including finance charges, and ANYBANK can apply any unpaid amount against your credit limit. You do not have to pay any questioned amount while ANYBANK is investigating, but you are still obligated to pay the parts of your bill that are not in question.

If ANYBANK finds that ANYBANK made a mistake on your bill, you will not have to pay any finance charges related to any questioned amount. If ANYBANK did not make a mistake, you may have to pay finance charges, and you will have to make up any missed payments on the questioned amount. In either case, ANYBANK will send you a statement of the amount you owe and the date that it is due.

If you fail to pay the amount that ANYBANK thinks you owe, ANYBANK may report you as delinquent. However, if ANYBANK's explanation does not satisfy you and you write to ANYBANK within ten days telling ANYBANK that you still refuse to pay, ANYBANK must tell anyone ANYBANK reports you to that you have a question about your bill. And, ANYBANK must tell you the name of anyone ANYBANK reported you to. ANYBANK must tell anyone ANYBANK reports you to that the matter has been settled between you and ANYBANK when it finally is.

If ANYBANK does not follow these rules, ANYBANK cannot collect the first $50 of the questioned amount, even if your bill was correct.

EQUITY LINE ACCOUNT DISCLOSURE AND AGREEMENT

ANYBANK AUTOMATIC ACCOUNT DEDUCT AUTHORIZATION

As an option and not a condition to the Agreement, ANYBANK has offered you the convenience of making payments using pre- authorized payments from a checking or savings account as described. In consideration of your voluntary election to make these automatic payments, ANYBANK agrees to reduce the Regular Margin by 1/4 of 1%. A price discount will only be included if ANYBANK Auto Deduct is from a ANYBANK Account.

This reduction will remain in effect so long as you are enrolled for the auto-deduct service and comply with all terms and conditions of the Agreement. If your enrollment is terminated for any reason, or if you fail to comply with any terms or conditions of the Agreement, your Regular Margin will revert to the non-discounted rate that is provided in the Agreement.

By signing below, you authorize ANYBANK to charge your account below to pay the minimum payments due to ANYBANK under the above Equity Line Account Disclosure and Agreement.

Name: _____

Address: _____

_____

_____

Account Type: [ ] Checking   [ ] Money Market
[ ] Savings
Account Number:
Routing Number:

_____   _____
Authorized Signature   Date   Authorized Signature   Date

ANYBANK Auto Deduct payment can only be made from a ANYBANK Checking, Savings or Insured Money Market Account. I authorize ANYBANK, N.A., ANYBANK, F.S.B., ANYBANK (New York State), or ANYBANK (Nevada), N.A., to initiate withdrawals from my ANYBANK account for payment of my ANYBANK loan listed below. The amount of the payment withdrawn will be the minimum payment due, as specified on my loan statement. If there are insufficient funds in the account, I understand that ANYBANK may debit my account when sufficient funds are available.

Loan Account Number: 428931212

EQUITY LINE ACCOUNT DISCLOSURE AND AGREEMENT

ANYBANK Automatic Account Deduct Terms and Conditions

Your payment will be made automatically on your current due date from your designated ANYBANK account. If your due date falls on a weekend or holiday, your payment will be deducted on the last business day before your due date. If there are insufficient funds in the account, we may debit your account for the payment when sufficient funds are available. Your payment will be made automatically at the minimum payment due amount, as indicated on your loan statement.

Payments will be listed on your ANYBANK Checking, Savings, or Money Market Account statement, to help with record keeping. Even after signing up for ANYBANK Auto Deduct, continue to make payments with your statement until ANYBANK Auto Deduct is in place for your account, and until you see the deduction on your Checking, Savings or Money Market Account statement.

ANYBANK reserves the right to cancel the terms of this Agreement if there are insufficient funds in your ANYBANK account for any three consecutive scheduled debits or if any payment is 60 days in arrears. ANYBANK also reserves the right to change the terms and conditions of this Agreement after 21 days prior notice to you.

PLEASE ATTACH VOIDED CHECK HERE

In addition to this form, please ATTACH a copy of a voided check or pre-printed deposit or withdrawal slip showing the account number from which funds are to be debited.

When Recorded mail to:
ANYBANK Document Administration
10000 Duquense Drive
Anytown, MO 63011

THIS INSTRUMENT WAS PREPARED BY:
MARGIE DOMINIA

ANYBANK, F.S.B.
15851 Duquense Road
Anytown, MO 63011

ACCOUNT NO.: 4212121212

Equity Line Account DEED OF TRUST

In this Deed, "You", "Your" and "Yours" means, AMANDA T GEORGE, A MARRIED WOMAN AS HER SOLE AND SEPARATE PROPERTY, each person signing as trustor. "We," "Us" and "Our" means ANYBANK, FEDERAL SAVINGS BANK ("beneficiary"), One Handsome St., San Francisco, CA 94104. The "Trustee" means ANYBANK Service Corporation, One Handsome St., San Francisco, CA 94104 or any successor appointed pursuant to Paragraph 26 of this Deed of Trust. The "Borrower" means AMANDA T GEORGE.

The "Agreement" means the Equity Line Account Agreement and Disclosure of even date herewith signed by the Borrower in connection with this Deed of Trust. The "Property" means the real estate, including the leasehold (if any), located at 8941 SMITH ST. LOS ANGELES. CA 90034 and having the legal description attached to and made a part of this Deed of Trust.

THIS MORTGAGE between You, Trustee and Us is made as of the date next to Your first signature below and has a final maturity date 30 years from such date. The Agreement provides that the credit secured by the Property is an open-end revolving line of credit at a variable rate of interest. The maximum amount of all loan advances made to the Borrower under the Agreement and which may be secured by this Deed of Trust may not exceed $118.500.00 (the "Credit Limit"). At any particular time, the outstanding obligation of Borrower to Us under the Agreement may be any sum equal to or less than the Credit Limit plus interest and other charges owing under the Agreement and amounts owing under this Deed of Trust. Obligations under the Agreement, Deed of Trust and any riders thereto shall not be released even if all indebtedness under the Agreement is paid, unless and until We cause a reconveyance of the Property to be executed to You and such reconveyance is properly recorded.

TO SECURE to Us: (a) the payment and performance of all indebtedness and obligations of the Borrower under the Agreement or any modification or replacement of the Agreement; (b) the payment of all other sums advanced in accordance herewith to protect the security of this Deed of Trust, with finance charges thereon at the variable rate described in the Agreement; and (c) the payment of any future advances made by Us to Borrower (pursuant to Paragraph 16 of this Deed of Trust (herein "Future Loan Advances")) and, in consideration of the indebtedness herein recited and the trust herein created, You hereby irrevocably grant and covey to Trustee, in trust, with, if allowed by applicable law, power of sale, the Property.

TOGETHER WITH all the improvements now or hereafter erected on the Property, and all easements, rights, appurtenances, rents (subject however to the rights and authorities given herein to You to collect and apply such rents), royalties, mineral, oil and gas rights and profits, water, water rights and water stock, and all fixtures now or hereafter attached to the Property (which, if this Deed of Trust is on a unit in a condominium project or planned unit development, shall include the common elements in such project or development associated with such unit), all of which, including replacements and additions thereto, shall be deemed to be and remain a part of the Property.

IN WITNESS WHEREOF, YOU HAVE EXECUTED THIS DEED OF TRUST, AND AGREE TO BE BOUND BY ALL TERMS AND CONDITIONS STATED ON PAGES 2 THROUGH 6 FOLLOWING.

Trustor **AMANDA T GEORGE**

[ ] Married   [ ] Unmarried

Trustor

[ ] Married   [ ] Unmarried

Trustor

[ ] Married   [ ] Unmarried

Trustor

[ ] Married   [ ]

Trustor

[ ] Married   [ ]

Trustor

[ ] Married   [ ]

STATE OF
COUNTY OF LOS ANGELES

On **7/08/20XX** before me, _____, personally appeared _____ personally known to me (or proved to me on the basis of satisfactory evidence) to be the same person(s) whose name(s) is/are subscribed to the within instrument and acknowledged to me that he/she/they executed the same in his/her/their authorized capacity(ies), and that by his/her/their signature(s) on the instrument the person(s), or the entity upon behalf of which the person(s) acted, executed the instrument.

WITNESS my hand and official seal.

_____
(Signature of Person Taking Acknowledgment)

_____
(Signature of Person Taking Acknowledgment Typed, Printed or Stamped)

You covenant that You are lawfully seized of the estate hereby conveyed and have the right to mortgage, grant, and convey the Property, and that the Property is unencumbered, except for the encumbrances of record and any first deed of trust. You covenant that You warrant and will defend generally the title to the Property against all claims and demands, except those disclosed in writing to Us as of the date of this Deed of Trust.

You and We Covenant and agree as follows:

1. **Payment of Indebtedness.** Borrower shall promptly pay when due the indebtedness secured by this Deed of Trust including, without limitation, that evidenced by the Agreement.

2. **Application of Payments.** Unless applicable law provides otherwise, all payments received by Us under the Agreement will be applied to the principal balance and any finance charges, late charges, collection costs, and other charges owing with respect to the indebtedness secured by this Deed of Trust in such order as We may choose from time to time.

3. **Charges; Liens.** Except as expressly provided in this Paragraph 3, You shall pay all taxes, assessments and other charges, fines and impositions attributable to the Property which may attain a priority over this Deed of Trust, and leasehold payments or ground rents, if any, by Your making payments, when due, directly to the payee thereof. In the event You make payments directly to the payee thereof, upon Our request You shall promptly furnish to Us receipts evidencing such payment.

You shall make payments, when due, on any indebtedness secured by a deed of trust or other lien that is prior in right time to this Deed of Trust (a "Prior Deed of Trust"). You shall promptly discharge the lien of any Prior Deed of Trust not disclosed to Us in writing at the time of application for the Agreement, provided, however, that You shall not be required to discharge any such lien so long as You shall (a) in good faith contest such lien by, or defend enforcement of such lien in, legal proceedings which operate to prevent the enforcement of the lien or forfeiture of the Property or any part thereof, or (b) secure from the holder of such prior lien an agreement in form and substance satisfactory to Us subordinating such lien to the Deed of Trust.

You shall not enter into any agreement with the holder of a Prior Deed of Trust whereby such Prior Deed of Trust, or the indebtedness secured thereby is modified, amended, extended or renewed, without Our prior written consent. You shall neither request nor allow any future advances to be secured by a Prior Deed of Trust without Our prior written consent.

4. **Hazard Insurance.** You shall keep the improvements now existing or hereafter erected on the Property insured against loss by fire, hazards included within the term "extended coverage" and such other hazards as We may require (including flood insurance coverage, if required by Us) and in such amounts and for such periods as We may require. Unless We require in writing otherwise, the policy shall provide insurance on a replacement cost basis in an amount not less than that necessary to comply with any coinsurance percentage stipulated in the hazard insurance policy. All insurance policies and renewals thereof shall be in form and substance and with carriers acceptable to Us and shall include a standard mortgage clause in favor of and in form and substance satisfactory to Us. In the event of loss, You shall give prompt notice to the insurance carrier and Us. We may make proof of loss if not made promptly by You.

If the Property is abandoned by You, or if You fail to respond to Us within thirty (30) days from the date the notice is mailed by Us to You that the insurance carrier offers to settle a claim for insurance benefits, We are authorized to collect and apply the insurance proceeds at Our option either to restoration or repair of the Property, or to sums secured by this Deed if Trust.

If the Property is acquired by Us under Paragraph 14 of this Deed of Trust, all of Your right, title and interest in and to any insurance policies, and in and to the proceeds thereof resulting from damage to the Property prior to the sale or acquisition, shall pass to Us to the extent of the sums secured by this Deed of Trust immediately prior to such sale or acquisition.

The provisions of this Paragraph 4 shall be subject to the provisions project or planned unit development.

5. **Preservation and Maintenance of Property; Condominiums and Planned Unit Developments.** If this Deed of Trust is on a unit in a condominium or a planned unit development (herein "Condominium Project"), then: (a) You shall perform all of Your obligations under the declaration or covenants creating or governing the Condominium Project, the by-laws and regulations of the Condominium Project, and all constituent documents (herein "Project Documents"), including the payment when due of assessments imposed by the homeowners association or other governing body of the Condominium Project (herein "Owner's Association"); (b) You shall be deemed to have satisfied the insurance requirements under Paragraph 5 of this Deed of Trust if the Owners Association maintains in full force and effect a "master" or "blanket" policy on the Condominium Project which provides insurance coverage against fire, hazards included within the term "extended coverage" and such other hazards (including flood insurance) as We may require, and in such amounts and for such periods as We may require naming Us as additional loss payee; (c) the provisions of any Project Documents regarding the application of any insurance proceeds from "master" or "blanket" policies covering the Condominium Project shall supersede the provisions of Paragraph 4 of this Deed of Trust to the extent necessary to avoid conflict between the provisions thereof and hereof; (d) You hereby assign to Us the right to receive distributions on account of the Property under "master" or "blanket" policies covering the Condominium Project to the extent not applied to the restoration or repair of the Property, with any such distributions in excess of the amount necessary to satisfy in full the obligations secured by this Deed of Trust being paid to You; (e) You shall give Us prompt written notice of any lapse in any insurance coverage under a "master" or "blanket" policy on the Condominium Project; and (f) You shall not, without Our prior written consent, consent to either (i) the abandonment or termination of the Condominium Project (except for the abandonment or termination provided by law in the case of substantial destruction by fire or other casualty or in the case of a taking or condemnation or eminent domain), (ii) any material amendment to the Project Documents (including any change in the percentage interests of the unit owners in the Condominium Project), or (iii) the effectuation of any decision by the Owners Association to terminate professional management and assume self-management of the Condominium Project. If the Property has rental units, You shall maintain insurance against net loss in addition to the other hazards for which insurance is required herein.

6. **Protection of Our Security.** If You fail to perform Your obligations under this Deed of Trust, or if any action or proceedings adversely affects Our interest in the Property, We may, at Our option, take any action reasonably necessary (including, without limitation, paying expenses and attorney fees and to have entry upon the Property to make repairs) to perform Your obligations or to protect Our interests. Any amounts disbursed by Us pursuant to this Paragraph 6, with interest thereon at the variable rate described in the Agreement, shall become indebtedness secured by this Deed of Trust (except as expressly provided herein). Nothing contained in this Paragraph 6 shall require Us to incur any expense or take any action hereunder.

7. **Inspection.** We or Our agents may enter and inspect the Property, after giving You reasonable prior notice.

8. **Condemnation.** The proceeds of any award or claim for damages, direct or consequential, in connection with any condemnation or other taking of the Property, or part thereof, or for conveyance in lieu of condemnation, are hereby assigned and shall be paid to Us. Neither Borrower nor You will be relieved of any obligation to make payments if We apply the award received to the outstanding balance owed.

If You abandon the Property, or if, after notice by Us to You that the condemnor offers to make an award or settle a claim for damages, You fail to respond to Us within thirty (30) days after the date such notice is mailed, We are authorized to collect and apply the proceeds in the same manner as provided in Paragraph 4 hereof.

9. **Forbearance Not a Waiver.** Any forbearance by Us in exercising any right or remedy hereunder, or otherwise afforded by applicable law, shall not be a waiver of or preclude the exercise of any such right or remedy in the future. Any waiver by Us must be in writing and signed by Us.

10. **Successors and Assigns Bound; Joint and Several Liability; Captions.** The covenants and agreements herein contained shall bind, and the rights hereunder shall inure to, Your and Our respective successors and assigns, subject to the provisions of Paragraph 13 hereof. All Your covenants and agreements shall be joint and several. The captions and headings of the paragraphs of this Deed of Trust are for convenience only and are not to be used to interpret or define the provisions hereof.

11. **Notices.** Except for any notice required under applicable law to be given in another manner, (a) any notice to You provided for in this Deed of Trust shall be given by personal delivery or by mailing such notice by first-class postage paid, addressed to You at the address of the Property shown at the beginning of the Deed of Trust or at such other address as You may designate by notice to Us as provided herein, and (b) any notice to Us shall be given by personal delivery or by mailing such notice by certified mail, return receipt requested, to Our address stated herein or to such other address as We may designate by notice to You as provided herein.

12. **Severability.** If any term of this Deed of Trust is found to be unenforceable, all other provisions will remain in full force.

13. **Due on Transfer Provision - Transfer of the Property.** If all or any part of the Property or any interest in it is sold or transferred (or if a beneficial interest in You is sold or transferred and You are not a natural person) without Our prior written consent, We may, at Our option, require immediate payment in full of all sums secured by this Deed of Trust. However, We shall not exercise this option if the exercise is prohibited by applicable law as of the date of this Deed of Trust. If We exercise this option, We shall give You notice of acceleration. The notice shall provide a period of not less than 30 days from the date the notice is delivered or mailed within which all sums secured by this Deed of Trust must be paid. If these sums are not paid prior to the expiration of this period, We may invoke any remedies permitted by this Deed of Trust without further notice or demand on You.

14. **Default.** If You breach any term in this Deed of Trust, or if Borrower fails to perform any obligation under the Agreement, We may, at Our option, declare all sums secured by this Deed of Trust to be immediately due and payable without further demand and may invoke the power of sale under this Deed of Trust and any other remedies permitted by law. We may collect from You all reasonable costs incurred in enforcing the terms of this Deed of Trust, including attorney's fees and allocated costs of Our salaried employees.

15. **Assignment of Rents.** As additional security hereunder, You hereby assign to Us the rents of the Property; provided, however, that You shall have, prior to acceleration under Paragraph 14 hereof or abandonment of the Property, the right to collect and retain such rents as they become due and payable.

16. **Future Loan Advances.** Upon Your request, We at Our option may make Future Loan Advances to You or Borrower. Such Future Loan Advances, with interest thereon, shall be secured by this Deed of Trust when evidenced by a promissory note or agreement stating that said note or agreement is so secured.

17. **Release.** Upon payment of all sums secured by this Deed of Trust and upon (a) shall release this Deed of Trust and You shall pay all costs of recordation, if any.

18. **Appointment of Receiver; Lender in Possession.** Upon acceleration under this Deed of Trust or abandonment of the Property; We shall be entitled to have a receiver appointed by a court to enter upon, take possession of, and manage the Property and collect the rents of the Property including those past due. All rents collected by the receiver shall be applied first to payment of the costs of management of the Property and collection of rents, including but not limited to, receiver's fees and premiums on the receiver's bonds and reasonable attorneys' fees and then to the sums secured by this Deed of Trust. The receiver shall be liable to account only for those rents actually received.

19. **Statement of Obligation.** We may collect a fee for furnishing a statement of obligation in an amount permitted under applicable law.

20. **No Merger.** There shall be no merger of the interest or estate created by this Deed of Trust with any other interest or estate in the Property at any time held by or for Our benefit in any capacity, without Our prior written consent.

21. **Fixture Filing.** This Deed of Trust constitutes a financing statement filed as a fixture filing in the Official Records of the County Recorder of the county in which the Property is located with respect to any and all fixtures included within the term "Property" as used in this Deed of Trust and with respect to any goods or other personal property that may now or hereafter become such fixtures.

22. **Third Party Waivers.** In the event that any of You has not also signed the Agreement as Borrower, each of You: (a) agrees that We may, from time to time, without notice to, consent from or demand on You, and without affecting or impairing in any way any of Our rights or Your obligations, (i) renew, extend, accelerate, compromise or change the interest rate or other terms of the Agreement and any promissory note or agreement evidencing a Future Loan Advance, and (ii) accept, waive and release other security (including guarantees) for the obligations arising under the Agreement or any promissory note or agreement evidencing a Future Loan Advance, and (b) waives (i) any right to require Us to proceed against any Borrower or any other person, proceed against or exhaust any security for the obligations secured by this Deed of Trust or pursue any other remedy in Our power whatsoever, (ii) any defense or right against Us arising out of any disability or other defense or cessation of liability of any Borrower for any reason other than full payment, (iii) any defense or right against Us arising out of Our foreclosure upon the Property, even though such foreclosure results in the loss of any right of subrogation, reimbursement or other right You have against any Borrower, (iv) all presentments, diligence, protests, demands and notice of protest, dishonor, and nonperformance, (v) until payment in full of the indebtedness secured by this Deed of Trust, any right of subrogation or the benefit of any security for such indebtedness, and (vi) the benefit of the statute of limitations affecting the Property to the extent permitted by law. Any partial payment by Borrower or other circumstance that operates to toll any statute of limitations as to such person shall operate to toll such statute as to You.

23. **Choice of Law.** This Deed of Trust will be governed by and interpreted in accordance with the federal laws of the United States and where not inconsistent with the laws of the State of California, regardless of the state in which You or Borrower resides.

24. **Your Copy.** You shall be given one conformed copy of the Agreement and this Deed of Trust.

25. **Loan Charges Legislation Affecting Our Rights.** If the Agreement is subject to a law which sets maximum loan charges, and that law is finally interpreted so that the interest or other loan charges collected or to be collected in connection with the Agreement exceed the permitted limits, then (a) any such loan charge shall be reduced by the amount necessary to reduce the charge to the permitted limit; and (b) any such loan charge already collected from You or Borrower which exceeded permitted limits will be refunded to You or Borrower; We may choose to make this refund by reducing the principal owed under the Agreement or by making a direct payment to You or Borrower. If a refund reduces principal, the reduction will be treated as a partial prepayment without any prepayment charge due. If enactment or expiration of applicable laws has the effect of rendering any provision of the Agreement or this Deed of Trust unenforceable according to its terms, We may at Our option, require immediate payment in full of all sums secured by this Deed of Trust and may invoke any remedies permitted by Paragraph 14.

26. **Substitute Trustee.** We may, at our Option, from time to time remove the Trustee and appoint a successor Trustee to any Trustee appointed hereunder. Without conveyance of the Property, the successor Trustee shall succeed to all the title, power and duties conferred upon the Trustee herein and by applicable law.

27. **Reconveyance.** After compliance with all requirements of the Agreement, We shall request the Trustee to reconvey the Property to You. Trustee shall reconvey the Property without warranty. You shall pay any fee legally charged by the Trustee for the issuance of reconveyance and all costs of recordation.

REQUEST FOR NOTICE OF DEFAULT AND FORECLOSURE
UNDER SUPERIOR DEED OF TRUST OR MORTGAGE

We and You request the holder of any encumbrance with a lien which has priority over this Deed of Trust give notice to Us, at Our address set forth on page one of this Deed of Trust, of any default under the superior encumbrance and of any sale or other foreclosure action.

REQUEST FOR RECONVEYANCE

TO TRUSTEE:

The undersigned is the holder of the Agreement secured by this Deed of Trust. The Agreement together with all other indebtedness and obligations secured by this Deed of Trust have been paid and performed in full. Trustee is hereby directed to cancel the Agreement and this Deed of Trust, which are delivered hereby, and to reconvey, without warranty, all estate now held by Trustee to the persons entitled thereto.

Date: _____   _____

Our Privacy Policy Notice

Keeping customer information secure is a top priority for all of us at Anybank*. We are providing this privacy notice to individual clients who purchase products or receive services from us for personal, family or household purposes ("you"). We hope this helps you understand how we handle the personal information about you that we collect and may disclose. This notice also tells you how you can limit our disclosure of personal information about you. The provisions of this notice will apply to former clients as well as our current clients unless we state otherwise.

When Anybank shares personal information with the Anygroup family of companies it can make it easier when you apply for accounts or services from these companies. In addition, sharing personal information can help you receive timely notice about products, services or other special offers that may be of interest to you from companies in the Anygroup family or from nonaffiliated third parties.

Our Policies and Practices to Protect Your Personal Information

We protect personal information we collect about you by maintaining physical, electronic, and procedural safeguards that meet or exceed applicable law. Third parties who have access to personal information must agree to follow appropriate standards of security and confidentiality.

We train people who work for us how to properly handle personal information and we restrict access to it. And, as a current client, you can rely on the Anygroup Privacy Promise for Consumers that we follow as a member of the Anygroup family of companies. It is found on the reverse side of this notice.

Categories of Personal Information We Collect and May Disclose:

The personal information we collect about you comes from the following sources:

- Information we receive from you on applications or other forms, such as name, address, social security number, telephone number, occupation, assets and income,
- Information about your transactions with us, our affiliates, or nonaffiliated third parties, such as account balances, payment history, and account activity,
- Information we receive from a consumer reporting agency, such as your credit bureau reports and other information relating to your credit worthiness, and
- Information we receive about you from other sources, such as your employer and other third parties.

We may disclose any of the above information that we collect to affiliates and nonaffiliated third parties as described below.

Categories of Affiliates To Whom We May Disclose Personal Information

Our affiliates are the family of companies controlled by Anygroup Inc. We may share personal information about you with affiliates in several different lines of business including banking, credit cards, consumer finance, securities, and insurance. Our affiliates do business under names that include AnyFinancial, Travelers Insurance, Salomon Smith Barney, and Primerica.

* All references in this notice to Anybank refer to either Anybank, N.A., Anybank, F.S.B., Anybank (New York State) or Anybank (Nevada), NA., depending upon which bank is maintaining your account or providing you with products or services.

Categories of Nonaffiliated Third Parties To Whom We May Disclose Personal Information
Nonaffiliated third parties are those not part of the family of companies controlled by AnyGroup, Inc. We may disclose personal information about you, to the following types of nonaffiliated third parties:

- Financial services providers, such as companies engaged in banking, credit cards, consumer finance, securities, and insurance,
- Non-financial organizations, such as companies engaged in direct marketing and the selling of consumer products and services.

.If you check Box 1 on the Privacy Choices Form, we will not make these disclosures except as follows. First, we may disclose information about you, as described above in "Categories of Personal Information We Collect and May Disclose," to third parties that perform marketing services on our behalf or to other financial institutions with whom we have joint marketing agreements. Second, we may disclose personal information about you to third parties as permitted by law, including disclosures necessary to process and service your account, to protect against fraud, and to protect the security or confidentiality of our records.

YOUR PRIVACY CHOICES
This section describes your privacy choices. Please remember that we will continue to protect your personal information regardless of your privacy choices.

Disclosing to Nonaffiliated Third Parties (Box 1)

As described in this notice, we will limit the personal information we disclose about you to nonaffiliated third parties if you check Box 1 on the Privacy Choices Form.

Sharing with Our Affiliates (Box 2)

The law allows us to share with our affiliates any information about our transactions or experiences with you. Unless otherwise permitted by law, we will not share with our affiliates other information that you provide to us or that we obtain from third parties (for example, credit bureaus) if you check Box 2 on the Privacy Choices Form.

If you are also a customer of other Anygroup affiliates and you receive a notice of their intent to share certain information about you, you will need to separately notify them if you do not want such information shared.

Our Mailing and Telemarketing Lists (Boxes 3 and 4)

We would like to keep you informed about promotional offers from our affiliates and from nonaffiliated third parties. If you wish to be taken off our Anybank mailing and/or telephone lists that we use for such offers, please check Box 3 and/or Box 4 on the Privacy Choices Form.

We will continue to mail you information that you may fmd valuable in managing your Anybank account, such as the availability of special offers, credit line increases, and new or upgraded Anybank products or services even if you have checked Box 3. We may also send you promotional offers from third parties in communications that you receive from us concerning your Anybank account, such as your periodic statement.

Instructions for Vermont Customers
In response to a Vermont regulation, we will automatically treat accounts with Vermont statement addresses as if you checked Box 1 and Box 2 on the Privacy Choices Form without requiring you to return the form. And if we disclose information about you to nonaffiliated third parties with whom we have joint marketing agreements, we will only disclose your name, address, other contact information, and information about our transactions or experiences with you.

Anygroup Privacy Promise for Consumers

While information is the cornerstone of our ability to provide superior service, our most important asset is our customers' trust. Keeping customer information secure, and using it only as our customers would want us to, is a top priority for all of us at Anygroup. Here, then, is our promise to our individual customers:

1. We will safeguard, according to strict standards of security and confidentiality, any information our customers share with us.

2. We will limit the collection and use of customer information to the minimum we require to deliver superior service to our customers, which includes advising our customers about our products, services and other opportunities, and to administer our business.

3. We will permit only authorized employees, who are trained in the proper handling of customer information, to have access to that information. Employees who violate our Privacy Promise will be subject to our normal disciplinary process.

4. We will not reveal customer information to any external organization unless we have previously informed the customer in disclosures or agreements, have been authorized by the customer, or are required by law.

5. We will always maintain control over the confidentiality of our customer information. We may, however, facilitate relevant offers from reputable companies. These companies are not permitted to retain any customer information unless the customer has specifically expressed interest in their products or services.

6. We will tell customers in plain language initially, and at least once annually, how they may remove their names from marketing lists. At any time, customers can contact us to remove their names from such lists.

7. Whenever we hire other organizations to provide support services, we will require them to conform to our privacy standards and to allow us to audit them for compliance.

8. For purposes of credit reporting, verification and risk management, we will exchange information about our customers with reputable reference sources and clearinghouse services.

9. We will not use or share - internally or externally - personally identifiable medical inforn1ation for any purpose other than the underwriting or administration of a customer's policy, claim or account, or as disclosed to the customer when the information is collected, or to which the customer consents.

10. We will attempt to keep customer files complete, up to date, and accurate. We will tell our customers how and where to conveniently access their account information (except when we're prohibited by law) and how to notify us about errors which we will promptly correct.

AMANDA T GEORGE   Reference #: **4212121212**

PRIVACY CHOICES FORM

If you want to limit disclosures of personal information about you as described in this notice, just check the box or boxes below to indicate your privacy choices. Then send this form to the address listed below.

1.   [   ]   Limit the disclosure of personal information about me to nonaffiliated third parties.

2.   [   ]   Limit the personal information about me that you share with Anygroup affiliates.

3.   [   ]   Remove my name from your mailing lists used for promotional offers.

4.   [   ]   Remove my name from your telephone marketing lists used for promotional offers.

My Anybank account number is: **4212121212**

Name: _____

Address: _____

City: _____ State: _____ Zip: _____

Phone Number: _____

If you have checked any of the boxes above, please mail this form in a stamped envelope to:

Anybank Processing Center
AB 0987 Mail Stop XXX
South Anytown, NJ
07606

Please allow approximately 30 days from our receipt of your privacy choices for them to become effective. Your privacy instructions and any previous privacy instructions will remain in effect until you request a change.

Closing Instructions: <u>GEORGE</u>

Anytown Closer Name: **MARGIE DOMINIA**   Phone Number: **1-800-000-000**
Title Company: **ENTRUST TITLE USA**   Closing Agent: **ENTRUST TITLE USA**
ACAPS Number: **100000000000000**   Loan Number: **4212121212**

NOTES

Page 1 of the "Closing Instructions" conveniently indicates the documents that comprise the loan package. The Notary Signing Agent should ensure all checked documents are present in the package.

_____ Equity Line Account   _____ Fixed Rate Home Equity Loan

8931212

Borrower(s) Names:	Home Phone #:	Work Phone #:
GEORGE	(310) 123-4567	(310) 987-6543
4.		

Address: 8941 SMITH ST   Closing Date: 7/8/20XX
                            LOS ANGELES, CA 90034
Credit Limit / Loan Amount: $118.500.00   Funding Date: 7/12/20XX
Interest Rate: 2.740%   Lien Position: 2nd

A. Enclosed Documents: Please ensure all documents marked with an "X" have been enclosed and have the borrower(s) sign and notarize as appropriate.

X	Scheduling Notification		Affidavit of No Liens (Notarize)
X	Closing Instructions		Affidavit of Continuous Marriage (Notarize)
X	Agreement & Disclosure (ESA) / Note (FRHEL)		Insurance Disclosure Notice (Anti-Coercion)
X	Mortgage / Deed of Trust / Co-Op Loan Security Agreement (Notarize)		Request for Student's or Borrower's Social Security Number and Certification (Form W -9S)
	Hud 1-a		Security Affidavit Class 1 and Class 2
	Truth-in-Lending		Maryland Request for Notice of Foreclosure Sale
X	Anygroup Privacy Promise for Consumers		Force Placed Insurance Notice
X	Notice of Right to Cancel		Section 255 Affidavit (Notarize)
	Loan Servicing Notice		Recognition /Aztech Agreement (signed by Co-Op Board)
X	Affiliated Business Arrangement Disclosure (Chesapeake)		Affidavit of Seller/Owner of Co-Op (Notarize)
	Affiliated Business Arrangement Disclosure (SSB)		Assignment of Ownership Documents - Co-Op (Notarize)
	Quit Claim Deed (Notarize)		Assignment of Proprietary Lease (Notarize)
	Power of Attorney		Financing Statement - Co-Op
	Deceased Joint Tenancy Affidavit (Notarize)		Stock Power (Notarize)
	Declaration of Abandonment of Declared Homestead		UCC-l Filing Statement Rider - Co-Op
	Flood Disclosure Notice		Certificate of Trust / Trustee Affidavit
X	Account Payoff Authorization		Letter of Direction
	Tax Information Authorization (Form 8821)		Personal Guarantee
	Broker Point Program		Statement by Grantor and Grantee
	Combined Security Agreement and Collateral Assignment of Beneficial Interest in Land Trust		Facsimile Assignment of Beneficial Interest for Purposes of Recording (Cook County Only)

B. Conditions to Close: The following conditions/requirements MUST be met PRIOR to disbursement of loan proceeds.

1. ENTRUST TITLE USA **MUST** complete page 1 of the Agreement and Disclosure with the appropriate closing costs and totals.

2. The **"Funding Transmittal"** and the **"Loan Funding Options"** (Pages 2 and 3 of these Closing Instructions) and Pages 1 and 11 of the **"Equity Source Account Agreement and Disclosure"** are to be faxed to the St. Louis Closing Department, 1-800-909-9876, within 24 hours of Borrower(s) signing the closing documents. (Borrower(s) must sign page 11 of the **"Equity Source Account Agreement and Disclosure"** if they wish to participate in the Auto-Deduct service.)

3. Borrower(s) to bring photo I.D. to closing.

4. If the payoff amount(s) on page 2 of these closing instructions have changed, you must write in the correct amount(s) and total.

Closing Instructions: <u>GEORGE</u>
Funding Transmittal, Page 2 of 3
Equity Line Account

Fax to the Anytown Closing Department 1-800-909-9876 immediately upon loan closing.

ACAPS #: <u>**100000000000000**</u>   Loan #: <u>**4212121212**</u>
Address: 8941 SMITH ST.
            LOS ANGELES, CA 90034   **Credit Limit / Loan Amount: $118.500.00**

C. Payoffs: The following items will be paid with the proceeds of this loan.

Payee name	Account #	Amount	Check #
1. ANYBANK		$40,266.49	
2. N/A		$0.00	
3. N/A		$0.00	
4. N/A		$0.00	
5. N/A		$0.00	
6. N/A		$0.00	
7. N/A		$0.00	
8. N/A		$0.00	
9. N/A		$0.00	
10. N/A		$0.00	
11. N/A		$0.00	
12. N/A		$0.00	
13. N/A		$0.00	
14. N/A		$0.00	
15. N/A		$0.00	
Total Loan Advances / Payoff Amounts		$40,266.49	

Miscellaneous Fees / Refunds: (Not Paid by customer)

Fee / Refund Type	Amount	Check #
Title Fees		

D. Final Reminders:

Fax this page to the St. Louis Closing Department at 1-636-256-2261 immediately upon completion of the closing.

TO BE COMPLETED BY SIGNER/NOTARY

_____   _____
(Printed name of person taking acknowledgment)   (Signature of person taking acknowledgment)

Closing Date: _____

NOTES

Page 2 of the "Closing Instructions" is a form to be signed by the Notary Signing Agent. For the purpose of this form, the "Closing Date" is the actual date of the signing appointment.

Closing Instructions: <u>GEORGE</u>
Loan Funding Options, Page 3 of 3
Equity Line Account

Fax to the Anytown Closing Department 1-800-256-2261 immediately upon loan closing.

ACAPS #: <u>100000000000000</u>	Title Company: <u>ENTRUST TITLE USA</u>
Credit Limit / Loan Amount: $118,500.00	Loan #: <u>4212121212</u>

This loan cannot fund until the day after three (3) business days following the date the loan documents are signed. The fourth (4) business day is the loan funding day. On the fifth (5) business day following the loan closing you will receive an overnight package containing five (5) starter checks. Your official Equity Source Account checkbook will arrive approximately two to three (2-3) weeks after the loan closing. You may also indicate a specific amount of your proceeds to be disbursed by one of the three (3) methods detailed below.

I/We request and authorize by virtue of my/our signature below, the following amount to be disbursed as indicated by the box checked below (only one (1) box may be checked).

$ _____

Direct Deposit Authorization:
(Funds will be available from your ANYBANK checking or savings account on the fifth (5) business day following the date the loan documents are signed).

I/We authorize ANYBANK to deposit my/our loan proceeds to the account listed below.

Account Number: _____

Name(s) on Account: _____

Marketplace (INTERNAL USE ONLY): _____

Official ANYBANK check (proceeds check) mailed overnight to the following address. (To be delivered on the fifth (5) business day following the date the loan documents are signed).

Name(s): _____

Mailing Address: _____

_____

_____

Wire Transfer Authorization. (Funds to be transferred on the fourth (4) business day following the date the loan documents are signed).

I/We authorize ENTRUST TITLE USA to wire my/our loan proceeds into the account listed below. I/We understand that ENTRUST TITLE USA will deduct a fee of $20 from the loan proceeds for this service. I/We also understand that my/our bank may also charge an additional fee to receive a wire transfer.

Name of Bank: _____

Address of Bank: _____

ABA Number: _____

Account Number: _____

Name(s) on Account: _____

* All lien payoff checks secured by this property will be sent via overnight mail directly to the creditor.
** All other required payoff checks will be made payable to you and the checks to the appropriate creditor. You will be responsible for mailing the checks to the appropriate creditor. These checks will be sent to you via overnight mail to <u>8941 SMITH ST. LOS ANGELES CA 90034</u> unless otherwise specified. _____

_____

AMANDA T GEORGE

REFINANCING WITH ORIGINAL CREDITOR
EQUITY LINE ACCOUNT
NOTICE OF RIGHT TO CANCEL

Borrower's Name(s): AMANDA T GEORGE
Address: 8941 SMITH ST
LOS ANGELES, CA 90034

I. YOUR RIGHT TO CANCEL

We have agreed to increase the credit limit on your open-end credit account. We have a [mortgage/lien/security interest] [on/in] your home as security for your account. Increasing the credit limit will increase the amount of the [mortgage/lien/security interest] [on/in] your home. You have a legal right under federal law to cancel the increase in your credit limit, without cost, within three business days after the latest of the following events:

    (1) The date of the increase in your credit limit which is <u>7/8/20XX</u>; or
    (2) The date you received your Truth-in-Lending disclosures; or
    (3) The date you received this notice of your right to cancel the increase in your credit limit.

If you cancel, your cancellation will only apply to the increase in your credit limit and to the [mortgage/lien/se___] that resulted from the increase in your credit limit. It will not affect the amount you presently owe, and it will [mortgage/lien/security interest] we already have [on/in] your home. Within 20 calendar days after we receive cancellation, we must take the necessary steps to reflect the fact that any increase in the [mortgage/lien/securit_ ___] your home has been canceled. We must also return to you any money or property you have given to us or to anyone else in connection with this extension of credit.

You may keep any money or property we have given you until we have done the things mentioned above, but you must then offer to return tile money or property. If it is impractical or unfair for you to return the property, you must offer its reasonable value. You may offer to return the property at your home or at the location of the property. Money must be returned to the address shown below. I/we do not take possession of the money or property within 20 calendar days of your offer, you may keep it without further obligation.

II. HOW TO CANCEL

If you decide to cancel the increase in your credit limit, you may do so by notifying us, in writing, at:

      ANYBANK
      Home Equity Closing Department
      P.O. Box 10000
      Anytown, MO 63179-0047

You may use any written statement that is signed and dated by you and states your intention to cancel, or you may use this notice by dating and signing below. Keep one copy of this notice no matter how you notify us because it contains important information about your rights.

If you cancel by mail or telegram, you must send the notice no later than midnight of <u>7/11/20XX</u> (or midnight of the third business day following the latest of the three events listed above).

If you send or deliver your written notice to cancel some other way, it must be delivered to the above address no later than that time.

III. I WISH TO CANCEL

Consumer's Signature: _____   Date: _____

Acknowledgment of Receipt

I/We each acknowledge receipt of two copies of this Notice of Right to Cancel. **I/We understand that any one of us, acting alone, can exercise the right to cancel.**

_____   _____

AMANDA T GEORGE

_____   _____

_____   _____

Note: Each person having an ownership interest in the real estate being given as security in the transaction in connection with which this notice is being given must be given two copies of this notice properly completed.

NOTES

This particular lender has entered the proper dates into the "Notice of Right to Cancel" form.

Affiliated Business Arrangement Disclosure

To: AMADA T GEORGE

From: ANYBANK, FSB, ANYBANK, NA, ANYBANK (New York State) and ANYBANK (Nevada), NA (collectively, "ANYBANK")

Property: 8941 SMITH ST, LOS ANGELES, CA 90034

Date: 7/8/20XX

This is to give you notice that ANYBANK has a business relationship with the settlement service providers listed below. Each is a wholly owned subsidiary of Anygroup. Because of this relationship, this referral may provide ANYBANK a financial or other benefit.

Set forth below is the estimated charge or range of charges for the settlement services listed. You are NOT required to use the listed provider(s) as a condition for settlement of your loan or the purchase, sale or refinance of the subject property. THERE ARE FREQUENTLY OTHER SETTLEMENT SERVICE PROVIDERS AVAILABLE WITH SIMILAR SERVICES. YOU ARE FREE TO SHOP AROUND TO DETERMINE THAT YOU ARE RECEIVING THE BEST SERVICES AND THE BEST RATE FOR THESE SERVICES.

Provider	Settlement Services	Charge or range of charges
MOSAC Services, Inc.	Flood Determination and Certification	$22. Cost paid by lender.

Set forth below is the estimated charge or range of charges for the settlement services of an attorney, credit reporting agency, or real estate appraiser that we, as your lender, may require you to use, as a condition of your loan on this property, to represent our interests in the transaction.

Provider	Settlement Services	Charge or range of charges
Virginia Appraisal and Settlement Services[1]	Appraisal	$175 - $670. Appraisal cost paid by lender.

ACKNOWLEDGEMENT

I/we have read this disclosure form, and understand that ANYBANK is referring me/us to purchase the above-described settlement service(s) and may receive a financial or other benefit as a result of this referral.

Borrower: **AMANDA T GEORGE**   Borrower:

Borrower: Borrower:

---

[1] Not all of the above services are available from Virginia in all states. You may inquire of lender regarding the services of Virginia in your state.

3

Reverse Mortgages

Traditionally, most home loan marketing targets young families or established individuals seeking to purchase a home, refinance a mortgage, or access the equity accumulated in their property. Borrowers qualify based upon their creditworthiness and ability to repay the loan in regular monthly payments.

Home loan marketing solicitations all but ignore seniors on fixed incomes. In fact, in years past if a retired couple needed to access the equity in their home and could not meet the income requirements to qualify for a home equity loan, their only option was to sell their residence.

Increasingly, however, Notary Signing Agents are encountering a unique loan transaction catering to seniors called a "reverse" mortgage, or more technically, a Home Equity Conversion Mortgage (HECM). This innovative loan product — so named because it "reverses" the typical borrower-to-lender loan payment stream — allows qualified seniors to convert the equity in their homes into a regularly monthly source of income or a line of credit. In a reverse mortgage, seniors do not make regular monthly principal and interest payments to the lender; rather, the lender makes payments to the seniors who own their homes outright or have sufficient equity to tap.

Reverse mortgages differ from conventional loans in other ways as well. Unlike a conventional loan, repayment is postponed as long as the borrower lives in the home. The lender recoups its investment, plus accumulated interest and fees, from the proceeds of the sale at the time the home is sold.

In addition, default, eviction, or foreclosure is never a worry, since there are no monthly payments to miss.

Table 3.1 contrasts relevant features of conventional mortgages and HECM loans:

Provision	Conv. Loan	HECM
Income/credit requirements	Yes	No
Age requirement	None	Seniors 62 years and over
Credit Counseling	Not required	Required
Loan proceeds disbursed	Up front or as a line of credit	Up front, as a line of credit, in monthly payments, or as a line of credit and monthly payments
Repayment	Monthly payments over loan term	One payment at loan maturity
Fixed maturity date	Yes	No
Forced sale upon default	Yes	Not while senior lives in home

Table 3.2 summarizes comparable features of conventional mortgages and HECM loans:

Loan Provision	Conv. Loan	HECM
Security for loan	First or second mortgage	First and second mortgage
Property maintenance	Borrower's responsibility	Borrower's responsibility
Property taxes	Borrower's responsibility	Borrower's responsibility
Hazard insurance	Borrower's responsibility	Borrower's responsibility
Borrower accumulates equity	Yes	Yes

The original HECM program was made available for the first time in 1989. HECM loans are federally insured through the Federal Housing Administration (FHA), a part of the U.S. Department of Housing and Urban Development.

According to the U.S. Department of Housing and Urban Development, the general requirements for HECM loans are as follows:

Borrower Requirements

• Age 62 years of age or older

• Own the property outright or paid-down a considerable amount

• Occupy property as primary residence

• Participate in consumer information session led by an approved counselor

• Not be delinquent on any federal debt

• Have financial resources to continue to make timely payment of ongoing property charges such as property taxes, insurance and Homeowner Association fees, etc.

Financial Requirements

• Income, assets, monthly living expenses, and credit history will be verified

• Timely payment of real estate taxes, hazard and flood insurance premiums will be verified

Mortgage Amount Based On

• Age of the youngest borrower

• Current interest rate

• Lesser of the home's appraised value, HECM FHA mortgage limit of $679,650 or the sales price (only applicable to HECM for purchase)

Property Requirements

- Family home or 2-4 unit dwelling with one unit occupied by the borrower

- Condominiums or Planned Unit Developments (PUD) must be HUD-FHA approved

- Manufactured Homes that meet HUD guidelines

The amount a homeowner can borrow depends on his or her age, the current interest rate, other loan fees, and the appraised value of the home or FHA mortgage limits for their area, whichever is less. In general, the more valuable the home, the older the borrower, the lower the interest rate, the more that can be borrowed.

The chart below compares how regional differences affect the amount of loan proceeds seniors can obtain from a home equity conversion mortgage. Zip codes from Los Angeles, California (90034), Portland, Maine (04105), and Appleton, Wisconsin (54912) are compared. For the purpose of the calculation, in each instance the borrower's age is 69 and the value of the property is $350,000.

Loan Proceeds	90034	04105	54912
Single Lump Sum	$193,208	$151,367	$102,998
Credit Line Account	$193,208	$151,367	$102,998
Monthly Loan Advance	$1,136	$890	$605

As illustrated in the chart below, a borrower age 79 can receive the following loan amounts in each of the three regions.

Loan Proceeds	90034	04105	54912
Single Lump Sum	$220,895	$173,551	$118,623
Credit Line Account	$220,895	$173,551	$118,623
Monthly Loan Advance	$1,532	$1,204	$826

HECM borrowers must pay an up-front mortgage insurance premium equal to 2 percent of the loan, plus a yearly .5 percent insurance premium thereafter. Since HECM loans are federally insured, this insurance premium guarantees that the government will back up the loan in the event that the loan servicer managing the mortgage goes out of business. The insurance premium also guarantees that borrowers will never owe more than the value the home when the loan must be repaid.

While the original HECM program serves the needs of many seniors, there are limitations. First, no one gets to borrow against 100 percent of their home equity. That's because unlike traditional "forward" mortgages, reverse mortgage balances increase over time. If you were to borrow against all of your equity, your loan balance would soon outstrip your home value. So the amount you can borrow is determined by a "principal limit factor," or PLF. Your property value (or $625,000, which ever is lower) is multiplied by the PLF to come up with your maximum loan. For example, if your home is worth $500,000 and your PLF is .50, you can borrow $250,000.

Second, original HECM loans could not be used to purchase a home and seniors who owned certain property types could not obtain a reverse mortgage on their properties.

Fannie Mae now offers a program that enables seniors to use a reverse mortgage to purchase a single family residence. This program reduces the out-of-pocket cash needed to buy a home, eliminates any new monthly mortgage payment, and helps the consumer keep more of the sales proceeds from the sale of the previous home — or a larger amount of savings — to use for other purposes.

Now a senior wishing to move to a warmer climate, move closer to family, or "downsize" from a larger home into a more accessible residence can take advantage of the features of a HECM loan to meet these lifestyle objectives.

Fannie Mae's programs also allow seniors to use the HECM program to purchase a condominium, a unit in a qualified planned unit development, a property held in trust, or a qualified leasehold property.

Notary Signing Agents should be aware that in a reverse mortgage loan documentation package there are two promissory notes and security instruments. Both notes and security instruments are for the same loan amount, so the second note and security deed could be mistaken as copies of the first. A careful look at these documents will show that the first note and security instrument names the lender providing the loan, while the second note and security instrument names the Secretary of Housing and Urban Development.

Agents must return both properly executed promissory notes and properly signed and notarized security instruments with the rest of the documentation.

Notary Signing Agents also should be aware that while a reverse mortgage transaction includes two notes and security deeds, the second note and security instrument do not secure a second loan on the property. A reverse mortgage is one loan for which the Agent is entitled to one fee.

Notarized Forms in Sample Set   Pages

American Title Lenders
555 Makeway Blvd. Concord, CA 94555

Borrower's Estimated Settlement Statement

Property: **705 13TH STREET,
LOS ANGELES, CA 90055**

File No:	**2474642c**
Officer:	Lynn Law
New Loan No:	**0048382555**
Settlement Date:	01/04/20XX
Disbursement Date:	01/10/20XX
Print Date:	1/7/20XX, 4:31 PM

Buyer: **EVE DAVID**
Address: **705 13TH STREET, LOS ANGELES, CA 90055**
Seller:
Address:

Charge Descriptions	Borrower Charge	Borrower Credit
New Loan(s):		
Lender: WELL CITY BANK N.A.		
Loan Origination Fee 2.0000% - (POC $1,325.00) to WFBNA	5,300.00	
Appraisal Fee - RES	475.00	
Credit Report - RELS Reporting	14.00	
Document Preparation Fee - FAND	100.00	
Mortgage Insurance Premium for 2.000% months - HUD	5,300.00	
Closing Costs - WELL CITY BANK N.A.		13,189.33
HOMEQ. Servicing -- WELL CITY BANK N.A.		113,661.56
Repair Administration Fee -- WELL CITY BANK N.A.	141.33	
Life of Loan Flood Certificate -- WELL CITY BANK N.A.	16.00	
Payoff Loan(s):		
Lender: Waco **estimate**		
Principal Balance Of Payoff Loan - Waco **estimate**	112,099.96	
Interest Pad - Waco * * estimate * *	1,561.60	
Title/Escrow Charges to:		
Lender's Policy - First Title Lenders	742.00	
Signing/Notary Service - First Title Lenders	200.00	
Escrow Fee - First Title Lenders	350.00	
Courier Service - First Title Lenders	80.00	
Record First Deed of Trust/Mortgage - First Title Lenders	75.00	
Record First Grant/Warranty Deed - First Title Lenders	30.00	
Record Additional Deed of Trust/Mortgage - First Title Lenders	75.00	
Disbursements Paid:		
Hazard Insurance Premium	226.00	
Pest Inspection to Pest Control	65.00	
	126,850.89	126,850.89

Notice-This Estimated Settlement Statement is subject to changes, corrections or additions at the time of final computation of the Settlement Statement

Borrower

_____

EVE DAVID

Reverse Mortgages

American Title Lenders
555 Makeway Blvd. Concord, CA 94555

October 31, 20XX

AMERICAN NLA
255 FIFTH ST
SANTA ANA, CA 92755
Attn: PROCESSOR

Title Officer: Telephone:	**Dennis Baer** **(714) 800-4155**
Order No.: Escrow No.: Ref No.:	**2474655c** **2474655c** **0048382555(V)**
Escrow Officer: Telephone:	**Lon Lence** **(925) 688-3255**
Owner: Property:	**EVE DAVID and REGIE MAMS** **705 13TH STREET** **LOS ANGELES, CA 90055**

Attached please find the following item(s):

PRELIMINARY REPORT

All inquiries and correspondence regarding the above should be directed to the Title Officer/Escrow Officer listed above.

Thank you for your confidence and support. We at First Title Company maintain the fundamental principle:

First Title!

NOTE: THE FOLLOWING INFORMATION SHOULD BE USED FOR ALL FUNDS TO BE WIRED FOR THIS ORDER. PLEASE INCLUDE THE ESCROW OFFICER'S NAME AND ESCROW NUMBER WHEN WIRING FUNDS TO:

FIRST TRUST CO.
455 MAIN STREET
SANTA ANA, CA 92755
ABA# 122241555
ACCOUNTS 16717
CREDIT: FIRST LENDERS
ESCROW OFFICER: Lon Lence
ESCROWS: 2474655c

Order No: 2474655c
Reference No.: 0048382555(V)
Escrow Officer: Lon Lence
Escrow Number: 24746552c

First Title Company
555 Makeway Blvd., Concord, CA 94055
Ph: (800) 540-8455 Fax: (866) 242-8155

AMERICAN NLA
255 FIFTH ST
SANTA ANA, CA 92755
Attn: PROCESSOR

Property Address: **705 13TH STREET, LOS ANGELES, CA 90055**

In response to the above referenced application for a policy of title insurance, this company hereby reports that it is prepared to issue, or cause to be issued, as of the date hereof, a policy or policies of title insurance describing the land and the estate or interest therein hereinafter set forth, insuring against loss which may be sustained by reason of any defect, lien or encumbrance not shown or referred to as an exception below or not excluded from coverage pursuant to the printed schedules, conditions and stipulations of the policy forms.

The printed exceptions and exclusions from the coverage of the policy or policies are set forth in exhibit a attached. Copies of the policy forms should be read. They are available from the office which issued this report.

This report (and any supplements or amendments hereto) is issued solely for the purpose of facilitating the issuance of a policy of title insurance and no liability is assumed hereby. If it is desired that liability be assumed prior to the issuance of a policy of title insurance, a binder or commitment should be requested.

Please read the exceptions shown or referred to below and the exceptions and exclusions set forth in exhibit a of this report carefully. The exceptions and exclusions are meant to provide you with notice of matters which are not covered under the terms of the title insurance policy and should be carefully considered.

It is important to note that this preliminary report is not a written representation as to the condition of title and may not list all liens, defects, and encumbrances affecting title to the land.

Dated as of October 26, 20XX at 7:30 A.M.

First Title Company

By   Larry L. Kent - President

By   Debbi Barker - Assistant Secretary, Title Officer
        Phone: (714) 800-4155

The form of policy of title insurance contemplated by this report is: **American Land Title Association Loan Policy (Extended Coverage).**

Title to the estate or interest at the date hereof is vested in:

EVE DAVID, a widow and REGIE MAMS, an unmarried woman as joint tenants

The estate or interest in the land hereinafter described or referred to covered by this report is:

A Fee

At the date hereof exceptions to coverage in addition to the printed exceptions and exclusions in the policy form would be as follows:

1. General and special taxes for the fiscal year **20XX–20XX,**
   First installment: **$292.38, PAYABLE**
   Second installment: **$292.37, PAYABLE**
   Code area: **03797**
   A. P. No.;   **6134-012-055**
   Exemption: **$7,000.00**
   Land: **$10,160.00**
   Improvement: **$12,746.00**

2. The lien of supplemental taxes assessed pursuant to Chapter 3.5 commencing with Section 75 of the California Revenue and Taxation Code.

3. Covenants, conditions and restrictions in an instrument recorded **MARCH 03, 20XX** in **BOOK 21755, PAGE(S) 55** of Official Records, and any amendments and modifications thereto which provide that a violation thereof shall not defeat or render invalid the lien of any first mortgage or deed of trust made in good faith and for value, but deleting any covenant, condition or restriction indicating a preference, limitation or discrimination based on race, color, religion, sex, handicap, familial status, or national origin to the extent such covenants, conditions or restrictions violate 42 USC 3604(c).

4. A Deed of Trust to secure an original indebtedness of **$108,000.00,** and any amounts or obligations secured thereby, recorded **JANUARY 16, 20XX** as instrument no. **20040115355** of Official Records.
   Dated: **JANUARY 08, 20XX**
   Trustor: **EVE DAVID, A WIDOW AND REGIE MAMS, AN UNMARRIED WOMAN AS JOINT TENANTS**
   Trustee: **COAST TITLE**
   Beneficiary: **WORLD FINANCIAL**

5. We find various liens and judgments that are of record against persons with similar or the same name as that of the vestee(s) shown herein. In order to complete this report or commitment, the company requires a statement of identity to be provided for the vestee named below, which may allow and assist in elimination of some or all of said liens and judgments. After review of the requested item, the company reserves the right to add additional items or make further requirements prior to the issuance of any policy of title insurance.

Page 3

Vestee(s): **EVE DAVID**

6. Any right, title or interest of the spouse (if any) of any married vestee herein.

7. This report is preparatory to the issuance of an Alta Loan Policy. We have no knowledge of any fact which would preclude the issuance of the policy with CLTA Endorsement Forms 100 and 116 attached.

   When issued, the CLTA Endorsement Form 116 will reference a **SINGLE** family residence known as **705 13TH STREET, LOS ANGELES, California 90055.**

DESCRIPTION

All that certain land situated in the unincorporated area of the **County of LOS ANGELES, State of California,** and described as follows:

LOT 145 OF TRACT 9255, IN THE CITY OF LOS ANGELES AREA, COUNTY OF LOS ANGELES, STATE OF CALIFORNIA, AS PER MAP RECORDED IN BOOK 135, PAGE(S) 65 TO 66, INCLUSIVE OF MAPS IN THE OFFICE OF THE COUNTY RECORDER OF SAID COUNTY.

APN No: **6134-012-055**

Page 5

****

W A R N I N G

"The map attached hereto may or may not be a survey of the land depicted
thereon. You should not rely upon it for any purpose other than
orientation to the general location of the parcel or parcels depicted. First
American expressly disclaims any liability for alleged loss or damage which
may result from reliance upon this map."

****

PLATS (CC&R'S, if any) enclosed.

INFORMATIONAL NOTES:

1. According to the public records, there have been no deeds conveying the land described herein within a period of twenty-four months prior to the date of this report, except as follows:

None.

2. Short Term Rate: Yes

N O T I C E

Section 12413.1 of the California insurance code, effective January 1,1990, requires that any title insurance company, under-written title company, underwritten title company, or controlled escrow company handling funds in an escrow or sub-escrow capacity, wait a specified number of days after depositing funds, before recording any documents in connection with the trans-action or disbursing funds. This statute allows for funds deposited by wire transfer to be disbursed the same day as deposit. In the case of cashier's checks or certified checks, funds may be disbursed the next day after deposit. In order to avoid unnecessary delays of three to seven days, or more please use wire transfer, cashier's checks, or certified checks whenever possible.

****

N O T I C E

In accordance with sections 18805 and 26131 of the revenue and taxation code, a buyer may be required to withhold an amount equal to three and one-third percent of the sales price in the case of the disposition of California real property interest by either:

1. A seller who is an individual with a last known street address outside of California or when the disbursement instructions authorize the proceeds be sent to a financial intermediary of the seller, or

2. A corporate seller which has no permanent place of business in California.

The buyer may become subject to penalty for failure to withhold an amount equal to the greater of 10 percent of the amount required to be withheld or five hundred dollars ($500).

However, notwithstanding any other provision included in the California statutes referenced above, no buyer will be required to withhold any amount or be subject to penalty for failure to withhold if:

1. The sales price of the California real property conveyed does not exceed one hundred thousand dollars ($100,000), or

2. The seller executes a written certificate, under the penalty of perjury, certifying that the seller is a resident of California, or if a corporation, has a permanent place of business in California, or

3. The seller, who is an individual, executes a written certificate, under the penalty of perjury, that the California real property being conveyed is the seller's principal residence (as defined in section 1034 of the internal revenue code).

The seller is subject to penalty for knowingly filing a fraudulent certificate for the purpose of avoiding the withholding requirement.

The California statutes referenced above include provisions which authorize the franchise tax board to grant reduced withholding and waivers from withholding on a case-by-case basis.

The parties to this transaction should seek an attorney's, accountants, or other tax specialist's opinion concerning the effect of this law on this transaction and should not act on any statements made or omitted by the escrow or closing officer.

Page 7

DESCRIPTION

All that certain land situated in the unincorporated area of the **County of LOS ANGELES, State of California,** and described as follows:

LOT 145 OF TRACT 9255, IN THE CITY OF LOS ANGELES AREA, COUNTY OF LOS ANGELES, STATE OF CALIFORNIA, AS PER MAP RECORDED IN BOOK 135, PAGE(S) 65 TO 66, INCLUSIVE OF MAPS IN THE OFFICE OF THE COUNTY RECORDER OF SAID COUNTY.

APN No: **6134-012-055**

Reverse Mortgages

Page 8

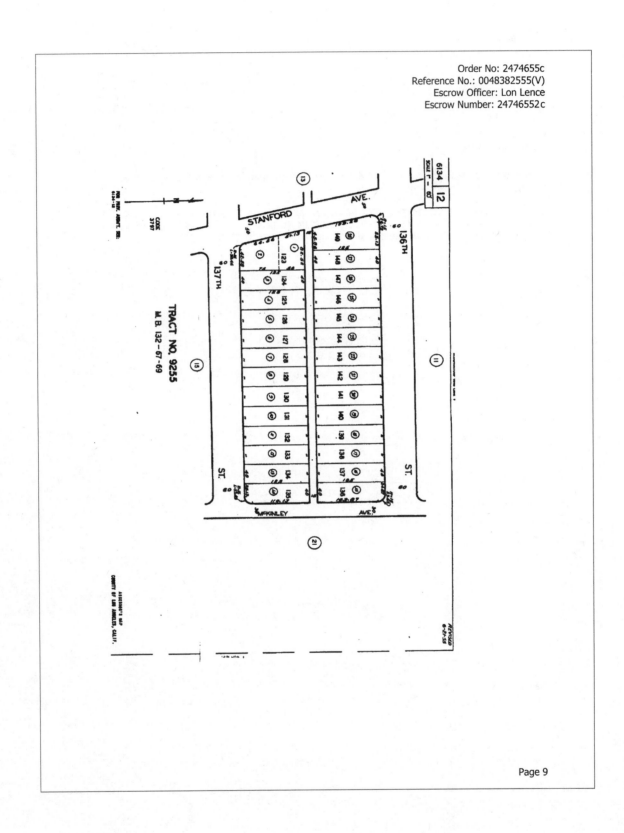

Page 9

RECORDING REQUESTED BY
FIRST TITLE CO.
WHEN RECORDED MAIL TO:
EVE DAVID
705 13TH STREET
LOS ANGELES, CA 90055
ORDER NO.: 2474655

SPACE ABOVE THIS LINE FOR RECORDER'S

MAIL TAX STATEMENTS TO:

SAME AS ABOVE

THE UNDERSIGNED GRANTOR(S) DECLA
DOCUMENTARY TRANSFER TAX IS $ 0.0(
[   ] computed on full value of property conveye
[   ] computed on full value less value of liens or encumbrances
         remaining at time of sale
[X] unincorporated area ___ city of LOS ANGELES AND

A.P.N.: 6134-012-055   Escrow No.: 2474655C

GRANT DEED

FOR A VALUABLE CONSIDERATION receipt of which is hereby acknowledged,

EVE DAVID, A WIDOW AND REGIE MAMS, AN UNMARRIED WOMAN AS JOINT TENANTS

hereby GRANT(S) to

EVE DAVID, A WIDOW

the following described real property in the City of **LOS ANGELES,** County of **LOS ANGELES,** State of California, described as

FOR LEGAL DESCRIPTION, SEE EXHIBIT "A" ATTACHED HERETO AND MADE A PART HEREOF

Dated: DECEMBER 9, 20XX
STATE OF   )
COUNTY OF   )   EVE DAVID

On _____ ,
Before me,_____ personally   REGIE MAMS
Appeared_____

personally known to me (or proved to me on the basis of satisfactory
evidence) to be the person(s) whose name(s) is/are subscribed to the
Within instrument and acknowledged to me that he/she/they executed the
Same in his/her/their authorized capacity(ies), and that by his/her/their
Signature(s) on the instrument the person(s) or the entity upon behalf of
Which the person(s) acted, executed the instrument.

WITNESS my hand and official seal.

Signature: _____

Exhibit A

LOT 145 OF TRACT 9255 IN THE CITY OF LOS ANGELES AREA, COUNTY OF LOS ANGELES, STATE OF CALIFORNIA, AS PER MAP RECORDED IN BOOK 135, PAGE(S) 65 TO 66, INCLUSIVE OF MAPS IN THE OFFICE OF THE COUNTY RECORDER OF SAID COUNTY.

PRELIMINARY CHANGE OF OWNERSHIP REPORT

To be completed by the transferee (buyer) prior to a transfer of subject property, in accordance with section 480.3 of the Revenue and Taxation Code. A *Preliminary Change of Ownership Report* must be **filed with each conveyance in the County Recorder's office for the county where the property is located.**

FOR ASSESSOR'S USE ONLY

ASSESSOR'S PARCEL NUMBER
6134-012-055

SELLER/TRANSFEROR
DAVID/MAMS

BUYER'S DAYTIME TELEPHONE NUMBER
(   )

BUYER'S EMAIL ADDRESS

STREET ADDRESS OR PHYSICAL LOCATION OF REAL PROPERTY
705 13th Street, Los Angeles, CA 90055

			MO	DAY	YEAR
☐ YES ☐ NO	This property is intended as my principal residence. If YES, please indicate the date of occupancy or intended occupancy.				

☐ YES ☐ NO Are you a disabled veteran or a unmarried surviving spouse of a disabled veteran who was compensated at 100% by the Department of Veterans Affairs?

MAIL PROPERTY TAX INFORMATION TO (NAME)
DAVID

MAIL PROPERTY TAX INFORMATION TO (ADDRESS)	CITY	STATE	ZIP CODE
705 13th Street	Los Angeles	CA	90055

PART 1. TRANSFER INFORMATION   *Please complete all statements.*

This section contains possible exclusions from reassessment for certain types of transfers.

YES NO

☐ ☐ A. This transfer is solely between spouses *(addition or removal of a spouse, death of a spouse, divorce settlement, etc.).*

☐ ☐ B. This transfer is solely between domestic partners currently registered with the California Secretary of State *(addition or removal of a partner, death of a partner, termination settlement, etc.).*

☐ ☐ *C. This is a transfer: ☐ between parent(s) and child(ren) ☐ from grandparent(s) to grandchild(ren).

☐ ☐ *D. This transfer is the result of a cotenant's death. Date of death _____

☐ ☐ *E. This transaction is to replace a principal residence owned by a person 55 years of age or older. Within the same county? ☐ YES ☐ NO

☐ ☐ *F. This transaction is to replace a principal residence by a person who is severely disabled as defined by Revenue and Taxation Code section 69.5. Within the same county? ☐ YES ☐ NO

☐ ☐ G. This transaction is only a correction of the name(s) of the person(s) holding title to the property *(e.g., a name change upon marriage).* If YES, please explain: _____

☐ ☐ H. The recorded document creates, terminates, or reconveys a lender's interest in the property.

☐ ☐ I. This transaction is recorded only as a requirement for financing purposes or to create, terminate, or reconvey a security interest *(e.g., cosigner).* If YES, please explain: _____

☐ ☐ J. The recorded document substitutes a trustee of a trust, mortgage, or other similar document.

K. This is a transfer of property:

☐ ☐ 1. to/from a revocable trust that may be revoked by the transferor and is for the benefit of ☐ the transferor, and/or ☐ the transferor's spouse ☐ registered domestic partner.

☐ ☐ 2. to/from an irrevocable trust for the benefit of the ☐ creator/grantor/trustor and/or ☐ grantor's/trustor's spouse ☐ grantor's/trustor's registered domestic partner.

☐ ☐ L. This property is subject to a lease with a remaining lease term of 35 years or more including written options.

☐ ☐ M. This is a transfer between parties in which proportional interests of the transferor(s) and transferee(s) in each and every parcel being transferred remain exactly the same after the transfer.

☐ ☐ N. This is a transfer subject to subsidized low-income housing requirements with governmentally imposed restrictions, or restrictions imposed by specified nonprofit corporations.

☐ ☐ *O. This transfer is to the first purchaser of a new building containing an active solar energy system.

☐ ☐ P. Other. This transfer is to _____

* Please refer to the instructions for Part 1.

Please provide any other information that will help the Assessor understand the nature of the transfer.

THIS DOCUMENT IS NOT SUBJECT TO PUBLIC INSPECTION

Reverse Mortgages

PART 2. OTHER TRANSFER INFORMATION   *Check and complete as applicable.*

A. Date of transfer, if other than recording date: _____

B. Type of transfer:

☐ Purchase   ☐ Foreclosure   ☐ Gift   ☐ Trade or exchange   ☐ Merger, stock, or partnership acquisition (Form BOE-100-B)

☐ Contract of sale. Date of contract: _____   ☐ Inheritance. Date of death: _____

☐ Sale/leaseback   ☐ Creation of a lease   ☐ Assignment of a lease   ☐ Termination of a lease. Date lease began: _____

Original term in years *(including written options)*: _____   Remaining term in years *(including written options)*: _____

☐ Other. Please explain: _____

C. Only a partial interest in the property was transferred. ☐ YES ☐ NO   If YES, indicate the percentage transferred: _____ %

PART 3. PURCHASE PRICE AND TERMS OF SALE   *Check and complete as applicable.*

A. Total purchase price $_____

B. Cash down payment or value of trade or exchange excluding closing costs   Amount $_____

C. First deed of trust @ _____% interest for _____ years.   Monthly payment $_____   Amount $_____

☐ FHA (___Discount Points)   ☐ Cal-Vet   ☐ VA (___Discount Points)   ☐ Fixed rate   ☐ Variable rate

☐ Bank/Savings & Loan/Credit Union   ☐ Loan carried by seller

☐ Balloon payment $_____   Due date: _____

D. Second deed of trust @ _____% interest for _____ years. Monthly payment $_____   Amount $_____

☐ Fixed rate   ☐ Variable rate   ☐ Bank/Savings & Loan/Credit Union   ☐ Loan carried by seller

☐ Balloon payment $_____   Due date: _____

E. Was an Improvement Bond or other public financing assumed by the buyer? ☐ YES ☐ NO   Outstanding balance $_____

F. Amount, if any, of real estate commission fees paid by the buyer which are not included in the purchase price $_____

G. The property was purchased: ☐ Through real estate broker. Broker name: _____ Phone number: (_____)_____

☐ Direct from seller   ☐ From a family member-Relationship _____

☐ Other. Please explain: _____

H. Please explain any special terms, seller concessions, broker/agent fees waived, financing, and any other information (e.g., buyer assumed the existing loan balance) that would assist the Assessor in the valuation of your property. _____

PART 4. PROPERTY INFORMATION   *Check and complete as applicable.*

A. Type of property transferred

☐ Single-family residence   ☐ Co-op/Own-your-own   ☐ Manufactured home

☐ Multiple-family residence. Number of units: _____   ☐ Condominium   ☐ Unimproved lot

☐ Other. Description: (i.e., timber, mineral, water rights, etc.)   ☐ Timeshare   ☐ Commercial/Industrial

B. ☐ YES ☐ NO   Personal/business property, or incentives, provided by seller to buyer are included in the purchase price. Examples of personal property are furniture, farm equipment, machinery, etc. Examples of incentives are club memberships, etc. Attach list if available.

If YES, enter the value of the personal/business property: $_____   Incentives $_____

C. ☐ YES ☐ NO   A manufactured home is included in the purchase price.

If YES, enter the value attributed to the manufactured home: $_____

☐ YES ☐ NO   The manufactured home is subject to local property tax. If NO, enter decal number: _____

D. ☐ YES ☐ NO   The property produces rental or other income.

If YES, the income is from: ☐ Lease/rent   ☐ Contract   ☐ Mineral rights   ☐ Other: _____

E. The condition of the property at the time of sale was: ☐ Good   ☐ Average   ☐ Fair   ☐ Poor

Please describe: _____

CERTIFICATION

I certify (or declare) that the foregoing and all information hereon, including any accompanying statements or documents, is true and correct to the best of my knowledge and belief.

| SIGNATURE OF BUYER/TRANSFEREE OR CORPORATE OFFICER ▶ | DATE | TELEPHONE (   ) |
| NAME OF BUYER/TRANSFEREE/PERSONAL REPRESENTATIVE/CORPORATE OFFICER (PLEASE PRINT) | TITLE | EMAIL ADDRESS |

The Assessor's office may contact you for additional information regarding this transaction.

Mail Package to
Well City Bank
FAX: 866-249-0155
Attn: KENNY WARD

Closing Instructions - HECM

Closing Agent:	**FIRST TITLE**	Document Date:	**01-07-2005**
		FHA Case #:	**196-3492489**
Borrower(s):	**EVE DAVID**		
Property Address	**705 13th STREET** **LOS ANGELES, CA. 90055**		
Loan Type:	Adjustable rate FHA "HECM"	Interest Rate: 5.79%	

IN CONNECTION WITH THE ABOVE REFERENCEDLOAN, WE REQUEST THE FOLLOW TO BE COMPLETED P
NOTE: HOME MORTGAGE MUST BE NOTIFIED OF ANY CHANGE IN PREARRANGED CHARGES IN CONNEC
PRIOR TO CLOSING. ISSUE ALTA LOAN POLICY (revision date 10/17/XX) WITH: ALTA 9 (Comprehensive), 116 Location Endorsement, ALTA 8.1 Environmental Endorsement AND FORM 9 Reverse Mortgage Endorsement OR ALTA 6.2 Adjustable Interest Rate Endorsement AND your endorsement for Open-Ended Mortgage Securing a Consumer Revolving Loan Agreement.

☒ Closing Package to be returned within **24 hours** after signing, mail to above address. Failure to return the closing package within 24 hours may delay or prevent disbursement of funds, could require re-execution of documents and may have a negative financial impact to the customer.

FINAL ALTA LOAN POLICY MUST BE IN OUR OFFICE WITHIN 5 DAYS OFAFTER CLOSING.

FUNDS MUST NOT BE DISBURSED UNTIL WELL HOME IS IN 1ST LIEN POSITION AND THE MOPRTGAGE HAS BEEN RECORED.

OTHER ENDORSEMENTS: **FORM** with liability in the amount of **$265,000.00** for the loan on the property describe herein. LIABILITY SUBJECT TO: (General and Special taxes) fiscal year CURRENT FISCAL YEAR

Funds may be used for the account of the vestees and you will record all instruments one you have complied with the following:
1. Issue said form of Policy showing title vested as shown on the attached Amendments to Escrow Instructions.
2. Issue said for of Policy free from encumbrances except item(s) **3** as shown on the preliminary Title report dated **10-26-20XX**. Secondary Financing not approved.
3. ALTA Policy must be in the amount of $265,000.00.

The following documents are enclosed for signatures:

X	FHA HECM First Note
X	FHA HECM First Deed of Trust/Mortgage
X	FHA HECM PUD or Condominium Rider, as applicable
X	FHA HECM Second Note
X	FHA HECM Second Deed of Trust/Mortgage
X	FHA HECM Loan Agreements (one original)
X	FHA HECM Repair Riders (one original)
X	FHAH Payment Plans (one original)
X	PHA HECM Federal Trust-in-Lending Closing Disclosure Statement
X	HUD-l Settlement Statement and Addendum
X	FHA Direct Endorsement Approval (HUD 92900-1, pages 3 & 4)
X	Personal Liability Notice
X	Tax/Insurance Payment Notice
X	Summary of Loan Terms and Benefits
X	Amortization Schedule
X	Total Annual Loan Cost Rate Disclosure
X	Request for Information Concerning the Borrower's Intent to Purchase an Annuity
X	Disclosure and Borrower Certification Regarding Third Party Fees
X	Compliance Agreement
X	Notice of Assignment, Sale of Transfer of Servicing Rights
X	Notice to Mortgagor at Loan Closing Regarding Prepayment
X	Flood Certification
X	Typed Uniform Residential Loan Application (FNMA 1009)
X	Name Affidavit
X	Electronics Funds Transfer Request
X	Acknowledgement of Federal Express Expense
X	W-9
X	Nearest Living Relative Information Sheet

Page 1 of 3

Mail all recorded documents and final title policy to: Wells City Bank, 3601 Wisconsin Dr., Bloomington MN 55435, ATTN; Doc Management Receiving MAC# X4701-022

REQUIREMENTS

This is a FHA "Home Equity Conversion Mortgage" ("HECM" or Reverse Mortgage) and is subject to non-standard requirements. Payments are made _from_ the Lender to the borrower as specified in the enclosed documents. **YOU MAY NOT ASSUME ANYTHING IN THE CLOSING OF THIS LOAN**. Please read and follow the instructions contained on these pages _very carefully_.

1. CORRECTIONS to any documents must be verified with Wells City prior to corrections and all documents with errors being **NEATLY BACK SLASHED AND TYPED - NOT WHITED OUT** and initialed by all borrowers.

2. Borrower(s) is/are to sign all documents **EXACTLY** as his/her name is typed on that document.

3. The lender must approve the use of a POWER OF ATTORNEY to sign loan documents. The Power of Attorney must be durable and survive the incapacity of the borrower. All documents must be signed as follows: **John Borrower by Joan Smith, as his attorney in fact.**

4. FANNIE MAE, currently the only secondary market investor for HECM loans, has imposed a strict time frame for the Lender to deliver documents to them. Therefore, the closed loan package, consisting of the documents in the order and quantity as listed on the "Closing Agent's Transmittal", **MUST** be returned to Wells City Home Mortgage within 24 hours of signing. In the event that the borrowers) has/have rescinded, you must advise us IMMEDIATELY in writing via fax to 336-854-0448.

5. **RECORDING** of documents should follow the proper chain of title. Please note that there are **TWO** Deeds of Trust/Mortgages with this transaction and they **MUST BE RECORDED IN THE PROPER ORDER**. The **first** Deed of trust/Mortgage in favor of Wells City Mortgage, N.A. **MUST** be recorded to reflect a first lien position. The **second** Deed of Trust/Mortgage in favor of HUD **MUST** be recorded immediately after the first Deed of Trust/Mortgage so it follows in a subordinate second lien position. It is **IMPERATIVE** that the first mortgage instrument be placed of record at the county **PRIOR** to the second mortgage instrument in favor of FHA, If the documents are not recorded in the correct order, we will rely on you, as the closing agent to re-record the documents at your expense.

    NOTE: Regardless of the amount shown on the Deed of Trust and Mortgage insured herein, the total liability of the Company under this policy of Title Insurance is hereby limited to the amount of insurance shown in Schedule A.

The recording language for the **first Deed of Trust/Mortgage** should be listed in **Schedule A** of the final policy and the recording language for the **second Deed of Trust/Mortgage (to HUD)** should be listed as a subordinate lien in **Schedule B-Part II**.

The following endorsement should also be made a part of the final tine policy;

X	ALTA 9 (comprehensive)
X	ALTA 8.1 Environmental Endorsement
X	116 Location Endorsement
X	Form 9 Reverse Mortgage Endorsement; or
X	ALTA 6.2 Adjustable Interest Rate, and Open-end Mortgage Securing a Consumer Revolving Loan Agreement Endorsements
___	ALTA 4 Condominium Endorsement
___	ALTA 5 Planned Unit Development Endorsement

Wells City Mortgagee clause for homeowners insurance is:
Wells City Bank, N. A. ISAOA
It's successors and/or assigns
P.O. Box 39457
Solon, Ohio 44139-9457

Lender:_____   Date: _____

Received by: _____   Date: _____
        Attorney/Closing Agent

Page 2 of 3

CLOSING AGENTS TRANSMITTAL

Re: Title Binder #: ___

Borrower(s): ___

The undersigned does hereby certify that he/she is the duly authorized closing agent for WELLS FARGO HOME MORTGAGE and that in such capacity accounted for and is transmitting (he following documents, as fully executed by the above referenced borrowers), **in the ORDER, type and quanties indicated below:**

Please stack the closing package as follows:

___ Form 928
___ Electronics Fund Transfer Request
   (If borrower does not want direct deposit, signature still required with "N/A" written across the form; If borrower does want direct deposit, form must be signed with "Voided" check attached. THIS APPLIES TO BORROWERS WITH PAYMENTS OR LINE-OF-CREDIT.)
___ First Note and 1 copy
___ Certified copy of the First Mortgage/Deed w/ Notary seal and Legal description
___ PUD or Condominium Rider, if applicable
___ Certified copy of the Second Mortgage/Deed w/ Notary seal and Legal description
___ PUD or Condominium Rider, if applicable
___ Second Note and 1 copy
___ HUD-1 and Addendum
___ Summary of Loan Terms and Benefits
___ Amortization Schedule
___ Total Annual Loan Cost Rate Disclosure
___ 1 original Loan Agreements and 1 original Schedule of Liens (2 certified copies)
___ 1 original Payment Plans (2 certified copies)
___ 1 original Repair Riders, if applicable (2 certified copies)
___ Final Truth and Lending Disclosure
___ Hazard insurance reflecting correct mortgagee clause
___ Flood insurance, if applicable
___ Nearest Living Relative Information Sheet
___ Final 1009 and pages 1,2, and 4 of the HUD 92900-A
___ Authorization to Waive FHA Homebuyer Summary 5-Day Notification Period
___ Notice to the Homebuyer
___ Closing Instructions, signed by closing agent
___ Notice of Right to Cancel
___ Federal Express Letter
___ Request for Information Concerning the Borrower's Intent to Purchase an Annuity
___ Disclosure and Borrower(s) Certification Regarding Third Party Fees
___ W-9
___ Tax/Insurance Payment Notice
___ Personal Liability Notice
___ Compliance Agreement
___ Name Affidavit with Notary Seal
___ Notice to Mortgagor at Loan Closing Regarding Prepayment
___ Notice of assignment. Sale, or Transfer of Servicing Rights
___ Flood Certification
___ Choice of Insurance, Notice to Borrower, Mortgagee, and Lender Certification
___ Any State Disclosures and/or Closing Conditions, and Miscellaneous forms

The above documents have been executed in accordance with the closing instructions and with state guidelines:

_____   _____
Closer Signature   Date

SUMMARY OF LOAN TERMS AND BENEFITS

Borrower(s): <u>EVE DAVID</u>   Loan No. _____

Youngest Borrower's Birth Date: <u>8/16/19XX</u>   Co-Borrower's Birth Date: _____

Property Appraised Value: <u>$265.000.00.</u>

Estimated Closing Date: <u>1/10/20XX</u>

	HECM Monthly	HECM Annual	Home Keeper®
Initial Interest Rate	4.270	5.870	5.750
Expected Average Interest Rate	5.790	7.3901	0.000
Maximum Lending Limit	265.000.00	265.000.00	265,000.00
Original Principal Limit	175.960.00	136,740.00	90,653.85
Upfront Premium	5,300.00	5,300.00	0.00
Other Closing Costs	7,889.33	7,889.33	7,889.33
Initial Draw	113,661.56	105,183.90	64.407.14
Servicing Fee/Set Asides	4,877.28	4,158.77	4,149.00
Net Principal Limit	30,023.83	0.00	0.00
Line of Credit	30,023,83	0.00	0.00
Monthly Payment	0.00	0.00	0.00
Length of Term			

We hereby acknowledge receipt of a copy of this Summary of Loan Terms and Benefits

_____   _____

Borrower   Date

_____   _____

Borrower   Date

OMB Approval No. 2502-0265

A. **Settlement Statement (HUD-1)**

B. Type of Loan

1. ☒ FHA	2. ☐ RHS	3. ☐ Conv. Unins.	6. File Number:	7. Loan Number: 0048382555	8. Mortgage Insurance Case Number: 197-3493819-955/956
4. ☐ VA	5. ☐ Conv. Ins.				

C. Note: This form is furnished to give you a statement of actual settlement costs. Amounts paid to and by the settlement agent are shown. Items marked "(p.o.c.)" were paid outside the closing; they are shown here for informational purposes and are not included in the totals.

D. Name & Address of Borrower:	E. Name & Address of Seller:	F. Name & Address of Lender:
EVE DAVID 705 13TH STREET LOS ANGELES, CA 90055	NA	WELL CITY BANK PO BOX 455 WEST COVINA, CA 91355

G. Property Location:	H. Settlement Agent:	I. Settlement Date:
705 13TH STREET LOS ANGELES, CA 90055	FIRST HERITAGE	
	Place of Settlement:	

J. Summary of Borrower's Transaction

100. Gross Amount Due from Borrower	
101. Contract sales price	
102. Personal property	
103. Settlement charges to borrower (line 1400)	$13,189.33
104.	
105.	
Adjustment for items paid by seller in advance	
106. City/town taxes to	
107. County taxes to	
108. Assessments to	
109.	$113,661.68
110.	
111.	
112.	
120. Gross Amount Due from Borrower	$126,850.89
200. Amount Paid by or in Behalf of Borrower	
201. Deposit or earnest money	
202. Principal amount of new loan(s)	
203. Existing loan(s) taken subject to	
204. CLOSING COSTS	$13,189.33
205.	
206.	
207.	
208.	
209.	
Adjustments for items unpaid by seller	
210. City/town taxes to	
211. County taxes to	
212. Assessments to	
213. HOME SERVICES	$113,661.56
214.	
215.	
216.	
217.	
218.	
219.	
220. Total Paid by/for Borrower	$126,850.89
300. Cash at Settlement from/to Borrower	
301. Gross amount due from borrower (line 120)	$126,850.89
302. Less amounts paid by/for borrower (line 220)	($126,850.89)
303. Cash ☐ From ☐ To Borrower	

K. Summary of Seller's Transaction

400. Gross Amount Due to Seller	
401. Contract sales price	
402. Personal property	
403.	
404.	
405.	
Adjustment for items paid by seller in advance	
406. City/town taxes to	
407. County taxes to	
408. Assessments to	
409.	$113,661.68
410.	
411.	
412.	
420. Gross Amount Due to Seller	
500. Reductions In Amount Due to seller	
501. Excess deposit (see instructions)	
502. Settlement charges to seller (line 1400)	
503. Existing loan(s) taken subject to	
504. Payoff of first mortgage loan	
505. Payoff of second mortgage loan	
506.	
507.	
508.	
509.	
Adjustments for items unpaid by seller	
510. City/town taxes to	
511. County taxes to	
512. Assessments to	
513.	
514.	
515.	
516.	
517.	
518.	
519.	
520. Total Reduction Amount Due Seller	
600. Cash at Settlement to/from Seller	
601. Gross amount due to seller (line 420)	
602. Less reductions in amounts due seller (line 520)	( )
603. Cash ☐ To ☐ From Seller	

The Public Reporting Burden for this collection of information is estimated at 35 minutes per response for collecting, reviewing, and reporting the data. This agency may not collect this information, and you are not required to complete this form, unless it displays a currently valid OMB control number. No confidentiality is assured; this disclosure is mandatory. This is designed to provide the parties to a RESPA covered transaction with information during the settlement process.

L. Settlement Charges

700. Total Real Estate Broker Fees		Paid From Borrower's Funds at Settlement	Paid From Seller's Funds at Settlement
Division of commission (line 700) as follows :			
701. $ to			
702. $ to			
703. Commission paid at settlement			
704.			

800. Items Payable in Connection with Loan			
801. Our origination charge	$ 5,300.00 (from GFE #1)		
802. Your credit or charge (points) for the specific interest rate chosen	$ (from GFE #2)		
803. Your adjusted origination charges	(from GFE #A)		
804. Appraisal fee to	(from GFE #3)	$475.00	
805. Credit report to	(from GFE #3)	$14.00	
806. Tax service to	(from GFE #3)		
807. Flood certification to	(from GFE #3)		
808. Repair Admin - WELL CITY		$141.33	
809. Courier Fee		$80.00	
810.			
811.			

900. Items Required by Lender to be Paid in Advance			
901. Daily interest charges from to @ $ /day	(from GFE #10)		
902. Mortgage insurance premium for months to	(from GFE #3)		
903. Homeowner's insurance for years to	(from GFE #11)		
904.			

1000. Reserves Deposited with Lender			
1001. Initial deposit for your escrow account	(from GFE #9)		
1002. Homeowner's insurance months @ $ per month $			
1003. Mortgage insurance months @ $ per month $			
1004. Property Taxes months @ $ per month $			
1005. months @ $ per month $			
1006. months @ $ per month $			
1007. Aggregate Adjustment -$			

1100. Title Charges			
1101. Title services and lender's title insurance	(from GFE #4)	$100.00	
1102. Settlement or closing fee	$		
1103. Owner's title insurance	(from GFE #5)	$742.00	
1104. Lender's title insurance	$		
1105. Lender's title policy limit $			
1106. Owner's title policy limit $			
1107. Agent's portion of the total title insurance premium to	$		
1108. Underwriter's portion of the total title insurance premium to	$		
1109. Notary Fees to First Title		$200.00	
1110. Escrow First Title		$350.00	
1111.			

1200. Government Recording and Transfer Charges			
1201. Government recording charges	(from GFE #7)	$75.00	
1202. Deed $ Mortgage $ Release $			
1203. Transfer taxes	(from GFE #8)	$75.00	
1204. City/County tax/stamps Deed $ Mortgage $			
1205. State tax/stamps Deed $ Mortgage $			
1206.		$30.00	

1300. Additional Settlement Charges			
1301. Required services that you can shop for	(from GFE #6)		
1302. Pest Inspection to Pest Control	$	$65.00	
1303.	$		
1304.			
1305.			

1400. Total Settlement Charges (enter on lines 103, Section J and 502, Section K)		$13,189.33	

Estimated Amortization Schedule for EVE DAVID

Age of Youngest Borrower: 70
Initial Interest Rate : 4.270%
Loan Limit: $265,000.00
Initial Principal Limit: $175,960.00
Initial Draw: $113,661.56
Financed Closing Costs: $13,189.33

Initial Property Value: $265,000.00
Beginning Mortgage Balance: $126,850.00
Expected Appreciation: 4.000%
Initial Line of Credit: $30,023.83
Monthly Payment: $0.00
Monthly Servicing Fee: $30.00

Year	Age	Service Fee	Monthly Payment	MIP	Interest	Loan Balance	Line of Credit	Property
1	71	360.00	0.00	649.29	5,544.98	133,405.16	31,487.70	275,600.00
2	72	360.00	0.00	682.79	5,831.04	140,278.99	33,022.93	286,624.00
3	73	360.00	0.00	717.94	6,131.08	147,488.01	34,633.03	298,088.96
4	74	360.00	0.00	754.77	6,445.70	155,048.48	36,321.62	310,012.52
5	75	360.00	0.00	793.42	6,775.70	162,977.60	38,092.55	322,413.02
6	76	360.00	0.00	833.93	7,121.78	171,293.31	39,949.82	335,309.54
7	77	360.00	0.00	876.43	7,484.75	180,014.49	41,897.64	348,721.92
8	78	360.00	0.00	920.99	7,865.36	189,160.84	43,940.44	362,670.80
9	79	360.00	0.00	967.75	8,264.57	198,753.16	46,082.83	377,177.63
10	80	360.00	0.00	1,016.79	8,683.25	208,813.20	48,329.68	392,264.74
11	81	360.00	0.00	1,068.21	9,122.30	219,363.71	50,686.08	407,955.32
12	82	360.00	0.00	1,122.11	9,582.82	230,428.64	53,157.37	424,273.54
13	83	360.00	0.00	1,178.65	10,065.74	242,033.03	55,749.15	441,244.48
14	84	360.00	0.00	1,237.95	10,572.22	254,203.20	58,467.30	458,894.26
15	85	360.00	0.00	1,300.18	11,103.42	266,966.80	61,317.98	477,250.03
16	86	360.00	0.00	1,365.40	11,660.49	280,352.69	64,307.65	496,340.03
17	87	360.00	0.00	1,433.81	12,244.73	294,391.23	67,443.08	516,193.63
18	88	360.00	0.00	1,505.58	12,857.47	309,114.28	70,731.39	536,841.38
19	89	360.00	0.00	1,580.81	13,500.05	324,555.14	74,180.02	558,315.03
20	90	360.00	0.00	1,659.72	14,173.99	340,748.85	77,796.80	580,647.63
21	91	360.00	0.00	1,742.48	14,880.77	357,732.10	81,589.92	603,873.54
22	92	360.00	0.00	1,829.28	15,622.03	375,543.41	85,567.99	628,028.48
23	93	360.00	0.00	1,920.30	16,399.42	394,223.13	89,740.01	653,149.62
24	94	360.00	0.00	2,015.79	17,214.70	413,813.62	94,115.44	679,275.60
25	95	360.00	0.00	2,115.89	18,069.76	434,359.27	98,704.21	706,446.63
26	96	360.00	0.00	2,220.90	18,966.48	455,906.65	103,516.71	734,704.49
27	97	360.00	0.00	2,331.02	19,906.95	478,504.62	108,563.85	764,092.67
28	98	360.00	0.00	2,446.51	20,893.27	502,204.40	113,857.07	794,656.38
29	99	360.00	0.00	2,567.65	21,927.68	527,059.73	119,408.38	826,442.63
30	100	360.00	0.00	2,694.68	23,012.51	553,126.92	125,230.35	859,500.34

Total Annual Loan Cost Rate

LOAN TERMS:
Age of Youngest Borrower: 70
Appraised Property Value: $265,000.00

Initial Interest Rate: 4.270%
Monthly Loan Advance: $0.00
Length of Term:

Initial Draw: $113,661.56
Line of Credit: $30,023.83

INITIAL LOAN CHARGES,
Closing costs: 7,889.33
Mortgage Insurance Premium: $5,300.00
Annuity Charges: $0. 00

MONTHLY LOAN CHARGES:
Servicing Fee: $30.00 ,
Mortgage Insurance: 0.5% annually

OTHER CHARGES: $0.00

REPAYMENT LIMITS: You have no personal liability for payment of the loan. The lender's recovery from you will be limited to the value of the property. Net proceeds are estimated at 93% of the projected home sale value.

Assumed Annual Home Appreciation	Total Annual Loan Cost Rate			
	2 - year loan term	8 - year loan term	15 - year loan term	21 - year loan term
0%	10.39%	6.38%	4.43%	3.14%
4%	10.39%	6.38%	5.75%	5.53%
8%	10.39%	6.38%	5.75%	5.53%

The cost of any reverse mortgage loan depends on how long you keep the loan and how much your house appreciates in value. Generally, the longer you keep 9 reverse mortgage, the lower the total annual loan cost rate will be.

This table shows the estimated cost of your reverse mortgage loan, expressed as an annual rate. It illustrates the cost for your age, that life expectancy, and 1.4 times that life expectancy. The table also shows the cost of the loan, assuming the value of your home appreciates at three different rates: 0%, 4%. and 9%.

The total annual cost rates in this table are based on the total charges associated with this loan. These charges typically include principal, interest, closing costs, mortgage insurance premiums, annuity costs, and servicing costs (but not disposition costs - costs when you sell the home).

The rates in this table are estimates. Your actual cost may differ if, for example, the amount of your loan advances varies or the interest rate on your mortgage changes. You may receive projections of loan balances from counselors or lenders that are based on an expected average mortgage rate that differs from the initial interest rate.

SIGNING AN APPLICATION OR RECEIVING THESE DISCLOSURES DOES NOT REQUIRE YOU TO COMPLETE THIS LOAN

_____   _____
Borrower   **EVE DAVID**   Date

_____   _____
Borrower   Date

HomEst Servicing Corporation
Post Office Box-13755
Sacramento. CA 95855
4855 Watts Avenue
North Highlands, CA 95655

```
*********************************************************************************
* Please contact Customer Service by calling 1.877-867-7355 with any    *
* questions concerning the payoff statement. Interest will accrue until  *
* the full amount is received.                                           *
*********************************************************************************
```

December 28, 20XX

Rob Wager
Well City Home Mortgage

Mortgagor Information
Eve David
Regie Mams

705 13TH STREET
LOS ANGELES CA 90055

Payoff Requestor
Rob Wager
Well City Home Mortgage

Loan Information
Loan Number: 0000321151655
Loan Type: 13 - Conventional Resid. w/o Principal

Property Address
705 13th Street
LOS ANGELS 90055

The payoff itemization amounts below are subject to final verification upon receipt of funds by HomEst.

This Payoff Quote is Good Through	01/28/2005
The Next Payment Due Is	01/28/2005
The Current Total Unpaid Principal Balance Is	$107,363.22
Interest At 6.95%	$3,062.33
Daily Per Diem	$20.65
Prepayment Penalty Charge	$2,980.27
Demand Fee	$60.00
Late Charge Fee	$9.00
Recording Fee	$71.50
Unpaid Other Fees	$100.00
Recoverable Corporate Advance Balance	$15.24
Total Amount To Pay This Account In FULL	**$113,661.56**

The current escrow balance of 103.06 may change due to receipt, and/or disbursements from the account prior to payment in full.

Issuance of this statement does not suspend the contract requirement to make the mortgage payments when due. A late charge of $35.75 will be assessed 15 days after a current payment is due.

Refer to the following Payoff Stipulations for additional information and instructions.

PAYOFF STIPULATIONS

Notice:
This payoff quote is subject to the conditions listed below. If you are acting as a payoff agent, you are responsible for providing this information to the mortgagor including all fees and costs. If you have any questions about HomEst payoff stipulations, please contact HomEst Customer Service by calling 1-877-867-7355.

Verify Information:
It is important that you verify this quote is for the correct account and property address. HomEst will not accept responsibility for a payoff received referencing the incorrect account number or property address.

Send Payoff Remittance To:
Payoff checks sent to locations other than the addresses listed above will be forwarded to the Payoff Processing Department and interest will continue to accrue until the: payoff funds are received at the North Highlands location.

1) Wire Transfers	2) Overnight Mail	3) US Postal Mail
Wachovia Bank, NA	HomEst Servicing Corporation	HomEst Servicing Corporation
301 College Street	Ann: Pay off Processing	Attn: Payoff Processing
Charlotte NC 28255	437 Watts Avenue	P.O. Box. 130055
ABA ff 053-000219	Highlands, CA 95655	Sacramento, CA 95855
Credit to: HomEst		
Account # 5000000021155		

Payoff Deadline:
Interest will accrue until the payoff funds arc received by the Payoff Processing Department Funds received after 11:00 AM PST will be processed the next business day and interest will be calculated accordingly. While we accept other forms of payment such as title company and closing attorney trust account. We request payoff funds be submitted in the form of a Cashier's Check, made payable to HomEst or a wire transfer to the above referenced account.

Insufficient Payoff Funds:
Any instrument received by HomEst fee an amount less than that required to pay the account in full, except in West Virginia, will be applied first to any payments delinquent or due, accrued interest repayable advances and fees. Any remaining funds will be applied to the principal balance of the account. The funds will be applied effective the day the instrument is received by HomEst The account will not be considered paid in full even if the instrument received contains or is accompanied by language: asserting such. By accepting and negotiating any instrument HomEst does not revoke its legal claim for collecting all outstanding amounts due on the account. Interest will continue to accrue on the principal balance remaining on the account until the entire outstanding amount is paid in full.

In the case of insufficient funds, the issuer of the instrument will be contacted (or the remaining amount due and payable. Written authorization is required to credit a positive escrow balance to the payoff amount.

For accounts secured by property in the state of West Virginia: if the instrument is for an amount less than what is required to pay the account in full, the issuer will be contacted prior to the application of the instrument to the account.

In the states of California, Indiana, Minnesota, New York, Ohio, and Virginia, a prepayment penalty may be waived when the payoff results from the sale of the property. The waiver may depend on lien position, and evidence of the sale (i.e., settlement statement/HUD1) must be presented to qualify for such waiver/refund.

DISPUTED DEBTS, INCLUDING INSTRUMENTS TENDERED AS FULL SATISFACTION OF A DEBT, MUST BE MAILED TO THE FOLLOWING ADDRESS:
HomEst Servicing Corporation
P.O. Box 13716
Attn: Account Research
Sacramento, CA 95816

<u>Automatic Draft Information:</u>
If the monthly payment is automatically draftee do not cancel a draft already applied to the account. To stop the next monthly draft, please contact HomEst Customer Service no later than 10 days before the draft date. If the draft is processed prior to receiving the payoff and the payment amount is also included in the payoff amount, the excess will be placed in escrow and refunded. A draft transaction rejected due to a NSF as stop-payment will delay the payoff process.

<u>Release/Reconveyance:</u>
Please include recording information on the mortgage by providing a copy of the appropriate schedule from the Title Commitment/Policy. The inclusion of the required information will accelerate the release/reconveyance process. Release/reconveyance documents will be sent to the county courthouse. Verification of the release will be sent to the borrower.

HOMEST SERVICING CORPORATION IS A DEBT COLLECTOR. HOMEST IS ATTEMPTING TO COLLECT A DEBT AND ANY INFORMATION OBTAINED: WILL BE USED FOR THAT PURPOSE.

IMPORTANT DISCLOSURES:

California
As required by law, you are hereby notified that a negative credit report reflecting on your credit record may be submitted to a credit reporting agency if you fail to fulfill the terms of your credit obligations.

Colorado
Collection agencies are licensed by the Colorado Collection Agency Board, 1525 Sherman Street, 5th Floor, Denver, Colorado 80203. Please do not send payments to the collection agency board.
      If you notify HomEst in writing that:
- You wish HomEst to cease contact by telephone at your residence or place of employment, then no such further contact by telephone shall be made,
- If you refuse to pay a debt or you wish HomEst to cease further communication with you, then HomEst shall not communicate further with you with respect to such debt, except for a written communication:
- To advise you that HomEst's further efforts are being terminated,
- To advise you that HomEst or your creditor may invoke specified remedies which are ordinarily invoked by HomEst or your creditor; or
- Where applicable, to notify you that HomEst or your creditor intends to invoke a specified remedy permitted by law.

Minnesota
This collection agency is licensed by the Minnesota Department of Commerce.
New York City
Collection Agency License; 1099500 - North Highlands, CA (Main Office)
              1099501 - Raleigh, NC (Branch)
              1099512 -Boone, NC (Branch)

North Carolina
Collection Agency Permit: 3677 - North Highlands, CA (Main Office)
              3676 - Raleigh, NC (Branch)
              3675 - Boone, NC (Branch)

Tennessee
This collection agency is licensed by the Collection Service Board, State Department of Commerce and Industry, 500 James Robertson Parkway, Nashville, Tennessee 37243

Premier Insurance
'You are First with us'

EVIDENCE OF INSURANCE

Coverage afforded by the policy is provided by Premier Insurance, Des Moines, Iowa

Premium NO.   909357W5
First Mortgage Loan Number: 000032115655

Insured's name, mailing address and zip code:
  EVE DAVID
  705 13 TH STREET
  LOS ANGELES
  CA   90055

Location of Premises (If different than shown above):
  SAME

First Mortgagee, address and zip code: Policy contains 438 BFU (AU359)
in favor of
  WELL CITY BANK NA ITS SUCCESSORS &/OR ASSIGNS
  P O BOX 39455
  SOLID, OH 44155 - 5106

The POLICY PERIOD will begin on the date shown and will continue with no fixed date of expiration. The PREMIUM PERIOD will be Annual and begins on the same date shown.	The POLICY PERIOD and PREMIUM PERIOD will begin at 12:01 a.m. Standard Time on 01/19/20XX to 01/19/20XX

Insurance 1s provided as follows;
    FIRE POLICY FORM - SPECIAL
    Policy Limit of Liability
    Section I/II Dwelling Protection $104,192.00
    Total Annual Policy Premium $226.00

Deductibles
  $500   to loss to the covered property front all insured perils.

Page 1 of 2

EVIDENCE OF INSURANCE

Number: 000032115655

PROVISIONS: This form is not the contract of insurance. The provisions of the policy shall prevail in all respects.

All premiums for the insurance policy shall be computed in accordance with Allstate's rules, forms, premiums and minimum premiums applicable to the insurance afforded which are in effect at the inception of the insurance and upon each anniversary thereof, including the date of interim changes.

It is understood that should the insurance protection evidenced herein terminate for any reason, due notice will be given to the Insured, to the mortgagee, and to all other interested parties in accordance with the standard mortgagee clause (438 BFU).

A copy of the Policy Declarations ref1ecting the annual premium will be sent, if required, to the mortgagee and to any other interested parties.

Authorized Agent: GABI MEJA
                     Exclusive Agent
                     445 N. Garey Ave.
                     Suite #7
                     Pomona   CA   91767
                     (909) 391-0987

Agent Signature: _____

Published 2/12/15. Please review Mortgagee Letters 2014-21 and 2015-02 for the effective dates of the new language in these model documents.

MODEL MORTGAGE FORM
ADJUSTABLE RATE
(HOME EQUITY CONVERSION)
[See Instructions Attached]

o.: **196-3492489-832**
     0048382555

[Space Above This Line For Recording Data]

MORTGAGE

THIS MORTGAGE ("Security Instrument") is given on **January 10, 20XX**. The mortgagor is **Eve David, a widow**, whose address is **705 13th Street, Los Angeles, CA 90055** ("Borrower"). The term "Borrower" does not include the Borrower's successors and assigns. This Security Instrument is given to **Well City Bank, N.A.**, which is organized and existing under the laws of **The United States of America**, and whose address is **P.O. Box 10000, Mediapolis, Iowa 50306-030** ("Lender"). Borrower has agreed to repay to Lender amounts which Lender is obligated to advance, including future advances made on the Borrower's behalf, under the terms of a Home Equity Conversion Mortgage Adjustable Rate Loan Agreement ("Loan Agreement") dated the same date as this Security Instrument. The agreement to repay is evidenced by Borrower's Note dated the same date as this Security Instrument ("Note"). This Security Instrument secures to Lender: (a) the repayment of the debt evidenced by the Note, with interest, and all renewals, extensions and modifications of the Note, up to a maximum principal amount of **Three Hundred Ninety Seven Thousand Five Hundred and 00/100 Dollars (U.S. $397,500.00)**; (b) the payment of all other sums, with interest, advanced under Paragraph 5 to protect the security of this Security Instrument or otherwise due under the terms of this Security Instrument; and (c) the performance of Borrower's covenants and agreements under this Security Instrument and the Note and Loan Agreement. For this purpose, Borrower does hereby mortgage, warrant, grant and convey to Lender, with power of sale, the following described property located in: **Los Angeles County, California**

LOT 145 OF TRACT 9255 IN THE CITY OF LOS ANGELES AREA, COUNTY OF LOS ANGELES, STATE OF CALIFORNIA, AS PER MAP RECOREDED IN BOOK 135, PAGES(S) 65 TO 66, INCLUSIVE OF MAPS IN THE OFFICE OF THE COUNTY RECORDER OF SAID COUNTY.

which has the address of   507 13th Street

Los Angeles	California	90055	("Property Address")
(City)	(State)	(Zip Code)	

TOGETHER WITH all the improvements now or hereafter erected on the property, and all easements, rights, appurtenances, and fixtures now or hereafter a part of the property. All replacements and additions shall also be covered by this Security Instrument. All of the foregoing is referred to in this Security Instrument as the "Property."

BORROWER COVENANTS that Borrower is lawfully seized of the estate hereby conveyed and has the right to mortgage, grant and convey the Property and that the Property is unencumbered. Borrower warrants and will defend generally the title to the Property against all claims and demands, subject to any encumbrances of record.

Page **1** of **14**

NOTES

This is the first "Deed of Trust" in this sample HECM package. It names the lender as beneficiary. The first deed secures the lender.

Published 2/12/15. Please review Mortgagee Letters 2014-21 and 2015-02 for the effective dates of the new language in these model documents.

THIS SECURITY INSTRUMENT combines uniform covenants for national use and non-uniform covenants with limited variations by jurisdiction to constitute a uniform security instrument covering real property.

UNIFORM COVENANTS. Borrower and Lender covenant and agree as follows:

1. **Payment of Principal and Interest.** Borrower shall pay when due the principal of $_____$, and interest on, the debt evidenced by the Note.

2. **Payment of Property Charges.** Borrower shall pay all property charges consisting of property taxes, hazard insurance premiums, flood insurance premiums, ground rents, condominium fees, planned unit development fees, homeowner's association fees, and any other special assessments that may be required by local or state law in a timely manner, and shall provide evidence of payment to Lender, unless Lender pays property charges as provided for in and in accordance with the Loan Agreement.

3. **Fire, Flood and Other Hazard Insurance.** Borrower shall insure all improvements on the Property, whether now in existence or subsequently erected, against any hazards, casualties, and contingencies, including but not limited to fire and flood, for which Lender requires insurance. Such insurance shall be maintained in the amounts and for the periods that Lender requires; Lender has the discretion to increase or decrease the amount of any insurance required at any time provided the amount is equal to or greater than any minimum required by the Secretary of Housing and Urban Development ("Secretary"). Whether or not Lender imposes a flood insurance requirement, Borrower shall at a minimum insure all improvements on the Property, whether now in existence or subsequently erected, against loss by floods to the extent required by the Secretary. If the Lender imposes insurance requirements, all insurance shall be carried with companies approved by Lender, and the insurance policies and any renewals shall be held by Lender and shall include loss payable clauses in favor of and in a form acceptable to Lender.

   In the event of loss, Borrower shall give Lender immediate notice by mail. Lender may make proof of loss if not made promptly by Borrower. Each insurance company concerned is hereby authorized and directed to make payment for such loss to Lender instead of to Borrower and Lender jointly. Insurance proceeds shall be applied to restoration or repair of the damaged Property, if the restoration or repair is economically feasible and Lender's security is not lessened. If the restoration or repair is not economically feasible or Lender's security would be lessened, the insurance proceeds shall be applied first to the reduction of any indebtedness under a Second Note and Second Security Instrument (as described in Paragraph 15) held by the Secretary on the Property and then to the reduction of the indebtedness under the Note and this Security Instrument. Any excess insurance proceeds over an amount required to pay all outstanding indebtedness under the Note and this Security Instrument shall be paid to the entity legally entitled thereto.

   In the event of foreclosure of this Security Instrument or other transfer of title to the Property that extinguishes the indebtedness, all right, title and interest of Borrower in and to insurance policies in force shall pass to the purchaser.

4. **Occupancy, Preservation, Maintenance and Protection of the Property; Borrower's Loan Application; Leaseholds.** Borrower shall occupy, establish, and use the Property as Borrower's Principal Residence after the execution of this Security Instrument and Borrower (or at least one Borrower, if initially more than one person are Borrowers) shall continue to occupy the Property as Borrower's Principal Residence for the term of the Security Instrument.

Page **2** of **14**

Published 2/12/15. Please review Mortgagee Letters 2014-21 and 2015-02 for the effective dates of the new language in these model documents.

Instructions for Model Adjustable Rate Mortgage Form (Home Equity Conversion)

HUD requires that a security instrument follow the form and content of the approved FNMA/FHLMC security instrument for the jurisdiction, except where HUD has determined that differences are needed to reflect HUD policy and practice. The following explains those differences. Additional instructions are found in Chapter 4, HUD Handbook 4155.2 and Chapter 6, HUD Handbook 4235.1.

1. Language Preceding Uniform Covenants

Use FNMA/FHLMC language but:

a. Add a box for the FHA Case No. as shown on the Model Form.

b. For a Mortgage, delete the language beginning with "THIS MORTGAGE" or "THIS DEED OF TRUST" through "covenants and agreements under this Security Instrument and Note." Substitute the language shown on the Model Form. The phrase "up to a maximum principal amount of Dollars _____(U.S. $_____)" should be omitted in jurisdictions where there is no legal requirement to state the maximum principal amount in a mortgage or deed of trust. If the phrase is used, the blank should be completed with an amount equal to or greater than 150% of the maximum claim amount.

c. For a Deed of Trust, follow the instructions in "b" above, except that the first three sentences of the Model Form must be further revised to read as follows:

> This DEED OF TRUST ("Security Instrument") is made on_____, 20__. The grantor [or trustor] is ("Borrower"). The trustee is _____ ("Trustee"). The beneficiary is_____, which is organized and existing under the laws of_____, and whose address is_____ ("Lender").

d. For Colorado deeds of trust, Georgia security deeds and Louisiana mortgages, the FNMA/FHLMC forms should be consulted for guidance regarding additional adaptation of the initial language of the Security Instrument, including language describing a note for Louisiana.

e. For Maine and New York in which FNMA and FHLMC use "plain English" forms, the format and language should be based on FNMA/FHLMC forms for other states provided that the language is in conformity with applicable law.

The Model Form uses the FNMA/FHLMC language for Michigan as an example. The form may include variations to the standard language that have been approved by FNMA and/or FHLMC.

2. Uniform Covenants

The form should designate the paragraphs preceding Paragraph 24 on foreclosure procedures as "Uniform Covenants". The text of these paragraphs must be used as presented in the Model Form without any change. FNMA/FHLMC language may not be substituted. If change is needed to make requirements of state or local law or practice, written approval from HUD is needed before the change is made.

Page **13** of **14**

Published 2/12/15. Please review Mortgagee Letters 2014-21 and 2015-02 for the effective dates of the new language in these model documents.

3. Non-Uniform Covenants

The form should designate the paragraphs beginning with Paragraph 23 on assignment of rents as "Non-Uniform Covenants".

a. The FNMA/FHLMC paragraph on foreclosure procedures will need adaptation to reflect HUD policy. The Model Form contains an adaptation of the FNMA/FHLMC language for Michigan as an example. Following the phrase "If Lender requires immediate payment in full under Paragraph 10" as shown in Paragraph 24 of the Model Form, the mortgage should use the foreclosure procedures paragraph of the current approved FNMA/FHLMC form (including language regarding payment of costs such as attorney's fees) as a guide with any necessary adaptation to conform to these instructions. Language in the FNMA/FHLMC paragraph regarding notice and acceleration should be omitted. For Maine and New York, Lenders should use foreclosure language based on these instructions and other FNMA/FHLMC forms that are not "plain English" forms provided that the language will authorize foreclosure in conformity with applicable law. The mortgage must include the Lender's right to a public sale of the Property, including a power of sale if legally permissible in the jurisdiction in which the property is located even if mortgages are usually foreclosed through a judicial proceeding.

b. The paragraphs following Paragraph 24 should contain provisions required to adapt the mortgage to the laws and practices of the particular jurisdiction in which the Property is located. The text of these paragraphs should be the same as the FNMA/FHLMC non-uniform covenants for the jurisdiction in which the Property is located. Changes to the FNMA/FHLMC paragraphs and additional material may be included if needed to conform to requirements of state law or practice. The paragraph entitled "Riders to this Security Instrument" should be used as shown in the Model Form instead of as shown in the FNMA/FHLMC forms.

c. Any special language or notices required by applicable law should appear following the non-uniform covenants using the FNMA/FHLMC form as a guide.

4. Signatures, etc.

Use the FNMA/FHLMC format at the end of the mortgage except that:

a. Witness lines may be omitted if state and local law does not require witnesses for mortgages.

b. HUD does not require the Borrower's social security number to appear on the mortgage.

Page **14** of **14**

Published 2/12/15. Please review Mortgagee Letters 2014-21 and 2015-02 for the effective dates of the new language in these model documents.

NOTES

This is the second "Deed of Trust." It names the applicable official of the U.S. HUD department field office as the trustee and the Secretary of HUD as the beneficiary. The second "Deed of Trust" must be executed in the event the original lender cannot continue to make payments to the borrower under the Note. The second deed secures FHA.

MODEL SECOND MORTGAGE FORM
ADJUSTABLE RATE
(HOME EQUITY CONVERSION)
[See Instructions Attached]

6-3492489-832
48382555

[Space Above This Line For Recording Data]

SECOND MORTGAGE

THIS MORTGAGE ("Security Instrument" or "Second Security Instrument") is given on **January 10, 20XX**. The mortgagor is **Eve David, a widow**, whose address is **705 13th Street, Los Angeles, CA 90055** ("Borrower"). The term "Borrower" does not include the Borrower's successors and assigns. This Security Instrument is given to the Secretary of Housing and Urban Development, whose address is 451 Seventh Street, S.W., Washington, DC 20410 ("Lender" or "Secretary"). Borrower has agreed to repay to Lender amounts which Lender is obligated to advance, including future advances, under the terms of a Home Equity Conversion Mortgage Adjustable Rate Loan Agreement dated the same date as this Security Instrument ("Loan Agreement"). The agreement to repay is evidenced by Borrower's Note dated the same date as this Security Instrument ("Second Note"). This Security Instrument secures to Lender: (a) the repayment of the debt evidenced by the Second Note, with interest, and all renewals, extensions and modifications of the Note, up to a maximum principal amount of **Three Hundered Ninety Seven Thousand Five Hundered and 00/100 Dollars (U.S.$397,500.00)**; (b) the payment of all other sums, with interest, advanced under Paragraph 5 to protect the security of this Security Instrument or otherwise due under the terms of this Security Instrument; and (c) the performance of Borrower's covenants and agreements under this Security Instrument and the Second Note. For this purpose, Borrower does hereby mortgage, warrant, grant and convey to Lender, with power of sale, the following described property located in **Los Angeles County,**

LOT 145 OF TRACT 9255 IN THE CITY OF LOS ANGELES AREA, COUNTY OF LOS ANGELES, STATE OF CALIFORNIA, AS PER MAP RECOREDED IN BOOK 135, PAGES(S) 65 TO 66, INCLUSIVE OF MAPS IN THE OFFICE OF THE COUNTY RECORDER OF SAID COUNTY.

which has the address of 507 13th Street [Street]

California	Los Angeles	90055	
[State]	[City]	[Zip Code]	("Property Address");

TOGETHER WITH all the improvements now or hereafter erected on the property, and all easements, rights, appurtenances, and fixtures now or hereafter a part of the property. All replacements and additions shall also be covered by this Security Instrument. All of the foregoing is referred to in this Security Instrument as the "Property."

BORROWER COVENANTS that Borrower is lawfully seized of the estate hereby conveyed and has the right to mortgage, grant and convey the Property and that the Property is only encumbered by a First Security Instrument given by Borrower and dated the same date as this Security Instrument ("First Security Instrument"). Borrower warrants and will defend generally the title to the Property against all claims and demands, subject to any encumbrances of record.

Page **1** of **14**

Published 2/12/15. Please review Mortgagee Letters 2014-21 and 2015-02 for the effective dates of the new language in these model documents.

Instructions for Model Adjustable Rate Second Mortgage Form (Home Equity Conversion)

HUD requires that a security instrument follow the form and content of the approved FNMA/FHLMC security instrument for the jurisdiction, except where HUD has determined that differences are needed to reflect HUD policy and practice. The following explains those differences. Additional instructions are found in Chapter 4, HUD Handbook 4155.2 and Chapter 6, HUD Handbook 4235.1.

1. **Language Preceding Uniform Covenants**

Use FNMA/FHLMC language but:

a. Add a box for the FHA Case No. as shown on the Model Form.

b. For a Mortgage, delete the language beginning with "THIS MORTGAGE" or "THIS DEED OF TRUST" through "covenants and agreements under this Security Instrument and Note." Substitute the language shown on the Model Form. The phrase "up to a maximum principal amount of Dollars _____(U.S. $_____)" should be omitted in jurisdictions where there is no legal requirement to state the maximum principal amount in a mortgage or deed of trust. If the phrase is used, the blank should be completed with an amount equal to or greater than 150% of the maximum claim amount.

c. For a Deed of Trust, follow the instructions in "b" above, except that the first three sentences of the Model Form must be further revised to read as follows:

> This DEED OF TRUST ("Security Instrument" or "Second Security Instrumnet") is made on_____, 20__. The grantor [or trustor] is ("Borrower"). The trustee is _____ ("Trustee"). The beneficiary is the Secretary of Housing and Urban Development, whose address is 451 Seventh Street, S.W., Washington, D.C. 20410 ("Lender" or "Secretary").

d. For Colorado deeds of trust, Georgia security deeds and Louisiana mortgages, the FNMA/FHLMC forms should be consulted for guidance regarding the initial language of the Security Instrument, including language describing a note for Louisiana.

e. For Maine and New York in which FNMA and FHLMC use "plain English" forms, the format and language should be based on FNMA/FHLMC forms for other states provided that the language is in conformity with applicable law.

The Model Form uses the FNMA/FHLMC language for Michigan as an example. The form may include variations to the standard language that have been approved by FNMA and/or FHLMC.

2. **Uniform Covenants**

The form should designate the paragraphs preceding Paragraph 25 on foreclosure procedures as "Uniform Covenants". The text of these paragraphs must be used as presented in the Model Form without any change. FNMA/FHLMC language may not be substituted. If change is needed to make requirements of state or local law or practice, written approval from HUD is needed before the change is made.

3. **Non-Uniform Covenants**

Page **13** of **14**

Published 2/12/15. Please review Mortgagee Letters 2014-21 and 2015-02 for the effective dates of the new language in these model documents.

The form should designate the paragraphs beginning with Paragraph 24 on assignment of rents as "Non-Uniform Covenants".

   a. The FNMA/FHLMC paragraph on foreclosure procedures will need adaptation to reflect HUD policy. The Model Form contains an adaptation of the FNMA/FHLMC language for Michigan as an example. Following the phrase "If Lender requires immediate payment in full under Paragraph 10" as shown in Paragraph 25 of the Model Form, the mortgage should use the foreclosure procedures paragraph of the current approved FNMA/FHLMC form (including language regarding payment of costs such as attorney's fees) as a guide with any necessary adaptation to conform to these instructions. Language in the FNMA/FHLMC paragraph regarding notice and acceleration should be omitted. For Maine and New York, Lenders should use foreclosure language based on these instructions and other FNMA/FHLMC forms that are not "plain English" forms provided that the language will authorize foreclosure in conformity with applicable law. The mortgage must include the Lender's right to a public sale of the Property, including a power of sale if legally permissible in the jurisdiction in which the property is located even if mortgages are usually foreclosed through a judicial proceeding.

   b. The paragraphs following Paragraph 25 should contain provisions required to adapt the mortgage to the laws and practices of the particular jurisdiction in which the Property is located. The text of these paragraphs should be the same as the FNMA/FHLMC non-uniform covenants for the jurisdiction in which the Property is located. Changes to the FNMA/FHLMC paragraphs and additional material may be included if needed to conform to requirements of state law or practice. The paragraph entitled "Riders to this Security Instrument" should be used as shown in the Model Form instead of as shown in the FNMA/FHLMC forms.

   c. Any special language or notices required by applicable law should appear following the non-uniform covenants using the FNMA/FHLMC form as a guide.

4. Signatures, etc.

Use the FNMA/FHLMC format at the end of the mortgage except that:

   a. Witness lines may be omitted if state and local law does not require witnesses for mortgages.

   b. HUD does not require the Borrower's social security number to appear on the mortgage.

Page **14** of **14**

Please review Mortgagee Letters 2014-21 and 2015-02 for the effective dates of the new language in these model documents.

FHA Case No.
197-3493819-955/956

**MODEL ADJUSTABLE RATE
NOTE FORM
(HOME EQUITY CONVERSION)**

[Date] September 19, 20XX

ADJUSTABLE RATE NOTE

[Property Address]

705 13th Street

Los Angeles, CA 90055

NOTES

The first Note goes to the Lender.

1. DEFINITIONS

"Allonge" means any Shared Appreciation Allonge executed by the Borrower as more fully described in Paragraph 12 below.

"Borrower" means each person signing at the end of this Note. The term does not include his or her successors or assigns.

"Change Date" means each date on which the interest rate could change.

"Current Index" means the most recent Index figure available thirty (30) days before the Change Date.

"Eligible Non-Borrowing Spouse" means a Non-Borrowing Spouse who meets, and continues to meet, the Qualifying Attributes requirements established by the Secretary that the Non-Borrowing Spouse must satisfy in order to be eligible for deferral of the due and payable status.

"Index" means the weekly average yield on United States Treasury Securities adjusted to a constant maturity of one year, as made available by the Federal Reserve Board, or the 1-Month or 1-Year LIBOR, as applicable, as made available by the *Wall Street Journal*[i].

"Ineligible Non-Borrowing Spouse" means a Non-Borrowing Spouse who does not meet the Qualifying Attributes requirements established by the Secretary that the Non-Borrowing Spouse must satisfy in order to be eligible for deferral of the due and payable status.

"Lender" means _____Well City Bank_____ and its successors and assigns.

"Loan Agreement" means the Home Equity Conversion Mortgage Adjustable Rate Loan Agreement dated __September 19_, 20XX by and between the Borrower and Lender.

"Non-Borrowing Spouse" means the spouse [Name], as determined by the law of the state in which the spouse [Name] and Borrower [Name] reside or the state of celebration, of the Borrower [Name] at the time of closing and who is not a Borrower.[ii]

Page **1** of **9**

Published 2/12/15. Please review Mortgagee Letters 2014-21 and 2015-02 for the effective dates of the new language in these model documents.

"Property" means Borrower's property identified in the Security Instrument.

"Property Address" means the address provided above.

"Qualifying Attributes" means those requirements established by the Secretary that the Non-Borrowing Spouse must satisfy in order to be eligible for deferral of the due and payable status.

"Secretary" means the Secretary of Housing and Urban Development or his or her authorized representatives.

"Security Instrument" means the mortgage, deed of trust, security deed or other security instrument which is signed by Borrower together with the Loan Agreement and which secures the amounts advanced under this Note.

2. BORROWER'S PROMISE TO PAY; INTEREST

In return for amounts to be advanced by Lender to or for the benefit of Borrower under the terms of the Loan Agreement, Borrower promises to pay to the order of Lender a principal amount equal to the sum of all Loan Advances made under the Loan Agreement with interest. Interest will be charged on unpaid principal at the rate of_6.5_ percent (_6.5_%) per year until the full amount of principal has been paid. The interest rate may change in accordance with Paragraph 5 of this Note. Accrued interest shall be added to the Principal Balance as a Loan Advance at the end of each month.

3. PROMISE TO PAY SECURED

Borrower's promise to pay is secured by the Security Instrument. The Security Instrument protects the Lender from losses which might result if Borrower defaults under this Note.

4. MANNER OF PAYMENT

(A) Time. Borrower shall pay all outstanding principal and accrued interest to Lender upon receipt of a notice by Lender requiring immediate payment in full, as provided in Paragraph 7 of this Note.

(B) Place. Payment shall be made at __P.O. Box 455 West Covina, CA 91355_ or any such other place as Lender may designate in writing by notice to Borrower.

(C) Limitation of Liability. Borrower shall have no personal liability for payment of the debt. Lender shall enforce the debt only through sale of the Property. If this Note is assigned to the Secretary, the Borrower shall not be liable for any difference between the mortgage insurance benefits paid to Lender and the outstanding indebtedness, including accrued interest, owed by Borrower at the time of the assignment.

Published 2/12/15. Please review Mortgagee Letters 2014-21 and 2015-02 for the effective dates of the new language in these model documents.

5. INTEREST RATE CHANGES[iii]

(A)   Change Date. The interest rate may change on the first day of _January 1_, 20xx , and on that day of each succeeding year.

(B)   The Index. Beginning with the first Change Date, the interest rate will be based on an Index chosen by the Borrower _____. If the Index is no longer available, Lender will use as a new Index any index prescribed by the Secretary. Lender will give Borrower notice of the new Index.

(C)   Calculation of Interest Rate Changes. Before each Change Date, Lender will calculate a new interest rate by adding a margin of percentage points (__%) to the current Index.iv Subject to the limits stated in Paragraph 5(D) of this Note, this amount will be the new interest rate until the next Change Date.

(D)   Limits on Interest Rate Changes. The interest rate will never increase or decrease by more than two percentage points (2.0%) on any single Change Date. The interest rate will never be more than five percentage points (5.0%) higher or lower than the initial interest rate stated in Paragraph 2 of this Note.

(E)   Notice of Changes. Lender will give notice to Borrower of any change in the interest rate. The notice must be given at least twenty-five (25) days before the new interest rate takes effect, and must set forth (i) the date of the notice, (ii) the Change Date, (iii) the old interest rate, (iv) the new interest rate, (v) the Current Index and the date it was published, (vi) the method of calculating the adjusted interest rate, and (vii) any other information which may be required by law from time to time.

(F)   Effective Date of Changes. A new interest rate calculated in accordance with paragraphs 5(C) and 5(D) of this Note will become effective on the Change Date, unless the Change Date occurs less than twenty-five (25) days after Lender has given the required notice. If the interest rate calculated in accordance with Paragraphs 5(C) and 5(D) of this Note decreased, but Lender failed to give timely notice of the decrease and applied a higher rate than the rate which should have been stated in a timely notice, then Lender shall recalculate the Principal Balance owed under this Note so it does not reflect any excessive interest.

6. BORROWER'S RIGHT TO PREPAY

A Borrower receiving monthly payments under the Loan Agreement has the right to pay the debt evidenced by this Note, in whole or in part, without charge or penalty. Any amount of debt prepaid will first be applied to reduce the Principal Balance of the Second Note described in Paragraph 11 of this Note and then to reduce the Principal Balance of this Note.

All prepayments of the Principal Balance shall be applied by Lender as follows:

Please review Mortgagee Letters 2014-21 and 2015-02 for the effective dates of the new language in these model documents.

FHA Case
No.197-3493819-955/956

**MODEL ADJUSTABLE RATE
SECOND NOTE FORM
(HOME EQUITY CONVERSION)**

19, 20XX

ADJUSTABLE RATE SECOND NOTE

705 13th Street

Los Angeles, CA 90055

1.DEFINITIONS

"Allonge" means any Shared Appreciation Allonge executed by the Borrower as more fully described in Paragraph 12 below.

"Borrower" means each person signing at the end of this Note. The term does not include his or her successors or assigns.

"Change Date" means each date on which the interest rate could change.

"Current Index" means the most recent Index figure available thirty (30) days before the Change Date.

"Eligible Non-Borrowing Spouse" means a Non-Borrowing Spouse who meets, and continues to meet, the Qualifying Attributes requirements established for deferral of the due and payable status.

"First Note" means the promissory note signed by Borrower together with the Loan Agreement and given to the holder of the First Note to evidence Borrower's promise to repay, with interest, Loan Advances made by the holder of the First Note and secured by the First Security Instrument.

"First Security Instrument" means the mortgage, deed of trust, security deed or other security instrument which is signed by Borrower together with this Loan Agreement and which secures the First Note.

"Index" means the weekly average yield on United States Treasury Securities adjusted to a constant maturity of one year, as made available by the Federal Reserve Board, or the 1-Month or 1-Year LIBOR, as applicable, as made available by the *Wall Street Journal*.

"Ineligible Non-Borrowing Spouse" means a Non-Borrowing Spouse who does not meet the Qualifying Attributes requirements for deferral of the due and payable status.

"Loan Agreement" means the Home Equity Conversion Mortgage Adjustable Rate Loan Agreement dated September 19, 20XX by and between the Borrower and holder of the First Note.

Page **1** of **9**

Published 2/12/15. Please review Mortgagee Letters 2014-21 and 2015-02 for the effective dates of the new language in these model documents.

"LIBOR" means the London Interbank Offered Rate.

"Non-Borrowing Spouse" means the spouse [Name], as determined by the law of the state in which the spouse [Name] and Borrower [Name] reside or the state of celebration, of the Borrower [Name] at the time of closing and who is not a Borrower.[ii]

"Property" means Borrower's property identified in the Security Instrument.

"Property Address" means the address provided above.

"Qualifying Attributes" means those requirements established by the Secretary that the Non-Borrowing Spouse must satisfy in order to be eligible for deferral of the due and payable status.

"Secretary" or "Lender" means the Secretary of Housing and Urban Development or his or her authorized representatives.

"Security Instrument" or "Second Security Instrument" means the mortgage, deed of trust, security deed or other security instrument which is signed by Borrower together with the Loan Agreement and which secures the amounts advanced under this Note.

2. BORROWER'S PROMISE TO PAY; INTEREST

In return for amounts to be advanced by Lender to or for the benefit of Borrower under the terms of a the Loan Agreement, Borrower promises to pay to the order of Lender a principal amount equal to the sum of all Loan Advances made by Lender under the Loan Agreement with interest. Interest will be charged on unpaid principal at the rate of_6.5_ percent (_6.5_%) per year until the full amount of principal has been paid. The interest rate may change in accordance with Paragraph 5 of this Note. Accrued interest shall be added to the Principal Balance as a Loan Advance at the end of each month.

3. PROMISE TO PAY SECURED

Borrower's promise to pay is secured by the "Security Instrument". The Security Instrument protects the Lender from losses which might result if Borrower defaults under this Note. Borrower also executed a First Security Instrument and First Note when the Second Security Instrument and this Note were executed.

4. MANNER OF PAYMENT

(A) <u>Time</u>. Borrower shall pay all outstanding principal and accrued interest to Lender upon receipt of a notice by Lender requiring immediate payment in full, as provided in Paragraph 7 of this Note.

(B) <u>Place</u>. Payment shall be made at the Office of the Housing-FHA Comptroller, Director of Mortgage Insurance Accounting and Servicing, 451 7th Street, S.W., Washington, DC 20410, or any such other place as Lender may designate in writing by notice to Borrower.

Published 2/12/15. Please review Mortgagee Letters 2014-21 and 2015-02 for the effective dates of the new language in these model documents.

(C) <u>Limitation of Liability</u>. Borrower shall have no personal liability for payment of the debt. Lender shall enforce the debt only through sale of the Property.

5. INTEREST RATE CHANGES[iii]

(A) <u>Change Date</u>. The interest rate may change on the first day of _January 1_, 20xx, and on that day of each succeeding year.

(B) <u>The Index</u>. Beginning with the first Change Date, the interest rate will be based on the [Index] chosen by the Borrower. If the Index is no longer available, Lender will use as a new Index Lender will use as a new Index any index prescribed by the Secretary. Lender will give Borrower notice of the new Index.

(C) <u>Calculation of Interest Rate Changes</u>. Before each Change Date, Lender will calculate a new interest rate by adding a margin of _____ percentage points (___%) to the current Index.[iv] Subject to the limits stated in Paragraph 5(D) of this Note, this amount will be the new interest rate until the next Change Date.

(D) <u>Limits on Interest Rate Changes</u>. The interest rate will never increase or decrease by more than two percentage points (2.0%) on any single Change Date. The interest rate will never be more than five percentage points (5.0%) higher or lower than the initial interest rate stated in Paragraph 2 of this Note.

(E) <u>Notice of Changes</u>. Lender will give notice to Borrower of any change in the interest rate. The notice must be given at least twenty-five (25) days before the new interest rate takes effect, and must set forth (i) the date of the notice, (ii) the Change Date, (iii) the old interest rate, (iv) the new interest rate, (v) the Current Index and the date it was published, (vi) the method of calculating the adjusted interest rate, and (vii) any other information which may be required by law from time to time.

(F) <u>Effective Date of Changes</u>. A new interest rate calculated in accordance with paragraphs 5(C) and 5(D) of this Note will become effective on the Change Date, unless the Change Date occurs less than twenty-five (25) days after Lender has given the required notice. If the interest rate calculated in accordance with Paragraphs 5(C) and 5(D) of this Note decreased, but Lender failed to give timely notice of the decrease and applied a higher rate than the rate which should have been stated in a timely notice, then Lender shall recalculate the Principal Balance owed under this Note so it does not reflect any excessive interest.

6. BORROWER'S RIGHT TO PREPAY

A Borrower receiving monthly payments under the Loan Agreement has the right to pay the debt evidenced by this Note, in whole or in part, without charge or penalty. Any amount of debt prepaid will first be applied to reduce the Principal Balance of this Note and then to reduce the Principal Balance of the First Note.

All prepayments of the Principal Balance shall be applied by Lender as follows:

Page **3** of **9**

FHA Case No. 197-3493819-955/956

HOME EQUITY CONVERSION MORTGAGE ADJUSTABLE RATE

LOAN AGREEMENT

THIS AGREEMENT is made this day of <u>September 19</u>, 20XX, among <u>Eve David</u> ("Borrower") and <u>Well City Bank</u> ("Lender").

Article 1 - Definitions

1.1. "Borrower" is defined above. The term does not include the Borrower's successors or assigns.

1.2 "Deferral Period" means the period of time following the death of the last surviving Borrower during which the due and payable status of a loan is further deferred based on the continued satisfaction of the requirements for an Eligible Non-Borrowing Spouse determined by the Secretary and all other FHA requirements.

1.3. "Eligible Non-Borrowing Spouse" means a Non-Borrowing Spouse who meets the Qualifying Attributes requirements established for a Deferral Period.

1.4. "Expected Average Mortgage Interest Rate" means the amount indicated on the Payment Plan. It is a constant interest rate used to calculate monthly payments to the Borrower throughout the life of the loan.

1.5. "First 12-Month Disbursement Period" means the period that begins on the day of loan closing and ends on the day before the anniversary date of loan closing. When the day before the anniversary date of loan closing falls on a Federally-observed holiday, Saturday or Sunday, the period end date will be on the next business day.

1.6. "Ineligible Non-Borrowing Spouse" means a Non-Borrowing Spouse who does not meet the Qualifying Attributes requirements established for a Deferral Period.

1.7. "Initial Disbursement Limit" means the maximum disbursement to the Borrower allowed at loan closing and during the First 12-Month Disbursement Period which is the greater of sixty percent (60%) of the Principal Limit; or the sum of Mandatory Obligations, plus an additional ten percent (10%) percent of the Principal Limit. The Initial Disbursement Limit shall not exceed the Principal Limit amount established at loan closing.

[1.8. "LA Property Charges" means certain Property Charges consisting of taxes, hazard insurance premiums, flood insurance premiums, ground rents, and any other assessments that may be required by local or state law if indicated on the Payment Plan.][i]

[1.8. "LESA Property Charges" means certain Property Charges consisting of property taxes including special assessments levied by Municipalities or State Law, hazard insurance premiums, and applicable flood insurance premiums.][ii]

Published 2/12/15. Please review Mortgagee Letters 2014-21 and 2015-02 for the effective dates of the new language in these model documents.

1.9. "Loan Advances" means all funds advanced from or charged to Borrower's account under conditions set forth in this Loan Agreement, whether or not actually paid to Borrower.

1.10. "Loan Documents" means the Note, Second Note, Security Instrument and Second Security Instrument.

1.11. "Mandatory Obligations" means only those charges, fees, amounts and expenses as authorized by the Secretary.

1.12. "Maximum Claim Amount" means the lesser of the appraised value of the Property, as determined by the appraisal used in underwriting the loan, or the sales price of the Property being purchased for the sole purpose of being the Principal Residence, or the national mortgage limit under Section 255(g) or (m) of the National Housing Act applicable to this Loan Agreement. Closing costs must not be taken into account in determining the appraised value.

1.13. "Non-Borrowing Spouse" means the spouse [Name], as determined by the law of the state in which the spouse [Name] and Borrower [Name] reside or the state of celebration, of the Borrower [Name] at the time of closing and who is not a Borrower.[1]

1.14. "Note" means the promissory note signed by Borrower together with this Loan Agreement and given to Lender to evidence Borrower's promise to repay, with interest, Loan Advances by Lender or Lender's assignees.

1.15. "Payment Plan" means the payment plan set forth in Exhibit 1, which is attached to and made a part of this Loan Agreement.

1.16. "Principal" or "Principal Balance" means the sum of all Loan Advances made as of a particular date, including interest and mortgage insurance premiums.

1.17. "Principal Limit" means the amount indicated on the Payment Plan when this Loan Agreement is executed, and increases each month for the life of the loan at a rate supplied by the Secretary that is listed on the Payment Plan. The Principal Limit is calculated by multiplying the Maximum Claim Amount by a factor supplied by the Secretary.

1.18. "Principal Residence" means the dwelling where a Borrower and, if applicable, a Non-Borrowing Spouse maintains his or her permanent place of abode, and typically spends the majority of the calendar year. A person may have only one Principal Residence at any one time. The Property shall be considered to be the Principal Residence of any Borrower who is temporarily in a health care institution provided the Borrower's residency in a health care institution does not exceed twelve (12) consecutive months. The Property shall be considered to be the Principal Residence of any Non-Borrowing Spouse, who is temporarily in a health care institution, as long as the Property is the Principal Residence of his or her Borrower spouse, who physically resides in the Property. During a Deferral Period, the Property shall continue to be considered to be the Principal Residence of any Eligible Non-Borrowing Spouse, who is temporarily in a health care institution, provided the Eligible

---

[1] If there is more than one Borrower and both and or all Borrowers have a spouse, add as needed, [the spouse [Name], as determined by the law of the state in which the spouse [Name] and Borrower [Name] reside or the state of celebration, of the Borrower [Name] at the time of closing and who is not a Borrower.]

Published 2/12/15. Please review Mortgagee Letters 2014-21 and 2015-02 for the effective dates of the new language in these model documents.

Non-Borrowing Spouse physically occupied the Property immediately prior to entering the health care institution and the Eligible Non-Borrowing Spouse's residency in a health care institution does not exceed twelve (12) consecutive months.

1.19. "Property" means Borrower's property identified in the Security Instrument.

1.20. "Property Charges" means property taxes, hazard insurance premiums, flood insurance premiums, ground rents, condominium fees, planned unit development fees, homeowner's association fees, and any other special assessments that may be required by local or state law.

1.21. "Qualifying Attributes" means those requirements established by the Secretary that the Non-Borrowing Spouse must satisfy in order to be eligible for the Deferral Period.

1.22. "Secretary" means the Secretary of the Department of Housing and Urban Development, his or her successors and assigns.

1.23. "Second Note" means the promissory note signed by Borrower together with this Loan Agreement and given to the Secretary to evidence Borrower's promise to repay, with interest, Loan Advances by the Secretary secured by the Second Security Instrument.

1.24. "Second Security Instrument" means the mortgage, deed of trust, security deed or other security instrument which is signed by Borrower together with this Loan Agreement and which secures the Second Note.

1.25. "Security Instrument" means the mortgage, deed of trust, security deed or other security instrument which is signed by Borrower together with this Loan Agreement and which secures the Note.

Article 2 - Loan Advances

2.1. General. Lender agrees to make Loan Advances under the conditions set forth in this Loan Agreement in consideration of the Note and Security Instrument given by Borrower on the same date as this Loan Agreement.

2.2. Initial Advances.

2.2.1. Loan Advances shall be used by Lender to pay, or reimburse Borrower for, closing costs listed in the Schedule of Closing Costs (Exhibit 2) attached to and made a part of this Loan Agreement, except that Loan Advances will only be used to pay origination fees in an amount not to exceed the greater of two thousand five hundred dollars ($2,500) or two percent (2%) of the Maximum Claim Amount, up to a Maximum Claim Amount of two hundred thousand dollars ($200,000), *plus* one percent (1%) of any portion of the Maximum Claim Amount that is greater than two hundred thousand dollars ($200,000). The Lender may not charge the Borrower an origination fee in excess of six thousand dollars ($6,000).

Page **3** of **15**

Published 2/12/15. Please review Mortgagee Letters 2014-21 and 2015-02 for the effective dates of the new language in these model documents.

2.2.2. Loan Advances shall be used by Lender to discharge those liens on the Property listed in the Schedule of Liens/HECM for Purchase Disbursements to Seller (Exhibit 2) attached to and made a part of this Loan Agreement.

2.2.3. Lender shall pay an initial Loan Advance to Borrower in the amount indicated on the Payment Plan.

2.2.4. Initial advances required by this Section 2.2. shall be made as soon as such advances are permitted by the applicable provisions of 12 CFR Part 226 (Truth in Lending) governing Borrower's right of rescission, but not before that time.

2.2.5. Borrower's aggregate initial advances and any subsequent advances made, except for any disbursements or accruals under 2.3.3, during the First 12-Month Disbursement Period may not exceed the Initial Disbursement Limit established at closing and in the amount indicated on the Payment Plan. In the event Borrower makes a payment towards the outstanding loan balance on the line of credit during the First 12-Month Disbursement Period, the Lender may make subsequent Loan Advances during the remainder of the First 12-Month Disbursement Period only to the extent Borrower's payment was applied to the outstanding Principal Balance.

2.2.6. If any requested Loan Advance would exceed the Initial Disbursement Limit established at closing, Lender must make a partial payment to the Borrower for the amount that would not exceed the limit. Prior to Lender paying a partial Loan Advance to avoid causing the aggregate initial advances to exceed the Initial Disbursement Limit within the First 12-Month Disbursement Period, Lender must provide Borrower with written notice about inability to exceed the threshold.

2.2.7. No Loan Advances are permitted during a Deferral Period, except for amounts disbursed or accrued from under 2.3.2, 2.3.3, 2.12.3, 2.13.3, and 2.15.3.

2.3. Set-Asides.

2.3.1. Amounts set aside from the Principal Limit shall be considered Loan Advances to the extent actually disbursed or earned by Lender.

2.3.2. Lender shall initially set aside from the Principal Limit the amount indicated on the Payment Plan for repairs to be made in accordance with a Repair Rider attached to and made a part of this Loan Agreement (Exhibit 3). This set-aside remains available for disbursement during any Deferral Period and the Lender may add such disbursements to the Principal Balance for the sole purpose of paying the cost of the repairs specifically identified in the Repair Rider. Additionally, such repairs may only be disbursed if the repairs are satisfactorily completed during the time period established in the Repair Rider.

2.3.3. Lender shall initially set aside from the Principal Limit the amount indicated on the Payment Plan to be applied to payment due for a fixed monthly charge for servicing activities of Lender or its servicer. Such servicing activities are necessary to protect Lender's interest in the Property. A servicing fee set-aside, if any, is not available to the Borrower for any purpose, except to pay for loan servicing. A servicing set-aside under this Section remains available for

Published 2/12/15. Please review Mortgagee Letters 2014-21 and 2015-02 for the effective dates of the new language in these model documents.

disbursement during any Deferral Period and the Lender may add such disbursements to the Principal Balance.

2.3.4. Lender shall set aside from the Principal Limit any amounts required by Section 2.10 as indicated on the Payment Plan.

2.4. Charges and Fees. Borrower shall pay to Lender reasonable and customary charges and fees as permitted under 24 CFR 206.207(a). Such amounts shall be considered Loan Advances when actually disbursed by Lender.

2.5. Monthly Payments.

2.5.1. Loan Advances paid directly to Borrower shall be made in equal monthly payments if requested by Borrower.

2.5.2. Monthly payments, if requested under 2.5.1, shall be calculated based on the payment option requested by Borrower.

2.5.3. Monthly payments under the term payment option are made only during a term chosen by Borrower and shall be calculated so that the sum of (i) or (ii) as applicable added to (iii), (iv), (v) and (vi) shall be equal to or less than the Principal Limit at the end of the term; except that during the First 12-Month Disbursement Period, the amount calculated shall not be greater than the Initial Disbursement Limit:

> (i) Initial advances under Section 2.2 plus any initial servicing fee set-aside under Subsection 2.3.3, or

> (ii) The Principal Balance at the time of a change in payments under Sections 2.8 and 2.9 plus any remaining servicing fee set-aside under Subsection 2.3.3, and

> (iii) The portion of the Principal Limit set aside as a line of credit under Section 2.7, including any set-asides for repairs (Subsection 2.3.2) [and first-year LESA Property Charges/LA Property Charges (Subsection 2.3.4 and Section 2.10)], and

> (iv) All monthly payments due through the payment term, including funds withheld for payment of Property Charges under Section 2.10, and

> (v) All mortgage insurance premiums, or monthly charges due to the Secretary in lieu of mortgage insurance premiums, which are due through the payment term (Subsection 2.13), and

> (vi) All interest through the payment term. The Expected Average Mortgage Interest Rate shall be used for this purpose.

Published 2/12/15. Please review Mortgagee Letters 2014-21 and 2015-02 for the effective dates of the new language in these model documents.

2.5.4. Monthly payments under the tenure payment option shall be calculated as in Subsection 2.5.3 as if there were a payment term with the number of months in the term equal to the sum of one hundred (100) minus the age of the youngest Borrower multiplied by twelve (12), but payments shall continue until the loan becomes due and payable as provided in the Loan Documents.

2.5.5. Monthly payments shall be paid to Borrower on the first business day of a month.

2.5.6. If Borrower has requested monthly payments, payments shall be indicated on the Payment Plan. The payment option may be changed by Borrower as provided in Sections 2.8 and 2.9.

2.6. Line of Credit without Monthly Payments.

2.6.1. Borrower can request Loan Advances under a line of credit payment option in amounts and at times determined by Borrower, if the Principal Balance of the loan after the Loan Advance is made is less than or equal to the applicable Principal Limit, except that during the First 12-Month Disbursement Period the amount available shall not be greater than the maximum amount permitted under 2.2.5, excluding any portion of the Principal Limit set aside under Sections 2.3.2, 2.3.3, 2.3.4 and 2.10. The line of credit amount increases at the same rate as the total Principal Limit under Section 1.17.

2.6.2. Line of credit payments shall be paid to Borrower within five business days after Lender has received a written request for payment by Borrower.

2.6.3. Lender may specify a form for line of credit payment requests.

2.6.4. Lender shall provide Borrower with a statement of the account every time a line of credit payment is made. The statement shall include the current interest rate, the previous Principal Balance, the amount of the current Loan Advance, the current Principal Balance after the Loan Advance, and the current Principal Limit.

2.7. Line of Credit with Monthly Payments.

2.7.1. Borrower may receive monthly payments under either a term or tenure payment option combined with a line of credit, as indicated on the Payment Plan.

2.7.2. Subsections 2.6.2, 2.6.3, and 2.6.4, apply to a line of credit combined with term or tenure payments.

2.7.3. If Borrower combines a line of credit with a term or tenure payment option, the Principal Limit is divided into: (a) an amount for the line of credit payments, including any repair set-aside as provided for in Subsection 2.3.3 and amounts set-aside or withheld for Property Charges as provided for in Subsection 2.3.4 and Section 2.10, (b) an amount for monthly payments which shall be calculated under Subsection 2.5.3 or 2.5.4 and (c) an amount for a servicing fee set-aside, if required by Lender under Subsection 2.3.3. Amounts designated for line of credit payments and monthly payments increase independently at the same rate as the total Principal Limit increases under Section 1.17. Borrower can request Loan Advances in amounts and at

Please review Mortgagee Letters 2014-21 and 2015-02 for the effective dates of the new language in these model documents.

EXHIBIT 1
HOME EQUITY CONVERSION ADJUSTABLE RATE MORTGAGE
PAYMENT PLAN

Date of Payment Plan: September 19, 20XX

FHA Case Number: 197-3493819-955/956___

Name of Lender: ___Well City Bank_____

Name of Borrower(s) and Eligible Non-Borrowing Spouse(s)

Birthdate(s)

_____Eve David_____

02/12/1956

_____

___/___/___

_____

___/___/___

First 12-Month Disbursement Period Expiration Date:
September 19, 20XX

_____

_____

_____

Expected Average Mortgage Interest Rate: 6.5%

Was the Expected Average Mortgage Interest Rate locked? Y

Date used to determine the Index to calculate
Expected Average Mortgage Interest Rate:

Provide the Initial Mortgage Interest (Accrual) Rate: Provide

the Margin:

_____

Borrower's Designation (only one may be checked):

__x__ 60% of Principal Limit; or

____ Mandatory Obligations, plus 10% of the Principal Limit

_____

1

0048382555
196-3492489-832

EXHIBIT 2

<u>Schedule of Closing Costs</u>

See HUD-1 Settlement Statement for Schedule of Closing Costs

<u>Schedule of Liens</u>

<u>Item</u>	<u>Amount</u>
HomEst Servicing	**$ 113,661.56**

Please review Mortgagee Letters 2014-21 and 2015-02 for the effective dates of the new language in these model documents.

EXHIBIT 3 - REPAIR RIDER

ADJUSTABLE RATE

THIS REPAIR RIDER is made this 19th day of September, 20XX, and is incorporated into and shall be deemed to supplement the Loan Agreement of the same date made by the undersigned Lender ("Lender") and the undersigned Borrower ("Borrower"). The term Borrower does not include the Borrower's successors or assigns.

I. Lender's Promises

A. The Lender shall set aside twenty thousand dollars ($20,000) from the Principal Limit under the Loan Agreement to be used for the purpose of bringing the Property up to the property standards required by the Secretary by repairing (List each item separately and estimated cost to repair):

_____

_____

_____

_____

[Use an additional page if needed]

B. The Lender may charge a repair administration fee not to exceed the greater of fifty dollars ($50) or one and one-half percent 1.5% of the amounts advanced by Lender under this Repair Rider. This fee shall be added to the Principal Balance as each Loan Advance is made.

C. The Lender shall require one or more inspections by a HUD-approved inspector during the course of the repair work. The Lender shall not release any funds for work which is not complete and which is not approved by a HUD-approved inspector. The Lender certifies by executing this Repair Rider that the repairs which are funded under this Repair Rider will be completed in a manner to meet property standards required by the Secretary as determined by a HUD-approved inspector.

D. The Lender shall ensure that all mechanic's liens and materialmen's liens are released of record prior to an advance of funds under this Repair Rider. The Lender may require the Borrower to obtain acknowledgment of payment and releases of lien from all contractors, subcontractors, and materialmen. Such acknowledgements and releases shall be in the form required by local laws and shall cover all work done, labor performed and materials (including equipment and fixtures) furnished for the project. During a Deferral Period, if any, the Lender may require the Borrower's estate to obtain the requisite acknowledgments, which otherwise would have been required of the Borrower.

E. Until a HUD-approved inspector finds that all repairs required by Section I.A. of this Repair Rider have been completed in a satisfactory manner, the Lender shall not release funds in excess of (i) the total value of work satisfactorily completed, and (ii) the value of

Page **1** of **3**

HOME EQUITY CONVERSION MORTGAGE
FEDERAL LOAN CLOSING TRUTH-IN-LENDING DISCLOSURE STATEMENT

FHA Case Number: 197-3060715-955

In this Disclosure the words you, your, and yours mean the Borrower(s), and the words we, us and our mean **WELL CITY MORTGAGE COMPANY,** a California Corporation.

The Home Equity Conversion Mortgage ("HECM" or "Account") will be governed by two Notes, a Loan Agreement and two Mortgages or Deeds of Trust (the "First Security Instrument" and the "Second Security Instrument", collectively, the "Security Instruments"). You will be able to obtain loan advances under a set schedule and/or by requesting advances up to the available Principal Limit.

SECURITY INTEREST. You are giving us and the Department of Housing and Urban Development ("HUD") a security interest in the residential property located at **705 13ᵀᴴ STREET,**
LOS ANGELES, CALIFORNIA 90055   (the "Property")
You could lose this Property if you do not meet the obligations in the Note(s) and Loan Agreement with us.

POSSIBLE ACTIONS: Under certain conditions discussed below, we may take certain actions including terminating your Account and accelerating your outstanding balance, suspending your credit privileges, and implementing certain changes to the Notes, Security Instruments and Loan Agreement.

We can terminate your Account and require immediate payment of the entire outstanding balance in one payment if:
- All of the Borrowers have died.
- All of the Borrowers have sold or conveyed title to the Property.
- The Property is no longer the principal residence of at least one Borrower.
- No Borrower maintains the Property as a principal residence for a period exceeding 12 consecutive months because of physical or mental illness.
- The Borrower violates any other covenants of the Security Instruments and has refused or is unable to comply with the violated conditions of the Security Instruments.

We can refuse to make additional extensions of credit during any period in which the following are in effect:
- The outstanding balance equals the credit limit ("Principal Limit").
- We have notified you that we will require immediate payment of the entire outstanding balance due to the occurrence of one of the events of termination listed above.
- The initial repairs required to bring the Property up to the property standards required by HUD are not completed by the time required in the Repair Rider to the Loan Agreement.
- We determine on the basis of title evidence that the Property securing the Account is encumbered by any liens that jeopardize the first lien status of the First Security Instrument or the second lien status of the Second Security Instrument, or if you refuse to execute any document necessary to extend the first and second lien status to an additional maximum principal balance or for an additional number of years.
- A petition for bankruptcy by or against you is filed.
- You have paid the Notes in full.

We are permitted to make certain changes to the terms of the Account. We may make changes to the Account if you agree to the change in writing at that time, if the change will unequivocally benefit you throughout the remainder of the Account if the change is insignificant (such as changes relating to our data processing system), or if the change involves the substitution of the index and margin if the current index becomes unavailable (as described below).

MINIMUM PAYMENT REQUIREMENTS: You can obtain advances of credit under one of several "payment plans" available under the HECM program. The length of time during which you can obtain advances depends upon the payment plan that you select. As long as the Account is not due and payable under the conditions set forth above, you may obtain advances under the following payment plans:
(a) Tenure plan: Under this plan, you will receive equal monthly payments from us for as long as you occupy the property as a principal residence.
(b) Term plan: Under this plan, you will receive equal monthly payments from us for a fixed period that you select.
(c) Line of Credit plan: Under this plan, you will receive advances in unscheduled payments or in installments, at times and in amounts that you choose until the line of credit is exhausted.
(d) Modified Term or Tenure plan: Under these plans, you may combine a line of credit with monthly payments. In exchange for reduced monthly payments, you will set aside a specified amount of money at closing for a line of credit, on which you can draw until the line of credit is exhausted.

The period during which you can obtain advances (the "Draw Period") is, therefore, indefinite under the Tenure and Line of Credit or Modified Term or Tenure plans. You can choose the length of the Draw Period under the Term or Tenure plan [If you have chosen a Term plan, you have elected a Draw Period of **N/A** years and **N/A** months.] You can

Page 1

switch from one plan to another at any time during the life of your Account. If you elect to change your payment plan, the length of your Draw Period may also change.

Repayment of all amounts outstanding under your HECM will be due in one single payment; therefore there will be no repayment period. Your payment will be due when: (a) a Borrower dies and the Property is not the principal residence of at least one surviving Borrower, (b) a Borrower conveys all of his or her title to the Property (other than a transfer of the Borrower's title into a trust that satisfies HUD's requirements or a transfer of title to the Property from such a trust to the Borrower) and no other Borrower retains title to the Property in fee simple or on a leasehold interest, or (c) upon approval by the Secretary of Housing and Urban Development, if: (i) the Property ceases to be the principal residence of a Borrower for reasons other than death and the Property is not the principal residence of at least one other Borrower, (ii) for a period longer than 12 consecutive months a Borrower fails to physically occupy the Property because of physical or mental illness and the Property is not the principal residence of at least one other Borrower, or (iii) an obligation of the Borrower under the Security Instruments is not performed. Your minimum payment will be equal to the amount of (1) all advances you have obtained, (2) all advances that we have made pay for repairs, escrows, monthly mortgage insurance premiums, servicing fees and other charges that you authorize us to pay or for which we are permitted to advance funds under the Notes, Security Instruments and Loan Agreement, (3) all interest that has accrued on the amount outstanding from time to time and (4) any other fees or charges that are due under your Notes, Security Instruments and Loan Agreement.

MINIMUM DRAW AND BALANCE REQUIREMENTS: The amount of your advances and any limitations on those advances will depend upon the payment plan that you select. If you have selected a Tenure or Term plan or a Modified Term or Tenure plan, then the amount of your advances (payments to you) will be set at $0.00 and will be paid to you on a monthly basis. If you have selected a Line of Credit plan or a Modified Term or Tenure plan (payment plans with monthly payments combined with a line of credit), there are no limitations on the amount of an advance or the number of advances you may obtain under the line of credit (as long as you remain within your Principal Limit). You may change the type of payment plan throughout the life of the Account (including switching to a Line of Credit plan). There are no minimum outstanding balance requirements under the Account.

FINANCE CHARGE: Each advance made to you or on your behalf under your HECM will be subject to a Finance Charge beginning on the day after each advance is made. A Finance Charge will continue to be assessed on the outstanding balance under your HECM until the entire outstanding balance and all interest and fees due under the Notes, Security Instruments and Loan Agreement are paid.

The interest portion of the Finance Charge on your Account is computed by (i) calculating the Finance Charge on the balance existing at the beginning of each month, taking into consideration any payments or credits to your account, (ii) calculating the Finance Charge on each advance made to you or on your behalf during the month and (iii) adding all of these sums together. We start with the outstanding principal balance on your Account at the beginning of each month, which includes Finance Charges from the prior month (the "Outstanding Principal Balance"). At the end of each month, we multiply the Outstanding Principal Balance by the then-current Annual Percentage Rate and then divide the result of this calculation by 12 (the "Monthly Periodic Rate"). At the end of each month in which any advances or payments have been made to you or on your behalf, we multiply the amount of the advance or payment by the number of days remaining in the month after that advance or payment was made (not including the day it was made) and then multiply this amount by the then-current Annual Percentage Rate and divide the result of this calculation by 365 (the "Daily Periodic Rate"). This calculation is repeated for each advance or payment made to you or on your behalf during the month. The sum of the final result of these calculations equals the interest portion of your Finance Charge for the month. Advances made to pay fees for Finance Charges due under the Account will also accrue Finance Charges as described above.

In addition, mortgage insurance premiums ("MIP"), which are a Finance Charge, are computed by calculating the MIP on the Outstanding Principal Balance, calculating the MIP on each advance made to you or on your behalf during the month, and then adding all of these sums together. At the end of each month, we multiply the Outstanding Principal Balance by 0.5% and then divide the result of this calculation by 12 (the "MIP Monthly Periodic Rate"). At the end of each month in which any advances have been made to you or on your behalf,. We multiply the amount of the advance by the number of days remaining in the month after that advance was made, (not including the day the advance was made) and then multiply this amount by the 0.5% and divide this calculation by 365 (the "MIP Daily Periodic Rate"). This calculation is repeated for each advance made to you or on your behalf during the month. The sum of the final result of these calculations equals the mortgage insurance portion of your Finance Charge for the month. The MIP Monthly Periodic Rate applicable to your Account to calculate the mortgage insurance premium on the Outstanding Principal Balance is 0.041667%. The MIP Daily Periodic Rate applicable to your Account to calculate the mortgage insurance premium on each advance made to you or on your behalf during the month is 0.001370%. The Corresponding Annual Percentage Rate to these MIP Periodic Rates is 0.5%.

Another Finance Charge in an amount not to exceed that determined by the Secretary will be imposed each time you elect to change your payment plan. You must also pay at settlement an Origination Fee and an Initial Mortgage Insurance Premium, which are Finance Charges. These fees must be paid in the amounts disclosed in the "Fees and Charges" section below.

☒　(The following paragraph is applicable only if the box at left is checked).

Because repairs that are necessary to bring the Property up to HUD's Minimum Property Standards will be completed after

Page 2

closing and because advances from the Account will be used to pay for these repairs, a Repair Administration Fee of $50 which is a **Finance Charge,** will be imposed when advances are made to pay for those repairs, or if permitted by HUD, at settlement.

RATE CHANGES: The Calculation of rate changes will depend on whether you select an annually adjustable or monthly adjustable variable rate account. The paragraph next to the checked box applies to your Account. ☐ The Annual Percentage Rate for the interest portion of your Finance Charge may increase or decrease annually based upon changes in the Weekly Average Yield on United States Treasury Securities Adjusted to a Constant Maturity of One Year ("Treasury Securities Index"). However, your first rate change can occur between twelve and eighteen months after the date of closing Rate changes can occur every twelve months thereafter. To determine the Annual Percentage Rate that will apply to your Account we add a margin to the value of the Treasury Securities Index. However, the Annual Percentage Rate cannot change by more than 2.0 percentage points at each rate change or by more than 5.0 percentage points over the life of the Account. Increases in the Annual Percentage Rate will result in larger advances made to pay the increased accrued interest portion of the Finance Charge and a larger Outstanding Principal Balance.

☒   The Annual Percentage Rate for the interest portion of your Finance Charge may increase or decrease monthly based upon changes in the Weekly Average Yield on United States Treasury Securities Adjusted to a Constant Maturity of One Year ("Treasury Securities Index"). However your first rate change can occur on the first day of the second month after closing. Rate changes can occur every month thereafter. To determine the Annual Percentage Rate that will apply to your Account, we add a margin to the value of the Treasury Securities Index. There are no limits on the amount of the rate change each month, however, the Annual Percentage Rate cannot increase by more than 10.0% over the life of the Account. Increases in the Annual Percentage Rate will result in larger advances made to pay the increased accrued interest portion of the Finance Charge and a larger Outstanding Principal Balance.

In the event the Index is no longer available, we will choose a new index and margin. The new index will have an historical movement substantially similar to the original index and the new index and margin will result in an Annual Percentage Rate that is substantially similar to the rate in effect at the time the original index becomes unavailable.

The initial Monthly Periodic Rate applicable to your Account to calculate the interest portion of the Finance Charge on the Outstanding Principal Balance is **0.3558** %. The initial Daily Periodic Rate applicable to your Account to calculate the interest portion of the Finance Charge on each advance or payment made to you or on your behalf during the month is **0.0117%.** The Corresponding **Annual Percentage Rate** to these periodic rates (relating to the interest portion of the Finance Charge) is **4.2700** %. The Margin, which is added to the value of the Index, will be **1.50000%.** The Annual Percentage Rate includes only interest and not other costs.

MAXIMUM RATE: The maximum Annual Percentage Rate (relating to the interest portion of the Finance Charge) that can apply to your Account is **14.27000** %.

NEGATIVE AMORTIZATION: Under the HECM, you do not make any payments until one of the conditions of termination described above occurs. Therefore, principal, along with the Finance Charges and other charges that accrue during the life of your HECM, are not paid as they are advanced or accrue, and "negative amortization" will occur. Negative amortization, under which the advances of credit and accrued Finance Charges and other charges are added to your outstanding loan balancer will increase the amount you owe us and reduce your equity in your home.

TAX DEDUCTIBILITY: You should consult a tax advisor regarding the deductibility of interest and charges for the Account.

FEES AND CHARGES: You must pay certain charges in connection with this Account as follows:

(a) Finance Charges: You must pay the following Finance Charges in connection with the opening of your Account at settlement:

(1) Origination Fee	$5,300.00
(2) Mortgage Insurance Premium (2% of HUD's maximum claim amount)	$5,300.00
Life of Loan Flood Cert	16.00
(3) Repair Administration Fee	$141.33

(b) Settlement Costs: You must pay the following charges •" connection with the opening of your Account:

(1) Title Insurance Premium	$742.00
(2) Recording Fees	$180.00
(3) Appraisal Fees	$475.00
(4) Credit Report Fee	$14.00
Hazard Insurance	$226.00
(5) Escrow Closing Fee	$350.00
(6) Document Preparation	$100.00
(7) Notary Fee	$200.00
(8) Termite Inspection/Pest Control Fee	$65.00
(9) Wire Fee	$0.00
(10) Courier Fee	$80.00

Page 3

Property Insurance: Property hazard insurance is required. You may obtain such insurance from any source you want that is acceptable to us.

YOUR BILLING RIGHTS

This notice contains important information about your rights and our responsibilities under the Fair Credit Billing Act.

<u>Notify Us in Case of Errors or Questions About Your Statement</u>

If you think your statement is wrong, or if you need more information about a transaction on your statement, write us [on a separatesheet] at

WELL CITY BANK, N. A.
P.O. BOX 26901
Attention: **Reverse Mortgage Department**   Write to us as soon as possible. We must hear from you no later than 60 day after we sent you the first statement on which the error or problem appeared. You can telephone us, but doing so will not preserve your rights.

In your letter, give us the following information:

- Your name and Account number.
- The dollar amount of the suspected error.
- Describe the error and explain, if you can, why you believe there is an error. If you need more information, describe the item you are not sure about.

<u>Your Rights and Our Responsibilities After We Receive Your Written Notice</u>

We must acknowledge your letter within 30 days, unless we have corrected the error by then. Within 90 days, we must either correct the error or explain why we believe the statement was correct.

After we receive your letter, we cannot try to collect any amount you question, or report you as delinquent. We can continue to bill you for the amount you question, including Finance Charges, and we can apply any unpaid amount against your credit limit. You do not have to pay any questioned amount while we are investigating, but you are still obligated to pay the parts of your statement that are not in question.

If we find that we made a mistake on your statement, you will not have to pay any Finance Charges related to any questioned amount. If we did not make a mistake, you may have to pay Finance Charges, and you will have to make any missed payments on the questioned amount. In either case, we will send you a statement of the amount you owe and the date that it is due.

If you fail to pay the amount that we think you owe, we may report you as delinquent. However, if our explanation does not satisfy you and you write us within ten days telling us that you still refuse to pay, we must tell anyone we report you to that you have a question about your statement. And, we must tell you the name of anyone we reported you to. We must tell anyone we report you to that the matter has been settled between us when it finally is.

If we don't follow these rules, we can't collect the first $50 of the questioned amount, even if your statement was correct.

Although all of your billing error rights apply, because of the way the Account is structured, some of the requirements discussed above (e.g. regarding payments to us) may not be relevant to the HECM.

I/We hereby acknowledge receipt of the Home Equity Conversion Mortgage Federal Truth-in-Lending Loan Closing Disclosure Statement and agree to its terms.

_____   _____
Borrower   Date
EVE DAVID

_____   _____
Borrower   Date

Page 4

STATE OF **CA.**)
)
COUNTY OF   )

E DAVID

LL CITY BANK, N. A.

PROPERTY: **705 13TH STREET,
LOS ANGELES, CALIFORNIA 90055**

LOAN NO.: **0048382555**

COMPLIANCE AGREEMENT

The undersigned borrower(s), in consideration of the lender disbursing funds today of the closing of property located at 705 13TH STREET, LOS ANGELES, CALIFORNIA 90055 agrees, if requested by lender or someone acting on behalf of said lender, to fully cooperate and adjust for clerical errors, any and all loan closing documentation deemed necessary or desirable in the reasonable discretion of lender to enable lender to sell, convey, seek guaranty or market said loan to any entity, including but not limited to, an investor, Federal National Mortgage Association (FNMA), Government National Mortgage Association (GNMA), Federal Home Loan Mortgage Corporation, Department of Housing and Urban Development, Department of Veterans Affairs, or any Municipal Bonding Authority, or to ensure enforceability of loan if kept in lender's own portfolio.

The undersigned borrower(s) do hereby so agree and covenant in order to assure that the loan documentation executed this date will conform and be acceptable in the market place in the instance of transfer, sale or conveyance by lender of its interest in and to said loan documentation.

The undersigned borrower(s) do hereby certify that no form or document was signed in blank relevant to the loan application process on the property referenced above.

Dated effective this   day of

_____

(Borrower)
EVE DAVID

_____

(Borrower)

0048382555

DAVID
705 13TH STREET
LOS ANGELES, CALIFORNIA 90055

WELL CITY BANK, N. A.

LENDER CERTIFICATION

I certify that no form or document was signed in blank by the applicant borrower(s) relevant to the loan origination process on the property located at:

705 13TH STREET,
LOS ANGELES, CALIFORNIA 90055

Date: <u>JANUARY 10, 20XX</u>

_____
Authorized Signature

<u>**WELL CITY BANK, N. A.**</u>
Lender Name

Beetles-Termite, Pest Control Co.
13455 S. Avalon Blvd
Los Angeles, CA 90061
Ph# (310) 516-1820

INVOICE:
Invoice Number: 20042
Invoice Date: 12/03/20XX

Bill to:

Eve David
704 E. 13th Street
Los Angeles, CA 90055

Address of property inspected:

704 E. 13TH Street
Los Angeles, CA 90055

Invoice Description

Date of Inspection: 12/04/20XX
Termite Inspection Fee: 85.00 (termite work not included)
Payments: 0.00
Total due   **85.00**

Escrow Number

Escrow officer:

TERMS: Net 30 days.
Inspection fee: Work associated with the inspection report that is completed by this firm within 90 days includes this inspection fee.
Fannie Mae No. _____
Federal Tax ID No. _____

Notice to owner of Mechanics Lien; Under the California Mechanics Lien Law any structural pest control company who contracts to do work for you, any contractor, subcontractor, laborer, supplier or other person who helps to improve your property, but is not paid for his work or supplies, has a right to enforce a claim against your property. This means that after a court hearing, your property could be sold by a court officer and the proceeds of the sale used to satisfy the indebtedness. This can happen even if you have paid your structural pest control company in full if the subcontractor, laborers or suppliers remain unpaid.

To preserve their right to file a claim or lien against your property, certain claimants such as subcontractors or material suppliers are required to provide you with a document entitled "Preliminary Notice". Prime contractors and laborers for wages do not have to provide this notice. A Preliminary Notice is no{ a lien against your properly. Its purpose is to notify you of persons who may have a right to file a lien against your property if they are not paid.

Work Authorization

Prepared by

BEETLES-TERMITE, PEST CONTROL CO.

ADDRESS OF PROPERTY INSPECTED

Building No. 704	Street 13th Street	City Los Angeles	Zip 90055	County Code 19	Date of Inspection 12/06/20XX

Ordered by: Eve David 704 13th Street Los Angeles, CA 90055	Property Owner: Eve David 704 13th Street Los Angeles, CA 90055	Report sent to: Eve David 704 13th Street Los Angeles, CA 90055

Compete Report ☒   Limited Report ☐   Supplemental Report ☐   Reinspection ☐

An inspection has been made of the structure9s) on the diagram in accordance with the Structural Pest Control Act. Detached porches, detached steps, detached decks and other structures not included in the diagram were not inspected.

NOTE: If diagram is not shown here, please see the report.

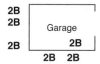

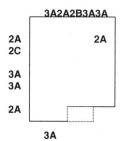

FRONT OF STRUCTURE

Page 1 of 3

Work Authorization

Prepared by

BEETLES-TERMITE, PEST CONTROL CO.

ADDRESS OF PROPERTY INSPECTED

Building No. 704	Street 13th Street	City Los Angeles	Zip 90055	County Code 19	Date of Inspection 12/06/20XX

Section: 1

2A =	1100.00	
2B =	See 2A ON REPORT	
2C =	1075.00	
3A =	COST SEE	

Section Total $ **2175.00**

Total (items quoted only):	**$2175** **.00**	Items to be completed by this company must be authorized on page three of this agreement.

Mechanic's Lien:

Notice to owner of Mechanics Lien; Under the California Mechanics Lien Law any structural pest control company who contracts to do work for you, any contractor, subcontractor, laborer, supplier or other person who helps to improve your property, but is not paid for his work or supplies, has a right to enforce a claim against your property. This means that after a court hearing, your property could be sold by a court officer and the proceeds of the sale used to satisfy the indebtedness. This can happen even if you have paid your structural pest control company in full if the subcontractor, laborers or suppliers remain unpaid.

To preserve their right to file a claim or lien against your property, certain claimants such as subcontractors or material suppliers are required to provide you with a document entitled "Preliminary Notice". Prime contractors and laborers for wages do not have to provide this notice. A Preliminary Notice is not a lien against your property. Its purpose is to notify you of persons who may have a right to file a lien against your property if they are not paid.

Page 2 of 3

Work Authorization

Prepared by

BEETLES-TERMITE, PEST CONTROL CO.

ADDRESS OF PROPERTY INSPECTED

Building No.	Street	City	Zip	County Code	Date of Inspection
704	13th Street	Los Angeles	90055	19	12/06/20XX

Total (items quoted only): **$2175.00**

1. If FURTHER INSPECTION is recommended, if additional work is required by any government agency, or if additional damage is discovered while performing the repairs, this company reserves the right to increase prices.

2. In the event that legal action is necessary to enforce the terms of this contract, reasonable attorney's fees may be awarded to the prevailing party.

3. This company will use due caution and diligence in their operations but assume no responsibility for matching existing colors and styles, or for incidental damage to roof coverings, TV. Antennas, solar panels, rain gutters, plant life, or paint.

4. This report is limited to the accessible areas shown on the diagram;. Please refer to the report for the areas not inspected.

5. If this contract is to be paid our of escrow impound the buyers and sellers agree to provide this company with all escrow billing information required to collect the amount due, The persons signing this contract are responsible for payment, and if the escrow does not close within 30 days after the date of completion of the work agree to pay in full the amount specified in this work authorization agreement.

6. If this agreement includes a charge for opening an area for FURTHER INSPECTION, it is for opening the area only and does not include making additional repairs, if needed, nor does it include replacing removed or damaged floor coverings, wall coverings, or painted exposed surfaces unless specifically stated.

This company is authorized to perform items:_____
Cost of work authorized: $_____

OWNER or Owner's Agent Date	BEETLES-TERMITES PEST CONTROL
x_____ _____ x_____ _____	BY: _____ ESCROW CO: _____ ESCROW CO: _____

Page 3 of 3

Report #:
200462

WOOD DESTROYING PESTS AND ORGANISMS INSPECTION REPORT

Building No.	Street	City	Date	No. of Pages
704	13th Street	Los Angeles	12/06/20XX	1of 6

Beetles-Termite, Pest Control Co.
13455 S. Avalon Blvd
Los Angeles, CA 90061
Ph# (310) 516-1820
PR 2422

Ordered by:	Property Owner:	Report sent to:
Eve David	Eve David	Eve David
704 13th Street	704 13th Street	704 13th Street
Los Angeles, CA 90055	Los Angeles, CA 90055	Los Angeles, CA 90055

Compete Report ☒   Limited Report ☐   Supplemental Report ☐   Reinspection ☐

General Description	Inspection Tag Posted:
One Story, single family residence with detached garage	Subarea
	Other Tags Posted:

An inspection has been made of the structure9s) on the diagram in accordance with the Structural Pest Control Act. Detached porches, detached steps, detached decks and other structures not included in the diagram were not inspected.

Subterranean Termites ☒   Dryrot Termites ☒   Fungus/Dryrot ☒

If any of the above boxes are checked, it indicates that there were visible problems in accessible areas. Read the report for details on checked items.

Key   1 = Subterranean Termites   2 = Dryrot Termites   3 = Fungus/Dryrot   4 = Other Findings   5 = Further Inspection

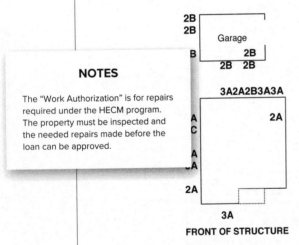

NOTES

The "Work Authorization" is for repairs required under the HECM program. The property must be inspected and the needed repairs made before the loan can be approved.

2B
2B

Garage   2B

B

2B   2B

3A2A2B3A3A

A
C

2A

A
A

2A

3A

FRONT OF STRUCTURE

Inspected by ____Steven Tonas____   License No ___OPR 2435___ Signature_____

You are entitled to obtain copies of all reports and completion notices on this property report to the Structural Pest Control Board during the two preceding years. To obtain copies contact: Structural Pest Control Board, 1418 Howe Ave. Suite 4, Sacramento, California, 16826

NOTE: Questions or problems concerning the above report should be directed to the manager of the company. Unresolved questions or problems with services performed may be directed to the or www.pestboard.ca.gov.

NOTES, CAUTIONS AND DISCLAIMERS

The pest control industry recognizes a structure to have certain areas both inaccessible and not Inspected. These areas include but are not limited to: Inaccessible and\or insulated attics or portions thereof, attics with less than 18" clear crawl space, the interior of hollow walls: the crawl space underneath a dock less than 12'; covered ceilings; spaces between a floor or porch deck and the ceiling below; areas where there is no access without defacing or tearing lumber, masonry, or finished work; areas underneath, behind or below appliances or beneath floor coverings or furnishings or storage, locked areas, and area's requiring an extension ladder; areas where encumbrances, storage, conditions, or locks make inspection impractical; and areas or timbers around eaves that would require use of an extension ladder.

Slab floor construction has become more prevalent in. recent years. Floor covering may conceal cracks in the slab that will allow infestations to enter. Infestations may be concealed by plaster, sheetrock or other wall coverings so that a diligent inspection may not uncover the true condition. The roof was not inspected due to lack of accessibility, qualification and licensing. These areas are not practical to inspect because of health hazards, damage, obstruction or inconvenience and unless specified or described in this wood destroying pests and organisms inspection report. This company shall exercise due care during inspections and treatments but assumes no liability for any damage to tiles, states, shingles or other roofing materials, including patio covers, aluminum awnings, solar heating, plants, shrubbery or paint during any type of treatment.

In the performance of corrective measures, ft may be necessary to drill into concealed areas and/or to cut or remove plants. The termite exterminator will not be liable for plumbing, heating, electrical, gas lines and equipment in or under a slab, nor to plants which may be damaged during treatments and/or repairs.

Guarantee policy:

This guarantee excludes structures with sub slab heating\air conditioning systems, plenum construction with air conditioning and heating duct in use, a well or cistern within fifty feet and areas that are inaccessible for treatment. Additional exclusions include structures with damage to or from excessive moisture, inadequate construction, areas of inaccessibility, deteriorating materials, masonry failure, grade alteration, pipes and conduits beneath concrete slab, furnishings or contents, etc. No guarantee will be issued for any work that is a secondary recommendation or work completed by others. Guaranteed for thirty days are any plumbing, grouting, caulking and resetting of commodes, sinks or enclosures. All other work performed by this company shall be guaranteed for the duration of one year.

This wood destroying pests and organisms inspection report does not include work which requires contact with materials containing asbestos. Termite inspectors have no expertise or license in asbestos analysis. Asbestos is a natural occurring mineral fiber used extensively in construction prior to 1978. The owner, employee or contractor must determine the asbestos status prior to the commencement of work on a project. Occupants and employees must be protected from asbestos fiber release. Should asbestos be observed during any construction or demolition, work must stop. The owner shall obtain the services of an asbestos abatement contractor to evaluate the situation, provide the necessary services and certify the area safe before work may resume. Asbestos statement ref: Ab2040, sb2Q72 and general industry safety order number 5208.

The purpose of this report is to document findings and recommendations which pertain to the absence or presence of wood destroying organisms and or conducive condition[s] at the time of inspection. This report should be read carefully and is not to be confused with a home maintenance survey. The client's cooperation and compliance to correct and or complete the recommendations documented in this report are obligatory. Without a mutual effort this company can not assure effective or satisfactory results.

The owner of this structure has certain obligations regarding maintenance and pertaining to the deterrence of wood destroying organisms. Maintenance procedures include; but are not limited to: Reasonable cleaning, upkeep of roofs, gutters and downspouts; painting and sealing of exposed surfaces: caulking about doors and windows or grouting about commodes, tub and shower enclosures, storing materials one foot away the structure's foundations; providing adequate ventilation, maintaining proper drainage away from structure (including sprinkler systems); keeping soil levels below the top of foundations and prohibiting earth contact with wood components of the structure(s).

Building No.	Street	City	Date	No. of Pages
704	13th Street	Los Angeles	12/06/20XX	3 of 6

Molds, sometime called mildew, are not wood-destroying organisms. Branch 3 licensees do not have A duty under the structural peat control act and related regulations to classify molds as harmful to human health or not harmful to human health.

THIS WOOD DESTROYING PESTS & ORGANISMS REPORT DOES NOT INCLUDE MOLD OR ANY MOLD LIKE CONDITIONS NO REFERENCE WILL BE MADE TO MOLD OR MOLD LIKE CONDITION. MOLD IS NOT A WOOD DESTORYING ORGANISM AND IS OUTSIDE TO SCOPE OF THIS REPORT AS DEFINED BY THE STRUCTURAL PEST CONTROL ACT. IF YOU WISH YOUR PROPERTY TO BE INSPECTED FOR MOLD LIKE CONDITIONS, PLEASE CONTACT THE APPROPRATE MOLD PROFESSIONAL.

THE ROOF WAS NOT INSPECTED. If roof Information is necessary, please contact the appropriate licensed tradesman.

The Structural Pest Control Board encourages competitive business practices among registered companies. Reports on this structure prepared by various registered companies should list the same findings (ie. Termite infestations, termite damage, fungus damage, etc.). However, recommendations to correct these findings may vary from company to company. Therefore, you may wish to seek a second opinion since there may be alternative methods of correcting the findings listed on this report that may be less costly.

SECTIONED REPORTING: This is a separated report which is defined as section 1 or section 2 conditions evident on the date of this inspection. Section 1 contains items where there is evidence of active infestation, infection or conditions that have resulted in or from infestation or infection on the date of inspection. Section 2 items are conditions deemed likely to lead to infestation or infection but where no visible evidence of such was found on the date of inspection. Further inspection items are defined as recommendations to inspect area(s) which during the original inspection did not allow the inspector access to complete his inspection and cannot be defined as Section 1 or Section 2.

2. DRYWOOD TERMITES
ITEM NO. 2A
FINDING:

(Section 1)
Evidence of DRYWOOD TERMITES as indicated by 2A on the diagram. Evidence noted in or near; WINDOW SILLS, FRAMING, SUBAREA AND EAVES.

RECOMMENDATION: 2A

Fumigate the structure with a fumigant lethal to DRYWOOD TERMITES, See the occupants fumigation notice for further details. This company is not responsible for delays or schedule changes due to inclement weather or other agencies, nor is it responsible for damage to roof or plants as a result of the fumigation. Refer to the occupant's fumigation notice/preparation sheet (sent separately) for additional information.

ITEM NO. 2B
FINDING:

(Section 1)
Evidence of DRYWOOD TERMITES as indicated by 2B on the diagram. Evidence noted in or near: ROOF SHEATHING, RAFTER TAIL AND STUDS OF GARAGE.

RECOMMENDATION: 2B

THIS RECOMMENDATION AND ITS COST ARE INCLUDED IN THE RECOMMENDATION FOR ITEM *2A ABOVE.

ITEM NO. 2C
FINDING.

(Section 1)
DRYWOOD TERMITE DAMAGE indicated by 2C on diagram. The damage was noted in or near: WINDOW SILL

RECOMMENDATION: 2C

Repair or reinforce as necessary with today's available widths and grades.

3. FUNGUS OR DRYROT
ITEM NO. 3A
RECOMMENDATION; 3A

(Section 1)
FUNGUS DAMAGE INDICATED 8Y 3A ON DIAGRAM. THE FUNGUS INFECTION WAS NOTED IN WINDOW AND BACK DOOR SILLS, STUCCO MOULDING AND ROOF SHEATHING.

RECOMMENDATION: 3A

Remove damaged materials and replace with similar materials in today's available selections. Match as close!) as practical, If owners desires a certain grade or color they are to specify their preferences prior to the commencement of the work and must be cautioned that additional charges may be necessitated depending upon the materials requested.

COMMENTS AND OTHER INFORMATION
This company is not responsible for damage found during the course of repairs nor damage In areas that were inaccessible at the time of inspection.

NOTE: FUMIGATION PERFORMED BY THIS COMPANY CARRIED TWO YEAR GUARANTEE. REPAIR(S), SUBTERRANEAN TERMITES AND LOCALIZED TREATMENT CARRIES ONE YEAR GUARANTEE, ON AREAS TREATED ONLY. SECONDARY RECOMMENDATION ARE CONSDERED BELOW STANDARD MEASURES AS PER STRUCTURAL PEST CONTROL ACT AND RULES AND REGULATION AND CARRIES NO GUARANTEE. HOWEVER PROTECTION MAYBE EXTENDED TO ENTIRE STRUCTURE BY PLACING IT ON A YEARLY CONTROL SERVICE WITHIN 45 DAYS AFTER THE COMPLETION OF WORK.

NOTE: THE EXTERIOR AREAS OF THIS STRUCTURE WERE VISUALLY INSPECTED FROM THE GROUND LEVEL.

Reverse Mortgages

Building No.	Street	City	Date	No. of Pages
704	13th Street	Los Angeles	12/06/20XX	5 of 6

NOTE: THIS COMPANY IS NOT RESPONSIBLE FOR DAMAGE FOUND DURING THE COURSE OF REPAIRS NOR DAMAGE IN AREAS THAT WERE INACCESSIBLE AT THE TIME OF INSPECTION. IF ANY INFESTATION, INFECTION OR DAMAGE IS DISCOVERED IN A CONCEALED AREA DURING THE COURSE OF PERFORMING ANY RECOMMENDATION IN THIS REPORT, THIS COMPANY WILL FILE A SUPPLEMENTAL REPORT.

NOTE: OUR INSPECTION IS LIMITED TO THE CONDITIONS WHICH ARE VISIBLE AND ACCESSIBLE AT THE TIME OF THIS INSPECTION. NO GUARANTEE IS IMPLIED OR EXPRESSED FOR CONDITIONS WHICH MAY BECOME APPARENT AFTER THE DATE OF THIS INSPECTION.

NOTE: THERE WILL BE NO CHARGE FOR THE INSPECTION FEE IF THE OUTLINED WORK IS COMPLETED BY OUR COMPANY WITHIN 30 DAYS OF THE INSPECTION.

NOTE: OUR COST DOES NOT INCLUDE PAINTING OR REDECORATING.

CALIFORNIA STATE LAW REQUIRES THAT YOU BE GIVEN THE FOLLOWING INFORMATION: "caution pesticides are toxic chemicals". Structural post control operators are licensed and regulated by the structural pest control board, and apply pesticides which are registered and approved for use by the California department of food and agriculture and the united states environmental protection agency. Registration is granted when the state finds that based en existing scientific evidence there are no appreciable risks if proper use conditions are followed or that risks are outweighed by the benefits. The degree of risk depends upon the degree of exposure, so exposure should be minimized.
If within twenty-four hours following application you experience symptoms similar to common seasonal illness comparable to the flu. Contact you physician or poison control center at: [(415) 428-3240] alameda [(415) 666-2845] San Francisco and your pest control operator immediately. For additional Information contact the county health department, county agricultural department and the structural pest control board: 1422 Howe Ave., Sacramento, CA. 95825-3280,

If we have recommended the use of a fungicide we will use:
TIM-BOR DISODIUM OCTABORATE TETRAHYDRATE...98%
If we have recommended the treatment of subterranean termites we will use:
PREMISE 75- IMIDACLOPRID,
1-[(6-CHLORO-3-PYRIDINYL)METHYL]-NITRO-2-IMIDAZOLIDINIMINE..75.0%
INVERT INGREDIENTS...........................25.0%

IF WE HAVE RECOMMENDED THE LOCALIZE TREATMENT OF DRYWOOD TERMITE WE WILL USE:
TIM-BOR-DISODIUMOCTABORATE-TETRAHYDRATE...98%

IF WE RECOMMEND FUMIGATION, THE FUMIGANT TO BE USED ON YOUR STRUCTURE WILL BE:
VIKANE-SULFURYL FLUORIDEAND CHLORPICRIN OR
METHYL BROMIDE AND CHLORICRIN

If we have recommended the treatment of wood boring beetles we will use:
TIM-BOR DISODIUM OCTABORATE TETRAHYDRATE...98%

For further information contact any of the following:

Building No.	Street	City	Date	No. of Pages
704	13th Street	Los Angeles	12/06/20XX	6 of 6

City	County Health Departments	Co. Agricultural Commissioner	Poison Control Center
San Francisco	(415) 554-2500	(415) 469-6301	(415) 476-6600
San Mateo	(415) 573-2222	(415) 363-4700	(415) 476-6600
Santa Clara	(408) 299-5858	(408) 299-2171	(408) 299-5112
Contra Costa	(510) 646-4416	(510) 646-5250	(510) 646-6600
Alameda	(510) 522-0889	(510) 670-5232	(800) 523-2222

NAME AFFIDAVIT

0048382555

NOTES

This "Name Affidavit" is required if the name of the borrower on the Firm Commitment, Title Insurance Policy, or Property Insurance Policy documents appear different.

The document must be notarized with a jurat.

be completed if there appear any discrepancies pertaining to the name(s) lowing documents: Firm Commitment, Title Insurance Policy, Property y.

y that

are one and the same person, and that I sign my name and am known by all above names.

This is to certify that

Are one and the same person, and that I sign my name and am known by all above names.

Dates this   day of

_____

Witness

_____

Borrower **EVE DAVID**

Sworn to and subscribed before me this   day of   ,   .

My commission expires:

_____

Notary Public

MORTGAGEE CERTIFICATION

Borrower: **EVE DAVID**

The mortgagee certifies that the authorized representative for the mortgagee executing form HUD-92900-A has personally reviewed the mortgage documents and the application for insurance endorsement and that the mortgage is eligible for mortgage insurance under HUD's Direct Endorsement program. The mortgagee has submitted all appropriate documents, properly executed, as required for the HECM program under all outstanding HUD handbooks and Mortgagee Letters. This mortgagee certification is in addition to any certifications required of the mortgagee, the mortgagor, or both on forms HUD-92800 or HUD-92900-A. The mortgagee certifies to the following additional matters:

(1) The mortgagor has executed a note, second note to the Secretary, security instrument (mortgage or deed of trust), second security instrument to the Secretary, and a loan agreement. The mortgagee has executed a loan agreement. All of these documents contain the provisions required by the Secretary.

(2) The payment plan attached to the loan agreement provides for monthly payments, a line of credit, or both in amounts calculated in accordance with the requirements of the Secretary.

(3) The security instrument is a first lien and the second security instrument given to the Secretary is a second lien.

(4) The security instrument is on real estate held in fee simple, or a life estate, or on a leasehold under a lease for not less than 99 years which is renewable, or under lease which otherwise meets the requirements of 24 CFR 206.45.

(5) If the mortgaged property is in a floodplain, the security instrument meets the flood insurance requirements of 24 CFR 206.45.

(6) If the property requires repair after closing to meet building standards of the Secretary, a repair rider to the loan agreement has been executed and the requirements of 24 CFR 206.47 will be complied with by the mortgagee.

WELL CITY BANK. N. A.
Lender Name:

_____
Lender Signature:

Lender:	**WELLS CITY BANK, N. A**.
Borrower:	**EVE DAVID**
Loan Number:	**0048382555**
Property Address:	**705 13TH STREET**
	LOS ANGELES, CALIFORNIA 90055

HOME EQUITY CONVERSION MORTGAGE
DISCLOSURE AND BORROWER CERTIFICATION REGARDING
THIRD PARTY FEES

Borrowers do not pay unnecessary or excessive costs for obtaining a Home Equity
~~tgage~~ ("HECM") loan. Federal law restricts the use of HECM loan proceeds, including
~~se~~ of such for payments to or on behalf of an "estate planning service firm" (as defined in
~~w~~). Further, HECM Borrowers must establish to the Lender that HECM loan proceeds will
~~ance~~ with law.

certifies to the Lender, and its successors and assigns:

~~sbursement~~ of loan proceeds by the Lender shall be used only for the following purposes:

a. the initial FHA mortgage insurance premium;

b. allowable fees and charges listed on the HUD-1 (or HUD-1A) Settlement Statement;

c. disbursements to Borrower(s), a relative or legal representative of the Borrower(s), or a trustee for the benefit of the Borrower(s);

d. amounts required to discharge any existing lien on the Property;

e. an annuity premium disclosed on the Federal Truth in Lending Disclosures; and

f. payment to contractors who performed repairs to the Property required as a condition of closing.

2   After the initial disbursement of loan proceeds for the purposes listed in Paragraph 1 above, all as disclosed on the HUD-1 (or HUD-1A) Settlement Statement, Borrower(s) will have no outstanding or unpaid obligations incurred in connection with the HECM loan, except for required repairs to the Property to be completed after loan closing and for monthly mortgage servicing fees to the Lender or servicer.

3   No portion of the initial disbursement of loan proceeds shall be used for any payment to or on behalf of an "estate planning service firm." [An "estate planning service firm" is an entity, other than the Lender or the housing counseling agency, which charges a fee not authorized by the Department of Housing and Urban Development which is 1) contingent on the homeowner obtaining a mortgage loan; 2) for initial information that the homeowner must, by regulation, receive from the housing counseling agency or Lender, except for information from an individual or company engaged in the bona fide business of providing tax or other legal or financial advice; or 3) for services for the purpose of improving an elderly homeowner's access to HECM loans.]

Page 1 of 2

NOTES

This disclosure form with reference to third party fees must be signed in two places. The second signature is required since the borrower is requesting a lump sum payment in excess of 25% of the net principal limit.

4.   Borrower(s) has received full disclosure of all costs of obtaining the HECM loan, including disclosure of which charges are required to obtain the HECM loan and which are not required to obtain the HECM loan.

_____	_____	_____	_____
Borrower	Date	Borrower	Date
EVE DAVID			

_____	_____	_____	_____
Borrower	Date	Borrower	Date

_____	_____	_____	_____
Borrower	Date	Borrower	Date

LUMP SUM DISBURSEMENT CERTIFICATION
(For Borrower(s) requesting at least 25% of the Net
Principal Limit as an initial lump sum disbursement.)

The Borrower(s) certifies to the Lender, and its successors and assigns, that the Borrower(s) ___ will ___ will not use any portion of the lump sum disbursement of HECM loan proceeds for payments to or on behalf of an "estate planning service firm," as that term is defined in Paragraph 3 above.

[Note: If you have checked the "will" box above, you are advised that Federal law prohibits any such payments to an "estate planning service firm."]

_____	_____	_____	_____
Borrower	Date	Borrower	Date
EVE DAVID			

_____	_____	_____	_____
Borrower	Date	Borrower	Date

_____	_____	_____	_____
Borrower	Date	Borrower	Date

NOTICE TO THE BORROWER

WHAT TO DO IN CASE OF LATE PAYMENTS OR NONPAYMENT
BY YOUR LENDER

FHA Case Number: **196-3492489-832**   Date of Mortgage: **January 10, 2005**

Borrower Name(s):   **EVE DAVID**
Property Address: **705 13th Street**
                            Los Angeles, CA 90055

lame: Well City Mortgage Company

of Housing and Urban Development (HUD) can help you if your lender fails to make payments to you on an only help you if you follow these instructions.

nversion Mortgage was insured on   [date] under a special law, Section 255 of Act, which makes HUD responsible for making any payments you have not received because the lender ocument explains the steps HUD will take if the lender fails to make its payments to you. The term "mortgage" in this Notice includes the loan agreement between you the lender and HUD.

2. HUD OFFICE

The HUD Field Office is located at **1516 S. BOSTON AVENUE, SUITE 100, TULSA, OKLAHOMA 74119.** Any letter addressed to that office should include your FHA case number, which appears at the top of this notice You should put "Home Equity Conversion Mortgage" on the envelope to ensure prompt and correct handling Telephone calls should be made to the **SINGLE FAMILY DIVISION** Branch at **(800) 594 - 9057** [telephone number]. You should inform the person answering the call that you are calling about your insured HECM. Please be prepared to provide your FHA case number.

3. METHOD OF PAYMENT

You may choose to receive payments through the "direct deposit" method of payment, where the lender automatically transfers money to your bank account, or you may receive checks through the mail. You may change your method of payment at any time during the loan.

4. PAYMENT OPTIONS

You can receive regular monthly payments, payments from a line of credit, or a combination of these payment options. You may change between these payment options. Please follow the instructions in this Notice which apply to the payment option that you have chosen.

5. REGULAR MONTHLY PAYMENTS

If you have chosen to receive regular monthly payments, the lender must transfer the full payment to your bank account by the first day of each month, or place your check in the mail by that day. If you do not receive payment on time (allowing sufficient time for mail delivery of the check, if applicable), your first contact should be with the lender's representative assigned to handle your account. HUD requires your lender to keep you informed of a current telephone number and address for the representative assigned to your account. If you can not contact your lender or if the account representative cannot help you, you should contact HUD.

HUD can help you with late payments in two circumstances. First, if the lender often makes payments which you receive late but before the 10th day of the month and this problem continues after you tell the lender about it, HUD will contact the lender at your request and require the lender to improve its performance and pay any late charges as required by your Loan Agreement. HUD will generally not be able to help with rare cases of late payment if the lender pays the late charge required by your Loan Agreement. Second, if any payment is not received before the 10th day of the month, you should immediately contact HUD (and the lender, if you have not done so). HUD will investigate the circumstances.

6. LINE OF CREDIT

If you have chosen to receive payments at your request from a line of credit, the lender should transfer the full amount requested, up to your principal limit, to your bank account or place your check in the mail within five business days after the lender receives your request. If you do not receive payment on time (allowing sufficient time for any mail delivery of your request to the lender, and any mail delivery of the check), your first contact should be with the lender representative assigned to handle your account. HUD requires your lender to keep you informed of a current telephone number and address for the representative assigned to your account. If you cannot contact your lender or if your account representative cannot help you, you should contact HUD. HUD can help you with late payments in two circumstances. First, if the lender often makes payments which your receive after you expect to receive them but fewer 10 days after you expect them, and this problem continues after you tell the lender about it, HUD will contact the lender and require the lender to improve its performance and pay late charges required by your Loan Agreement. HUD will generally not be able to help with rare cases of late payment if the lender pays the late charge required by your Loan Agreement. Second, if any payment has not been received 10 days after you expect to receive it, you should immediately contact HUD (and the lender if you have not already done so). HUD will investigate the circumstances.

7. HUD INVESTIGATION OF LATE LENDER PAYMENT: HUD PAYMENTS

A HUD investigation will begin with an immediate request to the lender for an explanation for the late or payment. If the lender does not provide a satisfactory explanation to HUD within 15 days of the request, or provide all funds due to you including any late charges), then HUD will begin arranging to make payments to you. Your HUD Field Office will keep you informed regarding the likely date for resumption of payments. The initial HUD payment will be equal to the total of all payments not made by the lender, including an amount equivalent to any late charge due from the lender. Subsequent HUD payments will be made in accordance with the timing required by the mortgage.

8. PAYMENT OF TAXES AND INSURANCE, OR OTHER PROPERTY CHARGES

If you elected to have the lender pay taxes, hazard insurance premiums, and certain other charges against the property using funds in your loan account, and you learn that the lender has not paid these items on time your should contact the lender's representative assigned to handle your account. If the lender does not correct the situation, you should contact the HUD office immediately.

9. HUD ASSUMPTION OF PAYMENT RESPONSIBILITY

Even if HUD is required to make some payments under the mortgage, we will try to have the lender resume making payments in accordance with the timing required by the mortgage. If HUD cannot arrange for the lender to resume payments HUD will demand assignment of the mortgage from the lender. If the mortgage is assigned to HUD you will deal with HUD as the new lender. If the lender cannot or will not assign the mortgage to HUD, you will receive no further payments from the lender under the first mortgage. No more interest or mortgage insurance premium will be added to the amount which you owe under the first mortgage. HUD will then make all future payments under the terms of a second mortgage which you gave to HUD when you gave the first mortgage to the original lender. The first and second mortgages will have to be repaid at the same time (for example, when you sell your home). Since you will not owe any interest under the first mortgage, the total debt under the first and second mortgages will be less than the amount you would have owed under the first mortgage if the lender had continued making payments. HUD may allow the lender to resume making payments after HUD has made payments. If that happens you will not owe anything to HUD but you will deal with the lender as if the lender had made all the payments under the first mortgage.

10. NO DEFICIENCY JUDGMENTS

When the mortgage loan becomes due and payable, you shall have no personal liability for payment of the mortgage. The lender's recovery from you will be limited to the value of the property. The lender may enforce the debt only through sale of the property, and the lender may not obtain a deficiency judgment against you if the Security Instrument securing the loan is foreclosed.

Signature of HUD Representative: _____

Title: _____

CHOICE OF INSURANCE OPTION

Date: **January 10, 20XX**

Loan No. : **0048382555**

Borrower: **EVE DAVID**

Property: **705 13th Street**
Los Angeles, CA 90055

With regard to the Home Equity Conversion Mortgage on the above referenced loan,
WELL CITY BANK

Chooses the Assignment Insurance Option.

_____

WELL CITY BANK   Date

NOTICE TO MORTGAGOR AT LOAN CLOSING
REGARDING PREPAYMENT

Date: **January 10, 20XX**

Loan No.:   **0048382555**

Mortgagor: **EVE DAVID**

Property: **705 13th Street,**
               Los Angeles, CA 90055

FHA No.:   **196-3492489-832**

This notice is to advise you of the requirements that must be followed to accomplish a prepayment of you mortgage, and to prevent accrual of any interest after the date of prepayment.

You may prepay any or all of the outstanding indebtedness due under you mortgage at any time, without penalty. However, to avoid the accrual of interest on any prepayment after the date of the prepayment, be sure the prepayment includes interest and finance charges through the date of the prepayment.

NOTE: Otherwise, you may be required to pay interest on the amount prepaid through the date when the prepayment was received.

WELL CITY BANK

By _____

_____
EVE DAVID   Borrower

HOME EQUITY CONVERSION MORTGAGE
NOTICE OF RIGHT TO CANCEL

Loan No.   **0048382555**   Date Notice Given: **JANUARY 10, 20XX**

Borrower(s):   **EVE DAVID**

1. YOUR RIGHT TO CANCEL

to establish an open-end credit account for you, and you have agreed to give us a mortgage on your
for the account. You have a legal right under federal law to cancel the account, without cost,
ness days after the latest of the following events:

opening date of your account which is **JANUARY 10, 20XX**   ;   or

date you received your Truth-in-Lending disclosures; or

(3) the date you received this notice of your right to cancel the account.

If you cancel the account, the mortgage on your home is also cancelled. Within 20 days of receiving you notice we must take the necessary steps to reflect the fact that the mortgage on your home has been cancelled. We must return to you any money or property you have given us or to anyone else in connection with the account.

You may keep any money or property we have given you until we have done the things mentioned above, but you must then offer to return the money or property. If it is impractical or unfair for you to return the property you must offer its reasonable value. You may offer to return the property at your home or at the location of the property Money must be returned to the address shown below. If we do not take possession of the money or property within 20 calendar days of your offer, you may keep it without farther obligation,

2. HOW TO CANCEL

If you decide to cancel the account, you may do so by notifying us, in writing, at

WELL CITY BANK, N.A.
2-D OAK BRANCH DRIVE, MAC: M5540-011
GREENSBORO, NORTH CAROLINA 27407

You may use any written statement that is signed and dated by you and states your intention to cancel, or you may use this notice by dating and signing below. Keep one copy of this notice because it contains important information about your rights

If you cancel by mail or telegram, you must send the notice no later than midnight of   **JANUARY 13, 20XX** (or midnight of the third business day following the latest of the three events listed above. If you send or deliver your written notice to cancel some other way, it must be delivered to the above address no later than that time.

I WISH TO CANCEL

_____   _____
Borrower's Signature   Date

ACKNOWLEDGEMENT OF RECEIPT

I hereby acknowledge receipt of two completed copies of the Home Equity Conversion Mortgage Notice of Right to Cancel and a copy of the Home Equity Conversion Mortgage Federal Truth-in-Lending Disclosure Statement.

_____   _____
Borrower's Signature   Date
EVE DAVID

NOTES

By law, the borrower must receive two executed copies of the Notice of Right to Cancel.

U.S.A. Patriot Act Customer Identification Program Disclosure

The U.S. Patriot Act, a federal law, requires all financial institutions to obtain sufficient information to verify your identity when creating a new reverse mortgage relationship. You may be asked several questions including your name, address, date of birth, and to provide one or more forms of identification to fulfill this requirement. In some instances, we require other identifying documents and/or use a third party information provider for verification purposes. All non-public information will be protected by our Privacy Policy and by federal law.

I/we acknowledge receipt of this disclosure.

_____   _____

Eve David   Date

NOTES

This U.S. Patriot Act disclosure form simply informs the borrower that the lender will require identification for new account holders. For this particular assignment, the Notary Signing Agent did not have to fill out an identification form.

WELL CITY BANK, N. A.
REVERSE MORTGAGE
ELECTRONICS FUND TRANSFER REQUEST

LOAN NUMBER: **0048382555**

I WOULD LIKE TO REQUEST THAT MY REVERSE MORTGAGE PAYMENT BE CREDITED DIRECTLY TO MY BANK ACCOUNT BY ELECTRONIC FUNDS TRANSFER. I UNDERSTAND THE MONTHLY PAYMENT WILL BE TRANSFERRED ON THE FIRST BUSINESS DAY OF EACH MONTH AND SHOULD BE AVAILABLE FOR WITHDRAWAL BY THE SECOND BUSINESS DAY.

SIGNATURE _____ DATE _____

SIGNATURE _____ DATE _____

SIGNATURE _____ DATE _____

SIGNATURE _____ DATE _____

EACH BORROWER MUST SIGN AND DATE ABOVE

ATTACH VOIDED CHECK WITH ALL BORROWERS' NAMES
HERE. COUNTER CHECKS ARE NOT ACCEPTABLE.

COMPLETE ONLY IF YOU WANT A DIRECT DEPOSIT ON YOUR MONTHLY PAYMENT OR LINE OF CREDIT ADVANCES.

PLEASE NOTE:
IF YOUR LOAN HAS MORE THAN ONE BORROWER OR A POWER OF ATTORNEY IS INVOLVED, ALL PARTIES' NAMES MUST APPEAR ON THE BANK ACCOUNT AND VOIDED CHECK ATTACHED.

WELL CITY BANK, N. A.
NEAREST LIVING RELATIVE INFORMATION SHEET

IN THE EVENT THAT WELL CITY BANK, N. A.
IS UNABLE TO REACH BORROWER(S) AS NEEDED, THE
PERSON WHOSE NAME APPEARS BELOW WILL BE
CONTACTED FOR ASSISTANCE.

NOTES

This information must be filled in by the borrower.

BORROWER NAME: _____

RELATIVE OR FRIEND: _____

RELATIONSHIP: _____

ADDRESS: _____

AREA CODE & PHONE #: _____

PLEASE COMPLETE THIS FORM

BY SIGNING BELOW, I AUTHORIZE WELL CITY TO RELEASE PERTINENT
INFORMATION REGARDING TO MY LOAN TO THE ABOVE MENTIONED PERSON(S)

_____
EVE DAVID

Reverse Mortgages

Correction Agreement Limited Power of Attorney

On **JANUARY 10 20XX**, the undersigned borrower(s), for and in consideration of the approval, closing and funding of their mortgage loan (**# 0048382555**) hereby grant as settlement agent and/or
WELL CITY BANK, N. A.

power of attorney to correct and/or execute or initial all typographical or clerical in any or all of the closing documentation required to be executed by the ttlement. In the event this limited power of attorney is exercised, the undersigned d receive a copy of the document executed or initialed on their behalf.

POWER OF ATTORNEY MAY NOT BE USED TO INCREASE THE TE THE UNDERSIGNED IS PAYING, INCREASE THE TERM OF THE D'S LOAN, INCREASE THE UNDERSIGNED'S OUTSTANDING LANCE OR INCREASE THE UNDERSIGNED'S MONTHLY D INTEREST PAYMENTS. Any of these specified changes must be executed dersigned.

er of attorney shall automatically terminate 120 days from the closing date of the undersigned's mortgage loan.

IN WITNESS WHEREOF, the undersigned have executed this Limited Power of Attorney as of the date and year first above referenced.

_____
Borrower
Typed Name: **EVE DAVID**

_____
Borrower
Typed Name:

_____
Borrower
Typed Name:

_____
Borrower
Typed Name:

State of _____)
_____)SS
County of _____)

This instrument was acknowledged before me on _____,

by _____ .

_____
Notary Public
My commission expires: _____

ADDENDUM TO HUD-1 SETTLEMENT STATEMENT

FHA Case Number: 197-3493819-955/956

Property Address: 705 13th Street Los Angeles, CA 90055

NOTICE TO ALL PARTIES: If information is obtained which indicates that the source of the borrower's financial investment is other than from the borrower or other than stated by the lender in its closing instructions, the settlement agent is to obtain written instructions from the lender before preceding with settlement.

CERTIFICATION OF BORROWER IN AN FHA-INSURED TRADITIONAL OR REFINANCE HECM LOAN TRANSACTION(s)

I (we) have carefully reviewed the HUD-1 Settlement Statement, and to the best of my knowledge and belief, it is a true and accurate statement of all receipts and disbursements made on my account or by me in this transaction. I further certify that I have received a copy of the HUD-1 Settlement Statement.

_____

Eve David
_____   _____

Borrower (s)   Date

_____
Power of Attorney

_____
Date

WARNING: Federal law provides that anyone who knowingly or willfully makes or uses a document containing any false, fictitious, or fraudulent statement or entry may be criminally prosecuted and may incur civil administrative liability.

CERTIFICATION OF BUYER IN AN FHA-INSURED HECM FOR PURCHASE LOAN TRANSACTION

I (we) certify that the sales price is _____. I (we) certify that I (we) have provided a down payment of _____ . I certify that the down payment has been provided by me (us) from my (our) own funds or from an approved FHA funding source as disclosed in my (our) mortgage application. I (we) certify that no part of the down payment has been provided by the seller or anyone else with a financial interest or financial connection to this transaction. I certify that I have no knowledge of any loans that have been or will be made to me (us) or loans that have been or will be assumed by me (us) for purposes of financing this transaction, other than those described in the sales contract dated _____(including addenda). I certify that I (we) have not been paid or reimbursed for any part of the monetary investment. I certify that I have not received and will not receive any payment or reimbursement for any of my (our) closing costs which have not been previously disclosed in the sales contract (including any addenda) and/or my application for mortgage insurance submitted to my (our) mortgage lender. I (we) certify that no cash or its equivalent, in whole or in part, was or will be received from the seller and/or other third party before, during, or after loan closing. I further certify that I (we) received a copy of the HUD-1 Settlement Statement.

_____

Eve David
_____   _____

Borrower (s)   Date

_____
Power of Attorney

_____
Date

WARNING: Federal law provides that anyone who knowingly or willfully makes or uses a document containing any false, fictitious, or fraudulent statement or entry may be criminally prosecuted and may incur civil administrative liability.

pg. 1

Notice of Special Flood Hazards and Availability of Federal Disaster Relief Assistance

Borrower Name: Eve David

Property Address: 705 13th Street

City, State, Zip: Los Angeles, CA 90055

Certificate Number:

We are giving you this notice to inform you that the building or mobile home securing the loan for which you have applied is or will be located in an area prone to high flood risks, also known as a Special Flood Hazard Area (SFHA).

"The area has been identified by the Director of the Federal Emergency Management Agency (FEMA) as a special flood hazard area using FEMA's Flood Insurance Rate Map or the Flood Hazard Boundary Map for the following community: _____
This area has at least a one percent (1%) chance of a flood equal to or exceeding the base flood elevation (a 100-year flood) in any given year. During the life of a 30-year mortgage loan, the risk of a 100-year flood in a special flood hazard area is 26 percent (26%)."

Federal law allows a lender and a borrower jointly to request the Administrator of FEMA to review the determination of whether the property securing the loan is located in an SFHA. If you would like to make such a request, please contact us for further information. Borrowers may also call a FEMA mapping specialist at (877) 336 2627 to discuss their concerns.

_____ The community in which the property securing the loan is located participates in the National Flood Insurance Program (NFIP). Federal law will not allow us to make you the loan that you have applied for if you do not purchase flood insurance on your property. The flood insurance must be maintained for the life of the loan. If you fail to purchase or renew flood insurance on your property, Federal law authorizes and requires us to purchase the flood insurance for you at your expense.

Flood insurance coverage under the NFIP may be purchased through an insurance agent who will obtain the policy either directly through the NFIP or through a Write Your Own (WYO) company that has agreed to write and service NFIP policies on Behalf of FEMA. Flood insurance also may be available from private insurers that are not federally backed.

At a minimum, flood insurance purchased must cover the lesser of: (1) the outstanding principal balance of the loan(s); or (2) the maximum amount of coverage allowed for the type of property under the NFIP; or (3) the full replacement cost value (RCV) of the building and/or contents securing the loan. The market value or land value on which the building is located has no bearing on the RCV of the building

Federal disaster relief assistance (usually in the form of a low-interest loan) may be available for damages incurred in excess of your flood insurance if your community's participation in the NFIP is in accordance with NFIP requirements.

_____ The community in which the property securing the loan is located does not participate in the National Flood Insurance Program (NFIP). Federal flood insurance is not available. However, private flood insurance may be available on a limited basis in the SFHAs of non-participating communities. Federal financial assistance including disaster assistance grants or loans and flood mitigation grants are not available in SFHAs of non-participating communities. For example, if the non-participating community has been identified for at least a year as containing an SFHA, properties located in the community will not be eligible for Federal disaster relief assistance in the event of a federally declared flood disaster.

Conventional loans, loans that are not federally backed can be made on buildings in SFHAs of non-participating communities, if authorized by the regulatory authority of the lending institution. However, government guaranteed or insured loans (e.g., SBA, VA, and FHA loans) are not permitted to be made in non-participating communities, if secured by structures in SFHAs.

We may assign, sell, or transfer the servicing of your mortgage loan. Your new lender/servicer may require more flood insurance coverage than the minimum amount that has been identified in your Notice of Special Flood Hazards (NSFH). The new lender may require coverage greater than the minimum and has the right to require flood coverage at least equal to 100% of the insurable value (also known as replacement costs value) of the building(s) used as collateral to secure the loan or the maximum allowable under the National Flood Insurance Program (NFIP) for the particular type of building. You should review your exposure to flood damage with your insurance provider, as you may wish to increase your coverage above the minimum amount required at the time of your loan closing versus what subsequently the new lender/servicer may require.

Received and acknowledged on this the _____ Day of _____, 20_____

_____   _____

Eve David   Date Mailed to Borrower

FannieMae

ARM Mortgage
HECM/HOME KEEPER
Loan Submission Schedule

	Fannie Mae Use Only
	Regional Receipt Date

	Fannie Mae Loan Number **6 -**	Date of Purchase	Home Office Receipt Date	Batch Control Number

1. Seller Number	2. Seller Contact Name	3. Phone	4. Fax

5. Servicer Number	6. Servicer Contact Name	7. Phone	8/ Fax

9. Subservicer Number	10. Subserivcer Contact Name	11. Phone	12. Fax

13. ABA Routing Number	14. Lender Loan ID **DAVID, E**	15. FHA Case Number **196-3492489-832**	16. Commitments Contract #	17.Period Contract **30 DAYS**

18. Property Street **704 13TH STREET**	19. Property City **LOS ANGELES**	20. Property State **CALIFORNIA**	21. Property Zip **90055**

22. No. of Units **1**	23. Type: Single Family **X** Condo Pud	24. Appraised Value **265,000.00**	25. Maximum Claim Amount **265,000.00**

26 Closing Date **01/10/XX**	27. Funding Date **01/14/XX**	28. Borrower's Birthdate **08/16/XX**	29. ARM PLAN Monthly **X** Yearly

30. Rounding Yes No **X**	31. Initial Rate: **4.2700**	32. Initial Index **2.7700**	33. Margin **1.50000**	34. Floor	35. Ceiling **14.270**	36. 1st Adjustment Date **APRIL, 20XX**

37. Expected Average Interest Rate **5.7900**	38. Expected Rate Index **4.29000**	**39. Monthly Service Fee** **30.00**	**40 Monthly Taxes & Insurance** **N/A**

41. Original Principal Limit	**175,960.00**

		Rate Lock	
42. Closing Costs	13,189.33	Application Date	
43. Lien Advances	113,661.56	Lock Expiration Date	
44. Other Draws		Lock Index	
45. Servicing Fee Set Aside	4,877.28	Lock Expected Rate	
46. Repair Set Aside	14,208.00	Lock Margin **0.00000**	
47. First Year Property Charges		HECM to HECM Refinance	

48. Net Principal Limit **30,023.83**	49. UPB **126,850.89**

50. Scheduled Payments to be Suspended	Yes	No
Suspension Start Date		
Suspension End Date		

LOAN TYPE

51. Term	Maturity	
	Monthly Payment Amount	
	First Disbursement Due Date	
52. Tenure	Monthly Payment Amount	
	First Disbursement Due Date	
53. Modified Term	Maturity	
	Monthly Payment Amount	
	Original Line of Credit Reserve	
	Net Line of Credit Reserve	
	First Disbursement Due Date	
54. Modified Tenure	Monthly Payment Amount	
	Original Line of Credit Reserve	
	Net Line of Credit Reserve	
	First Disbursement Due Date	
55. Line of Credit	Original Line of Credit Reserve	44,231.83
	Net Line of Credit Reserve	30,023.83

HECM/ HOME KEEPER

Addendum to Loan Submission
Schedule 928

56. Number of Borrowers	1
57. Gender of Borrower Male -- 1 Female -- 2	2
58. Race of Borrower * See Below	3
60. Race of Co-Borrower * See Below	
61. Age of Co-Borrower	0
62. Monthly Income	300.00
63. Year Built	20XX
64. Number of Bedrooms	2
Ethnicity of Borrower * See Below	2
Ethnicity of Co-Borrower * See Below	0

* Race Designations	
1 = American Indian/Alaskan	5 = White
2. = Asian	6. = Information not provided
3 = Black or African American	7 = Not applicable (ie Entity)
4 = Native Hawaiian or Other Pacific Islander	

* Ethnic Designations	
1 = Hispanic or Latino	
2 = Not Hispanic or Natino	
3 = Information not provided	
4 = Not Applicable (i.e. Entity)	

Authorized Signature	Name (Please Print

4

Sale and Purchase Transactions

INTRODUCTION

Occasionally a Notary Signing Agent may take on an assignment for a transaction involving the sale or purchase of real property. Since sale and purchase transactions have their own unique nuances, documentation for sale and purchase transactions differ from refinance and home equity line of credit assignments. The main differences can be noted as follows:

First, unlike refinance and HELOC transactions, there are two distinct parties signing documents in a sale or purchase transaction: the seller and buyer. Depending upon the circumstance, the Notary Signing Agent may handle the signing for the buyer, seller, or possibly both parties.

Second, if asked to handle the signing of papers for the seller, there will be a deed among the papers in the package. The seller must execute the deed to convey his or her ownership interest in the property. The presence of a deed in the package should not pose any particular challenge to the Notary Signing Agent because some refinance and home equity line of credit transactions include the execution of a deed for various purposes.

When signing papers for the seller, there will not be a promissory note or security instrument in the document package, or any other "lender" documents typically found in a refinance package. In fact, the typical "seller" package might appear slim compared to a refinance package.

Finally, there are a few forms in a sale or purchase documentation package that normally are not found in a typical set of refinance papers the Notary Signing Agent may encounter in a routine assignment. The unique forms contained in the seller's document package included in this chapter are as follows:

- Certification for No Information Reporting on the Sale or Exchange of a Principal Residence

- Transferor's (Seller's) Affidavit

- Notification to Buyer on Disposition of California Real Property (Seller)

- Notification from Buyer on Disposition of California Real Property

- Premium Invoice for a home warranty policy

- Residential Disclosure Report

The "Residential Disclosure Report" warrants special explanation. In this report, a seller of real property — or the agent for the seller — must disclose whether historical evidence indicates that an event of natural origin is likely to affect the desirability and value of the property. (California Civil Code Section 1102.)

The "Residential Disclosure Report," a document of several pages in length, includes disclosures in the following special subject areas:

- Special flood hazard areas, including areas of potential flooding from dam failure. The seller or seller's agent must disclose actual knowledge that the property is located within an area of potential flooding or a dam inundation area, or that the local jurisdiction has compiled a list of properties that are within an area of potential flooding or inundation, and the property appears on the parcel list.

- Very high hazard fire areas. The seller or seller's agent must disclose to a prospective buyer actual knowledge that the property is located within a very high fire hazard severity zone or the property appears on a map delineating such zones.

- Seismic activity. The seller or seller's agent must disclose to a prospective buyer if the seller or seller's agent has actual knowledge that the property is located within a delineated "Earthquake Fault Zone," provided that officially prepared maps, or the information contained in the maps, are "reasonably available."

- "Mello Roos" districts. A seller must make a good faith effort to obtain a "Notice of Special Lien" from each local agency which levies a special tax on the property providing for construction of a new school, sewage lines, streets, parks and other public improvements. Usually every homeowner in the district is assessed the same tax.

- <u>Proximity to military ordnance zone, industrial area and commercial airport</u>. The seller must inform the buyer of any former military training locations with potentially explosive munitions and districts allowing manufacturing or commercial airport use located within one mile of the subject property.

While the "Residential Disclosure Report" is a California form, other states require similar forms.

In keeping with all other transactions Notary Signing Agents regularly handle, there will be a settlement statement in a sale or purchase transaction, although it may be called "Seller's Estimated Closing Statement" or the like. In addition, closing or escrow instructions will be present (often titled "Joint Escrow Instructions") as well as loan payoff and disbursement instructions.

In handling the signing of papers for the buyer, Agents might expect to see many of the standard lender forms required in refinance transactions, except one: a "Notice of Right to Cancel" form. The three-day rescission period option common to refinance and home equity lines of credit transactions does not apply in purchase transactions. Agents must be careful not to misrepresent that a rescission option exists when in fact it may not. To avoid potential problems, it is always safest to check the document package for inclusion of the "Notice of Right to Cancel" form before the appointment and direct any questions about a rescission period to the escrow or title agent handling the closing.

Forms in Sample Set   **Pages**

The full list of documents comprising the sample seller's documentation package is as follows (borrower's documentation package is not provided). Refer to the marginal notes for additional comments on these forms.

Notarized Forms in Sample Set   Pages

The documents in the sample seller's documentation package that must be notarized are listed below. Refer to the marginal notes for additional comments and guidelines for notarizing these forms.

RIGHT CORP. TITLE COMPANY OF CALIFORNIA
2950 Mandrake Ave., Suite 122,
Walnut Creek, CA 94596
(925)287-4680

SELLER'S CLOSING STATEMENT
Estimated

Escrow No: 99988888-715 BR
Close Date: 09/30/20XX
Proration Date:
Date Prepared: 09/26/20XX

Property: 100 Goodfellow Drive
Pleasant Hill, CA 94523

Description	Debit	Credit
TOTAL CONSIDERATION:		
Total Consideration		399,000.00
PRORATIONS AND ADJUSTMENTS:		
County Taxes from 07/01/03 To 09/30/03	945.61	
Based on the Semi - Annual Amount of $1,912.46		
COMMISSIONS:	19,950.00	
Commission		
$9,975.00 to Kim Hong Realty		
$9,975.00 to Help U Sell - Heritage		
TITLE CHARGES:		
Overnight/Express Mail Fees to Right Corp. Title Company of California	75.00	
ESCROW CHARGES:		
Document Preparation to Right Corp. Title of California	100.00	
RECORDING FEES:		
County Transfer Tax to Right Corp. Title Company of California	438.90	
PAYOFFS:		
Payoff to Bank of United States	264,485	
$258,683.30 Principal Balance		
$5,366.74 Interest to 10/6/03		
$344.49 Prorated Mortgage Insurance Premium		
$16.00 Recording Fee		
$24.98 NSF Fees		
$30.00 Payoff Statement Fee		
$20.00 Misc. Fees		
Payoff to BANK OF UNITED STATES	98,629	
$316.94 Interest from 0910/2003 to 10/06/2003		
$97,837.66 Principal & Interest to 09/10/03		
$400.00 Early Closure Fee		
$75.00 Payoff Statement & Reconveyance Fee		
ADDITIONAL CHARGES:		
Home Warranty, #110-365-941 to New National Home Protection	330	
Natural Hazards Report to CGS Reports	49	
Termite Inspection to San Miguel - need invoice	205	
Termite Repairs Section I to San Miguel - need invoice	491	
Notary/Signing (seller package to Central Signing Service)	90	
Sub totals.	385,790	
Proceeds Due Seller 13,209.43	13,209	
Totals	$399,000	

_____
Kevin L. Paine

NOTES

The "Seller's Closing Statement" resembles the "Borrower's Estimated Closing Statement" found in most residential refinance packages.

However, unique line items in the "Seller's Closing Statement" include:

• Commissions paid to real estate agents

• Home warranty premium

• Natural hazards report

• Termite inspection

• Termite repairs

Since there is no new loan financing, notice the absence of new loan charges.

RIGHT CORP. TITLE COMPANY OF CALIFORNIA
Date: September 26, 20XX
Escrow No.: 99988888-715 BR
Escrow Officer: Maryanne Richards
Property Address: 100 Goodfellow Drive Pleasant Hill, CA 94523

2950 Mandrake Ave.. Suite 122 Walnut Creek, CA 94596 Telephone: (925) 287-4680 Fax:(925) 287-9105

SUPPLEMENTAL JOINT ESCROW INSTRUCTIONS

scrow are hereby, modified, amended and/or supplemented in the following particulars only.

any funds (in the form of wire transfer, certified check, cashiers check or teller's check payable to Right Corp.
rnia pursuant to the "Deposit of Funds", Paragraph 1 contained in the General Provisions attached hereto and
r instruments required from me to enable you to close in accordance with the estimated dosing statement and
cure/issue a coverage form Policy of Title Insurance from Chicago Title Insurance Company, with a liability
operty described property described in your Preliminary Report number 00028843, dated July 11, 20XX, a
read and hereby approve.

SELLER/TRANSFEROR STATES THAT PROPERTY ADDRESS IS:
100 Goodfellow Drive, Pleasant Hill, CA 94523

SHOWING TITLE VESTED IN:
John Buyer and Julie Buyer

FREE FROM ENCUMBRANCES EXCEPT:
1. Current general and special taxes for the fiscal year in which this escrow closes, and taxes for the ensuing year, if any, a lien not yet due and payable;
2. The lien of supplemental taxes, if any, assessed pursuant to the provisions of Chapter 3.5 (commencing with Section 751 of the Revenue and Taxation code of the State of California;
3. Bonds and Assessments with no delinquent payments, if any;
4. Covenants, conditions, restrictions, reservations, easements and rights of way now of record, if any;
5. Exceptions numbered 1,2,3,4, as shown on your preliminary report above referenced.
6. A first deed of trust to record, in the amount of $TBD in favor of TBD.

PRORATIONS: Prorate as of Close of Escrow, on the basis of a 30 day month
Taxes, Tax bill for 03/XX amounts are $1912.46

ADDITIONAL INSTRUCTIONS:
1. The receipt by escrow of all documents and monies required to transfer title in accordance with these instructions hall be deemed as sufficient indication that all contingencies and/or conditions contained in the purchase agreement by and between the within buyers and sellers have been removed, complied with, or will be satisfied outside of escrow.
2. Buyers and Sellers acknowledge receipt of Escrow Holder's Acceptance of Escrow and that all agreements, counter offers and/or any addendums to the Purchase Agreement have been deposited with Escrow Holder and that there are no other outstanding agreements, counter offers and/or addendums to the Purchase Agreement which affect the closing of this transaction. Right Corp. Title Company of California is relieved of any and all responsibility and/or liability and will be held harmless as it relates to said documents not deposited to escrow.
3. The undersigned hereby authorize and instruct Escrow Holder to charge each party to the escrow for their respective Federal Express and special mail handling/courier. Unless specified in writing by the undersigned, Escrow Holder is authorized to select special mail/delivery or courier service to be used.
4. Buyer agrees to provide new hazard insurance policy acceptable to lender and to authorize payment of premium through escrow unless a paid receipt is provided to escrow.
5. The undersigned Buyer hands you herewith Preliminary Change of Ownership Report as provided for in Section 480.34 of the Revenue and Taxation Code. State of California which you are to cause to be filed concurrently with the Deed in our favor. If form is rejected by the County, a surcharge may be imposed by said County and is to be paid by Buyer herein.

6. Escrow Holder is authorized to obtain demands and reconveyance and/or releases of existing encumbrances not to remain of record and to pay said demands at close of escrow from the account of Seller herein. Seller is aware that interest on the existing loan(s) does not stop accruing at close of escrow, but continues until the actual day of receipt of the payoff to lender(s). In the event an FHA loan is being paid off, interest may accrue past the date of receipt by lender pursuant to the terms of the note securing the loan. The undersigned acknowledges and understands that disbursement of any payoffs for encumbrances being paid off at dose of this escrow must be received by the lender by a specific date to avoid further accrual of interest either daily or monthly.

   You are instructed to forward payoff funds to the lender by express service of your choice and Charge my/our account any fees for overnight delivery at close of escrow. In the event the lender demands additional funds after the close of escrow, we agree to deposit any additional funds necessary to comply with lenders instructions immediately upon notice of same.

7. Close of escrow to be on or before _____ , or thereafter, unless revoked by written demand on you by the undersigned.

8. VESTING-BUYER TO COMPLETE: John Buyer and Julie Buyer

   Escrow Holder is authorized and instructed to insert same in the Grant Deed without ful1her instructions from the Buyer and/or Seller.

   PLEASE MARK ONE OF THE FOLLOWING:
   ____ Husband and Wife as Joint Tenants
   ____ Husband and Wife as Community Property
   ____ Husband and Wife as Community Property with Right of Survivorship
   ____ A Single Man (never been married)
   ____ A Single Woman (never been married)
   ____ An unmarried Man (divorced)
   ____ An unmarried Woman (divorced)
   ____ A Widow/Widower (spouse deceased)
   ____ A married Man/Woman as his/her sole and separate property**
         **Please indicate name of spouse so interspousal deed may be drawn:
         _____
   ____ Each as to an undivided _____ +% interests, as Tenants in Common
   ____ All as Joint Tenants
   ____ Other (Please explain) Escrow Holder advises the parties hereto to seek legal counsel with their attorney and/or accountant as to how they should hold title.

9. Escrow Holder is hereby authorized and Instructed that, in the event any party utilizes "facsimile" transmitted signed documents or instructions to Escrow Hokier, you are to rely on the same for all escrow instruction purposes and the closing of escrow as if they bore original signatures. Each party shall provide to the other party and to Escrow Holder within 72 hours after transmission, duplicate original documents or instructions bearing the original signatures. Not withstanding the foregoing, any and all escrow instructions pertaining to the release or disbursement of funds from escrow prior to close of escrow shall not be effective until Escrow Holder has received such instructions from all parties bearing original, NOTARIZED signatures. Each party further acknowledges and agrees that documents with non- original signatures may mot be accepted for recording by the County Recorder, therefore, no closing or recording may take place without the submission of the original documents.

10. Borrower/Buyer hereby agrees to provide escrow with an evidence of insurance, in compliance with the Lender's Instructions.
   Insurance Company: _____
   Agents Name: _____
   Telephone Number: _____
   Any additional coverage desired by Buyer shall be handled outside of this escrow and will be no conc[...] whatsoever.

11. As previously set forth herein, Escrow Holder is instructed to pro-rate taxes on the latest tax bill as of the [...] view of the change of ownership of the subject property which will take place on the close of this escrow [...] Chapter 498 and 1102, Statutes of 1983 of the State of California (commonly referred to as Senate Bill N[...] Bill No. 399 respectively), it is to be expected that the taxing authorities will re-assess the property and i[...] bin. Seller and Buyer acknowledge their awareness of the foregoing and hereby release and relieve Escr[...] in connection herewith and Escrow Holder shall not be further concerned with the above re- assessment [...]

12. The undersigned acknowledges that the tax proration set forth herein is based upon the 2002 - 2003 as[...] the 2002 - 2003 tax rate, and that the final tax liability may vary from that shown herein. It is further a[...] should any adjustment In tax proration be required after the 2003 - 2004 tax bills become available, said adjustment will be made between the Buyer and Seller without any responsibility therefore on the part of the Escrow Holder.

Continued on following page   Initials _____

NOTES

If conducting the signing of documents for one party, make sure that any paragraphs addressing the party are properly completed. (Note items #8 and #10 require the buyer to complete.)

Parties must initial the bottom of this form.

13. The undersigned hereby instruct and authorized Escrow Holder to disburse proceeds/refund as follows:
   ☐ TRANSFER ☐ All Net Proceeds/Refund. or ☐ $ _____ to
   _____
   ATTN: _____

   Escrow No: _____
   ☐ HOLD check for PICK UP
   ☐ CALL when check is ready for PICK UP, PHONE NUMBER _____
   ☐ WIRE funds to (Bank Name) _____
      Address _____
      Routing No. _____
      Account _____
   ☐ MAIL ☐ FEDERAL EXPRESS check to _____

14. Seller hereby acknowledges that Escrow will be required to send 3 1/3% ($13,167.00) of purchase should seller not qualify as principal residence sale.

   In accordance with Sections 18805 and 26131 of the Revenue and Taxation Code, a Buyer may be required to withhold an amount equal to 3 1/3rd per cent of the sales price in the case of a disposition of California real property interest by either.

   1. A seller who is an initial with a last known address outside of California or when the disbursement instructions authorize the proceeds be sent to a financial intermediary of the seller; OR

   [eller] which has no permanent place of business in California.

   [become] subject to penalty for failure to withhold an amount equal to the greater of 10% of the amount [withheld] or five hundred dollars ($500.00).

   [who] is an individual, executes a written certificate, under the penalty of perjury, that the California real [conveyed] is the Seller's principal residence (as defined In Section 1034 of the Internal Revenue Code).

   [subject] to penalty for knowingly filing a fraudulent certificate under the penalty of perjury, certifying that the [state] of California, or if a corporation, has a permanent place of business in California;

   [statutes] referenced above include provisions which authorize the Franchise Tax Board to grant reduced [waivers] from withholding on a case-by-case basis.

   THE PARTIES TO THIS TRANSACTION SHOULD SEEK THE PROFESSIONAL ADVICE AND COUNSEL OF AN ATTORNEY, ACCOUNTANT OR OTHER TAX SPECIALIST'S OPINION CONCERNING THE EFFECT OF THIS LAW ON THIS TRANSACTION AND SHOULD NOT ACT ON ANY STATEMENTS MADE OR OMITTED BY THE ESCROW OR CLOSING OFFICER.

   THIS AGREEMENT IN ALL PARTS APPLIES TO, INURES TO THE BENEFIT OF, AND BINDS ALL PARTIES HERETO, THEIR HEIRS, LEGATEES, DEVISEES, ADMINISTRATORS, EXECUTORS, SUCCESSORS AND ASSIGNS, AND WHENEVER THE CONTEXT SO REQUIRES THE MASCULINE GENDER INCLUDES THE FEMININE AND NEUTER, AND THE SINGULAR NUMBER INCLUDES THE PLURAL, THESE INSTRUCTIONS AND ANY OTHER AMENDMENTS MAY BE EXECUTED IN ANY NUMBER OF COUNTERPARTS, EACH OF WHICH SHALL BE CONSIDERED AS AN ORIGINAL AND BE EFFECTIVE AS SUCH.

   MY SIGNATURE HERETO CONSTITUTES INSTRUCTION TO ESCROW HOLDER OF ALL TERMS AND CONDITIONS CONTAINED IN THIS AND ALL PRECEDING PAGES AND FURTHER SIGNIFIES THAT I HAVE READ AND UNDERSTAND THESE GENERAL PROVISIONS.

   Right Corp. Title Company of California CONDUCTS ESCROW BUSINESS UNDER LICENSE NUMBER 371 ISSUED BY THE CALIFORNIA DEPARTMENT OF INSURANCE.

   BUYERS: SELLERS:

   _____   _____
   John Buyer   Kevin L. Paine

   _____
   Julie Buyer

NOTES

Seller must complete item #13 providing instruction for disbursement of proceeds and/or refunds.

Note item #14 requires the seller to initial in the "bubble."

GENERAL PROVISIONS

1. DEPOSIT OF FUNDS
The law dealing with the disbursement of funds requires that all funds be available for withdrawals a matter of right by the title entity's escrow and/or sub escrow account prior to disbursement of any funds, Only case or wire transferred funds can be given immediate availability upon deposit. Cashiers checks, teller's checks and Certified checks may be available one business day after deposit. All other funds such as personal, corporate or partnership checks and drafts are subject to mandatory holding periods which may cause delays, all funding should be wire transfer. Outgoing wire transfers will not be authorized until confirmation of this respective incoming wire transfer or of availability of deposited checks.

All funds received in this escrow shall be deposited with other escrow funds in a general escrow account or accounts of Right Corp. Title Company of California, with any state or national bank, or savings and loan association (the "depository institution") and may be transferred to any other such general escrow account or accounts The parties to this escrow acknowledge that the maintenance of such escrow accounts with some depository institutions may result in Escrow Holder's being provided with an array of bank services, accommodations or other benefits by the depository institution. Escrow Holder or its affiliates also may elect to enter into other business transactions with or obtain loans for investment or other purposes from the depository institution. All such services, accommodations and other benefits shall accrue to Escrow Holder and Escrow Holder shall have no obligation to account to the parties to this escrow for the value of such services, accommodations or other benefits. Said funds will not earn interest unless the instructions otherwise specifically state that funds shall be deposited in an interest bearing account. All disbursements shall be made by check of Right Corp. Title Company of California. The principals to this escrow are hereby notified that the funds deposited herein are insured only to the limit provided by the Federal Deposit Insurance Corporation. Any instruction for bank wire will provide reasonable time or notice for Escrow Holder's compliance with such instruction. Escrow Holder's sole duty and responsibility shall be to place said wire transfer instructions with its wiring bank upon confirmation of (1) satisfaction of conditions precedent or (2) document recordation at close of escrow. Escrow Holder will NOT be held responsible for lost interest due to wire delays caused by any bank or the Federal Reserve System, and recommends that all parties make themselves aware of banking regulations with regard to placement of wires.

In the event there is insufficient time to place a wire upon any such confirmation or the wires have closed for the day, the parties agree to provide written instructions for an alternative method of disbursement. WITHOUT AN ALTERNATIVE DISBURSEMENT INSTRUCTION, FUNDS WILL BE HELD IN TRUST IN A NON-INTEREST BEARING ACCOUNT UNTIL THE NEXT OPPORTUNITY FOR WIRE PLACEMENT.

To the extent provided by law, if for any reason funds are retained or remain in escrow following the close of escrow, you are to deduct therefrom a reasonable monthly charge as custodian thereof of not less than $10.00 per month.

2. PRORATIONS AND ADJUSTMENTS
All prorations and/or adjustments called for in this escrow are to be made on the basis of a thirty (30) day month unless otherwise instructed in writing. You are to use information contained on last available tax statement, rental statement as provided by the Seller, beneficiary's statement and fire insurance policy delivered into escrow for the prorations provided for herein.

3. SUPPLEMENTAL TAXES
The within described property may be subject to supplemental real property taxes due to the change of ownership taking place through this escrow. Any supplemental real property taxes arising as a result of the transfer of the property to Buyer shall be the sole responsibility of Buyer and any supplemental real property taxes arising prior to the closing date shall be the sole responsibility of the Seller. TAX BILLS ISSUED AFTER CLOSE OF ESCROW SHALL BE HANDLED DIRECTLY BETWEEN BUYER AND SELLER.

4. UTILITIES/POSSESSION
Transfer of utilities and possession of the premises are to be settled by the parties directly and outside of escrow.

5. PREPARATION AND RECORDATION OF INSTRUMENTS
Escrow holder is authorized to prepare, obtain, record and deliver the necessary instruments to carry out the terms and conditions of this escrow and to order the policy of title insurance to be issued at close of escrow as called for in these instructions. Close of escrow shall mean the date instruments are recorded

6. AUTHORIZATION TO FURNISH COPIES
You are authorized to furnish copies of these instructions, supplements, amendments, notices and cancellation and closing statements, to the Real Estate Broker(s) and lender(s) named in this escrow.

7. RIGHT OF CANCELLATION
Any principal instructing you to cancel this escrow shall file notice of cancellation in your office in writing. You shall, within two (2) working days thereafter, deliver, on copy of such notice to each of the other principals at the addresses stated in this escrow. UNLESS WRITTEN OBJECTION TO CANCELLATION IS FILED IN YOUR OFFICE BY A PRINCIPAL WITHIN TEN (10) DAYS AFTER DATE OF SUCH MAILING, YOU ARE AUTHORIZED TO COMPLY WITH SUCH NOTICE AND DEMAND PAYMENT OF YOUR CANCELLATION CHARGES. If written objection is filed, you are authorized to hold all money and instruments in this escrow and take no further action until otherwise directed, either by the principals' mutual written instructions, or by final order of a court of competent jurisdiction.

8. PERSONAL PROPERTY
No examination or insurance as to the amount or payment of personal property taxes is required unless specifically requested. By signing these General Provisions, the parties to the escrow hereby acknowledge that they are indemnifying the Escrow Holder against any and all matters relating to any "Bulk Sales" requirements, and instruct Escrow Agent to proceed with the closing of escrow without any consideration of matter of any nature whatsoever regarding "Bulk Sales" being handled through escrow.

9. RIGHT OF RESIGNATION
Escrow Holder has the right to resign upon ten (10) days written notice delivered to the principals herein. If such right is exercised, all funds and documents shall be returned to the party who deposited them and Escrow Holder shall have no liability hereunder.

10. AUTHORIZATION TO EXECUTE ASSIGNMENT OF HAZARD INSURANCE POLICIES
Either Buyer, Seller and/or Lender may hand you the insurance agent's name and insurance policy information, and you are to execute, on behalf of the principals hereto, from assignments of interest in any insurance policy (other than title insurance) called for in this escrow, forward assignment and policy to the insurance agent, requesting that the insurer consent to such transfer and/or attach a loss payable clause and/or such endorsements as may be required, and forward such policy(s) to the principals entitled thereto. It is not your responsibility to verify the information handed you or the assignability of said insurance. Your sole duty is to forward said request to insurance agent at close of escrow.

Further, there shall be no responsibility upon the part of Escrow Holder to renew hazard insurance policy(s) upon expiration or otherwise keep it in force either during or subsequent to the close of escrow. Cancellation of any xi sting hazard insurance policies is to be handled directly by the principals, and outside of escrow.

11. ACTION IN INTERPLEADER
The principals hereto expressly agree that you, as Escrow Holder, have the absolute right at your election to file an action in interpleader requiring the principals to answer and litigate their several claims and rights among themselves and you are authorized to deposit with the clerk of the court all documents and funds held in this escrow. In the event such action is filed, the principals jointly and severally agree: to pay your cancellation charges and costs, expenses and reasonable attorney's fees which you are required to expend or incur in such interpleader action, the amount thereof to be fixed and judgment therefor to be rendered by the court. Upon the filing of such action, you shall thereupon be fully released and discharged from all obligations imposed by the terms of this escrow or otherwise.

12. TERMINATION OF AGENCY OBLIGATION
If there is no action taken on this escrow within six (6) months after the "time limit date" as set forth in the escrow instructions or written extension thereof, our agency obligation shall terminate at your option and all documents, monies or other items held by you shall be returned to the parties depositing same. In the event of cancellation of this escrow, whether it be at the request of any of the principals or otherwise, the fees and charges due Right Corp. Title Company of California, including expenditures incurred and/or authorized shall be borne equally by the parties hereto (unless otherwise agreed to specifically).

13. CONFLICTING INSTRUCTIONS
Upon receipt of any conflicting instructions, you are to take no action in connection with this escrow until non-conflicting instructions are received from all of the principals to this escrow (subject to sections 7, 9, 11 and 12 above).

14. REIMBURSEMENT ATTORNEY FEES/ESCROW HOLDER
In the event that a suit is brought by any party or parties to these escrow instructions to which the Escrow Holder is named as a party which results in a judgment in favor of the Escrow Holder and against a principal or principals herein, the principals or principals' agent agree to pay said Escrow Holder all costs, expenses and reasonable attorney's fees which it may expend or incur in said suit, the amount thereof to be fixed and judgment therefore to be ordered by the court in said suit.

15. DELIVERY/RECEIPT
Delivery to principals as used in these instructions unless otherwise stated herein is to be by regular mail and receipt is determined to be 72 hours after such mailing. All documents, balances and statements due to the undersigned are to be mailed to the address shown herein.

16. STATE/FEDERAL CODE NOTIFICATIONS
According to Federal law, the Seller, when applicable, will be required to complete a sales activity report that will be utilized to generate a 1099 Statement to the Internal Revenue Service, oR provide Escrow Holder with a non-reporting affidavit.

Pursuant to State law prior to the close of escrow, Buyer will provide Escrow Holder with Preliminary Change of Ownership Report. In the event said report is not handed to Escrow Holder for submission to the County in which subject property is located, upon recording of the Grant Deed, Buyers acknowledge lat the applicable fee will be assessed by said County and Escrow Holder shall debit the account of Buyer for same at close of escrow. Buyer and Seller herein represent and warrant that they will seek and obtain dependent legal advice and counsel relative to their obligations under the "Foreign Investors In Real Property Act" and any other applicable federal and/or state laws regarding same, and will take all steps nec
requirements and hereby hold you harmless relative to their

17. ENCUMBRANCES
Escrow Holder Is to act upon any statements furnished by
liability or responsibility for the accuracy of such statement
because of a discrepancy between the information furnishe
later determined to be correct shall be settled between the

18. ENVIRONMENTAL ISSUES
Right Corp. Title Company of California has made no inves
to environmental/toxic waste issues. Any due diligence req
environmental impact as to forms of toxification, if applicab
principals outside of escrow. Right Corp. Title Company of California is released of any responsibility and/or liability in connection therewith

19. USURY
Escrow Holder is not to be concerned with any questions of usury in any loan encumbrance involved in the processing of this escrow and is hereby released of any responsibility of liability therefore.

20. DISCLOSURE
Escrow Holder's knowledge of matters affecting the property, provided such acts do not prevent compliance with these instructions, does not create any liability or duty in addition to these instructions

21. CLARIFICATION OF DUTIES
Right Corp. Title Company of California serve ONLY as an Escrow Holder in connection with these instructions and cannot give legal advice to any party hereto. Escrow Holder is not to be held accountable or liable for the sufficiency or correctness as to form, manner of execution, or validity of any instrument deposited in this escrow, not as to the identity, authority or rights of any person executing the same. Escrow Holder's duties hereunder shall be limited to the proper handling of such money and proper safekeeping of such instruments, or other documents received by Escrow Holder, and for the disposition of same in accordance with the written instructions accepted by Escrow Holder.

The agency and duties of Escrow Holder commence only upon receipt of copies of these Escrow instructions executed by all parties.

Initials ____________________

NOTES

Parties must initial the "General Provisions" section of the "Supplemental Joint Escrow Instructions."

Sale and Purchase Transactions

RECORDING REQUESTED BY
Right Corp. Title Company of California
WHEN RECORDED MAIL TO
AND MAIL TAX STATEMENTS TO
John Buyer and Julie Buyer

GRANT DEED

00028843   ESCROW NO. 999288888 BR 715   APN NO. 149-283-010-2

GRANTOR(s) DECLARE(s) DOCUMENTARY TRANSFER TAX is $ 438.90.

on full value of property conveyed, or
on full value less value of liens or encumbrances remaining at time of sale,
rated area: ☑ City of Pleasant Hill

FOR A VALUABLE CONSIDERATION, receipt of which is hereby acknowledged, Kevin L. Paine, a married woman, as her sole and separate property

hereby GRANT(s) to John Buyer and Julie Buyer

the following described real property in the City of Pleasant Hill
County of Contra Costa, State of California:

Lot 248, as designated on the Map entitled, "Pleasant Valley View Homes, Unit No. 3, Contra Costa County, California", which Map was filed in the office of the Recorder of the County of Contra Costa, State of California, on September 8, 20XX, in Volume 33 of Maps, at Page 44.

Date: Sepember 26, 20XX

_____
Kevin L. Paine

STATE OF   }
COUNTY OF   } ss.

On _____ before me, _____, (here
insert name and title of the officer), personally appeared _____
_____ ,
personally known to me (or proved to me on the basis of satisfactory evidence) to be the person(s) whose name(s) is/are subscribed to the within instrument and acknowledged to me that he/she/they executed the same in his/her/their authorized capacity(ies), and that by his/her/their signature(s) on the instrument the person(s), or the entity upon behalf of which the person(s) acted, executed the instrument.

WITNESS my hand and official seal.

Signature_____

CERTIFICATION FOR NO INFORMATION REPORTING
ON THE SALE OR EXCHANGE OF A PRINCIPAL RESIDENCE

This form may be completed by the seller of a principal residence. This information is necessary to determine whether the sale or exchange should be reported to the seller, and to the Internal Revenue Service on Form 1099-S, Proceeds form Real Estate Transaction. If the seller properly completes Parts I and III, and makes a "yes" response to assurance (1) through (4) in Part II, no information reporting to the seller or to the Service will be required for that seller. The term "seller" includes each owner of the residence that is sold or exchanged. Thus, if a residence has more than one owner, a real estate reporting person must either obtain a certification from each owner (whether married or not) or file an information return and furnish a payee statement for any owner that does not make the certification.

PART I. Seller Information

1. Name: <u>Kevin L. Paine</u>

2. Address or legal description (including city, state and ZIP code) of residence being sold or exchanged:
<u>100 Goodfellow Drive, Pleasant Hill, CA 94523</u>

3. Taxpayer Identification Number (TIN) _____

3. PART II. Seller Assurances

Check "yes" or "no" for assurances (1) through (4):

YES   NO

☐   ☐   (1) I owned and used the residence as my principal residence for periods aggregating 2 years or more during the 5-year period ending on the date of the sale or exchange of the residence.

☐   ☐   (2) I have not sold or exchanged another principal residence during the 2-year period ending on the date of the sale or exchange of the residence (not taking into account any sale or exchange before May 7, 1997).

☐   ☐   (3) No portion of the residence has been used for business or rental purposes by me (or my spouse if I am married) after May 6, 1997.

☐   ☐   (4) At least one of the following three statement applies: The sale or exchange is of for $250,000 or less.

OR

I am married, the sale or exchange is the entire residence for $500,000.00 or less, an or exchange on the entire residence is $250,000.00 or less.

OR

I am married, the sale or exchange is of the entire residence for $500,000 or less, and (a) I intend to file a joint return for the year of the sale or exchange, (b) my spouse also used the residence as his or her principal residence for periods aggregating 2 years or more during the 5-year period ending on the date of the sale or exchange of the residence, and (c) my spouse also has not sold or exchanged another principal residence during the 2-year period ending on the date of the sale or exchange of the residence (not taking into account any sale or exchange before May 7,1997).

PART III. Seller Certification

Under penalties of perjury, I certify that all of the above referenced information is true as of the end of the day of the sale or exchange.

_____   _____
Kevin L. Paine   Date

TRANSFEROR'S (SELLER'S) AFFIDAVIT
Pursuant to the
FOREIGN INVESTMENT IN REAL PROPERTY TAX ACT (FIRPTA)
Amended by the DEFICIT REDUCTION ACT of 1984 (DRA)

ESCROW NO.: 999288888-BR715
PROPERTY ADDRESS: 100 Goodfellow Drive Pleasant Hill, CA 94523

I/We the undersigned transferor/seller of real property subject of the above escrow do hereby state and swear under penalty of perjury that:

    1. My/Our tax identification number is set forth below;
    2. l/We am/are not (a) foreign person(s) as defined in the Internal Revenue Code as set forth in FJRPTA as amended;
    3. We are not a United States Real Property Holding Corporation as defined in the Internal Revenue Code.

I/We acknowledge that this statement will be forwarded to the Transferee/Buyer of the real property involved in this transaction.

Signed and subscribed under penalty of perjury this <u>September 26. 20XX</u>.

_____	_____
Transferor/Seller	Tax Identification Number
_____	_____
Transferor/Seller	Tax Identification Number

EFFECTIVE JANUARY 1, 20XX
NOTIFICATION TO BUYER
ON DISPOSITION OF CALIFORNIA REAL PROPERTY (Seller)

In accordance with Section 18662 of the Revenue and Taxation Code, a buyer may be required to withhold an amount equal to 3 and 1/3 per cent of the sales price in the case of a disposition of California real property interest by either:

1. A seller who is an individual or when the disbursement instructions authorize the proceeds to be sent to a financial intermediary of the seller, OR
2. A corporate seller that has no permanent place of business in California.

The buyer may become subject to penalty for failure to withhold an amount equal to the greater of 10 percent of the amount required to be withheld or five hundred dollars ($500).

However, notwithstanding any other provision included in the California statutes referenced above, no buyer will be required to withhold any amount or be subject to penalty for failure to withhold if:

1. The sales price of the California real property conveyed does not exceed one hundred thousand dollars ($100,000), OR
2. The seller executes a written certificate, under penalty of perjury, certifying that the seller is a corporation with a permanent place of business in California, OR
3. The seller, who is an individual, executes a written certificate, under penalty of perjury, certifying:
   a. That the California real property being conveyed is the seller's principal residence (within the meaning of Section 121 of the Internal Revenue Code).
   b. That the California real property being conveyed is or will be exchanged for property of like kind (within the meaning of Section 1031 of the Internal Revenue Code), but only to the extent of the amount of gain not required to be recognized for California income tax purposes under Section 1031 of the Internal Revenue Code.
   c. That the California real property has been compulsorily or involuntarily converted (within the meaning of Section 1033 of the Internal Revenue Code) and that the seller intends to acquire property similar or related in service or use so as to be eligible under Section 1033 of the Internal Revenue Code.
   d. That the California real property transaction will result in a loss for California income tax purposes.

The seller is subject to penalty for knowingly filing a fraudulent certificate for the purpose of avoiding the withholding requirement.

The California statutes referenced above include provisions which authorize the Franchise Tax Board to grant a reduced withholding and waivers from withholding on a case-by-case basis for corporations or other entities.

THE PARTIES TO THIS TRANSACTION SHOULD SEEK THE PROFESSIONAL ADVICE AND COUNSEL OF AN ATTORNEY, ACCOUNTANT OR OTHER TAX SPECIALIST'S OPINION CONCERNING THE EFFECT OF THIS LAW ON THIS TRANSACTION AND SHOULD NOT ACT ON ANY STATEMENTS MADE OR OMITTED BY THE ESCROW OR CLOSING OFFICER.

Receipt acknowledged this ____ day of _____, 20____.

_____   _____
(Buyer)   (Buyer)

_____   _____
(Seller)   (Seller)

NOTIFICATION FROM BUYER ON
DISPOSITION OF CALIFORNIA REAL PROPERTY

Date: September 26, 20XX
Escrow No.: 99988888 BR 715
Property Address: 100 Goodfellow Drive, Pleasant Hill, CA

I/We, the undersigned Buyer(s) hereby acknowledge that I/we have received, read and understand the Notification to Buyer on Disposition of California Real Property. I/We instruct escrow holder to:

- ☐ Withhold an amount equal to 3 and 1/3 percent of the sales price from the Seller's proceeds, according to seller's signatures on form FTB 597
- ☐ No funds are required to be held according to Seller's signature on form FTB 593-C.

_____   _____

John Buyer   Julie Buyer

_____   _____

I/We, the undersigned Seller(s) have handed the escrow holder FTB forms 597 or 593-C and instruct escrow holder to follow Buyer(s) instructions as set forth above.

_____   _____

Kevin L. Paine

_____   _____

RIGHT CORP. TITLE COMPANY OF CALIFORNIA

September 26, 20XX

BANK OF UNITED STATES
4161 Piedmont Parkway
Loan #68240039751000
Greensboro, NC 27410

CREDIT LINE AUTHORIZATION

ATTN: PAYOFF DEPARTMENT

RE: Account/Loan No: 68240039751000
Property Address: 100 Goodfellow Drive Pleasant Hill, CA 94523
Escrow No: 00028843-MR915

Dear Sir or Madam: The undersigned hereby authorize you to close the above referenced credit line account upon receipt of this notice.

I/we agree to pay any charges pending that may not be reflected on the demand for payoff issued to Right Corp. Title Company of California and/we agree to cease activity on this account.

Upon receipt of payoff, please send the release of lien/full reconveyance to:

Right Corp. Title Company of California
Attn: Maryanne Richards
2950 Mandrake Ave., Suite 122
Walnut Creek, CA 94596

as per their instructions.

Sincerely,
SELLER:

_____

Kevin L. Paine

(All borrowers must sign letter)

NOTES

The "Credit Line Authorization" is the seller's authorization to pay off a bank credit line account and is similar in form and function to a "Payoff Statement" found in refinance and HELOC loan packages.

---

950 Mandrake Ave., Suite 122, Walnut Creek, CA 94596
Phone: (925) 287-4680 Fax: (925) 287-9105

RIGHT CORP. TITLE COMPANY OF CALIFORNIA

TO: Maryanne Richards
Right Corp. Title Company of California
2950 Mandrake Ave., Suite 122
Walnut Creek, CA 94596

DATE: September 26, 20XX
Escrow No.: 99988888-715 BR
Proper1y Address: 100 Goodfellow Drive,
Pleasant Hill, CA 94523

PAYOFF DISBURSEMENT INSTRUCTIONS

The undersigned Kevin L. Paine acknowledge and understand that disbursement of any payoffs for encumbrances being paid off at close of this escrow must be received by the lender by a specific date to avoid further accrual of interest either daily or monthly.

You are instructed to forward payoff funds to the lender by express service of your choice and charge my/our account any fees for overnight delivery at close of escrow.

In the event the lender demands additional funds after the close of escrow, John Buyer and Julie Buyer agree to deposit any additional funds necessary to comply with lender's instructions immediately upon notice of same.

Sellers

_____   _____
Kevin L. Paine   Date   Date

RIGHT CORP. TITLE COMPANY OF CALIFORNIA

2950 Mandrake Ave., Suite 122
Walnut Creek, CA 94596
Phone: (925) 287-4680 Fax: (925) 287-9105

PRELIMINARY REPORT

WHEN REPLYING PLEASE CONTACT: Order No.: **99988888-BR -715**
Maryanne Richards at **(925) 287-4680**

TO: Help U Sell - Heritage
       1300 Contra Costa Blvd., #22
       Pleasant Hill, CA 94523
       Attn: Joseph Tanos

Your No.:   SHORT TERM RATE: YES

PROPERTY ADDRESS: 100 Goodfellow Drive, Pleasant Hill, CALIFORNIA

EFFECTIVE DATE: July 11, 20XX at 07:30 A.M.

The form of Policy or Policies of Title Insurance contemplated by this report is:

All American CLTA/ALTA Homeowners

ALTA Loan Policy (10-17-XX) W/Form 1 Cov.

1. THE ESTATE OR INTEREST IN THE LAND HEREINAFTER DESCRIBED OR REFERRED TO COVERED BY THIS REPORT IS:

    A FEE

2. TITLE TO SAID ESTATE OR INTEREST AT THE DATE HEREOF IS VESTED IN:

    Kevin L. Paine, a married man, as his sole and separate property

3.. THE LAND REFERRED TO IN THIS REPORT IS SITUATED IN THE CITY OF Pleasant Hill, COUNTY OF Contra Costa STATE OF CALIFORNIA, AND IS DESCRIBED AS FOLLOWS:

    SEE EXHIBIT "A" ATTACHED HERETO AND MADE A PART HEREOF.

                                        mf/mgb/September 4, 20XX

The undersigned hereby declares that there no other liens or encumbrances of record against subject property to the best of his or her knowledge.

_____

Kevin L. Paine

EXHBIT "A"

Lot 248, as designated on the Map entitled, "Pleasant Valley View Homes, Unit No.3, Contra Costa County, California", which Map was filed in the office of the Recorder of the County of Contra Costa, State of California, on September 8, 20XX, in Volume 33 of Maps, at Page 44.

Assessor's Parcel No.: 149-283-010-2

99988888-BR -715 2

AT THE DATE HEREOF, ITEMS TO BE CONSIDERED AND EXCEPTIONS TO COVERAGE IN ADDITION TO THE PRINTED EXCEPDONS AND EXCLUSIONS IN SAID POLICY FORM WOULD BE AS FOLLOWS:

1. Property taxes, including any assessments collected with taxes to be levied for the fiscal year 20XX - 20XX, a lien not yet due and payable.

2. Special Taxes which are now a lien levied under the Mello-Roos Community Facilities Act.

Such special tax is collected with property taxes.

The amount of such tax collected with the taxes for the CURRENT fiscal year is $67.00

Failure to pay said taxes prior to the delinquency date may result in the above assessment being removed from the County Tax Roll and subjected to Accelerated Judicial Bond Foreclosure.

3. The lien of supplemental taxes, if any, assessed pursuant to the provisions of Chapter 3.5 (commencing with Section 75) of the Revenue and Taxation Code of the State of California.

4. Covenants, Conditions and Restrictions, (deleting therefrom any restrictions indicating any preference, limitation or discrimination based on race, color, religion, sex, handicap, familial status or national origin), as set forth in the document

Recorded: September 3, 20XX, Book 1282, Page 563, of Official Records

NOTE: Section 12956.1 of the Government Code provides the following:

If this document or amendments thereto contain any restriction based on race, color, religion, sex, familial status, marital status, disability, national origin, or ancestry, that restriction violates state and federal housing laws and is void. Any person holding an interest in this property may request that the county recorder remove the restrictive language pursuant to subdivision (c) of Section 12956.1 of the Government Code.

 Said Covenants, Conditions and Restrictions lien of any Mortgage or Deed of Trust made in good faith and for value.

5. A Deed of Trust to secure an indebtedness of the amount stated below and any other obligations secured thereby

Dated : December 14, 20XX
Amount : $265,000.00
Trustor/Borrower : Kevin L. Paine, a married man as his sole and separate property
Trustee : Placer Title Co.
Beneficiary/Lender : Mortgage Electronic Registration Systems, Inc. ("MERS")
Loan No. : 891528
Recorded : December 21, 20XX as Instrument No. 2000-0286724, of Official Records

5. That a violation thereof shall not defeat the provide 28843-MR -915 3,

6. A Deed of Trust to secure an indebtedness of the amount stated below any other obligations secured thereby

Dated : August 09, 20XX
Amount : $98.000.00
Trustor/Borrower : Kevin L. Paine. a married person
Trustee : Equitable Deed Company
Beneficiary/Lender : Bank of United States, N .A.

Loan No. : 02502503620126998
Recorded : August 22, 20XX as Instrument No. 2002-0293984, Official Records

To avoid delays at the time of closing, if the above deed of trust is an equity Line/Line of Credit, it will be necessary that all checks, passbook, credit cards together with instructions to close the account be submitted prior to the close of escrow.

In order to expedite compliance with the above, please do the following:

a)   Request that the account be frozen
b)   Obtain a statement from the lender that no advances have been made after the issuance of the demand for payoff
c)   Upon delivery of the payoff check obtain a full reconveyance
d)   In that said deed of trust, under a design line agreement, may secure more than one note, make inquiry when requesting the demand as to the existence of more than one note.

END OF ITEMS

Note 1.   None of the items shown in this report will cause the Company to decline to attach CLTA Endorsement Form 100 to an Extended Coverage Loan Policy, when issued.

Note 2:   The Company is not aware of any matters which would cause it to decline to attach the CLTA Endorsement Form 116, indicating that there is located on said land a Single Family Dwelling known as 100 Goodfellow Drive, Pleasant Hill, CA 94523.

Note 3.   Property taxes for the fiscal year shown below are PAID. For prorating purposes the amounts are:

APN:	149-283-010-2
Fiscal Year:	2002-2003
1st Installment:	$1,874.01, PAID
2nd Installment:	$1,874.01, PAID
Exemption:	$0.00
Land:	$214,200.00
Improvements:	$90,780.00
Personal Property:	$0.00
Code Area:	12-018
Bill No.:	135316

Note 4.   There are NO deeds affecting said land, recorded within twenty-four (24) months of the date of this report. below and any other obligations stated

Note 5.   The name(s) of the buyer(s) furnished with this John Buyer and Julie Buyer.
If these names are incorrect, incomplete or misspelled, please notify the Company.

Note 6.   Section 12413.1, California Insurance Code became effective January 1, 20XX. This legislation deals with the disbursement of funds deposited with any title entity acting in an escrow or subescrow capacity. The law requires that all funds be deposited and collected by the title entity's escrow and/or subescrow account prior to disbursement of any funds. Some methods of funding may subject funds to a holding period which must expire before any funds may be disbursed. In order to avoid any such delays, all funding should be done through wire transfer, certified check or checks drawn on California financial institutions.

Note 7.   The charge where an order is cancelled after the issuance of the report of title, will be that amount which in the opinion of the Company is proper compensation for the services rendered or the purpose for which the report is used, but in no event shall said charge be less than the minimum amount required under Section 12404.1 of the Insurance Code of the State of California. If the report cannot be cancelled "no fee" pursuant to the provisions of said Insurance Code, then the minimum cancellation fee shall be that permitted by law.

Note 8.   California Revenue and Taxation Code Section 18662, effective January 1, 20XX and by amendment effective January 1, 20XX, provides that the buyer in all sales of California Real Estate may be required to withhold 3 and

1/3% of the total sales price as California State Income Tax, subject to the various provisions of the law as therein contained.

Note 9. In accordance with Section 18662 of the Revenue and Taxation code, effective January 1, 20XX a buyer may be required to withhold an amount equal to 3-1/3% of the sales price in the case of a disposition of California real property interest by either:

1. A seller who is an individual or when the disbursement instructions authorize the proceeds to be sent to a financial intermediary of the seller, OR A corporate seller that has no permanent place of business in California.

The buyer may become subject to penalty for failure to withhold an amount equal to the greater of 10 percent of the amount required to be withheld or five hundred dollars ($500).

However, notwithstanding any other provision included in the California statutes referenced above, no buyer will be required to withhold any amount or be subject to penalty for failure to withhold if:

1. The sales price of the California real property conveyed does not exceed one hundred thousand dollars ($100,000), OR the seller executes a written certificate, under penalty of perjury, certifying that the seller is a corporation with a permanent place of Business in California, OR

2. The seller, who is an individual, executes a written certificate, under penalty of perjury, of any of the following:

a. That the California real property being conveyed is the seller's principal residence (within the meaning of Section 121 of the Internal Revenue Code).

b. That the California real property being conveyed is or will be exchanged for property of like kind (within the meaning of Section 1031 of the Internal Revenue Code), but only to the extent of the amount of gain not required to be recognized for California income tax purposes under Section 103] of the Internal Revenue Code.

c. That the California real property has been compulsorily or involuntarily converted (within the meaning of Section 1033 of the Internal Revenue Code) and that the seller intends to acquire property similar or related in service or use so to be eligible under Section 1033 of the Internal Revenue Code.

d. That the California real property transaction will result in a loss for California income tax purposes.

The seller is subject to penalty for knowingly filing a fraudulent certificate for the purposes of avoiding the withholding requirements. The California statutes referenced above include provisions which authorize the Franchise Tax Board to grant reduced withholding and waivers from withholding on a case-by-case basis for corporations or other entities.

THE PARTIES TO THIS TRANSACTION SHOULD SEEK THE PROFESSIONAL ADVICE AND COUNSEL OF AN ATTORNEY, ACCOUNTANT OR OTHER TAX SPECIALIST'S OPINION CONCERNING THE EFFECT OF THIS LAW ON THIS TRANSACTION AND SHOULD NOT ACT ON ANY STATEMENTS MADE OR OMITTED BY THE ESCROW OR CLOSING OFFICER.

Note 10. Please be advised that the county recorder's office will no longer accept highlighted original documents for recording. This company requests that any documents sent here to be executed and recorded not have any highlighted areas.

NOTICE

If YOU BOUGHT, SOLD OR REFINANCED A HOME (RESIDENTIAL REAL PROPERTY) IN CALIFORNIA BETWEEN JULY 1, 20XX AND FEBRUARY 28, 20XX, PLEASE READ THE FOLLOWING:

Pursuant to a Settlement Agreement in a class action lawsuit filed in the Superior Court for Los Angeles County, a settlement agreement has been entered into that provides persons who bought, sold or refinanced residential real property in the State of California between July 1, 20XX and February 28, 20XX, with certain rights. If you are such a person and you are now engaged in an escrow transaction with Chicago Title Company, Gateway Title Company, Benefit Land Title Company or Trust American Title Insurance Company, you have the following rights:

If one of these companies previously handled a residential escrow transaction for you that involved residential real property in which a mortgage, promissory note, or similar debt instrument, repayment of which was secured by a duly recorded deed of trust, was fully paid, satisfied or discharged and a reconveyance of that deed of trust was executed and was delivered to one of those title companies for recording but was inadvertently not recorded, you have the right to request that a release of obligation or reconveyance be recorded in accordance with the terms of the Settlement Agreement.

To obtain this right you must:

(1) Establish to the satisfaction of the title company that you actually closed an escrow between July 1, 20XX and February 27, 20XX, which was handled by one of the above listed title insurance companies, in which a mortgage, promissory note, or similar debt instrument secured by a duly recorded deed of trust was fully paid, satisfied or discharged and a reconveyance of that deed of trust was executed and was delivered for recordation to the title company that handled the prior transaction. Proof of said transaction shall be made by presenting a closing statement, preliminary title report, title insurance policy or a paid escrow invoice which identifies you and the prior deed of trust; and

(2) Request in writing the recording of a reconveyance or release or obligation in the event that one inadvertently had not been previously recorded in the escrow transaction previously handled by one of the above-named title companies.

If you believe that you are entitled to benefits as a class member, please send your written requests or any questions concerning the foregoing to Janet Dorack, Legal Department, Trust American Title Insurance Company, 17911 Van Landingham Avenue, Suite 300, Irvine, California 92614.

Right Corp. Title Company of California
Trust American Financial Group of Companies' Privacy Statement
July 1, 20XX

We recognize and respect the privacy expectations of today's consumers and the requirements of applicable federal and state privacy laws. We believe that making you aware of how we use your non-public personal information ("Personal Information"), and to whom it is disclosed, will form the basis for a relationship of trust between us and the public that we serve. This Privacy Statement provides that explanation. We reserve the right to change this Privacy Statement from time to time consistent with applicable privacy laws.

In the course of our business, we may collect Personal Information about you from the following sources:
- From applications or other forms we receive from you or your authorized representative;
- From your transactions with, or from the services being performed by, us, our affiliates, or others;
- From our internet web sites;
- From the public records maintained by governmental entities that we either obtain directly from those entities, or from our affiliates or others; and
- From consumer or other reporting agencies.

Our Policies Regarding the Protection of the Confidentiality and Security of Your Personal Information.
We maintain physical, electronic and procedural safeguards to protect your Personal Information from unauthorized access or intrusion. We limit access to the Personal Information only to those employees who need such access in connection with providing products or services to you or for other legitimate business purposes.

Our Policies and Practices Regarding the Sharing of Your Personal Information
We may share your Personal Information with our affiliates, such as insurance companies, agents, and other real estate settlement service providers. We also may disclose your Personal Information:
- to agents, brokers or representatives to provide you with services you have requested;
- to third-party contractors or service providers who provide services or perform marketing or other functions on our behalf; and
- to others with whom we enter into joint marketing agreements for products or services that we believe you may find of interest.

In addition, we will disclose your Personal Information when you direct or give us permission, when we are required by law to do so, or when we suspect fraudulent or criminal activities. We also may disclose your Personal Information when otherwise permitted by applicable privacy laws such as, for example, when disclosure is needed to enforce our rights arising out of any agreement, transaction or relationship with you.

One of the important responsibilities of some of our affiliated companies is to record documents in the public domain. Such documents may contain your Personal Information.

Right to Access Your Personal Information and Ability to Correct Errors or Request Changes or Deletion Certain states afford you the right to access your Personal Information and, under certain circumstances, to find out to whom your Personal Information has been disclosed. Also, certain states afford you the right to request correction, amendment or deletion of you Personal Information. We reserve the right, where permitted by law, to charge a reasonable fee to cover the costs incurred in responding to such requests.

All requests must be made in writing to the following address:
Privacy Compliance Officer
Trust American Financial, Inc.
4050 Avenida Real, Suite 220
Santa Barbara, CA 93110

Multiple Products or Services
If we provide you with more than one financial product or service, you may receive more than one privacy notice from us. We apologize for any inconvenience this may cause you.

EXHIBIT A
AMERICAN LAND TITLE ASSOCIATION
RESIDENTIAL TITLE INSURANCE POLICY (6-1-87) EXCLUSIONS

In addition to the Exceptions in Schedule 8, you are not insured against loss, costs attorneys' fees, and expenses resulting from:

1. Governmental police power, and the existence or violation of any law or governmental regulation. This includes building and zoning ordinances and also laws and regulations concerning:
   - land use
   - improvements on the land
   - land division
   - environmental protection

This exclusion does not apply to violations or the enforcement of these matters which appear in the public records at Policy Date.
This exclusion does not limit the zoning coverage described in Items 12 and 13 d Covered Title Risks.

2. The right to take the land by condemning it, unless:
   - a notice of exercising the right appears in the public records on the Policy Date
   - the taking happens prior to the Policy Date and is binding on you if you bought the land without knowing of the taking

3. Title Risks:
   - that are created, allowed, or agreed to by you
   - that are known to you, but not to us, on the Policy Date - unless they appear in the public records
   - that result in no loss to you
   - that first affect your title after the Policy Date - this does not limit the labor and material lien
   - coverage in item 8 of Covered Title Risks

4. Failure to pay value for your title.

Lack of a right:
   - to any land outside the area specifically described and referred to in Item 3 of Schedule A
     OR
   - in streets, alleys, or waterways that touch your land.

This exclusion does not limit the access coverage in Item 5 of Covered Title Risks.

SCHEDULE B
EXCEPTIONS

In addition to the Exclusions, you are not insured against loss, costs, attorneys' fees, and the expenses resulting from:
1. Any rights, interests, or claims of parties in possession of the land not shown by the public records.
2. Any easements or liens not shown by the public records. This does not limit the lien coverage in Item 8 of Covered Title Risks.
3. Any facts about the land which a correct survey would disclose and which are not shown by the public records. This does not limit the forced removal coverage in item 12 of Covered Title Risks.
4. Any water rights or claims or title to water in or under the land, whether or not shown by the public records.

CALIFORNIA LAND TITLE ASSOCIATION STANDARD COVERAGE POLICY -1990
EXCLUSIONS FROM COVERAGE

The following matters are expressly excluded from the coverage of this policy and the Company will not pay loss or damage, costs, attorneys' fees or expenses which arise by reason of:
1. (a) Any law, ordinance or governmental regulation (including but not limited to building or zoning laws, ordinances, or regulations) restricting, regulating, prohibiting or relating (i) the occupancy, use, or enjoyment of the land; (ii) the character, dimensions or location of any improvement now or hereafter erected on the land; (ii) a separation in ownership or a change in the dimensions or area of the land or any parcel of which the land is or was a part; or (iv) environmental protection, or the effect of any violation of these laws, ordinances or governmental regulations, except to the extent that a notice of the enforcement there of or a notice of a defect, lien, or encumbrance resulting from a violation or alleged violation affecting the land has been recorded in the public records at Date of Policy.
(b) Any governmental police power not excluded by (a) above, except to the extent that a notice of the exercise thereof or notice of a defect, lien or encumbrance resulting from a violation or alleged violation affecting the land has been recorded in the public records at Date of Policy.
2. Rights of eminent domain unless notice of the exercise thereof has been recorded in the pubic records at Date of Policy, but not excluding from coverage any taking which has occurred prior to Date of Policy which would be binding on the rights of a purchaser for value without knowledge.
3. Defects, liens, encumbrances, adverse claims or other matters:
(a) whether or not recorded in the public records at Date of Policy, but created, suffered, assumed or agreed to by the insured claimant;
(b) not known to the Company, not recorded in the public records at Date of Policy, but known to the insured claimant and not disclosed in writing to the Company by the insured claimant prior to the date the insured claimant became an insured under this policy;
(c) resulting in no loss or damage to the insured claimant;
(d) attaching or created subsequent to Date of Policy; or
(e) resulting in loss or damage which would not have been sustained if the insured had paid value for the insured mortgage or for the estate or interest insured by this policy.
4. Unenforceability of the lien of the insured mortgage because of the inability or failure of the insured at Date of Policy, or the inability or failure of any subsequent owner of the indebtedness, to comply with the applicable doing business laws of the state in which the land is situated.
5.Invalidity or unenforceability of the lien of the insured mortgage, or claim thereof which arises out of the transaction evidenced by the insured mortgage and is based upon usury or any consumer credit protection or truth in lending law.
6. Any claim which arises out of the transaction vesting in the insured the estate of interest insured by this policy or the transaction creating the interest of the insured lender, by reason of the operation of federal bankruptcy, state insolvency or similar creditors' rights laws.

SCHEDULE B, PART 1
EXCEPTIONS FROM COVERAGE

This policy does not insure against loss or damage (and the Company will not pay costs, attorneys' fees or expenses) which arise by reason of:

PART 1

1. Taxes or assessments which are not shown as existing liens by the records of any taxing authority that levies taxes or assessments on real property or by the public records. Proceedings by a public agency which may result in taxes or assessments, or notices of such proceedings, whether or not shown by the records of such agency or by the public records.

2. Any facts, rights, interests. or claims which are not shown by the public records but which could be ascertained by an inspection of the land which or which may be asserted by persons in thereof.

3. Easements, liens or encumbrances, or claims thereof, which are not shown by the public records.

4. Discrepancies, conflicts in boundary lines, shortage in area, encroachments, or any other facts which a correct survey would disclose, and which are not shown by the public records.

5. (a) Unpatented mining claims; (b) reservations or exceptions in patents or in Acts authorizing the issuance thereof; (c) water rights, claims or title to water, whether or not the matters excepted under (a), (b) or (c) are shown by the public records.

AMERICAN LAND TITLE ASSOCIATION LOAN POLICY (10-17-92)
WITH ALTA ENDORSEMENT-FORM 1 COVERAGE and
AMERICAN LAND TITLE ASSOCIATION LEASEHOLD LOAN POLICY (10-17-92)
WITH ALTA ENDORSEMENT-FORM 1 COVERAGE
EXCLUSIONS FROM COVERAGE

The following matters are expressly excluded from the coverage of this policy and the Company will not pay loss or damage, costs, attorneys' fees or expenses which arise by reason of:
1. (a) Any law, ordinance or governmental regulation (including but not limited to building and zoning laws, ordinances, or regulations)restricting, regulating, prohibiting or relating to (i) the occupancy, use, or enjoyment of the land; (ii) the character, dimensions or location of any improvement now or hereafter erected on the land; (iii) a separation in ownership or a change in the dimensions or area of the land or any parcel of which the land is or was part; or (iv) environmental protection, or the effect of any violation of these laws, ordinances or governmental regulations, except to the extent that a notice of the enforcement thereof or a notice of a defect, lien or encumbrance resulting from a violation or alleged violation affecting the land has been recorded in the public records at Date of Policy.
(b) Any governmental police power not excluded by (a) above, except to the extent that a notice of the exercise thereof or a notice of a defect, lien or encumbrance resulting from a violation or alleged violation affecting the land has been recorded in the public records at Date of Policy.
2. Rights of eminent domain unless notice of the exercise thereof has been recorded in the public records at Date of Policy, but not excluding from coverage any taking which has occurred prior to Date of Policy which would be binding on the rights of a purchaser for value without knowledge.
3. Defects, liens, encumbrances, adverse claims or other matters:
(a) created, suffered, assumed or agreed to by the insured claimant;
(b) not known to the Company, not recorded in the public records at Data of Policy, but known to the insured claimant and not disclosed in writing to the Company by the insured claimant prior to the date the insured claimant became an insured under this policy;
(c) resulting in no loss or damage to the insured claimant;
(d) attaching or created subsequent to Date of Policy (except to the extent that this policy insures the priority of the lien of the insured mortgage over any statutory lien for services, labor or material or to the extent insurance is afforded herein as to assessments for street improvements under construction or completed at Date of Policy); or
(e) resulting in loss or damage which would not have been sustained if the insured claimant had paid value for the insured mortgage.
4. Unenforceability of the lien of the insured mortgage because of the inability or failure of the insured at Date of Policy, or the inability or failure of any subsequent owner of the indebtedness to comply with applicable doing business laws of the state in which the land b situated.
5. Invalidity or unenforceability of the lien of the insured mortgage, or claim thereof, which arises out of the transaction evidenced by the insured mortgage and is based upon usury or any consumer credit protection or truth in lending law.
6. Any statutory lien for services, labor or materials (or the claim of priority of any statutory lien for services, labor or materials over the lien of the insured mortgage)arising from an improvement or work related to the land which is contracted for and commenced subsequent to Date of Policy and is not financed in whole or in part by proceeds of the indebtedness secured by the insured mortgage which at Date of Policy the insured has advanced or is obligated to advance.
7. Any claim, which arises out of the transaction creating the interest of the mortgagee insured by this policy, by reason of the operation of federal bankruptcy, state insolvency, or similar creditors' rights laws, that is based on:
(i) the transaction creating the interest of the insured mortgagee being deemed a fraudulent conveyance or fraudulent transfer; or
(ii) the subordination of the interest of the insured mortgagee as a result of the doctrine of equitable subordination; or
(iii) the transaction creating the interest of the insured mortgagee being deemed a preferential transfer except where the preferential transfer results from the failure: to timely record the instrument of transfer; or of such recordation to impart notice to a purchaser for value or a judgment or lien creditor.

AMERICAN LAND TITLE ASSOCIATION OWNER'S POLICY (10-17-92) AND
AMERICAN LAND TITLE ASSOCIATION LEASEHOLD OWNER'S POLICY (10-17-92)
EXCLUSIONS FROM COVERAGE

The following matters are expressly excluded from the coverage of this policy and the Company will not pay loss or damage, costs, attorneys' fees or expenses which arise by reason of:
1. (a) Any law, ordinance or governmental regulation (including but not limited to building and zoning laws, ordinances, or regulations)restricting, regulating, prohibiting or relating to (i) the occupancy, use, or enjoyment of the land; (ii) the character, dimensions or location of any improvement now or hereafter erected on the land; (iii) a separation in ownership or a change in the dimensions or area of the land or any parcel of which the land is or was part; or (iv) environmental protection, or the effect of any violation of these laws, ordinances or governmental regulations, except to the extent that a notice of the enforcement thereof or a notice of a defect, lien or encumbrance resulting from a violation or alleged violation affecting the land has been recorded in the public records at Date of Policy.
(b) Any governmental police power not excluded by (a) above, except to the extent that a notice of the exercise thereof or a notice of a defect, lien or encumbrance resulting from a violation or alleged violation affecting the land has been recorded in the public records at Date of Policy.
2. Rights of eminent domain unless notice of the exercise thereof has been recorded in the public records at Date of Policy, but not excluding from coverage any taking which has occurred prior to Date of Policy which would be binding on the rights of a purchaser for value without knowledge.
3. Defects, liens, encumbrances, adverse claims or other matters:
(a) created, suffered, assumed or agreed to by the insured claimant;
(b) not known to the Company, not recorded in the public records at Data of Policy, but known to the insured claimant and not disclosed in writing to the Company by the insured claimant prior to the date the insured claimant became an insured under this policy;
(c) resulting in no loss or damage to the insured claimant;
(d) attaching or created subsequent to Date of Policy; or
(e) resulting in loss or damage which would not have been sustained if the insured claimant had paid value for the estate or interest insured by this policy.
4. Any claim which arises out of the transaction vesting in the insured of the estate or interest insured by this policy, by reason of the operation of federal bankruptcy, state insolvency, or similar creditors' rights laws, that is based on:
(i) the transaction creating the estate or interest insured by this policy being deemed a fraudulent conveyance or fraudulent transfer; or
(iii) the transaction creating the estate or interest insured by this policy being deemed a preferential transfer except where the preferential transfer results from the failure:
(a) to timely record the instrument of transfer; or
(b) of such recordation to impart notice to a purchaser for value or a judgment or lien creditor.

The above ALTA policy forms may be issued to afford either Standard Coverage or Extended Coverage. In addition to the above Exclusions from Coverage, the Exceptions from Coverage in a Standard Coverage policy will also include the following General Exceptions:

EXCEPTIONS FROM COVERAGE

This policy does not insure against loss or damage (and the Company will not pay costs, attorneys' fees or expenses) which arise by reason of:

1. Taxes or assessments which are not shown as existing liens by the records of any taxing authority that levies taxes or assessments on real property or by the public records. Proceedings by a public agency which may result in taxes or assessments, or notices of such proceedings, whether or not shown by the records of such agency or by the public records.
2. Any facts, rights, interest or claims which are not shown by the public records but which could be ascertained by an inspection of the land or which may be asserted by persons in possession thereof.

3. Easements, liens or encumbrances or claims thereof, which are not shown by the public records.
4. Discrepancies, conflicts in boundary lines, shortage in area, encroachments, or any other facts which a correct survey would disclose, and which are not shown by the public records.
5. (a) Unpatented mining claims; (b) reservations or exceptions in patents or in Acts authorizing the issuance thereof; (c) water rights, claims or title to water, whether or not the matters excepted under (a), (b), or (c) are shown by the public records.

CLTA HOMEOWNER'S POLICY OF TITLE INSURANCE (06-2-98)
ALTA HOMEOWNER'S POLICY OF TITLE INSURANCE (10-17-98)
EXCLUSIONS

In addition to the Exceptions in Schedule B, You are not insured against loss, costs, attorneys' fees, and expenses resulting from:

1. Governmental police power, and the existence or violation of any law or government regulation. This includes ordinances, laws and regulations concerning:
a. building
b. zoning.
c. Land us
d. improvements on Land
e. Land division
f. environmental protection
This exclusion does not apply to violations or the enforcement of these matters if notice of the violation or enforcement appears in the Public Records at the Policy Date.
This Exclusion does not limit the coverage described in Covered Risk 14, 15, 16, 17 or 24.
2. The failure of Your existing structures, or any part of them, to be constructed in accordance with applicable building codes. This Exclusion does not apply to violations of building codes if notice of the violation appears in the Public Records at the Policy Date.
3. The right to take the Land by condemning it, unless:
a. notice of exercising the right appears in the Public Records at the Policy Date; or

b. the taking happened before the Policy Date and is binding on Your if You bought the Land without Knowing of the taking.
4. Risks
a. that are created, allowed, or agreed to by You, whether or not they appear in the Public Records.
b. that are Known to You at the Policy Date, not to Us, unless unless they appear in the Public Records at the Policy Date;
c. that result in no loss to You, or
d. that first occur after the Policy Date-this does not limit the coverage described in Covered Risk 7, 8.d, 22, 23, 24 or 25.
e. Failure to pay value for Your Title.
6. Lack of a right:
a. to any Land outside the area specifically described and referred to in paragraph 3 of Schedule A; and
b. in streets, alleys, or waterways that touch the Land.
This Exclusion does not limit the coverage described in Covered Risk 11 or 18.

RESIDENTIAL TITLE INSURANCE POLICY
ONE-TO-FOUR FAMILY RESIDENCE
ENHANCED VERSION (1997)
EXCLUSIONS

In addition to the Exceptions in Schedule B, You are not insured against loss, costs, attorneys' fees, and expenses resulting from:

1. Governmental police power, and the existence or violation of any law or government regulation. This includes building and zoning ordinances and also laws and regulations concerning:
a. Land us
b. improvements on Land
c. Land division
d. environmental protection
This exclusion does not apply to violations or the enforcement of these matters if notice of the violation or enforcement appears in the Public Records at the Policy Date.
This Exclusion does not limit the coverage described in Item 12c and d, 13 and 18 of Covered Risks.
2. The right to take the Land by condemning it, unless:
a. notice of exercising the right appears in the Public Records at the Policy Date; or
b. the taking happened prior to the Policy Date and is binding on you if you bought the Land without knowing of the taking.
3. Title Risks:
a. that are created, allowed, or agreed to by you;
b. that are known to you, but not to us, on the Policy Date-unless they appear in the public records;
c. that result in no loss to You, or
d. that first occur after the Policy Date-this does not limit the coverage described in Items 3b, 8, 17 and 19 of the Covered Title Risks.
4. Failure to pay value for Your Title.
5. Lack of a right: (a) to any land outside the area specifically described and referred to in item 3 of Schedule A or (b) in streets, alleys, or waterways that touch the Land.
This Exclusion does not limit the coverage described in items 5 and 12a of the Covered Title Risks.

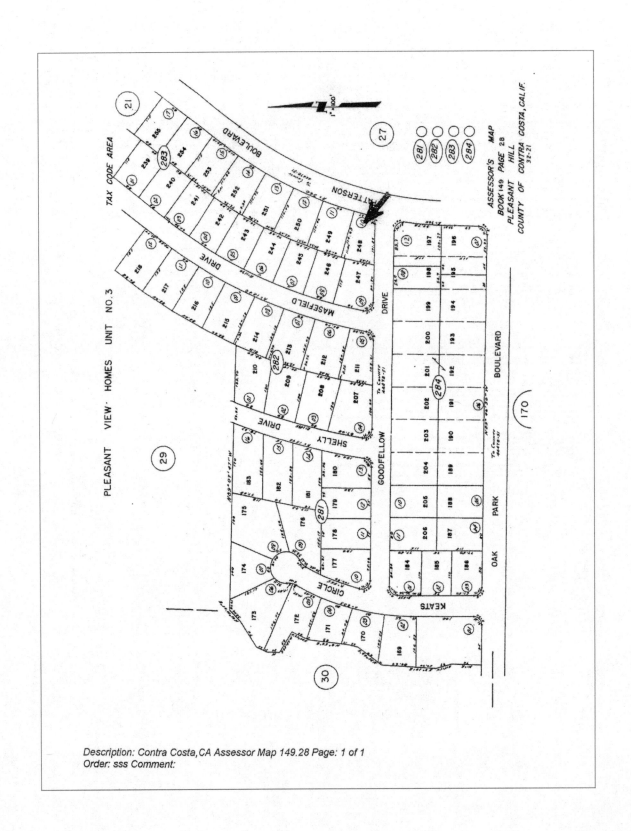

Description: Contra Costa, CA Assessor Map 149.28 Page: 1 of 1
Order: sss Comment:

Consumer Credit Services

SEPTEMBER 10, 20XX

RIGHT CORP. TITLE COMPANY
2950 MANDRAKE AVE. STE. 122
WALNUT CREEK, CA 94596

Escrow: 99988888-BR 715
Loan #:   86234009798100
Name: KEVIN L. PAINE
Property Address: 100 GOODFELLOW DR. PLEASANT HILL, CA 94523

Dear: MARY ANNE RICHARDS

Upon receipt of your request for payoff figures, we have frozen the customer's account to new activity. However, please note that all figures listed below are subject to change as this is a revolving line of credit and additional payments or advances may be applied to the account after this date. If adjustments must be made to the payoff balance due, we will attempt to advise you. Upon payment in full to us of the amount shown below as Total Amount Payable, plus any necessary additional interest, the above referenced account will be closed. The information contained in this document is current as of the close of business for the last business day preceding the date of this letter.

RELEASE OF APPLI CABLE COLLATERAL DOCUMENI'S, IF ANY, WILL NOT BE MADE UNTIL THE ACCOUNT IS PAID IN FULL.

Funds Required:

1. Principal & Interest	$97,837.66
2. Early Closure Fee **	400.00
3. Payoff Statement Fee & Reconveyance Fee	75.00
4. Other Contractual Fees	0.00
Amount Due to Payoff Loan and Subsequent RELEASE	**$98,312.66**
5. Misc. Fees	0.00
Total Amount Payable	**$98,312.66**
Disputed Transactions	$0.00
Electronic Transactions Authorized But Not Yet Received	$0.00
Daily Interest Per Diem * $ 12.19	

To avoid any processing delays please contact the number below for an updated payoff statement prior to forwarding funds. Bank of America reserves the right to adjust all these figures prior to closing and refuse any funds which are insufficient to ... any reason, including but not limited to error in calculation of payoff amount, previously dishonored check or mo... interest accruals, subsequent advances, intra day advances, payments, insurance, or fees on the account. Bank of Uni... loan production offices cannot accept payoff resulting from demands. Interest will continuo: to accrue until the payo... address below. Overnight/express mail delivery or Fed Wire Transfer is suggested for prompt receipt of funds.

Once the account has been paid in full, Release of Collateral Documents will be forwarded directly to the appro... recording.

* For each day after SEPTEMBER 10, 20XX to the date that payment reaches us, during regular banking hours, add the daily per diem listed above.

** If the account is being closed due to the !ale of property securing the account after it has been opened for one year the Early Closure Fee will be waived. A copy of the closing statement reflecting old/new owners will be required to support the waiver. If the escrow is canceled, the customer's account will not be reopened to new loan activity until we receive written notification of the cancellation from your office.

THIS DEMAND WILL EXPIRE ON NOVEMBER 09, 20XX AND A NEW DEMAND WILL BE REOUIRED.
PLEASE RETURN A COPY OF THIS DOCUMENT WITH YOUR REMITTANCE.

Read, approved & copy received

NOTES

Seller must sign in the stamped line to authorize payoff of the existing credit line.

```
                    New National Home Protection
                 P O Box 5017, San Ramon, CA 94583-0917
                 Phone (800)445-6999 Fax (877)445-6999

                          PREMIUM INVOICE
                             REVISED

     Date:       09/09/20XX
     Invoice to: MARION
                 T CORP. TITLE 2950 MANDRAKE AVE STE 122
                 UT CREEK, CA 94598-7779
                 88)

                 ional Home Warranty was ordered on Sep 9, 2003

                 R: 10-365-941
                 r: BUYER (Buyer)
          Covered property: 100 GOODFELLOW DR, PLEASANT HILL, CA 94523-4134

          PLEASE REMIT PREMIUM IN FULL AT CLOSE OF SALE AND INCLUDE OUR PLAN NUMBER
                    ON THE CHECK FOR PROPER PROCESSING.
```

NOTES

Seller must sign in the "stamped line" to authorize payment of home warranty premium.

Description				Premium
CA FSRE SFD 0031PA Premier Advantage	1	@	330.00	330.00
***Premier Coverage	1	@	0.00	0.00
***Air Conditioner	1	@	0.00	0.00
Additional air conditioner	____	@	55.00	_____
Pool/Spa Equipment	____	@	125.00	_____
Additional Pool/Spa Equipment	____	@	75.00	_____
Solar Pool/Spa Equipment	____	@	250.00	_____
Solar Hot Water System	____	@	250.00	_____
Well pump	____	@	100.00	_____
Well Pump Access	____	@	100.00	_____
Booster/Jet Pump	____	@	150.00	_____
Washer/Dryer	____	@	75.00	_____
Kitchen Refrigerator	____	@	25.00	_____
Wet bar refrigerator	____	@	25.00	_____
Kitchen Refrigerator (SubZero)	____	@	50.00	_____
Septic Tank Pumping	____	@	25.00	_____
Septic System	____	@	50.00	_____
Limited Roof Leak Repair	____	@	100.00	_____
Guest Home Under 1000 sq ft	____	@	145.00	_____
Vintage - FTCF - Fax Only	____	@	150.00	_____

```
                                        Premium        $ 330.00
                                Additional Options     _____
                                 Adjusted Premium       _____
                                                       _____

     If you add any additional options, please return a copy of this invoice with your
     payment. An original plan will be sent to the buyer upon receipt of the premium.

     Questions? Call (800) 445-6000 5 AM -- 5 PM (PST/PDT)
```

Read, approved & copy received

```
Payoff Statement                        Bank of United States
September 09, 20XX                      Attn: Payoff Dept. 173
                                        4161 Piedmont Parkway
                                        Greensboro, NC 27410
                                        NC4-10S-01-40
                                        1.800.285.6000

                                        Loan Number: 10076551000
                                        Loan Type Conventional Inv 026

Ph# 9252874680
(925)287-9105
                        ** You must verify the property address **
                             ** information prior to payoff **
Property Information:
Mortgagor: Kevin L. Paine
Property Address: 100 Goodfellow Drive Pleasant Hill, CA 94523

Calculation of amount required to satisfy loan and related fees:

Payoff figures void after 10-06-XX
This loan is due for the 08-01-XX payment.

Current Total Unpaid Principal Balance                  $       258,683.31
Accrued Interest to 10-06-XX                                      5,366.74
Pro Rata Mortgage Insurance Premium                                344.49
Recording Fee                                                       16.00
Amount Due to Payoff Loan by 10-06-XX and subsequent release:  $   264,410.53
NSF Fees                                                             24.98
Payoff Statement Fee(s)                                             30.00
Misc. Fees (i.e. Inspection and/or prior FAX Fees)                 20.00
* * TOTAL AMOUNT PAYABLE * *                            $       264,485.51
```

This calculation is void after 10-06-XX. A new payoff statement should be requested after this date. Interest is $55.07 per Day. Interest is $.00 per for the second mortgage. Funds received after the first date of the month will require an additional $114.83 for Mortgage Insurance which is paid in arrears.

If the current months payment has not been paid and the payoff is received aft[...] charge assessment date, a late charge of $ 96.07 will be assessed and must be [...] payoff amount.

These figures are subject to final verification upon receipt of funds. Bank of U[...] reserves the right to adjust these figures and refuse any funds which are insuff[...] loan in full for any reason, including but not limited to error in calculation o[...] amount, previously dishonored checks or money orders or additional reimbursement[...] date of this payoff statement and the receipt of funds.

To receive same day credit and avoid additional interest, payoff funds must be remitted in US Dollars by cashiers check, certified check, title company check or wire transfer. Funds must be received by 4:00 p.m. Eastern Standard Time. Payments will not be applied or credited on Saturdays, Sundays or holidays.

DELIVERY OF FUNDS: Bank of United States branches and loan production offices cannot accept or process mortgage loan payoffs. Interest will continue to accrue until the payoff funds are received at the address below. Overnight/Express mail or wire transfer is suggested for prompt receipt of funds.

SEE PAGE TWO FOR DELIVERY INSTRUCTIONS

Read, approved & copy received

NOTES

Seller must sign in the "stamped line" to authorize payoff of existing mortgage.

Remit funds to: Bank of United States, Attn: Payoff Dept 173, NC4-105-01-40 4161 Piedmont Parkway, Greensboro, NC 27410.

When remitting funds please include the mortgagor's name and loan number as well as remitter name and phone number. Please write the loan number on the check.

Wire Instructions: Bank of United States
                          Bank of United States NA
                          ABA or Routing Number   051000000
                          Wire Account Number   004131000000
                          Reference:
                          Mortgagor   Kevin L. Paine
                          Loan Number   1007651000
                          Remitter
                          Remitter Phone Number

A $10.00 Wire Fee must be included with the incoming wire. The wire must reference the above information. Incomplete information may cause the wired funds to be returned, lost or not applied timely to the loan.

SHORT PAYOFF FUNDS: If the remittance is insufficient, we will withdraw funds from the mortgagor's escrow account to complete the payoff. If there is no such account or the funds are insufficient we will return the funds with an updated payoff statement. Interest will continue to accrue until sufficient funds are received in our office.

To avoid a short payoff, please request an amended statement by contacting Customer Service at 1.800.285.6000 prior to remitting payoff funds.

AUTOMATIC DRAFT/PAYMENT BY CHECK: If a monthly payment was already sent or drafted electronically, do not place a stop payment on the check or automatic daft. For cancellation of automatic payment transfer service written notification must be received by this office at least seven (7) calendar days prior to the next draft date.

FORWARDING ADDRESS: It is important that the mortgagor(s) provide a forwarding address prior to or with the payoff funds. Failure to do so may result in a delay of the escrow or overage retund check (if applicable). Escrow refund checks or overage checks are normally ~end within two (2) weeks after the payoff.

MAILING ADDRESS: _____

*** PLEASE RETURN THIS PAGE WITH THE PAYOFF CHECK ***

CANCELLATION OF MORTGAGE: Bank of United States will forward satisfaction document directly to the county/trustee to be recorded and thereby release the lien on the property. The county/trustee will be instructed to return the recorded document to the mortgagor of record. If available, please, the title policy showing the recording information relating to our lien with your remittance.

ESCROW ACCOUNT: Issuance of this statement does not suspend the responsibility of Bank of United States to pay taxes and insurance. If a bill for these items is received prior to receipt of the payoff funds, we will pay it from the escrow account. If an escrow refund is due, it will be mailed to the mortgagor(s) of record. Bank of United States is not responsible for agreements between the mortgagor(s) and a third party with regard to the disposition of escrow funds.

CURRENT TAX AND INSURANCE INFORMATION

DUE DATE	AMOUNT	PAYABLE TO
03-XX	$ 1,874.01	Contra Costa County
11-XX	$ 1,874.01	Contra Costa County
08-XX	$ 114.83	Triano Guaranty Ins Corp
12-18-XX	$ 687.96	Bankers Insurance Group

CGS REPORTS
INVOICE

Property Address
100 Goodfellow Dr.
Pleasant Hill, CA 94523-4134
APN 149-283-010-2

BILL TO

Mary
Right Corp. Title
2950 Mandrake Ave #122
Walnut Creek, CA 94597-7773

Invoice #   1127706

Invoice Date   9/9/XX

ESCROW NUMBER	TERMS	ORDERED BY	FROM	PHONE
88888	Bill Escrow	Kim	Hong Realty	925.687.4664

DESCRIPTION	UNIT PRICE	DISCOUNT	EXTENDED
CGS Disclosure Report	$49.95		$49.95

Read, approved & copy received

TO ENSURE PROPER PROCESSING OF YOUR PAYMENT, PLEASE

1) Write the CGS Invoice Number on your check, and

2) Include the Tear-Off Remittance Stub with a your payment

Please return the portion below with your payment.

> **NOTES**
>
> Seller must sign in the "stamped line" to approve and authorize payment of the invoice.

REMITTANCE STUB

9/9/20XX	
Received From: RIGHT CORP. TITLE	149-283-010-2 100 GOODFELLOW DR. PLEASANT HILL, CA 94523-4134
Escrow Number: 88888	Invoice **1127706**
Make check payable to: **CGS REPORTS** P.O. Box 92431 Los Angeles, CA 90009-2431	**AMOUNT DUE** **$49.95**

RESIDENTIAL DISCLOSURE REPORT
FOR CONTRA COSTA COUNTY

Property: 100 Goodfellow Dr, Pleasant Hill, CA
APN: 94523-4134 149-283-010-2   **Transferor:** Paine Kevin L.

THIS PROPERTY IS REPORTED AS:

Natural Hazards Disclosure

Not Situated	in a special FLOOD HAZARD AREA (Any type Zone "A" or "V") designated by the Federal Emergency Management Agency;
Not Situated	in a DAM OR RESERVOIR INUNDATION AREA designated by the State Office of Emergency Services.
Not Situated	in a State of California VERY HIGH FIRE HAZARD SEVERITY ZONE; The owner of a property within a Very High Severity Zone is subject to the maintenance requirements of Section § 51182 of the Government Code;
Not Situated	in a State of California FIRE RESPONISBILITY AREA. The owner of a property in a State Fire Responsibility Area is subject to the maintenance requirements of Section § 4291 of the Public Resources Code;
Not Situated	in a State of California Alquist-Priolo EARTHQUAKE FAULT ZONE;
Not Mapped	by the State of California Division of Mines and Geology SEISMIC HAZARD MAPPING ACT program;
Not Mapped	in an Earthquake-Induced LANDSLIDE HAZARD ZONE on official maps of the Seismic Hazard Mapping Act;
Not Mapped	in a soil LIQUEFACTION HAZARD ZONE on official maps of the Seismic Hazard Mapping Act;

Prepared under the supervision of

Military Ordnance Disclosure

Not Situated	within one mile of a former federal or state ordnance location.

Commercial/Industrial Disclosure

Situated	within one mile of a zone or district allowing manufacturing, commercial or airport use. See Comm. Addendum on page 7.

Airport Proximity Disclosure

Situated	within five miles of a non-private airport. See Airport Proximity Addendum on page 8.

Database Disclosure (Megan's Law)

Notice	See Data Base Disclosure Addendum on page 9.

Mold Disclosure

Notice	See Mold Addendum on page 10.

Mello-Roos Disclosure

Situated	in a MELLO-ROOS COMMUNITY FACILITIES DISTRICT that is currently being assessed as reported by available records from the County Auditor-Controller as of the date of tax year of this report. Sellers of property in Mello-Roos Districts must provide a NOTICE OF SPECIAL TAXES to buyer. See Mello-Roos Addendum on page 12.

Special Assessment (1915 Bond) Addendum

Not Situated	in a SPECIAL ASSESSMENT DISTRICT (1915 Bond) that is currently being assessed as reported by available records from the County Auditor-Controller, as of the date of tax year of this report. Sellers of property in Special Assessment Districts must provide a NOTICE OF SPECIAL ASSESSMENTS to buyer.

NATURAL HAZARD DISCLOSURE STATEMENT

Property: 100 Goodfellow Dr, Pleasant Hill, CA 94523-4134   APN: 149-283-010-2   Transferor: Paine Kevin L.

The transferor and his or her agent(s) disclose the following information with the knowledge that even though this is not a warranty, prospective transferees may rely on this information in deciding whether and on what terms to purchase the subject property. Transferor hereby authorizes any agent(s) representing any principal(s) in this action to provide a copy of this statement to any person or entity in connection with any actual or anticipated sale of the property. The following are representations made by the transferor and his or her agent(s) based on their knowledge and maps drawn by the state and federal governments.

This information is a disclosure and is not intended to be part of any contract between the transferee and the transferor.

THIS REAL PROPERTY LIES WITHIN THE FOLLOWING HAZARDOUS AREA(S): (Check the answer that applies.)

A SPECIAL FLOOD HAZARD (Any type Zone "A" or V) designated by the Federal Emergency Management Agency.

Yes _____ No _____ (a) Do not know (b) Information not available from local jurisdiction

Only Check if BOTH (a) and (b) apply.

A SPECIAL FLOOD HAZARD (Any type zone "A" or "V") designated by the Federal Emergency Management Agency.

Yes _____ No _____ (a) Do not know (b) Information not available from local jurisdiction

Only Check if BOTH (a) and (b) apply.

AN AREA OF POTENTIAL FLOODING shown on a dam failure inundation map pursuant to Section 8589.5 of the Government Code.

Yes _____ No _____ (a) Do not know (b) Information not available from local jurisdiction

Only Check if BOTH (a) and (b) apply.

A VERY HIGH FIRE HAZARD SEVERITY ZONE pursuant to Section 51178 or 51179 of the Government Code. The owner of this property is subject to the maintenance requirements to Section 51182 of the Government Code.

Yes _____ No _____

A WILDLAND AREA THAT MAY CONTAIN SUBSTANTIAL FOREST FIRE RISKS AND HAZARDS pursuant to Section 4125 of the Public Resources Code. The owner of this property is subject to the maintenance requirements of Section 4291 of the Public Resources Code. Additionally, it is not the state's responsibility to provide fire protection servif2s to any building or structure located within the wildlands unless the Department of Forestry and Fire Protection has entered into a cooperative agreement with a local agency for those pursuant to Section 4142 of the Public Resources Code.

Yes _____   No _____

AN EARTHQUAKE FAULT ZONE pursuant to Section 2622 of the Public Resources Code.

Yes _____   No _____

A SEISMIC HAZARD ZONE pursuant to Section 2696 of the Public Resources Code.

Yes _____ (Landslide Zone) No _____

Yes (Liquefaction Zone)   No _____

THESE HAZARDS MAY LIMIT YOUR ABILITY TO DEVELOP THE REAL PROPERTY. TO OBTAIN INSURANCE, OR TO RECEIVE ASSISTANCE AFTER A DISASTER.

THE MAPS ON WHICH THESE DISCLOSURES ARE BASED ESTIMATE WHERE NATURAL HAZARDS EXIST. THEY ARE NOT DEFINITIVE INDICATORS OF WHETHER OR NOT A PROPERTY WILL BE AFFECTED BY A NATURAL DISASTER. TRΛNFEREE(S) AND TRANFEROR(S) MAY WISH TO OBTAIN PROFESSIONAL ADVICE REGARDING THOSE HAZARDS AND OTHER HAZARDS THAT MAY AFFECT THE PROPERTY.

The representations made in this NHD form and report are based upon information provided by an independent third party report provided as a substituted disclosure pursuant to California Civil Code § 1103.4. Neither the seller nor the seller's agent has (1) independently verified the information contained in this form and report or (2) is personally aware of any errors or inaccuracies in the information contained on the form.

Transferor represents that the information herein is true and correct to the best of the transferor's knowledge as of the date signed by the transferor.

Signature of Transferor _____ Date _____

Agent represents that the information herein is true and correct to the best of the agent's knowledge as of the date signed by the agent.

Signature of Agent _____ Date _____

Signature of Agent _____ Date _____

Transferee represents that he or she has read and understands this document

Signature of Transferor _____ Date _____

This form meets the standards of Civil Code §1103 transaction.

Natural Hazards Disclosure

This report is in conformance with California Civil Code § 1103 et seq. The maps and data cited herein were reviewed using the property address listed above (Property) in order to generate this report. The Certified Engineering Geologist who supervised the production of this report has provided his signature and State License number below to conform with Civil Code § 1103.4(c). There may exist other publicly available data regarding the Property, but this information is not included in this report. No visual or physical inspection of the Property has been conducted. Therefore, Reports, Inc. recommends a Certified Engineering Geologist or Professional Engineer be retained if specific information is desired, many cities and counties maintain additional geotechnical and other reports regarding specific properties located within their boundaries that should be reviewed if desired. The information contained in this report may be changed or altered by the aforementioned sources of site-specific information. Properties which contain significant natural or graded slopes have inherent risks not associated with flat sites. The evaluation of these slopes is beyond the scope of this report. Reports, Inc. recommends retaining a Certified Engineering Geologist to address any concerns regarding on-site slopes. This report was prepared in accordance with, and therefore is subject to, all of the conditions and limitations stated herein. A discussion of each category of disclosure is included later in this report.

EXPLANATION

SPECIAL FLOOD HAZARD AREAS

The Federal Emergency Management Agency (FEMA) has prepared Flood Insurance Rate Maps, which delineate flood zones based on estimated flood risk. The zones pertinent to the Natural Hazard Disclosure are Zones A and V (Special Flood Hazard Areas). Zone V is for coastal areas and Zone A is for inland areas. These zones are located within a 100-year flood plain. A 100-year flood has a one-percent chance of occurrence in any given year. Flood insurance is required by federally regulated lending institutions for properties located within Zones A or V. Local flood control projects to mitigate flood hazard potential can change the flood risk of a specific are or property. The flood risk of a specific area or property may be updated through a Letter of Map Change filed with FEMA. Specific updated flood risk information, not included on the Flood Insurance Rate Maps. Is not provide in our report. If a property is located within A Special Flood Hazard Area, Reports, Inc. recommends contacting FEMA for the update risk assessment of the property and the current flood insurance requirements. It should be noted that properties within a Special Flood Hazard Zone may never experience flooding, and conversely, properties not located within a Special Flood Hazard Zone may experience flooding. This disclosure is not meant to predict flooding, but rather to identify properties for which flood insurance may be required by federally regulated lending institutions.

AREAS OF POTENTIAL FLOODING FROM DAM FAILURES

The California Office of Emergency Services (CA OES) has provided Inundation Maps, which delineate areas subject to flooding from a sudden, catastrophic failure of a dam with a full reservoir. Maps are not available for all dams in the state. Additional maps may become available subsequent to approval by the OES. Inundation from reservoir, dam, or dike failure can pose serious risks to large segments of the population. Cities and counties within the mapped areas are required to adopt emergency procedures for the evacuation of populated areas.

VERY HIGH FIRE HAZARD SEVERITY ZONES

The California Department of Forestry and Fire Protection (CDF) under the Bates Bill (AB 337) established Very High Fire Hazard Severity Zones (VHFHSZ) in the Local Responsibility Areas (LRA) of California. The maps prepared by the CDF show zones based on State criteria. Local agencies, by law, are allowed to make changes to the zones. Fire defense improvements are mandated for properties located within the zones under Section 51182 of the Government Code. Mandated improvements include a Class A roof for new development or replacement of an existing roof and brush clearing within 30 feet of a structure. For a complete listing of the mandated fire defense improvements and local zone changes, contact the local fire department.

The Very High Fire Hazard Severity Zone Maps were prepared at a scale that does not always allow a conclusive determination to be made at zone boundaries. If a conclusive determination cannot be made, the property will be reported on the Natural Hazard Disclosure Statement as situated in the zone as mandated by Section § 1102.6C of the California Civil Code. Reports, Inc. will report the property as in a boundary condition on our Residential Disclosure Report. Therefore, the local fire department should be contacted to determine if the property is located within the zone.

STATE FIRE RESPONSIBILITY AREA

The California Depar1ment of Forestry and Fire Protection has established State Responsibility Areas (SRA) for which the primary financial responsibility for prevention and suppression of fires is that of the State. However, the State is not responsible for protecting structures within these areas. The proper1y owner is subject to cer1ain maintenance requirements and may be responsible for fire protection of structures under Section 4291 of the Public Resources Code. If the proper1y is located within a State Responsibility Area, CGS Repor1s, Inc. recommends contacting the county fire depar1ment to obtain a full listing of proper1y owner maintenance and fire protection requirements. Public Resources Code Section 4326 reads, "A seller of real property which is located within a state responsibility area determined by the board, pursuant to Section 4125, shall disclose to any prospective purchase the fact that the proper1y is located within a wildland area which may contain substantial forest fire risks and hazards and is subject to the requirements of Section 4291"

The State Responsibility Area Maps were prepared at a scale that does not always allow a conclusive determination to be made at zone boundaries. If a conclusive determination cannot be made, the proper1y will be repor1ed on the Natural Hazard Disclosure Statement as situated in the zone as mandated by Section 11 02.6C of the California Civil Code. CGS Repor1s, Inc. will report the proper1y as in a boundary condition on our Residential Disclosure Repor1. The county fire depar1ment should be contacted to determine if the proper1y is located within the zone.

ALQUIST-PRIOLO EARTHQUAKE FAULT ZONES

The State Geologist under the Alquist-Priolo Ear1hquake Fault Zoning Act has established regulatory zones around the mapped surface traces of active faults. These zones, typically one-quar1er mile or less in width, have been delineated on maps around "sufficiently active and well-defined" faults and fault segments that "constitute a potential hazard to structures from surface faulting or fault creep." Faults that demonstrate movement during the past 11,000 years are considered active. The purpose of the Act under Section 2621-2630 of the Public Resources Code is to assist cities and counties in land use planning and developing permit requirements. The State Mining and Geology Board provides additional regulations to guide cities and counties in their implementation of the law under California Code of Regulations, Title 14, Division 2. Local agencies must regulate most types of development projects located within the zones. The results of our search only indicate whether a proper1y is situated or not situated within an Ear1hquake Fault Zone, as shown on the Alquist-Priolo Ear1hquake Fault Zone Maps. Our search does not indicate whether or not a surface trace of an active fault is located on the proper1y. If this repor1 indicates the subject proper1y is located within an Earthquake Fault Zone, Reports, Inc. recommends consulting a Cer1ified Engineering Geologist to assess the site-specific potential for surface fault rupture. It should be noted that the State Ear1hquake Fault Zoning Program is ongoing and proper1ies currently not situated in a zone may be located in a zone established in the future.

SEISMIC HAZARD ZONES

The California Division of Mines and Geology under the Seismic Hazards Mapping Act has prepared maps delineating zones of potential seismic hazards. The legislation for this Act may be found in the California Public Resources Code" Division 2, Chapter 7.8, Sections 2690- 2699.6 and Chapter 8, Ar1icle 10, Sections 3720-3725. The purpose of the Act is to provide cities and counties with zones where site-specific geotechnical studies are required prior to development. Local agencies must regulate most types of development projects located within the zones. The currently available Official Maps of Seismic Hazard Zones contain zones 'for the seismic hazards of liquefaction and ear1hquake- induced landsliding for limited geographic areas only. However, future maps may contain additional seismic hazards and may cover the entire state. Our search indicates whether a proper1y is situated or not situated within a mapped Seismic Hazard Zone. If the proper1y is not located in an area mapped by the state Seismic Hazards Mapping Program, our repor1 indicates th3t the map for the site has not yet been released by the State. Due to the limitations of the state Seismic Hazards Mapping Program, CGS Reports, Inc. recommends hiring a Certified Engineering Geologist to address any concerns regarding the seismic hazard potential of the subject site.

The liquefaction Hazard Zones delineate areas where liquefaction has been recorded in the past End areas where local soil and groundwater conditions indicate a potential for permanent ground displacement from liquefaction that would require mitigation. Site specific geotechnical studies are required prior to new development. Liquefaction is a process whereby saturated, unconsolidated, sandy soils, temporarily become liquefied as a result of strong ground shaking. Liquefaction is considered most likely when the ground water table is located less than 50 feet below the ground surface. Ground displacement may occur and buildings may be damaged as a result of liquefaction.

Earthquake-Induced Landslide Zones include areas where geologic materials are considered susceptible to slope failure during strong ear1hquake ground shaking. Also included are areas with identified past landslide movement and areas with known ear1hquake-induced slope failure during historic ear1hquakes. Site specific geotechnical studies are required prior to new development.

It should be noted that the maps may not show all areas of potential liquefaction or earthquake-induced landsliding. In addition, the mapped areas within each zone will not be affected uniformly during an ear1hquake. As noted on the maps,' "liquefaction zones may also contain areas susceptible to the effects of ear1hquake-induced landslides. This situation typically exists at or near the toe of existing landslides, downslope from rockfall or debris flow source areas, or adjacent to steep stream beds."

Sale and Purchase Transactions

Military Ordnance Disclosure

California Civil Code §1102.15 requires the seller of residential real proper1y to disclose whether any former federal or state ordnance locations were located within one mile of the subject proper1y. For purposes of this law, "former federal or state ordnance locations" means an area identified by any agency or instrumentality of the federal or state governments as an area once used for military training purposes that may contain potentially explosive munitions.

Commercial/Industrial Disclosure

The disclosure regarding the Subject Property's proximity to a zone or district allowing manufacturing, commercial or airport use is based upon currently available public records and excludes entirely agricultural properties. A physical inspection of the Subject Property has not been made, The calculation of the one-mile proximity measurement is based upon the distance between the Subject Property's street address and the street address of the next closest property allowing manufacturing, commercial or airport use; the one-mile proximity measurement is not based upon a line of site measurement of the properties (e.g., "as the cross flies"). Therefore, it is possible for the Subject Property to be located immediately adjacent to a property allowing manufacturing, commercial or airport use, but because of the distance between the properties' street addresses, the Subject Property may be reported as not within one mile of a zone or district allowing manufacturing, commercial or airport use.

Airport Proximity Disclosure

This is not a noise (decibel level) disclosure and no disclosure is made regarding the proximity of private airports or landing strips. Rather, the airport proximity disclosure relates solely to the distance between the Subject Property's street address and the current boundaries of a non-private airport. The subject Property's proximity to a non-private airport is based upon currently available public records showing the present boundaries of the airport. No physical inspection of the Subject Property or the airport has been made, and this report does not consider the impact of any planned or approved airport expansion projects or modifications. The calculation of the five-mile proximity measurement is based upon the distance between the Subject Property's street address and present boundaries of the airport based upon curtly available public records. Therefore, it is possible for the Subject Property to be located immediately adjacent to an airport, but because of the distance between the airport's boundaries and the Subject Property's street address, the Subject Property may be reported as not within five miles of the airport. No finding or opinion is expressed or implied in this report regarding the take-off and landing patterns utilized by airports or the noise levels experienced at the Subject Property as a result therefore. Properties lying beneath or near airport take-off or landing routes often experience significant and disturbing noise levels notwithstanding that they are located more than five mile from the airport. In addition, take-off and landing patterns may change based upon weather conditions, wind conditions and airport expansion/modification projects. For more information, please contact the Federal Aviation Administration and/or the nearest airport of concern.

Mello-Roos and Special Assessments (1915 Bond) Determinations

This determination was made based on the Assessor's Parcel Number of the subject property as identified by the seller or seller's agent. Only Mello-Roos Community Facilities Districts and/or Special Assessment Districts (1915 Bond) which have actually levied a tax and/or assessment against properties are disclosed. Accurate Melio-Roos and Special Assessment information on a tax roll may not be available for a variety of reasons, such as if a property is in foreclosure for nonpayment of or delinquent in a f.1ello-Roos and/or Special Assessment. Under no circumstances will CGS Reports, Inc. be responsible for errors in the data provided by suppliers of the tax and/or data. Information is updated on a yearly basis as soon as reasonably possible after updated information is released. No study of the Assessor's or jurisdiction's files was made to determine the presence of any other tax or assessment, which may exist for the subject site. Due to changes in districts, this report cannot be relied upon for other nearby properties or future transactions of the subject property. All parties should be aware that the information is subject to change. Neither CGS nor the tax data supplier is responsible for advising parties of any changes that may occur after the date of this report. :

The purpose of this report is for preliminary disclosure. It is not a substitute for a Title Report or Title Insurance. The buyer must rely upon the seller's disclosure and a title report for final determination of whether the subject property is located within a Mello-Roos and/or a Special Assessment District (1915 Bond). This report is not a "Notice of Special Taxes. nor a "Notice of Special Assessments". The above explanation of Mello-Roos and/or Special Assessment Districts is intended to be brief and general in nature. CGS suggests that if any party to this transaction has any concerns or questions regarding Mello-Roos and/or Special Assessment. Districts, they contact an appropriate agent of the Community Facilities District and/or the Special Assessment District.

TERMS CONDITIONS AND LIMITATIONS OF LIABILITY

This report (Report) was prepared by CGS Reports, Inc. (CGS). This Report is for the exclusive use and reliance of the buyer, seller, listing agent and selling agent, if any. It may be used only in conjunction with a Natural Hazard Disclosure Statement, and then only in connection with the transaction contemplated by buyer and seller. This Report is not intended to be and may not be used for any other purposes, including but not limited to appraisal or valuation of the property.

This Report may not be used by or relied upon by any other parties, including but not limited to lenders or subsequent buyers, nor shall there be any third party beneficiaries regardless of their relationship with or to buyer, seller, or the property. CGS Reports, Inc. makes no representation or covenant as to the Report's effect on the value of the property as a result of the various disclosures contained in this Report.

This Report is valid solely for the transaction presently contemplated between this buyer and this seller relating to the property address and assessor's parcel number (APN) furnished by the seller as shown on page one .(1) of this Report. Seller is responsible for verifying the accuracy of the property address and APN within five (5) days of receipt of this Report. Upon notification of an inaccurate address or APN, CGS will issue a replacement report.

If multiple adjacent parcels are being transferred as a single property or in a single transaction, this Report treats them as if they were a single parcel. That is, hazards and locations that affect an individual parcel will be disclosed as affecting all parcels. Should seller or buyer desire a disclosure with regard to each parcel separately, a separate report must be ordered for each such parcel. The disclosures contained in this Report are valid only as of the date shown on page one (1) of this Report. CGS Reports, Inc. shall have no duty or obligation to inform buyer or seller, or their agents or lenders, of any changes or governmental actions pertaining to or affecting the property coming affective after the date shown on page one (1) of this report. It is recommended that a request for an updated Report be made if the property remains unsold for an extended period of time after this Report is issued.

CGS Reports, Inc. has relied solely upon records and information specifically referred to in this Report for preparation of this Report. These records and information were supplied by various governmental agencies. CGS Reports, Inc. assumes that the records and information supplied by various governmental agencies are complete and accurate. Consequently, CGS Reports, Inc. shall not be responsible for any inaccuracies or omissions in public records or in information reported by various governmental agencies. No physical inspection of the Property has been made.

CGS Reports, Inc. shall have no responsibility or liability for any costs or consequences arising due to the need, or lack of need, for earthquake insurance or flood hazard insurance. The National Flood Insurance or an insurance agent should be contacted for information regarding flood insurance. An insurance agent should be contacted for earthquake insurance information. Seller has requested that CGS Reports, Inc. provide the information contained in this Report. Delivery of this report is intended to assist the seller, and both agents, in availing themselves of the exemption from liability specified in Calif. Civil Code Section 1103.4(a), but CGS Reports, Inc. makes no representation or warranty, express or implied.. as to the actual availability of such exemption. CGS Reports, Inc. acknowledges that the information provided in this report will be used in fulfilling some of the disclosure requirements of Calif. Civil Code Section 11 02.6c and to no other items. The disclosures contained in this Report are applicable only to the items listed herein as they relate to the items listed in Calif. Civil Code Section 1102.6c and to no other items. CGS Reports, Inc. shall not be responsible for any items of information, or parts thereof, other than those expressly set forth in this Report.

ACCEPTANCE OR USE OF THIS REPORT, OR EXECUTION BY BUYER, SELLER, OR'THEIR RESPECTIVE AGENTS OF A NATURAL HAZARD DISCLOSURE STATEMENT IN CONJUNCTION WITH THIS REPORT, CONSTITUTES APPROVAL AND ACCEPTANCE OF THE TERMS, CONDITIONS, AND LIMITATIONS STATED HEREIN. UNDER NO CIRCUMSTANCES SHALL CGS BE LIABLE FOR LOST PROFITS OR ANY INDIRECT, INCIDENTAL, OR CONSEQUENTIAL DAMAGES IN CONNECTION WITH, OR ARISING OUT OF, THE PREPARATION, ISSUANCE, OR USE OF THIS REPORT.

Sale and Purchase Transactions

COMMERCIAL/INDUSTRIAL DISCLOSURE ADDENDUM
FOR CONTRA COSTA COUNTY

Property: 100 Goodfellow Dr, Pleasant Hill, CA 94523-4134

APN: 149-283-010-2

The Subject Property IS situated within one mile of a zone or district allowing manufacturing, commercial or airport use.

This Commercial/Industrial Disclosure is based upon currently available public records and excludes entirely agricultural properties. A physical inspection of the Subject Property has not been made. The calculation of the one-mile proximity measurement is based upon the distance between the Subject Property's street address and the street address of the next closest property allowing manufacturing, commercial or airport use; the one-mile measurement is not based upon a line of site measurement of the properties (e.g. "as the crow flies").

This Commercial/Industrial Disclosure Addendum can only be used in conjunction with the Residential Disclosure Report issued by CGS Reports, Inc. for the above referenced property dated as of the date of this report. The determination (s) made in this report is (are) based on data obtained from governmental authorities and pertains to the Assessor's Parcel Number of the subject property as identified by the seller or seller's agent. Information is updated as reasonably practical updated information is released by the cognizant governmental authorities. This addendum can not be relied upon for other nearby properties or for future transactions involving the same property. All parties should be aware that the information in this report is subject to change. CGS Reports, Inc. is not responsible for advising parties of any change or additional information that may arise after the date of this report.

_____   _____

AIRPORT PROXIMITY ADDENDUM
FOR CONTRA COSTA COUNTY

Property: 100 Goodfellow Dr, Pleasant Hill, CA 94523-4134

APN: 149-283-010-2   **Transferor:** Paine Kevin L.

The subject property is located within five miles of the following non-private airport(s);

AIRPORT	**LOCATION**
BUCHANAN FIELD	CONCORD

If you would like further information in connection with the above airport(s) please contact:

FAA Oakland Flight Standards District Office

8517 Earhart Rd.

Suite 100

Okland, CA (510) 273

This Airport Proximity addendum can only be used in conjunction with the Residential Disclosure Report issued by CGS Reports, Inc, for the above referenced property dated as of the date of this report, The determination(s) made in this report is(are) based on data obtained from governmental authorities and pertain to the Assessor's Parcel Number of the subject property as identified by the seller or seller's agent. Information is updated as reasonably practical after updated information is released by the cognizant governmental authorities. This addendum cannot be relied upon for other nearby properties or for future transactions involving the same property. All parties should be aware that the information in this report is subject to change. CGS Reports, Inc. is not responsible for advising parties of any change or additional information that may arise after the date of this report.

Sale and Purchase Transactions

Data Base Disclosure Addendum
(Megan's Law)
FOR CONTRA COSTA COUNTY

Property: 100 Goodfellow Dr, Pleasant Hill, CA 94523-4134

APN: 149-283-010-2   Transferor: Paine Kevin L.

NOTICE: The California Department of Justice, sheriff's departments, police departments serving jurisdictions of 200,000 or more and many other local law enforcement authorities maintain for public access a data base of the locations of persons required to register pursuant to paragraph (1) of subdivision (a) of Section 290.4 of the Penal Code. The data base is updated on a quarterly basis and a source of information about the presence of these individuals in any neighborhood. The Department of Justice also maintains a Sex Offender Identification Line through which inquiries about individuals may be made. This is a "900" telephone service. Callers must have specific information about individuals they are checking. Information regarding neighborhoods is not available through the "900" telephone service.

The form and content of the Megan's law disclosure notice is prescribed by statute. (California Civil Code § 2079.10a). No representation or warranty, express or implied, is made regarding the existence or non-existence of convicted sex offenders or other criminals in the neighborhood or area surrounding the Subject Property.

Prospective purchasers are encouraged to investigate web sites on the Internet Law, or for more information, please contact:

Contra Costa County Sheriff's Department
500 Court St. Martinez, CA 94553
(925) 335-1570
Mon-Fri; Barn - 5 pm, except holidays

_____   _____

Mold Addendum
Informational Statement Regarding Potential Mold Contamination
FOR CONTRA COSTA COUNTY

Property: 100 Goodfellow Dr, Pleasant Hill, CA 94523-4134

APN: 149-283-010-2   **Transferor:** Paine Kevin L.

All prospective home and condominium purchasers are advised to thoroughly inspect the subject property for mold. Mold may appear as discolored patches or cottony or speckled growth on walls: furniture or floors, and it often has an earthy or musty odor. Mold may also grow beneath water-damaged surfaces and floors, behind walls and above ceilings. Therefore, if you smell an earthy or musty odor, mold contamination may exist even if no actual mold growth is visible.

Mold only needs a food source (any organic material such as wood, paper, dirt or leaves) and moisture to grow. There are many potential food sources for mold in homes. Therefore, preventing excess moisture is the key to preventing mold growth. Excess moisture can come from many sources, including flooding, plumbing or roof leaks, lawn sprinklers hitting the house, air conditioner condensation, humidifiers, overflow from sinks and sewers, steam, and wet clothes drying indoors. Be sure to inspect the property for sources of excess moisture, current water leaks and evidence of past water damage. Once mold is found and the contaminated area properly cleaned up, mold growth is likely to recur unless the source of moisture is also eliminated.

If you suspect the subject property may have a mold problem, be sure to have a qualified inspector conduct a more thorough inspection. All areas contaminated with mold should be properly and thoroughly remediated.

Additional information about mold and what to do if you find mold in your home can be obtained from the following sources:

Sources	Publications Available
California Department of Health Services Indoor Air Quality Section and the Environmental Health Investigation Branch 2151 Berkeley Way (EHLB) Berkeley, CA 94704 Telephone: (510) 622-4500 Website: http://www.dhs.ca.gov/ps/deodc/ehib/ehib2/topics/mold.html	• Mold in My Home: What Can I Do? ¿ Moho en Mi Casa: Que Hago?
U.S. Environmental Protection Agency IAQ Information Clearinghouse Telephone: (800) 438-4318 Website: www.epa.gov/iaq/molds/moldguide.html	• " A Brief Guide to Mold, Moisture, and Your Home"
FEMA Website: http://www.fema.gov/diz02/d1419n40.shtm	• Mold Can Damage Home And Health

Local Hazards
Informational Statement Regarding Geologlic Hazards
FOR CONTRA COSTA COUNTY

Property: 100 Goodfellow Dr, Pleasant Hill, CA 94523-4134

APN: 149-283-010-2   Transferor: Paine Kevin L.

This Local Geologic Hazards Addendum has been provided for informational purposes only. The City and/or the County where the subject property is situated may have relevant information on liquefaction and landsliding in their General Plan. There may also be geologic, geotechnical, or grading reports that apply to the subject property. We suggest the Buyer thoroughly research the property with the City and/or the County as part of his or her due diligence. Local geologic hazards, liquefaction, landsliding, fault zones, geologic concerns, and permitting issues may be discovered that have not been disclosed due to the limited nature of the Natural Hazard Disclosure Statement.

For more information, please contact:

Contra Costa County, Community Development Department

651 Pine Street Martinez, CA 94553 (925) 335-1276 http://www.co.contra-costa.ca.us/deoartibi/comdev

Pleasant Hill Community Development Department

100 Gregory Lane Pleasant Hill, CA 94523

(925) 671-5208

http://www.ci.pleasant-hill.ca.us

MELLO ROOS ADDENDUM
FOR CONTRA COSTA COUNTY

Property: 100 Goodfellow Dr, Pleasant Hill, CA 94523-4134

APN: 149-283-010-2   **Transferor:** Paine Kevin L.

Fund Name	Purpose Of Fund	Yearly Levy	Beg Year	End Year
Community Facilities District No. 1	Schools	$67.00	1989	2026
For further Information please contact Joe Estrada				

This Mello-Roos addendum can only be used in conjunction with the Residential Disclosure Report issued by CGS Reports, Inc. for !he above referenced property dated as of !he date of this report; THIS ADDENDUM DOES NOT CONSTITUTE A NOTICE OF SPECIAL TAXES AND It CANNOT BE UTILIZED IN LIEU OF A NOTICE OF SPECIAL TAXES. Transferors of property must provide a NOTICE OF SPECIAL TAXES to their transferee. Only Mello-Roos/Community Facilities Districts that have actually levied a tax against the subject property are disclosed in this report. The determination(s) made in this report is(are) based on data provided by an independent electronic tax information service and pertains to the Assessor's Parcel Number of the subject property as identified by !he seller or seller's agent. Accurate Mello-Roos tax assessment information on a County Assessor's tax roll may not be available for a variety of reasons, such as if the property is in foreclosure or if there has been a nonpayment or delinquency in payment of a Mello- Roos Assessment. Under no circumstances will CGS Reports, Inc. be responsible for errors in the data provided by suppliers of the tax data, e.g., the electronic tax information service. Information is updated on a yearly basis as soon as reasonably practical after updated information is released by the cognizant governmental authorities. No study of the County Assessor's or other governmental files was made to determine the presence of any other tax or assessment that may affect the subject property. Due to changes in districts, this report cannot be relied upon for other nearby properties or for future transactions involving the same property. All parties should be aware that the information in this report is subject to change. Neither CGS nor its electronic tax information service is responsible for advising parties of any changed or additional information that may arise after the date of this report.

_____   _____

RECEIPT ACKNOWLEDGMENT

Property: 100 Goodfellow Dr, Pleasant Hill, CA 94523-4134

APN: 149-283-010-2   **Transferor:** Paine Kevin L.

Disclosures Received:

- ☑ Natural Hazards Disclosure
- ☑ Military Ordnance Disclosure
- ☑ Commercial/Industrial Disclosure
- ☑ Airport Proximity Disclosure
- ☑ Database Disclosure (Megan's Law)
- ☑ Mold Disclosure
- ☑ Local Disclosure
- ☑ Mello-Roos Disclosure
- ☑ Special Assessments Disclosure

_____	_____	_____	_____
Transferor (Seller)	**Date**	**Transferee (Buyer)**	**Date)**
_____	_____	_____	_____
Transferor (Seller)	**Date**	**Transferee (Buyer)**	**Date)**
_____	_____	_____	_____
Seller's Agent	**Date**	**Buyer's Agent**	**Date)**

CALIFORNIA FORM

2018 Real Estate Withholding Certificate

593-C

Part I – Seller/Transferor Information

Return this form to your escrow company

Name	SSN or ITIN
Kevin L. Paine	
Spouse's/RDP's name (if jointly owned)	Spouse's/RDP's SSN or ITIN (if jointly owned)

Address (apt./ste., room, PO box, or PMB no.)	☐ FEIN ☐ CA Corp no. ☐ CA SOS file no.
100 Goodfellow Dr.	

City (If you have a foreign address, see instructions.)	State	ZIP code	Ownership percentage
Pleasant Hill	C A	9 4 5 2 3	. %

Property address (if no street address, provide parcel number and county)

To certify that you qualify for a full or partial withholding exemption, check all boxes that apply to the property being sold or transferred. (See instructions)

Part II – Certifications which fully exempt the sale from withholding:

1. ☐ The property qualifies as the seller's/transferor's (or decedent's, if sold by the decedent's estate or trust) principal residence within the meaning of Internal Revenue Code (IRC) Section 121.

2. ☐ The seller/transferor (or decedent, if sold by the decedent's estate or trust) last used the property as the seller's/transferor's (decedent's) principal residence within the meaning of IRC Section 121 without regard to the two-year time period.

3. ☐ The seller/transferor has a loss or zero gain for California income tax purposes on this sale. To check this box you must complete Form 593-E, Real Estate Witholding-Computation of Estimated Gain or Loss, and have a loss or zero gain on line 16.

4. ☐ The property is being compulsorily or involuntarily converted and the seller/transferor intends to acquire property that is similar or related in service or use to qualify for nonrecognition of gain for California income tax purposes under IRC Section 1033.

5. ☐ The transfer qualifies for nonrecognition treatment under IRC Section 351 (transfer to a corporation controlled by the transferor) or IRC Section 721 (contribution to a partnership in exchange for a partnership interest).

6. ☐ The seller/transferor is a corporation (or a limited liability company (LLC) classified as a corporation for federal and California income tax purposes) that is either qualified through the California Secretary of State (SOS) or has a permanent place of business in California.

7. ☐ The seller/transferor is a California partnership or a partnership qualified to do business in California (or an LLC that is classified as a partnership for federal and California income tax purposes and is not a single member LLC that is disregarded for federal and California income tax purposes).

8. ☐ The seller/transferor is a tax-exempt entity under California or federal law.

9. ☐ The seller/transferor is an insurance company, individual retirement account, qualified pension/profit sharing plan, or charitable remainder trust.

Part III – Certifications that may partially or fully exempt the sale from withholding:

Real Estate Escrow Person (REEP): See instructions for amounts to withhold.

10. ☐ The transfer qualifies as a simultaneous like-kind exchange within the meaning of IRC Section 1031.

11. ☐ The transfer qualifies as a deferred like-kind exchange within the meaning of IRC Section 1031.

12. ☐ The transfer of this property is an installment sale where the buyer/transferee is required to withhold on the principal portion of each installment payment. Copies of Form 593-I, Real Estate Withhoiding Installment Sale Acknowledgement, and the promissory note are attached.

Seller/Transferor Signature

To learn about your privacy rights, how we may use your information, and the consequences for not providing the requested information, go to **ftb.ca.gov/forms** and search for **1131**. To request this notice by mail, call 800.852.5711.

Under penalties of perjury, I declare that I have examined the information on this form, including accompanying schedules and statements, and to the best of my knowledge and belief, it is true, correct, and complete. I further declare under penalties of perjury that if the facts upon which this form are based change, I will promptly notify the REEP.

Seller's/Transferor's Name and Title _____ Seller's/Transferor's Signature _____ Date _____

Spouse's/RDP's Name _____ Spouse's/RDP's Signature _____ Date _____

Seller/ Transferor

If you checked any box in Part II, you are exempt from real estate withholding.

If you checked any box in Part III, you may qualify for a partial or complete withholding exemption.

Except as to an installment sale, if the seller/transferor did not check any box in Part II or Part III of Form 593-C, the withholding will be 3¹/3% (.0333) of the total sales price or the optional gain on sale withholding amount from line 5 of Form 593, Real Estate Withholding Tax Statement. If the seller/transferor does not return the completed Form 593 and Form 593-C by the close of the real estate transaction, the withholding will be 3¹/3% (.0333) of the total sales price, unless the type of transaction is an installment sale. If the transaction is an installment sale, the withholding will be 3¹/3% (.0333) of the down payment.

If you are withheld upon, the REEP should give you one copy of Form 593. Attach a copy to the lower front of your California income tax return and make a copy for your records.

7131183

Form 593-C 2017

Midwest Title Company
HOMEOWNER'S POLICY OF TITLE INSURANCE AFFIDAVIT

Before me, the undersigned authority, on this day personally appeared ___Kevin L. Paine___ ("Affiants") personally known to me to be the persons whose names are subscribed hereto, who being by me first duly sworn, on their oaths stated the following to be true and correct:

1. We are the owners and occupants of the land commonly know as ___100 Goodfellow Drive Pleasant Hill. CA 94523___ (street address) described in Exhibit "An attached to this affidavit.

one-to-four family residence or a condominium and does not have a separate structure, garage or cond residence.

gainst the land and no judgments or tax liens against us, except those liens described in the (Title Co.)

ments by a taxing authority are paid through Contra Costa Tax Collector, there have been no special d on the land or tax exemptions that were not lawful.

essments by the homeowner's' association for the subdivision/condominium are paid current and ts are not yet payable.

improvements added to the land or construction on the land within the last year.

g repairs or improvements to the street(s) adjacent to the land.

ling permit from the proper government office authorized all improvements that we made to the

and have not been told that the improvements on the land violate any building , zoning ordinances/regulations, restrictions or covenants.

10. We are not aware of and have not been told that the improvements on the land described in Exhibit "A" encroach over any easement, property or building setback lines.

11. We are not aware of and have not been told that the improvements by our neighbors encroach over our property or building setback lines.

12. The land has actual pedestrian and vehicular access based on a legal right of access to the land.

13. The affiants indemnify and hold Midwest Title Insurance Company harmless from any loss, liability, costs, expenses, including attorney's fees, that Midwest Title Insurance Company may suffer from errors on incorrect statements in these representations, actually known to the affiant(s), upon which Midwest Title Insurance Company relies to issue the buyers an ALTA Homeowners Policy of Title Insurance for a one-to-four family residence (10/17/XX).

Dated: _____

_____
(Affiant)

STATE OF

COUNTY OF _____

Sworn to and subscribed before me, the undersigned, on this ____ day of _____, 20 ___.

_____
Notary Public

NOTES

The "Homeowner's Policy of Title Insurance Affidavit" is the only other document in the package that must be notarized besides the "Grant Deed."

Notice there are two lines in the affidavit that require completion. The title company has typed in the name of the seller and property address in these spaces. The document calls for a jurat notarization. The Notary must administer an oath to the seller that the representations contained in items #1-13 are true.

The seller signs in the space marked "Affiant."

MEMORANDUM

To Right Corp. Title Company of California, Escrow No. 99988888

The undersigned buyer in your captioned escrow has been informed by you of the availability of enhanced title insurance coverage in the form of the ALTA Homeowner's Policy of Title Insurance for a One-to-Four Family Residence, and I/we decline such insurance. Instead, I/we instruct that you issue a CLTA Standard coverage owner's policy of title insurance for my/out benefit.

DATE: _____   *BY:* _____

Please call with any questions. Thank you.

SUBSTITUTE FORM 1099-S
PROCEEDS FROM REAL ESTATE TRANSACTIONS
FOR THE TAX YEAR: 20XX
OMB No. 1545-0997

SETTLEMENT AGENT/FILER'S NAME AND ADDRESS
Right Corp. Title Company of California
2950 Mandrake Ave. Suite 122
Walnut Creek, CA 94596

Filer's Federal Tax ID Number:
FILE NUMBER:_____

SELLER/TRANSFEROR'S   NAME   AND   ADDRESS
_____
_____
_____

Transferor's Federal Tax ID Number:
_____

_____

1) Date of Closing:	2) Gross Proceeds:	4) X here if property or services received:	5) Buyer's part of real estate tax:
3) Address or Legal Description:			

THIS IS IMPORTANT TAX INFORMATION AND IS BEING FURNISHED TO THE INTERNAL REVENUE SERVICE. IF YOU ARE REQUIRED TO FILE A RETURN, A NEGLIGENCE PENALTY OR OTHER SANCTION WILL BE IMPOSED ON YOU IF THIS ITEM IS REQUIRED TO BE REPORTED AND THE IRS DETERMINES THAT IT HAS NOT BEEN REPORTED.

YOU ARE REQUIRED BY LAW TO PROVIDE US WITH YOUR CORRECT TAXPAYER IDENTIFICATION NUMBER. IF YOU DO NOT PROVIDE US WITH YOUR CORRECT TAXPAYER IDENTIFICATION NUMBER, YOU MAY BE SUBJECT TO CIVIL OR CRIMINAL PENALTIES IMPOSED BY LAW.

UNDER PENALTIES OF PERJURY, I CERTIFY THAT THE NUMBER SHOWN ABOVE ON THIS STATEMENT IS MY CORRECT TAX PAYER IDENTIFICATION NUMBER. I ACKNOWLEDGE RECEIPT OF A COPY OF THIS STATEMENT.

_____   _____
                                                                    Date

_____   _____
                                                                    Date

Instructions for Transferor

You MUST enter your Federal Tax Identification Number above.

Sign and return a copy of this form immediately

For sales or exchanges of certain real estate, the person responsible for closing a real estate transaction must report the real estate proceeds to the Internal Revenue Service and must furnish this statement to you. To determine if you have to report the sale or exchange of your main home on your tax return, see the 2002 Schedule D (Form 1040) instructions. If the real estate was not your main home, report the transaction on Form 4797, Sales of Business Property, Form 6252, Installment Sales Income, and/or Schedule D (Form 1040), Capital Gains and Losses.

You may have to recapture (pay back) all or part of a Federal mortgage subsidy if all the following apply:

- You received a loan provided from the proceeds of a qualified mortgage bond or you received a mortgage credit certificate.
- Your original mortgage loan was provided after 1990, and
- You sold or disposed of your home at a gain during the first 9 years after you received the Federal mortgage subsidy.

This will increase your tax. See Form 8828, Recapture of Federal Mortgage Subsidy, and Pub. 523, Selling Your Home.

If you have already paid the real estate tax for the period that includes the sale date, subtract the amount in box 5 from the amount already paid to determine your deductible real estate tax. But if you have already deducted the real estate tax in a prior year, generally report this amount as income on the "Other income" line of Form 1040. For more information, see Pub. 523.

For Paperwork Reduction Act Notice, see the 2002 Instructions for Forms 1099, 1098, 5498, and W-G2.

Department of the Treasury - Internal Revenue Service

5

Commercial Transactions

INTRODUCTION

Notary Signing Agents may be surprised when requested to appear at a signing for a corporation, partnership, or other legal entity purchasing or refinancing commercial real property. Consequently, they may feel unprepared when faced with an assignment that falls outside of the realm of their usual and ordinary experience of residential home loans.

The set of loan documents illustrated and discussed in this chapter represents a commercial real property loan transaction involving a corporation. While there are notable differences between commercial loans and residential loans, these differences can be grasped with a minimum of study and preparation.

Many Notaries already have experience notarizing documents for individuals signing as corporate officers and in other representative capacities. Depending upon the state where the Notary is commissioned, law may contain one or more statutory "representative" acknowledgment certificates for notarizing the signature of an agent signing on behalf of a corporation, partnership, trust, or other public or private legal entity. The representative acknowledgment form departs from the more common "individual" certificate in specifying the title of the person signing the document, the name of the person or entity represented, and a statement indicating that the agent executed the instrument under proper authority.

Familiarity with representative acknowledgment certificates in general will give a Notary Signing Agent a good basis for understanding the nature and complexities of commercial loan signings.

As defined under state law, a corporation can open a bank account, purchase goods and equipment, enter into contracts, operate a business, and finance or mortgage real property. In fact, a corporation can do things which most natural individuals can do and is often aptly described as an "artificial person" with rights, duties, and responsibilities similar to human persons. In addition to being an artificial person, a corporation is an entirely separate legal entity. One of the most important and attractive features of a corporation is that, generally, its owners are not individually liable for the debts of the corporation.

A corporation can only act through its members, directors, officers and agents. When the officers of the corporation sign papers, they must do so under specific authority. A specific corporate resolution authorizing the officers to act and duly recorded in the minutes of the corporation often constitutes such proof. In the sample set of loan documents under review in this chapter, the document entitled "Corporate Resolution to Borrow" provides this needed authorization.

Notary Signing Agents often ask whether they are responsible for determining that the individual signing papers in a representative capacity has the authority to act. This one question underscores what may be the single most defining difference between a corporate and a residential loan transaction.

The answer to this important question depends upon the state in which the Signing Agent is commissioned as a Notary. For example, in California, Notaries do not have a statutory obligation to verify the title or authority of a corporate officer. Notaries must only positively identify the signing corporate officer as an individual through the presentation of a state-approved identification document or the oath or affirmation of one or two credible witnesses. Since the sample transaction illustrated in this chapter was handled by a California Notary, a careful reading of the acknowledgment certificate wording on the "Deed of Trust and Fixture Filing," "Assignment of Rents," and "Subordination Agreement" will indicate that the Notary's only responsibility was to properly confirm the personal identity of each signing party.

If a California Notary Signing Agent encounters an out-of-state form containing acknowledgment wording that directs the Agent to confirm the signer's representative capacity, the Agent should complete and attach a California acknowledgment to the document.

However, Notary Signing Agents in other states may have a statutory responsibility to confirm the signing capacity of the transacting parties. One way to know if this is the case is to read the acknowledgment certificates on the instruments requiring notarization. Often, the acknowledgment wording will indicate that the signing corporate officer "acknowledged himself to be the president of XYZ Corporation, and that he, as such president, being authorized so to do, executed the foregoing instrument for the purposes therein contained." In other words, part of making an acknowledgment as a corporate officer involves acknowledging that he or she holds the capacity claimed.

Occasionally, as the following certificate from the state of Tennessee illustrates, proof of authority to act may involve the corporate officer making a sworn statement:

State of **TENNESSEE**

County of **DAVIDSON**

Before me, **JOHN Q. NOTARY** of the state and county mentioned, personally appeared **JANE C. OFFICER**, with whom I am personally acquainted (or proved to me on the basis of satisfactory evidence), and who, upon oath, acknowledged himself/herself to be **VICE PRESIDENT** of the **XYZ TEXTILES CORPORATION**, the within named bargainor, a corporation, and that he/she as such **VICE PRESIDENT**, executed the foregoing instrument for the purposes therein contained, by signing the name of the corporation by himself/herself as **VICE PRESIDENT**.

Witness my hand and seal, at office in Knoxville, TN, this **9TH** day of **JULY, 20XX**.

(SIGNATURE, SEAL, TITLE AND COMMISSION EXPIRATION DATE OF NOTARIZING OFFICER)

In reading this certificate carefully, the Notary's responsibility in taking the acknowledgment is twofold. The Notary must: (1) positively identify the signing officer through personal knowledge or satisfactory evidence, and the identification required of the Notary here does not include verification of the signing officer's official capacity; and (2) administer an oath to the officer. The words "and who, upon oath, acknowledged" is the Notary Signing Agent's cue that the Agent must administer an oath to the officer. The substance of the oath can be read aloud verbatim from the wording in the certificate.

The following acknowledgment certificate wording from the state of Washington illustrates that in some cases the Notary must certify that he or she has knowledge that the corporate officer holds a particular claimed signing capacity:

State of WASHINGTON   )

                                            ss.

County of PUGET SOUND)

On this **7TH** day of **SEPTEMBER, 20XX**, before me personally appeared **JOHN Q. OFFICER** to me known to be the **PRESIDENT** of the corporation that executed the within and foregoing instrument, and acknowledged said instrument to be the free and voluntary act and deed of said corporation, for the uses and purposes therein mentioned, and on oath stated that he was authorized to execute said instrument and that the seal affixed is the corporate seal of said corporation.

In Witness Whereof I have hereunto set my hand and affixed my official seal the day and year first above written.

(SIGNATURE AND TITLE OF OFFICER WITH PLACE OF RESIDENCE OF NOTARY PUBLIC.)

The words, "...to me known to be the PRESIDENT of the corporation..." clearly indicate the Notary must know that the signer holds the position of President. The law does not define what constitutes such proof, but the National Notary Association recommends that the Notary Signing Agent ask to view a copy of any corporate resolution designating the individual as the holder of a particular corporate office or title.

From the Notary Signing Agent's perspective, the matter of determining a corporate officer's representative signing capacity may be the only substantive difference between a commercial and residential loan transaction. In fact, in many other respects the sample commercial loan transaction is strikingly similar to a typical residential refinance transaction. The package contains a promissory note, deed of trust, hazard insurance disclosure, settlement statement, disbursement request and authorization, and escrow instructions — documents any borrower in a residential loan transaction must execute to obtain a loan.

While the similarities may be substantial, due to the unique features of commercial transactions there are several documents that may not be found in a typical residential refinance loan document package. The documents are (descriptions of each appear in the pages that follow):

1. Deed of Trust and Fixture Filing

2. Assignment of Rents

3. Commercial Security Agreement

4. Commercial Guaranty

First is the "Deed of Trust and Fixture Filing," a variation on the standard "Deed of Trust" that secures the residential property in a refinance, home equity line of credit, or reverse mortgage transaction. In addition to securing the lender's interest in the real property itself, the "Deed of Trust and Fixture Filing" secures the lender's right in buildings, improvements, easements, and mineral and oil rights.

In particular, the document defines these additional rights as follows:

> **CONVEYANCE AND GRANT. For valuable consideration, Trustor irrevocably grants, transfers and assigns to Trustee in trust, with power of sale, for the benefit of Lender as Beneficiary,** all of Trustor's right, title, and interest in and to the following described real property, together with all existing or subsequently erected or affixed buildings, improvements and fixtures; all easements, rights of way, and appurtenances; all water, water rights and ditch rights (including stock in utilities with ditch or irrigation rights); and all other rights, royalties, and profits relating to the real property, including without limitation all minerals, oil, gas, geothermal and similar matters..."

Most residential security instruments do not contain this additional language.

Second, an "Assignment of Rents" is a document that is executed by the borrower in favor of the lender and granting the lender the right to collect rents accruing from an income-producing property that is secured by a mortgage or deed of trust.

The need for an "Assignment of Rents" document is explained as follows:

> Traditionally, under the title theory of mortgages, a mortgage effected a transfer of legal title to real property as security for the mortgage debt. As an incident of this legal title, the mortgagee obtained the right to collect rents arising from the real property and apply them to the mortgage debt unless the mortgage stated otherwise. By contrast, in the majority of American states that follow the lien theory of mortgages, a mortgage grants the mortgagee only a right of security, capable of being enforced via foreclosure in the event of the mortgagor's default. Under the lien theory, until such enforcement occurs, a mortgage does not by itself convey to the mortgagee the right to collect rents accruing from the mortgaged real property.

Since completion of a foreclosure can take months, the "Assignment of Rents" precludes the possibility that the borrower can default on the mortgage and continue to collect rents. In a subsection entitled "Collect Rents" under "Rights and Remedies on Default (page 3), the document grants the lender the right to collect rents and apply them against the outstanding debt of the loan:

> Lender shall have the right, without notice to the Grantor, to take possession of the Property and collect the Rents, including amounts past due and unpaid, and apply the net proceeds, over and above Lender's costs, against the indebtedness.

The "Assignment of Rents" must be signed and acknowledged before a Notary Public. In some instances, a "Deed of Trust and Assignment of Rents" may incorporate into one document the security interest in the mortgaged property and rents accruing from the property.

Third, a word on the "Commercial Guaranty" contained in the sample set of documents. Fledgling or small corporations often have difficulty qualifying for loans due to their size, lack of money, or lack of credit history. Investors, banks, and lenders can sometimes be persuaded to lend if an individual or another company guarantees that the company will meet the loan obligation. In the "Commercial Guaranty" included in the sample documents, both corporate officers provide this guaranty individually. If the corporation does not meet the obligations of the loan, the individual executing the "Commercial Guaranty" becomes personally liable for the debt.

Finally, the "Commercial Security Agreement" is a form required under the Uniform Commercial Code that secures to the lender an additional interest in the "collateral" associated with the real property which is the subject of the commercial loan. In the form illustrated on pages 370–376, "Collateral" as defined includes "All Furniture, Fixtures, Equipment, Machinery, Accounts, Contracts, Inventory, General Intangibles, and Rental Income now owned and hereafter acquired located on the property…." In the same way that the "Assignment of Rents" gives the lender the right to collect rents to retire the debt, the "Commercial Security Agreement" gives the lender the right "to take possession of all or any part of the Collateral, with the power to protect and preserve the Collateral, to operate the Collateral preceding foreclosure or sale, and to collect the Rents from the Collateral and apply the proceeds, over and above the cost of the receivership, against the Indebtedness."

Forms in Sample Set   Pages

The full list of documents comprising the sample commercial documentation package is as follows. Refer to the marginal notes for additional comments on these forms.

Notarized Forms in Sample Set   **Pages**

The documents in the sample commercial documentation package that must be notarized are listed below. Refer to the marginal notes for additional comments and guidelines for notarizing these forms.

DISBURSEMENT REQUEST AND AUTHORIZATION

Principal	Loan Date	Maturity	Loan No	Call/Coll	Account	Officer	Initials
$400,000.00	02-16-XX	03-01-XX	9001	1C / 6520	0524840	***	

References in the shaded area are for Lender's use only and do not limit the applicability of this document to any particular loan or item.
Any item above containing "***" has been omitted due to text length limitations.

Borrower: DELKIM COMPANY, INC
10855 SAN PALO AVENUE
EL CERRITO, CA 94550

Lender: FIRST NATIONAL BANK
REAL ESTATE DEPARTMENT
ONE MAIN STREET
SALT LAKE CITY, UT 84155

LOAN TYPE. This is a Variable Rate Nondisclosable Loan to a Corporation for $400,000.00 due on March 1, 20XX. The reference rate (Prime Rate. Prime Rate means an index which is determined quarterly by the Prime Rate published in the Money Rate Section of the West Coast Edition of the Wall Street Journal, currently 5.500%) is added to the margin of 2.250%, resulting in an initial rate of 7.750.

PRIMARY PURPOSE OF LOAN. The primary purpose of this loan is for:
_____ Personal, Family, or Household Purposes or Personal Investment.
_____ Business (Including Real Estate Investment).

SPECIFIC PURPOSE. The specific purpose of this loan is: PROVIDE FINANCING FOR THE REFINANCE OF A 52-ROOM LIMITED SERVICE MOTEL

FLOOD INSURANCE. Some of the property that will secure the loan is not located in an area that has been identified by the Director of the Federal Emergency Management Agency as an area having special flood hazards. Therefore, although flood insurance may be available for the property, no special flood hazard insurance is required by law for this loan.

DISBURSEMENT INSTRUCTIONS. Borrower understands that no loan proceeds will be disbursed until all of Lender's conditions for making the loan have been satisfied. Please disburse the loan proceeds of $400,000.00 as follows:

Amount paid to others on Borrower's behalf:	$223,736.68
$223,736.68 to Wiring Loan Proceeds to Title Company	
Other Disbursements:	$164,832.00
$163,200.00 Tenant Improvements	
$1,632.00 Draw Fee	
Other Charges Financed:	$1,315.00
$200.00 Tax Monitoring Fee	
$100.00 Credit Report	
$50.00 Overnight Mail Fee	
$100.00 UCC Filing/Search Fees	
$100.00 UCC Filing/Search Fees	
$115.00 Environmental Vista Fee	
$750.00 Loan Documentation Fee	
Total Financed Prepaid Finance Charges:	$10,116.32
$1,116.32 Prepaid Interest	
$9,000.00 Loan Origination Fee (%)	
Note Principal:	$400,000.00

FINAL AGREEMENT. Borrower understands that the loan documents signed in connection with this loan are the final expression of the agreement between Lender and Borrower and may not be contradicted by evidence of any alleged oral agreement.

ERRORS AND OMISSIONS. Borrower hereby agrees that it will, within ten (10) days of a request by Lender, comply with any request by Lender to correct documentation errors, omissions or oversights, if any, that occur in any documentation relating to this loan.

FINANCIAL CONDITION. BY SIGNING THIS AUTHORIZATION, BORROWER REPRESENTS AND WARRANTS TO LENDER THAT THE INFORMATION PROVIDED ABOVE IS TRUE AND CORRECT AND THAT THERE HAS BEEN NO MATERIAL ADVERSE CHANGE IN BORROWER'S FINANCIAL CONDITION AS DISCLOSED IN BORROWER'S MOST RECENT FINANCIAL STATEMENT TO LENDER. THIS AUTHORIZATION IS DATED FEBRUARY 16, 2005.

BORROWER: DELKIM COMPANY, INC.

By: _____

JUAN HAN, President of DELKIM COMPANY INC.

By: _____

SUNNY HAN, Secretary of DELKIM COMPANY, INC.

PROMISSORY NOTE

Principal	Loan Date	Maturity	Loan No	Call/Coll	Account	Officer	Initials
$400,000.00	02-16-XX	03-01-XX	9001	1C / 6520	0524840	***	

References in the shaded area are for Lender's use only and do not limit the applicability of this document to any particular loan or item.
Any item above containing "***" has been omitted due to text length limitations.

Borrower:	DELKIM COMPANY, INC 10855 SAN PALO AVENUE EL CERRITO, CA 94550	Lender:	FIRST NATIONAL BANK REAL ESTATE DEPARTMENT ONE MAIN STREET SALT LAKE CITY, UT 84155

Principal Amount: $400,000.00   **Initial Rate: 7.750%**   **Date of Note: February 16, 20XX**

PROMISE TO PAY. DELKIM COMPANY, INC. ("Borrower") promises to pay to FIRST NATIONAL BANK ("Lender"), or order, in lawful money of the United States of America, the principal amount of Four Hundred Thousand & 00/100 Dollars ($400,000.00), together with interest on the unpaid principal balance from February 16, 20XX, until paid in full.

PAYMENT. Subject to any payment changes resulting from changes in the Index, Borrower will pay this loan in 240 payments of $3,312.30 each payment. Borrower's first payment is due April 1, 20XX, and all subsequent payments are due on the same day of each month after that. Borrower's final payment will be due on March 1, 20XX, and will be for all principal and all accrued interest not yet paid. Payments include principal and interest. Unless otherwise agreed or required by applicable law, payments will be applied first to any accrued unpaid interest; then to principal; then to any unpaid collection costs; and then to any late charges. The annual interest rate for this Note is computed on a 365/360 basis; that is, by applying the ratio of the annual interest rate over a year of 360 days, multiplied by the outstanding principal balance, multiplied by the actual number of days the principal balance is outstanding. Borrower will pay Lender at Lender's address shown above or at such other place as Lender may designate in writing.

VARIABLE INTEREST RATE. The interest rate on this Note is subject to change from time to time based on changes in an independent index which is the Prime Rate. Prime Rate means an index which is determined quarterly by the Prime Rate published in the Money Rate Section of the West Coast Edition of the Wall Street Journal (the "Index"). The Index is not necessarily the lowest rate charged by Lender on its loans. If the Index becomes unavailable during the term of this loan, Lender may designate a substitute index after notice to Borrower. Lender will tell Borrower the current Index rate upon Borrower's request. The interest rate change will not occur more often than each first calendar day of January, April, July and October. Borrower understands that Lender may make loans based on other rates as well. **The Index currently is 5.500% per annum. The interest rate to be applied to the unpaid principal balance of this Note will be at a rate of 2.250 percentage points over the Index, resulting in an initial rate of 7.750% per annum.** NOTICE: Under no circumstances will the interest rate on this Note be more than the maximum rate allowed by applicable law. Whenever increases occur in the interest rate, Lender, at its option, may do one or more of the following: (A) increase Borrower's payments to ensure Borrower's loan will pay off by its original final maturity date, (B) increase Borrower's payments to cover accruing interest, (C) increase the number of Borrower's payments, and (D) continue Borrower's payments at the same amount and increase Borrower's final payment.

PREPAYMENT PENALTY. Borrower agrees that all loan fees and other prepaid finance charges are earned fully as of the date of the loan and will not be subject to refund upon early payment (whether voluntary or as a result of default), except as otherwise required by law. **Upon prepayment of this Note, Lender is entitled to the following prepayment penalty: during the first five years from Date of Note, Borrower shall be subject to a prepayment penalty as follows: a declining 5%, 4%, 3%, 2%, 1% during Note years 1-5 respectively. Principal reductions are permitted without penalty provided such reductions do not exceed 20% of the original principal balance on the long term loan per Note year. (Said 20% allowance is non-cumulative from Note year to Note year.) However, if the loan is refinanced or repaid in full or in an amount exceeding the 20% paydown limitation, the applicable prepayment penalty shall apply to the entire prepaid principal amount at time of such prepayment (including any/all unscheduled principal reductions made during the previous twelve (12) month period).** Except for the foregoing, Borrower may pay all or a portion of the amount owed earlier than it is due. Early payments will not, unless agreed to by Lender in writing, relieve Borrower of Borrower's obligation to continue to make payments under the payment schedule. Rather, early payments will reduce the principal balance due and may result in Borrower's making fewer payments. Borrower agrees not to send Lender payments marked "paid in full", "without recourse", or similar language. If Borrower sends such a payment, Lender may accept it without losing any of Lender's rights under this Note, and Borrower will remain obligated to pay any further amount owed to Lender. All written communications concerning disputed amounts, including any check or other payment instrument that indicates that the payment constitutes "payment in full" of the amount owed or that is tendered with other conditions or limitations or as full satisfaction of a disputed amount must be mailed or delivered to: FIRST NATIONAL BANK, ONE MAIN SALT LAKE CITY, UT 84155.

LATE CHARGE. If a payment is 15 days or more late, Borrower will be charged **5.000% of the regularly scheduled payment or $50.00, whichever is greater.**

INTEREST AFTER DEFAULT. Upon default, including failure to pay upon final maturity, Lender, at its option, may, if permitted under applicable law, increase the variable interest rate on this Note to 5.250 percentage points over the Index. The interest rate will not exceed the maximum rate permitted by applicable law.

DEFAULT. Each of the following shall constitute an event of default ("Event of Default") under this Note:

Payment Default. Borrower fails to make any payment when due under this Note.

Other Defaults. Borrower fails to comply with or to perform any other term, obligation, covenant or condition contained in this Note or in any of the related documents or to comply with or to perform any term, obligation, covenant or condition contained in any other agreement between Lender and Borrower

Default in Favor of Third Parties. Borrower or any Grantor defaults under any loan, extension of credit, security agreement, purchase or sales agreement, or any other agreement, in favor of any other creditor or person that may materially affect any of Borrower's property or Borrower's ability to repay this Note or perform Borrower's obligations under this Note or any of the related documents.

False Statements. Any warranty, representation or statement made or furnished to Lender by Borrower or on Borrower's behalf under this Note or the related documents is false or misleading in any material respect, either now or at the time made or furnished or becomes false or misleading at any time thereafter.

Insolvency. The dissolution or termination of Borrower's existence as a going business, the insolvency of Borrower, the appointment of a receiver for any part of Borrower's property, any assignment for the benefit of creditors, any type of creditor workout, or the commencement of any proceeding under any bankruptcy or insolvency laws by or against Borrower.

Creditor or Forfeiture Proceedings. Commencement of foreclosure or forfeiture proceedings, whether by judicial proceeding, self-help, repossession or any other method, by any creditor of Borrower or by any governmental agency against any collateral securing the loan. This includes a garnishment of any of Borrower's accounts, including deposit accounts, with Lender. However, this Event of Default shall not apply if there is a good faith dispute by Borrower as to the validity or reasonableness of the claim which is the basis of the creditor or forfeiture proceeding and if Borrower gives Lender written notice of the creditor or forfeiture proceeding and deposits with Lender monies or a surety bond for the creditor or forfeiture proceeding, in an amount determined by Lender, in its sole discretion, as being an adequate reserve or bond for the dispute.

Events Affecting Guarantor. Any of the preceding events occurs with respect to any Guarantor of any of the indebtedness or any Guarantor dies or becomes incompetent, or revokes or disputes the validity of, or liability under, any guaranty of the indebtedness evidenced by this Note. In the event of a death, Lender, at its option, may, but shall not be required to, permit the Guarantor's estate to assume unconditionally the obligations arising under the guaranty in a manner satisfactory to Lender, and, in doing so, cure any Event of Default.

Change In Ownership. Any change in ownership of twenty-five percent (25%) or more of the common stock of Borrower.

Adverse Change. A material adverse change occurs in Borrower's financial condition, or Lender believes the prospect of payment or performance of this Note is impaired.

Insecurity. Lender in good faith believes itself insecure.

Cure Provisions. If any default, other than a default in payment is curable and if Borrower has not been given a notice of a breach of the same provision of this Note within the preceding twelve (12) months, it may be cured if Borrower, after receiving written notice from Lender demanding cure of such default: (1) cures the default within fifteen (15) days; or (2) if the cure requires more than fifteen (15) days, immediately initiates steps which Lender deems in Lender's sole discretion to be sufficient to cure the default and thereafter continues and completes all reasonable and necessary steps sufficient to produce compliance as soon as reasonably practical.

LENDER'S RIGHTS. Upon default, Lender may declare the entire unpaid principal balance on this Note and all accrued unpaid interest immediately due, and then Borrower will pay that amount.

ATTORNEYS' FEES; EXPENSES. Lender may hire or pay someone else to help collect this Note if Borrower does not pay. Borrower will pay Lender that amount. This includes, subject to any limits under applicable law, Lender's reasonable attorneys' fees and Lender's legal expenses, whether or not there is a lawsuit, including without limitation all reasonable attorneys' fees and legal expenses for bankruptcy proceedings (including efforts to modify or vacate any automatic stay or injunction), and appeals. If not prohibited by applicable law, Borrower also will pay any court costs, in addition to all other sums provided by law.

GOVERNING LAW. This Note will be governed by federal law applicable to Lender and, to the extent not preempted by federal law, the laws of the State of Utah without regard to its conflicts of law provisions. This Note has been accepted by Lender in the State of Utah.

CHOICE OF VENUE. If there is a lawsuit, Borrower agrees upon Lender's request to submit to the jurisdiction of the courts of SALT LAKE County, State of Utah.

RIGHT OF SETOFF. To the extent permitted by applicable law, Lender reserves a right of setoff in all Borrower's accounts with Lender (whether checking, savings, or some other account). This includes all accounts Borrower holds jointly with someone else and all accounts Borrower may open in the future. However, this does not include any IRA or Keogh accounts, or any trust accounts for which setoff would be prohibited by law. Borrower authorizes Lender, to the extent permitted by applicable law, to charge or setoff all sums owing on the indebtedness against any and all such accounts, and, at Lender's option, to administratively freeze all such accounts to allow Lender to protect Lender's charge and setoff rights provided in this paragraph.

COLLATERAL. Borrower acknowledges this Note is secured by the following collateral described in the security instruments listed herein:

(A) a Deed of Trust dated February 16, 20XX, to a trustee in favor of Lender on real property located in CONTRA COSTA County, State of California. That agreement contains the following due on sale provision: Lender may, at Lender's option, declare immediately due and payable all sums secured by the Deed of Trust upon the sale or transfer, without Lender's prior written consent, of all or any part of the Real Property, or any interest in the Real Property. A "sale or transfer" means the conveyance of Real Property or any right, title or interest in the Real Property; whether legal, beneficial or equitable; whether voluntary or involuntary; whether by outright sale, deed, installment sale contract, land contract, contract for deed, leasehold interest with a term greater than three (3) years, lease-option contract, or by sale, assignment, or transfer of any beneficial interest in or to any land trust holding title to the Real Property, or by any other method of conveyance of an interest in the Real Property. If any Borrower is a corporation, partnership or limited liability company, transfer also includes any change in ownership of more than twenty-five percent (25%) of the voting stock, partnership interests or limited liability company interests, as the case may be, of such Borrower.

(B) an Assignment of All Rents to Lender on real property located in CONTRA COSTA County, State of California.

ARBITRATION DISCLOSURES.

1. ARBITRATION IS FINAL AND BINDING ON THE PARTIES AND SUBJECT TO ONLY VERY LIMITED REVIEW BY A COURT.
2. IN ARBITRATION THE PARTIES ARE WAIVING THEIR RIGHT TO LITIGATE IN COURT, INCLUDING THEIR RIGHT TO A JURY TRIAL
3. DISCOVERY IN ARBITRATION IS MORE LIMITED THAN DISCOVERY IN COURT.
4. ARBITRATORS ARE NOT REQUIRED TO INCLUDE FACTUAL FINDINGS OR LEGAL REASONING IN THEIR AWARDS. THE RIGHT TO APPEAL OR SEEK MODIFICATION OF ARBITRATORS' RULINGS IS VERY LIMITED.
5. A PANEL OF ARBITRATORS MIGHT INCLUDE AN ARBITRATOR WHO IS OR WAS AFFILIATED WITH THE BANKING INDUSTRY.
6. ARBITRATION WILL APPLY TO ALL DISPUTES BETWEEN THE PARTIES, NOT JUST THOSE CONCERNING THE AGREEMENT.
7. IF YOU HAVE QUESTIONS ABOUT ARBITRATION, CONSULT YOUR ATTORNEY OR THE AMERICAN ARBITRATION ASSOCIATION.

(a) Any claim or controversy ("Dispute") between or among the parties and their employees, agents, affiliates, and assigns, including, but not limited to, Disputes arising out of or relating to this agreement, this arbitration provision ("arbitration clause"), or any related agreements or instruments relating hereto or delivered in connection herewith ("Related Agreements"), and including, but not limited to, a Dispute based on or arising from an alleged tort, shall at the request of any party be resolved by binding arbitration in accordance with the applicable arbitration rules of the American Arbitration Association (the "Administrator"). The provisions of this arbitration clause shall survive any termination, amendment, or expiration of this agreement or Related Agreements. The provisions of this arbitration clause shall supersede any prior arbitration agreement between or among the parties.

(b) The arbitration proceedings shall be conducted in a city mutually agreed by the parties. Absent such an agreement, arbitration will be conducted in Salt Lake City, Utah or such other place as may be determined by the Administrator. The Administrator and the arbitrator(s) shall have the authority to the extent practicable to take any action to require the arbitration proceeding to be completed and the arbitrators)' award issued within 150 days of the filing of the Dispute with the Administrator. The arbitrators) shall have the authority to impose sanctions on any party that fails to comply with time periods imposed by the Administrator or the arbitrator(s), including the sanction of summarily dismissing any Dispute or defense with prejudice. The arbitrator(s) shall have the authority to resolve any Dispute regarding the terms of this agreement, this arbitration clause, or Related Agreements, including any claim or controversy regarding the arbitrability of any Dispute. All limitations periods applicable to any Dispute or defense, whether by statute or agreement, shall apply to any arbitration proceeding hereunder and the arbitrators) shall have the authority to decide whether any Dispute or defense is barred by a limitations period and, if so, to summarily enter an award dismissing any Dispute or defense on that basis. The doctrines of compulsory counterclaim, res judicata, and collateral estoppel shall apply to any arbitration proceeding hereunder so that a party must state as a counterclaim in the arbitration proceeding any claim or controversy which arises out of the transaction or occurrence that is the subject matter of the Dispute. The arbitrator(s) may in the arbitrators)' discretion and at the request of any party: (1) consolidate in a single arbitration proceeding any other claim arising out of the same transaction involving another party to that transaction that is bound by an arbitration clause with Lender, such as borrowers, guarantors, sureties, and owners of collateral; and (2) consolidate or administer multiple arbitration claims or controversies as a class action in accordance with Rule 23 of the Federal Rules of Civil Procedure.

(c) The arbitrator(s) shall be selected in accordance with the rules of the Administrator from panels maintained by the Administrator. A single arbitrator shall have expertise in the subject matter of the Dispute. Where three arbitrators conduct an arbitration proceeding, the Dispute shall be decided by a majority vote of the three arbitrators, at least one of whom must have expertise in the subject matter of the Dispute and at least one of whom must be a practicing attorney. The arbitrator(s) shall award to the prevailing party recovery of all costs and fees (including attorneys' fees and costs, arbitration administration fees and costs, and arbitrators)' fees). The arbitrator(s), either during the pendency of the arbitration proceeding or as part of the arbitration award, also may grant provisional or ancillary remedies including but not limited to an award of injunctive relief, foreclosure, sequestration, attachment, replevin, garnishment, or the appointment of a receiver.

(d) Judgement upon an arbitration award may be entered in any court having jurisdiction, subject to the following limitation: the arbitration award is binding upon the parties only if the amount does not exceed Four Million Dollars ($4,000,000.00); if the award exceeds that limit, either party may demand the right to a court trial. Such a demand must be filed with the Administrator within thirty (30) days following the date of the arbitration award; if such a demand is not made with that time period, the amount of the arbitration award shall be binding. The computation of the total amount of an arbitration award shall include amounts awarded for attorneys' fees and costs, arbitration administration fees and costs, and arbitrator(s)' fees.

(e) No provision of this arbitration clause, nor the exercise of any rights hereunder, shall limit the right of any party to: (1) judicially or non-judicially foreclose against any real or personal property collateral or other security; (2) exercise self-help remedies, including but not limited to repossession and setoff rights; or (3) obtain from a court having jurisdiction thereover any provisional or ancillary remedies including but not limited to injunctive relief, foreclosure, sequestration, attachment, replevin, garnishment, or the appointment of a receiver. Such rights can be exercised at any time, before or after initiation of an arbitration proceeding, except to the extent such action is contrary to the arbitration award. The exercise of such rights shall not constitute a waiver of the right to submit any Dispute to arbitration, and any claim or controversy related to the exercise of such rights shall be a Dispute to be resolved under the provisions of this arbitration clause. Any party may initiate arbitration with the Administrator. If any party desires to arbitrate a Dispute asserted against such party in a complaint, counterclaim, cross-claim, or third-party complaint thereto, or in an answer or other reply to any such pleading, such party must make an appropriate motion to the trial court seeking to compel arbitration, which motion must be filed with the court within 45 days of service of the pleading, or amendment thereto, setting forth such Dispute. If arbitration is compelled after commencement of litigation of a Dispute, the party obtaining an order compelling arbitration shall commence arbitration and pay the Administrator's filing fees and costs within 45 days of entry of such order. Failure to do so shall constitute an agreement to proceed with litigation and waiver of the right to arbitrate. In any arbitration commenced by a consumer regarding a consumer Dispute, Lender shall pay one half of the Administrator's filing fee, up to $250.

(f) Notwithstanding the applicability of any other law to this agreement, the arbitration clause, or Related Agreements between or among the parties, the Federal Arbitration Act, 9 U.S.C. Section 1 et seq., shall apply to the construction and interpretation of this arbitration clause. If any provision of this arbitration clause should be determined to be unenforceable, all other provisions of this arbitration clause shall remain in full force and effect.

SUCCESSOR INTERESTS. The terms of this Note shall be binding upon Borrower, and upon Borrower's heirs, personal representatives, successors and assigns, and shall inure to the benefit of Lender and its successors and assigns.

GENERAL PROVISIONS. Lender may delay or forgo enforcing any of its rights or remedies under this Note without losing them. Borrower and any other person who signs, guarantees or endorses this Note, to the extent allowed by law, waive presentment, demand for payment, and notice of dishonor. Upon any change in the terms of this Note, and unless otherwise expressly stated in writing, no party who signs this Note, whether as maker, guarantor, accommodation maker or endorser, shall be released from liability. All such parties agree that Lender may renew or extend (repeatedly and for any length of time) this loan or release any party or guarantor or collateral; or impair, fail to realize upon or perfect Lender's security interest in the collateral; and take any other action deemed necessary by Lender without the consent of or notice to anyone. All such parties also agree that Lender may modify this loan without the consent of or notice to anyone other than the party with whom the modification is made. The obligations under this Note are joint and several.

PRIOR TO SIGNING THIS NOTE, BORROWER READ AND UNDERSTOOD ALL THE PROVISIONS OF THIS NOTE, INCLUDING THE VARIABLE INTEREST RATE PROVISIONS. BORROWER AGREES TO THE TERMS OF THE NOTE.

BORROWER ACKNOWLEDGES RECEIPT OF A COMPLETED COPY OF THIS PROMISSORY NOTE.

BORROWER: DELKIM COMPANY, INC.

By: _____

JUAN HAN, President of DELKIM COMPANY INC.

By: _____

SUNNY HAN, Secretary of DELKIM COMPANY, INC.

For space considerations, only pages 1, 9, 10, 11 of this Deed of Trust are reprinted.

FOR RECORDER's USE ONLY

DEED OF TRUST AND FIXTURE FILING

THIS DEED OF TRUST is dated February 16, 20XX, among DELKIM COMPANY, INC. ("Trustor"); FIRST NATIONAL BANK, whose address is REAL ESTATE DEPARTMENT, ONE MAIN STREET, SALT LAKE CITY, UT 84155 (referred to below sometimes as "Lender" and sometimes as "Beneficiary"); and FIRST NATIONAL BANK, whose address is ONE MAIN, SALT LAKE CITY, UT 84155 (referred to below as "Trustee").

CONVEYANCE AND GRANT. For valuable consideration, Trustor irrevocably grants, transfers and assigns to Trustee in trust, with power of sale, for the benefit of Lender as Beneficiary, all of Trustor's right, title, and interest in and to the following described real property, together with all existing or subsequently erected or affixed buildings, improvements and fixtures; all easements, rights of way, and appurtenances; all water, water rights and ditch rights (including stock in utilities with ditch or irrigation rights); and all other rights, royalties, and profits relating to the real property, including without limitation all minerals, oil, gas, geothermal and similar matters, **(the "Real Property") located in CONTRA COSTA County, State of California:**

See EXHIBIT "A", which is attached to this Deed of Trust and made a part of this Deed of Trust as if fully set forth herei

The Real Property or its address is commonly known as 10855 SAN PALO, EL CERRITO, CA 94550. The Assessor's P
Property is 558-340-006

Trustor presently assigns to Lender (also known as Beneficiary in this Deed of Trust) all of Trustor's right, title, and interest in and to of the Property and all Rents from the Property. This is an absolute assignment of Rents made in connection with an obligation secur to California Civil Code Section 2938. In addition, Trustor grants to Lender a Uniform Commercial Code security interest in the Perso

THIS DEED OF TRUST, INCLUDING THE ASSIGNMENT OF RENTS AND THE SECURITY INTEREST IN THE RENTS AND P GIVEN TO SECURE (A) PAYMENT OF THE INDEBTEDNESS AND (B) PERFORMANCE OF ANY AND ALL OBLIGATIONS (THE NOTE, THE RELATED DOCUMENTS, AND THIS DEED OF TRUST. THIS DEED OF TRUST IS GIVEN AND ACCEPTED ON T

PAYMENT AND PERFORMANCE. Except as otherwise provided in this Deed of Trust, Trustor shall pay to Lender all amounts secu they become due, and shall strictly and in a timely manner perform all of Trustor's obligations under the Note, this Deed of Trust, and

POSSESSION AND MAINTENANCE OF THE PROPERTY. Trustor agrees that Trustor's possession and use of the Property shall t provisions:

Possession and Use. Until the occurrence of an Event of Default, Trustor may (1) remain in possession and control of the Property; (2) use, operate or manage the Property; and (3) collect the Rents from the Property.

Duty to Maintain. Trustor shall maintain the Property in tenantable condition and promptly perform all repairs, replacements, and maintenance necessary to preserve its value.

Compliance With Environmental Laws. Trustor represents and warrants to Lender that: (1) During the period of Trustor's ownership of the Property, there has been no use, generation, manufacture, storage, treatment, disposal, release or threatened release of any Hazardous Substance by any person on, under, about or from the Property; (2) Trustor has no knowledge of, or reason to believe that there has been, except as previously disclosed to and acknowledged by Lender in writing, (a) any breach or violation of any Environmental Laws, (b) any use, generation, manufacture, storage, treatment, disposal, release or threatened release of any Hazardous Substance on, under, about or from the Property by any prior owners or occupants of the Property, or (c) any actual or threatened litigation or claims of any kind by any person relating to such matters; and (3) Except as previously disclosed to and acknowledged by Lender in writing, (a) neither Trustor nor any tenant, contractor, agent or other authorized user of the Property shall use, generate, manufacture, store, treat, dispose of or release any Hazardous Substance on, under, about or from the Property; and (b) any such activity shall be conducted in compliance with all applicable federal, state, and local laws, regulations and ordinances, including without limitation all Environmental Laws. Trustor authorizes Lender and its agents to enter upon the Property to make such inspections and tests, at Trustor's expense, as Lender may deem appropriate to determine compliance of the Property with this section of the Deed of Trust. Any inspections or tests made by Lender shall be for Lender's purposes only and shall not be construed to create any responsibility or liability on the part of Lender to Trustor or to any other person. The representations and warranties contained herein are based on Trustor's due diligence in investigating the Property for Hazardous Substances. Trustor hereby (1) releases and waives any future claims against Lender for indemnity or contribution in the event Trustor becomes liable for cleanup or other costs under any such laws; and (2) agrees to indemnify and hold harmless Lender against any and all claims, losses, liabilities, damages, penalties, and expenses which Lender

> **NOTES**
>
> The "Deed of Trust" and "Assignment of Rents" (see pages 343–353) reference an attached "Exhibit A" containing the property's legal description. This exhibit does not follow the "Deed of Trust" or "Assignment of Rents," but can be found at the end of the "Subordination Agreement" (page 384).

1980, as amended, 42 U.S.C. Section 9601, et seq. ("CERCLA"), the Superfund Amendments and Reauthorization Act of 1986, Pub. L No. 99-499 ("SARA"), the Hazardous Materials Transportation Act, 49 U.S.C. Section 1801, et seq., the Resource Conservation and Recovery Act, 42 U.S.C. Section 6901, et seq., Chapters 6.5 through 7.7 of Division 20 of the California Health and Safety Code, Section 25100, et seq., or other applicable state or federal laws, rules, or regulations adopted pursuant thereto.

Event of Default. The words "Event of Default" mean any of the events of default set forth in this Deed of Trust in the events of default section of this Deed of Trust.

Guarantor. The word "Guarantor" means any guarantor, surety, or accommodation party of any or all of the Indebtedness.

Guaranty. The word "Guaranty" means the guaranty from Guarantor to Lender, including without limitation a guaranty of all or part of the Note.

Hazardous Substances. The words "Hazardous Substances" mean materials that, because of their quantity, concentration or physical, chemical or infectious characteristics, may cause or pose a present or potential hazard to human health or the environment when improperly used, treated, stored, disposed of, generated, manufactured, transported or otherwise handled. The words "Hazardous Substances" are used in their very broadest sense and include without limitation any and all hazardous or toxic substances, materials or waste as defined by or listed under the Environmental Laws. The term "Hazardous Substances" also includes, without limitation, petroleum and petroleum by-products or any fraction thereof and asbestos.

Improvements. The word "Improvements" means all existing and future improvements, buildings, structures, mobile homes affixed on the Real Property, facilities, additions, replacements and other construction on the Real Property.

Indebtedness. The word "Indebtedness" means and includes without limitation all Loans, together with all other obligations, debts and liabilities of Borrower to Lender, or any one or more of them; as well as all claims by Lender against Borrower, or any one or more of them; whether now or hereafter existing, voluntary or involuntary, due or not due, absolute or contingent, liquidated or unliquidated; whether Borrower may be liable individually or jointly with others; whether Borrower may be obligated as a guarantor, surety, or otherwise; whether recovery upon such indebtedness may be or hereafter may become barred by any statute of limitations; and whether such indebtedness may be or hereafter may become otherwise unenforceable.

Lender. The word "Lender" means FIRST NATIONAL BANK, its successors and assigns.

Note. The word "Note" means the promissory note dated February 16, 20XX, **in the original principal amount of $400,000.00** from Trustor to Lender, together with all renewals of, extensions of, modifications of, refinancings of, consolidations of, and substitutions for the promissory note or agreement. **NOTICE TO TRUSTOR: THE NOTE CONTAINS A VARIABLE INTEREST RATE.**

Personal Property. The words "Personal Property" mean all equipment, fixtures, and other articles of personal property now or hereafter owned by Trustor, and now or hereafter attached or affixed to the Real Property; together with all accessions, parts, and additions to, all replacements of, and all substitutions for, any of such property; and together with all proceeds (including without limitation all insurance proceeds and refunds of premiums) from any sale or other disposition of the Property.

Property. The word "Property" means collectively the Real Property and the Personal Property. Real Property. The words "Real Property" mean the real property, interests and rights, as further described in this Deed of Trust.

Related Documents. The words "Related Documents" mean all promissory notes, credit agreements, loan agreements, environmental agreements, security agreements, mortgages, deeds of trust, security deeds, collateral mortgages, and all other instruments, agreements and documents, whether now or hereafter existing, executed in connection with the Indebtedness.

Rents. The word "Rents" means all present and future leases, rents, revenues, income, issues, royalties, profits, and other benefits derived from the Property together with the cash proceeds of the Rents.

Trustee. The word "Trustee" means FIRST NATIONAL BANK, whose address is ONE MAIN, SALT LAKE CITY, UT 84155 and any substitute or successor trustees.

Trustor. The word "Trustor" means DELKIM COMPANY, INC..

TRUSTOR ACKNOWLEDGES HAVING READ ALL THE PROVISIONS OF THIS DEED OF TRUST, AND TRUSTOR AGREES TO ITS TERMS, INCLUDING THE VARIABLE RATE PROVISIONS OF THE NOTE SECURED BY THIS DEED OF TRUST.

TRUSTOR: DELKIM COMPANY, INC.

By: _____

JUAN HAN, **President of DELKIM COMPANY, INC.**

By: _____

SUNNY HAN, **Secretary of DELKIM COMPANY, INC.**

Loan No: 9001

DEED OF TRUST
(Continued)

CERTIFICATE OF ACKNOWLEDGMENT

STATE OF _____)
　　　　　　　　　　　　　　　　　　) SS
COUNTY OF _____)

On _____, 20_____ before me, _____,
personally appeared **JUAN HAN,** personally known to me (or proved to me on the basis of satisfactory evidence) to be the person(s) whose name(s) is/are subscribed to the within instrument and acknowledged to me that he/she/they executed the same in his/her/their authorized capacity(ies), and that by his/her/their signature(s) on the instrument the person(s), or the entity upon behalf of which the person(s) acted, executed the instrument.

WITNESS my hand and official seal.

Signature _____　　　　　　　　　　　　　**(Seal)**

CERTIFICATE OF ACKNOWLEDGMENT

STATE OF _____)
　　　　　　　　　　　　　　　　　　) SS
COUNTY OF _____)

On _____, 20_____ before me, _____
personally appeared **SUNNY HAN,** personally known to me (or proved to me on the basis of satisfactory evidence) to be the pers subscribed to the within instrument and acknowledged to me that he/she/they executed the same in his/her/their authorized his/her/their signature(s) on the instrument the person(s), or the entity upon behalf of which the person(s) acted, executed the instrum

WITNESS my hand and official seal.

Signature _____　　　　　　　　　　　　　**(Seal)**

NOTES

The "Deed of Trust" and "Assignment of Rents" (see pages 343–353) contains acknowledgment certificates naming each borrower separately. While technically one form containing both names could be used, in this instance it is advisable that the Notary Signing Agent complete a form for each borrower, as requested.

DEED OF TRUST
(Continued)

(DO NOT RECORD)
REQUEST FOR FULL RECONVEYANCE

(To be used only when obligations have been paid in full)

To: _____, Trustee

The undersigned is the legal owner and holder of all Indebtedness secured by this Deed of Trust. All sums secured by this Deed of Trust have been fully paid and satisfied. You are hereby directed, upon payment to you of any sums owing to you under the terms of this Deed of Trust or pursuant to any applicable statute, to cancel the Note secured by this Deed of Trust (which is delivered to you together with this Deed of Trust), and to reconvey, without warranty, to the parties designated by the terms of this Deed of Trust, the estate now held by you under this Deed of Trust. Please mail the reconveyance and Related Documents to:

_____.

Date: _____   Beneficiary: _____

By: _____

Its: _____

RECORDATION REQUESTED BY:
  FIRST NATIONAL BANK
  REAL ESTATE DEPARTMENT
  ONE MAIN STREET
  SALT LAKE CITY, UT 84155

WHEN RECORDED MAIL TO:
  FIRST NATIONAL BANK
  REAL ESTATE DEPARTMENT
  ONE MAIN STREET
  SALT LAKE CITY, UT 84155

SEND TAX NOTICES TO:
  DELKIM COMPANY, INC.
  10855 SAN PABLO AVENUE
  EL CERRITO. CA 94550

FOR RECORDER'S USE ONLY

ASSIGNMENT OF RENTS

THIS ASSIGNMENT OF RENTS dated February 16, 20XX, is made and executed between DELKIM COMPANY, INC. (referred to below as "Grantor") and FIRST NATIONAL BANK, whose address is ONE MAIN STREET, SALT LAKE CITY, UT 84155 (referred to below as "Lender").

ASSIGNMENT. For valuable consideration, Grantor hereby assigns, grants a continuing security interest in, and conveys to Lender all of Grantor's right, title, and interest in and to the Rents from the following described Property located in CONTRA COSTA County, State of California:

See EXHIBIT "A" which is attached to this Assignment and made a part of this Assignment as if fully set forth herein.

The Property or its address is commonly known as 10855 SAN PALO, EL CERRITO, CA 94550. The Assessor's Parcel Number for the Property is 508-340-055

This is an absolute assignment of Rents made in connection with an obligation secured by property pursuant to California Civil Code section 2938.

THIS ASSIGNMENT IS GIVEN TO SECURE (1) PAYMENT OF THE INDEBTEDNESS AND (2) PERFORMANCE OF ANY AND ALL OBLIGATIONS OF GRANTOR UNDER THE NOTE, THIS ASSIGNMENT, AND THE RELATED DOCUMENTS. THIS ASSIGNMENT IS GIVEN AND ACCEPTED ON THE FOLLOWING TERMS:

PAYMENT AND PERFORMANCE. Except as otherwise provided in this Assignment or any Related Documents, Grantor shall pay to Lender all amounts secured by this Assignment as they become due, and shall strictly perform all of Grantor's obligations under this Assignment. Unless and until Lender exercises its right to collect the Rents as provided below and so long as there is no default under this Assignment, Grantor may remain in possession and control of and operate and manage the Property and collect the Rents, provided that the granting of the right to collect the Rents shall not constitute Lender's consent to the use of cash collateral in a bankruptcy proceeding.

GRANTOR'S REPRESENTATIONS AND WARRANTIES. Grantor warrants that:

  Ownership. Grantor is entitled to receive the Rents free and clear of all rights, loans, liens, encumbrances, and claims except as disclosed to and accepted by Lender in writing.

  Right to Assign. Grantor has the full right, power and authority to enter into this Assignment and to assign and convey the Rents to Lender.

  No Prior Assignment. Grantor has not previously assigned or conveyed the Rents to any other person by any instrument now in force.

No Further Transfer. Grantor will not sell, assign, encumber, or otherwise dispose of any of Grantor's rights in the Rents except as provided in this Assignment.

LENDER'S RIGHT TO RECEIVE AND COLLECT RENTS. Lender shall have the right at any time, and even though no default shall have occurred under this Assignment, to collect and receive the Rents. For this purpose, Lender is hereby given and granted the following rights, powers and authority:

  Notice to Tenants. Lender may send notices to any and all tenants of the Property advising them of this Assignment and directing all Rents to be paid directly to Lender or Lender's agent.

  Enter the Property. Lender may enter upon and take possession of the Property; demand, collect and receive from the tenants or from any other persons liable therefor, all of the Rents; institute and carry on all legal proceedings necessary for the protection of the Property, including such proceedings as may be necessary to recover possession of the Property; collect the Rents and remove any tenant or tenants or other persons from the Property.

  Maintain the Property. Lender may enter upon the Property to maintain the Property and keep the same in repair; to pay the costs thereof and of all services of all employees, including their equipment, and of all continuing costs and expenses of maintaining the Property in proper repair and condition, and also to pay all taxes, assessments and water utilities, and the premiums on fire and other insurance effected by Lender on the Property.

Compliance with Laws. Lender may do any and all things to execute and comply with the laws of the State of California and also all other laws, rules, orders, ordinances and requirements of all other governmental agencies affecting the Property.

Lease the Property. Lender may rent or lease the whole or any part of the Property for such term or terms and on such conditions as Lender may deem appropriate.

Employ Agents. Lender may engage such agent or agents as Lender may deem appropriate, either in Lender's name or in Grantor's name, to rent and manage the Property, including the collection and application of Rents.

Other Acts. Lender may do all such other things and acts with respect to the Property as Lender may deem appropriate and may act exclusively and solely in the place and stead of Grantor and to have all of the powers of Grantor for the purposes stated above.

No Requirement to Act. Lender shall not be required to do any of the foregoing acts or things, and the fact that Lender shall have performed one or more of the foregoing acts or things shall not require Lender to do any other specific act or thing.

APPLICATION OF RENTS. All costs and expenses incurred by Lender in connection with the Property shall be for Grantor's account and Lender may pay such costs and expenses from the Rents. Lender, in its sole discretion, shall determine the application of any and all Rents received by it; however, any such Rents received by Lender which are not applied to such costs and expenses shall be applied to the Indebtedness. All expenditures made by Lender under this Assignment and not reimbursed from the Rents shall become a part of the Indebtedness secured by this Assignment, and shall be payable on demand, with interest at the Note rate from date of expenditure until paid.

FULL PERFORMANCE. If Grantor pays all of the Indebtedness when due and otherwise performs all the obligations imposed upon Grantor under this Assignment, the Note, and the Related Documents, Lender shall execute and deliver to Grantor a suitable satisfaction of this Assignment and suitable statements of termination of any financing statement on file evidencing Lender's security interest in the Rents and the Property. Any termination fee required by law shall be paid by Grantor, if permitted by applicable law.

LENDER'S EXPENDITURES. If any action or proceeding is commenced that would materially affect Lender's interest in the Property or if Grantor fails to comply with any provision of this Assignment or any Related Documents, including but not limited to Grantor's failure to discharge or pay when due any amounts Grantor is required to discharge or pay under this Assignment or any Related Documents, Lender on Grantor's behalf may (but shall not be obligated to) take any action that Lender deems appropriate, including but not limited to discharging or paying all taxes, liens, security interests, encumbrances and other claims, at any time levied or placed on the Rents or the Property and paying all costs for insuring, maintaining and preserving the Property. All such expenditures incurred or paid by Lender for such purposes will then bear interest at the rate charged under the Note from the date incurred or paid by Lender to the date of repayment by Grantor. All such expenses will become a part of the Indebtedness and, at Lender's option, will (A) be payable on demand; (B) be added to the balance of the Note and be apportioned among and be payable with any installment payments to become due during either (1) the term of any applicable insurance policy; or (2) the remaining term of the Note; or (C) be treated as a balloon payment which will be due and payable at the Note's maturity. The Assignment also will secure payment of these amounts. Such right shall be in addition to all other rights and remedies to which Lender may be entitled upon Default.

DEFAULT. Each of the following, at Lender's option, shall constitute an Event of Default under this Assignment:

Payment Default. Grantor fails to make any payment when due under the Indebtedness.

Other Defaults. Grantor fails to comply with or to perform any other term, obligation, covenant or condition contained in this Assignment or in any of the Related Documents or to comply with or to perform any term, obligation, covenant or condition contained in any other agreement between Lender and Grantor.

Default on Other Payments. Failure of Grantor within the time required by this Assignment to make any payment for taxes or insurance, or any other payment necessary to prevent filing of or to effect discharge of any lien.

Default in Favor of Third Parties. Grantor defaults under any loan, extension of credit, security agreement, purchase or sales agreement, or any other agreement, in favor of any other creditor or person that may materially affect any of Grantor's property or Grantor's ability to perform Grantor's obligations under this Assignment or any of the Related Documents.

False Statements. Any warranty, representation or statement made or furnished to Lender by Grantor or on Grantor's behalf under this Assignment or the Related Documents is false or misleading in any material respect, either now or at the time made or furnished or becomes false or misleading at any time thereafter.

Defective Collateralization. This Assignment or any of the Related Documents ceases to be in full force and effect (including failure of any collateral document to create a valid and perfected security interest or lien) at any time and for any reason.

Insolvency. The dissolution or termination of Grantor's existence as a going business, the insolvency of Grantor, the appointment of a receiver for any part of Grantor's property, any assignment for the benefit of creditors, any type of creditor workout, or the commencement of any proceeding under any bankruptcy or insolvency laws by or against Grantor.

Creditor or Forfeiture Proceedings. Commencement of foreclosure or forfeiture proceedings, whether by judicial proceeding, self-help, repossession or any other method, by any creditor of Grantor or by any governmental agency against the Rents or any property securing the Indebtedness. This includes a garnishment of any of Grantor's accounts, including deposit accounts, with Lender. However, this Event of Default shall not apply if there is a good faith dispute by Grantor as to the validity or reasonableness of the claim which is the basis of the creditor or forfeiture proceeding and if Grantor gives Lender written notice of the creditor or forfeiture proceeding and deposits with Lender monies or a surety bond for the creditor or forfeiture proceeding, in an amount determined by Lender, in its sole discretion, as being an adequate reserve or bond for the dispute.

Property Damage or Loss. The Property is lost, stolen, substantially damaged, sold, or borrowed against.

Events Affecting Guarantor. Any of the preceding events occurs with respect to any Guarantor of any of the Indebtedness or any Guarantor dies or becomes incompetent, or revokes or disputes the validity of, or liability under, any Guaranty of the Indebtedness. In the event of a death, Lender, at its option, may, but shall not be required to, permit the Guarantor's estate to assume unconditionally the obligations arising under the guaranty in a manner satisfactory to Lender, and, in doing so, cure any Event of Default.

Adverse Change. A material adverse change occurs in Grantor's financial condition, or Lender believes the prospect of payment or performance of the Indebtedness is impaired. Insecurity. Lender in good faith believes itself insecure.

Cure Provisions. If any default, other than a default in payment is curable and if Grantor has not been given a notice of a breach of the same provision of this Assignment within the preceding twelve (12) months, it may be cured if Grantor, after receiving written notice from Lender demanding cure of such default: (1) cures the default within fifteen (15) days; or (2) if the cure requires more than fifteen (15) days, immediately initiates steps which Lender deems in Lender's sole discretion to be sufficient to cure the default and thereafter continues and completes all reasonable and necessary steps sufficient to produce compliance as soon as reasonably practical.

RIGHTS AND REMEDIES ON DEFAULT. Upon the occurrence of any Event of Default and at any time thereafter, Lender may exercise any one or more of the following rights and remedies, in addition to any other rights or remedies provided by law:

Accelerate Indebtedness. Lender shall have the right at its option without notice to Grantor to declare the entire Indebtedness immediately due and payable, including any prepayment penalty which Grantor would be required to pay.

Collect Rents. Lender shall have the right, without notice to Grantor, to take possession of the Property and collect the Rents, including amounts past due and unpaid, and apply the net proceeds, over and above Lender's costs, against the Indebtedness. In furtherance of this right, Lender shall have all the rights provided for in the Lender's Right to Receive and Collect Rents Section, above. If the Rents are collected by Lender, then Grantor irrevocably designates Lender as Grantor's attorney-in-fact to endorse instruments received in payment thereof in the name of Grantor and to negotiate the same and collect the proceeds. Payments by tenants or other users to Lender in response to Lender's demand shall satisfy the obligations for which the payments are made, whether or not any proper grounds for the demand existed. Lender may exercise its rights under this subparagraph either in person, by agent, or through a receiver.

Appoint Receiver. Lender shall have the right to have a receiver appointed to take possession of all or any part of the Property, with the power to protect and preserve the Property, to operate the Property preceding foreclosure or sale, and to collect the Rents from the Property and apply the proceeds, over and above the cost of the receivership, against the Indebtedness. The receiver may serve without bond if permitted by law. Lender's right to the appointment of a receiver shall exist whether or not the apparent value of the Property exceeds the Indebtedness by a substantial amount. Employment by Lender shall not disqualify a person from serving as a receiver.

Other Remedies. Lender shall have all other rights and remedies provided in this Assignment or the Note or by law.

Election of Remedies. Election by Lender to pursue any remedy shall not exclude pursuit of any other remedy, and an election to make expenditures or to take action to perform an obligation of Grantor under this Assignment, after Grantor's failure to perform, shall not affect Lender's right to declare a default and exercise its remedies.

Attorneys' Fees; Expenses. If Lender institutes any suit or action to enforce any of the terms of this Assignment, Lender shall be entitled to recover such sum as the court may adjudge reasonable as attorneys' fees at trial and upon any appeal. Whether or not any court action is involved, and to the extent not prohibited by law, all reasonable expenses Lender incurs that in Lender's opinion are necessary at any time for the protection of its interest or the enforcement of its rights shall become a part of the Indebtedness payable on demand and shall bear interest at the Note rate from the date of the expenditure until repaid. Expenses covered by this paragraph include, without limitation, however subject to any limits under applicable law, Lender's attorneys' fees and Lender's legal expenses, whether or not there is a lawsuit, including attorneys' fees and expenses for bankruptcy proceedings (including efforts to modify or vacate any automatic stay or injunction), appeals, and any anticipated post-judgment collection services, the cost of searching records, obtaining title reports (including foreclosure reports), surveyors' reports, and appraisal fees, title insurance, and fees for the Trustee, to the extent permitted by applicable law. Grantor also will pay any court costs, in addition to all other sums provided by law.

MISCELLANEOUS PROVISIONS. The following miscellaneous provisions are a part of this Assignment:

Amendments. This Assignment, together with any Related Documents, constitutes the entire understanding and agreement of the parties as to the matters set forth in this Assignment. No alteration of or amendment to this Assignment shall be effective unless given in writing and signed by the party or parties sought to be charged or bound by the alteration or amendment.

Arbitration Disclosures.

1. ARBITRATION IS FINAL AND BINDING ON THE PARTIES AND SUBJECT TO ONLY VERY LIMITED REVIEW BY A COURT.
2. IN ARBITRATION THE PARTIES ARE WAIVING THEIR RIGHT TO LITIGATE IN COURT, INCLUDING THEIR RIGHT TO A JURY TRIAL
3. DISCOVERY IN ARBITRATION IS MORE LIMITED THAN DISCOVERY IN COURT.
4. ARBITRATORS ARE NOT REQUIRED TO INCLUDE FACTUAL FINDINGS OR LEGAL REASONING IN THEIR AWARDS. THE RIGHT TO APPEAL OR SEEK MODIFICATION OF ARBITRATORS' RULINGS IS VERY LIMITED.
5. A PANEL OF ARBITRATORS MIGHT INCLUDE AN ARBITRATOR WHO IS OR WAS AFFILIATED WITH THE BANKING INDUSTRY.
6. ARBITRATION WILL APPLY TO ALL DISPUTES BETWEEN THE PARTIES, NOT JUST THOSE CONCERNING THE AGREEMENT.

7. IF YOU HAVE QUESTIONS ABOUT ARBITRATION, CONSULT YOUR ATTORNEY OR THE AMERICAN ARBITRATION ASSOCIATION.

(a) Any claim or controversy ("Dispute") between or among the parties and their employees, agents, affiliates, and assigns, including, but not limited to, Disputes arising out of or relating to this agreement, this arbitration provision ("arbitration clause"), or any related agreements or instruments relating hereto or delivered in connection herewith ("Related Agreements"), and including, but not limited to, a Dispute based on or arising from an alleged tort, shall at the request of any party be resolved by binding arbitration in accordance with the applicable arbitration rules of the American Arbitration Association (the "Administrator"). The provisions of this arbitration clause shall survive any termination, amendment, or expiration of this agreement or Related Agreements. The provisions of this arbitration clause shall supersede any prior arbitration agreement between or among the parties.

(b) The arbitration proceedings shall be conducted in a city mutually agreed by the parties. Absent such an agreement, arbitration will be conducted in Los Angeles, California or such other place as may be determined by the Administrator. The Administrator and the arbitrator(s) shall have the authority to the extent practicable to take any action to require the arbitration proceeding to be completed and the arbitrators)' award issued within 150 days of the filing of the Dispute with the Administrator. The arbitrators) shall have the authority to impose sanctions on any party that fails to comply with time periods imposed by the Administrator or the arbitrators), including the sanction of summarily dismissing any Dispute or defense with prejudice. The arbitrators) shall have the authority to resolve any Dispute regarding the terms of this agreement, this arbitration clause, or Related Agreements, including any claim or controversy regarding the arbitrability of any Dispute. All limitations periods applicable to any Dispute or defense, whether by statute or agreement, shall apply to any arbitration proceeding hereunder and the arbitrator(s) shall have the authority to decide whether any Dispute or defense is barred by a limitations period and, if so, to summarily enter an award dismissing any Dispute or defense on that basis. The doctrines of compulsory counterclaim, res judicata, and collateral estoppel shall apply to any arbitration proceeding hereunder so that a party must state as a counterclaim in the arbitration proceeding any claim or controversy which arises out of the transaction or occurrence that is the subject matter of the Dispute. The arbitrator(s) may in the arbitrator(s)' discretion and at the request of any party: (1) consolidate in a single arbitration proceeding any other claim arising out of the same transaction involving another party to that transaction that is bound by an arbitration clause with Lender, such as borrowers, guarantors, sureties, and owners of collateral; and (2) consolidate or administer multiple arbitration claims or controversies as a class action in accordance with Rule 23 of the Federal Rules of Civil Procedure.

(c) The arbitrator(s) shall be selected in accordance with the rules of the Administrator from panels maintained by the Administrator. A single arbitrator shall have expertise in the subject matter of the Dispute. Where three arbitrators conduct an arbitration proceeding, the Dispute shall be decided by a majority vote of the three arbitrators, at least one of whom must have expertise in the subject matter of the Dispute and at least one of whom must be a practicing attorney. The arbitrator(s) shall award to the prevailing party recovery of all costs and fees (including attorneys' fees and costs, arbitration administration fees and costs, and arbitrator(s)' fees). The arbitrator(s), either during the pendency of the arbitration proceeding or as part of the arbitration award, also may grant provisional or ancillary remedies including but not limited to an award of injunctive relief, foreclosure, sequestration, attachment, replevin, garnishment, or the appointment of a receiver.

(d) Judgement upon an arbitration award may be entered in any court having jurisdiction, subject to the following limitation: the arbitration award is binding upon the parties only if the amount does not exceed Four Million Dollars ($4,000,000.00); if the award exceeds that limit, either party may demand the right to a court trial. Such a demand must be filed with the Administrator within thirty (30) days following the date of the arbitration award; if such a demand is not made with that time period, the amount of the arbitration award shall be binding. The computation of the total amount of an arbitration award shall include amounts awarded for attorneys' fees and costs, arbitration administration fees and costs, and arbitrator(s)' fees.

(e) No provision of this arbitration clause, nor the exercise of any rights hereunder, shall limit the right of any party to: (1) judicially or non-judicially foreclose against any real or personal property collateral or other security; (2) exercise self-help remedies, including but not limited to repossession and setoff rights; or (3) obtain from a court having jurisdiction thereover any provisional or ancillary remedies including but not limited to injunctive relief, foreclosure, sequestration, attachment, replevin, garnishment, or the appointment of a receiver. Such rights can be exercised at any time, before or after initiation of an arbitration proceeding, except to the extent such action is contrary to the arbitration award. The exercise of such rights shall not constitute a waiver of the right to submit any Dispute to arbitration, and any claim or controversy related to the exercise of such rights shall be a Dispute to be resolved under the provisions of this arbitration clause. Any party may initiate arbitration with the Administrator. If any party desires to arbitrate a Dispute asserted against such party in a complaint, counterclaim, cross-claim, or third-party complaint thereto, or in an answer or other reply to any such pleading, such party must make an appropriate motion to the trial court seeking to compel arbitration, which motion must be filed with the court within 45 days of service of the pleading, or amendment thereto, setting forth such Dispute. If arbitration is compelled after commencement of litigation of a Dispute, the party obtaining an order compelling arbitration shall commence arbitration and pay the Administrator's filing fees and costs within 45 days of entry of such order. Failure to do so shall constitute an agreement to proceed with litigation and waiver of the right to arbitrate. In any arbitration commenced by a consumer regarding a consumer Dispute, Lender shall pay one half of the Administrator's filing fee, up to $250.

(f) Notwithstanding the applicability of any other law to this agreement, the arbitration clause, or Related Agreements between or among the parties, the Federal Arbitration Act, 9 U.S.C. Section 1 et seq., shall apply to the construction and interpretation of this arbitration clause. If any provision of this arbitration clause should be determined to be unenforceable, all other provisions of this arbitration clause shall remain in full force and effect.

Caption Headings. Caption headings in this Assignment are for convenience purposes only and are not to be used to interpret or define the provisions of this Assignment.

Governing Law. With respect to procedural matters related to the perfection and enforcement of Lender's rights against the Property, this Assignment will be governed by federal law applicable to Lender and to the extent not preempted by federal law, the laws of the State of California. In all other respects, this Assignment will be governed by federal law applicable to Lender and, to the extent not preempted by federal law, the laws of the State of Utah without regard to its conflicts of law provisions. However, if there ever is a question about whether any provision of this Assignment is valid or enforceable, the provision that is questioned will be governed by whichever state or federal law would find the provision to be valid and enforceable. The loan transaction that is evidenced by the Note and this Assignment has been applied for, considered, approved and made, and all necessary loan documents have been accepted by Lender in the State of Utah.

Choice of Venue. If there is a lawsuit, Grantor agrees upon Lender's request to submit to the jurisdiction of the courts of SALT LAKE County, State of Utah.

Merger. There shall be no merger of the interest or estate created by this assignment with any other interest or estate in the Property at any time held by or for the benefit of Lender in any capacity, without the written consent of Lender.

Interpretation. (1) In all cases where there is more than one Borrower or Grantor, then all words used in this Assignment in the singular shall be deemed to have been used in the plural where the context and construction so require. (2) If more than one person signs this Assignment as "Grantor," the obligations of each Grantor are joint and several. This means that if Lender brings a lawsuit, Lender may sue any one or more of the Grantors. If Borrower and Grantor are not the same person, Lender need not sue Borrower first, and that Borrower need not be joined in any lawsuit. (3) The names given to paragraphs or sections in this Assignment are for convenience purposes only. They are not to be used to interpret or define the provisions of this Assignment.

No Waiver by Lender. Lender shall not be deemed to have waived any rights under this Assignment unless such waiver is given in writing and signed by Lender. No delay or omission on the part of Lender in exercising any right shall operate as a waiver of such right or any other right. A waiver by Lender of a provision of this Assignment shall not prejudice or constitute a waiver of Lender's right otherwise to demand strict compliance with that provision or any other provision of this Assignment. No prior waiver by Lender, nor any course of dealing between Lender and Grantor, shall constitute a waiver of any of Lender's rights or of any of Grantor's obligations as to any future transactions. Whenever the consent of Lender is required under this Assignment, the granting of such consent by Lender in any instance shall not constitute continuing consent to subsequent instances where such consent is required and in all cases such consent may be granted or withheld in the sole discretion of Lender.

Notices. Any notice required to be given under this Assignment shall be given in writing, and shall be effective when actually delivered, when actually received by telefacsimile (unless otherwise required by law), when deposited with a nationally recognized overnight courier, or, if mailed, when deposited in the United States mail, as first class, certified or registered mail postage prepaid, directed to the addresses shown near the beginning of this Assignment. Any party may change its address for notices under this Assignment by giving formal written notice to the other parties, specifying that the purpose of the notice is to change the party's address. For notice purposes, Grantor agrees to keep Lender informed at all times of Grantor's current address. Unless otherwise provided or required by law, if there is more than one Grantor, any notice given by Lender to any Grantor is deemed to be notice given to all Grantors.

Powers of Attorney. The various agencies and powers of attorney conveyed on Lender under this Assignment are granted for purposes of security and may not be revoked by Grantor until such time as the same are renounced by Lender.

Severability. If a court of competent jurisdiction finds any provision of this Assignment to be illegal, invalid, or unenforceable as to any circumstance, that finding shall not make the offending provision illegal, invalid, or unenforceable as to any other circumstance. If feasible, the offending provision shall be considered modified so that it becomes legal, valid and enforceable. If the offending provision cannot be so modified, it shall be considered deleted from this Assignment. Unless otherwise required by law, the illegality, invalidity, or unenforceability of any provision of this Assignment shall not affect the legality, validity or enforceability of any other provision of this Assignment.

Successors and Assigns. Subject to any limitations stated in this Assignment on transfer of Grantor's interest, this Assignment shall be binding upon and inure to the benefit of the parties, their successors and assigns. If ownership of the Property becomes vested in a person other than Grantor, Lender, without notice to Grantor, may deal with Grantor's successors with reference to this Assignment and the Indebtedness by way of forbearance or extension without releasing Grantor from the obligations of this Assignment or liability under the Indebtedness.

Time is of the Essence. Time is of the essence in the performance of this Assignment.

WAIVER OF RIGHT OF REDEMPTION. NOTWITHSTANDING ANY OF THE PROVISIONS TO THE CONTRARY CONTAINED IN THIS ASSIGNMENT, GRANTOR HEREBY WAIVES ANY AND ALL RIGHTS OF REDEMPTION FROM SALE UNDER ANY ORDER OR JUDGMENT OF FORECLOSURE ON GRANTOR'S BEHALF AND ON BEHALF OF EACH AND EVERY PERSON, EXCEPT JUDGMENT CREDITORS OF GRANTOR, ACQUIRING ANY INTEREST IN OR TITLE TO THE PROPERTY SUBSEQUENT TO THE DATE OF THIS ASSIGNMENT.

DEFINITIONS. The following capitalized words and terms shall have the following meanings when used in this Assignment. Unless specifically stated to the contrary, all references to dollar amounts shall mean amounts in lawful money of the United States of America. Words and terms used in the singular shall include the plural, and the plural shall include the singular, as the context may require. Words and terms not otherwise defined in this Assignment shall have the meanings attributed to such terms in the Uniform Commercial Code:

Assignment. The word "Assignment" means this ASSIGNMENT OF RENTS, as this ASSIGNMENT OF RENTS may be amended or modified from time to time, together with all exhibits and schedules attached to this ASSIGNMENT OF RENTS from time to time.

Borrower. The word "Borrower" means DELKIM COMPANY, INC..

Default. The word "Default" means the Default set forth in this Assignment in the section titled "Default". Event of Default. The words "Event of Default" mean any of the events of default set forth in this Assignment in the default section of this Assignment.

Grantor. The word "Grantor" means DELKIM COMPANY, INC.

Guarantor. The word "Guarantor" means any guarantor, surety, or accommodation party of any or all of the Indebtedness.

Guaranty. The word "Guaranty" means the guaranty from Guarantor to Lender, including without limitation a guaranty of all or part of the Note.

Indebtedness. The word "Indebtedness" means and includes without limitation all Loans, together with all other obligations, debts and liabilities of Borrower to Lender, or any one or more of them, as well as all claims by Lender against Borrower, or any one or more of them; whether now or hereafter existing, voluntary or involuntary, due or not due, absolute or contingent, liquidated or unliquidated; whether Borrower may be liable individually or jointly with others; whether Borrower may be obligated as a guarantor, surety, or otherwise; whether recovery upon such indebtedness may be or hereafter may become barred by any statute of limitations; and whether such indebtedness may be or hereafter may become otherwise unenforceable.

Lender. The word "Lender" means FIRST NATIONAL BANK, its successors and assigns.

Note. The word "Note" means the promissory note dated February 16, 20XX, in the original principal amount of $400,000.00 from Grantor to Lender, together with all renewals of, extensions of, modifications of, refinancings of, consolidations of, and substitutions for the promissory note or agreement.

Property. The word "Property" means all of Grantor's right, title and interest in and to all the Property as described in the "Assignment" section of this Assignment.

Related Documents. The words "Related Documents" mean all promissory notes, credit agreements, loan agreements, environmental agreements, security agreements, mortgages, deeds of trust, security deeds, collateral mortgages, and all other instruments, agreements and documents, whether now or hereafter existing, executed in connection with the Indebtedness.

Rents. The word "Rents" means all of Grantor's present and future rights, title and interest in, to and under any and all present and future leases, including, without limitation, all rents, revenue, income, issues, royalties, bonuses, accounts receivable, cash or security deposits, advance rentals, profits and proceeds from the Property, and other payments and benefits derived or to be derived from such leases of every kind and nature, whether due now or later, including without limitation Grantor's right to enforce such leases and to receive and collect payment and proceeds thereunder.

THE UNDERSIGNED ACKNOWLEDGES HAVING READ ALL THE PROVISIONS OF THIS ASSIGNMENT, AND NOT PERSONALLY BUT AS AN AUTHORIZED SIGNER, HAS CAUSED THIS ASSIGNMENT TO BE SIGNED AND EXECUTED ON BEHALF OF GRANTOR ON FEBRUARY 16, 20XX.

GRANTOR: DELKIM COMPANY, INC.

By: _____

JUAN HAN, President of DELKIM COMPANY, INC.

By: _____

SUNNY HAN, Secretary of DELKIM COMPANY, INC.

CERTIFICATE OF ACKNOWLEDGMENT

STATE OF _____   )
) SS

COUNTY OF _____   )

On _____, 20_____ before me, _____,

personally appeared **JUAN HAN**, personally known to me (or proved to me on the basis of satisfactory evidence) to be the person(s) whose name(s) is/are subscribed to the within instrument and acknowledged to me that he/she/they executed the same in his/her/their authorized capacity(ies), and that by his/her/their signature(s) on the instrument the person(s), or the entity upon behalf of which the person(s) acted, executed the instrument.

WITNESS my hand and official seal.

Signature _____   **(Seal)**

ASSIGNMENT OF RENTS
(Continued)

CERTIFICATE OF ACKNOWLEDGMENT

STATE OF _____)
) SS
COUNTY OF _____)

On _____, 20_____ before me, _____,
personally appeared **SUNNY HAN,** personally known to me (or proved to me on the basis of satisfactory evidence) to be the person(s) whose name(s) is/are subscribed to the within instrument and acknowledged to me that he/she/they executed the same in his/her/their authorized capacity(ies), and that by his/her/their signature(s) on the instrument the person(s), or the entity upon behalf of which the person(s) acted, executed the instrument.

WITNESS my hand and official seal.

Signature _____   **(Seal)**

BUSINESS LOAN AGREEMENT

Principal	Loan Date	Maturity	Loan No	Call/Coll	Account	Officer	Initials
$400,000.00	02-16-20XX	03-01-20XX	9001	1C / 6520	0524840	***	

References in the shaded area are for Lender's use only and do not limit the applicability of this document to any particular loan or item.
Any item above containing "***" has been omitted due to text length limitations.

Borrower: DELKIM COMPANY, INC 10855 SAN PALO AVENUE EL CERRITO, CA 94550	Lender: FIRST NATIONAL BANK REAL ESTATE DEPARTMENT ONE MAIN STREET SALT LAKE CITY, UT 84155

THIS BUSINESS LOAN AGREEMENT dated February 16, 20XX, is made and executed between DELKIM COMPANY, INC. ("Borrower") and FIRST NATIONAL BANK ("Lender") on the following terms and conditions. Borrower has received prior commercial loans from Lender or has applied to Lender for a commercial loan or loans or other financial accommodations, including those which may be described on any exhibit or schedule attached to this Agreement ("Loan"). Borrower understands and agrees that: (A) in granting, renewing, or extending any Loan, Lender is relying upon Borrower's representations, warranties, and agreements as set forth in this Agreement; (B) the granting, renewing, or extending of any Loan by Lender at all times shall be subject to Lender's sole judgment and discretion; and (C) all such Loans shall be and remain subject to the terms and conditions of this Agreement.

TERM. This Agreement shall be effective as of February 16, 20XX, and shall continue in full force and effect until such time as all of Borrower's Loans in favor of Lender have been paid in full, including principal, interest, costs, expenses, attorneys' fees, and other fees and charges, or until March 1, 20XX.

CONDITIONS PRECEDENT TO EACH ADVANCE. Lender's obligation to make the initial Advance and each subsequent Advance under this Agreement shall be subject to the fulfillment to Lender's satisfaction of all of the conditions set forth in this Agreement and in the Related Documents.

Loan Documents. Borrower shall provide to Lender the following documents for the Loan: (1) the Note; (2) Security Agreements granting to Lender security interests in the Collateral; (3) financing statements and all other documents perfecting Lender's Security Interests; (4) evidence of insurance as required below; (5) guaranties; (6) together with all such Related Documents as Lender may require for the Loan; all in form and substance satisfactory to Lender and Lender's counsel.

Borrower's Authorization. Borrower shall have provided in form and substance satisfactory to Lender properly certified resolutions, duly authorizing the execution and delivery of this Agreement, the Note and the Related Documents. In addition, Borrower shall have provided such other resolutions, authorizations, documents and instruments as Lender or its counsel, may require.

Payment of Fees and Expenses. Borrower shall have paid to Lender all fees, charges, and other expenses which are then due and payable as specified in this Agreement or any Related Document.

Representations and Warranties. The representations and warranties set forth in this Agreement, in the Related Documents, and in any document or certificate delivered to Lender under this Agreement are true and correct. No Event of Default. There shall not exist at the time of any Advance a condition which would constitute an Event of Default under this Agreement or under any Related Document.

REPRESENTATIONS AND WARRANTIES. Borrower represents and warrants to Lender, as of the date of this Agreement, as of the date of each disbursement of loan proceeds, as of the date of any renewal, extension or modification of any Loan, and at all times any Indebtedness exists:

Organization. Borrower is a corporation for profit which is, and at all times shall be, duly organized, validly existing, and in good standing under and by virtue of the laws of the State of California. Borrower is duly authorized to transact business in all other states in which Borrower is doing business, having obtained all necessary filings, governmental licenses and approvals for each state in which Borrower is doing business. Specifically, Borrower is, and at all times shall be, duly qualified as a foreign corporation in all states in which the failure to so qualify would have a material adverse effect on its business or financial condition. Borrower has the full power and authority to own its properties and to transact the business in which it is presently engaged or presently proposes to engage. Borrower maintains an office at 10869 SAN PALO AVENUE, EL CERRITO, CA 94550. Unless Borrower has designated otherwise in writing, the principal office is the office at which Borrower keeps its books and records including its records concerning the Collateral. Borrower will notify Lender prior to any change in the location of Borrower's state of organization or any change in Borrower's name. Borrower shall do all things necessary to preserve and to keep in full force and effect its existence, rights and privileges, and shall comply with all regulations, rules, ordinances, statutes, orders and decrees of any governmental or quasi-governmental authority or court applicable to Borrower and Borrower's business activities.

Assumed Business Names. Borrower has filed or recorded all documents or filings required by law relating to all assumed business names used by Borrower. Excluding the name of Borrower, the following is a complete list of all assumed business names under which Borrower does business:

Borrower	Assumed Business Name	Filing Location	Date
DELKIM COMPANY, INC.	TERRACE MOTEL & APARTMENTS		

Authorization. Borrower's execution, delivery, and performance of this Agreement and all the Related Documents have been duly authorized by all necessary action by Borrower and do not conflict with, result in a violation of, or constitute a default under (1) any provision of (a) Borrower's articles of incorporation or organization, or bylaws, or (b) any agreement or other instrument binding upon Borrower or (2) any law, governmental regulation, court decree, or order applicable to Borrower or to Borrower's properties.

Financial Information. Each of Borrower's financial statements supplied to Lender truly and completely disclosed Borrower's financial condition as of the date of the statement, and there has been no material adverse change in Borrower's financial condition subsequent to the date of the most recent financial statement supplied to Lender. Borrower has no material contingent obligations except as disclosed in such financial statements.

Legal Effect. This Agreement constitutes, and any instrument or agreement Borrower is required to give under this Agreement when delivered will constitute legal, valid, and binding obligations of Borrower enforceable against Borrower in accordance with their respective terms.

Properties. Except as contemplated by this Agreement or as previously disclosed in Borrower's financial statements or in writing to Lender and as accepted by Lender, and except for property tax liens for taxes not presently due and payable, Borrower owns and has good title to all of Borrower's properties free and clear of all Security Interests, and has not executed any security documents or financing statements relating to such properties. All of Borrower's properties are titled in Borrower's legal name, and Borrower has not used or filed a financing statement under any other name for at least the last five (5) years.

Hazardous Substances. Except as disclosed to and acknowledged by Lender in writing, Borrower represents and warrants that: (1) During the period of Borrower's ownership of the Collateral, there has been no use, generation, manufacture, storage, treatment, disposal, release or threatened release of any Hazardous Substance by any person on, under, about or from any of the Collateral. (2) Borrower has no knowledge of, or reason to believe that there has been (a) any breach or violation of any Environmental Laws; (b) any use, generation, manufacture, storage, treatment, disposal, release or threatened release of any Hazardous Substance on, under, about or from the Collateral by any prior owners or occupants of any of the Collateral; or (c) any actual or threatened litigation or claims of any kind by any person relating to such matters. (3) Neither Borrower nor any tenant, contractor, agent or other authorized user of any of the Collateral shall use, generate, manufacture, store, treat, dispose of or release any Hazardous Substance on, under, about or from any of the Collateral; and any such activity shall be conducted in compliance with all applicable federal, state, and local laws, regulations, and ordinances, including without limitation all Environmental Laws. Borrower authorizes Lender and its agents to enter upon the Collateral to make such inspections and tests as Lender may deem appropriate to determine compliance of the Collateral with this section of the Agreement. Any inspections or tests made by Lender shall be at Borrower's expense and for Lender's purposes only and shall not be construed to create any responsibility or liability on the part of Lender to Borrower or to any other person. The representations and warranties contained herein are based on Borrower's due diligence in investigating the Collateral for hazardous waste and Hazardous Substances. Borrower hereby (1) releases and waives any future claims against Lender for indemnity or contribution in the event Borrower becomes liable for cleanup or other costs under any such laws, and (2) agrees to indemnify and hold harmless Lender against any and all claims, losses, liabilities, damages, penalties, and expenses which Lender may directly or indirectly sustain or suffer resulting from a breach of this section of the Agreement or as a consequence of any use, generation, manufacture, storage, disposal, release or threatened release of a hazardous waste or substance on the Collateral. The provisions of this section of the Agreement, including the obligation to indemnify, shall survive the payment of the Indebtedness and the termination, expiration or satisfaction of this Agreement and shall not be affected by Lender's acquisition of any interest in any of the Collateral, whether by foreclosure or otherwise.

Litigation and Claims. No litigation, claim, investigation, administrative proceeding or similar action (including those for unpaid taxes) against Borrower is pending or threatened, and no other event has occurred which may materially affect Borrower's financial condition or properties, other than litigation, claims, or other events, if any, that have been disclosed to and acknowledged by Lender in writing.

Taxes. To the best of Borrower's knowledge, all of Borrower's tax returns and reports that are or were required to be filed, have been filed, and all taxes, assessments and other governmental charges have been paid in full, except those presently being or to be contested by Borrower in good faith in the ordinary course of business and for which adequate reserves have been provided.

Lien Priority. Unless otherwise previously disclosed to Lender in writing, Borrower has not entered into or granted any Security Agreements, or permitted the filing or attachment of any Security Interests on or affecting any of the Collateral directly or indirectly securing repayment of Borrower's Loan and Note, that would be prior or that may in any way be superior to Lender's Security Interests and rights in and to such Collateral.

Binding Effect. This Agreement, the Note, all Security Agreements (if any), and all Related Documents are binding upon the signers thereof, as well as upon their successors, representatives and assigns, and are legally enforceable in accordance with their respective terms.

AFFIRMATIVE COVENANTS. Borrower covenants and agrees with Lender that, so long as this Agreement remains in effect, Borrower will:

Notices of Claims and Litigation. Promptly inform Lender in writing of (1) all material adverse changes in Borrower's financial condition, and (2) all existing and all threatened litigation, claims, investigations, administrative proceedings or similar actions affecting Borrower or any Guarantor which could materially affect the financial condition of Borrower or the financial condition of any Guarantor.

Financial Records. Maintain its books and records in accordance with GAAP, applied on a consistent basis, and permit Lender to examine and audit Borrower's books and records at all reasonable times.

Financial Statements. Furnish Lender with such financial statements and other related information at such frequencies and in such detail as Lender may reasonably request.

Additional Information. Furnish such additional information and statements, as Lender may request from time to time.

Insurance. Maintain fire and other risk insurance, public liability insurance, and such other insurance as Lender may require with respect to Borrower's properties and operations, in form, amounts, coverages and with insurance companies acceptable to Lender. Borrower, upon request of Lender, will deliver to Lender from time to time the policies or certificates of insurance in form satisfactory to Lender, including stipulations that coverages will not be cancelled or diminished without at least ten (10) days prior written notice to Lender. Each insurance policy also shall include an endorsement providing that coverage in favor of Lender will not be impaired in any way by any act, omission or default of Borrower or any other person. In connection with all policies covering assets in which Lender holds or is offered a security interest for the Loans, Borrower will provide Lender with such lender's loss payable or other endorsements as Lender may require.

Insurance Reports. Furnish to Lender, upon request of Lender, reports on each existing insurance policy showing such information as Lender may reasonably request, including without limitation the following: (1) the name of the insurer; (2) the risks insured; (3) the amount of the policy; (4) the properties insured; (5) the then current property values on the basis of which insurance has been obtained, and the manner of determining those values; and (6) the expiration date of the policy. In addition, upon request of Lender (however not more often than annually), Borrower will have an independent appraiser satisfactory to Lender determine, as applicable, the actual cash value or replacement cost of any Collateral. The cost of such appraisal shall be paid by Borrower.

Guaranties. Prior to disbursement of any Loan proceeds, furnish executed guaranties of the Loans in favor of Lender, executed by the guarantors named below, on Lender's forms, and in the amounts and under the conditions set forth in those guaranties.

Names of Guarantors	Amounts
Juan Han	$400,000
Sunny Han	$400,000

Other Agreements. Comply with all terms and conditions of all other agreements, whether now or hereafter existing, between Borrower and any other party and notify Lender immediately in writing of any default in connection with any other such agreements.

Loan Proceeds. Use all Loan proceeds solely for Borrower's business operations, unless specifically consented to the contrary by Lender in writing.

Taxes, Charges and Liens. Pay and discharge when due all of its indebtedness and obligations, including without limitation all assessments, taxes, governmental charges, levies and liens, of every kind and nature, imposed upon Borrower or its properties, income, or profits, prior to the date on which penalties would attach, and all lawful claims that, if unpaid, might become a lien or charge upon any of Borrower's properties, income, or profits.

Performance. Perform and comply, in a timely manner, with all terms, conditions, and provisions set forth in this Agreement, in the Related Documents, and in all other instruments and agreements between Borrower and Lender. Borrower shall notify Lender immediately in writing of any default in connection with any agreement.

Operations. Maintain executive and management personnel with substantially the same qualifications and experience as the present executive and management personnel; provide written notice to Lender of any change in executive and management personnel; conduct its business affairs in a reasonable and prudent manner.

Environmental Studies. Promptly conduct and complete, at Borrower's expense, all such investigations, studies, samplings and testings as may be requested by Lender or any governmental authority relative to any substance, or any waste or by-product of any substance defined as toxic or a hazardous substance under applicable federal, state, or local law, rule, regulation, order or directive, at or affecting any property or any facility owned, leased or used by Borrower.

Compliance with Governmental Requirements. Comply with all laws, ordinances, and regulations, now or hereafter in effect, of all governmental authorities applicable to the conduct of Borrower's properties, businesses and operations, and to the use or occupancy of the Collateral, including without limitation, the Americans With Disabilities Act. Borrower may contest in good faith any such law, ordinance, or regulation and withhold compliance during any proceeding, including appropriate appeals, so long as Borrower has notified Lender in writing prior to doing so and so long as, in Lender's sole opinion, Lender's interests in the Collateral are not jeopardized. Lender may require Borrower to post adequate security or a surety bond, reasonably satisfactory to Lender, to protect Lender's interest.

Inspection. Permit employees or agents of Lender at any reasonable time to inspect any and all Collateral for the Loan or Loans and Borrower's other properties and to examine or audit Borrower's books, accounts, and records and to make copies and memoranda of Borrower's books, accounts, and records. If Borrower now or at any time hereafter maintains any records (including without limitation computer generated records and computer software programs for the generation of such records) in the possession of a third party, Borrower, upon request of Lender, shall notify such party to permit Lender free access to such records at all reasonable times and to provide Lender with copies of any records it may request, all at Borrower's expense.

Environmental Compliance and Reports. Borrower shall comply in all respects with any and all Environmental Laws; not cause or permit to exist, as a result of an intentional or unintentional action or omission on Borrower's part or on the part of any third party, on property owned and/or occupied by Borrower, any environmental activity where damage may result to the environment, unless such environmental activity is pursuant to and in compliance with the conditions of a permit issued by the appropriate federal, state or local governmental authorities; shall furnish to Lender promptly and in any event within thirty (30) days after receipt thereof a copy of any notice, summons, lien, citation, directive, letter or other communication from any governmental agency or instrumentality concerning any intentional or unintentional action or omission on Borrower's part in connection with any environmental activity whether or not there is damage to the environment and/or other natural resources.

Additional Assurances. Make, execute and deliver to Lender such promissory notes, mortgages, deeds of trust, security agreements, assignments, financing statements, instruments, documents and other agreements as Lender or its attorneys may reasonably request to evidence and secure the Loans and to perfect all Security Interests.

LENDER'S EXPENDITURES. If any action or proceeding is commenced that would materially affect Lender's interest in the Collateral or if Borrower fails to comply with any provision of this Agreement or any Related Documents, including but not limited to Borrower's failure to discharge or pay when due any amounts Borrower is required to discharge or pay under this Agreement or any Related Documents, Lender on Borrower's behalf may (but shall not be obligated to) take any action that Lender deems appropriate, including but not limited to discharging or paying all taxes, liens, security interests, encumbrances and other claims, at any time levied or placed on any Collateral and paying all costs for insuring, maintaining and preserving any Collateral. All such expenditures incurred or paid by Lender for such purposes will then bear interest at the rate charged under the Note from the date incurred or paid by Lender to the date of repayment by Borrower. All such expenses will become a part of the Indebtedness and, at Lender's option, will (A) be payable on demand; (B) be added to the balance of the Note and be apportioned among and be payable with any installment payments to become due during either (1) the term of any applicable insurance policy; or (2) the remaining term of the Note; or (C) be treated as a balloon payment which will be due and payable at the Note's maturity.

NEGATIVE COVENANTS. Borrower covenants and agrees with Lender that while this Agreement is in effect, Borrower shall not, without the prior written consent of Lender:

Indebtedness and Liens. (1) Except for trade debt incurred in the normal course of business and indebtedness to Lender contemplated by this Agreement, create, incur or assume indebtedness for borrowed money, including capital leases, (2) sell, transfer, mortgage, assign, pledge, lease, grant a security interest in, or encumber any of Borrower's assets (except as allowed as Permitted Liens), or (3) sell with recourse any of Borrower's accounts, except to Lender.

Continuity of Operations. (1) Engage in any business activities substantially different than those in which Borrower is presently engaged, (2) cease operations, liquidate, merge, transfer, acquire or consolidate with any other entity, change its name, dissolve or transfer or sell Collateral out of the ordinary course of business, or (3) pay any dividends on Borrower's stock (other than dividends payable in its stock), provided, however that notwithstanding the foregoing, but only so long as no Event of Default has occurred and is continuing or would result from the payment of dividends, if Borrower is a "Subchapter S Corporation" (as defined in the Internal Revenue Code of 1986, as amended), Borrower may pay cash dividends on its stock to its shareholders from time to time in amounts necessary to enable the shareholders to pay income taxes and make estimated income tax payments to satisfy their liabilities under federal and state law which arise solely from their status as Shareholders of a Subchapter S Corporation because of their ownership of shares of Borrower's stock, or purchase or retire any of Borrower's outstanding shares or alter or amend Borrower's capital structure.

Loans, Acquisitions and Guaranties. (1) Loan, invest in or advance money or assets to any other person, enterprise or entity, (2) purchase, create or acquire any interest in any other enterprise or entity, or (3) incur any obligation as surety or guarantor other than in the ordinary course of business-

Agreements. Borrower will not enter into any agreement containing any provisions which would be violated or breached by the performance of Borrower's obligations under this Agreement or in connection herewith.

CESSATION OF ADVANCES. If Lender has made any commitment to make any Loan to Borrower, whether under this Agreement or under any other agreement, Lender shall have no obligation to make Loan Advances or to disburse Loan proceeds if: (A) Borrower or any Guarantor is in default under the terms of this Agreement or any of the Related Documents or any other agreement that Borrower or any Guarantor has with Lender; (B) Borrower or any Guarantor dies, becomes incompetent or becomes insolvent, files a petition in bankruptcy or similar proceedings, or is adjudged a bankrupt; (C) there occurs a material adverse change in Borrower's financial condition, in the financial condition of any Guarantor, or in the value of any Collateral securing any Loan; or (D) any Guarantor seeks, claims or otherwise attempts to limit, modify or revoke such Guarantor's guaranty of the Loan or any other loan with Lender; or (E) Lender in good faith deems itself insecure, even though no Event of Default shall have occurred.

RIGHT OF SETOFF. To the extent permitted by applicable law, Lender reserves a right of setoff in all Borrower's accounts with Lender (whether checking, savings, or some other account). This includes all accounts Borrower holds jointly with someone else and all accounts Borrower may open in the future. However, this does not include any IRA or Keogh accounts, or any trust accounts for which setoff would be prohibited by law. Borrower authorizes Lender, to the extent permitted by applicable law, to charge or setoff all sums owing on the Indebtedness against any and all such accounts, and, at Lender's option, to administratively freeze all such accounts to allow Lender to protect Lender's charge and setoff rights provided in this paragraph.

DEFAULT. Each of the following shall constitute an Event of Default under this Agreement;

Payment Default. Borrower fails to make any payment when due under the Loan.

Other Defaults. Borrower fails to comply with or to perform any other term, obligation, covenant or condition contained in this Agreement or in any of the Related Documents or to comply with or to perform any term, obligation, covenant or condition contained in any other agreement between Lender and Borrower.

Default in Favor of Third Parties. Borrower or any Grantor defaults under any loan, extension of credit, security agreement, purchase or sales agreement, or any other agreement, in favor of any other creditor or person that may materially affect any of Borrower's or any Grantor's property or Borrower's or any Grantor's ability to repay the Loans or perform their respective obligations under this Agreement or any of the Related Documents.

False Statements. Any warranty, representation or statement made or furnished to Lender by Borrower or on Borrower's behalf under this Agreement or the Related Documents is false or misleading in any material respect, either now or at the time made or furnished or becomes false or misleading at any time thereafter.

Insolvency. The dissolution or termination of Borrower's existence as a going business, the insolvency of Borrower, the appointment of a receiver for any part of Borrower's property, any assignment for the benefit of creditors, any type of creditor workout, or the commencement of any proceeding under any bankruptcy or insolvency laws by or against Borrower.

Defective Collateralization. This Agreement or any of the Related Documents ceases to be in full force and effect (including failure of any collateral document to create a valid and perfected security interest or lien) at any time and for any reason.

Creditor or Forfeiture Proceedings. Commencement of foreclosure or forfeiture proceedings, whether by judicial proceeding, self-help, repossession or any other method, by any creditor of Borrower or by any governmental agency against any collateral securing the Loan. This includes a garnishment of any of Borrower's accounts, including deposit accounts, with Lender. However, this Event of Default shall not apply if there is a good faith dispute by Borrower as to the validity or reasonableness of the claim which is the basis of the creditor or forfeiture proceeding and if Borrower gives Lender written notice of the creditor or forfeiture proceeding and deposits with Lender monies or a surety bond for the creditor or forfeiture proceeding, in an amount determined by Lender, in its sole discretion, as being an adequate reserve or bond for the dispute.

Events Affecting Guarantor. Any of the preceding events occurs with respect to any Guarantor of any of the Indebtedness or any Guarantor dies or becomes incompetent, or revokes or disputes the validity of, or liability under, any Guaranty of the Indebtedness. In the event of a death, Lender, at its option, may, but shall not be required to, permit the Guarantor's estate to assume unconditionally the obligations arising under the guaranty in a manner satisfactory to Lender, and, in doing so, cure any Event of Default.

Change in Ownership. Any change in ownership of twenty-five percent (25%) or more of the common stock of Borrower.

Adverse Change. A material adverse change occurs in Borrower's financial condition, or Lender believes the prospect of payment or performance of the Loan is impaired. Insecurity. Lender in good faith believes itself insecure. Right to Cure. If any default, other than a default on Indebtedness, is curable and if Borrower or Grantor, as the case may be, has not been given a notice of a similar default within the preceding twelve (12) months, it may be cured if Borrower or Grantor, as the case may be, after receiving written notice from Lender demanding cure of such default: (1) cure the default within fifteen (15) days; or (2) if the cure requires more than fifteen (15) days, immediately initiate steps which Lender deems in Lender's sole discretion to be sufficient to cure the default and thereafter continue and complete all reasonable and necessary steps sufficient to produce compliance as soon as reasonably practical.

EFFECT OF AN EVENT OF DEFAULT. If any Event of Default shall occur, except where otherwise provided in this Agreement or the Related Documents, all commitments and obligations of Lender under this Agreement or the Related Documents or any other agreement immediately will terminate (including any obligation to make further Loan Advances or disbursements), and, at Lender's option, all Indebtedness immediately will become due and payable, all without notice of any kind to Borrower, except that in the case of an Event of Default of the type described in the "Insolvency" subsection above, such acceleration shall be automatic and not optional. In addition, Lender shall have all the rights and remedies provided in the Related Documents or available at law, in equity, or otherwise. Except as may be prohibited by applicable law, all of Lender's rights and remedies shall be cumulative and may be exercised singularly or concurrently. Election by Lender to pursue any remedy shall not exclude pursuit of any other remedy, and an election to make expenditures or to take action to perform an obligation of Borrower or of any Grantor shall not affect Lender's right to declare a default and to exercise its rights and remedies.

FINANCIAL STATEMENT. BORROWER AND GUARANTORS COVENANTS AND AGREES WITH LENDER THAT, WHILE THIS AGREEMENT IS IN EFFECT, THEY WILL FURNISH LENDER WITH, UPON REQUEST, THEIR BUSINESS AND PERSONAL FINANCIAL STATEMENTS.

TAX RETURNS. BORROWER AND ALL GUARANTORS SHALL PROVIDE LENDER ON AN ANNUAL BASIS A COPY OF THEIR FEDERAL TAX RETURNS WITHIN 30 DAYS OF FILING.

CASH FLOW COVERAGE. BORROWER SHALL MAINTAIN A RATIO OF ANNUAL NET OPERATING INCOME BEFORE INCOME TAXES, DEPRECIATION AND AMORTIZATION EXPENSE AND INTEREST EXPENSE, LESS 3% OF GROSS ROOM REVENUES AS AN EXPENSE FOR REPLACEMENT RESERVE, (THE "NUMERATOR") GREATER THAN OR EQUAL TO 1.25 TIMES AGGREGATE ANNUAL DEBT SERVICE INCLUDING ZIONS AND ALL LOAN PAYMENTS

ON THE SUBJECT BUILDING (THE "DENOMINATOR"). MEASURED ANNUALLY BASED UPON BORROWER'S FISCAL YEAR END FINANCIAL STATEMENT. MONITORING TO BEGIN DECEMBER 31, 2005.

ENVIRONMENTAL REPRESENTATIONS AND WARRANTIES. BORROWER REPRESENTS AND WARRANTS THAT, EXCEPT AS LENDER HAS OTHERWISE PREVIOUSLY BEEN ADVISED BY BORROWER THROUGH THE ENVIRONMENTAL SENSITIVITY QUESTIONNAIRE, NO HAZARDOUS MATERIALS ARE NOW LOCATED ON, IN OR UNDER THE PROPERTY, NOR IS THERE ANY ENVIRONMENTAL CONDITION ON, IN OR UNDER THE PROPERTY AND NEITHER BORROWER NOR, TO BORROWER'S KNOWLEDGE, AFTER DUE INQUIRY AND INVESTIGATION, ANY OTHER PERSON HAS EVER CAUSED OR PERMITTED ANY HAZARDOUS MATERIALS TO BE PLACED, HELD, USED, STORED, RELEASED, GENERATED, LOCATED OR DISPOSED OF ON, IN OR UNDER THE PROPERTY, OR ANY PART THEREOF, NOR CAUSED OR ALLOWED AN ENVIRONMENTAL CONDITION TO EXIST ON, IN OR UNDER THE PROPERTY. BORROWER FURTHER REPRESENTS AND WARRANTS THAT NO INVESTIGATION, ADMINISTRATIVE ORDER, CONSENT ORDER AND AGREEMENT, LITIGATION, OR SETTLEMENT WITH RESPECT TO HAZARDOUS MATERIALS IS PROPOSED, THREATENED, ANTICIPATED, OR IN EXISTENCE WITH RESPECT TO THE PROPERTY.

HAZARDOUS MATERIALS. BORROWER SHALL NOT PERMIT THE PRESENCE, USE, DISPOSAL, STORAGE OR RELEASE OF ANY HAZARDOUS MATERIALS ON, IN OR UNDER THE PROPERTY, EXCEPT IN THE ORDINARY COURSE OF BORROWER'S BUSINESS UNDER CONDITIONS THAT ARE GENERALLY RECOGNIZED TO BE APPROPRIATE AND SAFE AND THAT ARE IN STRICT COMPLIANCE WITH ALL APPLICABLE ENVIRONMENTAL HEALTH AND SAFETY LAWS.

ENVIRONMENTAL INDEMNIFICATION. BORROWER SHALL INDEMNIFY LENDER, ITS AFFILIATES AND ASSIGNS, FROM AND AGAINST ANY AND ALL CLAIMS, DEMANDS, ACTIONS, PROCEEDINGS. LOSSES, LIABILITIES, DAMAGES, COSTS, AND EXPENSES WHICH ARE OR MAY BE AWARDED OR INCURRED BY LENDER, AND FOR ALL REASONABLE ATTORNEY FEES, LEGAL EXPENSES, AND OTHER OUT-OF-POCKET EXPENSES ARISING FROM OR RELATED IN ANY MANNER, DIRECT OR INDIRECT, TO (1) HAZARDOUS MATERIALS LOCATED ON, IN OR UNDER THE PROPERTY; (2) ANY ENVIRONMENTAL CONDITION ON, IN OR UNDER THE PROPERTY; (3) ANY BREACH OR VIOLATION OF THIS AGREEMENT AND/OR (4) ANY ACTIVITY OR OMISSION, WHETHER OCCURING ON OR OFF THE PROPERTY, WHETHER PRIOR TO OR DURING THE TERM OF THE LOANS SECURED HEREBY, AND WHETHER BY BORROWER OR ANY OTHER PERSON OR ENTITY, RELATING TO HAZARDOUS MATERIALS OR ENVIRONMENTAL CONDITION AND THE PROPERTY. THE INDEMNIFICATION OBLIGATIONS OF BORROWER UNDER THIS AGREEMENT SHALL SURVIVE ANY RECONVEYANCE, RELEASE, OR FORECLOSUIRE OF THE PROPERTY, ANY TRANSFER IN LIEU OF FORECLOSURE, AND SATISFACTION OF THE OBLIGATIONS SECURED HEREBY. LENDER SHALL HAVE THE SOLE AND COMPLETE CONTROL OF THE DEFENSES OF ANY SUCH CLAIMS. LENDER IS HEREBY AUTHORIZED TO SETTLE OR OTHERWISE COMPROMISE ANY SUCH CLAIMS AS LENDER IN GOOD FAITH DETERMINES SHALL BE IN ITS BEST INTERESTS. NOTWITHSTANDING ANYTHING TO THE CONTRARY IN THIS LOAN AGREEMENT, THE PROMISSORY NOTES, THE SECURITY DOCUMENTS, OR ANY OTHER AGREEMENT, ANY INDEMNIFICATION AMOUNT OWING PURSUANT TO THIS AGREEMENT SHALL NOT BE SECURED BY ANY PROPERTY WHICH IS THE SUBJECT OF ANY BREACH OR VIOLATION OF THIS AGREEMENT.

FAILURE TO PROVIDE ACCEPTABLE FINANCIAL STATEMENTS AS REQUIRED. FURNISHING FINANCIAL INFORMATION: DURING THE TERM OF THE NOTE AND ANY EXTENSIONS OR RENEWALS THEREOF, BORROWER/GUARANTOR SHALL FURNISH AN ANNUAL FINANCIAL STATEMENT PREPARED IN A FORM ACCEPTABLE TO THE BANK, AS SOON AS PRACTICABLE BUT NO LATER THAN 120 DAYS AFTER BORROWER/GUARANTOR'S YEAR END AND SUCH INTERIM FINANCIAL STATEMENTS AND ALL OTHER INFORMATION AND MATERIAL AS BANK MAY FROM TIME TO TIME REQUEST. IF AN EVENT OF DEFAULT (AS DEFINED BELOW AND IN THE NOTE) SHALL HAVE OCCURED AND BY CONTINUING FOR WHICH THE BANK DOES NOT ACCELERATE THE INDEBTEDNESS EVIDENCED BY THE NOTE, WHICH EVENT OF DEFAULT CONSISTS OF THE FAILURE OF BORROWER/ GUARANTOR TO PROVIDE FINANCIAL STATEMENTS AND OTHER INFORMATION AS REQUIRED BY THE TERMS OF THIS AGREEMENT, THE INTEREST RATE APPLICABLE TO THE NOTE, FOR A PERIOD BEGINNING THREE (3) DAYS AFTER WRITTEN NOTICE OF SUCH EVENT, OF DEFAULT IS GIVEN AND ENDING UPON THE CURING OF SUCH DEFAULT, SHALL AT BANK'S OPTION, BE INCREASED BY ONE QUARTER OF ONE PERCENT (.25%) FOR THE FIRST 30-DAYS OF SAID EVENT OF DEFAULT AND BY AN ADDITIONAL ONE QUARTER OF ONE PERCENT (.25%) DURING EACH 30-DAY PERIOD THEREAFTER DURING WHICH SUCH EVENT OF DEFAULT CONTINUES. SUCH RATES SHALL APPLY TO THE ENTIRE OUTSTANDING PRINCIPAL BALANCE OF THE NOTE. UPON CURING SUCH EVENT OF DEFAULT, THE INTEREST RATE ON THE NOTE SHALL REVERT TO THE APPLICABLE RATE THEREUNDER EFFECTIVE AS OF THE DATE ON WHICH SAID EVENT OF DEFAULT IS CURED. BORROWER ACKNOWLEDGES THAT SUCH INCREASE INTEREST RATE IS INTENDED TO COMPENSATE BANK FOR THE POTENTIALLY HIGHER CREDIT RISK AND INCREASED ADMINISTRATIVE COSTS ASSOCIATED WITH BORROWER/GUARANTOR'S FAILURE TO FURNISH TIMELY FINANCIAL INFORMATION.

MISCELLANEOUS PROVISIONS. The following miscellaneous provisions are a part of this Agreement:

Amendments. This Agreement, together with any Related Documents, constitutes the entire understanding and agreement of the parties as to the matters set forth in this Agreement. No alteration of or amendment to this Agreement shall be effective unless given in writing and signed by the party or parties sought to be charged or bound by the alteration or amendment.

Arbitration Disclosures.

1. ARBITRATION IS FINAL AND BINDING ON THE PARTIES AND SUBJECT TO ONLY VERY LIMITED REVIEW BY A COURT.
2. IN ARBITRATION THE PARTIES ARE WAIVING THEIR RIGHT TO LITIGATE IN COURT, INCLUDING THEIR RIGHT TO A JURY TRIAL.
3. DISCOVERY IN ARBITRATION IS MORE LIMITED THAN DISCOVERY IN COURT.
4. ARBITRATORS ARE NOT REQUIRED TO INCLUDE FACTUAL FINDINGS OR LEGAL REASONING IN THEIR AWARDS. THE RIGHT TO APPEAL OR SEEK MODIFICATION OF ARBITRATORS' RULINGS IS VERY LIMITED.
5. A PANEL OF ARBITRATORS MIGHT INCLUDE AN ARBITRATOR WHO IS OR WAS AFFILIATED WITH THE BANKING INDUSTRY.
6. ARBITRATION WILL APPLY TO ALL DISPUTES BETWEEN THE PARTIES, NOT JUST THOSE CONCERNING THE AGREEMENT.
7. IF YOU HAVE QUESTIONS ABOUT ARBITRATION, CONSULT YOUR ATTORNEY OR THE AMERICAN ARBITRATION ASSOCIATION.

(a) Any claim or controversy ("Dispute") between or among the parties and their employees, agents, affiliates, and assigns, including, but not limited to, Disputes arising out of or relating to this agreement, this arbitration provision ("arbitration clause"), or any related agreements or instruments relating hereto or delivered in connection herewith ("Related Agreements"), and including, but not limited to, a Dispute based on or arising from an alleged tort, shall at the request of any party be resolved by binding arbitration in accordance with the applicable arbitration rules of the American Arbitration Association (the

"Administrator"). The provisions of this arbitration clause shall survive any termination, amendment, or expiration of this agreement or Related Agreements. The provisions of this arbitration clause shall supersede any prior arbitration agreement between or among the parties.

(b) The arbitration proceedings shall be conducted in a city mutually agreed by the parties. Absent such an agreement, arbitration will be conducted in Salt Lake City, Utah or such other place as may be determined by the Administrator. The Administrator and the arbitrator(s) shall have the authority to the extent practicable to take any action to require the arbitration proceeding to be completed and the arbitrators)' award issued within 150 days of the filing of the Dispute with the Administrator. The arbitrator(s) shall have the authority to impose sanctions on any party that fails to comply with time periods imposed by the Administrator or the arbitrators), including the sanction of summarily dismissing any Dispute or defense with prejudice. The arbitrator(s) shall have the authority to resolve any Dispute regarding the terms of this agreement, this arbitration clause, or Related Agreements, including any claim or controversy regarding the arbitrability of any Dispute. All limitations periods applicable to any Dispute or defense, whether by statute or agreement, shall apply to any arbitration proceeding hereunder and the arbitrator(s) shall have the authority to decide whether any Dispute or defense is barred by a limitations period and, if so, to summarily enter an award dismissing any Dispute or defense on that basis. The doctrines of compulsory counterclaim, res judicata, and collateral estoppel shall apply to any arbitration proceeding hereunder so that a party must state as a counterclaim in the arbitration proceeding any claim or controversy which arises out of the transaction or occurrence that is the subject matter of the Dispute. The arbitrators) may in the arbitrators)' discretion and at the request of any party: (1) consolidate in a single arbitration proceeding any other claim arising out of the same transaction involving another party to that transaction that is bound by an arbitration clause with Lender, such as borrowers, guarantors, sureties, and owners of collateral; and (2) consolidate or administer multiple arbitration claims or controversies as a class action in accordance with Rule 23 of the Federal Rules of Civil Procedure.

(c) The arbitrator(s) shall be selected in accordance with the rules of the Administrator from panels maintained by the Administrator. A single arbitrator shall have expertise in the subject matter of the Dispute. Where three arbitrators conduct an arbitration proceeding, the Dispute shall be decided by a majority vote of the three arbitrators, at least one of whom must have expertise in the subject matter of the Dispute and at least one of whom must be a practicing attorney. The arbitrator(s) shall award to the prevailing party recovery of all costs and fees (including attorneys' fees and costs, arbitration administration fees and costs, and arbitrator(s)' fees). The arbitrator(s), either during the pendency of the arbitration
proceeding or as part of the arbitration award, also may grant provisional or ancillary remedies including but not limited to an award of injunctive relief, foreclosure, sequestration, attachment, replevin, garnishment, or the appointment of a receiver.

(d) Judgement upon an arbitration award may be entered in any court having jurisdiction, subject to the following limitation: the arbitration award is binding upon the parties only if the amount does not exceed Four Million Dollars ($4,000,000.00); if the award exceeds that limit, either party may demand the right to a court trial. Such a demand must be filed with the Administrator within thirty (30) days following the date of the arbitration award; if such a demand is not made with that time period, the amount of the arbitration award shall be binding. The computation of the total amount of an arbitration award shall include amounts awarded for attorneys' fees and costs, arbitration administration fees and costs, and arbitrator(s)' fees.

(e) No provision of this arbitration clause, nor the exercise of any rights hereunder, shall limit the right of any party to: (1) judicially or non-judicially foreclose against any real or personal property collateral or other security; (2) exercise self-help remedies, including but not limited to repossession and setoff rights; or (3) obtain from a court having jurisdiction thereover any provisional or ancillary remedies including but not limited to injunctive relief, foreclosure, sequestration, attachment, replevin, garnishment, or the appointment of a receiver. Such rights can be exercised at any time, before or after initiation of an arbitration proceeding, except to the extent such action is contrary to the arbitration award. The exercise of such rights shall not constitute a waiver of the right to submit any Dispute to arbitration, and any claim or controversy related to the exercise of such rights shall be a Dispute to be resolved under the provisions of this arbitration clause. Any party may initiate arbitration with the Administrator. If any party desires to arbitrate a Dispute asserted against such party in a complaint, counterclaim, cross-claim, or third-party complaint thereto, or in an answer or other reply to any such pleading, such party must make an appropriate motion to the trial court seeking to compel arbitration, which motion must be filed with the court within 45 days of service of the pleading, or amendment thereto, setting forth such Dispute. If arbitration is compelled after commencement of litigation of a Dispute, the party obtaining an order compelling arbitration shall commence arbitration and pay the Administrator's filing fees and costs within 45 days of entry of such order. Failure to do so shall constitute an agreement to proceed with litigation and waiver of the right to arbitrate. In any arbitration commenced by a consumer regarding a consumer Dispute, Lender shall pay one half of the Administrator's filing fee, up to $250.

(f) Notwithstanding the applicability of any other law to this agreement, the arbitration clause, or Related Agreements between or among the parties, the Federal Arbitration Act, 9 U.S.C. Section 1 et seq., shall apply to the construction and interpretation of this arbitration clause. If any provision of this arbitration clause should be determined to be unenforceable, all other provisions of this arbitration clause shall remain in full force and effect.

Attorneys' Fees; Expenses. Borrower agrees to pay upon demand all of Lender's costs and expenses, including Lender's reasonable attorneys' fees and Lender's legal expenses, incurred in connection with the enforcement of this Agreement. Lender may hire or pay someone else to help enforce this Agreement, and Borrower shall pay the costs and expenses of such enforcement. Costs and expenses include Lender's reasonable attorneys' fees and legal expenses whether or not Lender's salaried employee and whether or not there is a lawsuit, including reasonable attorneys' fees and legal expenses for bankruptcy proceedings (including efforts to modify or vacate any automatic stay or injunction), appeals, and any anticipated post-judgment collection services. Borrower also shall pay all court costs and such additional fees as may be directed by the court.

Caption Headings. Caption headings in this Agreement are for convenience purposes only and are not to be used to interpret or define the provisions of this Agreement.

Consent to Loan Participation. Borrower agrees and consents to Lender's sale or transfer, whether now or later, of one or more participation interests in the Loan to one or more purchasers, whether related or unrelated to Lender. Lender may provide, without any limitation whatsoever, to any one or more purchasers, or potential purchasers, any information or knowledge Lender may have about Borrower or about any other matter relating to the Loan, and Borrower hereby waives any rights to privacy Borrower may have with respect to such matters. Borrower additionally waives any and all notices of sale of participation interests, as well as all notices of any repurchase of such participation interests. Borrower also agrees that the purchasers of any such participation interests will be considered as the absolute owners of such interests in the Loan and will have all the rights granted under the participation agreement or agreements governing the sale of such participation interests. Borrower further waives all rights of offset or counterclaim that it may have now or later against Lender or against any purchaser of such a participation interest and unconditionally agrees that either Lender or such purchaser may enforce Borrower's obligation under the Loan irrespective of the failure or insolvency of any holder of any interest in the Loan. Borrower further agrees that the purchaser of any such participation interests may enforce its interests irrespective of any personal claims or defenses that Borrower may have against Lender.

Governing Law. This Agreement will be governed by federal law applicable to Lender and, to the extent not preempted by federal law, the laws of the State of Utah without regard to its conflicts of law provisions. This Agreement has been accepted by Lender in the State of Utah.

Choice of Venue. If there is a lawsuit, Borrower agrees upon Lender's request to submit to the jurisdiction of the courts of SALT LAKE County. State of Utah.

No Waiver by Lender. Lender shall not be deemed to have waived any rights under this Agreement unless such waiver is given in writing and signed by Lender. No delay or omission on the part of Lender in exercising any right shall operate as a waiver of such right or any other right. A waiver by Lender of a provision of this Agreement shall not prejudice or constitute a waiver of Lender's right otherwise to demand strict compliance with that provision or any other provision of this Agreement. No prior waiver by Lender, nor any course of dealing between Lender and Borrower, or between Lender and any Grantor, shall constitute a waiver of any of Lender's rights or of any of Borrower's or any Grantor's obligations as to any future transactions. Whenever the consent of Lender is required under this Agreement, the granting of such consent by Lender in any instance shall not constitute continuing consent to subsequent instances where such consent is required and in all cases such consent may be granted or withheld in the sole discretion of Lender.

Notices. Unless otherwise provided by applicable law, any notice required to be given under this Agreement or required by law shall be given in writing, and shall be effective when actually delivered in accordance with the law or with this Agreement, when actually received by telefacsimile (unless otherwise required by law), when deposited with a nationally recognized overnight courier, or, if mailed, when deposited in the United States mail, as first class, certified or registered mail postage prepaid, directed to the addresses shown near the beginning of this Agreement. Any party may change its address for notices under this Agreement by giving formal written notice to the other parties, specifying that the purpose of the notice is to change the party's address. For notice purposes, Borrower agrees to keep Lender informed at all times of Borrower's current address. Unless otherwise provided by applicable law, if there is more than one Borrower, any notice given by Lender to any Borrower is deemed to be notice given to all Borrowers.

Severability. If a court of competent jurisdiction finds any provision of this Agreement to be illegal, invalid, or unenforceable as to any circumstance, that finding shall not make the offending provision illegal, invalid, or unenforceable as to any other circumstance. If feasible, the offending provision shall be considered modified so that it becomes legal, valid and enforceable. If the offending provision cannot be so modified, it shall be considered deleted from this Agreement. Unless otherwise required by law, the illegality, invalidity, or unenforceability of any provision of this Agreement shall not affect the legality, validity or enforceability of any other provision of this Agreement.

Subsidiaries and Affiliates of Borrower. To the extent the context of any provisions of this Agreement makes it appropriate, including without limitation any representation, warranty or covenant, the word "Borrower" as used in this Agreement shall include all of Borrower's subsidiaries and affiliates. Notwithstanding the foregoing however, under no circumstances shall this Agreement be construed to require Lender to make any Loan or other financial accommodation to any of Borrower's subsidiaries or affiliates.

Successors and Assigns. All covenants and agreements by or on behalf of Borrower contained in this Agreement or any Related Documents shall bind Borrower's successors and assigns and shall inure to the benefit of Lender and its successors and assigns. Borrower shall not, however, have the right to assign Borrower's rights under this Agreement or any interest therein, without the prior written consent of Lender.

Survival of Representations and Warranties. Borrower understands and agrees that in making the Loan, Lender is relying on all representations, warranties, and covenants made by Borrower in this Agreement or in any certificate or other instrument delivered by Borrower to Lender under this Agreement or the Related Documents. Borrower further agrees that regardless of any investigation made by Lender, all such representations, warranties and covenants will survive the making of the Loan and delivery to Lender of the Related Documents, shall be continuing in nature, and shall remain in full force and effect until such time as Borrower's Indebtedness shall be paid in full, or until this Agreement shall be terminated in the manner provided above, whichever is the last to occur.

Time is of the Essence. Time is of the essence in the performance of this Agreement.

DEFINITIONS. The following capitalized words and terms shall have the following meanings when used in this Agreement. Unless specifically stated to the contrary, all references to dollar amounts shall mean amounts in lawful money of the United States of America. Words and terms used in the singular shall include the plural, and the plural shall include the singular, as the context may require. Words and terms not otherwise defined in this Agreement shall have the meanings attributed to such terms in the Uniform Commercial Code. Accounting words and terms not otherwise defined in this Agreement shall have the meanings assigned to them in accordance with generally accepted accounting principles as in effect on the date of this Agreement:

Advance. The word "Advance" means a disbursement of Loan funds made, or to be made, to Borrower or on Borrower's behalf on a line of credit or multiple advance basis under the terms and conditions of this Agreement.

Agreement. The word "Agreement" means this Business Loan Agreement, as this Business Loan Agreement may be amended or modified from time to time, together with all exhibits and schedules attached to this Business Loan Agreement from time to time.

Borrower. The word "Borrower" means DELKIM COMPANY, INC. and includes all co-signers and co-makers signing the Note.

Collateral. The word "Collateral" means all property and assets granted as collateral security for a Loan, whether real or personal property, whether granted directly or indirectly, whether granted now or in the future, and whether granted in the form of a security interest, mortgage, collateral mortgage, deed of trust, assignment, pledge, crop pledge, chattel mortgage, collateral chattel mortgage, chattel trust, factor's lien, equipment trust, conditional sale, trust receipt, lien, charge, lien or title retention contract, lease or consignment intended as a security device, or any other security or lien interest whatsoever, whether created by law, contract, or otherwise.

Environmental Laws. The words "Environmental Laws" mean any and all state, federal and local statutes, regulations and ordinances relating to the protection of human health or the environment, including without limitation the Comprehensive Environmental Response, Compensation, and Liability Act of 1980, as amended, 42 U.S.C. Section 9601, et seq. ("CERCLA"), the Superfund Amendments and Reauthorization Act of 1986, Pub. L. No. 99-499 ("SARA"), the Hazardous Materials Transportation Act, 49 U.S.C. Section 1801, et seq., the Resource Conservation and Recovery Act, 42 U.S.C. Section 6901, et seq., or other applicable state or federal laws, rules, or regulations adopted pursuant thereto.

Event of Default. The words "Event of Default" mean any of the events of default set forth in this Agreement in the default section of this Agreement.

GAAP. The word "GAAP" means generally accepted accounting principles.

Grantor. The word "Grantor" means each and all of the persons or entities granting a Security Interest in any Collateral for the Loan, including without limitation all Borrowers granting such a Security Interest.

Guarantor. The word "Guarantor" means any guarantor, surety, or accommodation party of any or all of the Loan. Guaranty. The word "Guaranty" means the guaranty from Guarantor to Lender, including without limitation a guaranty of all or part of the Note.

Hazardous Substances. The words "Hazardous Substances" mean materials that, because of their quantity, concentration or physical, chemical or infectious characteristics, may cause or pose a present or potential hazard to human health or the environment when improperly used, treated, stored, disposed of, generated, manufactured, transported or otherwise handled. The words "Hazardous Substances" are used in their very broadest sense and include without limitation any and all hazardous or toxic substances, materials or waste as defined by or listed under the Environmental Laws. The term "Hazardous Substances" also includes, without limitation, petroleum and petroleum by-products or any fraction thereof and asbestos.

Indebtedness. The word "Indebtedness" means and includes without limitation all Loans, together with alt other obligations, debts and liabilities of Borrower to Lender, or any one or more of them, as well as all claims by Lender against Borrower, or any one or more of them; whether now or hereafter existing, voluntary or involuntary, due or not due, absolute or contingent, liquidated or unliquidated; whether Borrower may be liable individually or jointly with others; whether Borrower may be obligated as a guarantor, surety, or otherwise; whether recovery upon such indebtedness may be or hereafter may become barred by any statute of limitations; and whether such indebtedness may be or hereafter may become otherwise unenforceable.

Lender. The word "Lender" means FIRST NATIONAL BANK, its successors and assigns.

Loan. The word "Loan" means any and all loans and financial accommodations from Lender to Borrower whether now or hereafter existing, and however evidenced, including without limitation those loans and financial accommodations described herein or described on any exhibit or schedule attached to this Agreement from time to time.

Note. The word "Note" means the Note executed by DELKIM COMPANY, INC. in the principal amount of $400,000.00 dated February 16, 2005, together with all renewals of, extensions of, modifications of, refinancings of, consolidations of, and substitutions for the note or credit agreement.

Permitted Liens. The words "Permitted Liens" mean (1) liens and security interests securing Indebtedness owed by Borrower to Lender; (2) liens for taxes, assessments, or similar charges either not yet due or being contested in good faith; (3) liens of materialmen, mechanics, warehousemen, or carriers, or other like liens arising in the ordinary course of business and securing obligations which are not yet delinquent: (4) purchase money liens or purchase money security interests upon or in any property acquired or held by Borrower in the ordinary course of business to secure indebtedness outstanding on the date of this Agreement or permitted to be incurred under the paragraph of this Agreement titled "Indebtedness and Liens"; (5) liens and security interests which, as of the date of this Agreement, have been disclosed to and approved by the Lender in writing; and (6) those liens and security interests which in the aggregate constitute an immaterial and insignificant monetary amount with respect to the net value of Borrower's assets.

Related Documents. The words "Related Documents" mean all promissory notes, credit agreements, loan agreements, environmental agreements, guaranties, security agreements, mortgages, deeds of trust, security deeds, collateral mortgages, and all other instruments, agreements and documents, whether now or hereafter existing, executed in connection with the Loan.

Security Agreement. The words "Security Agreement" mean and include without limitation any agreements, promises, covenants, arrangements, understandings or other agreements, whether created by law, contract, or otherwise, evidencing, governing, representing, or creating a Security Interest.

Security Interest. The words "Security Interest" mean, without limitation, any and all types of collateral security, present and future, whether in the form of a lien, charge, encumbrance, mortgage, deed of trust, security deed, assignment, pledge, crop pledge, chattel mortgage, collateral chattel mortgage, chattel trust, factor's lien, equipment trust, conditional sale, trust receipt, lien or title retention contract, lease or consignment intended as a security device, or any other security or lien interest whatsoever whether created by law, contract, or otherwise.

FINAL AGREEMENT. Borrower understands that this Agreement and the related loan documents are the final expression of the agreement between Lender and Borrower and may not be contradicted by evidence of any alleged oral agreement.

BORROWER ACKNOWLEDGES HAVING READ ALL THE PROVISIONS OF THIS BUSINESS LOAN AGREEMENT AND BORROWER AGREES TO ITS TERMS. THIS BUSINESS LOAN AGREEMENT IS DATED FEBRUARY 16, 20XX.

BORROWER: DELKIM COMPANY, INC.

By: _____   By: _____

JUAN HAN, President of DELKIM COMPANY, INC   SUNNY HAN, Secretary of DELKIM COMPANY, INC.

LENDER: FIRST NATIONAL BANK

By: _____

Authorized Signer

COMMERCIAL GUARANTY

Principal	Loan Date	Maturity	Loan No	Call/Coll	Account	Officer	Initials
$400,000.00	02-16-20XX	03-01-20XX	9001	1C / 6520	0524840	***	

References in the shaded area are for Lender's use only and do not limit the applicability of this document to any particular loan or item.
Any item above containing "***" has been omitted due to text length limitations.

Borrower:	DELKIM COMPANY, INC 10855 SAN PALO AVENUE EL CERRITO, CA 94550	Lender: FIRST NATIONAL BANK REAL ESTATE DEPARTMENT ONE MAIN STREET SALT LAKE CITY, UT 84155
Guarantor:	SUNNY HAN 20 ROOSTER DRIVE SAN RAFAEL, CA 94901	

AMOUNT OF GUARANTY. This is a guaranty of payment of the Note, including without limitation the principal Note amount of Four Hundred Thousand & 00/100 Dollars ($400,000.00).

GUARANTY. For good and valuable consideration, JUAN HAN ("Guarantor") absolutely and unconditionally guarantees and promises to pay to FIRST NATIONAL BANK ("Lender") or its order, in legal tender of the United States of America, the Indebtedness (as that term is defined below) of DELKIM COMPANY, INC. ("Borrower") to Lender on the terms and conditions set forth in this Guaranty.

MAXIMUM LIABILITY. The maximum liability of Guarantor under this Guaranty shall not exceed at any one time the amount of the Indebtedness described herein, plus all costs and expenses of (A) enforcement of this Guaranty and (B) collection and sale of any collateral securing this Guaranty. The above limitation on liability is not a restriction on the amount of the Indebtedness of Borrower to Lender either in the aggregate or at any one time. If Lender presently holds one or more guaranties, or hereafter receives additional guaranties from Guarantor, Lender's rights under all guaranties shall be cumulative. This Guaranty shall not (unless specifically provided below to the contrary) affect or invalidate any such other guaranties. Guarantor's liability will be Guarantor's aggregate liability under the terms of this Guaranty and any such other unterminated guaranties.

INDEBTEDNESS GUARANTEED. The Indebtedness guaranteed by this Guaranty includes the Note, including (a) all principal, (b) all interest, (c) all late charges, (d) all loan fees and loan charges, and (e) all collection costs and expenses relating to the Note or to any collateral for the Note. Collection costs and expenses include without limitation all of Lender's reasonable attorneys' fees.

DURATION OF GUARANTY. This Guaranty will take effect when received by Lender without the necessity of any acceptance by Lender, or any notice to Guarantor or to Borrower, and will continue in full force until all Indebtedness shall have been fully and finally paid and satisfied and all of Guarantor's other obligations under this Guaranty shall have been performed in full. Release of any other guarantor or termination of any other guaranty of the Indebtedness shall not affect the liability of Guarantor under this Guaranty. A revocation Lender receives from any one or more Guarantors shall not affect the liability of any remaining Guarantors under this Guaranty.

GUARANTOR'S AUTHORIZATION TO LENDER. Guarantor authorizes Lender, without notice or demand and without lessening Guarantor's liability under this Guaranty, from time to time: (A) to make one or more additional secured or unsecured loans to Borrower, to lease equipment or other goods to Borrower, or otherwise to extend additional credit to Borrower; (B) to alter, compromise, renew, extend, accelerate, or otherwise change one or more times the time for payment or other terms of the Indebtedness or any part of the Indebtedness, including increases and decreases of the rate of interest on the Indebtedness; extensions may be repeated and may be for longer than the original loan term; (C) to take and hold security for the payment of this Guaranty or the Indebtedness, and exchange, enforce, waive, subordinate, fail or decide not to perfect, and release any such security, with or without the substitution of new collateral; (D) to release, substitute, agree not to sue, or deal with any one or more of Borrower's sureties, endorsers, or other guarantors on any terms or in any manner Lender may choose; (E) to determine how, when and what application of payments and credits shall be made on the Indebtedness; (F) to apply such security and direct the order or manner of sale thereof, including without limitation, any nonjudicial sale permitted by the terms of the controlling security agreement or deed of trust, as Lender in its discretion may determine; (G) to sell, transfer, assign or grant participations in all or any part of the Indebtedness; and (H) to assign or transfer this Guaranty in whole or in part.

GUARANTOR'S REPRESENTATIONS AND WARRANTIES. Guarantor represents and warrants to Lender that (A) no representations or agreements of any kind have been made to Guarantor which would limit or qualify in any way the terms of this Guaranty; (B) this Guaranty is executed at Borrower's request and not at the request of Lender; (C) Guarantor has full power, right and authority to enter into this Guaranty; (D) the provisions of this Guaranty do not conflict with or result in a default under any agreement or other instrument binding upon Guarantor and do not result in a violation of any law, regulation, court decree or order applicable to Guarantor; (E) Guarantor has not and will not, without the prior written consent of Lender, sell, lease, assign, encumber, hypothecate, transfer, or otherwise dispose of all or substantially all of Guarantor's assets, or any interest therein; (F) upon Lender's request, Guarantor will provide to Lender financial and credit information in form acceptable to Lender, and all such financial information which currently has been, and all future financial information which will be provided to Lender is and will be true and correct in all material respects and fairly present Guarantor's financial condition as of the dates the financial information is provided; (G) no material adverse change has occurred in Guarantor's financial condition since the date of the most recent financial statements provided to Lender and no event has occurred which may materially adversely affect Guarantor's financial condition; (H) no litigation, claim, investigation, administrative proceeding or similar action (including those for unpaid taxes) against Guarantor is pending or threatened; (I) Lender has made no representation to Guarantor as to the creditworthiness of Borrower; and (J) Guarantor has established adequate means of obtaining from Borrower on a continuing basis information regarding Borrower's financial condition. Guarantor agrees to keep adequately informed from such means of any facts, events, or circumstances which might in any way affect Guarantor's risks under this Guaranty, and Guarantor further agrees that, absent a request for information, Lender shall have no obligation to disclose to Guarantor any information or documents acquired by Lender in the course of its relationship with Borrower.

GUARANTOR'S WAIVERS. Except as prohibited by applicable law, Guarantor waives any right to require Lender (A) to continue lending money or to extend other credit to Borrower; (B) to make any presentment, protest, demand, or notice of any kind, including notice of any nonpayment of the Indebtedness or of any nonpayment related to any collateral, or notice of any action or nonaction on the part of Borrower, Lender, any surety, endorser, or other guarantor in connection with the Indebtedness or in connection with the creation of new or additional loans or obligations; (C) to resort for payment or to proceed directly or at once against any person, including Borrower or any other guarantor; (D) to proceed directly against or exhaust any collateral held by Lender from Borrower, any other guarantor, or any other person; (E) to give notice of the terms, time, and place of any public or private sale of personal property security held by Lender from Borrower or to comply with any other applicable provisions of the Uniform Commercial Code; (F) to pursue any other remedy within Lender's power; or (G) to commit any act or omission of any kind, or at any time, with respect to any matter whatsoever. Guarantor also waives any and all rights or defenses arising by reason of (1) any election of remedies by Lender which destroys or otherwise adversely affects Guarantor's subrogation rights or Guarantor's rights to proceed against Borrower for reimbursement, including without limitation, any loss of rights Guarantor may suffer by reason of any law limiting, qualifying, or discharging the Indebtedness; (2) any disability or other defense of Borrower, of any other guarantor, or of any other person, or by reason of the cessation of Borrower's liability from any cause whatsoever, other than payment in full in legal tender, of the Indebtedness; (3) any right to claim discharge of the Indebtedness on the basis of unjustified impairment of any Collateral for the Indebtedness; or (4) any statute of limitations, if at any time any action or suit brought by Lender against Guarantor is commenced, there is outstanding Indebtedness of Borrower to Lender which is not barred by any applicable statute of limitations. Guarantor acknowledges and agrees that Guarantor's obligations under this Guaranty shall apply to and continue with respect to any amount paid to Lender which is subsequently recovered from Lender for any reason whatsoever (including without limitation as a result of bankruptcy, insolvency or fraudulent conveyance proceeding), notwithstanding the fact that all or a part of the Indebtedness may have been previously paid, or this Guaranty may have been terminated, or both. Guarantor also waives and agrees not to assert or take advantage of (1) any right (including the right, if any, under Utah's one-action rule as set forth in Utah Code Annotated, 1953, Section 78-37-1) to require Lender to proceed against or exhaust any security held by Lender at any time or to pursue any other remedy in Lender's power before proceeding against Guarantor; (2) the release or surrender of any security held for the payments of the Indebtedness: or (3) any defense based upon an election of remedies (including, if available, an election of remedies to proceed by non-judicial foreclosure) by Lender which destroys or otherwise impairs the subrogation rights of Guarantor or the right of Guarantor to proceed against Borrower for reimbursement, or both. Guarantor further waives and agrees not to assert or claim at any time any deductions to the amount guaranteed under this Guaranty for any claim of setoff, counterclaim, counter demand, recoupment or similar right, whether such claim, demand or right may be asserted by the Borrower, the Guarantor, or both.

Guarantor's Understanding With Respect To Waivers. Guarantor warrants and agrees that each of the waivers set forth above is made with Guarantor's full knowledge of its significance and consequences and that, under the circumstances, the waivers are reasonable and not contrary to public policy or law. If any such waiver is determined to be contrary to any applicable law or public policy, such waiver shall be effective only to the extent permitted by law or public policy.

Subordination of Borrower's Debts to Guarantor. Guarantor agrees that the Indebtedness of Borrower to Lender, whether now existing or hereafter created, shall be superior to any claim that Guarantor may now have or hereafter acquire against Borrower, whether or not Borrower becomes insolvent. Guarantor hereby expressly subordinates any claim Guarantor may have against Borrower, upon any account whatsoever, to any claim that Lender may now or hereafter have against Borrower. In the event of insolvency and consequent liquidation of the assets of Borrower, through bankruptcy, by an assignment for the benefit of creditors, by voluntary liquidation, or otherwise, the assets of Borrower applicable to the payment of the claims of both Lender and Guarantor shall be paid to Lender and shall be first applied by Lender to the Indebtedness of Borrower to Lender. Guarantor does hereby assign to Lender all claims which it may have or acquire against Borrower or against any assignee or trustee in bankruptcy of Borrower; provided however, that such assignment shall be effective only for the purpose of assuring to Lender full payment in legal tender of the Indebtedness. If Lender so requests, any notes or credit agreements now or hereafter evidencing any debts or obligations of Borrower to Guarantor shall be marked with a legend that the same are subject to this Guaranty and shall be delivered to Lender. Guarantor agrees, and Lender is hereby authorized, in the name of Guarantor, from time to time to file financing statements and continuation statements and to execute such other actions as Lender deems necessary or appropriate to perfect, preserve and enforce its rights under this Guaranty.

Miscellaneous Provisions. The following miscellaneous provisions are a part of this Guaranty:

Amendments. This Guaranty, together with any Related Documents, constitutes the entire understanding and agreement of the parties as to the matters set forth in this Guaranty. No alteration of or amendment to this Guaranty shall be effective unless given in writing and signed by the party or parties sought to be charged or bound by the alteration or amendment.

Arbitration Disclosures.

1. ARBITRATION IS FINAL AND BINDING ON THE PARTIES AND SUBJECT TO ONLY VERY LIMITED REVIEW BY A COURT.

2. IN ARBITRATION THE PARTIES ARE WAIVING THEIR RIGHT TO LITIGATE IN COURT, INCLUDING THEIR RIGHT TO A JURY TRIAL

3. DISCOVERY IN ARBITRATION IS MORE LIMITED THAN DISCOVERY IN COURT.

4. ARBITRATORS ARE NOT REQUIRED TO INCLUDE FACTUAL FINDINGS OR LEGAL REASONING IN THEIR AWARDS. THE RIGHT TO APPEAL OR SEEK MODIFICATION OF ARBITRATORS' RULINGS IS VERY LIMITED.

5. A PANEL OF ARBITRATORS MIGHT INCLUDE AN ARBITRATOR WHO IS OR WAS AFFILIATED WITH THE BANKING INDUSTRY.

6. ARBITRATION WILL APPLY TO ALL DISPUTES BETWEEN THE PARTIES, NOT JUST THOSE CONCERNING THE AGREEMENT.

7. IF YOU HAVE QUESTIONS ABOUT ARBITRATION, CONSULT YOUR ATTORNEY OR THE AMERICAN ARBITRATION ASSOCIATION.

(a) Any claim or controversy ("Dispute") between or among the parties and their employees, agents, affiliates, and assigns, including, but not limited to, Disputes arising out of or relating to this agreement, this arbitration provision ("arbitration clause"), or any related agreements or instruments relating hereto or delivered in connection herewith ("Related Agreements"), and including, but not limited to, a Dispute based on or arising from an alleged tort, shall at the request of any party be resolved by binding arbitration in accordance with the applicable arbitration rules of the American Arbitration Association (the "Administrator"). The provisions of this arbitration clause shall survive any termination, amendment, or expiration of this agreement or Related Agreements. The provisions of this arbitration clause shall supersede any prior arbitration agreement between or among the parties.

(b) The arbitration proceedings shall be conducted in a city mutually agreed by the parties. Absent such an agreement, arbitration will be conducted in Salt Lake City, Utah or such other place as may be determined by the Administrator. The Administrator and the arbitrator(s) shall have the authority to the extent practicable to take any action to require the arbitration proceeding to be completed and the arbitrators)' award issued within 150 days of the filing of the Dispute with the Administrator. The arbitrator(s) shall have the authority to impose sanctions on any party that fails to comply with time periods imposed by the Administrator or the arbitrators, including the sanction of summarily dismissing any Dispute or defense with prejudice. The arbitrator(s) shall have the authority to resolve any Dispute regarding the terms of this agreement, this arbitration clause, or Related Agreements, including any claim or controversy regarding the arbitrability of any Dispute. All limitations periods applicable to any Dispute or defense, whether by statute or agreement, shall apply to any arbitration proceeding hereunder and the arbitrator(s) shall have the authority to decide whether any Dispute or defense is barred by a limitations period and, if so, to summarily enter an award dismissing any Dispute or defense on that basis. The doctrines of compulsory counterclaim, res judicata, and collateral estoppel shall apply to any arbitration proceeding hereunder so that a party must state as a counterclaim in the arbitration proceeding any claim or controversy which arises out of the transaction or occurrence that is the subject matter of the Dispute. The arbitrator(s) may in the arbitrators)' discretion and at the request of any party: (1) consolidate in a single arbitration proceeding any other claim arising out of the same transaction involving another party to that transaction that is bound by an arbitration clause with Lender, such as borrowers, guarantors, sureties, and owners of collateral; and (2) consolidate or administer multiple arbitration claims or controversies as a class action in accordance with Rule 23 of the Federal Rules of Civil Procedure.

(c) The arbitrators) shall be selected in accordance with the rules of the Administrator from panels maintained by the Administrator. A single arbitrator shall have expertise in the subject matter of the Dispute. Where three arbitrators conduct an arbitration proceeding, the Dispute shall be decided by a majority vote of the three arbitrators, at least one of whom must have expertise in the subject matter of the Dispute and at least one of whom must be a practicing attorney. The arbitrator(s) shall award to the prevailing party recovery of all costs and fees (including attorneys' fees and costs, arbitration administration fees and costs, and arbitrator(s)' fees). The arbitrator(s), either during the pendency of the arbitration proceeding or as part of the arbitration award, also may grant provisional or ancillary remedies including but not limited to an award of injunctive relief, foreclosure, sequestration, attachment, replevin, garnishment, or the appointment of a receiver.

(d) Judgement upon an arbitration award may be entered in any court having jurisdiction, subject to the following limitation: the arbitration award is binding upon the parties only if the amount does not exceed Four Million Dollars ($4,000,000.00); if the award exceeds that limit, either party may demand the right to a court trial. Such a demand must be filed with the Administrator within thirty (30) days following the date of the arbitration award; if such a demand is not made with that time period, the amount of the arbitration award shall be binding. The computation of the total amount of an arbitration award shall include amounts awarded for attorneys' fees and costs, arbitration administration fees and costs, and arbitrator(s)' fees.

(e) No provision of this arbitration clause, nor the exercise of any rights hereunder, shall limit the right of any party to: (1) judicially or non-judicially foreclose against any real or personal property collateral or other security; (2) exercise self-help remedies, including but not limited to repossession and setoff rights; or (3) obtain from a court having jurisdiction thereover any provisional or ancillary remedies including but not limited to injunctive relief, foreclosure, sequestration, attachment, replevin, garnishment, or the appointment of a receiver. Such rights can be exercised at any time, before or after initiation of an arbitration proceeding, except to the extent such action is contrary to the arbitration award. The exercise of such rights shall not constitute a waiver of the right to submit any Dispute to arbitration, and any claim or controversy related to the exercise of such rights shall be a Dispute to be resolved under the provisions of this arbitration clause. Any party may initiate arbitration with the Administrator. If any party desires to arbitrate a Dispute asserted against such party in a complaint, counterclaim, cross-claim, or third-party complaint thereto, or in an answer or other reply to any such pleading, such party must make an appropriate motion to the trial court seeking to compel arbitration, which motion must be filed with the court within 45 days of service of the pleading, or amendment thereto, setting forth such Dispute. If arbitration is compelled after commencement of litigation of a Dispute, the party obtaining an order compelling arbitration shall commence arbitration and pay the Administrator's filing fees and costs within 45 days of entry of such order. Failure to do so shall constitute an agreement to proceed with litigation and waiver of the right to arbitrate. In any arbitration commenced by a consumer regarding a consumer Dispute, Lender shall pay one half of the Administrator's filing fee, up to $250.

(f) Notwithstanding the applicability of any other law to this agreement, the arbitration clause, or Related Agreements between or among the parties, the Federal Arbitration Act, 9 U.S.C. Section 1 et seq., shall apply to the construction and interpretation of this arbitration clause. If any provision of this arbitration clause should be determined to be unenforceable, all other provisions of this arbitration clause shall remain in full force and effect.

Attorneys' Fees; Expenses. Guarantor agrees to pay upon demand all of Lender's costs and expenses, including Lender's reasonable attorneys' fees and Lender's legal expenses, incurred in connection with the enforcement of this Guaranty. Lender may hire or pay someone else to help enforce this Guaranty, and Guarantor shall pay the costs and expenses of such enforcement. Costs and expenses include Lender's reasonable attorneys' fees and legal expenses whether or not Lender's salaried employee and whether or not there is a lawsuit, including reasonable attorneys' fees and legal expenses for bankruptcy proceedings (including efforts to modify or vacate any automatic stay or injunction), appeals, and any anticipated post-judgment collection services. Guarantor also shall pay all court costs and such additional fees as may be directed by the court.

Caption Headings. Caption headings in this Guaranty are for convenience purposes only and are not to be used to interpret or define the provisions of this Guaranty.

Governing Law. This Guaranty will be governed by federal law applicable to Lender and, to the extent not preempted by federal law, the laws of the State of Utah without regard to its conflicts of law provisions. This Guaranty has been accepted by Lender in the State of Utah.

Choice of Venue. If there is a lawsuit, Guarantor agrees upon Lender's request to submit to the jurisdiction of the courts of SALT LAKE County, State of Utah.

Integration. Guarantor further agrees that Guarantor has read and fully understands the terms of this Guaranty; Guarantor has had the opportunity to be advised by Guarantor's attorney with respect to this Guaranty; the Guaranty fully reflects Guarantor's intentions and parol evidence is not required to interpret the terms of this Guaranty. Guarantor hereby indemnifies and holds Lender harmless from all losses, claims, damages, and costs (including Lender's attorneys' fees) suffered or incurred by Lender as a result of any breach by Guarantor of the warranties, representations and agreements of this paragraph.

Interpretation. In all cases where there is more than one Borrower or Guarantor, then all words used in this Guaranty in the singular shall be deemed to have been used in the plural where the context and construction so require; and where there is more than one Borrower named in this Guaranty or when this Guaranty is executed by more than one Guarantor, the words "Borrower" and "Guarantor" respectively shall mean all and any one or more of them. The words "Guarantor," "Borrower," and "Lender" include the heirs, successors, assigns, and transferees of each of them. If a court finds that any provision of this Guaranty is not valid or should not be enforced, that fact by itself will not mean that the rest of this Guaranty will not be valid or enforced. Therefore, a court will enforce the rest of the provisions of this Guaranty even if a provision of this Guaranty may be found to be invalid or unenforceable. If any one or more of Borrower or Guarantor are corporations, partnerships, limited liability companies, or similar entities, it is not necessary for Lender to inquire into the powers of Borrower or Guarantor or of the officers, directors, partners, managers, or other agents acting or purporting to act on their behalf, and any indebtedness made or created in reliance upon the professed exercise of such powers shall be guaranteed under this Guaranty.

Notices. Unless otherwise provided by applicable law, any notice required to be given under this Guaranty or required by law shall be given in writing, and shall be effective when actually delivered in accordance with the law or with this Guaranty, when actually received by telefacsimile (unless otherwise required by law), when deposited with a nationally recognized overnight courier, or, if mailed, when deposited in the United States mail, as first class, certified or registered mail postage prepaid, directed to the addresses shown near the beginning of this Guaranty. Any party may change its address for notices under this Guaranty by giving formal written notice to the other parties, specifying that the purpose of the notice is to change the party's address. For notice purposes, Guarantor agrees to keep Lender informed at all times of Guarantor's current address. Unless otherwise provided by applicable law, if there is more than one Guarantor, any notice given by Lender to any Guarantor is deemed to be notice given to all Guarantors.

No Waiver by Lender. Lender shall not be deemed to have waived any rights under this Guaranty unless such waiver is given in writing and signed by Lender. No delay or omission on the part of Lender in exercising any right shall operate as a waiver of such right or any other right. A waiver by Lender of a provision of this Guaranty shall not prejudice or constitute a waiver of Lender's right otherwise to demand strict compliance with that provision or any other provision of this Guaranty. No prior waiver by Lender, nor any course of dealing between Lender and Guarantor, shall constitute a waiver of any of Lender's rights or of any of Guarantor's obligations as to any future transactions. Whenever the consent of Lender is required under this Guaranty, the granting of such consent by Lender in any instance shall not constitute continuing consent to subsequent instances where such consent is required and in all cases such consent may be granted or withheld in the sole discretion of Lender.

Successors and Assigns. Subject to any limitations stated in this Guaranty on transfer of Guarantor's interest, this Guaranty shall be binding upon and inure to the benefit of the parties, their successors and assigns.

FINANCIAL STATEMENT. BORROWER AND GUARANTORS COVENANTS AND AGREES WITH LENDER THAT, WHILE THIS AGREEMENT IS IN EFFECT, THEY WILL FURNISH LENDER WITH, UPON REQUEST, THEIR BUSINESS AND PERSONAL FINANCIAL STATEMENTS.

TAX RETURNS. BORROWER AND ALL GUARANTORS SHALL PROVIDE LENDER ON AN ANNUAL BASIS A COPY OF THEIR FEDERAL TAX RETURNS WITHIN 30 DAYS OF FILING.

CASH FLOW COVERAGE. BORROWER SHALL MAINTAIN A RATIO OF ANNUAL NET OPERATING INCOME BEFORE INCOME TAXES, DEPRECIATION AND AMORTIZATION EXPENSE AND INTEREST EXPENSE, LESS 3% OF GROSS ROOM REVENUES AS AN EXPENSE FOR REPLACEMENT RESERVE, (THE "NUMERATOR") GREATER THAN OR EQUAL TO 1.25 TIMES AGGREGATE ANNUAL DEBT SERVICE INCLUDING ZIONS AND ALL LOAN PAYMENTS ON THE SUBJECT BUILDING (THE "DENOMINATOR"), MEASURED ANNUALLY BASED UPON BORROWER'S FISCAL YEAR END FINANCIAL STATEMENT. MONITORING TO BEGIN DECEMBER 31, 20XX.

FAILURE TO PROVIDE ACCEPTABLE FINANCIAL STATEMENTS AS REQUIRED. FURNISHING FINANCIAL INFORMATION: DURING THE TERM OF THE NOTE AND ANY EXTENSIONS OR RENEWALS THEREOF, BORROWER/GUARANTOR SHALL FURNISH AN ANNUAL FINANCIAL STATEMENT PREPARED IN A FORM ACCEPTABLE TO THE BANK, AS SOON AS PRACTICABLE BUT NO LATER THAN 120 DAYS AFTER BORROWER/GUARANTOR'S YEAR END AND SUCH INTERIM FINANCIAL STATEMENTS AND ALL OTHER INFORMATION AND MATERIAL AS BANK MAY FROM TIME TO TIME REQUEST. IF AN EVENT OF DEFAULT (AS DEFINED BELOW AND IN THE NOTE) SHALL HAVE OCCURED AND BY CONTINUING FOR WHICH THE BANK DOES NOT ACCELERATE THE INDEBTEDNESS EVIDENCED BY THE NOTE, WHICH EVENT OF DEFAULT CONSISTS OF THE FAILURE OF BORROWER/ GUARANTOR TO PROVIDE FINANCIAL STATEMENTS AND OTHER INFORMATION AS REQUIRED BY THE TERMS OF THIS AGREEMENT, THE INTEREST RATE APPLICABLE TO THE NOTE, FOR A PERIOD BEGINNING THREE (3) DAYS AFTER WRITTEN NOTICE OF SUCH EVENT, OF DEFAULT IS GIVEN AND ENDING UPON THE CURING OF SUCH DEFAULT, SHALL AT BANK'S OPTION, BE INCREASED BY ONE QUARTER OF ONE PERCENT (.25%) FOR THE FIRST 30-DAYS OF SAID EVENT OF DEFAULT AND BY AN ADDITIONAL ONE QUARTER OF ONE PERCENT (.25%) DURING EACH 30-DAY PERIOD THEREAFTER DURING WHICH SUCH EVENT OF DEFAULT CONTINUES. SUCH RATES SHALL APPLY TO THE ENTIRE OUTSTANDING PRINCIPAL BALANCE OF THE NOTE. UPON CURING SUCH EVENT OF DEFAULT, THE INTEREST RATE ON THE NOTE SHALL REVERT TO THE APPLICABLE RATE THEREUNDER EFFECTIVE AS OF THE DATE ON WHICH SAID EVENT OF DEFAULT IS CURED. BORROWER ACKNOWLEDGES THAT SUCH INCREASE INTEREST RATE IS INTENDED TO COMPENSATE BANK FOR THE POTENTIALLY HIGHER CREDIT RISK AND INCREASED ADMINISTRATIVE COSTS ASSOCIATED WITH BORROWER/GUARANTOR'S FAILURE TO FURNISH TIMELY FINANCIAL INFORMATION.

Definitions. The following capitalized words and terms shall have the following meanings when used in this Guaranty. Unless specifically stated to the contrary, all references to dollar amounts shall mean amounts in lawful money of the United States of America. Words and terms used in the singular shall include the plural, and the plural shall include the singular, as the context may require. Words and terms not otherwise defined in this Guaranty shall have the meanings attributed to such terms in the Uniform Commercial Code:

Borrower. The word "Borrower" means DELKIM COMPANY, INC. and includes all co-signers and co-makers signing the Note.

Guarantor. The word "Guarantor" means each and every person or entity signing this Guaranty, including without limitation JUAN HAN .

Guaranty. The word "Guaranty" means the guaranty from Guarantor to Lender, including without limitation a guaranty of all or part of the Note.

Indebtedness. The word "Indebtedness" means Borrower's indebtedness to Lender as more particularly described in this Guaranty.

Lender. The word "Lender" means FIRST NATIONAL BANK, its successors and assigns.

Note. The word "Note" means the promissory note dated February 16, 20XX, in the original principal amount of $400,000.00 from Borrower to Lender, together with all renewals of, extensions of, modifications of, refinancings of, consolidations of, and substitutions for the promissory note or agreement.

Related Documents. The words "Related Documents" mean all promissory notes, credit agreements, loan agreements, environmental agreements, guaranties, security agreements, mortgages, deeds of trust, security deeds, collateral mortgages, and all other instruments, agreements and documents, whether now or hereafter existing, executed in connection with the Indebtedness.

EACH UNDERSIGNED GUARANTOR ACKNOWLEDGES HAVING READ ALL THE PROVISIONS OF THIS GUARANTY AND AGREES TO ITS TERMS. IN ADDITION, EACH GUARANTOR UNDERSTANDS THAT THIS GUARANTY IS EFFECTIVE UPON GUARANTOR'S EXECUTION AND DELIVERY OF THIS GUARANTY TO LENDER AND THAT THE GUARANTY WILL CONTINUE UNTIL TERMINATED IN THE MANNER SET FORTH IN THE SECTION TITLED "DURATION OF GUARANTY". NO FORMAL ACCEPTANCE BY LENDER IS NECESSARY TO MAKE THIS GUARANTY EFFECTIVE. THIS GUARANTY IS DATED FEBRUARY 16, 20XX.

GUARANTOR:

X _____

SUNNY HAN

COMMERCIAL GUARANTY

Principal	Loan Date	Maturity	Loan No	Call/Coll	Account	Officer	Initials
$400,000.00	02-16-20XX	03-01-20XX	9001	1C / 6520	0524840	***	

References in the shaded area are for Lender's use only and do not limit the applicability of this document to any particular loan or item.
Any item above containing "****" has been omitted due to text length limitations.

Borrower: DELKIM COMPANY, INC
10855 SAN PALO AVENUE
EL CERRITO, CA 94550

Lender: FIRST NATIONAL BANK
REAL ESTATE DEPARTMENT
ONE MAIN STREET
SALT LAKE CITY, UT 84155

Guarantor: JUAN HAN
20 ROOSTER DRIVE
SAN RAFAEL, CA 94901

AMOUNT OF GUARANTY. This is a guaranty of payment of the Note, including without limitation the principal Note amount of Four Hundred Thousand & 00/100 Dollars ($400,000.00).

GUARANTY. For good and valuable consideration, JUAN HAN ("Guarantor") absolutely and unconditionally guarantees and promises to pay to FIRST NATIONAL BANK ("Lender") or its order, in legal tender of the United States of America, the Indebtedness (as that term is defined below) of DELKIM COMPANY, INC. ("Borrower") to Lender on the terms and conditions set forth in this Guaranty.

MAXIMUM LIABILITY. The maximum liability of Guarantor under this Guaranty shall not exceed at any one time the amount of the Indebtedness described herein, plus all costs and expenses of (A) enforcement of this Guaranty and (B) collection and sale of any collateral securing this Guaranty. The above limitation on liability is not a restriction on the amount of the Indebtedness of Borrower to Lender either in the aggregate or at any one time. If Lender presently holds one or more guaranties, or hereafter receives additional guaranties from Guarantor, Lender's rights under all guaranties shall be cumulative. This Guaranty shall not (unless specifically provided below to the contrary) affect or invalidate any such other guaranties. Guarantor's liability will be Guarantor's aggregate liability under the terms of this Guaranty and any such other unterminated guaranties.

INDEBTEDNESS GUARANTEED. The Indebtedness guaranteed by this Guaranty includes the Note, including (a) all principal, (b) all interest, (c) all late charges, (d) all loan fees and loan charges, and (e) all collection costs and expenses relating to the Note or to any collateral for the Note. Collection costs and expenses include without limitation all of Lender's reasonable attorneys' fees.

DURATION OF GUARANTY. This Guaranty will take effect when received by Lender without the necessity of any acceptance by Lender, or any notice to Guarantor or to Borrower, and will continue in full force until all Indebtedness shall have been fully and finally paid and satisfied and all of Guarantor's other obligations under this Guaranty shall have been performed in full. Release of any other guarantor or termination of any other guaranty of the Indebtedness shall not affect the liability of Guarantor under this Guaranty. A revocation Lender receives from any one or more Guarantors shall not affect the liability of any remaining Guarantors under this Guaranty.

GUARANTOR'S AUTHORIZATION TO LENDER. Guarantor authorizes Lender, without notice or demand and without lessening Guarantor's liability under this Guaranty, from time to time: (A) to make one or more additional secured or unsecured loans to Borrower, to lease equipment or other goods to Borrower, or otherwise to extend additional credit to Borrower; (B) to alter, compromise, renew, extend, accelerate, or otherwise change one or more times the time for payment or other terms of the Indebtedness or any part of the Indebtedness, including increases and decreases of the rate of interest on the Indebtedness; extensions may be repeated and may be for longer than the original loan term; (C) to take and hold security for the payment of this Guaranty or the Indebtedness, and exchange, enforce, waive, subordinate, fail or decide not to perfect, and release any such security, with or without the substitution of new collateral; (D) to release, substitute, agree not to sue, or deal with any one or more of Borrower's sureties, endorsers, or other guarantors on any terms or in any manner Lender may choose; (E) to determine how, when and what application of payments and credits shall be made on the Indebtedness; (F) to apply such security and direct the order or manner of sale thereof, including without limitation, any nonjudicial sale permitted by the terms of the controlling security agreement or deed of trust, as Lender in its discretion may determine; (G) to sell, transfer, assign or grant participations in all or any part of the Indebtedness; and (H) to assign or transfer this Guaranty in whole or in part.

GUARANTOR'S REPRESENTATIONS AND WARRANTIES. Guarantor represents and warrants to Lender that (A) no representations or agreements of any kind have been made to Guarantor which would limit or qualify in any way the terms of this Guaranty; (B) this Guaranty is executed at Borrower's request and not at the request of Lender; (C) Guarantor has full power, right and authority to enter into this Guaranty; (D) the provisions of this Guaranty do not conflict with or result in a default under any agreement or other instrument binding upon Guarantor and do not result in a violation of any law, regulation, court decree or order applicable to Guarantor; (E) Guarantor has not and will not, without the prior written consent of Lender, sell, lease, assign, encumber, hypothecate, transfer, or otherwise dispose of all or substantially all of Guarantor's assets, or any interest therein; (F) upon Lender's request, Guarantor will provide to Lender financial and credit information in form acceptable to Lender, and all such financial information which currently has been, and all future financial information which will be provided to Lender is and will be true and correct in all material respects and fairly present Guarantor's financial condition as of the dates the financial information is provided; (G) no material adverse change has occurred in Guarantor's financial condition since the date of the most recent financial statements provided to Lender and no event has occurred which may materially adversely affect Guarantor's financial condition; (H) no litigation, claim, investigation, administrative proceeding or similar action (including those for unpaid taxes) against Guarantor is pending or threatened; (I) Lender has made no representation to Guarantor as to the creditworthiness of Borrower; and (J) Guarantor has established adequate means of obtaining from Borrower on a continuing basis information regarding Borrower's financial condition. Guarantor agrees to keep adequately informed from such means of any facts, events, or circumstances which might in any way affect Guarantor's risks under this Guaranty, and Guarantor further agrees that, absent a request for information, Lender shall have no obligation to disclose to Guarantor any information or documents acquired by Lender in the course of its relationship with Borrower.

GUARANTOR'S WAIVERS. Except as prohibited by applicable law, Guarantor waives any right to require Lender (A) to continue lending money or to extend other credit to Borrower; (B) to make any presentment, protest, demand, or notice of any kind, including notice of any nonpayment of the Indebtedness or of any nonpayment related to any collateral, or notice of any action or nonaction on the part of Borrower, Lender, any surety, endorser, or other guarantor in connection with the Indebtedness or in connection with the creation of new or additional loans or obligations; (C) to resort for payment or to proceed directly or at once against any person, including Borrower or any other guarantor; (D) to proceed directly against or exhaust any collateral held by Lender from Borrower, any other guarantor, or any other person; (E) to give notice of the terms, time, and place of any public or private sale of personal property security held by Lender from Borrower or to comply with any other applicable provisions of the Uniform Commercial Code; (F) to pursue any other remedy within Lender's power; or (G) to commit any act or omission of any kind, or at any time, with respect to any matter whatsoever. Guarantor also waives any and all rights or defenses arising by reason of (1) any election of remedies by Lender which destroys or otherwise adversely affects Guarantor's subrogation rights or Guarantor's rights to proceed against Borrower for reimbursement, including without limitation, any loss of rights Guarantor may suffer by reason of any law limiting, qualifying, or discharging the Indebtedness; (2) any disability or other defense of Borrower, of any other guarantor, or of any other person, or by reason of the cessation of Borrower's liability from any cause whatsoever, other than payment in full in legal tender, of the Indebtedness; (3) any right to claim discharge of the Indebtedness on the basis of unjustified impairment of any Collateral for the Indebtedness; or (4) any statute of limitations, if at any time any action or suit brought by Lender against Guarantor is commenced, there is outstanding Indebtedness of Borrower to Lender which is not barred by any applicable statute of limitations. Guarantor acknowledges and agrees that Guarantor's obligations under this Guaranty shall apply to and continue with respect to any amount paid to Lender which is subsequently recovered from Lender for any reason whatsoever (including without limitation as a result of bankruptcy, insolvency or fraudulent conveyance proceeding), notwithstanding the fact that all or a part of the Indebtedness may have been previously paid, or this Guaranty may have been terminated, or both. Guarantor also waives and agrees not to assert or take advantage of (1) any right (including the right, if any, under Utah's one-action rule as set forth in Utah Code Annotated, 1953, Section 78-37-1) to require Lender to proceed against or exhaust any security held by Lender at any time or to pursue any other remedy in Lender's power before proceeding against Guarantor; (2) the release or surrender of any security held for the payments of the Indebtedness: or (3) any defense based upon an election of remedies (including, if available, an election of remedies to proceed by non-judicial foreclosure) by Lender which destroys or otherwise impairs the subrogation rights of Guarantor or the right of Guarantor to proceed against Borrower for reimbursement, or both. Guarantor further waives and agrees not to assert or claim at any time any deductions to the amount guaranteed under this Guaranty for any claim of setoff, counterclaim, counter demand, recoupment or similar right, whether such claim, demand or right may be asserted by the Borrower, the Guarantor, or both.

Guarantor's Understanding With Respect To Waivers. Guarantor warrants and agrees that each of the waivers set forth above is made with Guarantor's full knowledge of its significance and consequences and that, under the circumstances, the waivers are reasonable and not contrary to public policy or law. If any such waiver is determined to be contrary to any applicable law or public policy, such waiver shall be effective only to the extent permitted by law or public policy.

Subordination of Borrower's Debts to Guarantor. Guarantor agrees that the Indebtedness of Borrower to Lender, whether now existing or hereafter created, shall be superior to any claim that Guarantor may now have or hereafter acquire against Borrower, whether or not Borrower becomes insolvent. Guarantor hereby expressly subordinates any claim Guarantor may have against Borrower, upon any account whatsoever, to any claim that Lender may now or hereafter have against Borrower. In the event of insolvency and consequent liquidation of the assets of Borrower, through bankruptcy, by an assignment for the benefit of creditors, by voluntary liquidation, or otherwise, the assets of Borrower applicable to the payment of the claims of both Lender and Guarantor shall be paid to Lender and shall be first applied by Lender to the Indebtedness of Borrower to Lender. Guarantor does hereby assign to Lender all claims which it may have or acquire against Borrower or against any assignee or trustee in bankruptcy of Borrower; provided however, that such assignment shall be effective only for the purpose of assuring to Lender full payment in legal tender of the Indebtedness. If Lender so requests, any notes or credit agreements now or hereafter evidencing any debts or obligations of Borrower to Guarantor shall be marked with a legend that the same are subject to this Guaranty and shall be delivered to Lender. Guarantor agrees, and Lender is hereby authorized, in the name of Guarantor, from time to time to file financing statements and continuation statements and to execute documents and to take such other actions as Lender deems necessary or appropriate to perfect, preserve and enforce its rights under this Guaranty.

Miscellaneous Provisions. The following miscellaneous provisions are a part of this Guaranty:

Amendments. This Guaranty, together with any Related Documents, constitutes the entire understanding and agreement of the parties as to the matters set forth in this Guaranty. No alteration of or amendment to this Guaranty shall be effective unless given in writing and signed by the party or parties sought to be charged or bound by the alteration or amendment.

Arbitration Disclosures.

1. ARBITRATION IS FINAL AND BINDING ON THE PARTIES AND SUBJECT TO ONLY VERY LIMITED REVIEW BY A COURT.

2. IN ARBITRATION THE PARTIES ARE WAIVING THEIR RIGHT TO LITIGATE IN COURT, INCLUDING THEIR RIGHT TO A JURY TRIAL

3. DISCOVERY IN ARBITRATION IS MORE LIMITED THAN DISCOVERY IN COURT.

4. ARBITRATORS ARE NOT REQUIRED TO INCLUDE FACTUAL FINDINGS OR LEGAL REASONING IN THEIR AWARDS. THE RIGHT TO APPEAL OR SEEK MODIFICATION OF ARBITRATORS' RULINGS IS VERY LIMITED.

5. A PANEL OF ARBITRATORS MIGHT INCLUDE AN ARBITRATOR WHO IS OR WAS AFFILIATED WITH THE BANKING INDUSTRY.

6. ARBITRATION WILL APPLY TO ALL DISPUTES BETWEEN THE PARTIES, NOT JUST THOSE CONCERNING THE AGREEMENT.

7. IF YOU HAVE QUESTIONS ABOUT ARBITRATION, CONSULT YOUR ATTORNEY OR THE AMERICAN ARBITRATION ASSOCIATION.

(a) Any claim or controversy ("Dispute") between or among the parties and their employees, agents, affiliates, and assigns, including, but not limited to, Disputes arising out of or relating to this agreement, this arbitration provision ("arbitration clause"), or any related agreements or instruments relating hereto or delivered in connection herewith ("Related Agreements"), and including, but not limited to, a Dispute based on or arising from an alleged tort, shall at the request of any party be resolved by binding arbitration in accordance with the applicable arbitration rules of the American Arbitration Association (the "Administrator"). The provisions of this arbitration clause shall survive any termination, amendment, or expiration of this agreement or Related Agreements. The provisions of this arbitration clause shall supersede any prior arbitration agreement between or among the parties.

(b) The arbitration proceedings shall be conducted in a city mutually agreed by the parties. Absent such an agreement, arbitration will be conducted in Salt Lake City, Utah or such other place as may be determined by the Administrator. The Administrator and the arbitrator(s) shall have the authority to the extent practicable to take any action to require the arbitration proceeding to be completed and the arbitrators)' award issued within 150 days of the filing of the Dispute with the Administrator. The arbitrator(s) shall have the authority to impose sanctions on any party that fails to comply with time periods imposed by the Administrator or the arbitrators), including the sanction of summarily dismissing any Dispute or defense with prejudice. The arbitrator(s) shall have the authority to resolve any Dispute regarding the terms of this agreement, this arbitration clause, or Related Agreements, including any claim or controversy regarding the arbitrability of any Dispute. All limitations periods applicable to any Dispute or defense, whether by statute or agreement, shall apply to any arbitration proceeding hereunder and the arbitrator(s) shall have the authority to decide whether any Dispute or defense is barred by a limitations period and, if so, to summarily enter an award dismissing any Dispute or defense on that basis. The doctrines of compulsory counterclaim, res judicata, and collateral estoppel shall apply to any arbitration proceeding hereunder so that a party must state as a counterclaim in the arbitration proceeding any claim or controversy which arises out of the transaction or occurrence that is the subject matter of the Dispute. The arbitrator(s) may in the arbitrators)' discretion and at the request of any party: (1) consolidate in a single arbitration proceeding any other claim arising out of the same transaction involving another party to that transaction that is bound by an arbitration clause with Lender, such as borrowers, guarantors, sureties, and owners of collateral; and (2) consolidate or administer multiple arbitration claims or controversies as a class action in accordance with Rule 23 of the Federal Rules of Civil Procedure.

(c) The arbitrators) shall be selected in accordance with the rules of the Administrator from panels maintained by the Administrator. A single arbitrator shall have expertise in the subject matter of the Dispute. Where three arbitrators conduct an arbitration proceeding, the Dispute shall be decided by a majority vote of the three arbitrators, at least one of whom must have expertise in the subject matter of the Dispute and at least one of whom must be a practicing attorney. The arbitrator(s) shall award to the prevailing party recovery of all costs and fees (including attorneys' fees and costs, arbitration administration fees and costs, and arbitrator(s)' fees). The arbitrator(s), either during the pendency of the arbitration proceeding or as part of the arbitration award, also may grant provisional or ancillary remedies including but not limited to an award of injunctive relief, foreclosure, sequestration, attachment, replevin, garnishment, or the appointment of a receiver.

(d) Judgement upon an arbitration award may be entered in any court having jurisdiction, subject to the following limitation: the arbitration award is binding upon the parties only if the amount does not exceed Four Million Dollars ($4,000,000.00); if the award exceeds that limit, either party may demand the right to a court trial. Such a demand must be filed with the Administrator within thirty (30) days following the date of the arbitration award; if such a demand is not made with that time period, the amount of the arbitration award shall be binding. The computation of the total amount of an arbitration award shall include amounts awarded for attorneys' fees and costs, arbitration administration fees and costs, and arbitrator(s)' fees.

(e) No provision of this arbitration clause, nor the exercise of any rights hereunder, shall limit the right of any party to: (1) judicially or non-judicially foreclose against any real or personal property collateral or other security; (2) exercise self-help remedies, including but not limited to repossession and setoff rights; or (3) obtain from a court having jurisdiction thereover any provisional or ancillary remedies including but not limited to injunctive relief, foreclosure, sequestration, attachment, replevin, garnishment, or the appointment of a receiver. Such rights can be exercised at any time, before or after initiation of an arbitration proceeding, except to the extent such action is contrary to the arbitration award. The exercise of such rights shall not constitute a waiver of the right to submit any Dispute to arbitration, and any claim or controversy related to the exercise of such rights shall be a Dispute to be resolved under the provisions of this arbitration clause. Any party may initiate arbitration with the Administrator. If any party desires to arbitrate a Dispute asserted against such party in a complaint, counterclaim, cross-claim, or third-party complaint thereto, or in an answer or other reply to any such pleading, such party must make an appropriate motion to the trial court seeking to compel arbitration, which motion must be filed with the court within 45 days of service of the pleading, or amendment thereto, setting forth such Dispute. If arbitration is compelled after commencement of litigation of a Dispute, the party obtaining an order compelling arbitration shall commence arbitration and pay the Administrator's filing fees and costs within 45 days of entry of such order. Failure to do so shall constitute an agreement to proceed with litigation and waiver of the right to arbitrate. In any arbitration commenced by a consumer regarding a consumer Dispute, Lender shall pay one half of the Administrator's filing fee, up to $250.

(f) Notwithstanding the applicability of any other law to this agreement, the arbitration clause, or Related Agreements between or among the parties, the Federal Arbitration Act, 9 U.S.C. Section 1 et seq., shall apply to the construction and interpretation of this arbitration clause. If any provision of this arbitration clause should be determined to be unenforceable, all other provisions of this arbitration clause shall remain in full force and effect.

Attorneys' Fees; Expenses. Guarantor agrees to pay upon demand all of Lender's costs and expenses, including Lender's reasonable attorneys' fees and Lender's legal expenses, incurred in connection with the enforcement of this Guaranty. Lender may hire or pay someone else to help enforce this Guaranty, and Guarantor shall pay the costs and expenses of such enforcement. Costs and expenses include Lender's reasonable attorneys' fees and legal expenses whether or not Lender's salaried employee and whether or not there is a lawsuit, including reasonable attorneys' fees and legal expenses for bankruptcy proceedings (including efforts to modify or vacate any automatic stay or injunction), appeals, and any anticipated post-judgment collection services. Guarantor also shall pay all court costs and such additional fees as may be directed by the court.

Caption Headings. Caption headings in this Guaranty are for convenience purposes only and are not to be used to interpret or define the provisions of this Guaranty.

Governing Law. This Guaranty will be governed by federal law applicable to Lender and, to the extent not preempted by federal law, the laws of the State of Utah without regard to its conflicts of law provisions. This Guaranty has been accepted by Lender in the State of Utah.

Choice of Venue. If there is a lawsuit, Guarantor agrees upon Lender's request to submit to the jurisdiction of the courts of SALT LAKE County, State of Utah.

Integration. Guarantor further agrees that Guarantor has read and fully understands the terms of this Guaranty; Guarantor has had the opportunity to be advised by Guarantor's attorney with respect to this Guaranty; the Guaranty fully reflects Guarantor's intentions and parol evidence is not required to interpret the terms of this Guaranty. Guarantor hereby indemnifies and holds Lender harmless from all losses, claims, damages, and costs (including Lender's attorneys' fees) suffered or incurred by Lender as a result of any breach by Guarantor of the warranties, representations and agreements of this paragraph.

Interpretation. In all cases where there is more than one Borrower or Guarantor, then all words used in this Guaranty in the singular shall be deemed to have been used in the plural where the context and construction so require; and where there is more than one Borrower named in this Guaranty or when this Guaranty is executed by more than one Guarantor, the words "Borrower" and "Guarantor" respectively shall mean all and any one or more of them. The words "Guarantor," "Borrower," and "Lender" include the heirs, successors, assigns, and transferees of each of them. If a court finds that any provision of this Guaranty is not valid or should not be enforced, that fact by itself will not mean that the rest of this Guaranty will not be valid or enforced. Therefore, a court will enforce the rest of the provisions of this Guaranty even if a provision of this Guaranty may be found to be invalid or unenforceable. If any one or more of Borrower or Guarantor are corporations, partnerships, limited liability companies, or similar entities, it is not necessary for Lender to inquire into the powers of Borrower or Guarantor or of the officers, directors, partners, managers, or other agents acting or purporting to act on their behalf, and any indebtedness made or created in reliance upon the professed exercise of such powers shall be guaranteed under this Guaranty.

Notices. Unless otherwise provided by applicable law, any notice required to be given under this Guaranty or required by law shall be given in writing, and shall be effective when actually delivered in accordance with the law or with this Guaranty, when actually received by telefacsimile (unless otherwise required by law), when deposited with a nationally recognized overnight courier, or, if mailed, when deposited in the United States mail, as first class, certified or registered mail postage prepaid, directed to the addresses shown near the beginning of this Guaranty. Any party may change its address for notices under this Guaranty by giving formal written notice to the other parties, specifying that the purpose of the notice is to change the party's address. For notice purposes, Guarantor agrees to keep Lender informed at all times of Guarantor's current address. Unless otherwise provided by applicable law, if there is more than one Guarantor, any notice given by Lender to any Guarantor is deemed to be notice given to all Guarantors.

No Waiver by Lender. Lender shall not be deemed to have waived any rights under this Guaranty unless such waiver is given in writing and signed by Lender. No delay or omission on the part of Lender in exercising any right shall operate as a waiver of such right or any other right. A waiver by Lender of a provision of this Guaranty shall not prejudice or constitute a waiver of Lender's right otherwise to demand strict compliance with that provision or any other provision of this Guaranty. No prior waiver by Lender, nor any course of dealing between Lender and Guarantor, shall constitute a waiver of any of Lender's rights or of any of Guarantor's obligations as to any future transactions. Whenever the consent of Lender is required under this Guaranty, the granting of such consent by Lender in any instance shall not constitute continuing consent to subsequent instances where such consent is required and in all cases such consent may be granted or withheld in the sole discretion of Lender.

Successors and Assigns. Subject to any limitations stated in this Guaranty on transfer of Guarantor's interest, this Guaranty shall be binding upon and inure to the benefit of the parties, their successors and assigns.

FINANCIAL STATEMENT. BORROWER AND GUARANTORS COVENANTS AND AGREES WITH LENDER THAT, WHILE THIS AGREEMENT IS IN EFFECT, THEY WILL FURNISH LENDER WITH, UPON REQUEST, THEIR BUSINESS AND PERSONAL FINANCIAL STATEMENTS.

TAX RETURNS. BORROWER AND ALL GUARANTORS SHALL PROVIDE LENDER ON AN ANNUAL BASIS A COPY OF THEIR FEDERAL TAX RETURNS WITHIN 30 DAYS OF FILING.

CASH FLOW COVERAGE. BORROWER SHALL MAINTAIN A RATIO OF ANNUAL NET OPERATING INCOME BEFORE INCOME TAXES, DEPRECIATION AND AMORTIZATION EXPENSE AND INTEREST EXPENSE, LESS 3% OF GROSS ROOM REVENUES AS AN EXPENSE FOR REPLACEMENT RESERVE, (THE "NUMERATOR") GREATER THAN OR EQUAL TO 1.25 TIMES AGGREGATE ANNUAL DEBT SERVICE INCLUDING ZIONS AND ALL LOAN PAYMENTS ON THE SUBJECT BUILDING (THE "DENOMINATOR"), MEASURED ANNUALLY BASED UPON BORROWER'S FISCAL YEAR END FINANCIAL STATEMENT. MONITORING TO BEGIN DECEMBER 31, 20XX.

FAILURE TO PROVIDE ACCEPTABLE FINANCIAL STATEMENTS AS REQUIRED. FURNISHING FINANCIAL INFORMATION: DURING THE TERM OF THE NOTE AND ANY EXTENSIONS OR RENEWALS THEREOF, BORROWER/GUARANTOR SHALL FURNISH AN ANNUAL FINANCIAL STATEMENT PREPARED IN A FORM ACCEPTABLE TO THE BANK, AS SOON AS PRACTICABLE BUT NO LATER THAN 120 DAYS AFTER BORROWER/GUARANTOR'S YEAR END AND SUCH INTERIM FINANCIAL STATEMENTS AND ALL OTHER INFORMATION AND MATERIAL AS BANK MAY FROM TIME TO TIME REQUEST. IF AN EVENT OF DEFAULT (AS DEFINED BELOW AND IN THE NOTE) SHALL HAVE OCCURED AND BY CONTINUING FOR WHICH THE BANK DOES NOT ACCELERATE THE INDEBTEDNESS EVIDENCED BY THE NOTE, WHICH EVENT OF DEFAULT CONSISTS OF THE FAILURE OF BORROWER/ GUARANTOR TO PROVIDE FINANCIAL STATEMENTS AND OTHER INFORMATION AS REQUIRED BY THE TERMS OF THIS AGREEMENT, THE INTEREST RATE APPLICABLE TO THE NOTE, FOR A PERIOD BEGINNING THREE (3) DAYS AFTER WRITTEN NOTICE OF SUCH EVENT, OF DEFAULT IS GIVEN AND ENDING UPON THE CURING OF SUCH DEFAULT, SHALL AT BANK'S OPTION, BE INCREASED BY ONE QUARTER OF ONE PERCENT (.25%) FOR THE FIRST 30-DAYS OF SAID EVENT OF DEFAULT AND BY AN ADDITIONAL ONE QUARTER OF ONE PERCENT (.25%) DURING EACH 30-DAY PERIOD THEREAFTER DURING WHICH SUCH EVENT OF DEFAULT CONTINUES. SUCH RATES SHALL APPLY TO THE ENTIRE OUTSTANDING PRINCIPAL BALANCE OF THE NOTE. UPON CURING SUCH EVENT OF DEFAULT, THE INTEREST RATE ON THE NOTE SHALL REVERT TO THE APPLICABLE RATE THEREUNDER EFFECTIVE AS OF THE DATE ON WHICH SAID EVENT OF DEFAULT IS CURED. BORROWER ACKNOWLEDGES THAT SUCH INCREASE INTEREST RATE IS INTENDED TO COMPENSATE BANK FOR THE POTENTIALLY HIGHER CREDIT RISK AND INCREASED ADMINISTRATIVE COSTS ASSOCIATED WITH BORROWER/GUARANTOR'S FAILURE TO FURNISH TIMELY FINANCIAL INFORMATION.

Definitions. The following capitalized words and terms shall have the following meanings when used in this Guaranty. Unless specifically stated to the contrary, all references to dollar amounts shall mean amounts in lawful money of the United States of America. Words and terms used in the singular shall include the plural, and the plural shall include the singular, as the context may require. Words and terms not otherwise defined in this Guaranty shall have the meanings attributed to such terms in the Uniform Commercial Code:

Borrower. The word "Borrower" means DELKIM COMPANY, INC. and includes all co-signers and co-makers signing the Note.

Guarantor. The word "Guarantor" means each and every person or entity signing this Guaranty, including without limitation JUAN HAN .

Guaranty. The word "Guaranty" means the guaranty from Guarantor to Lender, including without limitation a guaranty of all or part of the Note.

Indebtedness. The word "Indebtedness" means Borrower's indebtedness to Lender as more particularly described in this Guaranty.

Lender. The word "Lender" means FIRST NATIONAL BANK, its successors and assigns.

Note. The word "Note" means the promissory note dated February 16, 20XX, in the original principal amount of $400,000.00 from Borrower to Lender, together with all renewals of, extensions of, modifications of, refinancings of, consolidations of, and substitutions for the promissory note or agreement.

Related Documents. The words "Related Documents" mean all promissory notes, credit agreements, loan agreements, environmental agreements, guaranties, security agreements, mortgages, deeds of trust, security deeds, collateral mortgages, and all other instruments, agreements and documents, whether now or hereafter existing, executed in connection with the Indebtedness.

EACH UNDERSIGNED GUARANTOR ACKNOWLEDGES HAVING READ ALL THE PROVISIONS OF THIS GUARANTY AND AGREES TO ITS TERMS. IN ADDITION, EACH GUARANTOR UNDERSTANDS THAT THIS GUARANTY IS EFFECTIVE UPON GUARANTOR'S EXECUTION AND DELIVERY OF THIS GUARANTY TO LENDER AND THAT THE GUARANTY WILL CONTINUE UNTIL TERMINATED IN THE MANNER SET FORTH IN THE SECTION TITLED "DURATION OF GUARANTY". NO FORMAL ACCEPTANCE BY LENDER IS NECESSARY TO MAKE THIS GUARANTY EFFECTIVE. THIS GUARANTY IS DATED FEBRUARY 16, 20XX.

GUARANTOR:

X _____

JUAN HAN

COMMERCIAL SECURITY AGREEMENT

Principal	Loan Date	Maturity	Loan No	Call/Coll	Account	Officer	Initials
$400,000.00	02-16-20XX	03-01-20XX	9001	1C / 6520	0524840	***	

References in the shaded area are for Lender's use only and do not limit the applicability of this document to any particular loan or item.
Any item above containing "***" has been omitted due to text length limitations.

Grantor: DELKIM COMPANY, INC
10855 SAN PALO AVENUE
EL CERRITO, CA 94550

Lender: FIRST NATIONAL BANK
REAL ESTATE DEPARTMENT
ONE MAIN STREET
SALT LAKE CITY, UT 84155

THIS COMMERCIAL SECURITY AGREEMENT dated February 16, 20XX, is made and executed between DELKIM COMPANY, INC. ("Grantor") and FIRST NATIONAL BANK ("Lender").

GRANT OF SECURITY INTEREST. For valuable consideration, Grantor grants to Lender a security interest in the Collateral to secure the Indebtedness and agrees that Lender shall have the rights stated in this Agreement with respect to the Collateral, in addition to all other rights which Lender may have by law.

COLLATERAL DESCRIPTION. The word "Collateral" as used in this Agreement means the following described property, whether now owned or hereafter acquired, whether now existing or hereafter arising, and wherever located, in which Grantor is giving to Lender a security interest for the payment of the Indebtedness and performance of all other obligations under the Note and this Agreement:

> **All Furniture, Fixtures, Equipment, Machinery, Accounts, Contracts, Inventory, General Intangibles, and Rental Income now owned and hereafter acquired located on the property at: 10855 SAN PALO, EL CERRITO, CA 94550**

In addition, the word "Collateral" also includes all the following, whether now owned or hereafter acquired, whether now existing or hereafter arising, and wherever located:

> (A) All accessions, attachments, accessories, replacements of and additions to any of the collateral described herein, whether added now or later.

> (B) All products and produce of any of the property described in this Collateral section.

> (C) All accounts, general intangibles, instruments, rents, monies, payments, and all other rights, arising out of a sale, lease, consignment or other disposition of any of the property described in this Collateral section.

> (D) All proceeds (including insurance proceeds) from the sale, destruction, loss, or other disposition of any of the property described in this Collateral section, and sums due from a third party who has damaged or destroyed the Collateral or from that party's insurer, whether due to judgment, settlement or other process.

> (E) All records and data relating to any of the property described in this Collateral section, whether in the form of a writing, photograph, microfilm, microfiche, or electronic media, together with all of Grantor's right, title, and interest in and to all computer software required to utilize, create, maintain, and process any such records or data on electronic media.

Despite any other provision of this Agreement, Lender is not granted, and will not have, a nonpurchase money security interest in household goods, to the extent such a security interest would be prohibited by applicable law. In addition, if because of the type of any Property, Lender is required to give a notice of the right to cancel under Truth in Lending for the Indebtedness, then Lender will not have a security interest in such Collateral unless and until such a notice is given.

CROSS-COLLATERALIZATION. In addition to the Note, this Agreement secures all obligations, debts and liabilities, plus interest thereon, of Grantor to Lender, or any one or more of them, as well as all claims by Lender against Grantor or any one or more of them, whether now existing or hereafter arising, whether related or unrelated to the purpose of the Note, whether voluntary or otherwise, whether due or not due, direct or indirect, determined or undetermined, absolute or contingent, liquidated or unliquidated whether Grantor may be liable individually or jointly with others, whether obligated as guarantor, surety, accommodation party or otherwise, and whether recovery upon such amounts may be or hereafter may become barred by any statute of limitations, and whether the obligation to repay such amounts may be or hereafter may become otherwise unenforceable.

RIGHT OF SETOFF. To the extent permitted by applicable law, Lender reserves a right of setoff in all Grantor's accounts with Lender (whether checking, savings, or some other account). This includes all accounts Grantor holds jointly with someone else and all accounts Grantor may open in the future. However, this does not include any IRA or Keogh accounts, or any trust accounts for which setoff would be prohibited by law. Grantor authorizes Lender, to the extent permitted by applicable law, to charge or setoff all sums owing on the Indebtedness against any and all such accounts, and, at Lender's option, to administratively freeze all such accounts to allow Lender to protect Lender's charge and setoff rights provided in this paragraph.

GRANTOR'S REPRESENTATIONS AND WARRANTIES WITH RESPECT TO THE COLLATERAL. With respect to the Collateral, Grantor represents and promises to Lender that:

> **Perfection of Security Interest.** Grantor agrees to take whatever actions are requested by Lender to perfect and continue Lender's security interest in the Collateral. Upon request of Lender, Grantor will deliver to Lender any and all of the documents evidencing or constituting the Collateral, and Grantor will note Lender's interest upon any and all chattel paper and instruments if not delivered to Lender for possession by Lender. This is a continuing Security Agreement and will continue in effect even though all or any part of the Indebtedness is paid in full and even though for a period of time Grantor may not be indebted to Lender.

> **Notices to Lender.** Grantor will promptly notify Lender in writing at Lender's address shown above (or such other addresses as Lender may designate from time to time) prior to any (1) change in Grantor's name; (2) change in Grantor's assumed business name(s); (3) change in the management of the Corporation Grantor; (4) change in the authorized signer(s); (5) change in Grantor's principal office address; (6) change in Grantor's state of organization;

(7) conversion of Grantor to a new or different type of business entity; or (8) change in any other aspect of Grantor that directly or indirectly relates to any agreements between Grantor and Lender. No change in Grantor's name or state of organization will take effect until after Lender has received notice.

No Violation. The execution and delivery of this Agreement will not violate any law or agreement governing Grantor or to which Grantor is a party, and its certificate or articles of incorporation and bylaws do not prohibit any term or condition of this Agreement.

Enforceability of Collateral. To the extent the Collateral consists of accounts, chattel paper, or general intangibles, as defined by the Uniform Commercial Code, the Collateral is enforceable in accordance with its terms, is genuine, and fully complies with all applicable laws and regulations concerning form, content and manner of preparation and execution, and all persons appearing to be obligated on the Collateral have authority and capacity to contract and are in fact obligated as they appear to be on the Collateral. There shall be no setoffs or counterclaims against any of the Collateral, and no agreement shall have been made under which any deductions or discounts may be claimed concerning the Collateral except those disclosed to Lender in writing.

Location of the Collateral. Except in the ordinary course of Grantor's business, Grantor agrees to keep the Collateral at Grantor's address shown above or at such other locations as are acceptable to Lender. Upon Lender's request, Grantor will deliver to Lender in form satisfactory to Lender a schedule of real properties and Collateral locations relating to Grantor's operations, including without limitation the following: (1) all real property Grantor owns or is purchasing; (2) all real property Grantor is renting or leasing; (3) all storage facilities Grantor owns, rents, leases, or uses; and (4) all other properties where Collateral is or may be located.

Removal of the Collateral. Except in the ordinary course of Grantor's business, Grantor shall not remove the Collateral from its existing location without Lender's prior written consent. Grantor shall, whenever requested, advise Lender of the exact location of the Collateral.

Transactions Involving Collateral. Except for inventory sold or accounts collected in the ordinary course of Grantor's business, or as otherwise provided for in this Agreement, Grantor shall not sell, offer to sell, or otherwise transfer or dispose of the Collateral. Grantor shall not pledge, mortgage, encumber or otherwise permit the Collateral to be subject to any lien, security interest, encumbrance, or charge, other than the security interest provided for in this Agreement, without the prior written consent of Lender. This includes security interests even if junior in right to the security interests granted under this Agreement. Unless waived by Lender, all proceeds from any disposition of the Collateral (for whatever reason) shall be held in trust for Lender and shall not be commingled with any other funds; provided however, this requirement shall not constitute consent by Lender to any sale or other disposition. Upon receipt, Grantor shall immediately deliver any such proceeds to Lender.

Title. Grantor represents and warrants to Lender that Grantor holds good and marketable title to the Collateral, free and clear of all liens and encumbrances except for the lien of this Agreement. No financing statement covering any of the Collateral is on file in any public office other than those which reflect the security interest created by this Agreement or to which Lender has specifically consented. Grantor shall defend Lender's rights in the Collateral against the claims and demands of all other persons.

Repairs and Maintenance. Grantor agrees to keep and maintain, and to cause others to keep and maintain, the Collateral in good order, repair and condition at all times while this Agreement remains in effect. Grantor further agrees to pay when due all claims for work done on, or services rendered or material furnished in connection with the Collateral so that no lien or encumbrance may ever attach to or be filed against the Collateral.

Inspection of Collateral. Lender and Lender's designated representatives and agents shall have the right at all reasonable times to examine and inspect the Collateral wherever located.

Taxes, Assessments and Liens. Grantor will pay when due all taxes, assessments and liens upon the Collateral, its use or operation, upon this Agreement, upon any promissory note or notes evidencing the Indebtedness, or upon any of the other Related Documents. Grantor may withhold any such payment or may elect to contest any lien if Grantor is in good faith conducting an appropriate proceeding to contest the obligation to pay and so long as Lender's interest in the Collateral is not jeopardized in Lender's sole opinion. If the Collateral is subjected to a lien which is not discharged within fifteen (15) days, Grantor shall deposit with Lender cash, a sufficient corporate surety bond or other security satisfactory to Lender in an amount adequate to provide for the discharge of the lien plus any interest, costs, attorneys' fees or other charges that could accrue as a result of foreclosure or sale of the Collateral. In any contest Grantor shall defend itself and Lender and shall satisfy any final adverse judgment before enforcement against the Collateral. Grantor shall name Lender as an additional obligee under any surety bond furnished in the contest proceedings. Grantor further agrees to furnish Lender with evidence that such taxes, assessments, and governmental and other charges have been paid in full and in a timely manner. Grantor may withhold any such payment or may elect to contest any lien if Grantor is in good faith conducting an appropriate proceeding to contest the obligation to pay and so long as Lender's interest in the Collateral is not jeopardized.

Compliance with Governmental Requirements. Grantor shall comply promptly with all laws, ordinances, rules and regulations of all governmental authorities, now or hereafter in effect, applicable to the ownership, production, disposition, or use of the Collateral, including all laws or regulations relating to the undue erosion of highly-erodible land or relating to the conversion of wetlands for the production of an agricultural product or commodity. Grantor may contest in good faith any such law, ordinance or regulation and withhold compliance during any proceeding, including appropriate appeals, so long as Lender's interest in the Collateral, in Lender's opinion, is not jeopardized.

Hazardous Substances. Grantor represents and warrants that the Collateral never has been, and never will be so long as this Agreement remains a lien on the Collateral, used in violation of any Environmental Laws or for the generation, manufacture, storage, transportation, treatment, disposal, release or threatened release of any Hazardous Substance. The representations and warranties contained herein are based on Grantor's due diligence in investigating the Collateral for Hazardous Substances. Grantor hereby (1) releases and waives any future claims against Lender for indemnity or contribution in the event Grantor becomes liable for cleanup or other costs under any Environmental Laws, and (2) agrees to indemnify and hold harmless Lender against any and all claims and losses resulting from a breach of this provision of this Agreement. This obligation to indemnify shall survive the payment of the Indebtedness and the satisfaction of this Agreement.

Maintenance of Casualty Insurance. Grantor shall procure and maintain all risks insurance, including without limitation fire, theft and liability coverage together with such other insurance as Lender may require with respect to the Collateral, in form, amounts, coverages and basis reasonably acceptable to Lender and issued by a company or companies reasonably acceptable to Lender. Grantor, upon request of Lender, will deliver to Lender from time to time

---

the policies or certificates of insurance in form satisfactory to Lender, including stipulations that coverages will not be cancelled or diminished without at least ten (10) days' prior written notice to Lender and not including any disclaimer of the insurer's liability for failure to give such a notice. Each insurance policy also shall include an endorsement providing that coverage in favor of Lender will not be impaired in any way by any act, omission or default of Grantor or any other person. In connection with all policies covering assets in which Lender holds or is offered a security interest, Grantor will provide Lender with such loss payable or other endorsements as Lender may require. If Grantor at any time fails to obtain or maintain any insurance as required under this Agreement, Lender may (but shall not be obligated to) obtain such insurance as Lender deems appropriate, including if Lender so chooses "single interest insurance," which will cover only Lender's interest in the Collateral.

Application of Insurance Proceeds. Grantor shall promptly notify Lender of any loss or damage to the Collateral. Lender may make proof of loss if Grantor fails to do so within fifteen (15) days of the casualty. All proceeds of any insurance on the Collateral, including accrued proceeds thereon, shall be held by Lender as part of the Collateral. If Lender consents to repair or replacement of the damaged or destroyed Collateral, Lender shall, upon satisfactory proof of expenditure, pay or reimburse Grantor from the proceeds for the reasonable cost of repair or restoration. If Lender does not consent to repair or replacement of the Collateral, Lender shall retain a sufficient amount of the proceeds to pay all of the Indebtedness, and shall pay the balance to Grantor. Any proceeds which have not been disbursed within six (6) months after their receipt and which Grantor has not committed to the repair or restoration of the Collateral shall be used to prepay the Indebtedness.

Insurance Reserves. Lender may require Grantor to maintain with Lender reserves for payment of insurance premiums, which reserves shall be created by monthly payments from Grantor of a sum estimated by Lender to be sufficient to produce, at least fifteen (15) days before the premium due date, amounts at least equal to the insurance premiums to be paid. If fifteen (15) days before payment is due, the reserve funds are insufficient, Grantor shall upon demand pay any deficiency to Lender. The reserve funds shall be held by Lender as a general deposit and shall constitute a non-interest-bearing account which Lender may satisfy by payment of the insurance premiums required to be paid by Grantor as they become due. Lender does not hold the reserve funds in trust for Grantor, and Lender is not the agent of Grantor for payment of the insurance premiums required to be paid by Grantor. The responsibility for the payment of premiums shall remain Grantor's sole responsibility.

Insurance Reports. Grantor, upon request of Lender, shall furnish to Lender reports on each existing policy of insurance showing such information as Lender may reasonably request including the following: (1) the name of the insurer; (2) the risks insured; (3) the amount of the policy; (4) the property insured; (5) the then current value on the basis of which insurance has been obtained and the manner of determining that value; and (6) the expiration date of the policy. In addition, Grantor shall upon request by Lender (however not more often than annually) have an independent appraiser satisfactory to Lender determine, as applicable, the cash value or replacement cost of the Collateral.

Financing Statements. Grantor authorizes Lender to file a UCC financing statement, or alternatively, a copy of this Agreement to perfect Lender's security interest. At Lender's request, Grantor additionally agrees to sign all other documents that are necessary to perfect, protect, and continue Lender's security interest in the Property. This includes making sure Lender is shown as the first and only security interest holder on the title covering the Property. Grantor will pay all filing fees, title transfer fees, and other fees and costs involved unless prohibited by law or unless Lender is required by law to pay such fees and costs. Grantor irrevocably appoints Lender to execute documents necessary to transfer title if there is a default. Lender may file a copy of this Agreement as a financing statement. If Grantor changes Grantor's name or address, or the name or address of any person granting a security interest under this Agreement changes, Grantor will promptly notify the Lender of such change.

GRANTOR'S RIGHT TO POSSESSION. Until default, Grantor may have possession of the tangible personal property and beneficial use of all the Collateral and may use it in any lawful manner not inconsistent with this Agreement or the Related Documents, provided that Grantor's right to possession and beneficial use shall not apply to any Collateral where possession of the Collateral by Lender is required by law to perfect Lender's security interest in such Collateral. If Lender at any time has possession of any Collateral, whether before or after an Event of Default, Lender shall be deemed to have exercised reasonable care in the custody and preservation of the Collateral if Lender takes such action for that purpose as Grantor shall request or as Lender, in Lender's sole discretion, shall deem appropriate under the circumstances, but failure to honor any request by Grantor shall not of itself be deemed to be a failure to exercise reasonable care. Lender shall not be required to take any steps necessary to preserve any rights in the Collateral against prior parties, nor to protect, preserve or maintain any security interest given to secure the Indebtedness.

LENDER'S EXPENDITURES. If any action or proceeding is commenced that would materially affect Lender's interest in the Collateral or if Grantor fails to comply with any provision of this Agreement or any Related Documents, including but not limited to Grantor's failure to discharge or pay when due any amounts Grantor is required to discharge or pay under this Agreement or any Related Documents, Lender on Grantor's behalf may (but shall not be obligated to) take any action that Lender deems appropriate, including but not limited to discharging or paying all taxes, liens, security interests, encumbrances and other claims, at any time levied or placed on the Collateral and paying all costs for insuring, maintaining and preserving the Collateral. All such expenditures incurred or paid by Lender for such purposes will then bear interest at the rate charged under the Note from the date incurred or paid by Lender to the date of repayment by Grantor. All such expenses will become a part of the Indebtedness and, at Lender's option, will (A) be payable on demand; (B) be added to the balance of the Note and be apportioned among and be payable with any installment payments to become due during either (1) the term of any applicable insurance policy; or (2) the remaining term of the Note; or (C) be treated as a balloon payment which will be due and payable at the Note's maturity. The Agreement also will secure payment of these amounts. Such right shall be in addition to all other rights and remedies to which Lender may be entitled upon Default.

DEFAULT. Each of the following shall constitute an Event of Default under this Agreement;

Payment Default. Grantor fails to make any payment when due under the Indebtedness.

Other Defaults. Grantor fails to comply with or to perform any other term, obligation, covenant or condition contained in this Agreement or in any of the Related Documents or to comply with or to perform any term, obligation, covenant or condition contained in any other agreement between Lender and Grantor.

Default in Favor of Third Parties. Should Borrower or any Grantor default under any loan, extension of credit, security agreement, purchase or sales agreement, or any other agreement, in favor of any other creditor or person that may materially affect any of Grantor's property or Grantor's or any Grantor's ability to repay the Indebtedness or perform their respective obligations under this Agreement or any of the Related Documents.

False Statements. Any warranty, representation or statement made or furnished to Lender by Grantor or on Grantor's behalf under this Agreement or the Related Documents is false or misleading in any material respect, either now or at the time made or furnished or becomes false or misleading at any time thereafter.

Defective Collateralization. This Agreement or any of the Related Documents ceases to be in full force and effect (including failure of any collateral document to create a valid and perfected security interest or lien) at any time and for any reason.

Insolvency. The dissolution or termination of Grantor's existence as a going business, the insolvency of Grantor, the appointment of a receiver for any part of Grantor's property, any assignment for the benefit of creditors, any type of creditor workout, or the commencement of any proceeding under any bankruptcy or insolvency laws by or against Grantor.

Creditor or Forfeiture Proceedings. Commencement of foreclosure or forfeiture proceedings, whether by judicial proceeding, self-help, repossession or any other method, by any creditor of Grantor or by any governmental agency against any collateral securing the Indebtedness. This includes a garnishment of any of Grantor's accounts, including deposit accounts, with Lender. However, this Event of Default shall not apply if there is a good faith dispute by Grantor as to the validity or reasonableness of the claim which is the basis of the creditor or forfeiture proceeding and if Grantor gives Lender written notice of the creditor or forfeiture proceeding and deposits with Lender monies or a surety bond for the creditor or forfeiture proceeding, in an amount determined by Lender, in its sole discretion, as being an adequate reserve or bond for the dispute.

Events Affecting Guarantor. Any of the preceding events occurs with respect to any Guarantor of any of the Indebtedness or Guarantor dies or becomes incompetent or revokes or disputes the validity of, or liability under, any Guaranty of the Indebtedness.

Adverse Change. A material adverse change occurs in Grantor's financial condition, or Lender believes the prospect of payment or performance of the Indebtedness is impaired.

Insecurity. Lender in good faith believes itself insecure.

Cure Provisions. If any default, other than a default in payment is curable and if Grantor has not been given a notice of a breach of the same provision of this Agreement within the preceding twelve (12) months, it may be cured if Grantor, after receiving written notice from Lender demanding cure of such default: (1) cures the default within fifteen (15) days; or (2) if the cure requires more than fifteen (15) days, immediately initiates steps which Lender deems in Lender's sole discretion to be sufficient to cure the default and thereafter continues and completes all reasonable and necessary steps sufficient to produce compliance as soon as reasonably practical.

RIGHTS AND REMEDIES ON DEFAULT. If an Event of Default occurs under this Agreement, at any time thereafter, Lender shall have all the rights of a secured party under the California Uniform Commercial Code. In addition and without limitation, Lender may exercise any one or more of the following rights and remedies:

Accelerate Indebtedness. Lender may declare the entire Indebtedness, including any prepayment penalty which Grantor would be required to pay, immediately due and payable, without notice of any kind to Grantor.

Assemble Collateral. Lender may require Grantor to deliver to Lender all or any portion of the Collateral and any and all certificates of title and other documents relating to the Collateral. Lender may require Grantor to assemble the Collateral and make it available to Lender at a place to be designated by Lender. Lender also shall have full power to enter upon the property of Grantor to take possession of and remove the Collateral. If the Collateral contains other goods not covered by this Agreement at the time of repossession, Grantor agrees Lender may take such other goods, provided that Lender makes reasonable efforts to return them to Grantor after repossession.

Sell the Collateral. Lender shall have full power to sell, lease, transfer, or otherwise deal with the Collateral or proceeds thereof in Lender's own name or that of Grantor. Lender may sell the Collateral at public auction or private sale. Unless the Collateral threatens to decline speedily in value or is of a type customarily sold on a recognized market, Lender will give Grantor, and other persons as required by law, reasonable notice of the time and place of any public sale, or the time after which any private sale or any other disposition of the Collateral is to be made. However, no notice need be provided to any person who, after Event of Default occurs, enters into and authenticates an agreement waiving that person's right to notification of sale. The requirements of reasonable notice shall be met if such notice is given at least ten (10) days before the time of the sale or disposition. All expenses relating to the disposition of the Collateral, including without limitation the expenses of retaking, holding, insuring, preparing for sale and selling the Collateral, shall become a part of the Indebtedness secured by this Agreement and shall be payable on demand, with interest at the Note rate from date of expenditure until repaid.

Appoint Receiver. Lender shall have the right to have a receiver appointed to take possession of all or any part of the Collateral, with the power to protect and preserve the Collateral, to operate the Collateral preceding foreclosure or sale, and to collect the Rents from the Collateral and apply the proceeds, over and above the cost of the receivership, against the Indebtedness. The receiver may serve without bond if permitted by law. Lender's right to the appointment of a receiver shall exist whether or not the apparent value of the Collateral exceeds the Indebtedness by a substantial amount. Employment by Lender shall not disqualify a person from serving as a receiver.

Collect Revenues, Apply Accounts. Lender, either itself or through a receiver, may collect the payments, rents, income, and revenues from the Collateral. Lender may at any time in Lender's discretion transfer any Collateral into Lender's own name or that of Lender's nominee and receive the payments, rents, income, and revenues therefrom and hold the same as security for the Indebtedness or apply it to payment of the Indebtedness in such order of preference as Lender may determine. Insofar as the Collateral consists of accounts, general intangibles, insurance policies, instruments, chattel paper, choses in action, or similar property, Lender may demand, collect, receipt for, settle, compromise, adjust, sue for, foreclose, or realize on the Collateral as Lender may determine, whether or not Indebtedness or Collateral is then due. For these purposes, Lender may, on behalf of and in the name of Grantor, receive, open and dispose of mail addressed to Grantor; change any address to which mail and payments are to be sent; and endorse notes, checks, drafts, money orders, documents of title, instruments and items pertaining to payment, shipment, or storage of any Collateral. To facilitate collection, Lender may notify account debtors and obligors on any Collateral to make payments directly to Lender.

Obtain Deficiency. If Lender chooses to sell any or all of the Collateral, Lender may obtain a judgment against Grantor for any deficiency remaining on the Indebtedness due to Lender after application of all amounts received from the exercise of the rights provided in this Agreement. Grantor shall be liable for a deficiency even if the transaction described in this subsection is a sale of accounts or chattel paper.

Other Rights and Remedies. Lender shall have all the rights and remedies of a secured creditor under the provisions of the Uniform Commercial Code, as may be amended from time to time. In addition, Lender shall have and may exercise any or all other rights and remedies it may have available at law, in equity, or otherwise.

Election of Remedies. Except as may be prohibited by applicable law, all of Lender's rights and remedies, whether evidenced by this Agreement, the Related Documents, or by any other writing, shall be cumulative and may be exercised singularly or concurrently. Election by Lender to pursue any remedy shall not exclude pursuit of any other remedy, and an election to make expenditures or to take action to perform an obligation of Grantor under this Agreement, after Grantor's failure to perform, shall not affect Lender's right to declare a default and exercise its remedies.

MISCELLANEOUS PROVISIONS. The following miscellaneous provisions are a part of this Agreement:

Amendments. This Agreement, together with any Related Documents, constitutes the entire understanding and agreement of the parties as to the matters set forth in this Agreement. No alteration of or amendment to this Agreement shall be effective unless given in writing and signed by the party or parties sought to be charged or bound by the alteration or amendment.

Arbitration Disclosures.

1. ARBITRATION IS FINAL AND BINDING ON THE PARTIES AND SUBJECT TO ONLY VERY LIMITED REVIEW BY A COURT.

2. IN ARBITRATION THE PARTIES ARE WAIVING THEIR RIGHT TO LITIGATE IN COURT, INCLUDING THEIR RIGHT TO A JURY TRIAL.

3. DISCOVERY IN ARBITRATION IS MORE LIMITED THAN DISCOVERY IN COURT.

4. ARBITRATORS ARE NOT REQUIRED TO INCLUDE FACTUAL FINDINGS OR LEGAL REASONING IN THEIR AWARDS. THE RIGHT TO APPEAL OR SEEK MODIFICATION OF ARBITRATORS' RULINGS IS VERY LIMITED.

5. A PANEL OF ARBITRATORS MIGHT INCLUDE AN ARBITRATOR WHO IS OR WAS AFFILIATED WITH THE BANKING INDUSTRY.

6. ARBITRATION WILL APPLY TO ALL DISPUTES BETWEEN THE PARTIES, NOT JUST THOSE CONCERNING THE AGREEMENT.

7. IF YOU HAVE QUESTIONS ABOUT ARBITRATION, CONSULT YOUR ATTORNEY OR THE AMERICAN ARBITRATION ASSOCIATION.

(a) Any claim or controversy ("Dispute") between or among the parties and their employees, agents, affiliates, and assigns, including, but not limited to, Disputes arising out of or relating to this agreement, this arbitration provision ("arbitration clause"), or any related agreements or instruments relating hereto or delivered in connection herewith ("Related Agreements"), and including, but not limited to, a Dispute based on or arising from an alleged tort, shall at the request of any party be resolved by binding arbitration in accordance with the applicable arbitration rules of the American Arbitration Association (the "Administrator"). The provisions of this arbitration clause shall survive any termination, amendment, or expiration of this agreement or Related Agreements. The provisions of this arbitration clause shall supersede any prior arbitration agreement between or among the parties.

(b) The arbitration proceedings shall be conducted in a city mutually agreed by the parties. Absent such an agreement, arbitration will be conducted in Los Angeles, California or such other place as may be determined by the Administrator. The Administrator and the arbitrator(s) shall have the authority to the extent practicable to take any action to require the arbitration proceeding to be completed and the arbitrators)' award issued within 150 days of the filing of the Dispute with the Administrator. The arbitrator(s) shall have the authority to impose sanctions on any party that fails to comply with time periods imposed by the Administrator or the arbitrator(s), including the sanction of summarily dismissing any Dispute or defense with prejudice. The arbitrator(s) shall have the authority to resolve any Dispute regarding the terms of this agreement, this arbitration clause, or Related Agreements, including any claim or controversy regarding the arbitrability of any Dispute. All limitations periods applicable to any Dispute or defense, whether by statute or agreement, shall apply to any arbitration proceeding hereunder and the arbitrator(s) shall have the authority to decide whether any Dispute or defense is barred by a limitations period and, if so, to summarily enter an award dismissing any Dispute or defense on that basis. The doctrines of compulsory counterclaim, res judicata, and collateral estoppel shall apply to any arbitration proceeding hereunder so that a party must state as a counterclaim in the arbitration proceeding any claim or controversy which arises out of the transaction or occurrence that is the subject matter of the Dispute. The arbitrator(s) may in the arbitrators)' discretion and at the request of any party: (1) consolidate in a single arbitration proceeding any other claim arising out of the same transaction involving another party to that transaction that is bound by an arbitration clause with Lender, such as borrowers, guarantors, sureties, and owners of collateral; and (2) consolidate or administer multiple arbitration claims or controversies as a class action in accordance with Rule 23 of the Federal Rules of Civil Procedure.

(c) The arbitrator(s) shall be selected in accordance with the rules of the Administrator from panels maintained by the Administrator. A single arbitrator shall have expertise in the subject matter of the Dispute. Where three arbitrators conduct an arbitration proceeding, the Dispute shall be decided by a majority vote of the three arbitrators, at least one of whom must have expertise in the subject matter of the Dispute and at least one of whom must be a practicing attorney. The arbitrator(s) shall award to the prevailing party recovery of all costs and fees (including attorneys' fees and costs, arbitration administration fees and costs, and arbitrator(s)' fees). The arbitrator(s), either during the pendency of the arbitration proceeding or as part of the arbitration award, also may grant provisional or ancillary remedies including but not limited to an award of injunctive relief, foreclosure, sequestration, attachment, replevin, garnishment, or the appointment of a receiver.

(d) Judgement upon an arbitration award may be entered in any court having jurisdiction, subject to the following limitation: the arbitration award is binding upon the parties only if the amount does not exceed Four Million Dollars ($4,000,000.00); if the award exceeds that limit, either party may demand the right to a court trial. Such a demand must be filed with the Administrator within thirty (30) days following the date of the arbitration award; if such a demand is not made with that time period, the amount of the arbitration award shall be binding. The computation of the total amount of an arbitration award shall include amounts awarded for attorneys' fees and costs, arbitration administration fees and costs, and arbitrators)' fees.

(e) No provision of this arbitration clause, nor the exercise of any rights hereunder, shall limit the right of any party to: (T) judicially or non-judicially foreclose against any real or personal property collateral or other security; (2) exercise self-help remedies, including but not limited to repossession and setoff rights; or (3) obtain from a court having jurisdiction thereover any provisional or ancillary remedies including but not limited to injunctive relief, foreclosure, sequestration, attachment, replevin, garnishment, or the appointment of a receiver. Such rights can be exercised at any time, before or after initiation of an arbitration proceeding, except to the extent such action is contrary to the arbitration award. The exercise of such rights shall not constitute a waiver of the right to submit any Dispute to arbitration, and any claim or controversy related to the exercise of such rights shall be a Dispute to be resolved under the provisions of this arbitration clause. Any party may initiate arbitration with the Administrator. If any party desires to arbitrate a Dispute asserted against such party in a complaint, counterclaim, cross-claim, or third-party complaint thereto, or in an answer or other reply to any such pleading, such party must make an appropriate motion to the trial court seeking to compel arbitration, which motion must be filed with the court within 45 days of service of the pleading, or amendment thereto, setting forth such Dispute. If arbitration is compelled after commencement of litigation of a Dispute, the party obtaining an order compelling arbitration shall commence arbitration and pay the Administrator's filing fees and costs within 45 days of entry of such order. Failure to do so shall constitute an agreement to proceed with litigation and waiver of the right to arbitrate. In any arbitration commenced by a consumer regarding a consumer Dispute, Lender shall pay one half of the Administrator's filing fee, up to $250.

(f) Notwithstanding the applicability of any other law to this agreement, the arbitration clause, or Related Agreements between or among the parties, the Federal Arbitration Act, 9 U.S.C. Section 1 et seq., shall apply to the construction and interpretation of this arbitration clause. If any provision of this arbitration clause should be determined to be unenforceable, all other provisions of this arbitration clause shall remain in full force and effect.

Attorneys' Fees; Expenses. Grantor agrees to pay upon demand all of Lender's costs and expenses, including Lender's attorneys' fees and Lender's legal expenses, incurred in connection with the enforcement of this Agreement. Lender may hire or pay someone else to help enforce this Agreement, and Grantor shall pay the costs and expenses of such enforcement. Costs and expenses include Lender's attorneys' fees and legal expenses whether or not there is a lawsuit, including attorneys' fees and legal expenses for bankruptcy proceedings (including efforts to modify or vacate any automatic stay or injunction), appeals, and any anticipated post-judgment collection services. Grantor also shall pay all court costs and such additional fees as may be directed by the court.

Caption Headings. Caption headings in this Agreement are for convenience purposes only and are not to be used to interpret or define the provisions of this Agreement.

Governing Law. With respect to procedural matters related to the perfection and enforcement of Lender's rights against the Collateral, this Agreement will be governed by federal law applicable to Lender and to the extent not preempted by federal law, the laws of the State of California. In all other respects, this Agreement will be governed by federal law applicable to Lender and, to the extent not preempted by federal law, the laws of the State of Utah without regard to its conflicts of law provisions. However, if there ever is a question about whether any provision of this Agreement is valid or enforceable, the provision that is questioned will be governed by whichever state or federal law would find the provision to be valid and enforceable. The loan transaction that is evidenced by the Note and this Agreement has been applied for, considered, approved and made, and all necessary loan documents have been accepted by Lender in the State of Utah.

Choice of Venue. If there is a lawsuit, Grantor agrees upon Lender's request to submit to the jurisdiction of the courts of SALT LAKE County, State of Utah.

Preference Payments. Any monies Lender pays because of an asserted preference claim in Grantor's bankruptcy will become a part of the Indebtedness and, at Lender's option, shall be payable by Grantor as provided in this Agreement.

No Waiver by Lender. Lender shall not be deemed to have waived any rights under this Agreement unless such waiver is given in writing and signed by Lender. No delay or omission on the part of Lender in exercising any right shall operate as a waiver of such right or any other right. A waiver by Lender of a provision of this Agreement shall not prejudice or constitute a waiver of Lender's right otherwise to demand strict compliance with that provision or any other provision of this Agreement. No prior waiver by Lender, nor any course of dealing between Lender and Grantor, shall constitute a waiver of any of Lender's rights or of any of Grantor's obligations as to any future transactions. Whenever the consent of Lender is required under this Agreement, the granting of such consent by Lender in any instance shall not constitute continuing consent to subsequent instances where such consent is required and in all cases such consent may be granted or withheld in the sole discretion of Lender.

Notices. Any notice required to be given under this Agreement shall be given in writing, and shall be effective when actually delivered, when actually received by telefacsimile (unless otherwise required by law), when deposited with a nationally recognized overnight courier, or, if mailed, when deposited in the United States mail, as first class, certified or registered mail postage prepaid, directed to the addresses shown near the beginning of this Agreement. Any party may change its address for notices under this Agreement by giving formal written notice to the other parties, specifying that the purpose of the notice is to change the party's address. For notice purposes, Grantor agrees to keep Lender informed at all times of Grantor's current address. Unless otherwise provided or required by law, if there is more than one Grantor, any notice given by Lender to any Grantor is deemed to be notice given to all Grantors.

Power of Attorney. Grantor hereby appoints Lender as Grantor's irrevocable attorney-in-fact for the purpose of executing any documents necessary to perfect, amend, or to continue the security interest granted in this Agreement or to demand termination of filings of other secured parties. Lender may at any time, and without further authorization from Grantor, file a carbon, photographic or other reproduction of any financing statement or of this Agreement for use as a financing statement. Grantor will reimburse Lender for all expenses for the perfection and the continuation of the perfection of Lender's security interest in the Collateral.

Waiver of Co-Obligor's Rights. If more than one person is obligated for the Indebtedness, Grantor irrevocably waives, disclaims and relinquishes all claims against such other person which Grantor has or would otherwise have by virtue of payment of the Indebtedness or any part thereof, specifically including but not limited to all rights of indemnity, contribution or exoneration.

Severability. If a court of competent jurisdiction finds any provision of this Agreement to be illegal, invalid, or unenforceable as to any circumstance, that finding shall not make the offending provision illegal, invalid, or unenforceable as to any other circumstance. If feasible, the offending provision shall be considered modified so that it becomes legal, valid and enforceable. If the offending provision cannot be so modified, it shall be considered deleted from this Agreement. Unless otherwise required by law, the illegality, invalidity, or unenforceability of any provision of this Agreement shall not affect the legality, validity or enforceability of any other provision of this Agreement.

Successors and Assigns. Subject to any limitations stated in this Agreement on transfer of Grantor's interest, this Agreement shall be binding upon and inure to the benefit of the parties, their successors and assigns. If ownership of the Collateral becomes vested in a person other than Grantor, Lender, without notice to Grantor, may deal with Grantor's successors with reference to this Agreement and the Indebtedness by way of forbearance or extension without releasing Grantor from the obligations of this Agreement or liability under the Indebtedness.

Survival of Representations and Warranties. All representations, warranties, and agreements made by Grantor in this Agreement shall survive the execution and delivery of this Agreement, shall be continuing in nature, and shall remain in full force and effect until such time as Grantor's Indebtedness shall be paid in full.

Time is of the Essence. Time is of the essence in the performance of this Agreement.

DEFINITIONS. The following capitalized words and terms shall have the following meanings when used in this Agreement. Unless specifically stated to the contrary, all references to dollar amounts shall mean amounts in lawful money of the United States of America. Words and terms used in the singular shall include the plural, and the plural shall include the singular, as the context may require. Words and terms not otherwise defined in this Agreement shall have the meanings attributed to such terms in the Uniform Commercial Code:

Agreement. The word "Agreement" means this Commercial Security Agreement, as this Commercial Security Agreement may be amended or modified from time to time, together with all exhibits and schedules attached to this Commercial Security Agreement from time to time.

Borrower. The word "Borrower" means DELKIM COMPANY, INC. and includes all co-signers and co-makers signing the Note.

Collateral. The word "Collateral" means all of Grantor's right, title and interest in and to all the Collateral as described in the Collateral Description section of this Agreement.

Default. The word "Default" means the Default set forth in this Agreement in the section titled "Default".

Environmental Laws. The words "Environmental Laws" mean any and all state, federal and local statutes, regulations and ordinances relating to the protection of human health or the environment, including without limitation the Comprehensive Environmental Response, Compensation, and Liability Act of 1980, as amended, 42 U.S.C. Section 9601, et seq. ("CERCLA"), the Superfund Amendments and Reauthorization Act of 1986, Pub. L. No. 99-499 ("SARA"), the Hazardous Materials Transportation Act, 49 U.S.C. Section 1801, et seq., the Resource Conservation and Recovery Act, 42 U.S.C. Section 6901, et seq., Chapters 6.5 through 7.7 of Division 20 of the California Health and Safety Code, Section 25100, et seq., or other applicable state or federal laws, rules, or regulations adopted pursuant thereto.

Event of Default. The words "Event of Default" mean any of the events of default set forth in this Agreement in the default section of this Agreement.

Grantor. The word "Grantor" means DELKIM COMPANY, INC..

Guarantor. The word "Guarantor" means any guarantor, surety, or accommodation party of any or all of the Indebtedness. Guaranty. The word "Guaranty" means the guaranty from Guarantor to Lender, including without limitation a guaranty of all or part of the Note.

Hazardous Substances. The words "Hazardous Substances" mean materials that, because of their quantity, concentration or physical, chemical or infectious characteristics, may cause or pose a present or potential hazard to human health or the environment when improperly used, treated, stored, disposed of, generated, manufactured, transported or otherwise handled. The words "Hazardous Substances" are used in their very broadest sense and include without limitation any and all hazardous or toxic substances, materials or waste as defined by or listed under the Environmental Laws. The term "Hazardous Substances" also includes, without limitation, petroleum and petroleum by-products or any fraction thereof and asbestos.

Indebtedness. The word "Indebtedness" means and includes without limitation all Loans, together with all other obligations, debts and liabilities of Borrower to Lender, or any one or more of them, as well as all claims by Lender against Borrower, or any one or more of them; whether now or hereafter existing, voluntary or involuntary, due or not due, absolute or contingent, liquidated or unliquidated; whether Borrower may be liable individually or jointly with others; whether Borrower may be obligated as a guarantor, surety, or otherwise; whether recovery upon such indebtedness may be or hereafter may become barred by any statute of limitations; and whether such indebtedness may be or hereafter may become otherwise unenforceable.

Lender. The word "Lender" means FIRST NATIONAL BANK, its successors and assigns.

Note. The word "Note" means the Note executed by DELKIM COMPANY, INC. in the principal amount of $400,000.00 dated February 16, 20XX, together with all renewals of, extensions of, modifications of, refinancings of, consolidations of, and substitutions for the note or credit agreement.

Property. The word "Property" means all of Grantor's right, title and interest in and to all the Property as described in the "Collateral Description" section of this Agreement.

Related Documents. The words "Related Documents" mean all promissory notes, credit agreements, loan agreements, environmental agreements, security agreements, mortgages, deeds of trust, security deeds, collateral mortgages, and all other instruments, agreements and documents, whether now or hereafter existing, executed in connection with the Indebtedness.

GRANTOR HAS READ AND UNDERSTOOD ALL THE PROVISIONS OF THIS COMMERCIAL SECURITY AGREEMENT AND AGREES TO ITS TERMS. THIS AGREEMENT IS DATED FEBRUARY 16, 20XX.

GRANTOR: DELKIM COMPANY, INC.

By: _____
JUAN HAN, President of DELKIM COMPANY, INC.

By: _____
SUNNY HAN, Secretary of DELKIM COMPANY, INC.

CORPORATE RESOLUTION TO BORROW

Principal	Loan Date	Maturity	Loan No	Call/Coll	Account	Officer	Initials
$400,000.00	02-16-20XX	03-01-20XX	9001	1C / 6520	0524840	***	

References in the shaded area are for Lender's use only and do not limit the applicability of this document to any particular loan or item.
Any item above containing "***" has been omitted due to text length limitations.

Corporation: DELKIM COMPANY, INC
10855 SAN PALO AVENUE
EL CERRITO, CA 94550

Lender: FIRST NATIONAL BANK
REAL ESTATE DEPARTMENT
ONE MAIN STREET
SALT LAKE CITY, UT 84155

WE, THE UNDERSIGNED, DO HEREBY CERTIFY THAT:

THE CORPORATION'S EXISTENCE. The complete and correct name of the Corporation is DELKIM COMPANY, INC. ("Corporation"). The Corporation is a corporation for profit which is, and at all times shall be, duly organized, validly existing, and in good standing under and by virtue of the laws of the State of California. The Corporation is duly authorized to transact business in all other states in which the Corporation is doing business, having obtained all necessary filings, governmental licenses and approvals for each state in which the Corporation is doing business. Specifically, the Corporation is, and at all times shall be, duly qualified as a foreign corporation in all states in which the failure to so qualify would have a material adverse effect on its business or financial condition. The Corporation has the full power and authority to own its properties and to transact the business in which it is presently engaged or presently proposes to engage. The Corporation maintains an office at 10855 SAN PALO AVENUE, EL CERRITO, CA 94550. Unless the Corporation has designated otherwise in writing, the principal office is the office at which the Corporation keeps its books and records. The Corporation will notify Lender prior to any change in the location of The Corporation's state of organization or any change in The Corporation's name. The Corporation shall do all things necessary to preserve and to keep in full force and effect its existence, rights and privileges, and shall comply with all regulations, rules, ordinances, statutes, orders and decrees of any governmental or quasi-governmental authority or court applicable to the Corporation and The Corporation's business activities.

RESOLUTIONS ADOPTED. At a meeting of the Directors of the Corporation, or if the Corporation is a close corporation having no Board of Directors then at a meeting of the Corporation's shareholders, duly called and held on February 16, 20XX, at which a quorum was present and voting, or by other duly authorized action in lieu of a meeting, the resolutions set forth in this Resolution were adopted.

OFFICERS. The following named persons are officers of DELKIM COMPANY, INC.:

NAMES	TITLES	AUTHORIZED		ACTUAL SIGNATURES
JUAN HAN	President	Y	x	_____
SUNNY HAN	Secretary	Y	x	_____

ACTIONS AUTHORIZED. Any two (2) of the authorized persons listed above may enter into any agreements of any nature with Lender, and those agreements will bind the Corporation. Specifically, but without limitation, any two (2) of such authorized persons are authorized, empowered, and directed to do the following for and on behalf of the Corporation:

Borrow Money. To borrow, as a cosigner or otherwise, from time to time from Lender, on such terms as may be agreed upon between the Corporation and Lender, such sum or sums of money as in their judgment should be borrowed; however, not exceeding at any one time the amount of Four Hundred Thousand & 00/100 Dollars ($400,000.00), in addition to such sum or sums of money as may be currently borrowed by the Corporation from Lender.

Execute Notes. To execute and deliver to Lender the promissory note or notes, or other evidence of the Corporation's credit accommodations, on Lender's forms, at such rates of interest and on such terms as may be agreed upon, evidencing the sums of money so borrowed or any of the Corporation's indebtedness to Lender, and also to execute and deliver to Lender one or more renewals, extensions, modifications, refinancings, consolidations, or substitutions for one or more of the notes, any portion of the notes, or any other evidence of credit accommodations.

Execute Security Documents. To execute and deliver to Lender the forms of mortgage, deed of trust, pledge agreement, hypothecation agreement, and other security agreements and financing statements which Lender may require and which shall evidence the terms and conditions under and pursuant to which such liens and encumbrances, or any of them, are given; and also to execute and deliver to Lender any other written instruments, any chattel paper, or any other collateral, of any kind or nature, which Lender may deem necessary or proper in connection with or pertaining to the giving of the liens and encumbrances. Notwithstanding the foregoing, any one of the above authorized persons may execute, deliver, or record financing statements.

Negotiate Items. To draw, endorse, and discount with Lender all drafts, trade acceptances, promissory notes, or other evidences of indebtedness payable to or belonging to the Corporation or in which the Corporation may have an interest, and either to receive cash for the same or to cause such proceeds to be credited to the Corporation's account with Lender, or to cause such other disposition of the proceeds derived therefrom as they may deem advisable.

Further Acts. In the case of lines of credit, to designate additional or alternate individuals as being authorized to request advances under such lines, and in all cases, to do and perform such other acts and things, to pay any and all fees and costs, and to execute and deliver such other documents and agreements, including agreements requiring disputes with Lender to be submitted to binding arbitration for final resolution, as the officers may in their discretion deem reasonably necessary or proper in order to carry into effect the provisions of this Resolution.

ASSUMED BUSINESS NAMES. The Corporation has filed or recorded all documents or filings required by law relating to all assumed business names used by the Corporation. Excluding the name of the Corporation, the following is a complete list of all assumed business names under which the Corporation does business:

Assumed Business	Name Filing Location	Date
TERRACE APARTMENTS		

NOTICES TO LENDER. The Corporation will promptly notify Lender in writing at Lender's address shown above (or such other addresses as Lender may designate from time to time) prior to any (A) change in the Corporation's name; (B) change in the Corporation's assumed business name(s); (C) change in the management of the Corporation; (D) change in the authorized signer(s); (E) change in the Corporation's principal office address; (F) change in the Corporation's state of organization; (G) conversion of the Corporation to a new or different type of business entity; or (H) change in any other aspect of the Corporation that directly or indirectly relates to any agreements between the Corporation and Lender. No change in the Corporation's name or state of organization will take effect until after Lender has received notice.

CERTIFICATION CONCERNING OFFICERS AND RESOLUTIONS. The officers named above are duly elected, appointed, or employed by or for the Corporation, as the case may be, and occupy the positions set opposite their respective names. This Resolution now stands of record on the books of the Corporation, is in full force and effect, and has not been modified or revoked in any manner whatsoever.

NO CORPORATE SEAL. The Corporation has no corporate seal, and therefore, no seal is affixed to this Resolution.

CONTINUING VALIDITY. Any and all acts authorized pursuant to this Resolution and performed prior to the passage of this Resolution are hereby ratified and approved. This Resolution shall be continuing, shall remain in full force and effect and Lender may rely on it until written notice of its revocation shall have been delivered to and received by Lender at Lender's address shown above (or such addresses as Lender may designate from time to time). Any such notice shall not affect any of the Corporation's agreements or commitments in effect at the time notice is given. IN

TESTIMONY WHEREOF, We have hereunto set our hand.

We each have read all the provisions of this Resolution, and we each personally and on behalf of the Corporation certify that all statements and representations made in this Resolution are true and correct. This Corporate Resolution to Borrow is dated February 16, 20XX.

CERTIFIED TO AND ATTESTED BY:

By: _____

         JUAN HAN, President of DELKIM COMPANY, INC.

By: _____

         SUNNY HAN, Secretary of DELKIM COMPANY, INC.

HAZARD INSURANCE DISCLOSURE

Principal	Loan Date	Maturity	Loan No	Call/Coll	Account	Officer	Initials
$400,000.00	02-16-20XX	03-01-20XX	9001	1C / 6520	0524840	***	

References in the shaded area are for Lender--s use only and do not limit the applicability of this document to any particular loan or item.
Any item above containing "***" has been omitted due to text length limitations.

Borrower: DELKIM COMPANY, INC
10855 SAN PALO AVENUE
EL CERRITO, CA 94550

Lender: FIRST NATIONAL BANK
REAL ESTATE DEPARTMENT
ONE MAIN STREET
SALT LAKE CITY, UT 84155

HAZARD INSURANCE DISCLOSURE

Made Pursuant to California Civil Code Section 2955.5

IMPORTANT

DO NOT SIGN THIS FORM UNTIL YOU CAREFULLY
READ IT AND UNDERSTAND ITS CONTENT

You have applied for a loan or credit accommodation that will be secured by real property. As a condition of the loan or credit accommodation, Lender may require you to maintain hazard insurance coverage for the real property. California law provides that Lender cannot require you, as a condition of receiving or maintaining a loan secured by real property, to provide hazard insurance coverage against risks to the property (such as fire and other perils) in an amount exceeding the replacement value of the building or structures attached to the property.

BY SIGNING BELOW, YOU ACKNOWLEDGE THAT YOU HAVE READ, RECEIVED AND UNDERSTAND THIS HAZARD INSURANCE DISCLOSURE. THIS DISCLOSURE IS DATED FEBRUARY 16, 20XX.

BORROWER:

By: _____
JUAN HAN, President of DELKIM COMPANY, INC.

By: _____
SUNNY HAN, Secretary of DELKIM COMPANY, INC.

GRANTOR: DELKIM COMPANY, INC.

By: _____   By: _____

JUAN HAN, President of DELKIM COMPANY, INC.   SUNNY HAN, Secretary of DELKIM COMPANY, INC.

FOR LENDER USE ONLY
INSURANCE VERIFICATION

Date_____   Phone _____

Agent's Name: _____

Agency: _____

Insurance Company: _____

Policy Number:

Effective Dates: _____
_____

Comments: _____
_____

FOR LENDER USE ONLY
INSURANCE VERIFICATION

Date_____   Phone _____

Agent's Name: _____

Agency: _____

Insurance Company: _____

Policy Number:

Effective Dates: _____
_____

Comments: _____
_____

RECORDING REQUESTED BY:
American Title Company

WHEN RECORDED MAIL TO:
LeAnn T. Wang and Joan L. Wang
424 Corvelle St.
El Cerrito, CA 94530

ESCROW NO: 3649573-FS
TITLE ORDER NO: 54702552

SPACE ABOVE THIS LINE FOR RECORDER'S USE

APN: Title Order No. 54702552   Escrow No. 3649573-FS

SUBORDINATION AGREEMENT

NOTICE: THIS SUBORDINATION AGREEMENT RESULTS IN YOUR SECURITY INTEREST IN THE PROPERTY BECOMING SUBJECT TO AND OF LOWER PRIORITY THAN THE LIEN OF SOME OTHER OR LATER SECURITY INSTRUMENT.

THIS AGREEMENT, made on November 22, 20XX, by Delkim Company, Inc. owner(s) of the land hereinafter described and hereinafter referred to as "Owner," and, and LeAnn T. Wang and Joan L. Wang, Trustees of the LeAnn T. Wang and Joan L. Wang 20XX Revocable Intervivos Trust, present owner and holder of the deed of trust and note first hereinafter described and hereinafter referred to as "Beneficiary;"

WITNESSETH

THAT WHEREAS, Juan Han and Sunny Han, husband and wife did execute a deed of trust, dated ~~~ National Title Insurance Company, a California corporation, as trustee, covering:

LEGAL DESCRIPTION ATTACHED HERETO AS EXHIBIT A AND MADE A PART HEREOF

to secure a note in the sum of $ 1,3000,000.00, dated June 4, 20XX, in favor of LeAnn T. Wang ~~~ Trustees of the LeAnn T. Wang and Joan L. Wang 20XX Revocable Intervivos Trust, which deed ~~~ on June 17, 20XX, in book NA, page NA, Official Records of said county; and

WHEREAS, Owner has executed, or is about to execute, a deed of trust and note in the sum of $ 400,000.00, Dated February 16, 20XX, in favor of First National Bank, hereinafter referred to as "Lender," payable with interest and upon the terms and conditions described therein, which deed of trust is to be recorded concurrently herewith; and

WHEREAS, it is a condition precedent to obtaining said loan that said deed of trust last above mentioned shall unconditionally be and remain at all times a lien or charge upon the land hereinbefore described, prior and superior to the lien or charge of the deed of trust first above mentioned; and

WHEREAS, lender is willing to make said loan provided the deed of trust securing the same is a lien or charge upon the above described property prior and superior to the lien or charge of the deed of trust first above mentioned and provided that Beneficiary will specifically and unconditionally subordinate the lien or charge of the deed of trust first above mentioned to the lien or charge of the deed of trust in favor of Lender; and

WHEREAS, it is to the mutual benefit of the parties hereto that Lender make such loan to Owner; and Beneficiary is willing that the deed of trust securing the same shall, when recorded, constitute a lien or charge upon said land which is unconditionally prior and superior to the lien or charge of the deed of trust first above mentioned.

NOTES

See page 78 for a description of the "Subordination Agreement." The form must be notarized (see page 383).

Make sure the borrowers properly initial each page of the "Subordination Agreement."

CLTA SUBORDINATION "A"
(EXISTING DEED OF TRUST TO NEW DEED OF TRUST)

INITIALS: _____ _____ _____ _____

Page No. 1 of 3

NOW, THEREFORE, in consideration of the mutual benefits accruing to the parties hereto and other valuable consideration, the receipt and sufficiency of which consideration is hereby acknowledged, and in order to induce Lender to make the loan above referred to, it is hereby declared, understood and agreed as follows:

(1) That said deed of trust securing said note in favor of Lender, and any renewals or extensions thereof, shall unconditionally be and remain at all times a lien or charge on the property therein described, prior and superior to the lien or charge of the deed of trust above mentioned.

(2) That Lender would not make its loan above described without this subordination agreement.

(3) That this agreement shall be the whole and only agreement with regard to the subordination of the lien or charge of the deed of trust first above mentioned to the lien or charge of the deed of trust in favor of Lender above referred to and shall supersede and cancel, but only insofar as would affect the priority between the deeds of trust hereinbefore specifically described, any prior agreement as to such subordination including, but not limited, those provisions, if any, contained in the deed of trust first above mentioned, which provide for the subordination of the lien or charge thereof to another deed or deeds of trust or to another mortgage or mortgages.

Beneficiary declares, agrees and acknowledges that:

(a) He consents to and approves (i) all provisions of the note and deed of trust in favor of Lender above referred to, and (ii) all agreements, including but not limited to any loan or escrow agreements, between Owner and Lender for the disbursement of the proceeds of Lender's loan;

(b) Lender in making disbursements pursuant to any such agreement is under no obligation or duty to, nor has Lender represented that it will, see to the application of such proceeds by the person or persons to whom Lender disburses such proceeds and any application or use of such proceeds for purposes other than those provided for in such agreement or agreements shall not defeat the subordination herein made in whole or in part;

(c) He intentionally and unconditionally waives, relinquishes and subordinates the lien or charge of the deed of trust first above mentioned in favor of the lien or charge upon said land of the deed of trust in favor of Lender above referred to and understands that in reliance upon, and in consideration of, this waiver, relinquishment and subordination, specific loans and advances are being and will be made and, as part and parcel thereof, specific monetary and other obligations are being and will be entered into which would not be made or entered into but for said reliance upon this waiver, relinquishment and subordination; and

(d) An endorsement has been placed upon the note secured by the deed of trust first above mentioned that said deed of trust has by this instrument been subordinated to the lien or charge of the deed of trust in favor of Lender above referred to.

NOTICE: THIS SUBORDINATION AGREEMENT CONTAINS A PROVISION WHICH ALLOWS THE PERSON OBLIGATED ON YOUR REAL PROPERTY SECURITY TO OBTAIN A LOAN, A PORTION OF WHICH MAY BE EXPENDED FOR OTHER PURPOSES THAN IMPROVEMENT OF THE LAND.

Beneficiary

Beneficiary:
LeAnn T. Wang and Joan L. Wang, Trustees of the
Trustees of the LeAnn T. Wang and Joan L. Wang
1993 Revocable Intervivos Trust

_____
LeAnn T. Wang, Trustee

_____
Juan Han, Owner

_____
Joan L. Wang, Trustee

_____
Sunny Han, Owner

CLTA SUBORDINATION "A"
(EXISTING DEED OF TRUST TO NEW DEED OF TRUST)

INITIALS: _____ _____ _____ _____

Page No. 2 of 3

IT IS RECOMMENDED THAT, PRIOR TO THE EXECUTION OF THIS SUBORDINATION AGREEMENT, THE PARTIES CONSULT WITH THEIR ATTORNEYS WITH RESPECT THERETO.

(ALL SIGNATURES MUST BE ACKNOWLEDGED)

STATE OF
COUNTY OF _____

ON _____ before me, _____ personally appeared

personally known to me (or proved to me on the basis of satisfactory evidence) to be the person(s) whose name(s) is/are subscribed to the within instrument and acknowledged to me that he/she/they executed the same in his/her/their authorized capacity(ies), and that by his/her/their signature(s) on the instrument the person(s), or the entity upon behalf of which the person(s) acted, executed the instrument.

Witness my hand and official seal.

Signature _____

STATE OF
COUNTY OF _____

ON _____ before me, _____ personally appeared

personally known to me (or proved to me on the basis of satisfactory evidence) to be the person(s) whose name(s) is/are subscribed to the within instrument and acknowledged to me that he/she/they executed the same in his/her/their authorized capacity(ies), and that by his/her/their signature(s) on the instrument the person(s), or the entity upon behalf of which the person(s) acted, executed the instrument.

Witness my hand and official seal.

Signature _____

CLTA SUBORDINATION "A"
(EXISTING DEED OF TRUST TO NEW DEED OF TRUST)

INITIALS: _____ _____ _____ _____
Page No. 3 of 3

EXHIBIT A

Description:

The land referred to herein is situated in the State of California, County of Contra Costa, City of Richmond, and is described as follows:

PORTION OF LOTS 53 AND 54 IN BLOCK 31 AS SHOWN ON THE AMENDED MAP OF ALTA PUNTA TRACT, FILED IN BOOK D OF MAPS, AT PAGE 90, IN THE OFFICE OF THE COUNTY RECORDER OF CONTRA COSTA COUNTY, DESCRIBED AS FOLLOWS: BEGINNING ON THE SOUTHWESTERN LINE OF SAN PABLO AVENUE AT THE MOST EASTERN CORNER OF LOT 54, AS SAID AVENUE AND LOT ARE SHOWN ON SAID MAP; THENCE NORTH 29° 01' WEST ALONG SAID SOUTHWESTERN LINE 150 FEET TO THE NORTHWESTERN LINE OF THE PARCEL OF LAND DESCRIBED IN THE DEED FROM ESTHER LAMAR SUNDGRON TO MARTHA J. MASTERSON, RECORDED DECEMBER 13, 20XX, BOOK 1455 OF OFFICIAL RECORDS OF CONTRA COSTA AT PAGE 355; THENCE SOUTHWESTERLY ALONG SAID NORTHWESTERN LINE TO THE NORTHEASTERN LINE OF THE PARCEL OF LAND DESCRIBED IN THE DEED FROM MARTHA J. MASTERSON TO JOHN D. GERLATTI, ET UX, RECORDED FEBRUARY 6, 20XX, IN BOOK 1555 OF OFFICIAL RECORDS OF CONTRA COSTA COUNTY AT PAGE 129; THENCE SOUTH 28° 18' EAST ALONG SAID NORTHEASTERN LINE 150 FEET TO THE SOUTHEASTERN LINE OF SAID LOT 54; THENCE NORTH 61° 42' EAST, ALONG SAID SOUTH LINE 321.76 FEET TO THE POINT OF BEGINNING.

APN: 508-340-006

CLTA SUBORDINATION "A"
(EXISTING DEED OF TRUST TO NEW DEED OF TRUST)

INITIALS: _____ _____ _____ _____
Page No. 4 of 3

BANK BUSINESS LOAN REQUEST

Business: <u>Delkim Company. Inc.</u>

Contact Person(s): <u>Juan Han . Sunny Han</u>

Address: <u>10855 San Palo Ave, E1 Cerrito, CA 94550</u>

Phone (day/evening): <u>510-235-8558</u> SSN or Fed. Tax# _____

LOAN INFORMATION

Amount: $ 400,000 Purpose: To provide financing for the refinance of a limited service motel along the 12 apartment units located in El Cerrito, CA

Type: ____ Line of credit; ____ Single payment, due: _____; ____ Term Loan, _____ years; ____ Other

Sources of repayment: 1. <u>Cash flow from the operations of Terrace Apts.</u>

                        2. <u>Liquidation of Collateral</u>

                        Alimony, child support, or separate maintenance income need not be revealed if you do not wish it considered as a basis for repaying this obligation.

Collateral offered/value: <u>1st Deed of Trust and Assignment of Rents on a limited service motel along with 12 apartment units located in El Cerrito, CA $1,900,000.</u>

Guarantors: <u>Juan Han, Sunny Han</u>

BACKGROUND

Date business started: <u>20XX</u>   Present management since: <u>Juan Han, Sunny Han</u>

Current legal form: ___ Sole Proprietor ___ DBA ___ Partnership ___ Limited Partnership ___ Corporation ___ LLC

Owners/percent owned: <u>Juan Han, Sunny Han</u>

Type of business/product or service: _____

_____

____ Own plant   ____ Lease plant   ____ Own equipment   ____ Lease equipment

Insurance agent and phone number:_____

Accountant and phone number: _____

Major customers: _____

Market area: _____

Competition: _____

ATTACHMENT CHECKLIST

____ Year-end business sheets and income statements for one to three years, depending on request.
____ Income tax returns for one to three years, depending on request.
____ Current interim balance sheet and income statement.
____ Financial statements and resumes of principal owners and guarantors.
____ Projected balance, income statement, and cash flow (for larger loans).
____ Business plan, if available.

I have read and agree with the Statement of Accuracy and Permission to Verify paragraphs on the reverse side, and I have read and understand the Rights of Credit Applications on the reverse side. I have retained a copy of this loan request.

_____   _____   _____
Signature   Title   Date

DELKIM COMPANY, INC.
271-0524840-9551

WHAT ADDRESS SHOULD BORROWER'S MONTHLY BILLING STATEMENT BE SENT TO?

Street Address: _____

_____

City/State/Zip Code: _____

E-Mail Address: _____

STATEMENT OF ACCURACY

The statements made here and in all attached documents are true and represent the total disclosure of the information pertaining to our/my credit worthiness. I agree to promptly notify Bank of any material changes in the information. I understand that additional information may be required.

PERMISSION TO VERIFY

I understand that all loans are subject to credit approval, and I authorize Bank to investigate and verify this information. I authorize any person or agency to disclose related credit information to Bank or its agents.

RIGHTS OF CREDIT APPLICANTS

Credit Denial

If the application for business credit is denied, you have the right to a written statement of the specific reasons for denial. To obtain the statement, please contact the office from which you obtained this request within 60 days from the date you are notified of our decision. We will send you a written statement of reasons for the denial within 30 days of receiving your request for the statement.

Equal Credit Opportunity

The federal Equal Opportunity Act prohibits creditors from discriminating against credit applicants on the basis of race, color, religion, national origin, sex, marital status, age (provided the applicant the capacity to enter into a binding contract); because al or part of the applicant's income derives from any public assistance program; or because the applicant has in good faith exercised any right under the Consumer Credit Protection Act. The federal agency administers compliance with this law concerning this creditor is the Office of the Comptroller of the Currency, Western Division, 50 Fremont Street, Suite #3900, San Francisco, California 94105.

Right to Appraisal

In the event you have applied for a loan that might or will secured by residential real property, you have the right to a copy of the appraisal report used in connection with your application for credit. If you would like a copy, please write to us at the office from which you obtained this request. In order to comply with your request, please provide us with the following information: Name used on this application for credit, your complete address, your phone number and your application or loan number, if known. If you wish to have a copy, you must notify us no later than 90 days after we notify you about the action taken on your credit applications or 90 days from the date you withdraw you request. This is to advise you that the sole purpose of the appraisal is to establish the adequacy of the property as security for the loan. Bank, the appraiser, any inspector retained by Bank and any agency insuring the loan make no representations or warranties of any kind or nature as to the market value of the property or its improvements.

Alimony

Alimony, child support, or separate maintenance income need not be revealed if you do not wish to have it considered as a basis for repaying this obligation.

LOAN EXPENSE LOG

Borrower: Delkim Co, inc dba Terrance Apts

Date	Expense Description	Billed	Paid
10-25-XX	Check from Borrower		$10,000
11-08-XX	Appraisal (Acme)	$4,200	
10-22-XX	Packaging	$1,500	
11-03-XX	Prelim UCC/Corp/Lien	$250	
	D&B@ $55	$0	
11-02-XX	TRW 2 @ $25	$50	
11-02-XX	Flood Search	$40	
11-03-XX	Fed Ex (9@$30)	$270	
	Misc. Copying	$50	
	SubTotals	$6360	$10,000
	Excess to be refunded	$3640	
	Totals	$10,000	$10,000

MONB will refund to Borrower
Mission Bank
Attn: C. Deets
5555 Mission Road
Sansai, CA 92055

Reviewed and Approved

_____

C Deets   **Date**

This log is to be used to keep track of all borrower loan related expenses incurred and collected during the life of the loan

This document is mandatory and must stay in the file at all times.

Read and Approved
Dated:
By: _____
By: _____

STATE BANK
601 Montry Street
San Francisco, CA 94111
Phone: (415)399-8000
Fax: (415)421-3257

BENEFICIARY DEMAND STATEMENT

TO: American Title Company
     Fax: (818) 773-6855
Attn: Jerry Spender

Date____02/03/XX_____
Our Loan No.: 16803855
Borrower(s): Juan Han
Escrow#: 3649655-TS
Property Address: 10855 San Palo Avenue
El Cerrito, CA 94550

Dear Mr. Jerry Spender,

In compliance with your telephone and facsimile request(s) for demand, we are pleased to supply the following information and documents:

Full Reconveyance will be forwarded upon receipt of funds

1. Your remittance "*MUST BE FORWARDED BY WIRE TRANSFER*. Wiring Instructions are as follows:**
     For credit to the account of:

     PACIFIC BANK
     501 Montry Street
     San Francisco, CA 94155
     ABA no.121038255
     ATTN: Note Department

FOUR ADDITIONAL DAYS OF INTEREST WILL BE ACCRUED If fund Is sent in the form of cashier check.

***S15.00 Wire Fee Charged *** If fund is sent in the form of wire.

Please submit to Bank the amount of $ 125.00   plus any accrued interest of $0.00 per day from 02/03/XX to the date payment is received at our address above. Interest is also calculated on a 365/360 day basis. Please telephone Will King at (925)287-1755 prior to payoff to verify these figures.

These demand figures were allocated in the following manner:

Principal as of 02/03/XX	0.00
Interest to 02/03/XX	0.00
Notary Fee	10.00
Transmittal Fee	25.00
Demand Fee	30.00
Reconveyance Fee	45.00
Wire in Fee	15.00
*Net Amount Due Pacific Bank:	**125.00**

Read and Approved

Dated:

By: _____

By: _____

AMERICAN TITLE COMPANY
21550 Plum Street
Chatsworth, CA, 91355
PHONE: (818)773-6855 • FAX: (818)773-6553

Borrower Closing Statement
Estimated

Borrower DELKIM COMPANY, INC.

Escrow No: 3649553-TS
Escrow Branch: LAST Escrow Department
Escrow Officer: T. SPENDER
Preparer: T. SPENDER
Date Prepared: 2/16/20XX 3:23:19 PM
Est. Close: 12/6/20XX

Property: 10855 SAN PALO AVE.
EL CERRITO, CA 94550

Description	Debit	Credit
Encumbrances		
1st New Loan from BANK		$400,000.00
Loan Charges		
BANK Total Charges $176,263.32		
1st Interest in Advance to National Bank		
Flat Amount of $1116.32	$1,116.32	
1st Tenant Improvements to holdback	$163,200.00	
1st Tax Monitoring Fee to BANK	$200.00	
1st Draw Fee to BANK	$1,632.00	
1st Credit Report Fee to BANK	$100.00	
1st overnight Mail fee to BANK	$50.00	
1st UCC filing/search fees to BANK	$100.00	
1st Environmental Vista Fee to BANK	$115.00	
1st Loan Doc fee to BANK	$750.00	
1st Origination Fee to BANK	$9,000.00	
1st Flood Search to 1 @ $40	$40.00	
1st Fed exp to 9 @ $30	$270.00	
1st Misc. copying to MISSION BANK	$50.00	
1st Bal. of funds to be refunded to Borr. to MISSION	$3,540.00	
1st Borrower's deposit to MISSION BANK		$10,000.00
1st Appraisal Fee to Acme Corp	$4,200.00	
1st packaging to MISSION BANK	$1,600.00	
1st Preliminary UCC/corp./lien search to MISSION	$250.00	
1st TRW to 2 @ $25	$50.00	
Payoffs		
CALIFORNIA BANK Total Charges $125.00	$125.00	
$30.00 Statement Fee		
$45.00 Reconveyance Fee		
$15.00 Wire in fee		
$25.00 Transmittal fee		
$10.00 Notary fee		
Additional Charges		
Notary/Signing Fee to CENTRAL SIGNING	$125.00	
Messenger fee to NC - CHATSWORTH	$100.00	
Title Charges		
Property Tax Due- 2nd half 04/05 to AMERICAN TITLE	$15,942.96	
Lenders Policy to AMERICAN TITLE COMPANY	$980.35	
Wire Fee to AMERICAN TITLE COMPANY	$40.00	

AMERICAN TITLE COMPANY
21550 Plum Street
Chatsworth, CA, 91355
PHONE: (818)773-6855 • FAX: (818)773-6553

Borrower Closing Statement
Estimated

Borrower DELKIM COMPANY, INC.

Property: 10855 SAN PALO AVE.
EL CERRITO, CA 94550

Escrow No: 3649553-TS
Escrow Branch: LAST Escrow
Department
Escrow Officer: T. SPENDER
Preparer: T. SPENDER
Date Prepared: 2/16/20XX 3:23:19 PM
Est. Close: 12/6/20XX

Description	Debit	Credit
Recording Fees		
AMERICAN TITLE COMPANY	$165.00	
$125.00 Recording Deed of Trust to AMERICAN TITLE		
$40.00 Misc. Recording Fee- Subord. Agreement to AMERICAN TITLE		
Escrow Charges		
Settlement Fee to AMERICAN TITLE ESCROW	$550.00	
Document Preparation- Subord. Agreement to AMERICAN TITLE	$75.00	
Subtotals	$204,366.63	$410,000.00
Proceeds Due Borrower	$205,633.37	
Totals	$410,000.00	$410,000.00

Buyers/Borrowers understand and agree that this is an estimated settlement statement only and all items shown are subject to change at closing.

Read and approved:

_____
Juan Han

_____
Sunny Han

AMERICAN TITLE COMPANY
21550 Plum Street
Chatsworth, CA, 91355
PHONE: (818) 773-6855 · FAX: (818) 773-6553

AMENDED AND/OR SUPPLEMENTED
ESCROW INSTRUCTIONS

November 22, 20XX   Escrow No: 3649553-TS
RE: 10855 SAN PALO AVE. EL CERRITO, CALIFORNIA 94550

TO: American Title Company

My previous instructions in the above numbered escrow are hereby amended and/or supplemented in the following particulars only:

Escrow is instructed to type and record a subordination agreement in the content and form handed into escrow. Said subordination agreement will subordinate that certain Trust Deed executed by

JUAN HAN AND SUNNY HAN (trustor) in favor of LeAnn Wang and Joan L Wang, TRUSTEES (beneficiary) in the amount of $1,3000,000.00 (SUBORDINATED TRUST DEED) to a Trust Deed executed by JUAN HAN AND SUNNY HAN (trustor) in favor of FIRST NATIONAL BANK (beneficiary) in the amount of $400,000.00 (SENOR TRUST DEED). Escrow makes no representations regarding the terms of the loan now being made as being in accordance with any previous agreements to subordinate.

The beneficiary under the SUBORDINATED TRUST DEED has read and approves the SENIOR TRUST DEED, the note which it secures and the building loan agreement, if applicable.

If the SENIOR TRUST DEED is for construction purposes, the undersigned acknowledges that the property is over-encumbered. FURTHER, American Title Insurance Company HAS NO CONTROL OVER THE DISBURSEMENT OF PROCEEDS OF THE LOAN AND MAKES NO REPRESENTATIONS OR ASSURANCES THAT THE CONSTRUCTION LOAN PROCEEDS WILL BE USED TO IMPROVE THE SUBJECT PROPERTY.

The beneficiary under the SUBORDINATED TRUST DEED understands that should a foreclosure action being on the SENIOR TRUST DEED, his security would be at risk unless funds were advanced to bring the SENIOR TRUST DEED current. The beneficiary under the SUBORDINATED TRUST DEED also understands that should they complete a foreclosure action, they would acquire the property subject to the SENIOR TRUST DEED and would be responsible for that obligation.

The undersigned acknowledge that American Title Company has recommended that they consult with legal counsel regarding the Subordination Agreement/priority of the trust deeds referenced herein and the matters addressed in these instructions, and that American Title Company has given no advice of any nature with respect to said subordination.

The following fees will be incurred in regards to said subordination:
Doc prep fee $75.00
Overnight mail fee(s) $50.00
Approx recording fee $25.00

*****ALL OTHER TERMS AND CONDITIONS SHALL REMAIN THE SAME.*****

EACH OF THE UNDERSIGNED STATES THAT HE/SHE HAS READ THE FOREGOING INSTRUCTIONS AND UNDERSTANDS THEM AND DOES HEREBY ACKNOWLEDGE RECEIPT OF A COPY OF THESE INSTRUCTIONS. EACH OF THE UNDERSIGNED UNDERSTANDS THESE INSTRUCTIONS MAY BE EXECUTED IN COUNTERPARTS, ALL OF WHICH WHEN TAKEN TOGETHER SHALL BE DEEMED TO BE THE INSTRUMENT.

BORROWERS:

_____
Juan Han

_____
Sunny Han

Part II
COMMON SIGNING AGENT FORMS

The chapters in Part I of this book illustrated loan document packages from refinance loans, home equity lines of credit, reverse mortgages, purchase and sale and commercial transactions. The reader may have discovered that many of the same forms appear in each of the sample sets with little or no variation. Common forms include the "Closing Disclosure," the Internal Revenue Service "Form W-9 Request for Taxpayer Identification Number and Certification," and uniform notes and security instruments.

Part II of this *Handbook* discusses additional common forms found in loan packages. The reader will learn that many of the commonly notarized forms — occupancy affidavits, compliance agreements, and signature/name affidavits — appear at times with alternative titles and minor changes in substance. Some will not even require notarization at all.

Part II also includes chapters on the common deeds used to convey an interest in real property, and the promissory notes and security instruments which underlie most residential loan transactions. There are separate chapters devoted to discussing "Notice of Right to Cancel" and U.S. PATRIOT Act Customer Identification Program (CIP) forms. A final chapter presents various affidavits used in a variety of circumstances that Notary Signing Agents may be asked to notarize.

Chapter

6

Occupancy Affidavits

INTRODUCTION

An often seen form found in residential home loan packages is the occupancy affidavit. This document is known by many different titles, including "Statement of Occupancy" or "Occupancy Statement," "Occupancy Certification," "Owner Occupancy Letter" and "Residency Affidavit."

In certain FHA loans, the form is titled "Occupancy Affidavit and Financial Status." In addition to certifying residency of the property, this form also requires the borrower to certify that the homeowner's place of employment and financial condition have not materially changed since the time the borrower first applied for the loan.

There are even instances in which an occupancy statement is one of several certifications contained in a single form. A sample generic "Disclosure" form containing several borrower certifications, including owner-occupancy of the subject property, is illustrated on page 404.

The purpose of the occupancy affidavit is to obtain the homeowner's certification and assurance at the settlement or closing that the property being financed serves as the homeowner's principal residence. When the borrower is presented with this form it will not be the first time the borrower is asked to indicate whether he or she will reside in the home. In applying for the loan, the borrower had answered questions on the "Universal Residential Loan Application" related to the occupancy of the subject property and whether the home would serve as the primary residence.

Lenders typically offer a lower interest rate to homeowners who intend to occupy the property because there is less risk to the property when the owner resides in the home. Lenders know from experience that most homeowners take pride in their homes, perform regular upkeep and maintenance on their properties, and take precautions to secure and protect their investment.

When the property will serve as a second home or investment property, lenders offer loans at higher rates because these properties are at greater risk than owner-occupied homes, and with income properties in particular, have higher maintenance costs that are associated with tenant turnover. Also, since the property is used as an investment, lenders up the rate to "get their slice of the pie."

To obtain a lower interest rate for residential, owner-occupied homes, the occupancy affidavit requires borrowers to state that they presently occupy the property or intend to do so upon close of escrow. A terse warning is included in the form to remind borrowers that misrepresenting facts can lead to criminal prosecution. An example of a warning found on most occupancy affidavits is as follows:

> Non-compliance by me may also result in fines or imprisonment as more fully described in section 1010 of title 18, U.S.C., Department of Housing and Urban Development which provides as follows, "whoever, for the purpose of...influencing in any way the action of such departments... makes, passes, utters or publishes any statement knowing the same to be false...shall be fined not more than $5,000 or imprisoned not more than two years, or both."

Given the often serious penalties for falsehoods, it is not surprising that most lenders require the occupancy affidavit and its derivatives to be notarized with a jurat requiring the borrower to sign a sworn statement. As there are cases in which this so-called affidavit will require a simple acknowledgment, Notary Signing Agents will need to check the form to ensure that the proper notarial act is performed.

While the occupancy affidavit is notarized routinely, there are forms that do not require notarization. Samples of non-notarized occupancy statements are included in the sample forms which follow.

Forms in Sample Set   **Pages**

OCCUPANCY STATEMENT

Lender: LIBERTY LENDING CORPORATION
Borrower Name: William and Mary Hoskins
Loan #:
Date: September 14, 20XX
Property Address: 19087 Fair Park Road
Aurora, Colorado

Borrower hereby declares, under penalty of perjury, as follows:

☐   **Owner Occupied**

I/We will occupy the subject property as my/our principal residence within 60 days after the date of closing as required by, and in compliance with, the terms of the Deed of Trust/Mortgage/Security Instrument relating to the subject property. I/We will continue to occupy the property as my/our principal residence for at least one year after the date of occupancy, unless Lender otherwise agrees in writing.

☐   **Occupied as a Second Home**

I/We will occupy the subject property as my/our second residence as required by, and in compliance with, the terms of the Deed of Trust/Mortgage/Security Instrument relating to the subject property.

☐   **Investment Property - Will Not Occupy**

I/We will not occupy the subject property.

I/We are aware of and understand that if at any time it is determined that the foregoing statement is untrue, I/We will be subject to prosecution for fraud under applicable state laws.

I certify under penalty of Chapter 18, U.S.C. 1010 to 1014 that the statement contained herein is true and correct.

_____   _____
- BORROWER -   - DATE -

STATE OF _____

COUNTY OF: _____

Subscribed and sworn to before me this   day of   .

WITNESS my hand and official seal.   Signature: _____
                                            Name (typed or printed)
                                            My Commission Expires:

AFFIDAVIT OF OCCUPANCY

Personally appeared before the undersigned officer authorized by law to administer oaths

came   **William and Mary Hoskins**   , who after being duly sworn

does depose and affirm to the following facts:

1. My name(s) is/are: **William and Mary Hoskins**   .

2. I/We am/are the same person(s) who executed a Mortgage to secure debt to:

   Liberty Lending Corporation in the principal amount of $ **2,500,000**

   on **August 31, 20XX.**

3. A condition precedent to **Liberty Lending Corporation**   funding   the

   referenced loan is that I occupy the premises at the following address: **19087 Fair**

   Park Road East, Aurora, Colorado as my principal residence.

4. All bills for utilities, water and/or sewerage are in my name.

Dated this _____ day of _____, 20____.

_____   _____

Borrower **William Hoskins**   Borrower **Mary Hoskins**

State of

County of

Sworn to and subscribed before me this _____ day of _____, 20____.

_____

NOTARY PUBLIC

AFFIDAVIT OF OCCUPANCY

Lender: West Coast Lenders, LLC

STATE OF _____   }

                                      }SS

COUNTY OF _____   }

PROPERTY ADDRESS: 455   Howard   Avenue
Las Vegas, NV 89109

Before me, the undersigned authority, personally appeared the undersigned **Borrowers**, (herein so called, whether one or more) who, upon being duly sworn on oath stated the following:

1.1   ☐   The **Property** is or will be **Borrowers'** Primary Residence. This means at least one of the **Borrowers** who executes the **Note** and **Deed of Trust** or **Mortgage** will take title to and occupy the **Property**. The **Property** is now occupied as the **Borrowers'** principal residence or will be occupied as **Borrowers'** principal residence no later than sixty (60) days after this date or sixty days after the **Property** shall first become ready for occupancy as a habitable dwelling, whichever is later. The **Borrowers** have no present intention that is contrary to this representation.

1.2   ☐   The **Property** is or will be the **Borrowers'** Secondary Residence. A secondary residence is a single family property that either is currently or will be occupied by at least one of the **Borrowers** in addition to their primary residence. It will not be income producing.

1.3   ☐   The **Property** is or will be Investment Property. The **Property** will not be occupied or claimed as a primary or secondary residence by any of the **Borrowers**, and may produce revenue. Each **Borrower** now owns, resides on, uses and claims another property or properties which, under the laws of the state in which such properties are located, are entitle to receive homestead exemptions for taxes and/or creditor claims.

2. If the **Borrowers** have indicated that the **Property** is their primary residence, the **Borrowers** represent that (i) they have no present intent to sell, lease, rent or otherwise dispose of said Property, (ii) upon occupancy of the Property they will not have any other permanent and primary residence, and (iii) the Property is not to be used for investment purposes. The **Borrowers** agree to furnish to
    , it's successors and/or assigns
(the "Lender") upon **Lender's** request, evidence satisfactory to **Lender** of their continuing occupancy of the **Property** as their permanent full time residence.

Initials: _____

AFFIDAVIT OF OWNER-OCCUPANCY

In addition to the representations in section 21 of Addendum #1 of the Contract of Sale dated October 15, 20XX, between the Federal Home Loan Mortgage Corporation (Seller, sometimes described as Freddie Mac or HomeSteps) and Purchaser and any and all other contractual documents, for the property located at _____123 Elm Street St. Louis, Missouri_ ("Property"), I certify, agree, represent and acknowledge that:

1. All of the information provided in this Affidavit of Owner-Occupancy and any supporting documents requested by Seller and provided to Seller by me are truthful and accurate.
2. I understand that Seller will rely upon the information provided by me in determining whether to complete that sale of the Property to me.
3. I will occupy, establish and use the Property as my residence as soon as possible after closing and I will continue to occupy the Property as my residence for at least one year after the first date of occupancy.
4. I agree and understand that any misstatement or misrepresentation in this Affidavit of Owner-Occupancy will constitute a breach by me of the Contract of Sale, and will permit Seller the right to cancel the Contract of Sale and to exercise any remedies available under the Contract of Sale and applicable law.
5. I understand that any misstatement or misrepresentation in this Affidavit of Owner-Occupancy may subject me to criminal and/or civil liability.

_____   _____
Purchaser Signature   Date

_____   _____
Purchaser Signature   Date

Statement of Selling Agent

Selling Agent agrees and represents that to the best of Selling Agent's knowledge the Purchaser intends to occupy the Property after closing as Purchaser's residence. Selling Agent acknowledges that Seller is relying on this representation.

_____   _____
Selling Agent   Date

0867831

Statement of Occupancy

DATE: **09/28/XX**
BORROWERS: **RIK HUON AND GIDGET MANN**
PROPERTY ADDRESS: **6155 NARROWS DRIVE, LOS ANGELES, CA 90055**

I hereby acknowledge and understand that I am executing this Statement of Occupancy which provides that if my loan application on the above described property is approved, I will occupy the same as my principal residence within sixty (60) days of the loan closing.

It is understood and agreed that:
a. You intend to sell the Note to an Investor;
b. You would not make the loan unless you are able to sell the Note; and
c. The Investor would not buy the Note unless I occupy the property as my principal residence.

I further confirm my understanding and agreement that if I fail to occupy the property as my principal residence as provided above, such failure shall constitute a default under the terms and conditions of my loan, and upon the occurrence of such default, the whole sum of principal and interest shall immediately become due and payable at the option of the holder of my Note.

You have advised me that you intend to sell said loan and that you may not be able to do so or may be required to repurchase the same and may be damaged in certain other respects if I fail to occupy said property as my principal residence as provided above. This will also confirm our agreement that I shall indemnify you and hold you harmless from and against any and all loss, damage, liability or expense, including costs and reasonable attorney's fees, to which you may be put or which you may incur by reason of or in connection with my failure to so occupy said property as my principal residence as provided above.

Borrower	*Date*	*Borrower*	*Date*
Rik Huon		**Gidget Mann**	

Borrower	*Date*	*Borrower*	*Date*

OCCUPANCY STATEMENT

OCCS/0140674060

Property Address: <u>5105 CORTNEY DRIVE</u>

<u>BOSTON, MA 02108</u>

Please complete the following, indicating the purpose of this transaction. If for any reason, you are uncertain which purpose to indicate, please request assistance from your settlement agent.

☐ I hereby certify that I am purchasing the above referenced property as:

    ☐ a primary and principal residence which I intend to occupy within sixty (60) days after loan closing, and for at least one year after the date of occupancy.

    ☐ a second/vacation home.

    ☐ an investment/rental property.

☐ I hereby certify that I am refinancing the above referenced property as:

    ☐ a primary and principal residence which I intend to occupy within sixty (60) days after loan closing, and for at least one year after the date of occupancy.

    ☐ a second/vacation home.

    ☐ an investment/rental property.

I/we have read this disclosure form, understood its contents and indicated the appropriate information, as evidenced by my/our signature(s) below. I/we understand that this acknowledgement is a required part of the mortgage loan transaction.

_____   _____
Signature JAVIER RAMIREZ   Date

_____   _____
Signature MARIA B RAMIREZ   Date

_____   _____
Signature   Date

_____   _____
Signature   Date

DISCLOSURE NOTICE

Applicant(s) __LAWRENCE JOHNSON__   Property Address __678 STORY ST.__

__MINDY JOHNSON__   __APPLETON, WI 54914__

AFFIDAVIT OF OCCUPANCY

The Applicant(s) hereby certify and acknowledge that, upon taking title to the real property described above, their occupancy status will be as follows:

☑ Primary Residence – Occupied by Applicant(s) within 30 days of closing.

☐ Secondary Residence – To be occupied by Applicant(s) at least 15 days yearly, as second home (vacation, etc.), while maintaining principal residence elsewhere. (Please check this box if you plan to establish it as your primary residence at a future date(i.e. retirement).

☐ Investment Property – Not owner occupied. Purchased as an investment to be held or rented.

The Applicant(s) acknowledge it is a federal crime punishable by fine or imprisonment, or both, to knowingly make any false statements concerning this loan application as applicable under the provisions of Title 18, United States Code, Section 1014.

APPLICANT _____   CO-APPLICANT _____

FAIR CREDIT REPORTING ACT

An investigation will be made as to the credit standing of all individuals seeking credit in this application. The nature and scope of any investigation will be furnished to you upon written request made within a reasonable period of time. In the event of denied credit due to an unfavorable consumer report, you will be advised of the identity of the Consumer Reporting Agency making such report and of right to request within sixty (60) days the reason for the adverse action, pursuant to provisions of section 615 (b) of the Fair Credit Reporting Act.

EQUAL CREDIT OPPORTUNITY ACT

The Equal Credit Opportunity Act prohibits creditors from discriminating against credit applicants on a basis of race, color, religion, national origin, sex, marital status, age (provided that the applicant has the capacity to enter into a binding contract); because all or part of the applicant's income derives from any public assistance program; or because the applicant has in good faith exercised any right under the Consumer Credit Protection Act. Income which you receive as alimony, child support or separate maintenance need not be disclosed to this creditor unless you choose to rely on such sources to qualify for the loan. Income from these and other sources, including part time or temporary employment, will not be discounted by this lender because of your sex or marital status. However, we will consider very car3efully the stability and probable continuity of any income you disclose to us. The Federal Agency that administers compliance with this law concerning this creditor is:

_____

_____

_____

FHA LOANS ONLY

IF YOU PREPAY YOUR LOAN ON OTHER THAN THE REGULAR INSTALLMENT DATE, YOU MAY BE ASSESSED INTEREST CHARGES UNTIL THE END OF THAT MONTH.

GOVERNMENT LOANS ONLY

RIGHT TO FINANCIAL PRIVACY ACT OF 1978 – This is notice to you as required by the Right to Financial Privacy Act of 1978 that the Department of Housing and Urban Development or Department of Veterans Affairs has a right of access to financial records held by a financial institution in connection with the consideration of administration of assistance to you. Financial records involving your transaction will be available to the Department of Housing and Urban Development or Department of Veterans Affairs without further notice or authorization but will not be disclosed or released to another Government agency or Department without your consent except as required or permitted by law.

EMPLOYMENT CERTIFICATION

An approval for a loan is based upon employment, income and obligations as shown on the loan application. At closing, the applicant and co-applicant/spouse, if applicable, are required to execute a sworn statement affirming that they are currently working as previously reported, have not received notice of layoff nor have knowledge of pending layoff, and that outstanding obligations are substantially the same as reported on the application. Should a change occur in your employment or financial status prior to loan closing, immediately notify your loan officer, as it will be necessary to obtain approval of any changes.

ANTI-COERCION STATEMENT/ INSURANCE STATEMENT

The insurance laws of this state provide that the lender may not require the applicant to take insurance through any particular insurance agent or company to protect the mortgaged property. The applicant, subject to the rules adopted by the Insurance Commissioner, has the right to have the insurance placed with an insurance agent or company of his choice, provided the company meets the requirements of the lender. The lender has the right to designate reasonable financial requirements as to the company and the adequacy of the coverage.

I have read the foregoing statement, or the rules of the Insurance Commissioner relative thereto, and understand my rights and privileges and those of the lender relative to the placing of such insurance.

I have selected the following agencies to write the insurance covering the property described above:

__ACME HOME INSURANCE CORPORATION__   __SAM INSURED__
Insurance Company Name   Agent
__123 COLLEGE AVE., APPLETON, WI 54911__   __(920) 876-0987__
Agent's Address   Agent's Telephone Number

FLOOD INSURANCE NOTIFICATION

Federal regulations require us to inform you that the property used as security for this loan is located in an area identified by the U.S. Secretary of Housing & Urban Development as having special flood hazards and that in the event of damage to the property caused by flooding in a Federally declared disaster, Federal disaster relief assistance, if authorized, will be available for the property. At the closing you will be asked to acknowledge your receipt of this information. If you have any questions concerning this notice, kindly contact your loan officer.

IMPORTANT: Please notify your insurance agent that the "loss payee" clause for the mortgagee on both the hazard and flood insurance must read as follows, unless otherwise advised: American Financial Resources, Inc. its successors and/or assigns, 3770 N. 7th St. Suite A, Phoenix AZ 85014

The undersigned applicant(s) certify that they have been furnished with the "Settlement Cost Booklet" on this date and, if applicable, the booklet "Consumer Handbook on Adjustable Rate Mortgages" (CHARM booklet) which was presented to me/us along with the residential loan application form.

I/We hereby certify that I/we have read the Notices set forth above and fully understand all of the above.

APPLICANT _____ DATE _____   APPLICANT _____ DATE _____

APPLICANT _____ DATE _____   APPLICANT _____ DATE _____

Chapter

7

Compliance Agreements

INTRODUCTION

The compliance agreement is found in many loan documentation packages under a variety of titles, including "Errors and Omissions Compliance Agreement," "Document Correction and Re-Execution Agreement," and "Document Correction Agreement."

As with occupancy affidavits, there are cases in which a compliance agreement statement is one of several certifications contained in a single form. A sample "Borrower Certifications" form containing such a certification is illustrated on page 414.

In executing the document, a borrower pledges to "comply" with requests from the lender or closing agent to correct typographical or clerical errors and inadvertent mistakes in the loan documentation. Securing the cooperation of the borrower to adjust the documentation is often necessary for originating lenders to sell, convey, or market the loan to a secondary market investor, including Fannie Mae, Freddie Mac, and the Department of Veteran Affairs.

A key paragraph in one such agreement reads:

> The undersigned borrower(s) do hereby agree and covenant in order
> to assure that this loan documentation executed this date will conform

and be acceptable in the marketplace in the instance of transfer, sale or conveyance by Lender of its interest in and to said loan documentation, and to assure marketable title in the said borrower(s).

A borrower promises to reply to a lender's written request for assistance in correcting errors within a period of time specified by the lender, usually 30 days, although lenders may require response within a shorter time frame. For example, one lender requires a response within seven days. (See the "Document Correction and Re-Execution Agreement" on page 410.) Failure to respond in a timely manner or to cooperate fully can result in the borrower being liable for actual expenses, legal fees and marketing losses caused by such failure, or constitute an actual default on the loan.

Compliance agreements are routinely notarized with a jurat or acknowledgment, and, like the occupancy affidavit, may not require notarization at all.

A related form is the "Correction Agreement Limited Power of Attorney." Used for the same general purpose as the compliance agreement, the borrower names an agent to make the actual corrections in the borrower's place. If a potential investor is available and time is of the essence, having of an attorney-in-fact with authorization to make the necessary corrections can significantly reduce the time the lender holds the loan before it is sold or transferred to the investor.

Since executing a power of attorney document is a significant personal legal decision, many powers of attorney specifically state that an agent cannot make changes to the loan that will affect the loan amount and terms. The following paragraph extracted from the sample illustrated on page 439 reads as follows:

> **THIS LIMITED POWER OF ATTORNEY MAY NOT BE USED TO INCREASE THE INTEREST RATE THE UNDERSIGNED IS PAYING, INCREASE THE TERM OF THE UNDERSIGNED'S LOAN, INCREASE THE UNDERSIGNED'S OUTSTANDING PRINCIPAL BALANCE OR INCREASE THE UNDERSIGNED'S MONTHLY PRINCIPAL AND INTEREST PAYMENTS.** Any of these specified changes must be executed directly by the undersigned.

The sample document also states that the borrower will receive a photocopy of any documents corrected by the agent.

In what sense is the above-described power of attorney "limited"? The borrower gives authority to the lender's agent to act subject to two primary limitations. First, a limitation in scope; the appointed agent may only make corrections to documents executed at the closing appointment and the corrections made by the agent cannot materially affect the loan amount or terms. Second, a limitation in duration; the agent's authority expires 180 days following the date of closing.

A comparison of the "Errors and Omissions Compliance Agreement" and "Correction Agreement Limited Power of Attorney" is presented in the table below.

Errors and Omissions Compliance Agreement	Correction Agreement Limited Power of Attorney
Facilitates marketability of loan in secondary market	Facilitates marketability of loan in secondary market
Borrower agrees to adjust errors personally	Borrower appoints agent to adjust errors
May be notarized or only signed	Must be notarized
Borrower presented written request for assistance	Borrower provided written copy of changes made
Borrower must act within specified time period	Agent may act only for duration of specified time period
Borrower may be penalized for non-compliance	Penalties not applicable

Forms in Sample Set

LENDER: **LIBERTY AMERICAN MORTGAGE CORP.**
BORROWER(S): **ERNIE HALL AND TERRIE HALL**

PROPERTY ADDRESS: **855 RIVER STREET, PHOENIX, AZ 85007**
LOAN NO.: **04110551**

ERROR AND OMISSIONS / COMPLIANCE AGREEMENT

STATE OF   **ARIZONA**
COUNTY OF   **MARICOPA**

The undersigned borrower(s) for and in consideration of the above-referenced Lender funding the closing of this loan agrees, if requested by Lender or Closing Agent for Lender, to fully cooperate and adjust for clerical errors, any or all loan closing documentation if deemed necessary or desirable in the reasonable discretion of Lender to enable Lender to sell, convey, seek guaranty or market said loan to any entity, including but not limited to an investor, Federal National Mortgage Association, Federal Home Loan Mortgage Corporation, Government National Mortgage Association, Federal Housing Authority or the Department of Veterans Affairs, or any Municipal Bonding Authority.

The undersigned borrower(s) agree(s) to comply with all above noted requests by the above-referenced Lender within 30 days from date of mailing of said requests. Borrower(s) agree(s) to assume all costs including, by way of illustration and not limitation, actual expenses, legal fees and marketing losses for failing to comply with correction requests in the above noted time period.

The undersigned borrower(s) do hereby so agree and covenant in order to assure that this loan documentation executed this date will conform and be acceptable in the marketplace in the instance of transfer, sale or conveyance by Lender of its interest in and to said loan documentation, and to assure marketable title in the said borrower(s).

DATED effective this   **13th**   day of **DECEMBER, 20XX**

_____		_____	
ERNIE HALL	Borrower	**TERRIESA HALL**	Borrower
_____		_____	
	Borrower		Borrower

Sworn to and subscribed before me this   day of

_____
(Notary Public)

My Commission Expires:

0003725428

National Complete Loan

DOCUMENT CORRECTION AND RE-EXECUTION AGREEMENT

National Complete Loan is a registered trademark of National Corporation.

In consideration of a certain loan or line of credit ("Loan") made by National Bank ("National"), which is secured by a certain mortgage/deed of trust ("Mortgage") given by the undersigned (collectively the "Mortgagors") to National, Mortgagors agree as follows:

1. National is hereby expressly authorized to complete on Mortgagors' behalf all portions of the Mortgage or other Loan documentation that were not completed by Mortgagors at the closing of the Loan.

2. National is hereby expressly authorized to correct on Mortgagors' behalf all inadvertent errors in the Mortgage or Loan documentation.

3. Upon request by National, Mortgagors will re-execute the Mortgage and other Loan documentation reasonable required by National if any document is lost, misplaced or inaccurate for any reason or if the document was incorrectly drafted and/or signed. All such requests shall receive the full cooperation and compliance by the Mortgagors within seven (7) days of National's request. Any request under this Agreement may be made by National (including assignees and persons acting on behalf of National) or Settlement Agent and shall be prima facie evidence of the necessity for same. A written statement addressed to Mortgagors at the address indicated in the Loan documentation shall be considered conclusive evidence of the necessity for re-execution of any documents. Failure to do so shall constitute an additional event of default under Mortgagors' promissory note and Mortgage. In addition, Mortgagors agree to be liable for any loss or damage which National reasonable sustains by Mortgagors' failure to timely execute and return any such documentation, including reasonable attorney's fees and costs incurred by National.

This Agreement shall survive the closing of the Loan and inure to the benefit of National, its successors and assigns, and be binding upon the heirs, devisees, personal representatives, successors, and assigns of Mortgagors.

Dated: **12/07/20XX**   **MORTGAGORS:**

X _____
    AHMEAD RODAR

X _____
    PERRY RODAR

X _____

X _____

STATE OF _____

COUNTY OF _____

BEFORE ME, a Notary Public in and for said County and State, personally appeared the above named Mortgagors who acknowledged that they did sign the foregoing instrument, and that the same is their free act and deed.

IN TESTIMONY WHEREOF, I have hereunto set my hand and official seal, this _____ day of _____

_____
Notary Public

Errors and Omissions Correction Agreement   MECA/0140574055

TRUST MORTGAGE, INC.

Date: 09/03/XX   Loan No: 0140674055

Borrower(s): JAVIER RAMIREZ

MARIA B RAMIREZ

Property Address: 5105 PINE COVE DRIVE

LA JOLLA CA 92039

The undersigned borrower(s) (whether one or more, collectively referred to herein as the "Borrower"), for and in consideration of   **TRUST MORTGAGE, INC.,** ("Lender"), funding the closing of the loan, on the above described property, agree to the following:

1. After settlement of the loan and upon the request of settlement agent or Lender, Borrower agrees to reexecute and/or initial any and all loan closing documentation in order to correct for any clerical or other similar errors contained therein.

2. After settlement of the loan and upon the request of the Lender, Borrower agrees to pay the Lender any closing or other costs erroneously not collected at the time of closing. Borrower further agrees to refund any excess funds erroneously paid to borrower at the time of closing.

3. Borrower agrees to cooperate with Lender's reasonable requests in accomplishing any and all clerical corrections required by governmental authorities or secondary market investors.

JAVIER RAMIREZ   Borrower

MARIA B RAMIREZ   Borrower

Borrower

Borrower

Lender: **MANHATTAN MORTGAGE CORPORATION**
Loan Number: **1595436855**

DOCUMENT CORRECTION AGREEMENT

AGREEMENT TO CORRECT MISSTATED OR PROVIDE ADDITIONAL DOCUMENTATION OR FEES:
In consideration of Lender disbursing funds for the closing of the Loan secured by the Property being encumbered, and regardless of the reason for any loss, misplacement, or inaccuracy in any Loan documentation, Borrower(s) agrees as follows: If any document is lost, misplaced, misstated or inaccurately reflects the true and correct terms and conditions of the Loan, upon request of the Lender, Borrower(s) will comply with Lender's request to execute, acknowledge, initial and deliver to Lender any documentation Lender deems necessary to replace or correct the lost, misplaced, misstated or inaccurate document(s). If the original promissory note is replaced, the Lender hereby indemnifies the Borrower(s) against any loss associated with a demand on the original note. All documents Lender requests of Borrower(s) shall be referred to as "Replacement Documents". Borrower(s) agrees to deliver the Replacement Documents within ten (10) days after receipt by Borrower(s) of a written request for such replacement. Borrower(s) also agrees that upon request Borrower(s) will supply additional amounts and/or pay to Lender any additional sum previously disclosed to Borrower(s) as a cost or fee associated with the Loan, which for whatever reason was not collected at closing.

REQUEST BY LENDER: Any request under this Agreement may be made by the Lender, (including assignees and persons acting on behalf of the Lender) or Settlement Agent, and shall be prima facie evidence of the necessity for same. A written statement addressed to Borrower(s) at the address indicated in the Loan documentation shall be considered conclusive evidence of the necessity for Replacement Documents.

FAILURE TO DELIVER REPLACEMENT DOCUMENTS CAN CONSTITUTE DEFAULT: If the Loan is to be guaranteed by the Department of Veterans Affairs ("VA") or insured by the Federal Housing Administration ("FHA"), Borrower(s) failure or refusal to comply with the terms of the correction request may constitute a default under the note and/or deed of trust, and may give Lender the option of declaring all sums secured by the loan documents immediately due and payable.

BORROWER LIABILITY: If Borrower(s) fails or refuses to execute, acknowledge, initial and deliver the Replacement Documents or provide the Additional Documents or Fees to Lender more than ten (10) days after being request to do so by Lender, and understanding that Lender is relying on these representations, Borrower(s) agree(s) to be liable for any and all loss or damage which Lender reasonably sustains thereby, including, but not limited to all reasonable attorney's fees and costs incurred by Lender.

This agreement shall survive the closing of the Loan, and inure to the benefit of Lender's successors and assigns and be binding upon the heirs, devisees, personal representatives, successors and assigns of Borrower(s).

_____   _____
DARLENE ALICIA   DATE

0867831

Compliance Agreement

State of **OKLAHOMA**

County of **POTTAWATOMIE**

Borrower(s): **RIF HATTON AND BRIDGET HATTON**

Lender: **PRIME ONE HOME MORTGAGE, INC.**

Property: **6155 BARROWS DRIVE, SHAWNEE OK 74804**

The undersigned Borrower(s), in consideration of the lender disbursing funds today for the closing of the property listed above agrees, if requested by the lender or someone acting on behalf of the lender, to fully cooperate and adjust for errors and omissions, any and all loan closing documentation deemed necessary or desirable in the reasonable discretion of the lender to sell, convey, seek guaranty or market said loan to any entity including but not limited to any investor, Federal National Mortgage Association (FNMA), Government National Mortgage Association (GNMA), Federal Home Loan Mortgage Corporation, Department of Housing and Urban Development, Veterans Administration or any Municipal Bonding Authority.

The undersigned Borrower(s) do hereby so agree and covenant in order to assure that the loan documentation executed this date will conform and be acceptable in the marketplace in the instance of transfer, sale or conveyance by the Lender of its interest in and to said loan documentation.

Dated effective this **28TH** *day of* **SEPTEMBER** *,* 20**XX** *.*

(Borrower)

(Borrower) **RIF HATTON**

(Borrower)

(Borrower) **BRIDGET HATTON**

Point Mortgage Funding, Inc.

BORROWER CERTIFICATIONS

BORROWER: **SHAHAN NORAN**   LOAN#: **0080644455**
PROPERTY ADDRESS: **455 Laurel Avenue, Huntingdon, TN 38344**

☐ <u>SALES CONTRACT:</u> All of the conditions, including but not limited to inspections, of the Contract/Offer to Purchase signed and executed by me have been satisfactorily met.

☐ <u>TERMITE CERTIFICATION:</u> I have received a copy of the Termite Report or Termite Soil Treatment Guaranty on new construction, and have read, understand, and accept it.

☐ <u>NAME CERTIFICATIONS:</u> With reference to the subject loan application, the following names appearing in the loan file are one and the same person.
SHAHAN Z. NORAN; SHAHAN S. NORAN; SHAHAN N. NORAN; SHAHAN E. NORAN

☑ <u>JUDGMENTS:</u> There are no judgments against (me) (us) (it) unsatisfied of record in the courts of this state or of the United States. No Federal Tax Claims or liens have been assessed or filed against (me) (us) (it). (I) (we) have not made an assignment of rents of said premises or made an assignment for the benefit of creditors.

☑ <u>COMPLIANCE AGREEMENT:</u> The undersigned Borrower(s) are receiving a loan secured by the above referenced property. In consideration of Lender making said loan and disbursing the loan proceeds for the refinance, construction or purchase of the above-referenced property, Borrower(s) consent and agree, if requested, to promptly and fully cooperate, BEFORE AND AFTER LOAN CLOSING, with Lender, its agents, its representatives or assigns in the correction or completion of loan closing documents or other items if deemed reasonably necessary by Lender.

Borrower(s) understand that pursuant to this covenant, Borrower(s) may be requested to execute a new promissory note, Security Instrument, Riders to such Note or Security Instrument and such other documents as Lender may reasonably request. Borrower(s) acknowledge that Lender may sell the above-captioned loan to a public or private investor and to the extent the documents for the loan are incorrect or incomplete, the loan will not be saleable to said Investor and Lender will suffer substantial irreparable damages. Such damages include but are not limited to the proceeds of the loan, fees and costs incurred in connection with the loan and interest on such loan proceeds.

Accordingly, Borrower(s) agree that in the event (I) (we) fail within seven (7) days of their receipt to execute and return to Lender such documents as Lender may request, such failure shall be a material default under the loan. Borrower(s) agree that in the event of such a default Lender shall be entitled to declare the loan immediately due and payable and to seek specific enforcement of this Agreement, unless otherwise prohibited by applicable law. In the event Lender institutes an Action to enforce this agreement or to pursue a default under this agreement, Lender shall be entitled to receive from (me) (us) all of Lender's costs and expenses including but not limited to attorney's fees.

☐ <u>MANUFACTURED HOUSING:</u> The building on the subject property is a manufactured housing unit. It is (my) (our) intent that the unit will be attached to and made a part of the real property.

☐ <u>OTHER</u>
_____
_____
_____

(I) (we) certify that the above applicable representations are true and correct as of this _____ day of _____

_____
SHAHAN NORAN

IMPORTANT: BORROWER MUST SIGN AND SIGNATURE MUST BE NOTARIZED

STATE OF _____   County of _____

Sworn to and subscribed before me this _____ day of _____, _____.

_____
Notary

_____
My commission expires

COMPLIANCE AGREEMENT

LENDER: LIBERTY MORTGAGE CORP.

ADDRESS: 2255 RIDGE COURT, 2ND FLOOR, ROSE, CA 95655

BORROWER(S): ERIE HALL AND TERRIE HALL

PROPERTY: 855 RIVER STREET, SIMI VALLEY, CA 93055

LOAN NO.:   04110551

FHA/VA CASE NO.:

DATED effective this __13th__ day of ____DECEMBER____ , __20XX__

The undersigned borrower(s), in consideration of Lender disbursing loan proceeds for the purchase or refinance of, or construction of improvements on the aforementioned property, agree(s), if requested by the Lender or someone acting on behalf of said Lender, to fully co-operate in adjusting for clerical errors, and all loan closing documentation deemed necessary or desirable, in the reasonable discretion of Lender, to enable Lender to sell, convey its interest in, seek guaranty of, or market said loan to any entity, including but not limited to, a secondary investor, the Federal National Mortgage Association (FNMA), Government National Mortgage Association (GNMA), the Federal Home Loan Mortgage Corporation (FHLMC), Department of Housing and Urban Development (HUD), the Department of Veterans Affairs (VA), or any Municipal Bonding Authority.

In order to assure that the loan documentation executed this date will conform and be acceptable in the market place in the instance of transfer, sale, or the conveyance by Lender of its interest in and to the above mentioned property evidenced by said loan documentation, the undersigned borrower(s) do hereby so agree and covenant as aforesaid herein.

_____   _____
ERIE HALL   Date   **TERRIE HALL**
    Date

_____   _____
             Date   Date

State of   )
County of   )

    On _____ , before me, a Notary Public in and for said County and State, personally appeared

ERIE HALL AND TERRIE HALL

personally known to me (or proved to me on the basis of satisfactory evidence) to be the person(s) whose name(s) is/are subscribed to the within instrument and acknowledged to me that he/she/they executed the same in his/her/their authorized capacity(ies), and that by his/her/their signature(s) on the instrument the person(s) or the entity upon behalf of which the person(s) acted, executed the instrument.

    Witness my hand and official seal.   Signature _____

                                                _____
                                                Notary name

                                                  _____
                                                  Commission expiration date

Prepared by: A. SANTA

DATE: **11/05/20XX**
Borrower: **MIKE TAKAT**

AMERICA'S FINEST LENDER
BRANCH #955
915 HAMILTON AVENUE
CAMPBELLTOWN, CA 95055
(458)558-7750
Br Fax (458)369-8255

CASE#:
LOAN#: 021785576
PROPERTY ADDRESS: **11557 NEBRASKA AVENUE**
                  ABILENE, TX

DOCUMENT CORRECTION AND FEES DUE AGREEMENT

AGREEMENT TO CORRECT MISSTATED OR PROVIDE ADDITIONAL DOCUMENTATION OR FEES: In consideration of Lender disbursing funds for the closing of the Loan secured by the Property being encumbered, and regardless of the reason for any loss of, misplacement of, inaccuracy in, or failure to sign any Loan documentation, Borrower(s) agrees as follows: If any document is lost, misplaced, misstated, inaccurately reflects the true and correct terms and conditions of the Loan, or otherwise missing upon request of the Lender, Borrower(s) will comply with Lender's request to execute, acknowledge, initial and deliver to Lender any documentation Lender deems necessary to replace or correct the lost, misplaced, misstated, inaccurate or otherwise missing document(s). If the original promissory note is replaced, the Lender hereby indemnifies the Borrower(s) against any loss associated with a demand on the original note. All documents Lender requests of Borrower(s) shall be referred to as "Documents." Borrower(s) agrees to deliver the Documents within ten (10) days after receipt by Borrower(s) of a written request for such replacement. Borrower(s) also agrees that at any time, upon request by Lender, including at the time of loan pay-off, Borrower(s) will supply additional amounts and/or pay to Lender any additional sum previously disclosed to Borrower(s) as a cost or fee associated with the Loan, which for whatever reason was not collected at closing ("Fees"). Such amount due from Borrower(s) may also be off-set by Lender from any funds held by Lender, for Borrower's benefit, after loan pay-off. Borrower(s) further agrees that if funds are collected by Lender at closing to pay any outstanding Escrow Items for (a) taxes and assessments; (b) hazard or property insurance premiums; (c) leasehold payments or ground rents on the property; (d) flood insurance premiums; or (e) mortgage insurance premiums, and if those Escrow Items have been or are paid by Lender from Borrower's old escrow account, then Lender may retain those funds to reimburse Lender for any shortage in Borrower's old escrow account that results from such payment.

REQUEST BY LENDER: Any request under this Agreement may be made by the Lender, (including assignees and persons acting on behalf of the Lender) or Settlement Agent, and shall be prima facie evidence of the necessity for same. A written statement addressed to Borrower(s) at the address indicated in the Loan documentation shall be considered conclusive evidence of the necessity for the Documents.

FAILURE TO DELIVER DOCUMENTS CAN CONSTITUTE DEFAULT: If the Loan is to be guaranteed by the Department of Veterans Affairs ("VA") or insured by the Federal Housing Administration ("FHA"), Borrower(s) failure or refusal to comply with the terms of the correction request may constitute a default under the note and/or deed of trust, and may give Lender the option of declaring all sums secured by the loan documents immediately due and payable. If applicable, Borrower(s) further acknowledges that Lender estimated the amount of the one-time FHA Mortgage Insurance Premium (MIP) or VA Funding Fee at the time the loan was made. Borrower(s) hereby agrees and consents that Lender has the right to apply to the debt any amount held by the Lender in excess of the actual MIP or VA Funding Fee, as an offset against the debt.

BORROWER LIABILITY: If Borrower(s) fails or refuses to execute, acknowledge, initial and deliver the Documents or pay the Fees to Lender more than ten (10) days after being requested to do so by Lender, and understanding that Lender is relying on these representations, Borrower(s) agree(s) to be liable for any and all loss or damage which Lender reasonably sustains thereby, including but not limited to all reasonable attorney's fees and costs incurred by Lender.

RETURNED PAYMENTS: For the life of the loan, Borrower agrees to pay a fee of up to $25.00 ($40.00 in FL) for each returned payment, except as otherwise limited by law.

This agreement shall survive the closing of the Loan, and inure to the benefit of Lender's successors and assigns and be binding upon the heirs, devisees, personal representatives, successors and assigns of Borrower(s).

_____
Refinance

      (Seller/Contractor)

_____

      (Seller/Contractor)

_____
MICHAEL T. TAKATA   (Borrower)

_____
(Borrower)

_____
(Borrower)

_____
(Borrower)

Correction Agreement
Limited Power of Attorney

On   **FEBRUARY 20, 20XX** , the undersigned borrower(s), for and in consideration of the approval, closing and funding of their mortgage loan   **(# 20000000000),** hereby grant **PMAC MORTGAGE CORPORATION DBA LOANTECH.COM**   as settlement agent and/OR **PMAC MORTGAGE CORPORATION DBA LOANTECH.COM** as lender limited power of attorney to correct and/or execute or initial all typographical or clerical errors discovered in any or all of the closing documentation required to be executed by the undersigned at settlement. In the event this limited power of attorney is exercised, the undersigned will be notified and receive a copy of the document executed or initialed on their behalf.

THIS LIMITED POWER OF ATTORNEY MAY NOT BE USED TO INCREASE THE INTEREST RATE THE UNDERSIGNED IS PAYING, INCREASE THE TERM OF THE UNDERSIGNED'S LOAN, INCREASE THE UNDERSIGNED'S OUTSTANDING PRINCIPAL BALANCE OR INCREASE THE UNDERSIGNED'S MONTHLY PRINCIPAL AND INTEREST PAYMENTS. Any of these specified changes must be executed directly by the undersigned.

This limited power of attorney shall automatically terminate 180 days from the closing date of the undersigned's mortgage loan.

IN WITNESS WHEREOF, the undersigned have executed this Limited Power of Attorney as of the date and year first above referenced.

_____   _____
RANDALL STEINBECK — BORROWER

_____   _____
MAUREEN STEINBECK — BORROWER

State of

County of

On _____ before me, _____
                 Date   Name and Title of Officer (e.g. Jane Doe. Notary Public")

personally appeared _____

Personally known to me - OR - proved to me on the basis of satisfactory evidence to be the person(s) whose
                                              name(s) is/are subscribed to the within instrument and
                                              acknowledged to me that he/she/they executed the same in
                                              his/her/their authorized capacity(ies), and that by his/her/their
                                              signature(s) on the instrument the person(s), or the entity upon
                                              behalf of which the person(s) acted, executed the instrument.

                                              WITNESS my hand and official seal.

                                              _____

Chapter

8

Signature and Name Affidavits

INTRODUCTION

Of the individual loan documents presented in Part II of this volume, the signature and name affidavit is by far the most common, appearing in approximately 90% of all loan documentation packages. It also happens to be the most commonly notarized form outside of the security instrument (deed of trust or mortgage).

It is no surprise to discover that there are more variations of the signature and name affidavit than any of the common loan documents. Versions of the document include forms with such titles as: "Signature/Name Affidavit," "Signature Statement," "Signature Certification," "Name/AKA Affidavit," "AKA Statement," "Affidavit of Common Identity," "Identity Certificate," "One and the Same Certification," and the more generic "Borrower Affidavit," a title that departs from the standard practice of naming this document by its function.

IDENTITY THEFT AND MORTGAGE FRAUD

Despite the wide variations in title, these documents share a common goal: to protect the lender and title company from identity related real property frauds. The real property industry is particularly vulnerable to increasingly innovative identity frauds spawned from within the real property and lending industry itself. Examples of these frauds include:

- **Fraudulent loan originations:** When real estate professionals or lender-insiders help unqualified buyers obtain funds for a mortgage loan by using the identities of highly qualified individuals. When identities cannot be "stolen," con artists seek out actual persons with exceptional credit histories and enlist them as "straw buyers" who knowingly or unknowingly "sell" their identities for use in a fraudulent loan application. When the loan is uncovered as a fraud, unsuspecting straw buyers typically aren't prosecuted. But by that time their credit histories are adversely damaged as a result of participating in the scheme.

- **Home improvement scams:** When industry professionals obtain loans in the names of fictitious borrowers, or by assuming the identities of innocent victims who are unaware their identities are being used. Victims later discover a lien on their property they did not know existed, only to learn that a scammer has used their personal identifying information to secure a home equity loan on their property and to strip their hard-earned equity.

Technology in particular has been a double-edged sword to the industry. The explosion in the Notary Signing Agent field can be attributed in part to the technology innovations that enabled lenders, closing agents, and title companies to process and close more loans than ever before and made it more economically viable to farm out the responsibilities for the loan signing ceremony to Notary Signing Agents.

At the same time, experts say mortgage fraud is becoming more sophisticated because a highly educated and trained criminal element is also using technology to its advantage. Perpetrators use technology to produce bogus bank statements, tax records, ID documents, closing documents, appraisals, and proofs of employment that are virtually indistinguishable from real documents. Criminals use computer technology to steal identities, making it easier to obtain a home loan in an unsuspecting borrower's name.

Proper execution of the signature and name affidavit at the signing appointment is an important tool should the lender later discover that the loan was conceived in fraud.

The purposes of the signature and name affidavit are to obtain the borrower's acknowledgment or sworn statement to one or more of the following guarantees:

1. The borrower is signing documents with his or her correct legal name.

2. The signature used in executing the loan documents is the borrower's true and correct signature.

3. The borrower is one and the same person as any additional names documented in credit or title reports and other financial transactions that have been disclosed to the lender and which appear on the affidavit. The "one and the same" certification often appears as an additional document in the loan package alongside a "Signature Affidavit" or related form.

Name Affidavit

MNA2/0142944655

State of _____

City of _____

Before me, a Notary Public in and for the State and City aforesaid, personally appeared

BARRY B RABAB _____ who after being by me first duly sworn, upon his/her

oath depose and say that: BARRY B RABAB _____ as his/her name is signed

on the Note and Security Instruments in connection with the purchase/refinance of the property

known as:

1338 STANFORD STREET #C

SANTA MONICA, CA 90404

is one and the same as BARRY RABAB

_____

_____

Signature   **BARRY B. RABAB**

Subscribed to and sworn to before me this _____ day of _____,

_____.

My commission expires: _____

_____

Notary Public

NAME/AKA AFFIDAVIT

TLC Mortgage, Inc.
10555 Vista Parkway
San Diego, CA 92155-2799

LOAN NUMBER   **02-0955**

On this   day of   ,   before me, the undersigned, a Notary
Public in and for said State, personally appeared

Rika Snow

known to me, or proved to me on the basis satisfactory evidence, to be the person who, after being duly sworn by
me, upon his/her oath, does affirm that he/she is also known as:

Erika Ramirez

and is the same person who executed a Promissory Note dated   **November 5, 20XX**   in the
amount of $ **375,000.00**   and Deed of Trust of the same date securing property located at:

5355 Hart Street
Escondido, CA 92026

_____
RIKA SNOW   Date

Dated

State of   )
) ss.
County of   )

WITNESS my hand and official seal.

_____ (Seal)

<table>
<tr><td>FOR NOTARY SEAL OR STAMP</td></tr>
</table>

NOTES

The notarial act to be performed on this "Name/AKA Affidavit" is an oath (not a jurat). Since most states do not specify an exact Notary certificate form for an oath, the substance of the actual document itself serves as the Notary certificate. No other form need be completed by the Notary and attached.

O'DOWELL SAVINGS
and Loan Association, F.A.

9031634955

SIGNATURE STATEMENT

I, MICHAYLE J BERTMAN
hereby certify that I sign my name as indicated below, and said signature is my legal name.

_____

I,

hereby certify that I sign my name as indicated below, and said signature is my legal name.

_____

I,

hereby certify that I sign my name as indicated below, and said signature is my legal name.

_____

I,

hereby certify that I sign my name as indicated below, and said signature is my legal name.

_____

I,

hereby certify that I sign my name as indicated below, and said signature is my legal name.

_____

I,

hereby certify that I sign my name as indicated below, and said signature is my legal name.

_____

I,

hereby certify that I sign my name as indicated below, and said signature is my legal name.

_____

I,

hereby certify that I sign my name as indicated below, and said signature is my legal name.

_____

I,

hereby certify that I sign my name as indicated below, and said signature is my legal name.

_____

I,

hereby certify that I sign my name as indicated below, and said signature is my legal name.

_____

EXP29-4255F
416-1014556

SIGNATURE CERTIFICATION

THIS IS TO CERTIFY THAT MY SIGNATURE AS SIGNED ON THE LOAN DOCUMENTS AND THIS CERTIFICATION REPRESENTS MY COMPLETE AND LEGAL/NORMAL SIGNATURE FOR MY NAME ___ALBERT C. BOYER_____.

_____
Borrower's Signature

THIS IS TO CERTIFY THAT MY SIGNATURE AS SIGNED ON THE LOAN DOCUMENTS AND THIS CERTIFICATION REPRESENTS MY COMPLETE AND LEGAL/NORMAL SIGNATURE FOR MY NAME ___DEBBIE D. BOYER_____.

_____
Borrower's Signature

STATE OF
COUNTY OF

On _____ before me, _____ , notary public, personally appeared _ALBERT C. BOYER and DEBBIE D. BOYER_____
☐ personally known to me,- OR - ☐ proved to me on the basis of satisfactory evidence to be the person(s) whose name(s) is/are subscribed to the within instrument and acknowledged to me that he/she/they executed the instrument.

WITNESS my hand and official seal.

Signature _____   Seal:

AKA STATEMENT

Date: 9/16/XX

Borrower name: DEBBIE D. BOYER

Property Address: 4557 SUTTON AVENUE, BOWLING GREEN, MO 63334

This is to certify that the following names represent one and the same person.

DEBBIE D. BOYER

DEBBIE BOYER

D. BOYER

D. D. BOYER

_____
Borrower's Signature

STATE OF

COUNTY OF _____

On _____ before me, _____,
a notary public in and for said state, personally appeared DEBBIE D. BOYER,
known to me to be the person(s) who executed the within instrument, and acknowledged to me
that he/she/they executed the same for the purposes therein stated..

WITNESS my hand and official seal.

Signature _____   Seal:

SIGNATURE AFFIDAVIT

TLC Mortgage, Inc.
10555 Haven Parkway
Orlando, FL 32801
LOAN NUMBER: **02-0955**

On this _____ day of _____, _____ before me, the undersigned, a Notary Public in and for said State, personally appeared

DAVID BRUCE AND ERICKA BRUCE, HUSBAND AND WIFE AS JOINT TENANTS

known to me; or proved to me on the basis satisfactory evidence, to be the person who, after being duly sworn by me, upon his/her oath, does affirm that he/she is the person who executed a Promissory Note dated **November 5, 20XX**   in the amount of $ **375,000.00**   and Deed of Trust of the same date securing property located at:

5355 Bart Street
Orlando, FL 82301

by affixing their signature as indicated below on said statements.

Borrower's Legal Signature(s):

_____   _____
DAVID BRUCE   Date   ERICKA BRUCE   Date

_____   _____
                             Date   Date

Dated : _____
)
State of _____   ) ss.
County of _____   )

Subscribed and sworn to (or affirmed) before me on _____ by _____
_____ .

WITNESS my hand and official seal

☐ Personally known to me; or
☐ Produced identification
Type of identification produced:
_____

FOR NOTARY SEAL OR STAMP

SIGNATURE AFFIDAVIT AND AKA STATEMENT

SIGNATURE STATEMENT

I   **ERIN HILLMAN**
certify that this my true and correct signature

ERIN HILLMAN
Borrower   Sample Signature

AKA STATEMENT

_____ further certify that I am also known as:

NOTES

Borrower should write "Never known as" on variation lines he/she doesn't agree is their name.

Name Variation (Print)   Sample Signature (Variation)

Name Variation (Print)   Sample Signature (Variation)

Name Variation (Print)   Sample Signature (Variation)

Name Variation (Print)   Sample Signature (Variation)

Name Variation (Print)   Sample Signature (Variation)

State of
County of

On _____ , before me,
personally appeared **ERIN HILLMAN**
personally known to me (or proved to me on the basis of satisfactory evidence) to be the person(s) whose name(s) is/are subscribed to the within instrument and acknowledged to me that he/she/they executed the same in his/her/their authorized capacity (ies), and that by his/her/their signature(s) on the instrument the person(s), or the entity upon behalf of which the person(s) acted, executed the instrument.

WITNESS my hand and official seal

Signature_____

AFFIDAVIT OF COMMON IDENTITY

Loan No.: **73821255**
Lender Name: **MORTGAGE LENDERS, INC.**
9055 WASHINGTON DR
TIGARD, OR 97255

STATE OF

COUNTY OF

Before me, the undersigned authority, personally appeared **GEORGE R. WRANK**
who after being duly sworn deposes and says that (s)he is one and the same person as:

and that (s)he makes this statement with the expressed purpose of inducing the above named lender to accept a mortgage on the following described property:

SEE ATTACHED EXHIBIT "A"

APN#: 6210-050-555

(Legal Description Above)

Further affiant saith not.

_____ (Seal)
GEORGE R. WRANK   -Borrower

STATE OF

COUNTY OF

The foregoing instrument was acknowledged before me this   day of   , 20   , by;

known to me to be the person whose name is subscribed the within instrument, and I acknowledge that executed the same.

_____
Notary Public

Date: **JULY 16, 20XX**
Loan Number: **625287255**
Borrowers: **JOHN ABRAMS**

IDENTITY CERTIFICATE/NAME AFFIDAVIT

THE STATE OF

COUNTY OF

BEFORE ME, the undersigned authority, a Notary Public in and for said County and State, on this day personally appeared

JOHN ABRAMS

who after being by me first duly sworn, upon oath depose and say:

     THAT, **JOHN ABRAMS**

as the name is signed on the note and security instrument and all other closing documents is one and the same person as

     JOHN ABRAMS

as the name appears on the various papers in the loan application.

Property Address: **6255 55TH PL
HARRISON, MI 48625**

_____   _____
JOHN ABRAMS   **DATE**

SUBSCRIBED AND SWORN TO BEFORE ME this   day of

_____

Notary Public in and for

_____

BORROWER AFFIDAVIT

LOAN NO.: **1595436855**   FEDERAL TAX ID NO.: **534-66-1255**

PROPERTY ADDRESS: **5520 GRACIOS STREET**
                              CONCORD, NH 03301

The undersigned does hereby certify that: **ARLENE ALICIA**

1. He/She is one and the same person as: **ARLENE ALICIA-ROJAS, ARLENE A. ALICIA**

2. The number shown above is my correct taxpayer identification number.

3. The following signature is my legal signature for my full name as it appears on the documents executed in connection with this transaction.

_____   _____
ARLENE ALICIA   **DATE**

NOTARY AFFIDAVIT

State of

County of

On   before me, the undersigned, a Notary Public in and for said state personally appeared

personally known-to me (or proved to me on the basis of satisfactory evidence) to be the person(s) whose name(s) is/are subscribed to the within instrument and acknowledged to me that he/she/they executed the same in his/her/their authorized capacity(ies), and that by his/her/their signature(s) on the instrument the person(s), or the entity upon behalf of which the person(s) acted, executed the instrument.

_____
Signature   Witness by hand and official seal.
                                                  (Reserved for official seal)

_____
Name (typed or printed)

LENDER: **PRIME FINANCIAL LENDING, INC.**

LOAN: **9879994444999999999**   DATE: **JULY 7, 20XX**

PROPERTY ADDRESS: **897 WEATHERSPOON AVE., BEVERLY HILLS, CA 90211**

SIGNATURE CERTIFICATION/AFFIDAVIT

I HEREBY CERTIFY THAT I, _____**JOSEPH ROHEN**_____, DO SIGN MY NAME
AS FOLLOWS. THIS IS MY TRUE AND ACCURATE SIGNATURE:

_____
BORROWER

State of _____

County of _____

_____scribed before me, a notary for the jurisdiction given this ____ day of _____.

_____
Notary Public

My Commission Expires: _____

_____CERTIFY THAT I HAVE REVIEWED THE SIGNATURE ON THE ABOVE CAPTIONED
_____ND HE/SHE HAS CONSISTENTLY SIGNED HIS/HER NAME ON ALL DOCUMENTS WITHIN
_____HE/SHE DID ON THE NOTE.

_____
Lender Representative   Title

- -

NAME AFFIDAVIT
Complete if AKA (also known as) is required.

THIS IS TO CERTIFY THAT:

JACK ROHEN_____,

JOSEPH E. ROHEN_____,

& _____**JOSEPH ROHEN**_____ ARE ONE AND THE SAME PERSON.
THIS NAME AFFIDAVIT IS COMPLETED IN CONNECTION WITH DOCUMENTS TO OBTAIN A FIRST
MORTGAGE LOAN ON THE SUBJECT PROPERTY.

Please sign each way name appears.

_____
BORROWER:

_____
BORROWER:

_____
BORROWER:

State of _____

County of _____

Sworn and Subscribed before me, a notary for the jurisdiction given this ____ day of _____.

_____
Notary Public

(Seal)

My Commission Expires: _____

SIGNATURE/NAME AFFIDAVIT
C- 7039 (12/97) (replaces C-7035 1/97 & C-7039 12/95)

NOTES

The "Signature Certification/Affidavit" requires 2 notarizations (jurats). At the top of the form, the borrower certifies under oath or affirmation that the signed name is the borrower's official signature. At the bottom of the form, the borrower similarly vouches the same for each name listed.

Chapter

9

Conveyance Instruments

INTRODUCTION

Notary Signing Agents often handle home loan transactions in which the homeowner retains ownership of the property or possibly conveys the title to a trustee by signing a deed of trust.

Agents also will encounter sale or purchase transactions in which a property is being sold to a new owner or buyer, or a transaction in which the title is being transferred to a spouse or a family member. In states that allow individuals to place their homes in a living trust (as in California), a step in the refinance transaction will require that the home be taken out of the trust to consummate the transaction and then be placed back into the trust afterward. When this occurs, Notary Signing Agents might see one or more deeds among the documents in a loan package.

A deed is a document that conveys title to real or personal property. In this chapter, the types of deeds used to convey title, the form a deed must take, and the signing formalities (including notarization) required will be discussed. Following this discussion several sample deeds will be illustrated.

CONVEYANCE INSTRUMENTS BY STATE

State law or customary practice dictates the type of deed used to convey title to real property. The most common instrument used by the majority of states is the warranty deed or special warranty deed. The quitclaim deed is also commonly used, but as the ensuing discussion in the following pages will demonstrate, it is used for a different purpose. Bargain and sale and grant deeds are less frequently employed.

TYPES OF DEEDS

General Warranty Deed

A deed which conveys not only all the grantor's interests in and title to the property, but also warrants that if the title is defective or has a "cloud" on it (such as mortgage claims, tax liens, title claims, judgments, or mechanic's liens), the grantee may hold the grantor liable. A general warranty deed provides five typical guarantees:

1. **Guarantee against encumbrances.** The grantor covenants that the title has no encumbrances other than those expressly stated in the deed.

2. **Guarantee of further assurance.** If title defects are subsequently found, the grantor promises or agrees to perform any acts required to correct those defects, within reason.

3. **Guarantee of quiet enjoyment.** This covenant is the grantor's assurance that no other person or party has claims to the property that are superior to the grantee, except as spelled out in the deed. The grantee can "rest easy" without worry of eviction or disturbance by a third party claiming title.

4. **Guarantee of seisin.** The legal term "seisin" or "seizin" means the grantor actually possesses ownership and has the right, authority, and legal capacity to convey that ownership.

5. **Guarantee of warranty forever (warranty of title).** The grantor covenants that if in the future the title conveyed is challenged, the grantor will pay the expenses required to defend the title against that challenge.

Special Warranty Deed

In a special warranty deed, the grantor conveys title to the grantee and agrees to protect the grantee against title defects or claims asserted by the grantor and those persons whose right to assert a claim against the title arose during the period the grantor held title to the property. The grantor guarantees against defects and adverse claims to title during the time the grantor held title to the property. Under a special warranty deed, the seller is not liable for defects in the title attributable to prior owners.

Quitclaim Deed

A quitclaim deed transfers the owner's interest to a buyer but does not guarantee against other claims to the property. A quitclaim deed offers no guarantee that the grantor actually possesses any ownership interest or ability to convey title. In fact, the quitclaim normally only conveys the grantor's current interest, if any, and not the property itself.

If the grantor's purported interest is false, invalid, or fraudulent, no ownership interests or property are conveyed.

Quitclaim deeds are often used in corrective or simple situations or if the grantor is unsure about the quality of the title he or she possesses. For example, if the grantor obtained a property through a foreclosure sale, the grantor may choose to use a quitclaim deed.

Grant Deed

A grant deed transfers title to real property or a real property interest from grantor to grantee and warrants that the grantor actually owned the title to transfer. A grant deed is similar to a special warranty deed and is the main conveyance instrument used in a few states, notably California, Maryland, and New Hampshire.

Bargain and Sale Deed

A contract resulting from a "bargain" between a buyer and a seller of real property that transfers title to the buyer by operation of law, without the grantor warranting title. In offering no warranties, a bargain and sale deed is similar to a quitclaim deed. Unlike a quitclaim deed, a bargain and sale deed clearly assumes the grantor owns the property and has the legal ability to convey title.

Fiduciary Deed

The fiduciary deed is used to transfer real estate from a grantor who is a "fiduciary" — a person in a position of trust. A fiduciary could be an executor, administrator, trustee, guardian, receiver, or commissioner. The fiduciary warrants only that the fiduciary is duly appointed and acting with proper authority. In other ways, the fiduciary deed is similar to the quitclaim deed.

Corporate Deed

In Idaho, a corporate deed is used where the grantor is a corporation. The corporation can convey title to another corporation or to one or more individuals as grantees. Many states have a single "all-purpose" warranty deed containing uniform or statutory covenants to which a corporate acknowledgment certificate is attached.

Authentic Act

In addition to employing a warranty deed as the instrument of conveyance, property titles may be transferred by an "authentic act" or "act of sale." An authentic act is the central distinguishing power of a Louisiana civil law Notary. Due to its French civil law heritage, Louisiana's civil law Notaries have considerably more education, authority, and responsibility than do Notaries in the rest of the United States. In an authentic act, a civil law Notary has the power to draft deeds, confirm all necessary matters incident to the transaction, and archive the original documentation. In many countries around the world with similar notarial systems, persons wishing to convey property seek out the local Notary, who sees the transaction through from beginning to end.

REQUIREMENTS

While state and local laws may prescribe additional requirements for conveyance deeds, the following conditions are almost universally present:

1. A deed must be in writing.

2. A deed must identify the full names of both the grantor and grantee.

3. The grantor must possess legal ability to convey title, and be of legal age and competence.

4. "Consideration" (i.e., purchase price) must be included, although in some transactions it may be viewed as a formality (e.g., "in consideration of zero dollars and other good and valuable considerations in hand paid").

5. A deed must contain clear language that it is the grantor's intention to convey the title to the grantee. For example, warranty deeds typically use the phrase "convey and warrant," while bargain and sale deeds contain the verbiage "bargains, sells, and conveys." Quitclaim deeds incorporate the phrase "convey and quitclaim" or "remise, release, and quitclaim."

6. The deed must describe the estate (interest) conveyed, for example "fee simple," life estate," "leasehold," etc.

7. The deed must contain the property's legal description, a method of geographically identifying a parcel of land by survey, which is represented in a graphic drawing of the parcel and acceptable in a court of law.

8. The deed must contain the grantor's signature. The grantee's signature is not required.

9. The deed must be notarized (acknowledged) before a Notary Public or other notarial officer. A few states allow a proof of execution by subscribing witness when the principal grantor cannot personally appear before a Notary to make acknowledgment. Absence of an acknowledgment or proof may invalidate a deed.

10. The deed must be legally delivered by the grantor — and in some states, formally accepted by the grantee. The acts of delivery and acceptance are often symbolic, occurring whenever the grantor has executed the deed (delivery) and when the deed is recorded (acceptance).

11. The deed must be publicly recorded in the local land records office. Recordation provides public notice of the conveyance. Recording was initiated so that all matters pertaining to property would be "out in the open" for everyone to know and to fend off challenges to ownership.

Recorded at the Request of:
When Recorded, mail to:

Order No:

Warranty Deed

For the consideration of _____ Dollars, and other valuable consideration, I, or we,

do hereby convey to

the following real property located in _____ County, Arizona:

Subject to current taxes and other assessments, reservations in patents and all easements, rights-of-way, encumbrances, liens, covenants, conditions, restrictions, obligations and liabilities as may appear of record, the Grantor warrants the title against all persons whomsoever.

Dated: _____

_____   _____

_____   _____

State of _____
County of _____ } ss.   Date of Acknowledgement _____

Acknowledgement of

This instrument was acknowledged before me this date by the persons above-subscribed and if subscribed in a representative capacity, then for the principal named and in the capacity indicated.

_____
Notary Public
My Commission Expires: _____

State of _____
County of _____ } ss.   Date of Acknowledgement _____

Acknowledgement of

This instrument was acknowledged before me this date by the persons above-subscribed and if subscribed in a representative capacity, then for the principal named and in the capacity indicated.

_____
Notary Public
My Commission Expires: _____

NOTE; The parties are cautioned that by completing and executing this document, legal rights, duties and obligations are created. By signing, the parties acknowledge that they have been advised to seek and obtain independent legal counsel as to all matters contained in the within document prior to signing same and that said parties have obtained advice or choose to proceed without same.

Recorded at the Request of:
When Recorded, mail to:

_____

Order No:

Special Warranty Deed

For the consideration of   Dollars, and other valuable considerations, I or we,

does hereby convey to

the following real property located in

Subject to current taxes and other assessments, reservations in patents and all easements, rights-of-way, encumbrances, liens, covenants, conditions, restrictions, obligations and liabilities as may appear of record, the Grantor hereby binds itself to warrant and defend the title as against all acts of the Grantor herein and not other.

Dated: _____

_____   _____

_____   _____

State of _____ }ss.   Date of Acknowledgement _____
County of _____

Acknowledgement of

This instrument was acknowledged before me this date by the persons above-subscribed and if subscribed in a representative capacity, then for the principal named and in the capacity indicated.

_____
                                                        Notary Public
My Commission Expires: _____

State of _____ }ss.   Date of Acknowledgement _____
County of _____

Acknowledgement of

This instrument was acknowledged before me this date by the persons above-subscribed and if subscribed in a representative capacity, then for the principal named and in the capacity indicated.

_____
                                                        Notary Public
My Commission Expires: _____

NOTE; The parties are cautioned that by completing and executing this document, legal rights, duties and obligations are created. By signing, the parties acknowledge that they have been advised to seek and obtain independent legal counsel as to all matters contained in the within document prior to signing same and that said parties have obtained advice or choose to proceed without same.

RECORDING REQUESTED BY

WHEN RECORDED MAIL TO
AND MAIL TAX STATEMENTS TO

NAME

ADDRESS

CITY
STATE & ZIP

TITLE ORDER NO.	ESCROW OR LOAN NO.	APN NO.

QUITCLAIM DEED

THE UNDERSIGNED GRANTOR(s) DECLARE(s)
DOCUMENTARY TRANSFER TAX is $_____ CITY TAX $_____
   ☐ computed on full value of property conveyed, or ☒ computed on full value less value of liens or encumbrances remaining at time of sale,
   ☐ Unincorporated area: ☐ City of _____, and

FOR A VALUABLE CONSIDERATION, receipt of which is hereby acknowledged,

hereby remise, release and forever quitclaim to

the following described real property in the County of _____, State of California:

Dated_____   _____

                                                                 _____

                                                                  _____

                                                                    _____

STATE OF
COUNTY OF _____ } **S.S.**

On _____ before me, _____,
(here insert name and title of the officer), personally appeared _____
_____,
personally known to me (or proved to me on the basis of satisfactory evidence) to be the person(s) whose name(s) is/are subscribed to the within instrument and acknowledged to me that he/she/they executed the same in his/her/their authorized capacity(ies), and that by his/her/their signature(s) on the instrument the person(s), or the entity upon behalf of which the person(s) acted, executed the instrument.

WITNESS my hand and official seal.

Signature_____

AFTER RECORDING MAIL TO:

Name

Address

City, State, Zip

Filed for Record at Request of:

_____

BARGAIN AND SALE DEED

THE GRANTOR(S)   ,

for and in consideration of   Dollars ($),

in hand paid, bargains, sells, and conveys to

the following described estate, situated in the County of   , state of Washington:

Assessor's Property Tax Parcel/Account Number:

The Grantor(s) for himself/herself/themselves and for his/her/their successors in interest do(es) by these presents expressly limit the covenants of the deed to those herein expressed, and exclude all covenants arising or to arise by statutory or other implication, and do(es) hereby covenant that against all persons whomsoever lawfully claiming or to claim by, through, or under said Grantor(s) and not otherwise, he/she/they will forever warrant and defend the said described real estate.

Dated:

STATE OF   )
) ss
COUNTY OF   )

I certify that I know or have satisfactory evidence that _____
(is/are) the person(s) who appeared before me, and said person(s) acknowledged that (he/she/they) signed this instrument and acknowledged it to be (his/her/their) free and voluntary act for the uses and purposes mentioned in this instrument.

Dated: _____   _____
                                         Notary Public in and for the state of
                                         My appointment expires:

FIDUCIARY DEED

KNOW ALL MEN BY THESE PRESENTS, that on _____ day of _____, 20 ____

for the sum of

whose address is

CONVEY TO

whose address is

The following described premises situated in the County, _____ , to wit:

Subject to

Together with all and singular the tenements, hereditaments and appurtenances thereto belonging or in anywise appertaining.

SIGNED IN THE PRESENCE OF: SIGNED BY:

_____   _____

_____   _____

STATE OF _____
                                        -ss-
COUNTY OF _____

The foregoing instrument was acknowledged before me this _____ day of _____, 20 ____

By _____

_____

Notary Public

_____ County, _____

My Commission expires: _____

Tax Code No. _____

Transfer Tax $ _____

DRAFTED BY:

WHEN RECORDED RETURN TO:

This is to certify that there are no liens or titles on the property and that the taxes are paid for FIVE YEARS previous to the date of this instrument. This certification does not include taxes, if any, now in the process of collection by the City, Village or Township Treasurer.

COUNTY TREASURER.

By: _____

This document prepared by (and after recording   )
return to):   )
Name:)
Firm/Company:)
Address:)
Address 2:   )
City, State, Zip:)
Phone:)
)
)
)

------Above This Line Reserved For Official Use Only------

WARRANTY DEED
(Corporation to Individual)

KNOW ALL MEN BY THESE PRESENTS THAT:

FOR VALUABLE CONSIDERATION OF _____($_____),
and other good and valuable consideration, cash in hand paid, the receipt and sufficiency of which is
hereby acknowledged, _____, a Corporation organized
under the laws of the state of _____, hereinafter referred to as "Grantor", does
hereby grant, bargain, sell, convey, and warrant unto _____,
☐ married ☐ unmarried, hereinafter "Grantee", the following lands and property, together with all
improvements located thereon, lying in the County of _____, State of _____, to-wit:

Describe Property of State "SEE DESCRIPTION ATTACHED"

Prior instrument reference: Book _____, Page _____, Document No. _____, of the Recorder
of _____ County, _____ .

LESS AND EXCEPT all oil, gas and minerals, on and under the above described property owned
by Grantor, if any, which are reserved by Grantor.

SUBJECT to all easements, rights-of-way, protective covenants and mineral reservations of
record, if any.

TO HAVE AND TO HOLD same unto Grantee, and unto Grantee's heirs and assigns forever,
with all appurtenances thereunto belonging.

GRANTOR does for Grantor and Grantee's heirs, personal representatives, executors and assigns
forever hereby covenant with GRANTEE that Grantor is lawfully seized in fee simple of said premises;
that the premises are free from all encumbrances, unless otherwise noted above; that Grantor has a good
right to sell and convey the same as aforesaid; and to forever warrant and defend the title to the said lands
against all claims whatsoever.

Taxes for tax year _____ shall be ☐ prorated between Grantor and Grantee as of the date selected by Grantor and Grantee, or ☐ paid by Grantee, or ☐ paid by Grantor.

IN WITNESS WHEREOF, this deed was executed by the undersigned on this the _____ day of _____, 20_____.

{Name of Corporation]

_____

BY: {Type Name}
TITLE: {Title with Corporation}

State of _____

County of _____ ss.

On this_____ day of _____, in the year _____, before me _____, a Notary Public, personally appeared _____ known or identified to me (or proved to me on the oath of _____) to be the president, or vice-president, or secretary or assistant secretary, of the corporation that executed the instrument or the person who executed the instrument on behalf of said corporation, and acknowledged to me that such corporation executed the same.

{Seal}

_____

Notary Public

Printed Name: _____

My Commission Expires: _____

Grantor(s) Name, Address, Phone: **Grantee(s) Name, Address, Phone:**

SEND TAX STATEMENTS TO GRANTEE

—————————————————————————— Space Above This Line For Recorder's Use ——————————————————————————
Title Order No.: _____ **Escrow No.:** _____

INTERSPOUSAL TRANSFER GRANT DEED
(COMMUNITY PROPERTY WITH RIGHT OF SURVIVORSHIP)

THE UNDERSIGNED GRANTOR(s) DECLARE(s):
DOCUMENTARY TRANSFER TAX is $ _____. CITY TAX $ _____.
☐ Computed on full value of property conveyed, or ☐ Computed on full value less value of liens or encumbrances remaining at time of sale or transfer.
☐ Unincorporated area: ☐ City of _____, and
☐ This conveyance is exempt from Documentary Transfer Tax:
    ☐ "This is a bona fide gift and the grantor received nothing in return, R & T 11911".
    ☐ "This conveyance changes the manner in which title is held, grantor(s) and grantee(s) remain the same and continue to hold the same proportionate interest, R & T 11911".
    ☐ "This conveyance confirms a community property interest, which was purchased with community property funds, R & T 11911".
☐ Excluded from Reappraisal Under Proposition 13, California Constitution Article 13A § 1, et seq.
☐ This conveyance does not constitute a "change of ownership", R & T 63.
☐ Check when grantees are expressly declaring that the transfer of the property is to be community property with right of survivorship.

FOR A VALUABLE CONSIDERATION, receipt of which is hereby acknowledged,

hereby GRANT(s) to

_____, Husband and Wife, as Community Property with Right of Survivorship,

the following described real property in the County of _____, State of _____
(Assessor's Parcel No. _____):

Dated: _____   _____
                                        (Grantor)

Dated: _____   _____
                                        (Grantor)

STATE OF _____ }
COUNTY OF _____ } *SS*

On _____ before me, _____

_____ (here insert name and title of the officer),

personally appeared _____

_____,

personally known to me (or proved to me on the basis of satisfactory evidence) to be the person(s) whose name(s) is/are subscribed to the within instrument and acknowledged to me that he/she/they executed the same in his/her/their authorized capacity(ies), and that by his/her/their signature(s) on the instrument the person(s), or the entity upon behalf of which the person(s) acted, executed the instrument.

WITNESS my hand and official seal.

Signature _____

DEED WITH MORTGAGE ASSUMPTION

State of

County of

     KNOW ALL MEN BY THESE PRESENTS:

That for and in consideration of the sum of _____ Dollars and other good and valuable

consideration paid to me/us by and the assumption and agreement by _____

to pay the balance of the mortgage indebtedness due _____

the receipt of which is hereby acknowledged, I the undersigned _____

married person, do grant, bargain and sell and convey unto the said _____

all of my right, title, claim and interest, present and prospective, including every contingent remainder and right of

reversion, in the following described real property, situated, lying and being in _____, County, _____,

viz.

     REAL PROPERTY DESCRIBED IN EXHIBIT A, WHICH IS ATTACHED HERETO
     AND INCORPORTATED HEREIN BY REFERENCE.

     This conveyance is made subject to the indebtedness secured by the mortgage of to _____,

which mortgage the Grantee by the acceptance by this deed assumes and agrees to pay.

     TO HAVE AND TO HOLD the same unto the said _____,his/her/

their heirs and assigns, in fee simple forever, together with every contingent remainder and right of reversion owned

by me in said real property.

     IN WITNESS WHEREOF, I have hereunto set my hand and seal on this _____ day of _____,

_____.

                    (SEAL) _____

Grantee's Address

_____

_____

_____

State of

County of

     I, the undersigned authority, a Notary Public in and for said County, in said State, do hereby certify that

_____ whose name(s) is/are signed to the foregoing

conveyance, and who is/are known to me, acknowledged before me on this day, that, being informed of the contents

of the conveyance, he/she/they executed the same voluntarily on the day the same bears date.

     Given under my hand and official seal, this _____ day of _____, _____.

                       _____

                                        Notary Public

Recorded at the Request of:

When Recorded, mail to:

_____

Order No: _____

Joint Tenancy Deed

For the consideration of Ten Dollars, and other valuable consideration, I or we,

do hereby convey to

as joint tenants with right of survivorship and not as a community property estate and not as tenants in common, the following-described property located in _____ County, Arizona:

Subject to current taxes and other assessments, reservations in patents and all easements, rights-of-way, encumbrances, liens, covenants, conditions, restrictions, obligations and liabilities as may appear of record, the Grantor warrants the title against all persons whomsoever.

The undersigned Grantees accept delivery of this deed as joint tenants with right of survivorship and not as a community property estate and not as tenants in common.

Dated: _____

Accepted and approved:

_____   _____

_____   _____

_____

State of _____ }ss.   Date of Acknowledgement _____
County of _____

Acknowledgement of

This instrument was acknowledged before me this date by the persons above-subscribed and if subscribed in a representative capacity, then for the principal named and in the capacity indicated.

_____
                                    Notary Public
My commission expires

State of _____ }ss.   Date of Acknowledgement _____
County of _____

Acknowledgement of

This instrument was acknowledged before me this date by the persons above-subscribed and if subscribed in a representative capacity, then for the principal named and in the capacity indicated.

_____
                                    Notary Public
My commission expires

NOTE; The parties are cautioned that by completing and executing this document, legal rights, duties and obligations are created. By signing, **the parties** acknowledge that they have been advised to seek and obtain **independent legal counsel** as to all matters contained in the within **document prior** to signing same and that said parties have obtained advice or choose to proceed without same.

Chapter

10

Notes and Security Instruments

INTRODUCTION

Few persons can afford to purchase a home without a loan. In every loan transaction there is a promissory note, the actual instrument of indebtedness obligating the borrower to repay the loan amount according to its stated terms. In simplest terms, the note is the borrower's "I.O.U."

However, no lender would approve a loan for thousands of dollars with merely an I.O.U. as evidence that the loan one day would be repaid. A security instrument — either a mortgage or deed of trust — also accompanies the note in every loan package. The mortgage or deed of trust "secures" repayment by pledging the property as collateral for the loan. In the event a borrower is unable to make payments on the note, the lender has a claim on the property to recover its investment.

This chapter will discuss common features of promissory notes and security instruments. Various note addenda and riders to the security instrument will also be discussed, since these documents surface in loan packages frequently.

THE PROMISSORY NOTE

The note is the written evidence of a loan. It is the contract between lender and borrower.

While the majority of loans that Notary Signing Agents handle are for refinancing the primary mortgage on residential properties, occasionally Agents might handle a signing appointment for a "purchase" or "construction" loan. A purchase loan, as the name implies, is used for buying a new or existing home. Construction loans provide financing for the addition or renovation of buildings and structures. Construction loans differ from refinance and purchase loans in that the "collateral" which these loans finance does not exist at the time the loan is extended. Purchase, refinance, and construction loans have a note, although the note's provisions will vary by loan type.

An expansive array of options for repaying mortgage loans now exist and more are added all the time. In addition to traditional regularly amortizing fixed and adjustable rate loans, some of the more popular programs include:

- Accelerated payback loans with 10-, 15- and even 20-year terms.

- Biweekly payment loans, which add an additional monthly payment each year, allowing a 30-year mortgage to be paid off completely in 26 years.

- "Balloon" loans, which have a shorter term than the amortized loan, resulting in the principal balance of the loan becoming due in full after five or seven years. Balloon loans are an attractive loan option for borrowers who know they will likely move before the balloon payment is due.

- Buy-Down loans, whereby a borrower can "buy down" the interest rate either temporarily (1–3 year period) or permanently.

- Interest-only loans, where only interest payments are made on the loan for a specified period (from 6 months to 10 years) before both interest and principal payments become due.

- Reverse mortgage loans, targeted specifically at seniors age 62 and older who nearly or fully own their homes. These loans allow seniors to tap the equity built up in their residences without having to repay the loan amount as long as they live in their homes.

The promissory notes found in most loan packages are fairly straightforward in their language. The note typically contains the following elements and provisions:

1. **Promise to Pay:** A statement whereby the borrower pledges to repay the note holder the full amount of principal and interest.

2. **Interest Rate:** If the loan has an adjustable interest rate feature, there will be reference to the date the interest rate changes, the financial index upon which the adjustable rate is based, the calculation of changes, and the cap or limits on interest rate increases.

3. **Payments:** A separate clause will specify the exact amount of monthly payments and the time and place where payments are made.

4. **Prepayments:** The payment clause states the terms under which the borrower may make a partial or full prepayment of principal. It is not unusual for the borrower to ask about the loan's prepayment clause. Agents should not attempt to explain prepayment terms, but they can point the borrower to the applicable paragraph within the note containing the prepayment provisions.

5. **Default:** The note will outline the remedies available to the lender when the borrower fails to make a timely payment or defaults on the loan, including imposition of late charges, delivery of notices, demand for payoff, and payment of the note holder's costs.

6. **Transfers:** A clause in the note will state that the lender may require the principal amount of the loan to be immediately repaid upon sale or transfer of the property. This clause also will often mention the circumstances under which the loan may be transferred to or assumed by another party.

7. **Liability:** The note contains a liability clause binding all persons signing the note individually and severally.

8. **Link to Security Instrument:** The note will make reference to the security instrument which provides security for the loan.

SECURITY INSTRUMENTS

The etymology of the term "mortgage" is fascinating. Derived from the Old French words mort ("dead") and gage ("pledge"), it has been variously understood. In one view, from the perspective of the borrower, a failure to carry through with the "pledge" to repay meant that the land pledged as security would be taken away forever, becoming "dead" to the borrower. From the lender's perspective, the right or pledge to the land was "dead" if the borrower performed his obligation to repay the loan.

Taken another way, a mortgage allows the obligation of the loan to be "killed off" gradually over time, usually a period of about 30 years, through a combination of principal and interest payments. The mortgagor (borrower) "kills" the debt; the mortgagee's (lender) loan is "killed off."

As mentioned earlier, the note and security instrument are tied together. Technically, it is possible to execute a note without a security instrument; the result would be a loan without security or collateral (possible, but highly unlikely). However, it would be meaningless to execute a security instrument without a note, since the mortgage or deed of trust secures an actual debt.

In a mortgage, the borrower promises to repay the loan by pledging the property as collateral. A lien is placed on title in favor of the lender until the debt is repaid. If the borrower defaults on the loan, the lender must initiate a legal foreclosure in the courts to recoup its investment, a process called "judicial" foreclosure. A mortgage is a two-party contract.

In a deed of trust, the borrower grants and conveys the property to a third party (the "trustee"). The trustee holds title to the property until the loan obligation is fully satisfied. If the borrower defaults on the loan, the lender (the "beneficiary") informs the trustee of the default, and the trustee can then invoke the power of sale on the property, a process called "nonjudicial" foreclosure. Unlike a mortgage, a judicial foreclosure is not necessary, since the borrower grants to the trustee the ability to sell the property to recover the lender's losses.

It is the process of foreclosure which constitutes the most significant difference between a mortgage and a deed of trust. Also of interest is the fact that the deed of trust involves three parties — the borrower (trustor), trustee, and the lender — while the mortgage involves only the borrower (mortgagor) and lender (mortgagee). A summary of the essential differences between these two security instruments is presented in the table below:

Mortgage	Deed of Trust
Two-party agreement	Three-party agreement
Lien placed on title in favor of lender	Title granted to trustee with power of sale
Judicial foreclosure	Non-judicial foreclosure

The exact nature of the claim a lender has upon the borrower's property depends upon whether the mortgage (or deed of trust) is drafted as a conveyance or a transfer of title to the lender, or as a lien to secure payment of the loan. In "title theory states," the lender takes actual title to the property, although the lender's ownership interest is limited to securing the title as collateral for the loan. In "lien theory states," the borrower retains ownership of the property throughout the loan repayment term; the lender does not gain title, but obtains a lien against the property. There is even an "intermediate title theory," which holds to lien theory until default, and then reverts to title theory.

While it is generally accepted that most states follow lien theory, there is varied opinion on whether certain states follow a particular theory.

Title Theory	Lien Theory	Intermediate Theory
Mortgage conveys title to lender	Mortgage creates a lien on title	Mortgage creates a lien on title
Lender holds legal title	Borrower holds legal title	Borrower holds legal title
Borrower has right of possession and use	Borrower has right of possession and use	Borrower has right of possession and use
Lender returns title upon payment	Lien is removed upon payment	Lien is removed upon payment
Lender has immediate title upon default	Lender must foreclose to obtain title	Lender has immediate title upon default

UNIFORM SECURITY INSTRUMENT

Most notes and security instruments found in loan packages today are "multi-state uniform instruments." Found on both the Fannie Mae (FNMA) and Freddie Mac (FHLMC) web sites, these state-specific forms are used for the majority of loans.

Why are uniform instruments used? Standardized forms minimize consumer costs for drawing up the note, any addenda to the note, the security instrument, and any riders to the security instrument for typical loan transactions. It would be prohibitively expensive for consumers to pay attorneys' fees to draft these documents. By containing large sections of "boilerplate text," the amount of data entry necessary to complete these forms is reduced to a few lines with blank spaces.

Uniform loan documents also facilitate the buying and selling of loans in the secondary mortgage market. Investors would face the same high legal expenses as consumers were it necessary to employ attorneys to review the hundreds of substantially diverse notes and security instruments found in a typical investment portfolio. However, when all mortgages contain the same uniform documentation, the cost of purchasing these mortgages is significantly less.

The standard uniform security instruments are used for almost all types of regularly amortizing mortgages. There are certain transactions wherein a standard uniform instrument cannot be used (in Texas Section 50(a)(6) mortgages, New York consolidated mortgages, Puerto Rico direct mortgages, and reverse mortgages). However, special uniform instruments are available for these unique loans.

SECURITY INSTRUMENT PROVISIONS

Most security instruments contain many, if not most, of the following covenants and provisions:

1. **Mortgagor or Trustor Covenants**

   a. Payment of the debt in accordance with the terms of the note.

   b. Payment of all real estate taxes on the property given as security.

   c. Maintenance of all required insurance to protect the lender if the property is destroyed or damaged by fire, windstorm, or other hazard.

   d. Maintenance of the property in good repair at all times.

   e. Securing lender authorization before making major alterations on the property.

   f. Occupation and use of the property as the borrower's principal residence.

2. **Provisions for Default:** If a borrower defaults, the lender has the right to accelerate the maturity of the debt.

3. **Assignment of the Mortgage:** There is a provision in most security instruments that the note may be sold to a third party, such as an investor or another mortgage company, who becomes the owner of the debt and security instrument.

4. **Release of the Mortgage:** A clause requires the lender to execute a satisfaction of mortgage when the note has been fully paid.

5. **Escrow Items:** Many lenders require borrowers to provide a fund (called an "impound" or "escrow" account) to meet future real estate taxes and property insurance premiums.

6. **Mortgage Insurance:** Mortgage insurance reimburses the lender for certain losses it may incur if the borrower does not repay the loan. If a lender requires the borrower to purchase mortgage insurance as a condition for extending the loan, the borrower agrees to pay all premiums.

7. **Flood Insurance Reserves:** The National Flood Insurance Reform Act of 1994 imposes certain mandatory obligations on lenders and loan services to set aside funds for flood insurance on new loans.

8. **Buying or Assuming a Seller's Mortgage or Deed of Trust:** The purchaser is responsible for making payments on the preexisting debt but is not personally liable. Upon default, if the sale does not pay off the entire debt, the purchaser is not liable for the difference. If the mortgage is assumed, the buyer becomes personally obligated for the payment of the entire debt.

9. **Alienation clause:** Provides that when the property is sold, the lender may either declare the entire debt due immediately or permit the buyer to assume the loan at the current market interest rate.

10. **Recording a Mortgage or Deed of Trust:** The mortgage document or deed of trust must be recorded in the recorder's office of the county in which the real estate is located.

RIDERS AND ADDENDA

It is sometimes necessary to amend or supplement special provisions to a promissory note or security instrument that apply to a particular loan or delete standard sections which may not apply in a given case. The amendments are accomplished through the use of a rider or an addendum. Occasionally, an addendum is also used to amend a rider.

According to Fannie Mae and Freddie Mac, uniform covenants must be modified by a "rider" containing additional stipulations and covenants for the following circumstances:

- Adjustable-rate mortgages;

- A balloon mortgage;

- A biweekly payment mortgage;

- Second home mortgages;

- Investment properties;

- Two- to four-family properties;

- Planned Unit Development (PUD); and

- Condominium mortgages.

Forms in Sample Set   **Pages**

Due to their prevalence and length, sample notes and security instruments are not reproduced here. We refer the reader to the complete sample sets reproduced in Part I of this book for examples of these forms.

The following addenda and riders are included in the pages which follow:

ADDENDUM TO ADJUSTABLE RATE RIDER
(Fixed Rate Conversion Option)

THIS ADDENDUM TO ADJUSTABLE RATE RIDER is made this ____ day of _____, ____, and is incorporated into and shall be deemed to amend and supplement the Adjustable Rate Rider (the "Rider") to the Mortgage, Deed of Trust, or Security Deed (the "Security Instrument"), each dated the same date as this Addendum and given by the undersigned ("Borrower") to secure Borrower's Adjustable Rate Note, with Addendum To Adjustable Rate Note, to _____ ("Lender") and dated the same date as this Addendum (the "Note"), covering the property described in the Security Instrument and located at:

_____
[Property Address]

ADDITIONAL COVENANTS. In addition to the covenants and agreements made in the Security Instrument and the Rider, Borrower and Lender further covenant and agree as follows:

A.   FIXED INTEREST RATE OPTION

The Note provides for Borrower's option to convert from an adjustable interest rate to a fixed interest rate, as follows:

1.   Option to Convert to Fixed Rate

I have a Conversion Option that I can exercise unless I am in default or this Section A1 will not permit me to do so. The "Conversion Option" is my option to convert the interest rate I am required to pay by the Note from an adjustable rate to the fixed rate calculated by the Note Holder under Section A2 below.

The conversion can only take place on (a) if the first Change Date is 21 months or less from the date of the Note, the third, fourth or fifth Change Date, or (b) if the first Change Date is more than 21 months from the date of the Note, the first, second or third Change Date. Each Change Date on which my interest rate can convert from an adjustable rate to a fixed rate also is called the "Conversion Date." **I can convert my interest rate only on one of the three Conversion Dates.**

If I want to exercise the Conversion Option, I must first meet certain conditions. Those conditions are that: (i) I must give the Note Holder notice that I want to do so at least 15 days before the next Conversion Date; (ii) on the Conversion Date, I must not be in default under the Note or the Security Instrument; (iii) by a date specified by the Note Holder, I must pay the Note Holder a conversion fee of U.S. $_____; and (iv) I must sign and give the Note Holder any documents the Note Holder requires to effect the conversion.

2.   Calculation of Fixed Rate

My new, fixed interest rate will be determined by the Note Holder based on Fannie Mae's required net yield as of a date and time of day specified by the Note Holder for: (i) if the original term of the Note is greater than 15 years, 30-year fixed rate mortgages covered by applicable 60-day mandatory delivery commitments, plus five-eighths of one percentage point (0.625%), rounded to the nearest one-eighth of one percentage point (0.125%); or (ii) if the original term of the Note is 15 years or less, 15-year fixed rate mortgages covered by applicable 60-day mandatory delivery commitments, plus five-eighths of one percentage point (0.625%), rounded to the nearest one-eighth of one percentage point (0.125%). If this required net yield cannot be determined because the applicable commitments are not available, the Note Holder will determine my interest rate by using comparable information. My new rate calculated under this Section A2 will not be greater than the Maximum Rate stated in the Note.

3.   New Payment Amount and Effective Date

If I am permitted to exercise the Conversion Option, the Note Holder will determine the amount of the monthly payment that would be sufficient to repay the unpaid principal I am expected to owe on the Conversion Date in full on the Maturity Date of the Note at my new fixed interest rate in substantially equal payments. The result of this calculation will be the new amount of my monthly payment. Beginning with my first monthly payment after the Conversion Date, I will pay the new amount as my monthly payment until the Maturity Date of the Note.

B.   TRANSFER OF THE PROPERTY OR A BENEFICIAL INTEREST IN BORROWER

If Borrower's adjustable interest rate is converted to a fixed rate as stated in Section A of this Addendum To Adjustable Rate Rider, the amendment to Uniform Covenant 18 of the Security Instrument contained in the Rider shall cease to be in effect, and the provisions of Uniform Covenant 18 of the Security Instrument shall instead read as follows:

FIXED RATE OPTION ADDENDUM (SECURITY INSTRUMENT)—Single Family—Fannie Mae Uniform Instrument   Form 3109   1/01   (page 1 of 2)

Transfer of the Property or a Beneficial Interest in Borrower. As used in this Section 18, "Interest in the Property" means any legal or beneficial interest in the Property, including, but not limited to, those beneficial interests transferred in a bond for deed, contract for deed, installment sales contract or escrow agreement, the intent of which is the transfer of title by Borrower at a future date to a purchaser.

If all or any part of the Property or any Interest in the Property is sold or transferred (or if Borrower is not a natural person and a beneficial interest in Borrower is sold or transferred) without Lender's prior written consent, Lender may require immediate payment in full of all sums secured by this Security Instrument. However, this option shall not be exercised by Lender if such exercise is prohibited by Applicable Law.

If Lender exercises this option, Lender shall give Borrower notice of acceleration. The notice shall provide a period of not less than 30 days from the date the notice is given in accordance with Section 15 within which Borrower must pay all sums secured by this Security Instrument. If Borrower fails to pay these sums prior to the expiration of this period, Lender may invoke any remedies permitted by this Security Instrument without further notice or demand on Borrower.

BY SIGNING BELOW, Borrower accepts and agrees to the terms and covenants contained in this Addendum To Adjustable Rate Rider.

.... (Seal)
-Borrower

.... (Seal)
-Borrower

Form 3109   1/01   *(page 2 of 2)*

BALLOON NOTE ADDENDUM
(CONDITIONAL RIGHT TO REFINANCE)

THIS BALLOON NOTE ADDENDUM is made this ____ day of _____, ____, and is incorporated into and shall be deemed to amend and supplement the Balloon Note made by the undersigned ("Borrower") in favor of _____ ("Lender") and dated as of even date herewith (the "Note"). The interest rate stated on the Note is called the "Note Rate." The date of the Note is called the "Note Date."

I understand Lender may transfer the Note, the related Mortgage, Deed of Trust, or Security Deed (the "Security Instrument"), and this Addendum. Lender or anyone who takes the Note, Security Instrument, and this Addendum by transfer and who is entitled to receive payments under the Note is called the "Note Holder."

ADDITIONAL COVENANTS. In addition to the covenants and agreements in the Security Instrument, Borrower and Lender further covenant and agree as follows (despite anything to the contrary contained in the Security Instrument or the Note):

1. CONDITIONAL RIGHT TO REFINANCE

At the Maturity Date of the Note and Security Instrument (the "Maturity Date"), I will be able to obtain a new loan ("New Loan") with a new Maturity Date of _____, ____, and with an interest rate equal to the "New Note Rate" determined in accordance with Section 3 below if all the conditions provided in Section 2 and 5 below are met (the "Conditional Refinancing Option"). If those conditions are not met, I understand that the Note Holder is under no obligation to refinance or modify the Note, or to extend the Maturity Date, and that I will have to repay the Note from my own resources or find a lender willing to lend me the money to repay the Note.

2. CONDITIONS TO OPTION

If I want to exercise the Conditional Refinancing Option at maturity, certain conditions must be met as of the Maturity Date. These conditions are: (a) I must still be the owner of the Property subject to the Security Instrument (the "Property"); (b) I must be current in my monthly payments and cannot have been more than 30 days late on any of the 12 scheduled monthly payments immediately preceding the Maturity Date; (c) the New Note Rate cannot be more than five percentage points above the Note Rate; and (d) I must make a written request to the Note Holder as provided in Section 5 below.

3. CALCULATING THE NEW NOTE RATE

The New Note Rate will be a fixed rate of interest equal to Fannie Mae's required net yield for 30-year fixed-rate mortgages subject to a 60-day mandatory delivery commitment, plus one-half of one percentage point (0.5%), rounded to the nearest one-eighth of one percentage point (0.125%) (the "New Note Rate"). The required net yield shall be the applicable net yield in effect on the date and time of day that the Note Holder receives notice of my election to exercise the Conditional Refinancing Option. If this required net yield is not available, the Note Holder will determine the New Note Rate by using comparable information.

4. CALCULATING THE NEW PAYMENT AMOUNT

Provided the New Note Rate as calculated in Section 3 above is not greater than five percentage points above the Note Rate and all other conditions required in Section 2 above are satisfied, the Note Holder will determine the amount of the monthly payment that will be sufficient to repay in full (a) the unpaid principal, plus (b) accrued but unpaid interest, plus (c) all other sums I will owe under the Note and Security Instrument on the Maturity Date (assuming my monthly payments then are current, as required under Section 2 above), over the term of the New Note at the New Note Rate in equal monthly payments. The result of this calculation will be the amount of my new principal and interest payment every month until the New Note is fully paid.

MULTISTATE BALLOON NOTE ADDENDUM—Single Family—**Fannie Mae Uniform Instrument**   Form 3266   1/01 (rev. 9/01)   *(page 1 of 2)*

5.   EXERCISING THE CONDITIONAL REFINANCING OPTION

The Note Holder will notify me at least 60 calendar days in advance of the Maturity Date and advise me of the principal, accrued but unpaid interest, and all other sums I am expected to owe on the Maturity Date. The Note Holder also will advise me that I may exercise the Conditional Refinancing Option if the conditions in Section 2 above are met. The Note Holder will provide my payment record information, together with the name, title, and address of the person representing the Note Holder that I must notify in order to exercise the Conditional Refinancing Option. If I meet the conditions of Section 2 above, I may exercise the Conditional Refinancing Option by notifying the Note Holder no later than 45 calendar days prior to the Maturity Date. The Note Holder will calculate the fixed New Note Rate based upon Fannie Mae's applicable published required net yield in effect on the date and time of day notification is received by the Note Holder and as calculated in Section 3 above. I will then have 30 calendar days to provide the Note Holder with acceptable proof of my required ownership. Before the Maturity Date, the Note Holder will advise me of the new interest rate (the New Note Rate), new monthly payment amount, and a date, time, and place at which I must appear to sign any documents required to complete the required refinancing. I understand the Note Holder will charge me a $250 processing fee and the costs associated with updating the title insurance policy, if any.

BY SIGNING BELOW, Borrower accepts and agrees to the terms and covenants contained in this Balloon Note Addendum.

....… (Seal)   ……………………………………………………….. (Seal)
                                    -Borrower   -Borrower

..…………………………….……………….. (Seal)
                                    -Borrower   *[Sign Original Only]*

Form 3266   1/01 (rev. 9/01)   *(page 2 of 2)*

CONSTRUCTION LOAN ADDENDUM AMENDING NOTE

THIS CONSTRUCTION LOAN ADDENDUM (the "Addendum") is made this _____ day of _____, _____, and is incorporated into and shall be deemed to amend and supplement the note made by the undersigned Borrower, ("I", "me", "my") to evidence my indebtedness (the "Loan") to _____ and its successors and assigns (the "Note Holder") and dated the same date as this Addendum (the "Note"). The Note is secured by a security instrument, as modified or amended, in favor of the Lender dated the same date as this Addendum (the "Security Instrument"). All terms defined in the Note shall have the same meaning in this Addendum.

ADDITIONAL COVENANTS. In addition to the covenants and agreements made in the Note, Note Holder and I further covenant and agree as follows:

1. **CONSTRUCTION/PERMANENT LOAN.** The Note, as amended by this Addendum, is for a construction loan and a permanent mortgage loan. During the Construction Phase of the Loan, Note Holder will advance funds in accordance with the Construction Loan Agreement dated the same date as this Addendum (the "Construction Loan Agreement"). The "Construction Phase" is the period beginning on the date the Loan consummates (the "Closing Date") until the first day of the month following the Completion Date specified in the Construction Loan Agreement. The Completion Date is _____, _____. The "Permanent Phase" is the period beginning on the first day of the month following the Completion Date specified in the Construction Loan Agreement. On the first day of the month following the Completion Date ("Permanent Mortgage Date"), the Loan will be a permanent mortgage loan. The Permanent Mortgage Date for my Loan is _____, _____. My first payment of principal and interest during the Permanent Phase will be due on the first day of the second month following the Completion Date which is _____, _____, as stated in Section 3(A) of the Note.

2. **INTEREST AND PAYMENTS.**

   (A)   Construction Phase Interest Rate.

   During the Construction Phase of the Loan, I will pay interest only on the amount of the Loan proceeds Lender disburses under the Construction Loan Agreement (each, an "Advance"). I will pay interest at the rate:

   Check applicable box:
   ❑ stated in Section 2 of the Note ("Note Rate")
   ❑ at _____ % per annum

   (B) Permanent Phase Rate

   During the Permanent Phase, I will pay interest ("Permanent Phase Rate") at the rate stated in Section 2 of the Note ("Note Rate").

MULTISTATE CONSTRUCTION LOAN ADDENDUM TO NOTE – Single-Family – **Fannie Mae HOMESTYLE MODEL DOCUMENT**   **Form 3736   11/01**
(page 1 of 2 pages)

Chapter 10: Notes and Security Instruments | 463

(C) Interest Only Payments

Interest on Advances shall be calculated from the date each Advance is made. My Construction Phase interest payments will be:

Check applicable box:
- ❏   due and payable fifteen (15) days after being billed by Note Holder, or
- ❏   paid directly from the "Interest Reserve Account" established at the time of closing in the amount reflected in Schedule of Advances, attached as Exhibit "B" to the Construction Loan Agreement.

(D) Interest Reserve Payments

If I choose to establish an Interest Reserve Account, (1) Construction Phase interest will be advanced by Note Holder from the Interest Reserve Account on the first day of the month following the month in which the interest is billed, (2) Construction Phase interest advanced will be added to Principal and (3) I:

Check applicable box:
- ❏   will pay interest on all Principal, including Advances from the Interest Reserve Account.
- ❏   will pay interest on all Principal, other than Advances from the Interest Reserve Account.

In the event that the Interest Reserve Account is depleted prior to the Completion Date, I agree to pay directly to Note Holder from my own funds any and all interest, which accrues prior to the Completion Date.

Note Holder shall pay no interest on the Interest Reserve Account.

(E) Principal Prepayments; Permanent Phase Interest and Principal Payments

Any portion of a payment Note Holder receives in excess of the interest due during the Construction Phase or any funds Note Holder does not advance under the Construction Loan Agreement may, at Note Holder's option, be used to pay costs associated with the Construction Phase or may be credited as a partial prepayment of the Principal amount of the Loan. The partial prepayment will reduce the ❏ amount of ❏ number of my monthly payments.

Beginning on the Permanent Mortgage Date, principal and interest will be due and payable as set forth in the Note.

3.   **NOTICE OF NO ORAL AGREEMENT**. THE NOTE, THIS ADDENDUM, THE CONSTRUCTION LOAN AGREEMENT, AND THE SECURITY INSTRUMENT, AS AMENDED, REPRESENT THE FINAL AGREEMENT BETWEEN THE PARTIES AND TO THE EXTENT PERMITTED BY LAW, MAY NOT BE CONTRADICTED BY EVIDENCE OF PRIOR, CONTEMPORANEOUS, OR SUBSEQUENT ORAL AGREEMENT OF THE PARTIES. THERE ARE NO ORAL AGREEMENTS BETWEEN THE PARTIES.

BY SIGNING BELOW, I accept and agree to the terms and covenants contained in this Addendum.
DATED this _____ day of _____, _____.

_____   _____
Borrower   Borrower

_____   _____
Borrower   Borrower

MULTISTATE CONSTRUCTION LOAN ADDENDUM TO NOTE – Single-Family – **Fannie Mae HOMESTYLE MODEL DOCUMENT**   **Form 3736**   **11/01**
(page 2 of 2 pages)

464 | The Notary Signing Agent's Loan Documents Sourcebook

CONDOMINIUM RIDER

THIS CONDOMINIUM RIDER is made this _____ day of _____, _____, and is incorporated into and shall be deemed to amend and supplement the Mortgage, Deed of Trust, or Security Deed (the "Security Instrument") of the same date given by the undersigned (the "Borrower") to secure Borrower's Note to _____ _____ (the "Lender") of the same date and covering the Property described in the Security Instrument and located at:

_____

[Property Address]

The Property includes a unit in, together with an undivided interest in the common elements of, a condominium project known as:

_____

[Name of Condominium Project]

(the "Condominium Project"). If the owners association or other entity which acts for the Condominium Project (the "Owners Association") holds title to property for the benefit or use of its members or shareholders, the Property also includes Borrower's interest in the Owners Association and the uses, proceeds and benefits of Borrower's interest.

CONDOMINIUM COVENANTS. In addition to the covenants and agreements made in the Security Instrument, Borrower and Lender further covenant and agree as follows:

A. Condominium Obligations. Borrower shall perform all of Borrower's obligations under the Condominium Project's Constituent Documents. The "Constituent Documents" are the: (i) Declaration or any other document which creates the Condominium Project; (ii) by-laws; (iii) code of regulations; and (iv) other equivalent documents. Borrower shall promptly pay, when due, all dues and assessments imposed pursuant to the Constituent Documents.

B. Property Insurance. So long as the Owners Association maintains, with a generally accepted insurance carrier, a "master" or "blanket" policy on the Condominium Project which is satisfactory to Lender and which provides insurance coverage in the amounts (including deductible levels), for the periods, and against loss by fire, hazards included within the term "extended coverage," and any other hazards, including, but not limited to, earthquakes and floods, from which Lender requires insurance, then: (i) Lender waives the provision in Section 3 for the Periodic Payment to Lender of the yearly premium installments for property insurance on the Property; and (ii) Borrower's obligation under Section 5 to maintain property insurance coverage on the Property is deemed satisfied to the extent that the required coverage is provided by the Owners Association policy.

What Lender requires as a condition of this waiver can change during the term of the loan.

Borrower shall give Lender prompt notice of any lapse in required property insurance coverage provided by the master or blanket policy.

In the event of a distribution of property insurance proceeds in lieu of restoration or repair following a loss to the Property, whether to the unit or to common elements, any proceeds payable to Borrower are hereby assigned and shall be paid to Lender for application to the sums secured by the Security Instrument, whether or not then due, with the excess, if any, paid to Borrower.

C. Public Liability Insurance. Borrower shall take such actions as may be reasonable to insure that the Owners Association maintains a public liability insurance policy acceptable in form, amount, and extent of coverage to Lender.

D. Condemnation. The proceeds of any award or claim for damages, direct or consequential, payable to Borrower in connection with any condemnation or other taking of all or any part of the Property, whether of the unit or of the common elements, or for any conveyance in lieu of condemnation, are hereby assigned and shall be paid to Lender. Such proceeds shall be applied by Lender to the sums secured by the Security Instrument as provided in Section 11.

E. Lender's Prior Consent. Borrower shall not, except after notice to Lender and with Lender's prior written consent, either partition or subdivide the Property or consent to: (i) the abandonment or termination of the Condominium Project, except for abandonment or termination required by law in the case of substantial destruction by fire or other casualty or in the case of a taking by condemnation or eminent domain; (ii) any amendment to any provision of the Constituent Documents if the provision is for the express benefit of Lender; (iii) termination of professional management and assumption of self-management of the Owners Association; or (iv) any action which would have the effect of rendering the public liability insurance coverage maintained by the Owners Association unacceptable to Lender.

F. Remedies. If Borrower does not pay condominium dues and assessments when due, then Lender may pay them. Any amounts disbursed by Lender under this paragraph F shall become additional debt of Borrower secured by the

MULTISTATE CONDOMINIUM RIDER--Single Family--**Fannie Mae/Freddie Mac UNIFORM INSTRUMENT**   **Form 3140   1/01** *(page 1 of 2 pages)*

Security Instrument. Unless Borrower and Lender agree to other terms of payment, these amounts shall bear interest from the date of disbursement at the Note rate and shall be payable, with interest, upon notice from Lender to Borrower requesting payment.

BY SIGNING BELOW, Borrower accepts and agrees to the terms and covenants contained in this Condominium Rider.

_____(Seal)
-Borrower

_____(Seal)
-Borrower

MULTISTATE CONDOMINIUM RIDER--Single Family--**Fannie Mae/Freddie Mac UNIFORM INSTRUMENT**   **Form 3140**   **1/01** *(page 2 of 2 pages)*

1-4 FAMILY RIDER
(Assignment of Rents)

THIS 1-4 FAMILY RIDER is made this _____ day of _____, _____, and is incorporated into and shall be deemed to amend and supplement the Mortgage, Deed of Trust, or Security Deed (the "Security Instrument") of the same date given by the undersigned (the "Borrower") to secure Borrower's Note to _____ _____ (the "Lender") of the same date and covering the Property described in the Security Instrument and located at:

_____
[Property Address]

1-4 FAMILY COVENANTS. In addition to the covenants and agreements made in the Security Instrument, Borrower and Lender further covenant and agree as follows:

A. **ADDITIONAL PROPERTY SUBJECT TO THE SECURITY INSTRUMENT.** In addition to the Property described in Security Instrument, the following items now or hereafter attached to the Property to the extent they are fixtures are added to the Property description, and shall also constitute the Property covered by the Security Instrument: building materials, appliances and goods of every nature whatsoever now or hereafter located in, on, or used, or intended to be used in connection with the Property, including, but not limited to, those for the purposes of supplying or distributing heating, cooling, electricity, gas, water, air and light, fire prevention and extinguishing apparatus, security and access control apparatus, plumbing, bath tubs, water heaters, water closets, sinks, ranges, stoves, refrigerators, dishwashers, disposals, washers, dryers, awnings, storm windows, storm doors, screens, blinds, shades, curtains and curtain rods, attached mirrors, cabinets, paneling and attached floor coverings, all of which, including replacements and additions thereto, shall be deemed to be and remain a part of the Property covered by the Security Instrument. All of the foregoing together with the Property described in the Security Instrument (or the leasehold estate if the Security Instrument is on a leasehold) are referred to in this 1-4 Family Rider and the Security Instrument as the "Property."

B. **USE OF PROPERTY; COMPLIANCE WITH LAW.** Borrower shall not seek, agree to or make a change in the use of the Property or its zoning classification, unless Lender has agreed in writing to the change. Borrower shall comply with all laws, ordinances, regulations and requirements of any governmental body applicable to the Property.

C. **SUBORDINATE LIENS.** Except as permitted by federal law, Borrower shall not allow any lien inferior to the Security Instrument to be perfected against the Property without Lender's prior written permission.

D. **RENT LOSS INSURANCE.** Borrower shall maintain insurance against rent loss in addition to the other hazards for which insurance is required by Section 5.

E. **"BORROWER'S RIGHT TO REINSTATE" DELETED.** Section 19 is deleted.

F. **BORROWER'S OCCUPANCY.** Unless Lender and Borrower otherwise agree in writing, Section 6 concerning Borrower's occupancy of the Property is deleted.

G. **ASSIGNMENT OF LEASES.** Upon Lender's request after default, Borrower shall assign to Lender all leases of the Property and all security deposits made in connection with leases of the Property. Upon the assignment, Lender shall have the right to modify, extend or terminate the existing leases and to execute new leases, in Lender's sole discretion. As used in this paragraph G, the word "lease" shall mean "sublease" if the Security Instrument is on a leasehold.

H. **ASSIGNMENT OF RENTS; APPOINTMENT OF RECEIVER; LENDER IN POSSESSION.** Borrower absolutely and unconditionally assigns and transfers to Lender all the rents and revenues ("Rents") of the Property, regardless of to whom the Rents of the Property are payable. Borrower authorizes Lender or Lender's agents to collect the Rents, and agrees that each tenant of the Property shall pay the Rents to Lender or Lender's agents. However, Borrower shall receive the Rents until (i) Lender has given Borrower notice of default pursuant to Section 22 of the Security Instrument and (ii) Lender has given notice to the tenant(s) that the Rents are to be paid to Lender or Lender's agent. This assignment of Rents constitutes an absolute assignment and not an assignment for additional security only.

If Lender gives notice of default to Borrower: (i) all Rents received by Borrower shall be held by Borrower as trustee for the benefit of Lender only, to be applied to the sums secured by the Security Instrument; (ii) Lender shall be entitled to collect and receive all of the Rents of the Property; (iii) Borrower agrees that each tenant of the Property shall pay all Rents due and unpaid to Lender or Lender's agents upon Lender's written demand to the tenant; (iv) unless applicable law provides otherwise, all Rents collected by Lender or Lender's agents shall be applied first to the costs of

MULTISTATE 1-4 FAMILY RIDER--Fannie Mae/Freddie Mac UNIFORM INSTRUMENT Form 3170 1/01 *(page 1 of 2 pages)*

taking control of and managing the Property and collecting the Rents, including, but not limited to, attorney's fees, receiver's fees, premiums on receiver's bonds, repair and maintenance costs, insurance premiums, taxes, assessments and other charges on the Property, and then to the sums secured by the Security Instrument; (v) Lender, Lender's agents or any judicially appointed receiver shall be liable to account for only those Rents actually received; and (vi) Lender shall be entitled to have a receiver appointed to take possession of and manage the Property and collect the Rents and profits derived from the Property without any showing as to the inadequacy of the Property as security.

If the Rents of the Property are not sufficient to cover the costs of taking control of and managing the Property and of collecting the Rents any funds expended by Lender for such purposes shall become indebtedness of Borrower to Lender secured by the Security Instrument pursuant to Section 9.

Borrower represents and warrants that Borrower has not executed any prior assignment of the Rents and has not performed, and will not perform, any act that would prevent Lender from exercising its rights under this paragraph.

Lender, or Lender's agents or a judicially appointed receiver, shall not be required to enter upon, take control of or maintain the Property before or after giving notice of default to Borrower. However, Lender, or Lender's agents or a judicially appointed receiver, may do so at any time when a default occurs. Any application of Rents shall not cure or waive any default or invalidate any other right or remedy of Lender. This assignment of Rents of the Property shall terminate when all the sums secured by the Security Instrument are paid in full.

I. CROSS-DEFAULT PROVISION. Borrower's default or breach under any note or agreement in which Lender has an interest shall be a breach under the Security Instrument and Lender may invoke any of the remedies permitted by the Security Instrument.

BY SIGNING BELOW, Borrower accepts and agrees to the terms and covenants contained in this 1-4 Family Rider.

_____(Seal)
-Borrower

_____(Seal)
-Borrower

MULTISTATE 1-4 FAMILY RIDER--Fannie Mae/Freddie Mac UNIFORM INSTRUMENT   **Form 3170**   **1/01** *(page 2 of 2 pages)*

PLANNED UNIT DEVELOPMENT RIDER

THIS PLANNED UNIT DEVELOPMENT RIDER is made this _____ day of _____, _____, and is incorporated into and shall be deemed to amend and supplement the Mortgage, Deed of Trust, or Security Deed (the "Security Instrument") of the same date, given by the undersigned (the "Borrower") to secure Borrower's Note to _____ _____ (the "Lender") of the same date and covering the Property described in the Security Instrument and located at:

_____
[Property Address]
The Property includes, but is not limited to, a parcel of land improved with a dwelling, together with other such parcels and certain common areas and facilities, as described in _____ _____ _____ (the "Declaration"). The Property is a part of a planned unit development known as _____ _____
[Name of Planned Unit Development]
(the "PUD"). The Property also includes Borrower's interest in the homeowners association or equivalent entity owning or managing the common areas and facilities of the PUD (the "Owners Association") and the uses, benefits and proceeds of Borrower's interest.

PUD COVENANTS. In addition to the covenants and agreements made in the Security Instrument, Borrower and Lender further covenant and agree as follows:

A. PUD Obligations. Borrower shall perform all of Borrower's obligations under the PUD's Constituent Documents. The "Constituent Documents" are the (i) Declaration; (ii) articles of incorporation, trust instrument or any equivalent document which creates the Owners Association; and (iii) any by-laws or other rules or regulations of the Owners Association. Borrower shall promptly pay, when due, all dues and assessments imposed pursuant to the Constituent Documents.

B. Property Insurance. So long as the Owners Association maintains, with a generally accepted insurance carrier, a "master" or "blanket" policy insuring the Property which is satisfactory to Lender and which provides insurance coverage in the amounts (including deductible levels), for the periods, and against loss by fire, hazards included within the term "extended coverage," and any other hazards, including, but not limited to, earthquakes and floods, for which Lender requires insurance, then: (i) Lender waives the provision in Section 3 for the Periodic Payment to Lender of the yearly premium installments for property insurance on the Property; and (ii) Borrower's obligation under Section 5 to maintain property insurance coverage on the Property is deemed satisfied to the extent that the required coverage is provided by the Owners Association policy.

What Lender requires as a condition of this waiver can change during the term of the loan.

Borrower shall give Lender prompt notice of any lapse in required property insurance coverage provided by the master or blanket policy.

In the event of a distribution of property insurance proceeds in lieu of restoration or repair following a loss to the Property, or to common areas and facilities of the PUD, any proceeds payable to Borrower are hereby assigned and shall be paid to Lender. Lender shall apply the proceeds to the sums secured by the Security Instrument, whether or not then due, with the excess, if any, paid to Borrower.

C. Public Liability Insurance. Borrower shall take such actions as may be reasonable to insure that the Owners Association maintains a public liability insurance policy acceptable in form, amount, and extent of coverage to Lender.

D. Condemnation. The proceeds of any award or claim for damages, direct or consequential, payable to Borrower in connection with any condemnation or other taking of all or any part of the Property or the common areas and facilities of the PUD, or for any conveyance in lieu of condemnation, are hereby assigned and shall be paid to Lender. Such proceeds shall be applied by Lender to the sums secured by the Security Instrument as provided in Section 11.

MULTISTATE PUD RIDER--Single Family--**Fannie Mae/Freddie Mac UNIFORM INSTRUMENT**   Form 3150   1/01 *(page 1 of 2 pages)*

E.   Lender's Prior Consent. Borrower shall not, except after notice to Lender and with Lender's prior written consent, either partition or subdivide the Property or consent to: (i) the abandonment or termination of the PUD, except for abandonment or termination required by law in the case of substantial destruction by fire or other casualty or in the case of a taking by condemnation or eminent domain; (ii) any amendment to any provision of the "Constituent Documents" if the provision is for the express benefit of Lender; (iii) termination of professional management and assumption of self-management of the Owners Association; or (iv) any action which would have the effect of rendering the public liability insurance coverage maintained by the Owners Association unacceptable to Lender.

F.   Remedies. If Borrower does not pay PUD dues and assessments when due, then Lender may pay them. Any amounts disbursed by Lender under this paragraph F shall become additional debt of Borrower secured by the Security Instrument. Unless Borrower and Lender agree to other terms of payment, these amounts shall bear interest from the date of disbursement at the Note rate and shall be payable, with interest, upon notice from Lender to Borrower requesting payment.

BY SIGNING BELOW, Borrower accepts and agrees to the terms and covenants contained in this PUD Rider.

_____(Seal)
                                                                          -Borrower

_____(Seal)
                                                                          -Borrower

MULTISTATE PUD RIDER--Single Family--**Fannie Mae/Freddie Mac UNIFORM INSTRUMENT**   **Form 3150   1/01** *(page 2 of 2 pages)*

SECOND HOME RIDER

THIS SECOND HOME RIDER is made this _____ day of _____, _____, and is incorporated into and shall be deemed to amend and supplement the Mortgage, Deed of Trust, or Security Deed (the "Security Instrument") of the same date given by the undersigned (the "Borrower," whether there are one or more persons undersigned) to secure Borrower's Note to _____ _____ (the "Lender") of the same date and covering the Property described in the Security Instrument (the "Property"), which is located at:

_____

[Property Address]

In addition to the covenants and agreements made in the Security Instrument, Borrower and Lender further covenant and agree that Sections 6 and 8 of the Security Instrument are deleted and are replaced by the following:

6. Occupancy. Borrower shall occupy, and shall only use, the Property as Borrower's second home. Borrower shall keep the Property available for Borrower's exclusive use and enjoyment at all times, and shall not subject the Property to any timesharing or other shared ownership arrangement or to any rental pool or agreement that requires Borrower either to rent the Property or give a management firm or any other person any control over the occupancy or use of the Property.

8. Borrower's Loan Application. Borrower shall be in default if, during the Loan application process, Borrower or any persons or entities acting at the direction of Borrower or with Borrower's knowledge or consent gave materially false, misleading, or inaccurate information or statements to Lender (or failed to provide Lender with material information) in connection with the Loan. Material representations include, but are not limited to, representations concerning Borrower's occupancy of the Property as Borrower's second home.

BY SIGNING BELOW, Borrower accepts and agrees to the terms and covenants contained in this Second Home Rider.

_____(Seal)
-Borrower

_____(Seal)
-Borrower

MULTISTATE SECOND HOME RIDER--Single Family--**Fannie Mae/Freddie Mac UNIFORM INSTRUMENT   Form 3890   1/01** *(page 1 of 1 page)*

Chapter

11

Notice of Right
to Cancel Forms

INTRODUCTION

There is perhaps no more important — and potentially more confusing —
document than the "Notice of Right to Cancel" (NRTC) form.

The NRTC is an important form for a borrower, since it helps allay pres-
sure to understand every tiny detail of the loan transaction at the signing
appointment. With knowledge that federal law provides a three-day "cooling off" period to thoroughly review documents, the borrower can rest
assured that there is sufficient time to take up any questions or concerns
with the loan agent or title company representative before the loan closes.

For the Notary Signing Agent, the presence of the NRTC form in the loan
documentation helps move the signing along at a speedier pace than would
be the case if the transaction had no rescission provision.

The confusion surrounding the form stems from three factors; first, whether
a particular loan transaction has a rescission provision. Not all mortgage
loans do. Second, there can be confusion surrounding how to calculate the
commencement and termination dates of the rescission period. Finally, the
forms can vary widely and are often difficult to decipher.

This chapter will provide clarifying background on the rescission feature
of real property loans under the federal Truth in Lending Act (TILA), and
then will present seven different NTRC forms from a number of different
lending institutions.

TRUTH IN LENDING ACT

History and Background

The Truth in Lending Act became law on May 29, 1968, as Title I of the Consumer Credit Protection Act. As is the case with many laws, the TILA is implemented by accompanying regulations issued after enactment of the legislation. TILA is implemented by Regulation Z, which became effective July 1, 1969.

The TILA has been modified several times since its enactment. It was first amended in 1970 to prohibit unsolicited credit cards. Additional major amendments to the TILA and Regulation Z were made by the Fair Credit Billing Act of 1974, the Consumer Leasing Act of 1976, the Truth in Lending Simplification and Reform Act of 1980, the Fair Credit and Charge Card Disclosure Act of 1988, the Home Equity Loan Consumer Protection Act of 1988, the Home Ownership and Equity Protection Act of 1994, and the Truth in Lending Act Amendments of 1995.

In addition to these changes, Regulation Z was amended to implement section 1204 of the Competitive Equality Banking Act of 1987, and in 1988, to include adjustable rate mortgage loan disclosure requirements. All consumer leasing provisions were deleted from Regulation Z in 1981 and transferred to other applicable regulations.

Purpose

The Truth in Lending Act is a consumer protection statute intended to ensure that credit terms are disclosed in a meaningful way so that consumers can compare credit terms between competing lenders. Before its enactment, consumers were faced with a bewildering assortment of credit terms and rates and comparing loans was challenging because lenders seldom presented loan information in the same format. As a result of the TILA, all creditors must use the same credit terminology. However, effective July 21, 2011, TILA's general rule-making authority was transferred to the Consumer Financial Protection Bureau (CFPB), whose authority was established pursuant to provisions enacted by the passage of the Dodd–Frank Wall Street Reform and Consumer Protection Act in July 2010.

In real property loan transactions, the CFPB requires lenders to make certain disclosures at various points throughout the loan process. Within three days of receipt of a written loan application, an early disclosure statement ("Loan Estimate" form) must be issued. At the loan closing, a final statement ("Closing Disclosure" form) containing the following information must be supplied:

- Name and address of creditor

- Amount financed

- Itemization of amount financed

- Finance charge

- Annual percentage rate (APR)

- Variable rate information

- Payment schedule

- Total payments

- Demand feature

- Total sales price

- Prepayment policy

- Late payment policy

- Security interest

- Insurance requirements

- Certain security interest charges

- Contract reference

- Assumption policy

- Required deposit information

The presence of multiple disclosure forms in a loan document package with differing dates can be traced to this federal requirement. Lenders must have signed copies of all disclosures throughout the process of the loan, and these multiple copies appear in instances in which the lender does not have an earlier signed disclosure on file. Also, if during the loan process the interest rate changes or the borrower opts for a different type of loan program (changing from an adjustable rate to a fixed rate loan, for example), new disclosure forms must be generated and signed.

In addition to providing a uniform system for disclosures, the CFPB protects consumers against inaccurate and unfair credit billing and credit card practices, provides for rate caps on certain dwelling-secured loans, and imposes limitations on home equity lines of credit and certain closed-end home mortgages.

The CFPB does more than simply shield borrowers from smooth-talking loan officers and unscrupulous lenders. The law also protects consumers from their own hasty decisions. A borrower who takes out a loan and then has second thoughts can rescind the loan. Also, a homeowner who takes out a refinance loan and then finds a better deal a day or two later, can rescind the first deal within three business days and then take the better loan.

When the Rescission Right Applies

The primary scenarios wherein a rescission right applies are those most often encountered by Notary Signing Agents: refinance loans in which the borrower is changing lenders, home equity loans or lines of credit, and "cash-out" refinance loans (loans for more than the current loan balance, and taking the difference in cash) with a different lender.

In practical terms, a Notary Signing Agent will discover that the right of rescission is not available for a particular loan when the Agent discovers that the NRTC form is not included in the loan documentation.

However, Agents should be aware that a mortgage loan has no right of rescission in the following circumstances:

- When the loan is used to buy a house (known as a "purchase" transaction).

- For refinance loans with the same lender.

- When the home is not a primary residence (e.g., vacation home or investment property).

- When the money borrowed is used for a private business.

- When the lender is a state agency.

- For "piggyback loans" — taking out a first and second mortgage loan — intended to avoid incurring private mortgage insurance.

- For "cash-out" refinance loans with the same lender, only the cash-out portion can be rescinded.

Notary Signing Agents should be aware whether the rescission right applies, since this could affect how the signing is conducted. If the loan does not contain a rescission right, Agents should plan for borrowers taking more time to sign documents. Most importantly, Agents should not assume that every loan contains a rescission feature. It would be embarrassing at least — and at worst misleading — to misrepresent to borrowers that a loan does contain a rescission right when in fact it does not. The latter is especially dangerous if the Agent has not had time to review the document prior to the signing or if the documents were delivered to the borrower instead of to the Agent.

Calculating Rescission Dates

It is expected that Notary Signing Agents understand the formula for calculating the rescission period commencement and termination dates and either enter the dates into the applicable spaces or guide the borrowers in doing so.

Fortunately, the process is not difficult to master. The CFPB gives borrowers three (3) business days beginning with the first business day following the date of signing and ending at midnight on the third business day. In general, every day is a business day except Sundays and federal holidays. Saturday counts as a business day, even if the lender's office is closed on Saturdays.

The federal holidays that do not count as a business day include:

- New Year's Day

- Martin Luther King Jr.'s Birthday

- Presidents Day

- Memorial Day

- Independence Day

- Labor Day

- Columbus Day

- Veterans Day

- Thanksgiving Day

- Christmas Day

Confusion can arise when one of these holidays falls on a weekend. For example, if Christmas Day falls on a Saturday, many Agents have wondered whether the date the holiday is observed by government and business offices should be considered a legal holiday for the purpose of calculating the rescission date. To make matters even more confusing, professionals in the mortgage lending industry often do not know the answer to this question.

In point of fact, the official commentary on Regulation Z, which provides the interpretations of the TILA regulations, contains an interpretation on this very point.

In the actual law itself (5 U.S.C. 6103(a), four of the 10 federal holidays listed are date-specific: New Year's Day — January 1; Independence Day — July 4; Veterans Day — November 11; and Christmas Day — December 25. The other six holidays affected in rescission period calculations do not have a specific date assigned. For example, the birthday of Martin Luther King, Jr. is observed on the third Monday in January and Columbus Day, the second Monday in October.

The Federal Reserve Board issued an important official interpretation of the term "business day" in relation to these four date-specific holidays. According to the commentary, the only date that counts when computing the rescission period is the date of the actual holiday itself. Using the previous example of Christmas Day falling on a Saturday, the Monday following would count as a business day for rescission period calculations — even if the holiday is nationally observed on Monday, with government office closures, etc.

Therefore, Notary Signing Agents can no longer assume that if banks, the post office, and other state and federal government offices are closed on a weekday in observance of a holiday falling on a weekend, the day of observance would not count as one of the three business days.

A note about the termination date. To rescind a loan transaction, a borrower must deliver written notice within the specified three-day rescission period. The notification to cancel need not be received by the lender or even postmarked by the deadline; it only must be mailed by the deadline. For example, if the rescission period ends at midnight on Saturday and a rescission notice is mailed on Saturday, the loan is canceled even though the notice will not be postmarked until Monday.

Due to this, many loan agents, escrow officers, and title company representatives will place a phone call to the borrower after the rescission period has officially ended to ask if the loan was canceled.

It is also possible to waive the right of rescission, but typically it is permitted only in emergencies at the discretion of the lender.

Forms in Sample Set   **Pages**

NOTICE OF RIGHT TO CANCEL
(General)

Borrower:
Ronald Hollenbeck, Marjorie Hollenbeck

Loan Number: **1111652927890**
Lender: **GTAC Mortgage Corporation**

Property Address: **1000 Amazola Anvenue**
Torrance, CA 90501

Tax I.D. No.:

---

1. YOUR RIGHT TO CANCEL
You are entering into a transaction that will result in a lien on your home. You have a legal right under federal law to cancel this transaction, without cost, within three business days from whichever of the following events occurs last:

(1) the date of the transaction, which is the date the promissory note and mortgage or deed of trust are actually signed and acknowledged by you (you have indicated that this will occur on) **February 20, 20XX** ; or
(2) the date you received your Truth in Lending disclosures; or
(3) the date you received this notice of your right to cancel.

Initial _____   Initial _____

Initial _____   Initial _____

If you cancel the transaction, the (mortgage/lien/security interest) is also canceled. Within 20 calendar days after we receive your notice, we must take steps necessary to reflect the fact that the (mortgage/lien/security interest) (on/in) your
~~~~~~~~ canceled, and we must return to you any money or property you have given to us or to anyone else in
~~~ this transaction.
~~~ any money or property we have given you until we have done the things mentioned above, but you must
~~~turn the money or property. If it is impractical or unfair for you to return the property, you must offer its
~~~e. You may offer to return the property at your home or at the location of the property. Money must be
~~~address below. If we do not take possession of the money or property within 20 calendar days of your
~~~keep it without further obligation.

~~~~CANCEL
~~~ cancel this transaction, you may do so by notifying us in writing, at:

~~~e Corporation, 3200 Park Center Dr. Suite 150, Costa Mesa, CA 92626
(creditor's name and business address)

You may use any written statement that is signed and dated by you and states your intention to cancel, and/or you may use this notice by dating and signing below. Keep one copy of this notice because it contains important information about your rights.

If you cancel by mail or telegram, you must send the notice no later than midnight of _____
(date)

Initial _____   Initial _____

Initial _____   Initial _____

(or midnight of the third business day following the latest of the three events listed above). If you send or deliver your written notice to cancel some other way, it must be delivered to the above address no later than that time.

_____   **I WISH TO CANCEL** _____
(Consumer's Signature)   (Date)

ON THE DATE LISTED ABOVE, I/WE THE UNDERSIGNED EACH RECEIVED TWO (2) COMPLETED COPIES OF THE NOTICE OF THE RIGHT TO CANCEL IN THE FORM PRESCRIBED BY LAW ADVISING ME/US OF MY/OUR RIGHT TO CANCEL THIS TRANSACTION.

_____   _____
Ronald Hollenbeck   Date   **Marjorie Hollenbeck**   Date

_____   _____
Date   Date

NOTES

Some NRTC forms require the borrower to initial the commencement and termination rescission dates. This is one such form. Note: If a form does not ask for initials, do not have borrowers initial the dates.

INSTRUCTIONS TO CLOSING AGENT An extra set of this Notice is provided. Please provide an original and copy to each Individual with an Ownership interest in the property (non-applicants vested on title, including a non-applicant spouse when required by law). The dates appearing in (1) and (3) below must be calculated based on the date the signing occurs.

American City

NOTICE OF RIGHT TO CANCEL
CUSTOMER'S NAME AND ADDRESS

JOHN DAY III
(NAME)
215 S CANON AVE
(STREET)
SIERRA MADRE, California 91024
(CITY)   (STATE)   (ZIP)

Your Right to Cancel

We: have agreed to establish an open-end credit account for you and you have agreed to give us a mortgage on your home as security for the account. The account includes the right to obtain non-purchase money advances und it may include a purchase money advance, as described in the Equity Line of Credit (Purchase Money Transactions) section below. You have a legal right under federal law to cancel the non purchase money part of the transaction without cost, within three Business days* from whichever of the following events occurs last:

  1)   the opening date of your account, which is _____ 11/01/20XX _____ ; or
  2)   the dale you received your Truth in Lending disclosures; or
  3)   the date you receive this notice of your right to cancel.

Three business days from the last of the above events is _____

EQUITY LINE OF CREDIT (PURCHASE MONEY TRANSACTIONS):

A right to rescind does not apply to the amount of advances used to finance the purchase or initial construction of you ("purchase advance"). However, the Equity Line of Credit is a revolving line of credit and you have a contractual rig to the extent you have not advanced all of the lint: or as the line becomes available to you as you pay down any purc Therefore you have the right to rescind access to non- purchase money advances. Because of this right, **all individua_ interest in the subject property must be provided with an original and copy of this Notice of Right to Cancel for this line of credit.**

If you cancel, your cancellation will apply only to the non-purchase part of the transaction and to the portion of the mortgage that resulted from the non-purchase part of the transaction. It will not affect the amount that you owe for the purchase advance, and it will not affect the mortgage we have on your home to secure the purchase advance. If you cancel, your line privileges for non-purchase money credit advances will be cancelled. Within 20 calendar days after we receive your notice of cancellation, we must take the necessary steps to reflect the fact that that your home does not secure the non-purchase part of the transaction. After we do this, your home will secure the purchase advance. We must also return to you any money or property you have given to us, or anyone else in connection with the non-purchase part of the transaction.

You may keep any non-purchase credit advance money or property given you until we have done the things mentioned above, but you must then offer to return the money or property. If it is impractical or unfair for you to return the property, you must offer its reasonable value. You may offer to return the property at your home or at the location of the property. Money must be returned to the address shown below. If we do not take possession of the money or property within 20 calendar days of your offer, you may keep it without further obligation.

How to Cancel

If you decide to cancel the non-purchase part of the transaction, you may do so by notifying us in writing at:

AMERICAN CITY BANK
AMERICAN HOME EQUITY
P.O. BOX 94991, LOCATOR #01-7180
CLEVELAND, OH 44101-8981
Attention: NHE OPERATIONS DEPARTMENT

You may use any written statement that is signed and dated by you and states your intention to cancel and/or you may use this notice by dating und signing below. Keep one copy of this notice no matter how you notify us because it contains important information about your rights.

If you cancel by mail or telegram, you must send the notice no later than midnight of date stated in the top portion of this notice (or midnight of the third business day following the latest of the three events listed above). If you send or deliver your written notice to cancel some other way, it must he delivered to the above address no later than that time.

*Business day means all calendar days except Sundays and legal public holidays as specified in 5 U.S.C. 6103(a): New Year's Day, Martin Luther King Day, President's Day, Memorial Day, Independence Day, Labor Day, Columbus Day, Veteran's Day, Thanksgiving Day and Christmas Day.

Sign below, ONLY if you wish to cancel the Transaction
(if part of the transaction is purchase money that part cannot be cancelled):

I WISH TO CANCEL:

_____   _____
(Customer's Signature)   (Date)

NOTES

This form is unique in requiring the borrower to sign only if the borrower intends to cancel the loan.

NOTICE OF RIGHT TO CANCEL

CUSTOMER NAME	LOAN NUMBER
W. PATRICIA TRYLIS	02-1400-009837678-0

MAILING ADDRESS

4900 E TWINING ST

CITY/STATE/ZIP

EL SERENO CA 90032

Your Right To Cancel

You are entering into a transaction with _____Montana Mutual Bank, FA_____ that will result in a deed of trust/security interest on your home. You have a legal right under federal law to cancel this transaction, without cost, within three business days from whichever of the following events occurs last:

(1) The date of the transaction, which is _____; or
(2) The date you received your Truth in Lending disclosures; or

ou received this notice of your right to cancel.

he transaction, the deed of trust/security interest is also cancelled. Within 20 calendar days after we
your desire to cancel, we must take the steps necessary to reflect the fact the deed of trust/security
has been cancelled, and we must return to you any money or property you have given to us or to
tion with this transaction.

any money or property we have given you until we have done the things mentioned above, but you
rn the money or property. If it is impractical or unfair for you to return the property, you must offer its
may offer to return the property at your home or at the location of the property. Money must be
s below. If we do not take possession of the money or property within 20 calendar days of your
offer, you may keep it without further obligation.

How To Cancel

If you decide to cancel this transaction, you may do so by notifying us in writing, at:

Montana Mutual Bank, FA
Attn: FRANCISCO AYALA   (714) 987-7416
100 S VINCENT AVE/1580FCCA
WEST COVINA, CA 91790

You may use any written statement that is signed and dated by you and states your Intention to cancel, or you may use this Notice by dating and signing below. Keep one copy of this Notice because it contains important information about your rights.

If you cancel by mail or telegram, you must send the notice no later than midnight of _____
(or midnight of the third business day following the latest of the three events listed above). If you send or deliver your written notice to cancel some other way, it must be delivered to the above address no later than that time.

I WISH TO CANCEL.

SIGNATURE _____   DATE _____

I hereby acknowledge receipt in duplicate of this Notice of Right to Cancel. _____
                                                                                    (INITIALS)

BANK

NOTES

This unique NRTC form requires the borrower to acknowledge receipt of the copies of the NRTC by providing initials only. The borrower does not sign the form.

WORLDWIDE SAVINGS	NOTICE OF RIGHT TO CANCEL (EQUITY LINE OF CREDIT)

0018365504

YOUR RIGHT TO CANCEL

We have agreed to establish an open-end credit account for you, and you have agreed to give us a security interest in your home as security for the account. You have a legal right under federal law to cancel the account, without cost, within three business days after the latest of the following events:

(1) the opening date of your account which is **JUNE 27, 20XX** : or

(2) the date you received your Truth-in-Lending disclosures; or

(3) the date you received this notice of your right to cancel the account.

If you cancel the account, the security interest in your home is also cancelled. Within 20 days of receiving your notice, we must take the necessary steps to reflect the fact that the security interest in your home has been cancelled. We must return to you any money or property you have given to us or to anyone else in connection with the account.

You may keep any money or property we have given you until we have done the things mentioned above, but you must then offer to return the money or property. If it is impractical or unfair for you to return the property, you must offer its reasonable value. You may offer to return the property at your home or at the location of the property. Money must be returned to the address below. If we do not take possession of the money or property within 20 calendar days of your offer, you may keep it without further obligation.

Joint owners of your home also have the right to cancel the account. If one joint owner cancels the account, cancellation is effective for all owners.

HOW TO CANCEL

If you decide to cancel the account, you may do so by notifying us in writing, at: WORLDWIDE SAVINGS, FINAL DOCUMENTATION, ATTN: CLOSING DEPARTMENT, 4155 WISE BOULEVARD, BUILDING #205, SAN ANTONIO, TEXAS 78255, FAX NUMBER (210) 509-1255. (No other office or representative of WorldWide Savings is authorized to accept your written notice to cancel.)

You may use any written statement that is signed and dated by you and states your intention to cancel, or you may use this notice by dating and signing below. Keep one copy of this notice no matter how you notify us because it contains important information about your rights.

If you cancel by mail or telegram (or fax), you must send the notice no later than midnight of **JULY 02, 20XX** (or midnight of the third business day following the latest of the three events listed above). If you send or deliver your written notice to cancel some other way, it must be delivered to the above address no later than that time.

I WISH TO CANCEL (DO NOT SIGN HERE UNLESS YOU WISH TO CANCEL)

Consumer's Signature _____ Date _____

Please advise the Closing Agent if you decide to cancel.

ACKNOWLEDGEMENT OF RECEIPT OF COPIES

BY MY SIGNATURE WHICH FOLLOWS, I acknowledge that I received two copies of this Notice of Right to Cancel to keep (plus one to sign and return to WorldWide).

Consumer's Signature _____ Date _____

Property Address:

Please return a signed copy of this Notice of Right to Cancel to the address shown above. Keep the other two copies.

NOTICE OF RIGHT OF
RESCISSION

Each Customer Must Sign
Each Customer Must Receive Two Copies

Account Number: 625287255
Customer(s): JACK ABRAM AND ANNE ABRAM

Identification of Transaction: A mortgage in which a security interest is retained or
acquired in real property used as principal residence of the customer and located:
6550 W 55TH PL
LOS ANGELES, CA 90055

NOTICE OF RIGHT TO CANCEL

You are entering into a transaction that will result in a lien, mortgage or other security
interest on your home. You have a legal right under federal law to cancel this transaction,
without cost, within three business days from whichever of the following events occur
last:
(1) the date of the transaction, which is JULY 16, 20XX OR
(2) the date you received your Truth-In-Lending disclosures OR
(3) the date you received this notice of your right to cancel.

EFFECT OF RESCISSION

If you cancel this transaction, the lien, mortgage or other security interest is also
cancelled. Within 20 calendar days after we receive your notice, we must take the steps
necessary to reflect the fact that the lien, mortgage or security interest on your home has
been cancelled, and we must return to you any money or property you have given us or to
anyone else in connection with this transaction. You may keep any money or property we
have given you until we have done the things mentioned above, but you must then offer
to return the money or property. If it is impractical or unfair for you to return the
property, you must offer its reasonable value. You may offer to return the property at
your home or at the location of the property. Money must be returned to the address
below. If we do not take possession of the money or property within 20 calendar days of
your offer, you may keep it without further obligation.

HOW TO CANCEL

If you decide to cancel this transaction, you may do so by notifying us in writing,

Name: UNITED TITLE ESCROW
At: 12550 BLUFF DRIVE 550
        SAN DIEGO, CA 92550

You may use any written statement that is signed and dated by you and states your intention to cancel, and/or you may use this notice by dating and signing below. Keep one copy of this notice because it contains important information about your rights. If you cancel by mail, telegram or fax, you must send the notice no later than midnight of JULY 19, 20XX (or midnight of the third business day following the latest of the three events listed above). For fax cancellations, please fax this signed notice to 734-557-2952 and contact your settlement agent. If you send or deliver your written notice to cancel some other way, it must be delivered to the above address no later than that time.

I WISH TO CANCEL

_____

JACK ABRAM   Date

_____

ANNE ABRAM   Date

RECEIPT OF NOTICE OF RIGHT OF RESCISSION

Receipt is herewith acknowledged of the foregoing notice, each of the undersigned customers having received two copies thereof, as well as one copy of the Truth-In-Lending Disclosures required by law. Undersigned warrant that they are all Customers obligated under this transaction who own or use as their principal residence the real property securing said obligation; this _____ day of _____, _____.

_____

JACK ABRAM   Date

_____

ANNE ABRAM   Date

CERTIFICATION OF CONFIRMATION

Whereas more than 3 business days have elapsed since the undersigned received the above and foregoing Notice of Right of Rescission and other Truth-In-Lending Disclosures concerning the transaction identified above; the undersigned do herewith warrant, covenant and certify that they, and neither of them, have not exercised their right to rescind; that they do not wish to and will not rescind said transaction; and that they do hereby ratify and confirm the same in all respects. They further represent that the undersigned are the only persons entitled to rescind, in that they are all the owners of the real property securing said obligation.

_____   _____

JACK ABRAM   Date

_____   _____

ANNE ABRAM   Date

NOTICE OF RIGHT TO CANCEL

LENDER: Quest Mortgage Company

DATE: June 14, 20XX
LOAN NO.: 0035671320 - 9551
TYPE: ADJUSTABLE RATE

BORROWER(S):   JANE WEBBER
ADDRESS: 857 EAST 152ND STREET
CITY/STATE/ZIP: LOS ANGELES, CA 90002

PROPERTY: 857 EAST 152ND STREET
LOS ANGELES, CA 90002

You are entering into a transaction that will result in a mortgage/lien/security interest on your home. You have a legal right under federal law to cancel this transaction, without cost, within THREE BUSINESS DAYS from whichever of the following events occurs last:

1. The date of the transaction, which is

> ENTER DOCUMENT SIGNING DATE
> _____

; or

2. The date you received your Truth in Lending disclosures; or
3. The date you received this notice of your right to cancel.

If you cancel the transaction, the mortgage/lien/security interest is also cancelled. Within 20 CALENDAR DAYS after we receive your notice, we must take the steps necessary to reflect the fact that the mortgage/lien/security interest on your home has been cancelled, and we must return to you any money or property you have given to us or anyone else in connection with this transaction.

You may keep any money or property we have given you until we have done the things mentioned above, but you must then offer to return the money or property. If it is impractical or unfair for you to return the property you must offer its reasonable value. You may offer to return the property at your home or at the location of the property. Money must be returned to the address below. If we do not take possession of the money or property within 20 CALENDAR DAYS of your offer, you may keep it without further obligation.

HOW TO CANCEL
If you decide to cancel this transaction, you may do so by notifying us in writing, at:

Quest Mortgage Company
5500 Town Rd, Suite 900
Orange, California 92868

ATTN: FUNDING
PHONE: (714) 479-0355
FAX: (714)347-1555

You may use any written statement that is signed and dated by you and states your intention to cancel, or you may use this notice by dating and signing below. Keep one copy of this notice because it contains important information about your rights.

If you cancel by mail or telegram, you must send the notice no later than MIDNIGHT of

> ENTER FINAL DATE TO CANCEL
> _____

(or MIDNIGHT of the THIRD BUSINESS DAY following the latest of the three events listed above). If you send or deliver your written notice to cancel some other way, it must be delivered to the above address no later than that time.
I WISH TO CANCEL

_____
SIGNATURE

_____
DATE

The undersigned each acknowledge receipt of two copies of this NOTICE OF RIGHT TO CANCEL and one copy of the Federal Truth in Lending Disclosure Statement, all given by lender in compliance with Truth in Lending Simplification and Reform Act of 1980 (Public Law 96-221).

Each borrower in this transaction has the right to cancel. The exercise of this right by one borrower shall be effective to all borrowers.

_____   _____
BORROWER/OWNER JANE WEBBER   Date

_____   _____
BORROWER/OWNER   Date

_____   _____
BORROWER/OWNER   Date

_____   _____
BORROWER/OWNER   Date

LENDER COPY

NOTICE OF YOUR RIGHT TO CANCEL
CREDIT TRANSACTION SECURED BY YOUR HOME

CREDITOR: JARDAN LOANS, INC.

TO: DAVID COLE AND RACHEL COLE

SPECIFIC INFORMATION REGARDING YOUR RIGHT TO CANCEL

☑ **This Is An Original Extension Of Credit:**

You are entering into a transaction that will result in a security interest in your home. You have a legal right under federal law to cancel this transaction, without cost, within three business days from whichever of the following events occurs last:

(1.) The date of the transaction, which is _____

(2.) The date you received your Truth-In-Lending Disclosures.

(3.) The date you received this notice of your Right-To-Cancel.

If you cancel the transaction, the security interest is also cancelled. Within 20 calendar days after we receive your notice, we must take the steps necessary to reflect the fact that the security interest in your home has been cancelled, and we must return to you any money you have given to us or to anyone else in connection with this transaction.

You may keep any money we have given you until we have done the things mentioned above, but you must then offer to return the money. Money must be returned to the address below. If we do not take possession of the money within 20 calendar days of your offer, you may keep it without further obligation.

☐ **This Is An Addition Credit Transaction:**

You are entering into a new transaction to increase the amount of credit provided to you. We acquired a security interest in your home under the original transaction and will retain that security interest in the new transaction. You have a legal right under federal law to cancel the new transaction, without cost, within three business days from whichever of the following three events occurs last:

(1.) The date of the transaction, which is _____

(2.) The date you received your Truth-In-Lending Disclosures.

(3.) The date you received this notice of your Right-To-Cancel.

If you cancel the new transaction, your cancellation will apply only to the increase in the amount of credit. It will not affect the amount that you presently owe or the security interest we already have in your home. If you cancel, the security interest as it applies the increased amount is also cancelled. Within 20 calendar days after we receive your notice of cancellation of the new transaction, we must take the steps necessary to reflect the fact that our security interest in your home no longer applies to the increase of credit. We must also return any money you have given to us or anyone else in connection with the new transaction.

You may keep any money we have given you in the new transaction until we have done the things mentioned above, but you must then offer to return the money at the address below. If we do not take possession of the money within 20 calendar days of your offer, you may keep it without further obligation.

☐ **The Creditor Is Requiring Additional Collateral In Connection With An Existing Transaction:**

On _____ you entered into a credit transaction with the Creditor. The Creditor has now requested additional collateral in the form of a security interest in your home. This new transaction will result in a security interest in your home. No new money or credit will be advanced to you in this transaction. You have a legal right under the federal law to cancel this transaction, without cost, within three business days of when you received this notice of your Right-To-Cancel.

If you cancel the transaction, the security interest is also cancelled. Within 20 calendar days after we receive your notice, we must take the steps necessary to reflect the fact that the security interest in your home has been cancelled. Because no money or credit will be advanced to you in this new transaction, no money will be returned to you if you cancel.

HOW TO CANCEL

If you decide to cancel this transaction, you may do so by notifying us in writing at:

JARDIN LOANS, INC.
3255 DANE BLVD, ALAMO, CA 94557

Page 1 of 2

You may use any written statement that is signed and dated by you and states your intention to cancel, or you may use this notice by signing and dating below. Keep one copy of this notice because it contains important information about your rights.

If you cancel by mail or telegram, you must send the notice no later than midnight of _____ (or midnight of the third business day following the latest of the three events listed above). If you send or deliver your written notice to cancel some other way, it must be delivered to the above address not later than that time.

I WISH TO CANCEL THE TRANSACTION DESCRIBED ABOVE.

_____		_____	
DAVID COLE	Date	RACHEL COLE	Date

Acknowledgment of Receipt
I hereby acknowledge receipt of two copies of this Notice of my right to cancel the credit transaction described above.

_____		_____	
DAVID COLE	Date	RACHEL COLE	Date

Page 2 of 2

Chapter

12

USA Patriot Act
CIP Forms

INTRODUCTION

At first, it may seem unfathomable that a law targeting terrorism, such as the "Uniting and Strengthening America by Providing Appropriate Tools Required to Intercept and Obstruct Terrorism" (USA PATRIOT) Act, could possibly affect Notary Signing Agents working in the field.

Signed into law on October 26, 2001, in the aftermath of the 9/11 attacks, the U.S. PATRIOT Act established enhanced measures to prevent, detect, and prosecute persons engaging in money laundering and terrorism. Effective October 1, 2003, regulations implementing Section 326 of the Act required all financial institutions to establish a Customer Identification Program (CIP) for identifying all new account holders.

To meet the minimum standards required by the Act, a qualifying financial institution's Customer Identification Program must:

- Collect identifying information about new account holders;

- Verify that the customers are who they say they are;

- Maintain records used to verify identity;

- Determine whether the customer appears on any list of suspected terrorists or terrorist organizations; and

- Obtain the identifying information on new account holders within a reasonable time after opening the account.

According to CIP regulations, every qualifying financial institution must have a written procedure for establishing the true identity of its customers approved by the institution's board of directors. The regulations enjoin financial institutions to conduct a risk assessment to determine whether their business practices meet the minimally acceptable compliance standards. The regulations do not impose specific methods, policies, or business rules to achieve these objectives, but leave it up to the individual institution to develop its own program.

The regulations also require that institutions implement procedures for collecting standard information such as a customer's name, address, date of birth, and a taxpayer identification number (for U.S. citizens, typically a Social Security number and for non-U.S. citizens, a similar number from a government-issued document).

Many are of a mistaken belief that only banks fall under the definition of "financial institution." In fact, the term is more broadly defined under the law to include (31 U.S.C. 5312(a)(2) and (c)(1)):

- An insured bank;

- A commercial bank or a trust company;

- Private bankers;

- An agency or branch of a foreign bank in the United States;

- Any credit union;

- A thrift institution;

- A broker or dealer registered with the SEC under the Securities Exchange Act of 1934;

- A broker or dealer in securities or commodities (whether registered with the SEC or not);

- An investment banker or investment company;

- A currency exchange;

- An issuer, redeemer, or cashier of traveler's checks, checks, money orders, or similar instruments;

- An operator of a credit card system;

- An insurance company;

- A dealer in precious metals, stones, or jewels;

- A pawnbroker;

- A loan or finance company;

- A travel agency;

- A licensed sender of money or any other person who engages as a business in the transmission of funds, formally or informally;

- A telegraph company;

- A business engaged in vehicle sales, including automobile, airplane, and boat sales;

- Persons involved in real state closings and settlements;

- The United States Postal Service;

- An agency of the federal or any state or local government carrying out a duty or power of a business described in the definition of a "financial institution";

- A state-licensed or Indian casino with annual gaming revenue of more than $1,000,000; and

- Certain other businesses designated by the Treasury.

Every type of entity appearing on the list is responsible for implementing a CIP program. It is immediately evident that a number of the listed entities provide mortgage loans or settlement services for these loans.

And this is where Notary Signing Agents enter the picture.

In carrying out their risk assessment, lenders, banks, savings and loan institutions, credit unions, mortgage brokers, and other lending institutions providing home loans did not have to think long to determine that the most effective, most cost-conscious, and least intrusive method for obtaining new customer identifying information was to employ Notary Signing Agents to complete this task at the loan signing appointment.

Since making a positive identification is the hallmark of the Notary Public office, and in the typical loan signing a Notary Signing Agent must positively identify the borrower to execute the acknowledgment on the mortgage or deed of trust, asking Agents to complete an additional form requesting the identifying information from any written identification document presented by the borrower for the notarizations seemed to be the perfect solution.

On October 1, 2003, Notary Signing Agents began informing the National Notary Association that "Patriot Act CIP" forms were appearing in loan document packages and raised a number of questions about these forms. Among the comments and questions were the following:

- Agents were unsure if they or the borrower were responsible for completing and signing the form.

- Agents asked if the form needed to be notarized.

- Agents asked to know more about the Patriot Act.

- Agents expressed alarm at wording on one form mentioning the need to prevent terrorism and money laundering.

Since that day, it has become almost second nature that Notary Signing Agents will complete a form on behalf of the lender certifying that the Agent properly identified the borrower at the signing appointment.

VERIFICATION OF CUSTOMER IDENTITY
Sign-up Service

Loan No.: _____

Escrow No.: _____

NOTICE: Under Section 326 of the USA Patriot Act (31 U.S.C. 531(1)) and regulations enacted pursuant to that statute (31 C.F.R. Part 103), certain lenders are required to follow specified procedures to verify the identity of their customers. This verification is intended to comply with that requirement.

Acceptable evidence of identity is a driver's license, passport, green card, alien identification card or other government-issued identification bearing a photograph of the person.

I, _____ declare:

1. I performed a sign-up service in this transaction.

2. I have done <u>one</u> of the following:

     a. I made a copy, which is attached, of the original identification card provided to me by the person representing himself/herself to me to be the borrower.

     b. I have taken the following information from such identification card:

BORROWER 1:

Name: _____

Date of Birth: _____

Address: _____

Type of Identification: _____

Issuer of Identification: _____

Identification Card No.: _____

BORROWER 2:

Name: _____

Date of Birth: _____

Address: _____

Type of Identification: _____

Issuer of Identification: _____

Identification Card No.: _____

I declare under penalty of perjury that the foregoing is true and correct.

_____

Print Name: _____

BROKER CERTIFICATION
Personal Customer Identification Record Validation

Effective October 1, 2003, in order to comply with Section 326 of the U.S. Patriot Act, FNBA/FNBN is required to verify the identity of EACH borrower. At a Brokers option, they can collect this information at the time of loan application. Any information not obtained at application will be collected at loan closing.

To complete this requirement, the Broker must:
1. Complete Section 1 by obtaining copies of one (1) primary and one (1) secondary form of identification from EACH borrower. Acceptable forms of identification are listed below.
    a. "See attached" may be indicated in the blank spaces (Issuer/Number/Expiration), when copies of the identification are attached.
    b. Record the Issuing Company, Document Number and Expiration when copies of the customers' identification are not retained. All fields of information must be documented on each piece of ID used to identify the customer.
2. Complete Section 2, indicating who collected the data on behalf of the bank.
3. Include this document (and copies of the customer's identification when obtained) with the loan file presented to Operations.

Borrowers Name_____

FNBA Loan Number: _____

One (1) primary and one (1) secondary form of identification are required for each borrower. Separate forms must be used for each borrower.

SECTION 1

Identification Documentation Detail

Information Requested	Issuing State / Country / County / Company	Number	Expiration Date	Date of Birth
Primary				
Driver's License				
State Identification Card				
Passport				
Alien Identification Card				
Matricula Consular Card				

Secondary				
Information Requested	Issuing State / Country / County / Company	Number	Expiration Date	Date of Birth
Employee ID Card				
Major Credit Card				
College Student ID Card				
Voter's Registration Card				
Firearm Owner's Registration Card				
Military Identification Card				
Public Assistance Card				
Current utility bill with place of residence				

SECTION 2

Signature: _____

Printed Name: _____

Title/Position: _____

PATRIOT ACT - CUSTOMER IDENTIFICATION PROGRAM (C.I.P.)
BORROWER NOTIFICATION AND IDENTIFICATION FORM

BORROWER'S NOTIFICATION FORM

We _____ (Lender) respect and protect the confidentiality of customer information. We only request information that is necessary to process and service your account/loan. Some of the information we request is required by a Federal law under the "Patriot Act". This law requires us to obtain, verify and record information that identifies each person or entity that is opening an account or applying for a loan. This information helps the government fight the funding of terrorism and money laundering activities. When you open an account or apply for a loan (new business transaction), we will ask you for your name, address, identification number (social security or tax identification number), and date of birth, which will allow us to properly identify you. We will request to see your driver's license and/or other forms of identification, if deemed necessary. Please rest assured that all customer information is kept in the strictest confidence.

Borrower to execute below, acknowledging receipt of notification addressing the Patriot Act – Customer Identification Program requirements. **Note**: Each individual Borrower must be provided with a separate Notification Form, to be completed and fully executed.

_____   _____
Borrower Signature   Date

LENDER IDENTIFICATION FORM

Lender to complete the following Sections listed below (Sections 1 and 2). **Note:** A separate "Lender Identification Form" must be completed for **each** Borrower and **two (2) forms of identification** evidencing the Borrowers name is required to comply with Section 326 of the Patriot Act.

SECTION 1

_____   _____   _____
Borrower Name   Social Security # -Tax ID #   Date of Birth

_____   _____
Borrower's Current Property Address   City, State, and Zip Code

SECTION 2

Lender to complete the following identifying the two (2) forms of identification used to verify the Borrower's identity.

Primary Forms

DOCUMENT	STATE OF ISSUANCE	DATE OF BIRTH	IDENTIFICATION NUMBER	DATE OF ISSUANCE	DATE OF EXPIRATION
Driver License					
Tax ID Card					
Passport					
Alien Registration Card					
Military ID Card					N/A

Secondary Forms

DOCUMENT	NAME OF ISSUER (State, Co., Tax Office, Employer)	IDENTIFICATION NUMBER	DATE OF ISSUANCE	DATE OF EXPIRATION
Social Security Card				N/A
Birth Certificate				N/A
Recent Signed Tax Returns				N/A
Most Recent W2				N/A
Most Recent Paycheck Stub				N/A
Most Recent Financial Statements				N/A
Insurance Documents				N/A
Most Recent Utility Bills				N/A
Most Recent Property Tax Bill				N/A
Government Issued Visa				
Non US Drivers License				
Voter Registration Card				
Organizational Membership Card				

Lender to execute below, acknowledging that they have personally viewed and accurately recorded all of the information documented on this form, and in doing so, has reasonably confirmed the identity of Borrower.

_____   _____
Lender Signature   Title

_____   _____
Printed Name   Date

CIP – Form 09/03

PATRIOT ACT INFORMATION FORM

Loan Number: _____

To help the government fight the funding of terrorism and money laundering activities, Federal law requires all financial institutions to obtain, verify, and record information that identifies every customer. When applying for a loan, applicants will be asked for their name, address, date of birth, and other information that will allow lenders to identify them. Applicants will also be asked to show their driver's license or other identifying documents.

COMPLETION OF THIS FORM IS REQUIRED IN ORDER TO COMPLY WITH THE PATRIOT ACT. A COPY OF THIS COMPLETED FORM MUST BE PLACED IN THE LOAN FILE.

Required Information:

Borrower Name: _____

Co-Borrower Name: _____

Borrower Date of Birth: _____

Co-Borrower Date of Birth: _____

Borrower Current Physical Address: _____

Co-Borrower Current Physical Address: _____

Method Of Identification For Borrower (Only <u>One</u> Form Of Verification Is Required):

(1) Driver's License: State____ #_____ Issue Date: _____ Expir. Date: _____
(2) Passport: #_____ Country: _____ Issue Date: _____ Expir. Date: _____
(3) Military ID: Country: _____ Expir. Date: _____
(4) State ID: #_____ Issue Date: _____ Expir. Date: _____
(5) Green Card: Country: _____ #: _____ Expir. Date: _____
(6) Immigration Card: Country: _____ # _____ Expir. Date: _____
(7) Gov't ID (Visa): #_____ Expir. Date: _____ Gov't Branch: _____
(8) Other Document: _____ Issue Date: _____ Expir. Date: _____

Method Of Identification For Co-Borrower (Only <u>One</u> Form Of Verification Is Required):

(1) Driver's License: State____ #_____ Issue Date: _____ Expir. Date: _____
(2) Passport: #_____ Country: _____ Issue Date: _____ Expir. Date: _____
(3) Military ID: Country: _____ Expir. Date: _____
(4) State ID: #_____ Issue Date: _____ Expir. Date: _____
(5) Green Card: Country: _____ #: _____ Expir. Date: _____
(6) Immigration Card: Country: _____ # _____ Expir. Date: _____
(7) Gov't ID (Visa): #_____ Expir. Date: _____ Gov't Branch: _____
(8) Other Document: _____ Issue Date: _____ Expir. Date: _____

Resolution Of Any Discrepancy:

_____

_____

_____

_____

_____

_____

Completed By: _____   **Date:** _____
PATRIOT Act Information Form

Patriot Act Disclosure
Borrower Identification

To help the government fight the funding of terrorism and money laundering activities, federal law requires all financial institutions to obtain, verify and record information that identifies each person who opens an account.

What this means for you: When you open an account we will ask for your name, address, date of birth and other information that will allow us to identify you. We may also ask to see your driver's license or other identifying documents.

Please provide the following information. We require two forms of identification for each borrower to comply with section 326 of the Act.

_____
Loan Number

_____   _____   _____
Borrower's Signature   Date of Birth   Social Security # / Tax ID #[1]

_____   _____   _____
Borrower's Signature   Date of Birth   Social Security # / Tax ID #[1]

_____   _____   _____
Borrower's Signature   Date of Birth   Social Security # / Tax ID #[1]

IMPORTANT - Information listed below must be exactly as indicated on the document.

Primary Forms of Identification-must display Borrower's name

Document	Country/State of Origin	ID Number	Date of Birth	Expiration Date
☐State Issued Driver License				
☐State Issued ID Card				
☐Military ID Card				
☐Passport				
☐US Alien Registration Card				
☐Canadian Driver License				

Secondary Forms of Identification-must display Borrower's name

Document	Name of Issuer on Form	ID Number	Issuance Date	Expiration Date
☐Social Security Card	U.S. Govt.			
☐Government Issued Visa				
☐Birth Certificate				
☐Non-US/Canadian Driver License				
☐Most Recent Signed Tax Returns	☐Fed ☐State	TIN:		
☐Property Tax Bill		APN:		
☐Voter Registration Card				
☐Organizational Membership Card				
☐Bank/Investment/Loan Statements				
☐Paycheck stub with name				
☐Most Recent W-2				
☐Home/car/renter insurance papers				
☐Recent utility bill				

Comments:_____
_____
_____

I certify that I have personally viewed and accurately recorded the information from the documents identified above, and have reasonably confirmed the identity of the applicant.

_____   _____
Signature   Title

_____   _____
Printed Name   Date

1 For persons without a SSN/TIN, the ID number must be from one of the following: passport, alien ID card, or any other government issued document evidencing nationality or residence and bearing a photograph or similar safeguard.

NOTES

The Notary Signing Agent will need to sign this disclosure at the bottom of the form.

USA PATRIOT ACT
CUSTOMER IDENTIFICATION PROGRAM (CIP)

Loan Number: _____

To help the government fight the funding of terrorism and money laundering activities, the *USA Patriot Act* requires all financial institutions to obtain, verify and record information that identifies each person who applies for a loan.

The following information must be obtained from the borrower(s) prior to funding.
IMPORTANT: If the borrower or co-borrower does not have a current street address, you must obtain a <u>military P.O.</u> Box (AFO/FPO), the street address of the borrower's next of kin or another contact individual.

Please Print:

Borrower's Information

☐Borrower's Name : (first, middle initial, last)	☐Date of Birth:
☐Current Address: (street, city, state, zip code)	
☐Next of Kin Name: (first, middle initial, last)	
☐Next of Kin Current Address: (street, city, state, zip code)	
For a Non-U.S. Citizen (Taxpayer I.D.#, passport # w/ country of issuance, alien ID, or other government issued ID w/ photo or similar safeguard.)	
☐I.D. Information	☐Expiration Date:

Co-Borrower's Information

☐Co-Borrower's Name : (first, middle initial, last)	☐Date of Birth:
☐Current Address: (street, city, state, zip code)	
☐Next of Kin Name: (first, middle initial, last)	
☐Next of Kin Current Address: (street, city, state, zip code)	
For a Non-U.S. Citizen (Taxpayer I.D.#, passport # w/ country of issuance, alien ID, or other government issued ID w/ photo or similar safeguard.)	
☐I.D. Information	☐Expiration Date:

Additional Borrower's Information*

☐Additional Borrower's Name : (first, middle initial, last)	☐Date of Birth:
☐Current Address: (street, city, state, zip code)	
☐Next of Kin Name: (first, middle initial, last)	
☐Next of Kin Current Address: (street, city, state, zip code)	
For a Non-U.S. Citizen (Taxpayer I.D.#, passport # w/ country of issuance, alien ID, or other government issued ID w/ photo or similar safeguard.)	
☐I.D. Information	☐Expiration Date:

Broker's **Signature**: _____

Broker's Name - **Printed**: _____ Date: _____

*If there are any additional borrowers, you may attach additional sheets to this form. (10/03)

Chapter

13

Affidavits

INTRODUCTION

Some of the most interesting — and unique — documents found in loan packages are affidavits used for a certain purpose.

On the occasion when the Notary Signing Agent is asked to conduct a signing for a purchase transaction, the Agent may discover a "Seller's Affidavit" among the documents. Or, in assisting a widow or widower in signing refinance papers, an "Affidavit of Death of Spouse" may appear in the package, a form needed to remove the deceased spouse's name from the title.

Since many of the affidavits presented in this chapter are used for a narrow purpose, a brief description of each of the affidavits follows.

Assumptor Affidavit

In transactions where a party is assuming an existing mortgage note, the "Assumptor Affidavit" assures that the provisions of federal law have been met for the legal act of assumption. The "Assumptor Affidavit" is executed only by those persons who are assuming the mortgage note and who are to reside in the property as their principal residence. The "Assumptor Affidavit" is to be executed by the assumptor no later than the date the transaction is closed. No other party but the assumptor may sign, regardless of whether another party may have power of attorney to do so.

Of particular interest to the Notary Signing Agent is the note at the end of the "Assumptor Affidavit" calling for the Notary to administer an oath to each person signing as Assumptor, having each signer raise his or her hand in a pledging gesture, and eliciting an affirmative response from each person.

Identification Affidavit

The "Identification Affidavit" is a form that assists "in determining whether certain matters of record affect the title under consideration, or whether they relate to other persons whose names are similar to those of the owner or owners or former owners or prospective owners." In function it serves a purpose similar to the "Statement of Information" form found in many loan packages. However, unlike the "Statement of Information" form, the "Identification Affidavit" must be signed and sworn to (or affirmed), and notarized with a jurat.

Address Certification

The "Address Certification" is a three-part form which requests a borrower to provide a current mailing address to receive billing information and correspondence. If a borrower wishes to list an alternative mailing address (Part II) or agent to receiving billing and correspondences (Part III), the form must be notarized. Although the title of the document does not contain the term "affidavit," the form clearly requires the Notary to administer an oath or affirmation, making it an "affidavit" in function, if not in name.

Affidavit of Income/Credit/Employment

The "Affidavit of Income/Credit/Employment" is a form which requires a borrower to vouch under oath or affirmation that the borrower's income, credit worthiness, and employment have not materially changed since making the initial application for the loan. Since the closing of a loan may take days, and even weeks to consummate, the lender would want to know that the borrower has not suffered loss or change of income, credit, or employment in the intervening time that would adversely affect the borrower's ability to qualify for the loan.

The Notary certificate wording contained in this document is somewhat confusing (see page 513). For all intents and purposes it reads like a standard acknowledgment certificate, but at the end includes the words, "and who did take an oath." These words indicate the Notary Signing Agent must administer an oath or affirmation as part of the notarization procedure.

Affidavit of Title

The "Affidavit of Title" is a written statement, made under oath by a seller or grantor of real property, in which the grantor (1) identifies himself or herself and indicates marital status; (2) certifies that since the examination of the title on the date of the contracts no defects have occurred in the title; and (3) certifies that he or she is in possession of the property (if applicable).

Affidavit and Indemnity (and similar forms)

The "Affidavit and Indemnity," "Borrower's Loan Affidavit," "Mortgagor's Affidavits," "Closing Affidavit," and "Occupancy, Misrepresentation, Nondisclosure Affidavit and Agreement" serve a similar function. The element common to all five — that each document must be sworn to under oath before a Notary Public — underscores the seriousness with which these forms are handled. To quote one instrument verbatim, "... the Lender shall make such Loan in reliance upon my representations, warranties and agreements stated herein and that I make such representations and warranties in order to induce the Lender to make the Loan; ...." That is, the borrower's sworn statements induce the lender to lend the money.

The exact Notary certificate wording for the "Affidavit and Indemnity" reads, "The foregoing instrument was acknowledged, subscribed and sworn to before me...." The word "acknowledged" should be understood in the broader sense of the term, and not in the sense of a Notary "acknowledgment." Since the wording clearly states that the instrument was "subscribed and sworn to," the proper notarial act is a jurat.

The "Borrower's Loan Affidavit" is a form similar to the "Affidavit of Title." A borrower must certify that he or she has clear ownership of the property and that there are no additional mechanic's or material liens against the property (with the exception of future real property taxes not yet due or payable). In addition, the borrower is asked to list the existing loans against the property and any loans or liens which will be satisfied with the proceeds of the loan.

The Notary certificate wording indicates the signer must take an oath administered by the Notary Signing Agent.

Two "Mortgagor's Affidavits" are illustrated in this chapter. These forms contain several certifications a borrower must make to receive a loan, including verification of occupancy, income, employment, and that the borrower does not intend to lease, sell, assign, or transfer interest in the subject property to another party.

In addition to containing several features of the "Borrower's Loan Affidavit" and "Mortgagor's Affidavit," the "Closing Affidavit" includes hold-harmless and waiver provisions, an errors and omissions agreement to correct typographical errors, an escrow disclosure notice, and a consent to all of the financial terms of the transaction.

The "Occupancy, Misrepresentation, Nondisclosure Affidavit and Agreement" is the lengthiest of the four forms. The instruction above the title alerts the borrower to read the document carefully before signing it under oath. In the interest of both lender and borrower, Notary Signing Agents should give a borrower time to read the document prior to administering the oath.

The form is lengthy, but upon examination there are certain representations (indicated by the repetitive use of the word "THAT") which may not apply to a borrower in a given case. For example, if the transaction is not a "purchase" transaction (see page 1 of the form), the borrower may skim over this section. Similarly, if the loan is not government-funded, the borrower can skip over the sections which pertain to VA and FHA loans.

The "Affidavit of Surviving Spouse Succeeding to Title" represents a class of affidavits which may accompany a loan document package. Under California law, after 40 days from the death of a spouse, the surviving spouse or the surviving spouse's personal representative has full power to sell, convey, lease, and mortgage the real property held as community property. The facts in this affidavit establish the right of the surviving spouse to make the disposition of real property and may be filed with the county recorder's office separately or in conjunction with any document that makes a disposition of property, such as a grant deed or deed of trust.

The "Seller's Affidavit" is a form required by the Nevada Housing Division. The Division is authorized to issue bonds and use the proceeds to purchase mortgage loans from certain participating lending institutions to benefit persons and families of low or moderate income. The "Seller's Affidavit" requires the seller of real property to certify the financial and other terms of the sales contract governing the transaction.

The "Seller's Affidavit" contains Notary certificate wording indicating that the signer "who, being duly sworn, did depose and say that he executed the above affidavit." Although the signer vouches in the oath that he or she executed the document, this wording does not say that the signer signed the document in the Notary's presence. Therefore, technically, the notarial act is an oath, not a jurat.

The "Affidavit (Grantor)" is a declaration made by the grantor and acknowledged before a Notary Public for the protection of the grantee named in a conveyance deed and the title company insuring the title of the real property conveyed. The grantor certifies that possession of the property has passed to the grantee and that the grantor was not acting under duress in executing and delivering the deed to the property.

Although the document bears the title "Affidavit (Grantor)," the Notary wording calls for an acknowledgment as the notarial act, not a jurat.

AFFIDAVIT AND INDEMNITY

TO SECOND NATIONAL TITLE INSURANCE COMPANY

1. This is written evidence to you that there are no unpaid bills, and to the extent there may be unpaid bills that the undersigned undertakes and agrees to cause the same to be paid such that there shall be no mechanics or materialmen's liens affecting the property for materials or labor furnished for construction and erection, repairs or improvements contracted by or on behalf of the undersigned on property located at

_____ and legally described as:

2. We further represent that to the actual knowledge and belief of the undersigned there are no public improvements affecting the property prior to the date of closing that would give rise to a special property tax assessment against the property after the date of closing.

3. We further represent that to the actual knowledge and belief of the undersigned there are no pending proceedings or unsatisfied judgments of record, in any Court, State or Federal, nor any tax liens filed against us, and that if there are judgments, bankruptcies, probate proceedings, state or federal tax liens of record against parties with same or similar names, they are not against us.

4. We further represent that there are no unrecorded contracts, leases, easements or other agreements or interests relating to said premises of which we have knowledge.

5. We further represent that to the actual knowledge and belief of the undersigned we are in sole possession of the real property described herein other than lease hold estates reflected as recorded items under the subject commitment for title insurance.

6. We further represent that there are no unpaid charges and assessments that could result in a lien in favor of any association of homeowners which are provided for in any document referred to in Schedule B. The undersigned affiant(s) know the matters herein stated are true and indemnifies SECOND NATIONAL TITLE INSURANCE COMPANY against loss, costs, damages and expenses of every kind incurred by it by reason of its reliance on the statements made herein. This agreement is executed with and forms a part of the sale and/or financing of the above described premises, and is given in addition to the conveyance and/or financing, and forms a complete agreement by itself for any action thereon.

SELLER(s): _____

By: _____, Attorney-in-fact

_____

By: _____, Attorney-in-fact

_____

STATE OF _____) ss.

COUNTY OF _____)

The foregoing instrument was acknowledged, subscribed and sworn to before me this _____ day of

_____, 20 _____, by _____

_____

My commission expires: _____

_____
Notary Public

ASSUMPTOR AFFIDAVIT

This Assumptor Affidavit shall be considered part of the application for the assumption, and is incorporated therein.

If any of the facts contained in the Assumptor Affidavit are found by MHFA to be incorrect, MHFA may exercise its right under the Mortgage Note and Mortgage to declare the remaining principal balance of the loan immediately due and payable. In addition, under the Minnesota Criminal Code, a person who obtains funds through sworn false representation is guilty of perjury and theft and may be sentenced accordingly.

State of _____

County of _____ ss.

The undersigned, hereinafter collectively referred to as "the Borrower," after being first duly sworn, state as follows:

    1. The Assumptor is purchasing the property located in _____ (city or

town), _____ County, in the State of Minnesota at the following street address (if

any) _____ and on land legally described as follows (the "Property"):

Assumptor specifically promises the following: Assumptor (i) intends to occupy the Property as a principal residence promptly after closing of the Mortgage Loan but in no event more than 60 days after such closing, (ii) has no present intent to lease, sell, assign or transfer any interest of the Assumptor in the Property to another, and (iii) has not entered into any agreements, understanding or other arrangement to lease, sell, assign or transfer the referenced Property.

    2. If the Property contains more than one dwelling unit, there are no more than two units, at least one of which will be occupied by the Assumptor within 60 days after closing of the Mortgage Loan, and the Property was first occupied as a residence at least five years before the date on which the Note is executed.

    3. The Assumptor does not now and does not intend to use more than 15 percent of the total area of the Property primarily in a trade or business in a manner which would permit the Assumptor to take a deduction for any portion of the costs of the Property for expenses incurred in connection with such trade or business use of the Property on the Assumptor's federal income tax return.

    4. The Assumptor does not now and does not intend to use the Property as an investment Property (except with respect to the rental of units in a two-unit residence) or as a recreational home.

    5. During the last three years the Assumptor did not have any present ownership interest in a principal residence including an interest in a factory made house, such as a mobile home permanently affixed to land owned by the Borrower. The Assumptor understands that "present ownership interest" includes the following types of interest: (i) a fee simple interest, (ii) a joint tenancy, a tenancy in common or tenancy by the entirety, (iii) the interest of a tenant-stockholder in a cooperative, (iv) a life estate, (v) a contract to purchase residential real estate, or (vi) an interest in a trust established by Assumptor or some other person. The Assumptor further understands that a "present ownership interest" does not include (i) a remainder interest, (ii) an ordinary lease, with or without an option to purchase, (iii) a mere expectancy to inherit an interest in a principal residence, (iv) the interest that a purchaser of a residence acquires on the execution of a purchase contract and (v) an interest in other than a principal residence during the previous three years.

    6. A true and correct copy of the complete agreement with the Seller for the purchase of the Property has been provided to the Lender and the purchase price stated herein is true, correct and complete as stated.

    7. The Assumptor has not assumed or incurred any indebtedness to anyone relating to the acquisition of the Property other than to the seller as shown in the agreement, referred to in paragraph 6 hereof.

8. With respect to the Acquisition Cost of the Property; the price stated in the agreement between the Assumptor and the seller of the Property is true and correct and represents the complete agreement between the purchaser or purchasers (or a related party for the benefit of the purchaser) and the seller (or a related party to or for the benefit of the seller) including the price of all fixtures, and reflects any indebtedness assumed or incurred by the mortgagor or anyone active on his or her behalf directly or indirectly (including any special assessments) except as otherwise provided in the Acquisition Cost Worksheet attached hereto and the information on the Acquisition Cost Worksheet is true and correct.

9. The Property includes a complete dwelling unit and the Assumptor has not entered into any contract or agreement to modify the Property beyond its physical condition at the time of closing for at least the next six months.

10. The Assumptor has provided the Lender with true and correct signed copies of his or her federal income tax returns for the last three years as filed with the Internal Revenue Service or as certified in accordance with the procedures set forth in Section 6103, Internal Revenue Code of 1954, as amended; or in lieu thereof, was not required to file a federal income tax return for one or more of the preceding three years.

11. The undersigned agrees to notify the Lender and MHFA immediately in the event that he or she vacates the Property, and to keep the Lender and MHFA informed of his or her current mailing address.

12. The undersigned will not reasonably withhold his or her consent to any inspection of the Property (the exterior and interior thereof) conducted by the Lender or its agents and/or the MHFA or its agents, for the purpose of verifying the truth of any of the statements contained in this Assumptor Affidavit, provided the inspection is conducted at a reasonable time and in a reasonable manner.

13. If the Property is prefab or manufactured housing or any other factory-made building, it is permanently fixed to land owned by the Assumptor by way of a foundation and is taxed as real property.

14. The Assumptor made no material misstatements in connection with the application for the assumption evidenced by the Note and Mortgage.

15. The Assumptor has duly executed either FNMA Form 1003/FHLMC Form 65, Residential Loan Application, or HUD Form 92900/VA form 26-1802A, HUD/FHA Application for Insurance under the National Housing Act/VA Application for Home Loan Guaranty, as applicable, within the four-month period ending on the date of the closing of the Mortgage Loan assumption, states that all information on the applicable form was true and correct as of the date of execution, and states that on said form all sources of Assumptor income have been disclosed and recited, including salary, commissions, bonuses, earnings from part-time employment, interest, dividends, tips, gains on sales of securities, annuities, pensions, royalties, Veterans Administration compensation, net rental income from all sources, alimony, child support, public assistance, sick pay, social security benefits, income received from business activities or investments, estate or trust income, unemployment compensation and miscellaneous income.

_____
Assumptor

_____
Assumptor

Subscribed and sworn to before this ___ day of _____, _____.

_____
Notary Public

The Notary Public signing the Assumptor's Affidavit must administer the oath required of affiants by the Procedural Manual and Minnesota Statutes Chapter 358, by having each person signing as Assumptor raise their hand and by eliciting an affirmative response from each person so signing to the following oath: "YOU DO SWEAR THAT THE STATEMENTS IN THIS AFFIDAVIT, BY YOU SUBSCRIBED, ARE TRUE. SO HELP YOU GOD."

Major City Title Insurance Company

IDENTIFICATION AFFIDAVIT

This affidavit - for the confidential use of the Major City Title Insurance Company - will assist in determining whether certain matters of record affect the title under consideration, or whether they relate to other persons whose names are similar to those of the owner or owners or former owners or prospective owners.

STATE OF INDIANA   )
) SS   S.S.# _____

COUNTY OF _____)

I, _____,being duly sworn, upon oath state that I am the _____
                                                                                     (owner, former owner to

_____of the premises described in the application hereinabove referred
for contract purchaser, perspective owner, etc.)

issuance of Guarantee Policy or Policies. I am _____ years of age. Affiant further states the following under oath:

1. A. HAVE YOU EVER BEEN MARRIED? Yes ☐ No ☐ If the answer is Yes please complete Item B.
    B. I was married to _____in the year _____.

2. HAVE YOU EVER BEEN WIDOWED?   Yes ☐ No ☐ Yes If the answer is Yes please list the name of your former spouse: _____

3. HAVE YOU EVER BEEN A PARTY TO A DIVORCE PROCEEDING: Yes ☐ No ☐ If the answer is Yes please complete Item B.

    B. I was divorced from_____in 20 _____in _____
                                                                          (Case No., Co. State)
         I was divorced from_____in 20 _____in _____
                                                                             (Case No., Co. State)

4. HAVE YOU EVER BEEN KNOWN BY ANY OTHER NAME?   Yes ☐ No ☐ If the answer is Yes please complete Items B and C if applicable.

    B. I have been known by the following names: (a) _____

        (b) _____ (c) _____

    C. I changed my name from _____ to _____

        in _____19____

5. A. HAVE YOU EVER BEEN ADJUDGED BANKRUPT? Yes ☐ No ☐ If the answer is Yes please complete Item B.

    B. I was adjudged bankrupt in Case No. _____ in 20 _____.

6. ARE YOU SUBJECT TO ANY UNSATISFIED OR UNRELEASED JUDGEMENTS, DECREES, FEDERAL OR STATE TAX LIENS, PERSONAL PROPERTY TAX LIENS OR OTHER LIENS OF RECORD IN _____COUNTY, INDIANA?

   Yes ☐ No ☐ If the answer is Yes please list them below:

7. PLEASE LIST ALL THE ADDRESSES AT WHICH YOU HAVE RESIDED IN THE LAST TEN (10) YEARS:

8. PLEASE LIST ALL PLACES OF EMPLOYMENT AND ADDRESSES FOR SAME FOR THE LAST TEN (10) YEARS:

       I understand that this affidavit is for the purpose of inducing the Major City Title Insurance Company to issue its Title Insurance Policy or Commitment free and clear of all judgements, decrees, Federal tax liens, State tax liens, bankruptcy, divorce and change of name and any other proceedings against persons whose names are the same as mine or similar thereto.

_____

Subscribed and sworn to before me by the said _____ this _____ day of _____ 20 ____.

My commission expires _____

                                          _____
                                          Notary Public

                                          Resident of _____ County

RESIDENTIAL MORTGAGE SURVEY AFFIDAVIT

Subject property (Street Address) _____

Owned by: _____

Now, therefore, the Seller(s)/Owner(s), for the purpose of inducing First American to remove exceptions from the lender's title insurance policy to be issued in this transaction, on oath depose(s) and say(s) as follows: I/We have owned the property now being sold or mortgaged by me/us continuously for _____ years last past, and my/our enjoyment thereof has been peaceable and undisturbed and the title to said property has never been disputed or questioned to my/our knowledge, nor do we know of any facts by reason of which the title to, or possession of, said property might be disputed or questioned, or by reason of which any claim to any of said property might be asserted adversely to me/us, and more particularly:

1. No party other than the Seller(s)/Owner(s) Is/are In possession of all or any portion of the premises above described under any unrecorded leases, tenancy at will or otherwise. I/we have not leased, contracted or granted an option to other parties.

2. The Seller(s)/Owner(s) during the time of ownership of the premises above described has/have conveyed no portion of the premises nor done any act or allowed any act to be done which has changed or could change the boundaries of the premises. The Seller(s)/Owner(s) has/have allowed no encroachments on the premises above described by any adjoining land owners nor has/have the undersigned encroached upon any property of adjoining land owners. The Seller(s)/Owner(s) has/have allowed no easements, rights of way, continuous driveway usage, drain, sewer, water, gas or oil pipeline or other rights of passage to others over the premises above described and has/have no knowledge of such adverse rights. The Seller(s)/Owner(s) has/have no knowledge of any discontinued highways, abandoned roads, lanes, cemetery or family burial grounds, springs, streams, rivers, ponds, or lakes bordering or running through said premises, other than those shown in the title search.

3. The Seller(s)/Owner(s), at present, and for a period of 180 days past, has/have caused no construction erection, alteration or repairs of any structures or improvements on the premises above cited to be done, nor has/have contracted for any materials to be delivered to the premises for which charges remain unpaid.

4. The Undersigned has/have no knowledge of any taxes or special assessments which are not shown as existing liens by the public records other than as shown in the title insurance binder and/or attorney's title opinion.

5. The Undersigned has/have not allowed and know(s) of no violation of any covenants, restrictions, agreements, conditions or zoning ordinances affecting the premises. I/we have obtained all required Building Permits and Town/City Approvals for past construction, remodeling, etc.

6. The following is true. The property is; 1-4 Family Owner-Occupied Dwelling, or Condominium: is in a Residential Zone: has frontage on a public street and I/we have vehicular and pedestrian access to get to and from my/our property.

_____   _____
Seller/Owner   Seller/Owner

Subscribed and sworn to before me this _____ day of _____ , 20 _____.

_____
Notary Public

Note: If this transaction includes a transfer of title, then Buyer(s) must sign below.
In order to induce First American to remove exceptions from the Lenders Title Insurance Policy Only, the undersigned (Buyer(s) of subject property) on oath depose and say(s) that _____ have read the contents of the above, have viewed the property, and know of no facts which would contradict the contents of said Affidavit.

_____   _____
Buyer   Buyer

Subscribed and sworn to before me this _____ day of _____ , 20 _____.

_____
Notary Public

ADDRESS CERTIFICATION
(TO BE COMPLETED BY THE BORROWER)

IMPORTANT: This form cannot be used to correct the property address on any recording instrument, such as the mortgage or Deed of Trust. Recording Instruments must contain the correct property address.

BORROWER: _____

1. **THIS IS TO CERTIFY THAT THE PROPERTY ADDRESS FOR THIS LOAN OR LINE IS:**

   _____

   COMPLETE ONLY IF APPLICABLE (if above address is incorrect): **THIS IS TO CERTIFY THAT THE CORRECT PROPERTY ADDRESS FOR THIS LOAN OR LINE IS:**

   _____
   STREET ADDRESS (No P.O. Box)

   _____
   CITY   STATE   ZIP CODE

2. **COMPLETE ONLY IF APPLICABLE (if desired). NOTARY IS REQUIRED IF COMPLETED.**
   ALTERNATE MAILING ADDRESS:
   I WOULD LIKE MY CORRESPONDENCE/BILLING FOR THIS LOAN OR LINE
   BE SENT TO THE FOLLOWING ADDRESS:

   _____
   NAME

   _____
   STREET ADDRESS (No P.O. Box)

   _____
   CITY   STATE   ZIP CODE

3. **COMPLETE ONLY IF APPLICABLE (if desired).** NOTARY IS REQUIRED IF COMPLETED.
   AGENT AND ALTERNATE MAILING ADDRESS:
   I AUTHORIZE NATIONAL CITY TO SEND MY CORRESPONDENCE/BILLING FOR THIS LOAN OR LINE TO MY/OUR AGENT OR NAME OF PERSON AS IDENTIFIED BELOW. THIS AUTHORIZATION SURVIVES MY INCAPACITY OR DEATH.

   _____
   NAME

   _____
   STREET ADDRESS (No P.O. Box)

   _____
   CITY   STATE   ZIP CODE

I acknowledge that there is potentially a greater security risk in having my private and confidential information sent to another person and/or another address and I agree to release American City from any claims that arise out of American City's following my instructions in this regard.

BORROWER'S SIGANTURE: _____
(Notary required if section 2 or 3 is completed)   Date

Sworn to before me this _____ day of _____, _____.

_____
Notary Public

AFFIDAVIT OF INCOME/CREDIT/EMPLOYMENT

I/We hereby certify that there has been no material change in my/our income, credit, or financial status since the time of application for this loan.

I/We further certify that my/our employer is the same as that shown on my/our loan application.

_____   _____
(Name of Borrower)   (Signature of Borrower)

_____
(Date)

_____   _____
(Name of Borrower)   (Signature of Borrower)

_____
(Date)

_____   _____
(Name of Borrower)   (Signature of Borrower)

_____
(Date)

_____   _____
(Name of Borrower)   (Signature of Borrower)

_____
(Date)

STATE OF

COUNTY OF

The foregoing instrument was acknowledged before me this _____ by
_____ who is
personally known to me or who has produced _____
as identification and who did take an oath.

_____
Notary Public
My Commission Expires:

AFFIDAVIT OF TITLE

STATE OF NEW JERSEY,
COUNTY OF _____ SS.:

_____ say(s) under oath:

1. Representations. If only one person signs this affidavit the words "we", "us" and "our" shall mean "I", "me" and "my". The statements in this affidavit are true to the best of our knowledge, information and belief.

2. Name, Age and Residence. We have never changed our names or used any other names. We are citizens of the United States and at least 18 years old. After today, we will live at _____.

3. Ownership and Possession. We are the only owners of Property located at _____ _____ called "this Property". We now mortgage this Property to _____ _____.

The date of the mortgage is the same as this Affidavit. This mortgage is given to secure a loan of $_____. We are in sole possession of this Property. There are no tenants or other occupants of this Property. We have owned this Property since _____. Since then no one has questioned our ownership or right to possession. We have never owned any property which is next to this Property.

4. Improvements. No additions, alterations or improvements are now being made or have been made to this Property since _____ _____. We have always obtained all necessary permits and certificates of occupancy. All charges for municipal improvements such as sewers, sidewalks, curbs or similar improvements benefiting this Property have been paid in full. No building, addition, extension or alteration on this Property has been made or worked on within the past four months. We are not aware that anyone has filed or intends to file a mechanic's lien, Notice of Unpaid Balance and Right to File Lien Claim, construction lien or building contract relating to this Property. No one has notified us that money is due and owing for construction, alteration or repair work on this Property.

5. Liens or Encumbrances. We have not allowed any interests (legal rights) to be created which affects our ownership or use of this Property. No other persons have legal rights in this Property, except the rights of utility companies to use this Property along the road or for the purpose of serving this Property. There are no pending lawsuits or judgments against us or other legal obligations which may be enforced against this Property. No bankruptcy or insolvency proceedings have been started by or against us. We have never been declared bankrupt. No one has any security interest in any personal Property or fixtures on this Property. All liens (legal claims, such as judgments) listed on the attached judgments or lien search are not against us, but against others with the same or similar names.

6. Marital History. (Check where appropriate)
    (   ) We are not married.
    (   ) We are married to each other. We were married on since _____. The maiden name of
    _____ was since _____.
    (   ) This Property has never been occupied as the principal matrimonial residence of any of us. (If it has, or if it was acquired
         before May 28, 1980, each spouse must sign the mortgage and affidavit N.J.S.A. 3B:28- 2,3.).
    (   ) Our complete marital history is listed above.
    (   ) Our complete marital history is listed below under paragraph number 7. This includes all marriages not listed above and
         any pending matrimonial actions. We include how each marriage ended. We have attached copies of any death certificates
         and judgments for divorce or annulment including any provisions in these judgments which relate to this Property.

7. Exceptions and Additions. The following is a complete list of exceptions and additions to the above statements. This includes all liens or mortgages which are not being paid off as a result of this mortgage, as well as marital information not particularly set forth in paragraph 6 above.

8. Child Support
    (   ) There are no outstanding child support orders or judgments against this deponent.
    (   ) There is a child support order outstanding, Docket no. since _____ against this
         deponent. All payments, however, are current as of this date.

9. Reliance. We make this affidavit in order to obtain the mortgage loan. We are aware that our lender will rely on our truthfulness and the statements made in this affidavit.

_____   _____
Borrower   Borrower

Signed and sworn to before me on _____.

_____
Notary Public

BORROWER'S LOAN AFFIDAVIT

Borrower(s): _____

Property Address: _____

Property Description:_____

_____

Lender: _____

Loan #: _____

Loan Amount: _____

Closing Date: _____

I (we) ("Borrower") do solemnly swear that to the best of my/our knowledge:

(A) I (we) are the exclusive fee simple owner(s) of the property above-described (the "Property") and that no one has questioned our ownership or right to possession.

(B) There is/are no lien(s) or encumbrance(s) on the Property except (1) ad valorem real estate taxes which are not yet due and payable, (2) First Mortgage loan and/or other loan(s) listed on next page which have a higher lien priority than loan being applied for (3) any assessment for municipal improvements such as sewers, sidewalks, curbs or similar improvements benefiting the property and (4) any mortgage loan listed on next page which is being subordinated to this loan. No other lien or encumbrance upon the Property has been given, executed, contracted for or agreed to be given or executed by Borrower to any other person.

(C) All labor and material used in the construction of improvements on the above-described property have been paid for and there are now no unpaid labor or material claims against the improvements of the property and that all sums of money due for the erection of improvements have been fully paid and satisfied. We are not aware that anyone has filed or intends to file a mechanic's lien relating to this property.

(D) I (we) have not applied for protection under Bankruptcy statutes or any state creditor's rights laws.

(E) The above-described property is not in violation of any building restriction lines; that the dwelling, outbuildings and all driveways and fences are located entirely within the lines of the legal description of the property; that no permanent structures encroach upon any drainage and utility or other easements, and that no structure, driveway or fence belonging to others encroaches onto the above-described property.

First Mortgage Loan:

Lender/Creditor:_____
Loan # /Account Balance: _____

Other Mortgage Liens or encumbrances:

Lender/Creditor:_____
Loan # /Account Balance: _____

Lender/Creditor:_____
Loan # /Account Balance: _____

Liens or encumbrances being subordinated to Lender's Loan:

Lender/Creditor:_____
Loan # /Account Balance: _____

Lender/Creditor:_____
Loan # /Account Balance: _____

Liens or encumbrances being paid in full from Lender's Loan:

Lender/Creditor:_____
Loan # /Account Balance: _____

Lender/Creditor:_____
Loan # /Account Balance: _____

(List any additional liens on separate page)

Borrower agrees to subrogate and assign any rights or payments which Borrower may have or receive which compensates Borrower for a loss and such loss would also cause a loss to the Lender.

Borrower hereby acknowledge(s) (1) that this Loan Affidavit and Indemnity is executed under oath for the purpose of inducing the Lender named above to make the Loan, (2) that the Lender will rely upon this Loan Affidavit in making the Loan and MORTGAGE INFORMATION SOURCE will rely on this Loan Affidavit in issuing guarantee thereon, (3) the information set out above is correct and complete, and (4) that I (we) understand that I (we) can be criminally liable for falsely so swearing.

BORROWER (S):

Signature: _____   Date: _____

Print Name: _____

Signature: _____   Date: _____

Print Name: _____

Sworn to, by the above named Borrower(s), on this _____ day of _____, _____ before me a Notary Public for the County of _____ and State of _____.

_____

My Commission Expires: _____

(Notary Seal)

Closing Affidavit

Closing Date: _____

BLF No: _____

Lender: _____

Loan No: _____

Property Address: _____

STATE OF _____, **COUNTY OF _____**

PERSONALLY APPEARED before me the undersigned authority in and for the aforesaid jurisdiction, the within named: _____ and _____, (hereinafter "Borrower"), who, after being duly deposed, did state and acknowledge that they have read each of the following items as may be appropriate and that they fully understand each item which they have initialed. BORROWER affirms the following representations and understands that these representations jointly benefit the CLOSING AGENT and any title insurance company involved in this transaction. Any numbered item not applying to this transaction may be crossed out. Singular references to "BORROWER" include multiple individuals and/or entities identified above.

1. **MARITAL STATUS:** As of the date of closing, BORROWER is Married ___ Single _____

2. **TRANSACTION:** The BORROWER has checked, reviewed and approved the figures appearing on the settlement statement, and to the best of my knowledge, it is a true and accurate statement of all receipts and disbursements made on my account or by me in this transaction and accurately reflects the terms of the agreement between the parties. BORROWER acknowledges receipt of the payment of the loan proceeds in full. We further certify that we have received a copy of the settlement statement.

3. **ACKNOWLEDGMENT OF FLOOD ZONE:** BORROWER acknowledges that a flood certification has been obtained in connection with this transaction and that BORROWER has been advised that the certification reflects that the property is in a flood zone, which is zone A__ B __ C or X __ Unknown ____.

4. **WAIVER OF INSPECTION:** BORROWER hereby waives any obligation on the part of the CLOSING AGENT to either inspect the property or have an inspection conducted. BORROWER agrees to be fully responsible for inspection of the Property to determine the rights of parties in possession and assumes full responsibility for obtaining possession from its present occupants. If an Owners Title Policy is purchased, BORROWER agrees to accept such policy with a "Rights of Parties in Possession" exception in Schedule "B" of the policy. Within the meaning of this exception, "possession" includes open acts or visible evidence of occupancy and any visible and apparent roadway or easement on or across all or any part of the property, but this exception does not extend to any right, claim or interest evidenced by a document recorded in the real estate records maintained by the Chancery Clerk of the county in which the Property is located.

5. **AD VALOREM TAXES:** BORROWER has been advised that in order to obtain homestead exemption, if applicable, it will be necessary to file for the exemption between January 1 and April 1 of next year. Filings should be made with the tax assessor's office in the county in which the property is

located. Further, the tax assessor should be contacted in advance of filing to determine what documents will be needed at the time of filing. If this is new construction, BORROWER acknowledges being advised that the Ad valorem taxes are currently estimated on an unimproved basis. For next year, the property will be assessed as improved property and there will be a significant increase in taxes. In order to avoid a deficiency in the escrow account at the end of next year, BORROWER should notify the mortgage company of the new amount of taxes at the first of next year.

6. **ERRORS AND OMISSIONS:** In the event that any of the documents prepared in connection with the closing of this transaction contain errors which misstate or inaccurately reflect the true and correct terms, conditions and provisions of this closing, and the inaccuracy or misstatement is due to a clerical error or to a unilateral mistake on the part of the CLOSING AGENT, or to a mutual mistake on the part of the CLOSING AGENT and/or the BORROWER, and/or the LENDER, the undersigned agree to execute, in a timely manner, such correction documents as CLOSING AGENT or LENDER may deem necessary to remedy such inaccuracy or misstatement.

7. **PAYOFF OF BORROWER'S EXISTING LIENS:** BORROWER agrees to hold CLOSING AGENT harmless from any liability with respect to the amount of monies collected at closing to pay off BORROWER's existing mortgage(s) on the Property. Upon notification by CLOSING AGENT that the payoff amount collected by CLOSING AGENT to pay off the existing mortgage(s) was deficient, BORROWER agrees to immediately forward a money order or cashier's check to CLOSING AGENT, payable to the appropriate mortgage company, for the balance of the payoff. BORROWER acknowledges that the amount of money collected for payoff of the mortgage(s) seems reasonable, but BORROWER understands that since CLOSING AGENT cannot rely on the payoff statement to be completely accurate, and since the mortgage lender will not be held responsible for the accuracy of the figures on said statement, BORROWER agrees to make any adjustments necessary to payoff all mortgages, as stated above.

8. **NO ESCROW ACCOUNT:** If the new lender does not require an escrow of money for the future payment of taxes, hazard or flood insurance, ground rent or homeowner assessments, the BORROWER acknowledges that it has been explained to him/her that it is his/her responsibility to pay said items as and when they come due. Further, BORROWER agrees to hold CLOSING AGENT harmless from any liability with respect to any non payment of any items listed herein.

9. **HOLD HARMLESS:** If the CLOSING AGENT has ordered the survey, home inspection or wood infestation report for BORROWER, said party understands that CLOSING AGENT does not endorse the party from which the service was ordered and has no financial interest in the said company. Further, BORROWER hereto agree to hold CLOSING AGENT harmless from any liability with respect to any of said items.

DATED this the _____ day of _____, 20_____. _____

_____   _____
BORROWER'S SIGNATURE   **BORROWER'S SIGNATURE**

SWORN TO AND SUBSCRIBED before me on this the _____ day of _____, 20____.

_____
NOTARY PUBLIC

My commission expires: _____

Member Name: _____

Account Number: _____

Property Address: _____

_____

RE: Mortgage Account Number: _____

Dear Member-Owner,

In order to expedite the processing of your insurance proceeds, please provide the following information:

1. MORTGAGOR'S AFFIDAVIT (attached)
    This form must be signed and notarized.

2. COPY of the Insurance Worksheets, Contractor's Bid or the Invoices/Receipts for supplies/repairs.

If you need additional information or have any questions, please contact our office at (800) 533-0035.

Best regards,
Mortgage Servicing Department

P.O. Box 619001
MD 2100
DFW Airport, Texas 75261-9001
(800) 533-0035 Main
AACreditUnion.org

Federally insured by NCUA

MORT CONT AFF 04/2017

MORTGAGOR'S AFFIDAVIT

STATE OF	COUNTY (OR PARISH) OF

PROPERTY ADDRESS

LOSS AMOUNT	ACCOUNT NUMBER

_____, the owner(s) of the above-described property, being first duly sworn, depose and state:

That on or about _____, the structure on said property was damaged by _____, but that said damage has been or will be fully repaired and that the property and structure are now or will be in as good condition as prior to the damage. The owner further states that the repairs to said property have been or will be fully paid. The owner agrees to pay for all materials and labor used in connection with said repairs and affirms that no mechanic's or materialmen's lien will be affixed by subcontractors or suppliers of materials.

X _____

       Owner's Signature

SUBSCRIBED, ACKNOWLEDGED AND SWORN TO BEFORE ME ON ___/___/____ (month/day/year) by _____, personally known to me (or proved to me on the basis of satisfactory evidence) to be the person whose name is subscribed to above.

_____

Notary Public, State of   _____

My Commission expires on   _____

Federally insured by NCUA

MORT CONT AFF 04/2017

11/2017

PHFA FORM 3

PENNSYLVANIA HOUSING FINANCE AGENCY
MORTGAGOR'S REAFFIRMATION AT LOAN CLOSING

If any information of representations contained in the Mortgagor's Affidavit have changed since the affidavit was completed, the information must be corrected or a new affidavit must be completed as of the date of closing (or conversion if a C/P loan).

BORROWER NAME(S): _____

ADDRESS OF HOME
BEING PURCHASED: _____

ORIGINATING LENDER: _____

I/we as Purchasers of the Residence indicated herein have reviewed all of the information, representations and warranties contained in the original Affidavit of Eligibility and Acknowledgement of Program Requirements and I/we do hereby reaffirm all information, representations and warranties made therein. I/we understand and acknowledge that this affidavit is being made under penalties of perjury and that if I/we have made any fraudulent statements or material misstatements in the representations contained in any part of this document, or failed to state any of the information requested, the following may occur:

1. I/we could be imprisoned for up to 30 years pursuant to Section 1014 of Title 18 of the United States Code.

2. The Office of the Attorney General of the Commonwealth may be contacted for investigation regarding perjury, misrepresentation and false swearing.

3. The outstanding principal balance of the loan, if financed by mortgage revenue bonds, will be immediately due and payable together with accrued interest and foreclosure costs, legal fees and applicable expenses. All application fees and other costs and/or charges paid in connection with the application will be nonrefundable.

4. If applicable, PHFA will revoke the MCC.

5. If applicable, I/we will be subject to a $10,000 penalty under section 6709 of the Internal Revenue Code in addition to the other monetary penalties permissible under Section 6709(a) of the Internal Revenue Code.

6. I/we may be subject to criminal penalties.

_____   _____
Signature of Borrower   Date

_____   _____
Signature of Co-Borrower   Date

Commonwealth of Pennsylvania

County of _____

This   record   was   acknowledged   before   me   on   _____,   20____,   by
_____, who
represents he/she executed the record for the purposes stated in the record.

_____
Signature of Notarial Officer

Page **5** of **8**

Read this document carefully before you sign it under oath. (False swearing may constitute perjury under applicable laws, and misrepresentations in this document may constitute fraud.)

OCCUPANCY, MISREPRESENTATION AND NONDISCLOSURE AFFIDAVIT AND AGREEMENT

BEFORE ME, the undersigned authority, a Notary Public in and for said (County and) State, on this day personally appeared Affiant(s): **MARTHA T. ARMENTHAL**

who after being duly sworn agree and say on oath, with respect to the loan to them from the Lender of approximately the same date as this document (the "Loan"):

THAT if the Loan is made by the Lender, the Lender shall make such Loan in reliance upon my representations, warranties and agreements stated herein and that I make such representations and warranties in order to induce the Lender to make the Loan;

THAT I (whether one or more) am the owner of and am in possession of (or are being tendered possession of) the following described property (the "Property"):

    5132 ROCKLAND AVENUE
    LOS ANGELES, CA 90041

THAT upon taking title to the Property, my occupancy status will be as follows:

    [x] if I represented in my application to the Lender (or to its predecessor, if my application was transferred to the Lender) that I intend to occupy the Property as my principal residence and my application has been processed as a loan for owner-occupied property, I shall occupy the Property as my principal residence, with occupancy to begin within sixty (60) days after loan funding.

    [   ] if I represented in my application to the Lender (or to its predecessor, if my application was transferred to the Lender) that I intend to occupy the Property as my second home and my application has been processed as a loan for a secondary residence, I shall not rent the Property and shall occupy the Property.

    [   ] if I represented in my application to the Lender (or to its predecessor, if my application was transferred to the Lender) that I will not occupy the Property as my principal residence and my application has been processed as a loan for investment property, I shall rent the Property and shall not occupy the Property.

THAT if the current transaction is for the purchase of the Property and not a refinance of existing indebtedness, I represent:

    (a) that the Real Estate Purchase Contract and Receipt for Deposit, Earnest Money Contract, Purchase and Sale Agreement, Escrow Instructions or other contract for the purchase of the Property (the "Contract") presented to the Lender (or its predecessor) as a part of the application process is the complete agreement between the seller and the buyer and that no other version of

Page 1 of 5   _____ Initial

the Contract or modification of the Contract exists which has not been presented to the Lender (or its predecessor);

(b) that the true and correct sales price of the Property is $ _____ .00 and we have paid in cash the down payment specified in the Contract;

(c) that the seller or its agent has neither paid nor orally, by implication, or in writing promised to pay, arranged for or agreed to arrange for any gift, payment, allowance, rebate, kickback, subsidy, assumption of indebtedness or other liability, or any other thing of value in connection with the purchase of the Property or with respect to the sale or other disposition of our existing residence, except as may be specified in the Contract presented to the Lender (or its predecessor); and

(d) if the Property represents new construction (i) the house and the improvements have been completed, (ii) I am fully satisfied with the construction and condition of the same, (iii) I do hereby accept the house and the improvements as being constructed according to the terms of the Contract, and (iv) I do accept the size of the lot on which such improvements are situated according to the records thereof. (The foregoing representations shall benefit solely the Lender and those claiming under or through it.)

THAT if the loan is a REFINANCE loan:

No additions, alterations or improvements are now being made to this property. I have always obtained all necessary permits and certificates of occupancy. All charges for municipal improvements such as sewers, sidewalks, curbs or similar improvements benefiting this Property have been paid in full. I am not aware that anyone has filed or intends to file a mechanic's lien or building contract relating to this Property. No one has notified me that money is due and owing for construction, alteration or repair work on this Property.

I have not allowed any interest (legal rights) to be created which affect my ownership or use of this Property. No other persons have legal rights in this Property, except the rights of utility companies to use this Property along the road or for the purpose of serving this Property.

THAT if the loan is an FHA loan:

(a) the utilities have been connected to the Property at no additional cost to me;

(b) I have not paid more than one percent (1.0%) origination fee to obtain this loan; and

(c) I am aware of, and have read and understood, the following statement of federal law:

Section 1010 of Title 18, V.S.C., "Federal Housing Administration Transactions" provides: "Whoever, for the purpose. . . influencing in any way the action of such Administration. . . makes, passes, utters or publishes any statement, knowing the same to be false. . . shall be fined not more than $5,000.00 or imprisoned not more than two years or both."

THAT if the loan is a VA loan:

(a) the utilities have been connected to the Property at no additional cost to me;

(b) I have not paid more than one percent (1.0%) origination fee to obtain this loan;

Page 2 of 5   _____ Initial

(c) I have paid no commission of any character in connection with the purchase Property; and

(d) I will occupy as my homestead and am aware of the following VA policy:

TO THE VETERAN: In connection with the Certificate of Eligibility which has been issued in your name, your attention is directed to the following: "While you may use your benefits for the purchase or construction of a dwelling, you must intend to occupy the dwelling as your home. You may not use your entitlement for the sole purpose of obtaining a GI loan to purchase a home if you arrange in advance of the closing of the loan to sell or convey the home to a third party. . . . You will be required, when obtaining a loan to buy or construct a dwelling, to certify on the loan report or loan application that you intend to occupy the dwelling as your home. A false statement on a loan application or loan report can make a veteran subject to penalties provided by law. In addition, a false certification may result in the forfeiture of all other veterans benefits to which you may be entitled, such as vocational training, subsistence allowance, and disability compensation."

THAT except as represented by me in writing and approved by the Lender, no liens upon the Property, other than the first and/or second lien I am granting to the Lender, have been contracted for or agreed to be given.

THAT except as provided in writing in either the Note, the Security Instrument, an addendum or rider to either, or by applicable Federal law, including FHA and VA regulations, I acknowledge the loan I am receiving from the Lender may not be assumed by anyone. (Such a non-assumable loan, however, may become assumable at the sole option of the Note Holder under whatever terms it deems to be in its best interest.)

THAT the employment, credit and other information contained in our loan application was accurate and correct; and as of this date, when compared with the information in our loan application:

(a) I am working for the same employer(s) at the same job(s);

(b) there has been no material change in my credit obligations;

(c) there has been no decrease in my income;

(d) I have received no notice of nor have any knowledge of a pending layoff or other termination of my employment.

THAT I have not discussed with any agent or employee of the Lender (or its predecessor) any matter which would tend to make the representation of (a), (b) or (c) or (d) above, or of any other provision of this document untrue.

THAT all representations and warranties made to Lender by any third party in connection with the Loan, are to the best of my knowledge true and correct as of the date hereof and shall be, to the best of my knowledge, true and correct as of the date the loan is made.

THAT all of the representations and warranties made by me herein are true and correct as of the date hereof and shall be true and correct as the date the Loan is made.

THAT, if as the result of a clerical error, omission or other mistake, corrections need to be made to my loan documentation or any additional documents that may be required to enable Lender to sell to a government agency or other Investor, upon the request of Lender or the Closing Agent, I shall, as

Page 3 of 5 _____ Initial

applicable: i) authorize Lender or Closing Agent to make such correction{s} and indicate on the modified document that a correction was made; ii) initial any correction{s} made to any loan documentation; and iii) re-execute corrected loan documentation. I agree to comply with such request within fifteen (15) days of receipt. I understand and agree that any failure to comply with my obligations described above shall constitute an event of default under any loan documentation and shall entitle Lender, or any successor to Lender, to pursue any remedies available to it for such default.

THAT I am not aware of any present or intended future use or condition of the Property which is in violation of any law or regulation regarding toxic or hazardous substances or that may require cleanup or disposal of any such substances located or to be located on the Property.

THAT I have not and shall not use funds derived, in whole or in part, directly, from any criminal activity, including, without limitation, the sale of controlled substances, to pay any part of the purchase price for the Property and that no subsequent payments by me with respect to the Loan will be made with such funds.

THAT in connection with Lender's review of the application, Lender may obtain reports of appraisals and other investigations made at Lender's request regarding the Property, and/or the value of the Property. I shall not rely upon such reports for any reason, and I do hereby waive, release, relinquish and discharge any and all claims against Lender, its employees and/or agents now existing or as may hereafter arise based upon any alleged errors or omissions in such reports or any alleged negligence or other misconduct with respect to any such investigation or the preparation of any such report.

THAT I represent there are no unpaid or unsatisfied judgements, liens, or encumbrances, and no pending lawsuits, judgements, federal tax liens, parking violation judgements, state tax warrants/liens, environmental liens, or any other lien or encumbrances against me or affecting the premises except the mortgage permitted by the first mortgage Lender.

No Bankruptcy or insolvency proceedings have been started by or against me. No one has any security interest in any personal property or fixtures on this Property. All liens {legal claims, such as judgements} listed on the lien search or Title Policy are not against me, but against others with similar names. I have been known by no other name for at least 10 years, except:

and there are no judgements or liens against me using said other name(s).

I agree not to permit any judgement, lien or encumbrances to be placed against the Property prior to the recording of the Mortgage given to Lender.

I make this Affidavit to induce Lender to grant this Security Instrument to me. I am aware that Lender and any subsequent holders of the Note/Agreement and Mortgage, will rely upon the truthfulness and the statements made in this Affidavit.

THAT I and/or my agent have made certain representations and disclosures in order to induce Lender to make the Loan, and that my execution of this document, including my agreements and representations in it, is a material inducement to the Lender to make the Loan and that all the agreements and representations made and sworn to in this document shall survive closing and continue until the Loan is paid in full. If I have made any material misrepresentations or failed to disclose any material fact either in this document, or in my loan application, or supplied to Lender in any other form, or should I breach any agreement I have made in this document, I acknowledge that, at the option of the Lender:

(a) to the extent not prohibited by applicable federal regulations. such misrepresentation or breach shall constitute an event of default under the terms of the Note and the Security Instrument and under any loan

Page 4 of 5   _____ Initial

made by Lender in reliance upon the information contained in my loan application and/or reliance upon my representations in this document;

(b) in case of such default, the Lender, at its option (except as provided in the Security Instrument) and without prior notice or demand; shall have the right to accelerate and declare immediately due and payable the indebtedness evidenced by the Note and secured by the Security Instrument, irrespective of the maturity date specified in the Note;

I shall be liable to Lender for all costs, expenses, and damages arising out of or resulting from any such misrepresentations or failures to disclose, including all litigation costs and attorneys' fee incurred by Lender in connection with any lawsuit or other proceeding by Lender to recover costs, expenses, or damages.

BY SIGNING BELOW, I accept and agree to the terms and provisions contained in this Affidavit and Agreement. In the event this document is executed by an Attorney-in-Fact in my behalf, the recitations herein shall be contractual and binding upon the absent principal without regard to any assertion of the lack of authority of such agent to give an affidavit on behalf of the principal.

_____   _____
Borrower **MARTHA T. ARMENTHAL**   Borrower

_____   _____
Borrower   Borrower

STATE OF _____)
) SS.
COUNTY OF _____)

SUBSCRIBED AND SWORN TO BEFORE ME, the ____ day of _____, _____

                                   _____

                                   Notary Public in and for said County and State

                                   My Commission Expires: _____

RECORDING REQUESTED BY

AND WHEN RECORDED MAIL TO

NAME

ADDRESS

CITY
STATE & ZIP

TITLE ORDER NO   ESCROW NO.   APN NO.

AFFIDAVIT

Surviving Spouse Succeeding to Title to Community Property
(Section 13540 Probate Code of the State of California)

STATE OF
COUNTY OF   } SS.

                                        , of legal age, being first duly sworn, deposes and says:
that   , the decedent mentioned in the attached certified copy
of Certificate of Death, is the same person as
named as one of the parties in that certain
executed by   dated
to

as community property, recorded as Instrument No.   on
in Book   , Page   , of Official Records of
County, California, covering the following described property situated in the
County of   , State of California

      That he/she was married to   at the time of the death of the decedent.

      That the above-described property has been at all times since acquisition considered the community property of him/her and decedent. More than forty (40) days have passed since the death of the above named decedent, and no notice has been recorded pursuant to Section 13541 of the Probate Code.

      That, with respect to the above-described property, there has not been nor will there be an election filed pursuant to Probate Code Sections 13502 or 13503 in any probate proceedings in any court of competent jurisdiction.

      That the above described property has not passed to someone other than the affiant under the decedent's will or by intestate succession. That the property has not been disposed of in trust under the decedent's will. That the decedent's will does not limit the affiant to a qualified ownership.

      That this Affidavit is made for the protection and benefit of the surviving spouse, his/her successors, assigns and personal representatives and all other parties hereafter dealing with or who may acquire an interest in the above described property.

Dated_____   _____

SUBSCRIBED AND SWORN TO before me

this _____ day of _____

Signature_____

                                                  (This area for official notarial seal)

THIS AFFIDAVIT WHEN COMPLETED IS TO BE SIGNED AND NOTARIZED. BEFORE RETURNING BE SURE TO COMPLETE ALL THE REQUESTED INFORMATION TO ENABLE THIS COMPANY TO PROPERLY PROCESS THE TRANSACTION PRESENTLY PENDING.

AFFIDAVIT

_____ **EACH FOR HIMSELF AND HERSELF,**

DECLARE: That they are the identical parties who made, executed and delivered that certain deed to _____, dated _____ and recorded _____, conveying the following property, to wit:

MORE COMMONLY KNOWN AS _____
(STREET ADDRESS)

That no consideration or minimal consideration was paid therefor;

That possession of said premises has been surrendered to the grantee;

That in the execution and delivery of said deed I was not acting under any misapprehension as to the effect thereof, and acted freely and voluntarily and was not acting under coercion or duress;

That this declaration is made for the protection of the grantee in said deed, his successors and assigns, and all other parties dealing with or who may acquire an interest in the property described herein, and particularly for the benefit of STEWART TITLE OF CALIFORNIA, INC., which is about to insure the title to said property in reliance thereon, and any other title company which may hereafter insure the title to said property;

That I will testify, declare, depose, or certify before any competent tribunal, officer, or person, in any case now pending or which may hereafter be instituted, to the truth of the particular facts hereinabove set forth.

TITLE ORDER NO._____   **APN NO.** _____

_Dated_____   _____

                                              _____

STATE OF
COUNTY OF _____ } SS.

On _____ before me, _____,
personally appeared _____
personally known to me (or proved to me on the basis of satisfactory evidence) to the person(s) whose name(s) is/are subscribed to the within instrument and acknowledged to me that he/she/they executed the same in his/her/their authorized capacity(ies), and that by his/her/their signature(s) on the instrument the person(s), or the entity upon behalf of which the person(s) acted, executed the instrument.

WITNESS my hand and official seal.

Signature_____

SELLER'S AFFIDAVIT

The undersigned seller(s) ("Seller") of the residence described below (the "Residence") swears under penalty of perjury that the assertions set forth in this Seller's Affidavit are true:

1. The address of the Residence to be sold is:

   _____   State _____

2. The Buyer(s) purchasing the Residence being sold is:

   _____

3. The Residence is a single family residence and is new construction (never has been occupied)_____ or is existing (has been previously occupied) _____ .

4. The sales price set forth in the Sales Contract represents the entire cost of the Residence to be paid by the Buyer (or any person acting on behalf of the Buyer) to or for the benefit of the Seller.

5. Except for the Sales Contract, neither the Seller nor any person acting on behalf of the Seller has entered into any contract, arrangement or understanding with the Buyer, or any person acting on behalf of the Buyer, which relates to: (a) the sale of the Residence and any related personal property or fixtures, (b) the furnishing of any services with respect to the Residence which are to be performed by any person other than the spouse, parent, brother, sister, or child of the Buyer, (c) the completion, addition, or re-equipping of the Residence, and (d) the purchase of any other real or personal property in connection with the purchase and occupancy of the Residence.

6. The values allocated in the Sales Contract to items of personal property (other than fixtures) to be acquired by the Buyer from the Seller are to be paid by the Buyer to the Seller in connection with the sale of the Residence are true and correct and are not in excess of the fair market value of such personal property.

7. Under the terms of the Sales Contract, the Seller is obligated to surrender possession of the Residence to the Buyer within thirty (30) days after the closing of the sale transaction.

8. In connection with the sale of the Residence, neither the undersigned nor anyone acting on behalf of the Seller (directly or indirectly) has entered into any contract, arrangement or understanding to make any payment to any real estate broker, agent or finder other than to _____ in the amount of $ _____

Seller(s) Initials

Complete all blank spaces, initial, sign on last page, notary required.

9.   The Sellers certify that in the event there are changes in the circumstances of the transaction described in this affidavit prior to the closing the Nevada Housing Division will be so informed.

By our signatures hereunder, and under penalty of perjury, we certify to the accuracy of each item in this affidavit.

Date: _____

_____
Seller(s) Signature

Date: _____

_____
Seller(s) Signature

STATE OF   )

)

COUNTY OF   )

On this _____ day of _____, 20_____, before me personally came _____, to me known who, being duly sworn, did depose and say that __he__ executed the above affidavit.

IN WITNESS WHEREOF, I have hereunto set my hand and affixed my official seal.

_____
NOTARY PUBLIC

My Commission Expires:_____

Appendix

Notary Signing Agent Code of Conduct

CONTENTS

Notary Signing Agent Code of Conduct   ii

Notary Signing Agent Code of Conduct

v

Version 1.01 was approved September 24, 2013.
Version 1.02 was approved October 9, 2013.
Version 2.0 approved June 3, 2014.
Version 3.0 was approved January 21, 2016.

For the list of amendments, visit www.signingprofessionalsworkgroup.org.

Notary Signing Agent Code of Conduct

vi

INTRODUCTION

Purpose of the Code

The Notary Signing Agent's pivotal role in lending integrity to mortgage finance and real property transactions necessitates sound standards for the performance of signing services.

While many occupations pose professional and ethical norms for their practitioners, the need for guidelines for Notary Signing Agents is necessary given the fact that the vocation of Notary Signing Agent is largely an unregulated profession. While state Notary Public laws and regulations apply to the notarial acts performed by NSAs, these laws offer no guidance to the non-notarial services rendered by NSAs.

The purpose of *The Notary Signing Agent Code of Conduct (Code)* is to enable Notary Signing Agents to operate according to the highest standards of practice expected of like professionals in the settlement services industry.

The *Code* Standards are of two types. Most are principles, policies and practices that have proven to be effective in helping Notary Signing Agents perform their primary function of witnessing the proper execution of loan and real estate documents. The rest address and guide the NSA's supportive duties, such as advertising services, charging and collecting fees, and demonstrating responsible conduct with contracting companies and customers.

Because the acts of Notary Signing Agents affect property, and most importantly, personal rights, it is imperative that standards of practice for NSAs be widely acknowledged as just, fair and well-developed. To that end, the Standards in this *Code* were drafted with input from representatives of occupational fields which employ NSAs, business professionals and NSAs themselves.

Organization of the Code

This *Notary Signing Agent Code of Conduct* is divided into ten sections or "Guiding Principles" to enumerate the essential roles of the Notary Signing Agent. They are general rules for responsible conduct.

Each Guiding Principle in turn sets forth particular "Standards of Practice" for the Notary Signing Agent. Each Standard clarifies the NSA's many duties.

Basis of the Code

The Guiding Principles and Standards of Practice are the distillation of interaction between the National Notary Association, thousands of Notary Signing Agents from every state and U.S. jurisdiction, lenders and the companies that employ NSAs. They address the common problems, issues and questions encountered by NSAs.

The Principles and Standards reflect the conviction that Notary Signing Agents must operate in a professional and businesslike fashion and always carefully document their official activities.

Notary Signing Agent Code of Conduct

1

Statutory Requirements

In some jurisdictions, a particular Standard Practice may already be a requirement of statute, such as the universal legal mandate to identify document signers when performing notarial acts. For the overwhelming majority of Notary Signing Agents, no statute or administrative rule will prevent adherence to the Standards of Practice in the *Code*. If adherence to a Guiding Principle or Standard would result in violation of the law, the NSA should always comply with the law.

Contracting Company Expectations

The Standards may contradict the policies or expectations of the Notary Signing Agent's contracting company, especially with regard to notarial practices. The point of conflict often surfaces due to the unique pressures inherent in the settlement services industry to close loans and transactions as quickly as possible.

Notary Signing Agents should understand that the *Code* is a model for preferred conduct. A NSA should never violate the law if compliance with the law is against the wishes of the contracting company or any other party to the transaction.

Uses and Benefits of the Code

This *Code* may serve as a tool to guide and educate not only Notary Signing Agents, but also contracting companies employing NSAs and any users of NSA services.

Widespread implementation of the *Code* will reduce fraud and litigation.

Any Notary Signing Agent's adherence to the *Code's* Standards brings confidence that he or she is acting in accord with the highest standards of the vocation.

Widespread adherence to the Standards by Notary Signing Agents will engender heightened respect and recognition for NSAs.

Revision of the Code

The *Notary Signing Agent Code of Conduct* is not intended to be static and unchangeable. Its organization allows the separable Standards to be added, deleted or amended with little or no disruption of other elements in the *Code*.

While the 10 Guiding Principles of the *Code* are sufficiently general to embrace considerable change in the duties and practices of Notary Signing Agents without amendment to their current form, it is likely that the *Code's* Standards may in time need revision or supplement to accommodate technological developments.

Periodic review and revision of the *Code* is intended. The most current version of the *Code* and a list of version changes will be made available upon release.

Notary Signing Agent Code of Conduct

2

DEFINITIONS

In this *Notary Signing Agent Code of Conduct* the following terms have the meaning ascribed:

D.1. Close Relative
"Close relative" means the Notary Signing Agent's spouse, domestic partner, parent, grandparent, sibling, child, stepchild, stepsibling, stepparent, step-grandparent, step-grandchild or in-law.

D.2. Closing
"Closing" means the consummation of a transaction involving the purchase, sale or financing of real property.

D.3. Closing Agent
"Closing agent" means a third party, including, but not limited to, an attorney, title agent or escrow officer, that performs duties incident to the consummation of a transaction involving the purchase, sale, or financing of an interest in real property.

D.4. Closing Documents
"Closing documents" mean the agreements, authorizations, contracts, disclosures, instructions, notices and statements executed to consummate the purchase, sale or financing of an interest in real property.

D.5. Contracting Company
"Contracting company" means an individual or entity that enters into an agreement with and hires Notary Signing Agents to perform signing services.

D.6. Critical Documents
"Critical documents" mean the Note, Deed of Trust or Mortgage, and, as applicable, the Truth in Lending Disclosure, HUD-1 Settlement Statement, Closing Disclosure and Notice of Right to Cancel form contained in the closing documents, and other documents specified by the lender.

D.7. Journal
"Journal" means a book or electronic medium to create and preserve a chronological record of notarizations maintained and retained by a Notary Signing Agent in his or her capacity as a Notary Public.

D.8. Lender's Representative
"Lender's representative" means an individual who acts on behalf of a lender, including, but not limited to, a loan officer, mortgage broker, banker, or loan closer or processor.

D.9. Non-Public Personal Information
"Non-public personal information" means personally identifiable data provided by a customer on a form or application, information about a customer's transactions, or any other information about a customer which is otherwise unavailable to the general public, and

Notary Signing Agent Code of Conduct   3 includes a customer's first name or first initial and last name coupled with any of the following: Social Security number, driver's license number, state-issued ID number, credit card number, debit card number, or other financial account numbers.

D.10. Notarial Evidence Form

"Notarial Evidence Form" means a record of notarizations performed in a transaction involving the purchase, sale or financing of real estate that is completed by a Notary Signing Agent and retained by the lender or closing agent.

D.11. Notary Signing Agent or NSA

"'Notary Signing Agent' or 'NSA'" means an individual who has fulfilled all requirements to earn and maintain the Notary Signing Agent designation prescribed by the Signing Professionals Workgroup, and provides signing services as an independent contractor.

D.12. Settlement Services

"Settlement services" has the meaning ascribed in 12 USC § 2602, and includes any of the following when performed in connection with a real property closing: title searches, title examinations, the provision of title certificates, title insurance, services rendered by an attorney, the preparation of documents, property surveys, the rendering of credit reports or appraisals, pest and fungus inspections, services rendered by a real estate agent or broker, the origination of a federally related mortgage loan (including, but not limited to, the taking of loan applications, loan processing, and the underwriting and funding of loans), and the handling of the processing, and closing or settlement.

D.13. Signer

"Signer" means an individual who is a buyer, seller or borrower in a transaction to purchase, sell or finance an interest in real property.

D.14. Signing Assignment

"Signing assignment" means an engagement to provide signing services.

D.15. Signing Presentation Guidelines

"Signing presentation guidelines" means standardized written copy or answers used by a Notary Signing Agent in providing signing services.

D.16. Signing Services

"Signing services" means performance by a Notary Signing Agent of any of the following: coordination of the appointment at which closing documents are signed; receipt, duplication, transportation to the parties for signatures, transmission by fax, and delivery to a shipping carrier, of closing documents; care, custody, and control of closing documents while in the possession of a NSA; presentation of closing documents to the parties for signatures; notarization of closing documents; and supervision of the signing of documents by the parties.

THE GUIDING PRINCIPLES

1. Qualifications

The Notary Signing Agent will satisfactorily meet and maintain all qualifications necessary to perform signing services.

2. Notarization

The Notary Signing Agent will follow all laws, rules and best practices that apply to the notarizing of closing documents.

3. Impartiality

The Notary Signing Agent will remain impartial to the transaction at all times.

4. Unauthorized Advice or Services

The Notary Signing Agent will not provide legal, personal, financial or other advice or services to the signer in connection with a signing assignment nor explain the terms of any closing document presented to the signer.

5. Illegal and Suspicious Activity

The Notary Signing Agent will not perform an illegal, deceptive or harmful act in connection with a signing assignment and will report any suspicious activity to the NSA's contracting company.

6. Privacy and Confidentiality

The Notary Signing Agent will respect the privacy of each signer and protect closing documents from unauthorized disclosure.

7. Fees

The Notary Signing Agent will follow all contractual obligations in charging and collecting fees for services rendered.

8. Advertising

The Notary Signing Agent will not advertise signing services in a manner that is unprofessional, false, misleading or deceptive.

9. Professionalism

The Notary Signing Agent will always act in a responsible manner towards contracting companies and parties to the transaction.

10. Standards

The Notary Signing Agent will endeavor to maintain and raise standards of practice amongst practitioners in the signing services industry.

GUIDING PRINCIPLE 1: QUALIFICATIONS

The Notary Signing Agent will satisfactorily meet and maintain all qualifications necessary to perform signing services.

Standards of Practice

1.1. Background Screening

The Notary Signing Agent will submit to a background screening of the NSA's identity, residence, record of state or federal criminal arrests and convictions, and state motor vehicle record, and to a check of the NSA's name against pertinent lists as required by rules implementing the USA PATRIOT Act.

1.2. Professional Licenses

The Notary Signing Agent will obtain and maintain all licenses and commissions required to perform signing services in the NSA's state or jurisdiction.

1.3. Notary Laws and Rules

The Notary Signing Agent will keep current on all laws and official regulations that affect the performance of notarial acts in the NSA's state or jurisdiction.

1.4. Federal Laws

The Notary Signing Agent will demonstrate an understanding of the provisions of any relevant federal laws and official regulations that pertain to the performance of signing services, including, but not limited to, the Gramm-Leach-Bliley Act (GLBA), Truth in Lending Act (TILA), Real Estate Settlement Procedures Act (RESPA), Fair and Accurate Credit and Transactions Act (FACTA) and the Uniting and Strengthening America by Providing Appropriate Tools Required to Intercept and Obstruct Terrorism (USA PATRIOT) Act.

1.5. Certification

The Notary Signing Agent will earn and maintain any relevant certifications needed to service contracting companies and parties to the transaction.

1.6. Closing Documents

The Notary Signing Agent will become familiar with the closing documents for each assignment but will not use this knowledge to provide unauthorized counsel or advice to signing parties.

1.7. Ongoing Learning

The Notary Signing Agent will keep informed on any technical matters, legal requirements and other developments that affect the NSA's competence or responsibilities in rendering signing services.

1.8. Supervising Attorney

The Notary Signing Agent will willingly submit to the supervision of an attorney if required by law or rule in the NSA's state or jurisdiction.

GUIDING PRINCIPLE 2: NOTARIZATION

The Notary Signing Agent will follow all laws, rules and best practices that apply to the notarizing of closing documents.

Standards of Practice

2.1. Standard of Care
The Notary Signing Agent will exercise reasonable care in the performance of notarial duties generally and will exercise a high degree of care in verifying the identity of any person whose identity is the subject of a notarial act.

2.2. Improper Identification
The Notary Signing Agent will not accept an unauthorized identification document or other means of identification as satisfactory evidence of identity in order to expedite the closing of the transaction or for any other reason, and will ensure that any identification document presented has not expired, unless expressly authorized by law.

2.3. Discrepancies in Names
The Notary Signing Agent will not notarize the signature of a signing party whose name on the document cannot be verified with reasonable certainty by examining a written identification document or by the oaths of credible witnesses.

2.4. Notary Seal
The Notary Signing Agent will authenticate each notarial act performed on closing documents with the NSA's Notary seal, even if not required by law.

2.5. Seal Misuse
The Notary Signing Agent will not use the NSA's Notary seal for any purpose other than performing authorized notarial acts.

2.6. Journal of Notarial Acts
The Notary Signing Agent will record each notarial act performed on closing documents in a journal of notarial acts even if not required by law.

2.7. Notarial Evidence Form
The Notary Signing Agent will complete and promptly return a Notarial Evidence Form for each assignment when requested or required by a lender, title company, closing agent or contracting company.

2.8. Control of Seal and Journal
The Notary Signing Agent will keep the NSA's Notary seal and journal in a locked and secure area when not in use and not allow any other person to possess or use them.

Notary Signing Agent Code of Conduct   8

2.9. Legibility

The Notary Signing Agent will ensure that the NSA's handwriting and Notary seal on all closing documents are legible and photographically reproducible.

2.10. Completion of Notarial Acts

The Notary Signing Agent will complete the notarial acts on all closing documents and the journal entries for the notarizations in the presence of the signer at the appointment when the documents are signed.

2.11. Notary Public Code of Professional Responsibility

The Notary Signing Agent will comply with all standards set forth in *The Notary Public Code of Professional Responsibility* as adopted and amended by the National Notary Association.

2.12. Undue Cause for Refusal

The Notary Signing Agent will not refuse to perform a notarial act solely because a signer refuses to comply with a practice that is not a legal requirement for notarization in the NSA's state or jurisdiction.

GUIDING PRINCIPLE 3: IMPARTIALITY

The Notary Signing Agent will remain impartial to the transaction at all times.

Standards of Practice

3.1. Personal Interest
The Notary Signing Agent will not provide signing services for a transaction in which the NSA or the NSA's close relative is directly or indirectly involved as a party.

3.2. Professional Interest
The Notary Signing Agent will not provide signing services for a transaction in which the NSA or NSA's close relative is the loan officer, real estate agent, mortgage broker, or a settlement services provider.

3.3. Notary Signing Agent and Attorney in Fact
The Notary Signing Agent will not sign documents in the capacity of Notary Signing Agent and as attorney in fact for a principal in the same transaction.

3.4. Notary Signing Agent and Witness
The Notary Signing Agent will not perform signing services in the capacity of Notary Signing Agent and witness to a deed, Deed of Trust or Mortgage in the same transaction unless expressly allowed by law.

3.5. Appearance of Partiality
The Notary Signing Agent will refrain from performing signing services in any transaction that would raise the appearance of or the potential for a conflict of interest.

3.6. Personal Opinion
The Notary Signing Agent will not offer a personal opinion to a signer about executing or not executing closing documents or consummating or not consummating a transaction.

3.7. Exercise of Rescission Option
The Notary Signing Agent will not recommend that a borrower proceed with the signing of any closing document on the grounds that the rescission option provides three business days to thoroughly read loan documents, ask questions of the lender and decide whether to consummate the transaction, but will recommend that the borrower contact the lender's representative immediately before signing the documents.

GUIDING PRINCIPLE 4: UNAUTHORIZED ADVICE OR SERVICES

The Notary Signing Agent will not provide legal, personal, financial or other advice or services to the signer in connection with a signing assignment nor explain the terms of any closing document presented to the signer.

Standards of Practice

4.1. Legal Advice

The Notary Signing Agent will not offer legal advice to a signer during an assignment to provide signing services unless the NSA is an attorney representing a party in the transaction.

4.2. Role and Limitations

The Notary Signing Agent will clearly explain to the signing parties that the NSA is solely responsible for providing signing services connected with the transaction and cannot answer specific questions about the transaction or the legal effect of the closing documents.

4.3. Response to Questions

The Notary Signing Agent may respond to a signer's specific question by directing the individual to read the provisions in the critical or other closing documents identified by the NSA that may answer the question or by referring the individual to the lender's representative or closing agent associated with the transaction.

4.4. Presentation of Documents

The Notary Signing Agent will present each closing document to a signer in conformance with a signing presentation guidelines authorized by the contracting company, and by naming and stating the general purpose of the document, specifying the number of pages and indicating where signatures, dates or initials are to be placed.

4.5. Loan Terms

The Notary Signing Agent may identify and provide a general description of a loan or payment amount, interest rate, annual percentage rate, finance charge, payment schedule, assumption option, prepayment penalty or any other loan term to a borrower in the closing documents, but may not explain, interpret or provide legal advice about the loan terms.

4.6. Settlement Fees

The Notary Signing Agent may identify and provide a general description of a fee or charge appearing on a signer's HUD-1, Closing Disclosure or other closing statement, as applicable, but may not explain, interpret or provide legal advice about the fee or charge.

4.7. Disbursement or Funding Date

The Notary Signing Agent will neither attempt to forecast nor disclose an actual disbursement or funding date to a signer unless expressly requested in writing by a lender's representative or closing agent or the date is clearly identified in a closing document the NSA can present to the individual.

4.8. Loan Programs and Professionals

The Notary Signing Agent will not advise a borrower on loan products, programs, competitive rates or mortgage loan professionals at a signing appointment or in any verbal or written communication in connection with an assignment.

4.9. Contact Sources

A Notary Signing Agent will not commence a signing appointment without having obtained the contact information of the lender's representative and closing agent associated with the transaction.

4.10. Disclosure of Contact Sources

The Notary Signing Agent will provide the borrower with the contact information of the lender's representative and closing agent who may answer questions about the loan and explain the terms of the loan or any closing document presented to the borrower.

GUIDING PRINCIPLE 5: ILLEGAL AND SUSPICIOUS ACTIVITY

The Notary Signing Agent will not perform an illegal, deceptive or harmful act in connection with a signing assignment and will report any suspicious activity to the NSA's contracting company.

Standards of Practice

5.1. Absent Signer
The Notary Signing Agent will not comply with a request to notarize the signature of a signer who does not personally appear before the NSA.

5.2. Pre- or Post-dated Certificate
The Notary Signing Agent will not pre- or post-date a notarial certificate in order to meet a funding deadline, avoid an expiring rate lock or for any other reason.

5.3. False Document or Certificate
The Notary Signing Agent will not comply with a request of a lender's representative, contracting company, closing agent, signer or any other person to falsify information in a closing document or certificate of a notarial act.

5.4. Extra Certificate
The Notary Signing Agent will not comply with a request of a lender's representative, contracting company or closing agent to mail a signed and sealed notarial certificate that is not securely attached to an actual closing document notarized by the NSA.

5.5. Approval of Power of Attorney Signing
The Notary Signing Agent will not commence an appointment involving an attorney in fact signing for an absent principal unless specifically approved by the lender's representative or closing agent for the transaction.

5.6. Signer Awareness, Willingness and Disability
The Notary Signing Agent will immediately contact the NSA's contracting company if the NSA has a reasonable belief that a signer is not aware of the loan or the significance of the transaction at the time closing documents are signed, possesses a physical disability requiring accommodation that the NSA has not been trained or authorized to perform, or the person is being overtly influenced or pressured into signing or not signing the documents.

5.7. Inconsistent Signatures or Handwriting
The Notary Signing Agent will immediately contact the NSA's contracting company if the NSA has a reasonable belief that a person's signature or handwriting appears to be overtly inconsistent with any identification card, journal entry or document presented or signed in connection with the transaction.

5.8. Incomplete Documents

The Notary Signing Agent will immediately contact the NSA's contracting company if any closing document required to be notarized is incomplete or contains blank spaces.

5.9. Presentation of Entire Document

The Notary Signing Agent will present all pages of a closing document, and not just the signature page, to a signer for signature.

5.10. Potential or Actual Misrepresentation

The Notary Signing Agent will immediately report any potential or actual misrepresentation or falsehood known or witnessed by the NSA in connection with a transaction to the NSA's contracting company.

5.11. Unlawful Transaction

The Notary Signing Agent will immediately contact the NSA's contracting company if the NSA has knowledge or a reasonable belief that a transaction is unlawful.

5.12. Evidence of Tampering

The Notary Signing Agent will immediately contact the NSA's contracting company if the NSA has knowledge or a reasonable belief that a closing document or notarial certificate has been tampered with or altered.

5.13. Disclosure of Wrongdoing

The Notary Signing Agent will not conceal knowledge of a criminal act committed in connection with a signing assignment but will immediately notify a lawful authority as soon as the NSA becomes aware that a criminal act has been committed.

5.14. Cooperation with Authorities

The Notary Signing Agent will fully cooperate with law enforcement investigating an allegation of criminal activity of which the NSA has knowledge or that implicates the NSA.

GUIDING PRINCIPLE 6: PRIVACY AND CONFIDENTIALITY

The Notary Signing Agent will respect the privacy of each signer and protect closing documents from unauthorized disclosure.

Standards of Practice

6.1. Nondisclosure of Signer Information
The Notary Signing Agent will not disclose the transaction or personal information of a signer to any person not directly a party to the transaction.

6.2. Journal Entries
The Notary Signing Agent will take reasonable steps to prevent other parties from viewing completed entries in the NSA's Notary journal.

6.3. Scrutiny of Documents
The Notary Signing Agent will not inspect or examine the closing documents beyond what is needed to determine the requirements and conditions for the assignment and to complete any journal entries for notarizations on the documents.

6.4. Reception and Delivery of Documents
The Notary Signing Agent will reasonably attempt to receive and deliver all closing document packages in person or via secure means.

6.5. Printing of Documents
The Notary Signing Agent will personally download and print all closing documents and not assign this responsibility to any other person.

6.6. Compromised Documents
The Notary Signing Agent will ensure that any package of closing documents is properly sealed upon reception and delivery and will immediately report to the contracting company any circumstance leading the NSA to reasonably believe that the contents of the package have been compromised.

6.7. Security of Documents
The Notary Signing Agent will keep all closing documents committed to the NSA under personal control or lock and key before and during the appointment, and until delivering them via secure means to a reliable delivery service, including but not limited to a secured drop box location or hand delivery at a facility or office, or the closing agent for the transaction.

6.8. Request for Electronic Documents
The Notary Signing Agent will not comply with a request from a signer to provide electronic closing documents, but will notify the NSA's contracting company of the individual's request for documents.

6.9. Return of Documents

The Notary Signing Agent will return all executed or unexecuted closing documents in compliance with instructions from the contracting company or closing agent for the transaction in the event that an assignment is postponed or canceled.

6.10. Access Instructions

The Notary Signing Agent will not share with any person the logon credentials or access instructions to a website for the purpose of viewing, downloading or printing closing documents.

6.11. Unprotected Network

The Notary Signing Agent will not use a public or unsecured computer network to retrieve electronic communications in connection with a signing assignment, to access, download or print closing documents, or to fax signed documents to a lender's representative, contracting company or closing agent.

6.12. Transmission or Reception of Non-public Personal Information

The Notary Signing Agent will use encryption, strong passwords and other secure delivery methods to send or receive closing documents or communications containing a signer's non-public personal information, whether by fax, email or other means.

6.13. Deletion of Electronic Documents

The Notary Signing Agent will permanently erase any files containing electronic closing documents from the NSA's personal or a shared computer immediately upon conclusion of an assignment.

GUIDING PRINCIPLE 7: FEES

The Notary Signing Agent will follow all contractual obligations in charging and collecting fees for services rendered.

Standards of Practice

7.1. Confirmation of Fee in Writing
The Notary Signing Agent will confirm the fee to be paid by the contracting company for an assignment to provide signing services in writing prior to the appointment with the signer.

7.2. Performance for Fee
The Notary Signing Agent will not refuse to perform services for an assignment that the NSA has previously accepted in dispute over a negotiated fee unless the requirements for the assignment materially change after the NSA has accepted the assignment.

7.3. Referral Fee
The Notary Signing Agent will only charge and receive the fee for rendering signing services in connection with a transaction and will not accept, charge or pay an illegal referral fee, rebate, fee-split, unearned fee or kickback.

7.4. Collusion
The Notary Signing Agent will not collude with other NSAs to set fees for signing services.

7.5. Submission of Invoice
The Notary Signing Agent will submit an invoice for payment to the contracting company for each completed assignment in a form that complies with the terms of the written agreement between the NSA and contracting company.

7.6. Invoice for Contracted Fee
The Notary Signing Agent will invoice the contracting company for the exact fee negotiated between the NSA and company and will not over- or understate this fee.

7.7. Collection of Fee from Contracting Company
The Notary Signing Agent will not attempt to collect on a nonpaying account without first establishing that the contracting company has failed to fulfill its contractual obligations.

7.8. Collection of Fee from Signer
The Notary Signing Agent will not attempt to collect the signing fee from the signer in the event that the contracting company fails to remit timely payment.

7.9. Separate Financial Records
The Notary Signing Agent will keep a separate and detailed record of all fees received for each assignment.

GUIDING PRINCIPLE 8: ADVERTISING

The Notary Signing Agent will not advertise signing services in a manner that is unprofessional, false, misleading or deceptive.

Standards of Practice

8.1. Truthful Personal Assessment

The Notary Signing Agent will not misrepresent the NSA's background, education, training or expertise in an application or interview to provide signing services, on a website or in any promotional materials distributed by the NSA.

8.2. False or Misleading Claims

The Notary Signing Agent will not make exaggerated or excessive claims, promises or guarantees about the NSA's services.

8.3. Use of Professional Designation

The Notary Signing Agent will not advertise or promote the NSA's services by using professional designations or certifications the NSA has not received or earned.

8.4. Observation of Rules for Use

The Notary Signing Agent will comply with all requirements governing the use of membership and professional designations, logos and marks as may be required by the issuing, certifying or accrediting entity.

8.5. Use of Improper Designation

The Notary Signing Agent will not use any false, misleading, nonexistent or meaningless designation to lend credence to the NSA's background, education, expertise or services.

8.6. Solicitation of Outside Business

The Notary Signing Agent will not directly or indirectly solicit a signer for products or services other than as a Notary Signing NSA or Notary Public at an appointment to provide signing services or in any written, verbal or electronic communication in connection with the assignment.

GUIDING PRINCIPLE 9: PROFESSIONALISM

The Notary Signing Agent will always act in a responsible manner towards contracting companies and parties to the transaction.

Standards of Practice

9.1. Refusal of Assignment

The Notary Signing Agent will refuse to accept an assignment if the NSA reasonably foresees that he or she will be unable to meet the contracting company's expectations for the assignment, including, but not limited to, arriving at the appointment at the set time, and printing and providing copies of closing documents.

9.2. Overbooked Appointments

The Notary Signing Agent will schedule appointments with sufficient time to complete the assignment and not so closely schedule same-day appointments that the NSA cannot reasonably meet the expectations for any prior or subsequent assignment.

9.3. Delegation of Duties

The Notary Signing Agent will not authorize another Notary Signing Agent to perform signing services on the NSA's behalf without the express approval of the contracting company providing the assignment.

9.4. Cancellation and Rescheduling of Appointments

The Notary Signing Agent will not cancel or attempt to reschedule an appointment with a signer once the appointment has been set, but will immediately notify the contracting company providing the assignment if an emergency prohibits the NSA from attending the appointment.

9.5. Signing Presentation Guidelines

The Notary Signing Agent will follow any signing presentation guidelines in performing signing services as may be required by the contracting company.

9.6. Assignment Requirements

The Notary Signing Agent will thoroughly review the requirements and expectations for a given assignment, noting in particular what stipulated documents and payments the NSA must receive from the signer, and what documents and copies the NSA must leave with that individual.

9.7. Contracting Company Instructions

The Notary Signing Agent will review each lender's and contracting company's instructions and signing presentation guidelines for the assignment prior to the signing appointment and follow such instructions and guidelines provided they do not violate a statute, regulation or official directive related to the performance of notarial acts.

9.8. Review of Documents

The Notary Signing Agent will review the closing documents prior to commencing the signing appointment to confirm the documents identify the correct signing party or parties and to determine which documents must be signed, dated, initialed and notarized.

9.9. Notification of Missing Documents

The Notary Signing Agent will immediately contact the closing agent for the transaction prior to the appointment if the NSA discovers that the Note, Mortgage or Deed of Trust, and, as applicable, the Truth in Lending Disclosure, Closing Disclosure, or other closing statement is either incomplete or missing from the closing package.

9.10. Appointment Confirmation

The Notary Signing Agent will confirm the appointment to sign closing documents with the signer, ensuring that all parties and witnesses signing documents, identification cards, stipulated documents and checks will be available upon the NSA's arrival, unless expressly prohibited by the contracting company.

9.11. Professional Communications

The Notary Signing Agent will ensure that the NSA's verbal and written communications, including, but not limited to, phone conversations, voicemail greetings, emails, faxes, Internet forum responses and social network postings, convey a professional tone and demeanor at all times.

9.12. Appropriate Attire

The Notary Signing Agent will dress for an assignment in a manner that conforms to the business requirements of the contracting company providing the assignment.

9.13. Notification of Late Arrival

The Notary Signing Agent will notify the signer and contracting company providing the assignment at least 30 minutes prior to the scheduled appointment time in the event that the NSA will arrive late to the appointment due to traffic, inclement weather or any other contingency.

9.14. Identifying Credentials

The Notary Signing Agent will present a government-issued identification document containing a photograph to identify the NSA upon meeting a signer at the appointment to sign closing documents.

9.15. Changes to Documents

The Notary Signing Agent will immediately inform the NSA's contracting company about any change to a closing document that is requested by a signer, and will not alter or add a document unless expressly authorized in writing by the lender's representative or contracting company; provided however, that a NSA may modify a notarial certificate on a document requiring notarization to comply with law in the NSA's state or jurisdiction.

9.16. Status Reporting

The Notary Signing Agent will immediately inform the NSA's contracting company about any development affecting the timely execution and return of the documents.

9.17. Quality Assurance Review

The Notary Signing Agent will ensure that closing documents are properly completed, signed and notarized, and that all stipulations are present, before adjourning the signing appointment and delivering the package of closing documents for shipment to the closing agent or lender for the transaction.

9.18. Observance of Deadlines

The Notary Signing Agent will perform each assignment in a timely manner, and timely return all expected documents, duly executed, to the contracting company or closing agent for the transaction according to the requirements of the lender.

GUIDING PRINCIPLE 10: STANDARDS

The Notary Signing Agent will endeavor to maintain and raise standards of practice amongst practitioners in the signing services industry.

Standards of Practice

10.1. Association with Practitioners

The Notary Signing Agent is encouraged to join and participate in national and regional associations of Notaries Public, Notary Signing Agents and real property services professionals.

10.2. Encouragement of Practitioners

The Notary Signing Agent will encourage signing services practitioners to aspire to the highest standards of professional practice and enhance their professional competencies.

10.3. Dispensing Knowledge

The Notary Signing Agent will provide expertise to less experienced Agents and assist them in their professional advancement.

10.4. Higher Standards

The Notary Signing Agent will support the development and improvement of laws, regulations and standards of practice as will foster competence and ethical conduct among NSAs and will benefit contracting companies and parties to the transaction.

NOTARY SIGNING AGENT'S ACKNOWLEDGMENT

I have read *The Notary Signing Agent Code of Conduct* and agree to perform signing services in conformance with the Standards of Practice of this *Code*.

_____
Date

_____
Notary Signing Agent's Signature

_____
Notary Signing Agent's Printed Name

The National Notary Association

Since 1957, The National Notary Association, a nonprofit educational organization, has served the nation's Notaries Public — today numbering nearly four and a half million — with a wide variety of instructional programs and services.

As the country's clearinghouse for information on notarial laws, customs and practices, the NNA educates Notaries through publications, seminars, its annual Conference and a NNA Hotline® that offers immediate answers to specific questions about notarization.

The Association is perhaps most widely known as the preeminent publisher of information for and about Notaries. NNA works include:

- *Notary Bulletin,* keeping NNA members up to date on developments affecting Notaries, especially new state laws and regulations.

- *The Complete How-To Guide for Notaries,* a thorough publication covering every facet of notarization.

- *The Notary Answer Book* that helps Notaries explain to customers and bosses why some requests for notarizations are improper and cannot be accommodated.

- *U.S. Notary Reference,* invaluable for any person relying on the authenticity and correctness of legal documents.

- ***Professor Closen's Notary Best Practices***, widely hailed as the Notary's bible, a definitive reference book on notarial procedures.

- ***Notary Primers***, explaining a state's notarial statutes in easy-to-understand language.

- ***The Q&A Success Handbook for Notary Signing Agents***, providing real-world answers to the Notary Signing Agent's most-asked questions.

- ***Model Notary Act***, prototype legislation conceived in 1973 and updated in 1984, 2002 and 2010 by an NNA-recruited panel of secretaries of state, legislators and attorneys, and regularly used by state legislatures in revising their notarial laws.

- ***The Notary Signing Agent Certification Course***, invaluable for candidates preparing to complete the Notary Signing Agent Certification Exam developed by the National Notary Association.

In addition, the National Notary Association offers the highest quality professional supplies, including official seals and stamps, embossers, record-keeping journals, affidavit stamps, thumbprinting devices and notarial certificates.

Though dedicated primarily to educating and assisting Notaries, the National Notary Association devotes part of its resources to helping lawmakers draft effective notarial statutes and to informing the public about the Notary's vital role in modern society. ■

Notes

Notes

Notes

Notes